Author Index (Volumes I-II)

AUTHOR
PRICE GUIDES

AUTHOR PRICE GUIDES

Volume Two

Compiled by

Allen Ahearn

and

Patricia Ahearn

Q&B

Rockville, Maryland

ISBN: 1-883060-00-1

Q&B

Quill & Brush
Box 5365
Rockville, MD 20848

For
Our Grandchildren
(the collectors, dealers, librarians,
writers and publishers
of the future)

Ariana
Jacqueline
John
Justin
Kelley
Matthew
Michael
Noelle
Stephanie
and
Thomas

CONTENTS

ACKNOWLEDGMENTS

First and foremost we wish to thank Carl Hahn. He has put in untold hours reading catalogs and auction records to record prices for titles covered by the price guides for use as we update. He has also pointed out variants, new titles by the authors, errors, and omissions based on these catalogs or records.

Second, we wish to thank the dealers whose catalogs we have used not only in compiling these guides initially, but in improving them over the years. These dealers are listed in the last section of this book. We want to specifically thank those dealers, collectors, librarians and publishers who took the time to provide additional detailed information to us - Alan Andres, Allan Asselstine, David Axelrod, George Banister, Audrey Bell, Bill Berger, Seth Berner, Christiana Blake, Kay Bourne, Chris Bready, Matt Bruccoli, Jackson Bryer, Robert Crass, John Crutcher, Randy Himmel, Robert Hittel, William Holland, Ann Nichols-Jones, Robert Kent, Jeff Klaess, John Knott, David MacLean, Phil McComish, Charles Michaud, Hans Petzoldt, Len Rzepczynski, Andre Rombs, Daren Salter, Clair Schulz, Jim Trepanier, Robert Van Norman, David Van Vactor, Jim Visbeck and Floyd Watkins and all those cited in the preambles to the individual guides.

Third, we wish to thank Elizabeth Jones, Suzanne Kalk, Dyanne Ahearn and Elizabeth Ahearn for the hours they put in working on our various projects.

Without the help of all of these people, the guides would not be possible.

INTRODUCTION

The *Author Price Guides* (APG) are intended to provide sufficient information to identify the first edition (first printing) of particular books (in hand) and provide estimates for these books as of the date of this book.

The *Author Price Guides* are prepared based on available information in bibliographies, dealer catalogs, auction records and our personal experience buying and selling first editions through our store, the Quill & Brush.

The series was started because there are few price guides covering all of an individual author's books; and the basic information necessary to identify first editions is not always available, even when "complete" bibliographies have been published.

In order to arrive at the price estimates we have used all catalogs received over the last five years and auction records for the last ten years. We realize that it is possible that some of the estimates may be unrealistically low or high but we believe that the vast majority of the estimates are in the ball park, plus or minus 20%. Some of the prices may seem high in relation to a particular bookseller's personal experience, however, the estimated prices are for copies without defects, and unfortunately most copies do have some defects. Booksellers usually rationalize these defects as minimal, but collectors find any defect is a good excuse not to buy. This is the reason we have provided estimates with and without dustwrappers. The point is that a copy in a well worn and chipped dustwrapper may not be worth much more than the APG estimate for a very good to fine copy without dustwrapper. Conversely, a very fine to mint copy of a book may be worth considerably more than the APG estimate.

The price estimates included in the APG's reflect current estimates and not projections. As such the APG's price estimates are not intended to place an upper limit on what a collector or librarian should pay for a fine copy, the estimates are, after all, just a guide based on an informed opinion. We have published a price guide to the identification and price of first books (1975, 1978, 1982, 1985 and 1989 {Putnams}). The analysis for the next edition is not complete, however, an initial spot check indicates only about one percent of the titles decreased in price over a ten year period while some increased 30 times in value. This is not a sales pitch for investing in first editions, (or perhaps it is if you are willing to wait ten years), but is only mentioned to make the point that historically the prices of first editions have risen and we do not believe it would be reasonable to expect the APG price estimates to hold steady when dealers find the demand for certain titles indicate higher prices. It should also be understood that in most cases these dealers have paid higher prices in order to purchase the books for resale.

Many, or perhaps most books were preceded by proofs or advance copies in paperwraps. Therefore, we include uncorrected proofs or advance reading copies in the guides only when we can indicate the color of the cover.

"A" items are the primary works of an author and we include all books, pamphlets and broadsides. In addition, we might occasionally include books edited by the authors and books that include introductions or forewords by the author. We do not include anthologies which include the author's work or magazine appearances.

The number of copies in the first printing will be included if known. We are attempting to collect this information but must admit it is not easy. Our experience thus far indicates that the most effective way to obtain the quantities is to find someone who works for the publishing house and is willing to take the time to locate the records (if they still exist) or have them located. We have had some success with Delacorte, Knopf, Little Brown, Houghton Mifflin, New Directions, Norton, Putnams, Simon & Schuster, and Viking but would appreciate assistance with other publishers. Our goal, over time, is to obtain the quantities, ascertain that records do not exist or that the information will not be released by the publisher. We have started recording data from *Publishers Weekly* and will put (PW) after the quantities derived from this source. We believe the users should be aware these quantities may be overstated in some cases. The differences in the initial quantity announced in *Publishers Weekly* and the actual production quantity, if reduced, reflects the fact that the advance orders from book sellers did not support the larger print run. We are keeping records of our sources for the quantities and would be happy to furnish this information to bibliographers who have legitimate need.

We plan to regularly update the APG's and believe this will afford an opportunity not only to update price estimates but also increase the accuracy of the information contained in each APG.

We hope the guides prove useful and that their content and accuracy will improve over succeeding years.

INSTRUCTIONS FOR USE

NUMBER - The individual numbered entries are entered chronologically based on the information available to the compilers at the time of preparation. Within each individual numbered entry the various printings are also listed chronologically with the following arbitrary sequence given to books that were published *simultaneously*:

signed lettered copy
signed numbered copy
hardbound trade edition
trade edition in paperwraps

TITLE - The first entry after the number is the title of the book in capital letters. The titles of the individual books are shown as they appear on the title pages (some abbreviations were used in the titles).

PUBLISHER - The second entry is the name of the publisher as it appears on the title page. If the publisher's name does not appear on the title page, the publisher's entry is enclosed in parenthesis, e.g. (Viking).

PLACE OF PUBLICATION - The third entry is the city of publication as it appears on the title page. If the city does not actually appear on the title page this entry is included in parenthesis, e.g. (NY). If more than one place is listed on the title page only the primary location, usually New York or London will be shown.

DATE - The fourth entry is the year the book was published. If the date of publication is not actually printed on the title page, the year will appear in this entry in parenthesis, e.g. (1971). Dates in parenthesis will be the date the book was copyrighted unless other information is available. If the date of publication or copyright date do not appear in the book "no-date" or the abbreviation "n-d" will appear and the date will be in parenthesis if known.

EDITION - The fifth entry is a code number which provides information on how to identify the first printing (first edition) of the particular book:

[ ] The open bracket after a title means the bibliography does not include enough information to identify the first edition; and we have not actually seen a copy. It will be noted that in many cases where there is an open bracket, the place or date may be in parenthesis on the title page. In these cases, we obtained this information from other dealer catalogs, as most dealers are conscientious in putting the place and date in parenthesis if they do not appear on the title page. Specific information to fill in these blanks would, of course, be welcomed.

[0] The book contains *no* statement of printing or edition

[1] The copyright page actually states the edition -"First Printing," "First Edition," "First Impression," "Published 19--," "First Published in 19--," and *does not* indicate any later printing. The important thing is that it actually indicates it is a first and/or includes the date.

[2] This entry is for limited editions. In addition to any of the other methods of indicating the edition, these

books contain a separate page, which furnishes any or all of the following detailed information - publisher, printer, date of publication, type of paper used, number of copies, the number of the particular book and the author's signature. These separate pages are bound either in the front of the book preceding the text or immediately following the last page of text. The inclusion of this page in the book is the most important factor in identifying these particular editions.

[3] The copyright page may or may not state "First Edition." "First Printing," etc. (as in [1] above) but more importantly it has a series of numbers or letters containing either a "1" or an "A"; i.e., "1 2 3 4 5...," "1 3 5 7 9 11 10 8 6 4 2," or "A B C D E F.." etc. All books (with the exceptions noted in [4] below) containing a series of numbers or letters without the "1" or "A," are later printings, even if the book states "First Edition."

[4] This designation is for either Random House or Harcourt up until the last few years. Both state "First Edition" on the copyright page. Random House includes a series of numbers starting with "2" and Harcourt a series of letters starting with "B." Both publishers remove the statement "First Edition" on the second printing of the book. Harcourt has recently changed to using "A B C D ..." on their first editions.

[5] This designates methods used by the following publishers. The user will be able to tell which of the following is applicable for a particular book by checking under the publisher of the book in the second entry of the guide (publisher).

APPLETON - Used the numerical identification "(1)" at the foot of the last text page of the book. This was changed to a "(2)" on the second printing, "(3)" on the third printing, etc.

GEORGE H. DORAN - Placed a design "GHD" on the copyright page of the first printing and removed it on later printings.

FARRAR & RINEHART - Placed "FR" on the copyright page of the first printing and removed it on later printings.

FARRAR & STRAUS - Placed the letters "FS" on the copyright page of the first printing and removed it on later printings.

RINEHART & CO. - Placed an "R" in a circle on the copyright page of the first printing and removed it on later printings.

CHARLES SCRIBNER'S SONS - Placed the letter "A" on the copyright page of the first printing and removed it on later printings, starting in 1930. In the 1950's Scribner started using a letter and a series of numbers starting with an "A" on the First Printings [e.g. A-6.65(v)] and changing to a "B" on the Second Printings [e.g. B-8.66(v)]. This code, [5], applies to any book Scribner published using either the "A" alone or in a series.

PAPERWRAPS (wr) - The inclusion of "wr" indicates this edition of the book was not hardbound, but issued in paperwraps. Alternatively, if "wr" does not appear, the book is hardbound and has a dustwrapper unless otherwise stated.

NUMBER OF COPIES - This entry indicates the total number of copies (cc) in the particular edition, if known. It also indicates if the book is a numbered (no) or lettered (ltr) copy and if it was signed (sgd) by the author. If the number includes (PW) it means the source was *Publishers Weekly*, which means the number is usually a maximum as there are many instances where lower first printings were actually ordered based on advance sales.

ISSUE POINTS | OTHER DETAILS - If there is more than one issue of a particular first edition, the points necessary to identify the issue are furnished. This entry may also include a comment or other information.

PAGE NUMBERS - If page and line numbers are necessary to identify issues they are shown as follows - page 87 line 13 = "p.87:13."

REFERENCE - Each APG will list the bibliographical source or sources for that guide. If a particular APG has more than one reference, it can be assumed the primary source, reference (a) has been used for those books covered and Ref.b thereafter. In other words, if Ref.a was published in 1975, it was used for books up to 1975 unless otherwise stated; and if Ref.b was published in 1990, it would have been used from 1975 to 1990 unless otherwise stated. If certain editions or issue points were obtained from specific dealer catalogs, the names of the firm and catalog number or date will be shown.

PRICES - The prices after each entry are the compiler's estimates of the retail prices current as of the date of the price guide. The *first* number is the estimated price for the book without its dustwrapper or without the original box or slipcase. The *second* number is the estimated price of the book in its original dustwrapper or box/slipcase on books published in 1920 or later. If only one price is shown, the particular book was issued in paperwraps, or was published before 1920.

The prices shown are estimates based on the compiler's knowledge of the current market and should be considered as such. The first edition marketplace is a volatile one, based on supply and demand. The prices for certain books have risen greatly over the last few years, while the majority of books have shown only modest price rises, usually keeping pace with inflation but not doubling or tripling in price annually as (relatively) few books have done. The compilers make no pretensions that these guides are perfectly accurate. In the final analysis each user will have to make their own judgment in evaluating the book-in-hand. The guide, hopefully, will prove useful in arriving at an informed judgment.

No value has been assigned (NVA) to a title if the quantity was so small that a copy is truly rare; if we have not seen a copy or a recorded price and are not sure if it is common or scarce; or if we know a title has been sold at what appears to us to be a relatively high price, and we do not feel comfortable with that price as an accurate estimate.

ABBREVIATIONS:

cc	copies
dw	dustwrapper/dust jacket
ed	edition or edited
ltd	limited
no.	numbered
NVA	No Value Assigned
PW	*Publishers Weekly*
sgd	signed
( )	indicates that information contained therein is not on the title page of the book; or miscellaneous information
+	used at the end of a title which includes the words "And Other Stories (Poems/Essays)"
...	indicates that the complete title or other information has been abbreviated

Note: We have abbreviated the places of publication using standard abbreviations, i.e. NY=New York

EXAMPLE:

013a: DANTE Faber & Faber L (1929) [1] 2,000 cc. Gray dustwrapper printed in blue and black. Earliest state of dustwrapper has no review excerpts on front flap and back $50/250

Translation:

013a: {the author's 13th book} DANTE {title} Faber & Faber {publisher} L {London} (1929) {date not on title page} [1] {states "First printing"/"First published..." etc.} 2,000 cc {number of copies} Gray dustwrapper printed in blue... {issue points} $50/250 {$50 without a dw | $250 with dw}

The price estimates shown assume a tight, clean copy of the book with no major defects. Likewise the dustwrapper is assumed to be clean and complete. More to the point, there are no major defects in the book or dustwrapper. The book is square, not cocked or rolled over. There are no stains on the covers or visible wear to the cloth or boards, The cover lettering is still relatively bright and readable. The pages are clean. In other words, the prices shown are for very good to fine copies and copies which are not in this condition would be worth far less than the prices shown. On the other hand, the user should be aware that absolutely mint copies of books, particularly those published before 1960, could be valued at higher prices than shown in the guide.

THE AUTHORS

JOHN BARTH

John Barth was born in Cambridge, Maryland in May, 1930. He was educated at the Juilliard School of Music (New York) and Johns Hopkins University (Baltimore) where he is currently a Professor of English and Creative Writing. His first book, *The Floating Opera*, was set (loosely) in Cambridge, Maryland, which is the setting for many of his books. He received the National Book Award for Fiction in 1973 for *Chimera*.

References:

(a). Joseph Weixlmann JOHN BARTH: A Bibliography Garland Publ., Inc. New York/London 1976.

(b). FIRST PRINTINGS OF AMERICAN AUTHORS Vol. 2 Matthew J. Bruccoli and E.E. Frazer Clark, Jr., editors Gale Research Co. Detroit, Michigan (1978).

(c). Inventory or dealer catalogs.

001a: THE FLOATING OPERA Appleton NY (1956) [5] 1,682 cc (ref. a & b) $75/400

001b: THE FLOATING OPERA (REVISED) Doubleday GC 1967 [0] 4,500 cc. "This ... Edition ... Revised By Author" $15/75

001c: THE FLOATING OPERA (REVISED) Secker & Warburg L (1968) [] Uncorrected proof in orange and white wraps (Waiting For Godot 6/88) $100.

001d: THE FLOATING OPERA (REVISED) Secker & Warburg L (1968) [1] 4,000 cc. States "This edition first published..." (ref.c) $15/60

002a: THE END OF THE ROAD Doubleday GC 1958 [1] 3,500 cc $75/350

002b: THE END OF THE ROAD Secker & Warburg L 1962 [0] 3,000 cc $15/125

002c: THE END OF THE ROAD (REVISED) Doubleday GC 1967 [1] 4,500 cc. "Revised Edition" stated $10/40

003a: THE SOT WEED FACTOR Doubleday GC 1960 [1] 3,000 cc. Jacket design by Edward Gorey $75/400

003b: THE SOT WEED FACTOR Secker & Warburg L (1961) [0] 6,100 cc $25/125

003c: THE SOT WEED FACTOR (REVISED) Doubleday GC 1967 [1] 8,000 cc. "Revised Edition" stated. Bill Berger reports "$7.50" with "N22" on last page; $7.95" with "J45" and $10" with "H42." Assume these would be three different printings $15/60

003d: THE SOT WEED FACTOR Franklin Press Franklin Ctr 1980 [2] Sgd "limited" edition in full leather. First illustrated $100.

004a: GILES GOAT BOY or THE REVISED NEW SYLLABUS Doubleday GC (1966) [2] 250 sgd no. cc. Issued without dustwrapper in a mottled brown slipcase with a lilac-brown label (ref.a) $100/200

004b: GILES GOAT BOY Doubleday GC 1966 [0] 15,000 cc. First edition has "H18" on last page of text (ref. a&c) $15/75

004c: GILES GOAT BOY Secker & Warburg L (1967) [0] 8,500 cc $15/75

005a: LOST IN THE FUNHOUSE Doubleday GC (1968) [2] 250 sgd no. cc. Issued without dustwrapper in slipcase $75/150

005b: LOST IN THE FUNHOUSE Doubleday GC 1968 [1] 25,000 cc $10/50

005c: LOST IN THE FUNHOUSE Secker & Warburg L (1969) [0] 1,800 cc $10/75

006a: A CONVERSATION WITH JOHN BARTH (Union College Schenectady 1972) [0] Wraps. Edited by Frank Gado $50.

007a: CHIMERA Random House NY (1972) [] Uncorrected proof in narrow green wraps (William Reese Co. 4/90) $75.

007b: CHIMERA Random House NY (1972) [2] 300 sgd no. cc. Issued in clear acetate dustwrapper and slate-blue slipcase $75/125

007c: CHIMERA Random House NY (1972) [1] 24,982 cc. Winner of the National Book Award for 1973 $10/35

007d: CHIMERA Andre Deutsch (L 1974) [0] 2,500 cc $10/50

007e: NATIONAL BOOK AWARD IN FICTION, 1973 ..FOR CHIMERA ACCEPTANCE REMARKS Alice Tully Hall Lincoln Center 1973 [0] One xeroxed page, 27 lines of text. Not for sale. Published April 11, 1973. Number of copies unknown $75.

008a: TODD ANDREWS TO THE AUTHOR Lord John Press Northridge 1979 [2] 50 sgd no.

cc. Leather bound, issued without dustwrapper (ref.c) $150.

008b: TODD ANDREWS TO THE AUTHOR Lord John Press Northridge 1979 [2] 300 sgd no. cc. Issued without dustwrapper (ref.c) $75.

009a: LETTERS Putnam NY (1979) [0] Uncorrected proof in red-orange wraps. Also noted in plain blue dustwrapper and oversize proof dustwrapper (Ken Lopez 2/92) $75/150

009b: LETTERS Putnam NY (1979) [2] 500 sgd no. cc. Issued in slipcase issued without dustwrapper (ref.c). Also noted with "or" in place of number and complimentary slip laid-in $50/150

009c: LETTERS Putnam NY (1979) [0] Noted in dustwrappers lettered in gold (or copper) and silver (priority unknown) $7/40

009d: LETTERS Secker & Warburg L 1980 [1] American sheets with cancel title page, spine imprint still Putnam (Robert Temple #42) $7/40

010a: TWO MEDITATIONS Walker Art Center/Toothpaste Press Minn. [2] 85 sgd no. cc. Broadside $100.

011a: THE LITERATURE OF EXHAUSTION AND THE LITERATURE OF REPLENISHMENT Lord John Press Northridge 1982 [2] 100 sgd no. cc. Deluxe edition $125.

011b: THE LITERATURE OF EXHAUSTION AND THE LITERATURE OF REPLENISHMENT Lord John Press Northridge 1982 [2] 300 sgd no. cc $75.

012a: SABBATICAL Putnam NY (1982) [0] Uncorrected Proof in orange wraps (H.E. Turlington #28) $75.

012b: SABBATICAL Putnam NY (1982) [2] 750 sgd no. cc. Issued in slipcase without dustwrapper (ref.c) $50/90

012c: SABBATICAL Putnam NY (1982) [0] 31,000 cc $7/35

012d: SABBATICAL Secker & Warburg L (1982) [ ] 2,500 cc $8/40

013a: DON'T COUNT ON IT: A Note on the Number of the 1001 Nights Lord John Press Northridge 1984 [2] 50 sgd no. cc. Deluxe edition (ref.c) $125.

013b: DON'T COUNT ON IT: A Note on the Number of the 1001 Nights Lord John Press Northridge 1984 [2] 150 sgd no cc (ref.c) $75.

014a: THE FRIDAY BOOK: Essays & Other Non-Fiction Putnam NY (1984) [0] Uncorrected Proof in green wraps (ref.c) $75.

014b: THE FRIDAY BOOK: Essays & Other Non-Fiction Putnam NY (1984) [0] $7/35

015a: THE TIDEWATER TALES Putnam NY (1987) [] Uncorrected proof in yellow wraps (Waiting For Godot 6/88) $60.

015b: THE TIDEWATER TALES Putnam NY (1987) [3] 18,500 cc (publ. 6/22/87 @ $24.95) $7/35

015c: THE TIDEWATER TALES Methuen L (1988) [] $7/35

016a: THE LAST VOYAGE OF SOMEBODY THE SAILOR Little Brown Boston 1991 [] Advance Review Copy in pictorial wraps $50.

016b: THE LAST VOYAGE OF SOMEBODY THE SAILOR Little Brown Boston 1991 [3] Also states "First Edition" (Published 2/91 @ $22.95)

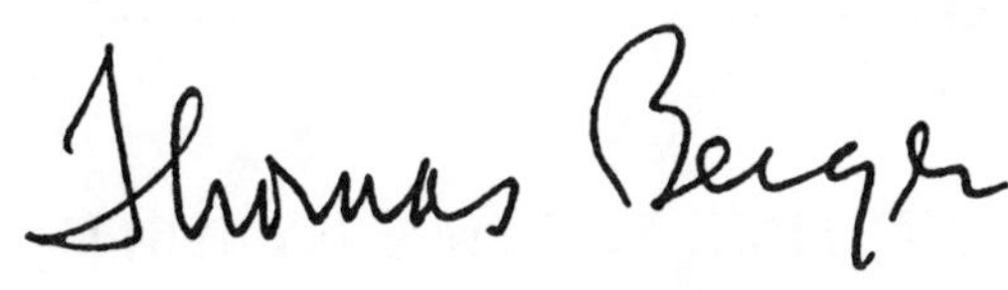

THOMAS BERGER

Berger was born in Cincinnati, Ohio in 1924. He was educated at the University of Cincinnati and Columbia University (New York). Berger served in the Army during WWII (1943-46). He has been employed as a professor and visiting lecturer at various universities over the years.

References:

(a) Lepper, Gary M. A BIBLIOGRAPHICAL REFERENCE TO SEVENTY-FIVE MODERN AMERICAN AUTHORS Serendipity Books Berkeley, 1976.

(b) FIRST PRINTINGS OF AMERICAN AUTHORS Vol. 2 Matthew J. Bruccoli and E.E. Frazer Clark, Jr., editiors Gale Research, Detroit (1978).

(c) Inventory.

001a: CRAZY IN BERLIN Scribners NY (1958) [5] (Ref.a states first issue lacks rear flyleaf but never seen) $40/175

002a: REINHART IN LOVE Scribners NY (1962) [5] $20/100

002b: REINHART IN LOVE Eyre and Spottiswoode London (1963) [1] Includes sentence (second from top of p.109) missing from U.S. edition (for what that is worth) $15/60

003a: LITTLE BIG MAN Dial Press NY 1964 [0] $30/150

003b: LITTLE BIG MAN Eyre and Spottiswoode London (1965) [] (ref.b) $20/75

004a: KILLING TIME Dial Press NY 1964 [1] $12/40

004b: KILLING TIME Eyre and Spottiswoode London (1968) [1] (ref.c) $10/40

005a: VITAL PARTS Baron NY 1970 [0] $8/40

005b: VITAL PARTS Eyre and Spottiswoode London 1971 [] (ref.b) $8/40

006a: REGIMENT OF WOMEN Simon & Schuster NY (1973) [1] $8/40

006b: REGIMENT OF WOMEN Eyre, Methuen London (1974) [1] (ref.c) $8/40

007a: SNEAKY PEOPLE Simon & Schuster NY (1975) [3] $7/35

007b: SNEAKY PEOPLE Magnum Books (L 1980) [1] Wraps $25.

008a: WHO IS TEDDY VILLANOVA? Delacorte (NY 1977) [1] $7/30

008b: WHO IS TEDDY VILLANOVA? Eyre Methuen London (1977) [] (ref.c) $7/30

009a: ARTHUR REX: A LEGENDARY NOVEL Delacorte (NY 1978) [] Uncorrected proof in mustard colored wraps $50.

009b: ARTHUR REX: A LEGENDARY NOVEL Delacorte (NY 1978) [1] $7/35

009c: ARTHUR REX: A LEGENDARY NOVEL Magnum Books (L 1980?) [] Wraps $25.

010a: NEIGHBORS Delacorte NY 1980 [1] $5/25

010b: NEIGHBORS Magnum Books (L 1981) [1] "Magnum edition published 1981" Wraps $25.

011a: REINHART'S WOMEN Delacorte NY (1981) [1] $5/25

011b: REINHART'S WOMEN Methuen L 1982 [] Using U.S. plates (Robert Loren Link 8/91) $7/35

012a: THE FEUD Delacorte NY 1983 [] Uncorrected proof in blue wraps $40.

012b: THE FEUD Delacorte NY 1983 [1] $5/20

012c: THE FEUD Methuen L 1984 [] $5/25

013a: GRANTED WISHES Lord John Press Northridge 1984 [2] 26 sgd ltr cc. Issued without dustwrapper or slipcase (in-print) $125.

013b: GRANTED WISHES Lord John Press Northridge 1984 [2] 250 sgd no. cc. Issued without dustwrapper or slipcase (in-print) $50.

014a: NOWHERE Delacorte (NY 1985) [] Uncorrected proof in blue wraps (Bev Chaney 6/91) $40.

014b: NOWHERE Delacorte (NY 1985) [1] $5/25

014c: NOWHERE Methuen L (1986) [] $5/25

015a: BEING INVISIBLE Little Brown Boston (1987) [1] (Published April 15, 1987 @ $16.95) $5/20

015b: BEING INVISIBLE Methuen L 1988 [] $5/25

016a: THE HOUSEGUEST Little Brown Boston (1988) [] Uncorrected proof in gold wraps (Waiting For Godot 10/90) $40.

016b: THE HOUSEGUEST Little Brown Boston (1988) [1] (Published April 1988 @ $16.95) $5/20

016c: THE HOUSEGUEST Weidenfeld & Nicolson L (1989) [] $6/30

017a: CHANGING THE PAST Little Brown B 1989 [] (Published September 1989 @ $18.95) $5/20

018a: ORRIE'S STORY Little Brown B (1990) [] (published October 1990 @ $18.95) $5/20

JOHN CHEEVER
1912-1984

John Cheever was born in Quincy, Massachusetts in 1912. He served in the Army during World War II and thereafter devoted himself primarily to writing short stories while occasionally teaching at various colleges. He was a consistently successful short story writer and was awarded a Pulitzer Prize for his collected stories in 1979.

We appreciate the assistance of John Crutcher in compiling this list.

REFERENCES:

(a) Lepper, Gary M., A BIBLIOGRAPHICAL INTRODUCTION TO SEVENTY-FIVE MODERN AMERICAN AUTHORS, Serendipity Books, Berkeley, 1976.

(b) Private Collection.

(c) JOHN CHEEVER: A BIBLIOGRAPHICAL CHECKLIST Compiled by Bev Chaney, Jr. and William Burton in the *American Book Collector*, August 1986.

(d) FIRST PRINTINGS OF AMERICAN AUTHORS, Vol. 5, Edited by Philip B. Eppard, Gale Research, Detroit (1987).

001a: THE WAY SOME PEOPLE LIVE Random House New York (1943) [1] $200/1,000

002a: THE ENORMOUS RADIO Funk & Wagnalls New York 1953 [1] "I" on copyright page. In dustwrapper priced $3.50 with "Funk & Wagnalls New York 10" on rear panel $50/250

002b: THE ENORMOUS RADIO Gollancz London 1953 [0] (ref.b) $25/125

003a: STORIES Straus & Cudahy New York (1956) [1] (Note: Jean Stafford, Daniel Fuchs and Wm. Maxwell also contributed) $15/75

003b: A BOOK OF STORIES Gollancz London 1957 [ ] (ref.d) $15/75

004a: THE WAPSHOT CHRONICLE Harper & Bros. New York (1957) [1] National Book Award Winner for 1958 (published March 25, 1957 @ $3.50) $25/125

004b: THE WAPSHOT CHRONICLE Gollancz London 1957 [0] (ref.b) (Also noted with Book Society wrap-around band) $25/75

004c: THE WAPSHOT CHRONICLE Time-Life New York (1965) [1] Wraps. Has "x" on last page, "xx" indicates second printing, etc. new introduction by author $20.

004d: THE WAPSHOT CHRONICLE Time Reading Program Alexandria (1982) [0] Simulated cloth without dustwrapper same introduction as 004c $20.

004e: THE WAPSHOT CHRONICLE Franklin Lib Franklin Ctr 1978 [2] Signed. Full leather with "Limited Edition" on title page. New note by Cheever (ref.b) $100.

005a: THE HOUSEBREAKER OF SHADY HILL Harper & Bros. New York (1958) [1] $20/100

005b: THE HOUSEBREAKER OF SHADY HILL Gollancz London 1958 [0] (ref.b) $15/75

006a: SOME PEOPLE, PLACES & THINGS THAT WILL NOT APPEAR IN MY NEXT NOVEL Harper & Bros. New York (1961) [1] $15/75

006b: SOME PEOPLE, PLACES & THINGS THAT WILL NOT APPEAR IN MY NEXT NOVEL Gollancz London 1961 [0] (ref.c) $15/75

007a: THE WAPSHOT SCANDAL Harper & Row New York (1964) [1] Wraps. (Tall) uncorrected proofs (ref.b) $250.

007b: THE WAPSHOT SCANDAL Harper & Row New York (1964) [1] $12/60

007c: THE WAPSHOT SCANDAL Gollancz London 1964 [0] Uncorrected proof in wraps (ref.b) $150.

007d: THE WAPSHOT SCANDAL Gollancz London 1964 [0] (ref.b) $12/60

008a: THE BRIGADIER AND THE GOLF WIDOW Harper & Row New York (1964) [1] Uncorrected proof in wraps (ref.b) $200

008b: THE BRIGADIER AND THE GOLF WIDOW Harper & Row New York (1964) [2] (Quantity unknown.) Signed by author on tipped-in sheet (before title page) $125/175

008c: THE BRIGADIER AND THE GOLF WIDOW Harper & Row New York (1964) [1] First issue dustwrapper with author's picture on back panel $10/60

008d: THE BRIGADIER AND THE GOLF WIDOW Harper & Row New York (1964) [1] Second issue dustwrapper with "From the Early

Reviews of ..." this book on back panel. Both have "01064" bottom of front flap $10/40

008e: THE BRIGADIER AND THE GOLF WIDOW Gollancz London 1965 [0] (ref.c) $10/50

009a: MIMI BOYER Bodley Gallery New York 1964 [0] (Folded sheet.) Exhibition brochure with text by Cheever $200.

010a: THE SWIMMER Stein & Day New York (1967) [0] By Eleanor Perry. Filmscript based on the story by Cheever (ref.b) $10/50

011a: SHADY HILL STORIES Eihosa Ltd. Tokyo (1965) [] Flex cover in dustwrapper (Glenn Horowitz #8) $175.

012a: THE SWIMMER Hoko-Shobo (Tokyo 1967) [] Wraps. Compiled with notes by Yoichiro Kobori (Waiting For Godot L-1) $60.

013a: THE ANGEL OF THE BRIDGE Hoko-Shobo (Tokyo 1967) [] Wraps. Compiled with notes by Yoichiro Kobori (Waiting For Godot L-1) $60.

013b: THE ANGEL OF THE BRIDGE Redpath Minn. 1987 [0] 5,000 cc. Wraps $25.

014a: HOMAGE TO SHAKESPEARE Country Squires Books Stevenson, CT (1968) [] Uncorrected proof in plain blue wraps $200.

014b: HOMAGE TO SHAKESPEARE Country Squires Books Stevenson, CT (1968) [2] 150 sgd no. cc in dustwrapper $175/250

015a: ELIZABETH AMES (The Corp of the Yaddo Saratoga Springs 1968) [0] Wraps. Two page tribute to founder of Yaddo. As few as 12 copies perhaps $1,500.

016a: BULLET PARK Knopf New York 1969 [1] Uncorrected proof in wraps $125.

016b: BULLET PARK Knopf New York 1969 [1] $8/40

016c: BULLET PARK Jonathan Cape London (1969) [1] (ref.b) $7/40

017a: THE WORLD OF APPLES Knopf New York 1973 [1] Uncorrected proof in wraps $125.

017b: THE WORLD OF APPLES Knopf New York [1] Noted in both white and black cloth (Waiting For Godot #11) $8/40

017c: THE WORLD OF APPLES Jonathan Cape London (1974) [1] (ref.b) $8/40

018a: FALCONER Knopf New York 1977 [1] Uncorrected proof in salmon colored wraps (Waiting For Godot #8). Also dated 1976 (Joseph The Provider #32) $175.

018b: FALCONER Knopf New York 1977 [1] (ref.b) $7/35

018c: FALCONER Jonathan Cape London (1977) [1] Uncorrected proof in wraps (ref.b) $125.

018d: FALCONER Jonathan Cape London (1977) [1] (ref.b) $8/40

019a: THE STORIES OF JOHN CHEEVER Knopf New York 1978 [1] Uncorrected proofs in green printed wraps. Winner of the Pulitzer Prize for 1979 and National Book Critics Circle Award for 1978 $200.

019b: THE STORIES OF JOHN CHEEVER Knopf New York 1978 [1] $15/60

019c: THE STORIES OF JOHN CHEEVER Jonathan Cape London (1979) [1] (ref.b) $10/50

019d: THE STORIES OF JOHN CHEEVER Franklin Lib Franklin Ctr 1980 [2] Signed (limitation not specified). Pulitzer prize series. Illustrated by Mitchell Hooks. Full leather (ref.b) $100.

020a: THE DAY THE PIG FELL IN THE WELL Lord John Press Northridge 1978 [2] 26 Sgd ltr cc. Issued without dustwrapper or slipcase (also at least one author's copy in different binding $350.

020b: THE DAY THE PIG FELL IN THE WELL Lord John Press Northridge 1978 [2] 275 sgd no. cc. Issued without dustwrapper or slipcase (ref.b) $150.

021a: WAPSHOT CHRONICLE, WAPSHOT SCANDAL Harper & Row New York (1979) [1] First combined edition (ref.d) $5/30

022a: OSSINING TOWN 22 KILOMETER ROAD RACE Ossining New York 1979 [0] Wraps. Large pamphlet, includes an introduction "The Ossining Marathon" by Cheever (ref.b) $100.

023a: THE LEAVES, THE LIONFISH AND THE BEAR Sylvester & Orphanos Los Angeles 1980 [2] 4 cc with printed name of recipient. Text is revised from previous magazine appearance (ref.c) $350.

023b: THE LEAVES, THE LIONFISH AND THE BEAR Sylvester & Orphanos Los Angeles 1980 [2] 26 sgd ltr cc (ref.b) $250.

023c: THE LEAVES, THE LIONFISH AND THE BEAR Sylvester & Orphanos Los Angeles 1980 [2] 300 sgd no. cc (ref.b) $100.

023d: THE LEAVES, THE LIONFISH AND THE BEAR Sylvester & Orphanos Los Angeles 1980 [2] Out-of-series (copies given as presentation) (ref.b). Number unknown $150.

024a: OH, WHAT A PARADISE IT SEEMS Knopf New York 1982 [1] Uncorrected proofs in cream colored wraps (also noted as white, but assume the same) $100.

024b: OH, WHAT A PARADISE IT SEEMS Knopf New York 1982 [1] (Published February 10, 1982 @ $10.) $5/30

024c: OH, WHAT A PARADISE IT SEEMS Jonathan Cape London (1982) [1] Uncorrected proofs in red printed wraps and oversize proof dustwrapper (Ian McKelvie 4/91) $75/125

024d: OH, WHAT A PARADISE IT SEEMS Jonathan Cape London (1982) [1] (ref.b) $6/30

025a: THE NATIONAL PASTIME Sylvester & Orphanos Los Angeles (1982) [2] 4 sgd no. cc with printed name of recipient $300.

025b: THE NATIONAL PASTIME Sylvester & Orphanos Los Angeles (1982) [2] 26 sgd ltr cc $200.

025c: THE NATIONAL PASTIME Sylvester & Orphanos Los Angeles (1982) [2] 300 sgd no. cc. Issued without dustwrapper or slipcase (ref.b) $100.

026a: CHRISTMAS IS A SAD SEASON FOR THE POOR Tales for Travellers (San Francisco 1982) [0] Wraps. No. 4 in Selected Short Stories Series. First separate appearance (ref.b) (The series was issued in a "map" folded format) $25.

027a: THE COUNTRY HUSBAND San Suya Tokyo (1983) [0] Wraps. Edited and notes by Haruma Okado $50.

028a: THE ENORMOUS RADIO Creative Education Mankato 1983 [] Pictorial boards without dustwrapper. First separate appearance $40.

029a: ATLANTIC CROSSING (Ex Ophidia Cottondale 1986) [2] 90 (99?) no. cc. Issued in full leather in drop-tray box (ref.c) $450.

030a: THE ANGEL OF THE BRIDGE Redpath Minn. 1987 [0] Wraps. 5,000 cc $25.

031a: EXPELLED Sylvestor & Orphanos (Los Angeles) 1988 [2] 9 cc with printed name of the recipient and signed by Malcolm Cowley (foreword), John Updike (afterword), Warren Chappell (illus) and Cheever. Miniature book issued without dustwrapper in slipcase $400/450

031b: EXPELLED Sylvestor & Orphanos (Los Angeles) 1988 [2] 26 sgd ltd cc $350/400

031c: EXPELLED Sylvestor & Orphanos (Los Angeles) 1988 [2] 150 sgd no. cc $275/325

032a: CONVERSATIONS WITH JOHN CHEEVER Univ. Press of Miss. Jackson (1988) [] $15/35

032b: CONVERSATIONS WITH JOHN CHEEVER Univ. Press of Miss. Jackson (1988) [] Wraps $15.

033a: THE UNCOLLECTED STORIES OF JOHN CHEEVER 1930-1981 Academy Chicago 1988 [ ] Uncorrected proof in wraps $2,000.

033b: THE UNCOLLECTED STORIES OF JOHN CHEEVER 1930-1981 Academy Chicago 1988 [] 22 page advance excerpt in wraps. Copies seen with and without sticker "This sampler is not authorized by the family of John Cheever" $40.

034a: THE LETTERS OF JOHN CHEEVER Simon & Schuster NY (1988) [3] Uncorrected proofs in yellow wraps. Edited by Benjamin Cheever $75.

034b: THE LETTERS OF JOHN CHEEVER Simon & Schuster NY (1988) [3] (published 11/88 @ $19.95) $5/20

034c: THE LETTERS OF JOHN CHEEVER Jonathan Cape L 1989 [] $5/25

035a: THE JOURNALS OF JOHN CHEEVER Knopf NY 1991 [] Uncorrected proof in white wraps $75.

035b: THE JOURNALS OF JOHN CHEEVER Knopf NY 1991 [1] (published 10/91 @ $25) Edited by Robert Gottlieb

035c: THE JOURNALS OF JOHN CHEEVER Jonathan Cape L 1991 [] Edited by Robert Gottlieb

SIR WINSTON S. CHURCHILL
(1874-1965)

For the English speaking world, at least, Winston Churchill dominated the first half of this century. He was the one man who served in important government positions during both the World Wars. As Prime Minister he was noted for his eloquence and memorable phrases. He was an international statesman, parlimentarian, prime minister, orator, war correspondent, historian, artist and Noble Prize Winner; but he was always proud of the fact that he earned his living as a writer. Before the turn of the century he was paid 5 pounds a column by the Daily Telegraph for his dispatches from the North West frontier and by the time he was 26 years old, while still serving as a cavalry officer, he had written five books. His collected works run to 38 volumes. An amazing output for a man so involved in day to day history.

Notes on pricing and identification:

The estimated prices are for very good to fine copies without dustwrapper before 1920 (both with and without dustwrapper from 1920 foreward). The Woods bibliography seems to state the fact that a particular book or pamphlet actually contains the wording "First Edition," therefore we have assumed that none of the numerous pamphlets actually state "First Edition." Further, we assume all of the pamphlets are in self-wraps unless "card-covers" or "paperwraps" are mentioned. By this we mean that the speech or statement begins on the first page and there is no other cover. We found very few data points for pricing these pamphlets and extrapolated from what little we found, which means that the estimated prices may be way out of line in some cases.

On the sets we priced the *First World War* individually and as a set, but on the others (*Marborough*, *WWII*, *English Speaking People*) we only priced the sets.

We are aware that we are far from Churchill experts, but still hope this guide will prove useful; and that errors and omissions will be pointed out so that the first revision will be even more accurate.

REFERENCES:

(a) Woods, Frederick A BIBLIOGRAPHY OF THE WORKS OF SIR WINSTON CHURCHILL Second Revised Edition St Paul's Bibliographies (Surrey 1979).

(b) Inventory, dealer catalogs, etc.

We would like to thank Jeff Klaess for laying out the bibliographical data from Woods, which was not as easy as it would seem. We also appreciate the clarification provided by Richard M. Langsworth (International Churchill Society) and Marvin Nicely.

001a: THE STORY OF THE MALAKAND FIELD FORCE Longmans, Green L 1898 [0] 2,000 cc (a&b). Published March 14. Apple green cloth, black endpapers frontis portrait sewn in and folding map tipped on to stub of frontis. 32 pages of ads at back on thinner paper, separately numbered. Author's name appears on spine as Winston L. Spencer Churchill $5,000.

001b: THE STORY OF THE MALAKAND FIELD FORCE Longmans, Green L 1898 [0] Second state. As above but with errata slip tipped-in immediately preceding first folding map $4,000.

001c: THE STORY OF THE MALAKAND FIELD FORCE Longmans, Green L 1898 [0] 2,000 cc. Colonial Library. "This edition intended for circulation ...India and the British Colonies". The front cover and spine have "1897" but actually distributed after 001a $2,000.

Note: No American edition. An unspecified number of copies were shipped to the U.S. to be sold by Longman's Green, NY, 1898

001d: THE STORY OF THE MALAKAND FIELD FORCE Longmans, Green L 1901 [] Second edition with substantial revisions and a new preface $1,250.

002a: THE RIVER WAR (2 vols) Longman's, Green L 1899 [0] 2,000 cc published November 6. Illustrated by Angus McNeill.

Vol. 1: folding maps facing pgs 146, 234, 308, 338, 402, 406, 420, 424, 430, 432 and 462.

Vol. 2: folding maps facing pgs 80, 98, 128, 144, 154, 156, 160, 172 and 224

The set $5,000.

002b: THE RIVER WAR (2 vols) Longman's, Green NY 1899 [0] Published December 9

$4,000.

002c: THE RIVER WAR Revised One Volume Edition Longmans, Green L 1902 [ ] 1,000 cc (c&d) published October 15. "New and Revised Edition" on title page. Folding maps facing pages 238, 256, 272, 284, 298 and 302. Text reduced and one chapter added. 40 page catalog at back on thinner paper and separately numbered (some copies issued without catalog) $1,000.

002d: THE RIVER WAR Longman Green NY 1902 [] Copies of 002c were exported to NY for American publication in Dec. 1 $750.

002e: THE RIVER WAR Thomas Nelson L (1915) [0] (First cheap edition.) Published in August. Blue cloth, top page edges gilt $200.

002f: THE RIVER WAR Eyre & Spottiswoode L 1933 [1] 3,000 cc. "First Cheap Edition 1933." New introduction. Brown cloth $150/350

002g: THE RIVER WAR Scribners NY 1933 [] (Glenn Horowitz #16) Not in ref.a $75/250

003a: SAVROLA Longmans, Green NY 1900 [0] 4,000 cc published Feb. 3 (although copyright copies were received in November 1899). Dark blue cloth. 24 un-numbered pages of advertisements $1,250.

Note: type-set in Boston. Two sets of Electroplates taken, one set sent to London, title page and c.page to be re-set in London, U.S. copyright notice removed, but not re-set, resulting in 2 states of first U.K. edition

003b: SAVROLA Longmans, Green L 1900 [0] 1,500 cc (b&c) published Feb. 13. Blue-green cloth, black endpapers. This issue has verso of title page blank (no copyright notice). Number of copies without copyright information unknown. Ref.a regards this as being simultaneous with 3c, but it would seem to us that it would more logically precede $1,000.

003c: SAVROLA Longmans, Green L 1900 [0] Blue-green cloth, black endpapers (issue with U.K. copyright notice on verso of title page) $900.

003d: SAVROLA (Colonial Edition) Longmans, Green L 1900 [0] 1,500 cc. Issued simultaneously with 003c $900.

003e: SAVROLA (First Illustrated Edition) George Newnes, Ltd. Strand, W.C. (1908) [0] Red and blue printed wraps. Published in May $350.

003f: SAVROLA Random House NY (1956) [1] "First printing/copyright 1956..." New short foreword by Churchill. Navy blue cloth and scarlet cloth (ref.b) $20/100

004a: LONDON TO LADYSMITH Longmans, Green L 1900 [0] 10,000 cc. Published May 15. Fawn pictorial cloth, black endpapers. Folding maps facing title, and pgs 366, 448; 32 pgs of ads on thinner paper, separately numbered $850.

004b: LONDON TO LADYSMITH Longmans, Green L 1900 [0] 500 cc. Published May 18. We have had a copy exactly the same as 004a but with "New Impression" added to title page, which we assume is this second printing $400.

004c: LONDON TO LADYSMITH Longmans, Green NY 1900 [0] 3,000 cc. Published June 16 $650.

004d: LONDON TO LADYSMITH Copp, Clark Toronto (1900) [] Smooth light brown cloth. Believe to be printed in the U.S. (Steven Temple 7/88) $250.

005a: IAN HAMILTON'S MARCH Longmans, Green L 1900 [0] 5,000 cc. Published October 12. Dark red cloth, black endpapers. Folding map tipped-in preceding 4 pages ads, then 32 page catalog on thinner paper, separately numbered $1,000.

005b: IAN HAMILTON'S MARCH Longmans, Green NY 1900 [0] 1,533 cc. Published December 1 $650.

006a: MR. WINSTON CHURCHILL ON THE EDUCATION BILL (no-publisher, no-place) 1902 [0] 8 page off-print reprinted from the

Lancashire Daily Post of November 11. (This is Woods first entry under 6) $1,500.

006b: MR. BRODRICK'S ARMY Arthur L. Humphreys L 1903 [0] 44 page, 8 3/8" x 5 1/2" pamphlet (Woods believes this to be the true first of 006c but, that it was not released. Identical text) $NVA

006c: MR. BRODRICK'S ARMY Arthur L. Humphreys L 1903 [0] Published in April. Publisher address as 187 Piccadilly, W. 8 13/16" x 6 3/8" pamphlet in dark red matt card cover, "Price One Shilling." (Richard Langworth in his article in *Antiquarian Bookman*, Jan. 16, 1989, mentions that a copy sold at auction for 10,000 pounds) $NVA

006d: MR. BRODRICK'S ARMY (Churchilliana Co. Sacramento 1977) [] (ref.b) $50.

007a: FREE TRADE LEAGUE. NORTH-WEST MANCHESTER DIVISION BRANCH Free Trade League Manchester 1904 [0] Pamphlet of speech given June 15. 20 pages plus covers $1,250.

008a: MR. WINSTON CHURCHILL ON THE ALIENS BILL Liberal Publications Department L 1904 [0] 2 pages. Reprinted from *The Liberal Magazine*, December 1904 $750.

009a: WHY I AM A FREE TRADER W.T. Stead L 1905 [0] Wraps. 24 pages plus cover $1,250.

010a: LORD RANDOLPH CHURCHILL Macmillan L 1906 [0] 2 vols. 8,000 cc. Plum cloth. Published January 2 $750.

010b: LORD RANDOLPH CHURCHILL Macmillan NY 1906 [] 2 vols. Published February 10 $600.

010c: LORD RANDOLPH CHURCHILL Macmillan L 1907 [1] 1 vol. 3,000 cc. Plum cloth. Published in May. "Second Edition...1907" (Ref.a has price of 7/6 while Any Amount of Books catalogued a copy in 1986 with price of 10s) $200.

010d: LORD RANDOLPH CHURCHILL Odhams Press L (1952) [0] Published February 5. Contains new introduction and Appendix V appears for first time. Red cloth $25/125

011a: FOR FREE TRADE Arthur L. Humphreys L 1906 [0] Dark red matt card cover. Published in April $1250.

011b: FOR FREE TRADE Churchilliana Co Sacramento 1977 [] $50.

012a: LIBERALISM AND SOCIALISM Scottish Liberal Assoc. Glasgow/Edinburgh 1906 [0] Wraps. 15(16) pages $1,000.

013a: TO THE ELECTORS OF NORTH-WEST MANCHESTER North-West Manchester Liberal Association 1906 [0] Wraps. 4 pages $850.

014a: NATIONAL DEMONSTRATIONS IN FAVOUR OF LAND AND HOUSING REFORM Liberal Publications Department L 1907 [0] Wraps. 20 pages $1,000.

015a: SPEECHES British Cotton Growing Association Manchester 1907 [0] 20 pages $1,000.

016a: FREE TRADE IN ITS BEARING ON INTERNATIONAL RELATIONS International Free Trade Congress L 1908 [0] 10 pages, plus cover $1,000.

017a: FOR LIBERALISM AND FREE TRADE John Leng Dundee 1908 [0] 32 pages $1,000.

018a: MY AFRICAN JOURNEY Hodder and Stoughton L 1908 [0] 12,500 cc Red pictorial cloth. Published in December. A later issue was issued without the illustration or lettering on front cover. Also "second binding in maroon cloth" (Bowie & Co. 8/92 but not in ref.a) $750.

018b: MY AFRICAN JOURNEY Hodder & Stoughton NY 1908 [] Few copies issued to protect copyright. Binding similiar to the later issue with plain vs. pictorial cover (Pepper & Stern 4/91) $2,000.

018c: MY AFRICAN JOURNEY Doubleday, Doran NY (1909) [0] Published on April 17. The only copy we've seen had a Doran tipped-in title page, blank on back, in later issue Hodder & Stoughton binding. Ref.a was incorrect in stating that Doubleday, Doran was the publisher as that firm didn't exist until the late 1920's. This issue is so scarce it would seem that it was not really "published" here $1,000.

019a: LIBERALISM AND SOCIALISM Liberal Publications Dept. L 1908 [0] 4 pages $850.

020a: BUDGET ISSUES Liberal Publications Dept. L 1909 [0] 16 pages $850.

021a: THE MENACE OF LAND MONOPOLY Free Trade and Land Values League Melbourne 1909 [0] 4 pages $850.

021b: THE MENACE OF LAND MONOPOLY Henry George Foundation Melbourne 1941 [0] 16 pages plus cover $500.

021c: ON HUMAN RIGHTS Henry George Foundation Melbourne 1942 [0] New title $400.

022a: LIBERALISM AND THE SOCIAL PROBLEM Hodder and Stoughton L 1909 [0] 5,000 cc in plum buckram. Published in November $1,000.

022b: LIBERALISM AND THE SOCIAL PROBLEM Hodder and Stoughton NY 1909 [] Few copies to protect copyright with tipped-in title page. Plum buckram lettered in gilt on spine (Pepper & Stern 4/91) $2,000.

022c: LIBERALISM AND THE SOCIAL PROBLEM Doubleday, Doran NY 1910 [ ] Published in February $750.

023a: TO THE ELECTORS OF DUNDEE John Leng Dundee 1909 [0] (Dated December 28, 1909 from the Board of Trade. Woods thinks may have been published in 1910) $750.

024a: THE PEOPLE'S RIGHTS Hodder and Stoughton L (1910) [0] Published January 14. Cherry red cloth, flecked with pink. Index at rear $1,000.

024b: THE PEOPLE'S RIGHTS Hodder and Stoughton L (1910) [0] Wraps. Issued simultaneously. First state with Index $600.

024c: THE PEOPLE'S RIGHTS Hodder and Stoughton L (1910) [0] Second issue with Index deleted and a second Appendix added $400.

024d: THE PEOPLE'S RIGHTS Taplinger NY (1971) [1] "First published in U.S. in 1971" $10/50

025a: PRISON AND PRISONERS A Speech in the House of Commons 20th July, 1910 Cassell and Company, Ltd. L 1910 [0] Grey wraps, printed in blue. Published August 6 $850.

026a: MR. CHURCHILL ON THE PEERS Liberal Publications Dept. L 1910 [0] 1(2) pages (from a letter to his constituents, November 14, 1910) $450.

027a: CHURCHILL SAID ... United Scotland Movement Glasgow 1911 [0] 2 pages $400.

028a: CHURCHILL SAID Scottish National Congress Glasgow 1911 [0] 2 pages (Note: both 027 and 028 quote from same speech but are entirely separate publications) $400.

029a: AN ADDRESS TO YOUNG LIBERALS National League of Young Liberals L 1912 [0] 12 pages (Young Liberals Pamphlet No. 7) $750.

030a: IRISH HOME RULE Liberal Publications Dept. L 1912 [0] 16 pages $750.

031a: MR. CHURCHILL'S MESSAGE TO ULSTER Home Rule Council L 1912 [0] 12 pages. Same speech as 030a $600.

032a: THE LIBERAL GOVERNMENT AND NAVAL POLICY Liberal Publications Dept. L 1912 [0] 24 pages $600.

033a: ON NAVAL ARMAMENTS American Assoc. For International Conciliation NY 1913 [0] 13(14) pages (an offprint from *The Times*) $600.

034a: THE TORIES AND THE ARMY Liberal Publications Dept L 1914 [0] 8 pages $500.

035a: NAVY ESTIMATES IN THE GREAT WAR Liberal Publications Dept. L 1915 [0] 20 pages $500.

036a: THE FIGHTING LINE Macmillan L 1916 [0] 32 pages $500.

037a: THE MUNITIONS MIRACLE National War Aims Committee L 1918 [0] 16 pages $500.

038a: THE RHINE ARMY Ministry of Information (H.M.S.O.) L 1919 [0] 8 pages $450.

039a: REASON AND REALITY Harrison and Sons L 1920 [0] 32 pages $450.

040a: THE POSITION ABROAD AND AT HOME (no-publ) L 1920 [0] 12 pages $400.

041a: ADDRESS H.M.S.O. L 1920 [0] 6 pages in wraps $400.

042a: DUNDEE PARLIAMENTARY ELECTION John Leng Dundee 1922 [0] 4 pages $400.

043a: INVITATION TO A POLITICAL MEETING Liberal Assoc Dundee 1922 [0] 8 pages $400.

044a: THE WORLD CRISIS - 1911-1914 Vol I Thornton Butter-worth Ltd L (1923) [1] 7,380 cc. Published April 10. Folding maps pages 304, 320, 376, 432 and 472. Errata slip tipped-in between p.(vi)-1 $75/250

044b: THE WORLD CRISIS - 1915 Vol I Scribners NY 1923 [1] "Published April 1923" (ref.b). This is the only U.S. edition mentioned in ref.a $60/200

044c: THE WORLD CRISIS - 1915 Vol II Thornton Butterworth Ltd L (1923) [1] 7,500 cc. Published October 30. Folding maps pages 144, 240, 328, two facing p.516 $75/250

044d: THE WORLD CRISIS - 1915 Vol II Scribners NY 1923 1923 [1] "Published April 1923" (ref.b) $60/200

044e: THE WORLD CRISIS - 1916-1918 Vol III (in 2 vols.) Thornton Butterworth Ltd L (1927) [1] Part 1: folding maps pages 82, 164, 206, two folding statistical tables with errata slip tipped-in, facing p.52; and

Part 2: Folding maps pgs 330, 368, 372, 374, 530 and 534.

7,523 cc of the pair published March 3 $125/300

044f: THE WORLD CRISIS - 1916-1918 Vol I (Vol III) Scribners NY 1927 [0] (ref.b) $50/150

044g: THE WORLD CRISIS - 1916-1918 Vol II (Vol IV) Scribners NY 1927 [0] (ref.b) $50/150

044h: THE WORLD CRISIS - THE AFTERMATH Vol IV Thornton Butterworth Ltd L (1929) [1] 7,500 cc. Published March 7. Folding maps pages 102, 230 276 and 438. Errata slip tipped-in between pages 10-11 $60/200

044i: THE WORLD CRISIS - THE AFTERMATH (Vol V) Scribners NY 1929 [0] (Ref.b) $40/125

044j: THE WORLD CRISIS - THE EASTERN FRONT Vol V Thornton Butterworth Ltd L (1931) [1] 5,150 cc. Published November 2.

Folding maps pages 98, 142, 156, 250, 256, 308, 324, 338, 346, 368 and one following the Index $75/200

044k: THE UNKNOWN WAR - THE EASTERN FRONT (Vol VI) Scribners NY 1931 [5] (ref.b) $40/125

The six London volumes together $750/2,500
The six American volumes together $600/2,000

044l: THE WORLD CRISIS 1911-1918 Thornton Butterworth Ltd L (1931) [0] 5,000 cc. Published February 26. One volume edition, abridged and revised with an additional chapter on "The Battle of the Marne" added $125/400

044m: THE WORLD CRISIS 1911-1918 Scribners NY 1931 [] Abridged and revised edition as above $100/300

044n: THE WORLD CRISIS The Sandhurst Edition Thornton Butterworth Ltd L (1933) [ ] 1,354 cc. Adds folding facsimile of a letter (facing p.426) $500.

045a: THE ALTERNATIVE TO SOCIALISM Harrison and Sons L 1924 [0] 16 pages $400.

046a: SHALL WE COMMIT SUICIDE? (Eilert Printing Co. NY) (back cover) 1924 [0] 11(12) pages. "Reprinted from Nash's *Pall Mall Magazine* of September 24, 1924." $400.

047a: ADDRESS Privately Printed L 1925 [0] 4 pages in wraps $400.

048a: CO-OPS AND INCOME TAX Conservative Party L 1927 [0] 3(4) pages $400.

049a: RINGING THE ALARM Anti-Socialist and Anti-Communist Union L 1929 [0] 12 pages $400.

050a: THE NAVY LEAGUE The Navy League L 1930 [0] 8 pages in wraps $400.

051a: PARLIAMENTARY GOVERNMENT AND THE ECONOMIC PROBLEM Clarendon Press Oxford 1930 [0] Bound in gray tinted laid paper, printed in green. 20 pages. Published July 11 $400.

052a: MY EARLY LIFE Thornton Butterworth Ltd L (1930) [1] 5,750 cc. (052a&b) Published October 20. Boxed list of 11 of Churchill's works on verso of half-title $300/1,250

052b: MY EARLY LIFE Thornton Butterworth Ltd L (1930) [1] Second issue adds 12th title *The World Crisis* $200/1,000

052c: A ROVING COMMISSION Scribners NY 1930 [5] New title Published October 31. Red cloth, covers and spine printed in gilt $75/350

052d: A ROVING COMMISSION Scribners NY 1939 [0] Introduction by Dorothy Thompson and a folding map facing p.352. Dark blue cloth, covers and spine printed in silver $40/150

053a: INDIA Thornton Butterworth Ltd L (1931) [1] Orange cloth. Published on May 27 $250/850

053b: INDIA Thornton Butterworth Ltd L (1931) [1] Orange wraps with price of 1/-net (Second printing in green wraps. No other difference) $450.

054a: THOUGHTS AND ADVENTURES Thornton Butterworth Ltd L (1932) [1] 4,000 cc. Published November 10. Sandy-brown cloth

$150/750

054b: AMID THESE STORMS Scribners NY 1932 [0] (Joel Sattler, Second Story Books.) No copy noted with Scribner "A" even though this was their normal designation on first editions after 1930 $100/400

055a: MARLBOROUGH: HIS LIFE AND TIMES 4 vols. George G. Harrap.

Vol. I: L (1933) [2] 155 sgd no. cc. (5 copies not for sale). Full orange morocco in slipcase with paper labels with number of the set. Folding map between pgs (16)-17. Also noted in black morocco (David Mayou 5/92).

Vol. II: L (1934) [2] 155 cc (5 copies not for sale). Binding as Vol. I but label of slipcase not numbered. 3 folding maps, sewn in between pgs 606-607, errata slip tipped-in facing p.434.

Vol. III: L (1936) [2] 155 cc (5 copies not for sale). Binding as Vol. I but label of slipcase not numbered.

Vol. IV: L (1938) [2] 155 cc (5 copies not for sale). Binding as Vol. I but label of slipcase not numbered

The set $7,500.

055b: MARLBOROUGH: HIS LIFE AND TIMES 4 vols. George G. Harrap Trade edition.

Vol. I: L(1933) [0] Plum buckram over bevelled boards. Folding map between pages 558-559, errata slip tipped-in between pgs (16)-17.

Vol. II: L (1934) [0] Binding as in Vol. I. 3 folding maps sewn in between pages 606-607, errata slip tipped-in facing p.434. Total of 15,000 copies in two impressions.

Vol. III: L (1936) [0] Binding as in Vol. I. 3 folding maps tipped-in between pages 556-557, errata slip tipped-in facing p.(18). 10,000 copies published Oct. 23.

Vol. IV: L (1938) [0] Binding as in Vol. I, but the color is much darker than preceding volumes. 10,000 copies published September 2.

The set $400/1,500

055c: MARLBOROUGH: HIS LIFE AND TIMES 6 vols. Scribners.

Vol. I and Vol. II (published as a set) NY 1933 [5] Deep green cloth, fore-edge lightly trimmed.

Vol. III and Vol. IV (published as a set) NY 1935 Binding as Vol. I. Folding maps (Vol. III) facing pages 98, 106 and 268; and (Vol. IV) pgs 40, 78, 106, 112 and three facing p.(256). The pair in a plain slipcase.

Vol. V NY 1937 Binding as Vol. I. Errata slip tipped-in between pgs (18)-19.

Vol. VI NY 1938 Binding as Vol. I. Folding maps facing p.166 and two facing p.656.

The 6 volume set $250/750

055d: MARLBOROUGH: HIS LIFE AND TIMES George G. Harrap L (1947) [1] New two-volume edition. Part I: folding maps facing pages 190, 484, 556, 564, 806 and 868; 3 folding maps facing p.900, folding facsimiles of letters, etc. facing pages 240, 382, 700, 838 and 855. Part II: folding maps facing pages 118, 380, (488) and 622; 3 folding maps facing pages 1040, folding facsimile of letter facing p.393 $100/300

056a: CHARLES IXth DUKE OF MARLBOROUGH Burns, Oates & Washbourne L (1934) [] Wraps. Tributes by Churchill and C.C. Martindale $300.

057a: THE GREAT WAR (George Newnes L 1933-34) First illustrated in 26 parts in illustrated wraps (Buddenbrooks 9/89) $650.

058a: INDIA: THE GREAT BETRAYAL The India Defence League L 1935 [0] 8 pages plus wrappers $350.

059a: A MESSAGE New Common Wealth Society L c.1935 [0] 4 pages (in the form of a postcard with a reply card attached) $250.

060a: THE TRUTH ABOUT HITLER Trustees for Freedom L 1936 [0] 11(12) pages plus yellow card wrappers $450.

061a: SPEECH The New Commonwealth L 1936 [0] 12 pages plus cream matt card wrappers. Speech given at a luncheon of the New Commonwealth $350.

062a: GREAT CONTEMPORARIES Thornton Butterworth Ltd L (1937) [1] 5,000 cc. Published October 4. Dark blue buckram, top edge stained blue $125/500

062b: GREAT CONTEMPORARIES Putnam NY 1937 [0] $40/200

062c: GREAT CONTEMPORARIES Thornton Butterworth Ltd L (1938) [1] "Revised Edition 1938." 5,000 cc. Includes 4 additional articles

$60/350

062d: GREAT CONTEMPORARIES Macmillan L 1943 [] Two articles about Trotsky and Roosevelt omitted for political reasons

$50/250

063a: HOMAGE TO KIPLING Rudyard Kipling Memorial Fund L 1937 [0] 12 pages

$350.

064a: COMMUNISM American Coalition Washington, D.C. (c. 1938) [] Broadside with an excerpt from *Great Contemporaries* (Glenn Horowitz #14) $300.

065a: ARMS AND THE COVENANT George G. Harrap L (1938) [0] Dark blue cloth, top edge stained blue. 3,381 cc. Published June 24 at 18s. First issue dustwrapper red on yellow

$175/850

065b: ARMS AND THE COVENANT George G. Harrap L (1938) [0] Second issue dustwrapper in blue $175/750

065c: ARMS AND COVENANT George G. Harrap L (1938) [0] 1,382 cc of first issue sheets were used in a "cheap" edition $100/500

065d: WHILE ENGLAND SLEPT Putnams NY 1938 [0] New title for U.S. edition. Blue cloth, top edge stained red. 5,000 cc published September 30 $50/250

066a: STEP BY STEP Thornton Butterworth Ltd. L (1939) [1] 7,500 cc. Green cloth. Published June 27 $150/750

066b: STEP BY STEP Putnam NY 1939 [0] 5,000 cc. Published August 25 $75/350

067a: U-BOAT WARFARE Ministry of Information L 1939 [0] 4 pages $300.

068a: THE WAR AT SEA Ministry of Information L 1939 [0] 4 pages $300.

069a: THE GLORIOUS BATTLE OF THE RIVER PLATE Ministry of Information L 1939 [0] 4 pages $300.

070a: ALLIES NOW IN THEIR STRIDE Ministry of Information L 1940 [0] 7(8) pages $300.

071a: THE STATE OF THE WAR Ministry of Information L 1940 [0] 4 pages $300.

072a: NAVY ESTIMATES Ministry of Information L 1940 [0] 7(8) pages $300.

073a: A STERNER WAR Ministry of Information L 1940 [0] 4 pages $300.

074a: THE WAR AT SEA Ministry of Information L 1940 [0] 8 pages $300.

075a: CONQUER WE SHALL Ministry of Information L 1940 [0] 4 pages $400.

076a: ADDRESS British Library of Information L 1940 [0] Speech delivered in House of Commons on June 4, 1940. 10(12) pages $300.

076b: ADDRESS British Library of Information NY 1940 [0] Priority unknown. Assume same number of pages as 076a $300.

076c: WINSTON SPENCER CHURCHILL SPEECH OF JUNE 4th, 1940 (no-publ) L.A. 1964 [] Bound in maroon morroco $300.

076d: A SPEECH Northern Educational Press Leeds 1972 [0] 10(12) pages plus card wrappers $300.

077a: SPEECH British Library of Information NY 1940 [0] Speech given by the Prime Minister in House of Commons on June 18, 1940. 8 pages $250.

078a: MESSAGE (M.O.I. or Ministry of Home Security?) L 1940 [0] 1(2) pages in the form of a letter from No. 10 Downing Street. Signed in facsimile (to Senior Officers of the Fighting and Civil Services) $250.

079a: SPEECH British Library of Information NY 1940 [0] 3 (4) pages. Speech broadcast July 14, 1940 $250.

080a: SPEECH British Library of Information NY 1940 [] 6 pages Speech delivered in House of Commons July 4, 1940 $250.

081a: A SPEECH Ministry of Information (L) 1940 [0] 16 pages, light blue matt card wrappers, printed in maroon. Speech given in the House of Commons on August 20, 1940. "Never in the field of human conflict was so much owed by so many to so few." Last page has "The Baynard Press." Also noted in light tan wraps printed in maroon $500.

082a: BRITAIN'S STRENGTH British Library of Information NY 1940 [0] 8 pages. Speech in the House of Commons on August 20, 1940 "Never in the field of human conflict was so much owed by so many to so few" $600.

083a: SPEECH TO THE PEOPLE OF FRANCE British Library of Information NY 1940 [0] 3(4) pages. Broadcast October 21, 1940 $150.

084a: WAR PROBLEMS FACING BRITAIN British Library of Information NY 1940 [0] 8 pages. Speech in House of Commons on November 5, 1940 $175.

085a: SPEECH TO THE ITALIAN PEOPLE British Library of Information NY 1940 [0] 7(8) pages. Broadcast December 23, 1940 $150.

086a: DO NOT DESPAIR Ministry of Information? L 1940 [0] 1(2) pages in the form of a postcard $100.

087a: ADDRESSES DELIVERED IN THE YEAR 1940 TO THE PEOPLE OF GREAT BRITAIN (Grabhorn Press) SF 1940 [2] 250 cc. Folio (ref.b) $450.

088a: BROADCAST ADDRESS TO THE PEOPLE OF GREAT BRITAIN (Grabhorn Press) SF 1941 [2] 250 cc (ref.b) $350.

089a: BLENHEIM George G. Harrap L (1941) [1] Red and black wraps. Published in February for the British Publishers Guild $175.

090a: SPEECH British Library of Information L 1941 [0] 3(4) pages in wraps. Speech by the Prime Minister to the Pilgrims $175.

091a: INTO BATTLE Cassell L (1941) [1] Light blue cloth (Woods notes there were perhaps 30,000 published but production records destroyed). First state lacks leaf 128 a/b with the speech "War With Germany" delivered Sept 3, 1939. First volume of *War Speeches* $100/250

091b: INTO BATTLE Cassell L (1941) [1] Contains leaf tipped-in in correct chronological order $50/200

091c: BLOOD, SWEAT, AND TEARS McClelland & Steward Toronto (1941) [0] 448 pages. Does not have the speech "War With Germany" which was tipped into the 2nd issue of the U.K. edition and also does not include January 1941 speech in the U.S. edition. Printed in Canada. We assume that this preceded the U.S. edition as it seems to be printed from the first state of the English edition (Steven Temple 5/92) $35/175

091d: BLOOD, SWEAT, AND TEARS McClelland & Steward Toronto (1941) [0] Presumed second issue with 525 pages with 3 speeches "The War Situation," "The Italian People" and "Give Us The Tools" added after p.488 (pages 505-520 tipped-in). (Steven Temple 5/92) $30/150

091e: BLOOD, SWEAT, AND TEARS Putnams NY (1941) [0] 50,000 cc Published April 14. Adds speech (of January 9, 1941) not in UK edition. Blue cloth, top edge stained red. (There was a Book-of-the-Month Club edition of this title. It does not have a price on the dustwrapper flap. It is in red cloth with top edge blue) $40/175

092a: SPEECH British Library of information NY 1941 [0] Broadcast February 9. 10(12) pages $175.

092b: SPEECH (Universal Life Winnipeg, Canada 1941) [0] Small pamphlet (about 3 1/2" x 6"). "Put Your Confidence in Us." Also contains Canadian Prime Minister King's "There is only one way to meet total war ..." broadcast Feb. 2. May precede 088a (ref.b) $175.

093a: SPEECH British Library of Information NY 1941 [0] Speech given to the Pilgrim Society on March 18. 3(4) pages in wraps $175.

094a: BEATING THE INVADER Ministry of Information in Cooperation with the War Office and Ministry of Home Security (L 1941) [0] Single leaf, printed on both sides. (There is a later issue, overprinted in red in the top left-hand corner, regarding the evacuation of invaded areas. Both issues dated 5/41) $400.

095a: SPEECH British Library of Information NY 1941 [0] Broadcast April 27. 7(8) pages $175.

096a: BROADCAST British Library of Information NY 1941 [0] Broadcast to the Polish people, May 3. 2 pages $150.

097a: ADDRESSES OF WINSTON CHURCHILL AND OTHERS AT NINETY-FIRST ANNUAL COMMENCEMENT OF THE UNIVER-SITY OF ROCHESTER Univ. of Rochester Rochester 1941 [1] Wraps (Pepper & Stern 5/92) $450.

098a: THE WAR IN THE MIDDLE EAST Ministry of Information L 1941 [0] Speech in the debate in the House of Commons, June 10. Printed in parallel texts (English and Chinese). 8 pages $250.

099a: FREEDOM'S CAUSE British Library of Information NY 1941 [0] Speech given on June 12. Together with Text of the Allied Resolution. 3(4) pages $200.

100a: SPEECH British Library of Information NY 1941 [0] Broadcast June 22. 4 pages $175.

101a: STATEMENT British Library of Information NY 1941 [0] Given to the House of Commons, June 29. 15(16) pages $175.

102a: THE ATLANTIC MEETING Ministry of Information L 1941 [0] Extracts from broadcast of August 24. 8 pages plus card wraps $250.

103a: THE ASSURANCE OF VICTORY Ministry of Information L 1941 [0] Broadcast following his meeting with President Roosevelt. Printed in parallel texts (English and Chinese). 4 pages $200.

104a: SPEECH British Library of Information NY (1941) [0] Broadcast of August 24. 7(8) pages $175.

105a: THE EUROPEAN WAR REVIEWED Ministry of Information L 1941 [0] Statement to the House of Commons, Sept. 9. Printed in parallel texts (English and Chinese). 6 pages $200.

106a: STATEMENT British Library of Information NY 1941 [0] Given to the House of Commons, September 30. 7(8) pages $175.

107a: SPEECH British Library of Information NY 1941 [0] Given at the Mansion House, November 10. 4 pages (also published in 3 leaflets by the Political Warfare Exec., 1941) $175.

108a: SPEECH British Library of Information NY 1941 [0] Given in the House of Commons, November 12. 8 pages $175.

109a: ADDRESS British Library of Information NY 1941 [0] Given December 2. 10(12) pages $175.

110a: SPEECH British Library of Information NY 1941 [0] Dec. 8th broadcast on the Far East War. 3(4) pages $175.

111a: SPEECH British Library of Information NY 1941 [0] Given to the House of Commons, December 11. 6(8) pages $175.

112a: ADDRESS British Library of Information NY 1941 [0] Given before the U.S. Congress, Dec. 26. 6(8) pages (Also printed by the Political Warfare Exec. in 1942) $250.

112b: ADDRESS ... BEFORE THE SENATE ... U.S. Government Printing Office Washington, D.C. 1941 [ ] Senate Document No. 153. 9(12) pages $250.

112c: ADDRESS Overbrook Press Stanford, Conn. 1942 [2] 1,000 cc. Red buckram with paper label on front board. Published January 4 $250.

112d: THE ADDRESS TO CONGRESS John Allen and Sons Oxford (1942) [0] 16 pages plus cream card wraps (some copies bound in dark brown suede wraps) $200.

THE MENACE OF LAND POLICY and ON HUMAN RIGHTS see entry 021.

113a: SPEECH British Library of Information NY 1942 [0] Given to the Canadian Parliament, December 30. 6(8) pages $175.

113b: CANADA AND THE WAR Director of Public Information Ottawa 1942 [0] 9(10) pages $175.

114a: WHAT KIND OF PEOPLE DO THEY THINK WE ARE? Daily Telegraph and

Morning Post L (1942) [0] Contains 2 speechs (110a and 111a). 8 pages $175.

115a: ADDRESS Bermuda Press Hamilton 1942 [0] Given to the House Assembly, January 15. 4 pages $150.

116a: ADDRESS British Library of Information NY 1942 [0] Broadcast of February 15. 6(8) pages $150

117a: SPEECH British Library of Information NY 1942 [0] Broadcast of May 10. 8 pages $150.

118a: THE UNRELENTING STRUGGLE Cassell L (1942) [1] 10,900 cc. Published September 24. Light blue cloth (*War Speeches*) $35/175

118b: THE UNRELENTING STRUGGLE Little, Brown B (1942) [1] 15,000 cc. Published October 21 $25/125

119a: SPEECH British Library of Information NY 1942 [0] Broadcast given November 29. 7(8) pages $150.

120a: A FOUR YEARS PLAN FOR BRITAIN Times Publishing Co. L 1943 [0] Speech broadcast March 22. 8 pages $250.

121a: ADDRESS U.S. Government Printing Office Washington, D.C. 1943 [0] Given to Joint Session of Congress, May 19. 10(12) pages. Also noted on legal size pulpy paper. 18 pages headed "British Information Service, Release No. A-24" $250.

121b: AN ADDRESS BY WINSTON S. CHURCHILL PRIME MINISTER OF GREAT BRITAIN Overbrook Press Stamford, Conn.

1943 [2] 600 cc. Published in September. Black paper-covered boards and red paper label $300.

121c: OUR CONTINENT REDEEMED Daily Telegraph L 1943 [0] 8 pages $150.

122a: THE END OF THE BEGINNING Cassell L (1943) [1] 16,000 cc. Published July 29. Light blue cloth (*War Speeches*) $30/150

122b: THE END OF THE BEGINNING Little, Brown B (1943) [1] 6,000 cc. Published August 19. $25/125

123a: THE LAST DAYS OF MARLBOROUGH Times Publ Co L 1943 [0] A broadsheet. 2 pages $175.

124a: LIBERALS' PART IN REBUILDING BRITAIN Liberal Publications Department L 1943 [0] Speech at the National Liberal Club. 4 pages $150.

124b: MR. CHURCHILL PAYS TRIBUTE TO THE LIBERAL PARTY Liberal Publications Department L 1943 [0] Excerpts from 121a 1(2) pages $100.

125a: THE PRIME MINISTER'S SPEECH ON THE HOUSE OF COMMONS REBUILDING, 28 OCTOBER 1943 The University Press Cambridge 1944 [0] 12 pages plus card wraps $250.

126a: PRIME MINISTER : A SELECTION FROM SPEECHES British Information Service NY 1943 [1] "Published December 1943." Stapled wraps. 52 pages illustrated with photographs (Glenn Horowitz #16) $100.

127a: A SPEECH Kingsport Press Tennessee 1943 [2] ltd to 400 cc. Blue wraps with printed label on front cover. Speech given before Parliament of England, November 11. 36 pages $350.

128a: THE EVE OF ACTION W. & G. Baird (Belfast Telegraph), Belfast 1944 [0] Speech to House of Commons, Feb. 22. 20 pages plus red card wraps $250.

129a: FOREIGN POLICY: THE PRIME MINISTER'S REVIEW Times Publishing Co L 1944 [0] 12 pages $175.

130a: THE TIDE OF TRIUMPH British Legation Press Department Berne 1944 [0] Speech in the House of Commons, September 28. 24 pages $200.

131a: ONWARDS TO VICTORY Cassell L 1944 [1] 15,000 cc. Published June 29. Light blue cloth (*War Speeches*) $30/125

131b: ONWARDS TO VICTORY Little, Brown B (1944) [1] 9,000 cc. Published July 13 $25/100

132a: COUNTRY BEFORE PARTY S.H. Benson L 1945 [ ] From a speech on March 15. 2 pages (3 variations at foot of p.2, "Vote Conservative", "Vote Unionist" or "Vote National") $100.

133a: OUR LAND OUR FOOD: MR. CHURCHILL'S DECLARATION S.H. Benson L 1945 [0] From speech to Conservative Party Congress, March 25. 4 pages $125.

133b: PREMIER'S PLEDGE TO FARMERS AND FARM WORKERS Conservative Party L 1945 [0] A shorter version of 128a. 2 pages $100.

134a: A TIMELY DELIVERANCE W. & G. Baird (Belfast Telegraph) Belfast 1945 [0] Broadcast to the Nation, May 13. 10 pages $200.

134b: VICTORY IN EUROPE British Legation Press Department Berne 1945 [0] Adds speech by George VI $150.

135a: MR. CHURCHILL'S DECLARATION OF POLICY TO THE ELECTORS S.H. Benson L 1945 [0] General Election 1945. 16 pages $150.

136a: "HERE IS THE COURSE WE STEER" Conservative Party L 1945 [0] 12 pages plus pictorial paper wraps $200.

137a: THE DAWN OF LIBERATION Cassell L (1945) [1] 14,250 cc. Published July 26. Light blue cloth *(War Speeches)* $25/125

137b: THE DAWN OF LIBERATION Little, Brown B (1945) [1] 3,500 cc. Published August 12 $20/100

137c: THE DAWN OF LIBERATION McClelland & Steward T 1945 [ ] (ref.b) $15/75

138a: A TRUE PEOPLE'S PARTY Conservative Party L 1945 [0] 12 pages $175.

139a: SUBALTERN'S READING Times Publishing Co. L 1945 [0] An extract from *My Early Life*. 2 pages $125.

140a: WE FIGHT FOR THE PEOPLE Conservative Party L 1945 [0] 16 pages $200.

141a: THE DAY WILL COME Conservative Party L 1946 [0] A speech at Edinburgh, April 29. 14(16) pages $200.

142a: VICTORY Cassell L (1946) [1] 38,000 cc. Published June 27. Light blue cloth (*War Speeches*) $15/75

142b: VICTORY Little, Brown B 1946 [ ] 5,000 cc. Published August 7 $12/60

143a: WAR SPEECHES 1940-1945 Cassell L (1946) [1] 20,000 cc. Published in July. Bound in white card wraps, printed black on a blue background $300.

144a: SECRET SESSION SPEECHES Cassell L (1946) [1] 48,500 cc. Published September 26. Light blue cloth (some copies simultaneously issued in full blue morocco) $25/100

144b: SECRET SESSION SPEECHES Simon and Schuster NY 1946 [0] 5,910 cc. Published in September. $15/75

145a: SPEECH Conservative Party L 1946 [ ] Speech given at Winter Gardes, Blackpool on October 5. 16 pages $150.

146a: UNITED EUROPE United Europe Movement L 1946 [0] A leaflet in the form of a letter from Churchill. 4 pages $200.

147a: A UNITED EUROPE: ONE WAY TO STOP A NEW WAR United Europe Movement L 1947 [0] 7(8) pages $200.

148a: MAXIMS AND REFLECTIONS Eyre and Spottiswoode L (1947) [ ] Arranged and introduction by Colin Coote $15/75

148b: MAXIMS AND REFLECTIONS Houghton Mifflin B 1949 [1] $12/60

149a: THE PEOPLE'S PERIL - AND THE WAY OUT Conservative Party L 1947 [0]

Speech in the House of Commons on March 12. 16 pages $175.

150a: "TRUST THE PEOPLE" Conservative Party L 1947 [0] A speech at Ayr, May 16. 16 pages $150.

151a: SET THE PEOPLE FREE Conservative Party L 1948 [0] A broadcast talk, February 14. 8 pages plus card wraps $150.

152a: "THIS COUNTRY NEEDS A NEW PARLIAMENT" Conservative Party L 1948 [0] Speech given April 21. 12 pages plus paper wraps $175.

153a: THE GRAND DESIGN United Europe Movement L 1948 [0] A speech at the Congress of Europe, May 7. 12 pages including cover $200.

154a: THE SECOND WORLD WAR 6 volumes Hougton Mifflin. All volumes preceded the comparable British editions (from four to ten months earlier); and did not incorporate all of Churchill's corrections or include the folding maps which were in the Cassell edition:

Vol. I: THE GATHERING STORM Boston 1948 [0] 75,000 cc. Published June 21. Red cloth, top edge yellow-brown, red and yellow imitation head and foot bands (a second state of this edition appeared without head and foot bands and without top edge stained).

Vol. II: THEIR FINEST HOUR Boston 1949 [0] 35,000 cc. Published March 29. Red cloth, top edge yellow-brown, stars on title page inverted in this volume only.

(Woods comments: "It is noticeable that the print-run of this volume is at least half that of any of the others. It may possibly be of significance that this is also the only volume in which Americans could not read about themselves.")

Vol. III: THE GRAND ALLIANCE Boston 1950 [0] 61,000 cc. Published April 24. Red cloth, top edge yellow-brown. (Stars inverted on dw of this volume only per Jeff Klaess.)

Vol. IV: THE HINGE OF FATE Boston 1950 [0] 70,000 cc. Published November 27. Red cloth, top edge yellow-brown.

Vol. V: CLOSING THE RING Boston 1951 [0] 60,000 cc. Published November 23. Red cloth, top edge yellow-brown.

Vol. VI: TRIUMPH AND TRADGEDY Boston 1953 [0] 60,000 cc. Published November 30. Red cloth, top edge yellow-brown.

The 6 volume set $100/350

(Note: leather presentation binding offered by James Cummins 2/92 $4,000)

154b: THE SECOND WORLD WAR 6 volumes Cassell & Co. Ltd.

Vol. I: THE GATHERING STORM L (1948) [1] 221,000 cc. Published October 4. Black cloth, top edge red. Un-numbered errata page and Corrigenda page tipped-in facing p.610, folding map facing p.496. This volume set in small type than all succeeding volumes.

(Woods notes that there were 100 sets bound in full black pebble-grain morocco for presentation, but does not clarify whether any of the other volumes were so bound. Vols I & II in dark blue morocco offered by Bertram Rota 7/90.)

Vol. II: THEIR FINEST HOUR L (1949) [1] 270,000 cc. Published June 27. Binding as Vol. I. Folding maps facing pgs 78, 174 and 462.

Vol. III: THE GRAND ALLIANCE L (1950) [1] 300,000 cc. Published July 20. Binding as Vol. I. Folding maps facing pgs 302, 366 and 526.

Vol. IV: THE HINGE OF FATE L (1951) [1] 275,000 cc. Published August 3. Binding as Vol. I. Folding maps facing pgs 174, 214 and 686. Folding facsimile of letter facing p.654.

Vol. V: CLOSING THE RING L (1952) [1] 275,000 cc. Published September 3. Binding as Vol. I. Folding maps facing pgs 494, 526 and 558. Folding facsimile of minute facing p.78.

Vol. VI: TRIUMPH AND TRAGEDY L (1954)[1] 200,000 cc. Published April 26. Binding as Vol. I. Folding maps facing pgs 22, 158, 160, 162, 246, 438, 454, 526, 542, 566 and (678).

The 6 volume set $150/450

154c: THE SECOND WORLD WAR Cassell L (1959) [1] 25,000 cc. Published February 5. Abridged one volume edition with Epilogue on the years 1945 to 1957 $35/125

154d: MEMOIRS OF THE SECOND WORLD WAR Houghton Mifflin B 1959 [1] (ref.b) $30/100

154e: THE SECOND WORLD WAR Time Ch/NY 1959 [0] Two vols in slipcase, with 10" recording of excerpts from Churchill's speechs (in pocket between the volumes). "By Winston Churchill and the Editors of *Life*" (Although the recording is not by Churchill) $50/100

155a: THE SINEWS OF PEACE Cassell L (1948) [1] 10,000 cc. Published August 19. Post-War speeches, edited by Randolph S. Churchill. Orange-brown cloth $15/75

155b: THE SINEWS OF PEACE Houghton Mifflin B 1949 [0] 3,000 cc $12/60

155c: THE SINEWS OF PEACE : A SPEECH Halcyon-Commonwealth Foundation NY 1965 [] Wraps. First separate edition with a preface by Harry S. Truman $50.

156a: PAINTING AS A PASTIME Odhams Press / Ernest Benn L (1948) [1] 25,000 cc. Published in December. Fawn cloth $25/100

156b: PAINTING AS A PASTIME Whittlesey House NY 1950 [0] 20,000 cc. from sheets of 3rd printing of U.K. edition. Published February 10, 1950 $12/60

157a: THE RIGHT ROAD FOR BRITAIN Conservative Party L 1949 [0] Speech at Wolverhampton on July 23. 19(20) pages plus card wrappers $175.

158a: CHURCHILL'S VISIT TO NORWAY : SPEECHES ... TOGETHER WITH ADDRESSES ... (others) Cappelens Oslo 1949 [] Pictorial wraps. Also noted in photographic wraps with "School Edition" on front (Glenn Horowitz #16) $100.

159a: EUROPE UNITE - SPEECHES 1947 AND 1948 Cassell L (1950) [1] 12,000 cc. Published February 3. Edited by Randolph S. Churchill. Dark green cloth $25/100

159b: EUROPE UNITE - SPEECHES 1947 AND 1949 Houghton Mifflin B 1950 [0] 2,500 cc from English sheets $25/100

160a: MR. CHURCHILL'S MESSAGE TO YOU Conservative Party L 1950 [0] 4 pages $125.

160b: MR. CHURCHILL'S MESSAGE TO YOU Conservative Party L 1950 [0] 1(2) pages $125.

161a: ELECTION ADDRESS Woodford Divisional Conservation Assoc. Woodford Green 1950 [0] 4 pages $100.

162a: AN ADDRESS Overbrook Press Stamford, Conn. 1950 [2] 1,000 cc only. Speech given in the House of Commons November 30, 1950. Printed for members of 82nd Congress $200.

163a: BROADCAST APPEAL ON BEHALF OF THE ROYAL AIR FORCE BENEVOLENT FUND R.A.F. Benevolent Fund L 1951 [0] 2 page $75.

164a: IN THE BALANCE - SPEECHES 1949 AND 1950 Cassell L (1951) [1] 8,200 cc (2,000 used for 160b). Published October 18. Edited by Randolph S. Churchill. Dark blue cloth. First issue has first gathering bound so that last leaf of contents appears prior to half title (Glenn Horowitz #16) $50/100

164b: IN THE BALANCE - SPEECHES 1949 AND 1950 Cassell L (1951) [1] Second issue. Corrected. $15/60

164c: IN THE BALANCE - SPEECHES 1949 AND 1950 Houghton Mifflin B 1952 [0] 2,000 cc from English sheets $15/75

165a: ELECTION SPEECH Woodford Divisional Conservative Association Woodford Green 1951 [0] 4 pages $100.

166a: THANKS TO THE BUNGLERS Charles Knight (Election Agent) Orpington (Kent) 1951 [0] 2 pgs $75.

167a: THE MANIFESTO OF THE CONSERVATIVE AND UNIONIST PARTY Conservative Party L 1951 [0] 7(8) pages plus paper wraps. Signed in facsimile at end of text $100.

168a: THE STATE OF THE NATION Conservative Party L 1952 [0] Broadcast of December 22. 8 pages plus paper wraps $100.

169a: MR. CHURCHILL'S SPEECH TO THE CONGRESS OF THE UNITED STATES OF AMERICA, January 17th, 1952 H.M.S.O. L 1952 [0] 8 pages $125.

170a: KING GEORGE VI Times Publishing Co L 1952 [0] Broadcast of February 7. 4 pages (issued unbound) $100.

170b: KING GEORGE VI Achille J. St. Onge Worcester (Mass) 1952 [2] ltd to 750 cc. Purple Nigerian goatskin, all edges gilt. Approximately 100 copies of total edition bound in red Nigerian Goatskin $300.

171a: THE WAR SPEECHES Cassell L (1952) [1] (Definitive edition) Compiled by Charles Eade. 3 volumes. 4,700 sets. Published September 3. (Woods notes that the three volumes were intended to be published separately, but printing difficulties delayed Vol. I for a year) (assume no slipcase) $300.

171b: THE WAR SPEECHES Houghton Mifflin B 1953 [0] (Definitive Edition) Compiled by Charles Eade. 3 volumes. 500 sets from English sheets. In slipcase (George Houle 10/88) $300/350

172a: STEMMING THE TIDE Speeches 1951 and 1952 Cassell L (1953) [1] 5,500 cc. Published June 25. Edited by Randolph S. Churchill $25/100

172b: STEMMING THE TIDE Speeches 1951 and 1952 Houghton Mifflin B 1954 [0] 1,850 cc from the English sheets $25/100

173a: A CHURCHILL READER. Houghton Mifflin B 1954 [] The Wit & Wisdom with intro by Colin R. Coote (Glenn Horowitz #16) $15/75

174a: DEFENCE THROUGH DETERRENTS Regional Information Office Singapore 1955 [0] Speech in House of Commons on March 1. 16 pages $125.

175a: ELECTION ADDRESS Woodford Divisional Conservative Assoc. Woodford Green 1955 [0] 4 pages $100.

176a: THE WISDOM OF WINSTON CHURCHILL ... 1900-1955 George Allen & Unwin L 1956 [] $15/60

177a: I SUPPORT Conservative Central Office L 1956 [0] 1(2) pages $75.

178a: A HISTORY OF THE ENGLISH-SPEAKING PEOPLES 4 vols.

Vol. I: THE BIRTH OF BRITAIN Cassell L (1956) [1] 130,000 cc. Published April 23. Red buckram, top edge red.

A HISTORY OF THE ENGLISH-SPEAKING PEOPLES Vol. I: THE BIRTH OF BRITAIN Dodd, Mead NY 1956 [1] Published simultaneously with 168a. Did not see variant but assume there is one like the other volumes (see below).

A HISTORY OF THE ENGLISH-SPEAKING PEOPLES Vol. II: THE NEW WORLD Cassell L (1956) [1] 150,000 cc. Published November 26. Binding as in Vol. I.

A HISTORY OF THE ENGLISH-SPEAKING PEOPLES Vol. II: THE NEW WORLD Dodd, Mead NY 1956 [0] Published December 3. Noted in two different bindings: (1) light to medium red panels on spine, bulking 42mm; and (2) dark red panels, bulking 35mm. Assume the first is first issue/state because the front dustwrapper flap did not have "BOMC" over printed, while the second did have BOMC printed on dustwrapper. Otherwise, no difference in dustwrappers. Both were priced.

A HISTORY OF THE ENGLISH-SPEAKING PEOPLES Vol. III: THE AGE OF REVOLUTION Cassell L (1957) [1] 150,000 cc. Published October 14. Binding as in Vol. I.

A HISTORY OF THE ENGLISH-SPEAKING PEOPLES Vol. III: THE AGE OF REVOLUTION Dodd, Mead NY 1957 [1] Published September 23 (if this publication date is correct, than this precedes the U.K. edition). See Vol. II above. These bulked 42mm vs 33mm.

A HISTORY OF THE ENGLISH-SPEAKING PEOPLES Vol. IV: THE GREAT DEMOCRACIES Cassell L (1958) [1] 150,000 cc. Published March 14. Binding as in Vol. I

A HISTORY OF THE ENGLISH-SPEAKING PEOPLES Vol. IV: THE GREAT DEMOCRACIES Dodd, Mead NY 1958 [1] See Vol. II above. These bulked 45mm vs 38mm.

The 4 UK volumes	$100/400
The 4 US volumes	$75/300

Note: There was an illustrated edition published simultaneously on a subscription basis, by The Educational Book Company Ltd (8 guineas the set); a 12 volume "Blenheim" edition issued by Cassell, 1965 and 1966; Dodd Mead, "Presentation Edition" (on copyright page) in black and gray cloth in dustwrappers (Glenn Horowitz #16); and a set of Cassell in publisher's leather presentation bindings (James Cummins 2/92).

179a: CATALOG OF AN EXHIBITION OF PAINTINGS BY RT. HON. SIR WINSTON CHURCHILL (Hallmark Cards, Kansas City, Mo.) 1958 [0] With Foreword by Dwight Eisenhower. Hardcover issued in tissue wraps (Joel Sattler, Second Story Books) $75

179b: CATALOG OF AN EXHIBITION OF PAINTINGS BY... (Hallmark Cards, Kansas City, Mo.) 1958 [] white wraps $35.

180a: ELECTION ADDRESS Woodford Divisional Conservative Association Woodford October, 1959 [ ] 4 pages $75.

181a: PAINTINGS BY THE RT. HON. SIR WINSTON CHURCHILL Royal Academy of Arts L 1959 [] Wraps (Dalian #49) $75.

182a: THE AMERICAN CIVIL WAR Cassell L (1961) [1] 10,000 cc Published March 23. "This Edition First Published 1961." From Vol.

IV of *A History of The English-Speaking Peoples.* Adds Civil War photographs $30/125

183a: LETTER TO ANTHONY WEDGWOOD BENN H.E. Rogers Briston 1961 [0] 10,000 cc. 1(2) pages $60.

184a: THE UNWRITTEN ALLIANCE Speeches 1953 to 1959 Cassell L (1961) [0] 5,000 cc. Published April 27 $25/100

185a: FRONTIERS AND WARS (Eyre & Spottiswoode L 1962) [] A condensation of Churchill's first four books (Glenn Horowitz #16) $15/75

185b: FRONTIERS AND WARS Harcourt Brace NY (1962) [] A condensation of Churchill's first four books (Glenn Horowitz #16) $12/60

186a: THE ISLAND RACE Cassell L (1964) [0] 42,500 cc. Published November 23. Abridged from *A History of The English-Speaking Peoples* $25/100

186b: THE ISLAND RACE Dodd, Mead NY 1964 [ ] 7,500 cc from the English sheets. Published simultaneously $15/75

187a: GREAT DESTINY Putnam NY (1965) [1] "Sixty Years of Memorable Events... in His Own Words." Edited by F.W. Heath (ref.b) $20/75

188a: CHURCHILL HIS PAINTINGS Hamish Hamilton L (1967) [0] Catalog compiled by David Coombs, Foreword by Lady Spencer Churchill (ref.b) $15/75

189a: YOUNG WINSTON'S WARS Leo Cooper Ltd. L (1972) [0] 5,000 cc. Published

July 20. Edited by Frederick Woods. Blue cloth $15/75

189b: YOUNG WINSTON'S WARS Viking NY (1972) [1] "Published in 1972 by Viking" (actually published 3/30/73 at $8.95) $12/60

190a: YOUNG WINSTON Ballantine NY 1972 [] Wraps. Screenplay by Carl Foreman $30.

191a: COLLECTED WORKS Library of Imperial History L (1973-1976) [2] 3,000 no. cc (1,000 for American market were planned). Centenary Limited Edition. Edited by Frederick Woods, preface by Clementine Churchill. Each bound in full white vellum and in separate green leatherette slipcases. 38 volumes (Collected Works - 34 volumes plus 4 volumes of the Collected Essays). According to Richard Langworth's article in the January 16, 1989 issue of *The Antiquarian Bookman*, there were only about 2,000 sets of sheets printed, of which about 1,750 sets were bound and numbered as above. There are 20 sets bound in full red morocco and apparently one can order a set in morocco or in the original binding and slipcase. The original price in 1973 was $2,500. but it was raised to $3,000 $6,000.

192a: WINSTON S. CHURCHILL : THE COMPLETE SPEECHES 1897-1963 Chelsea House/Bowker L/NY 1974 [] 8 volumes (Glenn Horowitz #16) $400.

193a: THE DREAM Churchill Foundation (L, NY, Australia, Canada, NZ 1987) [2] 500 cc. Issued without dustwrapper $125.

JAMES CLAVELL

Clavell was born in England in 1924. When he was 17 years old he went into the Royal Artillery as a Captain. He was captured by the Japanese in Java and spent the last three years of the war in the Changi Camp in Singapore, where only 10,000 of the 150,000 prisoners survived. This experience was the basis for his first book. In the 1950's he was a writer in Hollywood, and a very successful one, which led to his writing the screenplay, producing and directing *To Sir, With Love*. He made it for $625,000 and it grossed over $25,000,000. His books haven't done badly either.

We thank Atheneum, Delacorte and Little, Brown for providing the quantitles shown.

REFERENCE:

(a) Inventory.

(b) CUMULATIVE BOOK INDEX.

001a: KING RAT Little, Brown Boston (1962) [1] 7,500 cc $60/300

001b: KING RAT Michael Joseph London (1963) [] Uncorrected proof in blue wraps $150.

001c: KING RAT Michael Joseph London (1963) [1] $25/125

002a: TAI-PAN: A NOVEL OF HONG KONG Atheneum NY 1966 [1] Advance reading copy bound in dustwrapper (Reese #40) $175.

002b: TAI-PAN: A NOVEL OF HONG KONG Atheneum NY 1966 [1] 25,000 cc $25/125

002c: TAI-PAN: A NOVEL OF HONG KONG Michael Joseph London 1966 [] (ref.b) $15/75

003a: SHOGUN: A NOVEL OF JAPAN Atheneum NY 1975 [] Uncorrected proof in two volumes in plain wraps with labels on front and spines (Antic Hay 12/91) $200.

003b: SHOGUN: A NOVEL OF JAPAN Atheneum NY 1975 [1] 50,000 cc $15/75

003c: SHOGUN: A NOVEL OF JAPAN Hodder & Stoughton London 1975 [ ] Wraps (ref.b) $40.

004a: NOBLE HOUSE: A NOVEL OF CONTEMPORARY HONG KONG Delacorte NY (1980) [1] Manuscript proof pages in red 3-ring binder with label of "Localmedia" and title and author on front. According to publicity department there were 20 copies in this format for review: 4 were xeroxed on one side of paper only and 16 on both sides. Indicated an edition of 250,000 copies to be published 4/30/81) $250.

004b: NOBLE HOUSE: A NOVEL OF CONTEMPORARY HONG KONG Delacorte NY (1980) [2] 500 sgd no. cc. Issued without dustwrapper in slipcase $60/125

004c: NOBLE HOUSE: A NOVEL OF CONTEMPORARY HONG KONG Delacorte NY (1980) [1] 247,000 cc. Also a "Complimentary Edition" in red cloth (Heritage Bookshop), "6456" on front dustwrapper flap, "0481" on back flap. These numbers also appear on the priced ($19.95) dustwrapper. Also noted with "Special Edition." Also a variant in black cloth with numbers and no price (Steven Temple) $10/40

004d: NOBLE HOUSE Hodder & Stoughton London 1981 [] ref.b $10/40

005a: THE MAKING OF JAMES CLAVELL'S SHOGUN Delta/Dell NY 1980 [ ] Wraps (ref.b) $35.

005b: THE MAKING OF JAMES CLAVELL'S SHOGUN Cornet Books London 1981 [] Wraps (ref.b) $30.

006a: ART OF WAR Hodder & Stoughton London 1981 [] Wraps. A translation from the Chinese of Sun Tzu, edited by Clavell (British Books In Print, 1983) $40.

006b: ART OF WAR Delacorte NY (1983) [1] Uncorrected proof in peach colored printed wraps. Publication date: April, 1983 $75.

006c: ART OF WAR Delacorte NY (1983) [1] 25,000 cc $10/40

007a: THE CHILDREN'S STORY Delacorte (NY 1981) [1] 100,000 cc $5/25

008a: THRUMP-O-MOTO Hodder & Stoughton L (1986) [1] Reportedly precedes U.S. edition $8/40

008b: THRUMP-O-MOTO Delacorte NY (1986) [1] Illustrated by George Sharp $5/30

009a: WHIRLWIND Morrow NY 1986 [] Uncorrected proof in white wraps $150.

009b: WHIRLWIND Morrow NY 1986 [2] 75 sgd cc. "For Friends of the Publisher." Tipped-in leaf before half title. Red cloth ribbon. Issued in plain black cloth slipcase (Steven Temple 8/89) $150.

009c: WHIRLWIND Morrow NY 1986 [ ] 850,000 cc (PW). (Published November 10, 1986 @ $22.95) $5/25

009d: WHIRLWIND Hodder & Stoughton L (1986) [1] $6/30

009e: WHIRLWIND Macmillan of Canada T (1986?) [3] Also states"First published in U.S. in 1986 by William Morrow ..." $6/30

009f: WHIRLWIND Macmillan of Canada T (1986?) [3] Same as 009e except no price and the top edge yellow (Steven Temple 8/89) $6/30

HARRY CREWS

Crews was born in Alma, Georgia in 1935. He received his B.A. and Ms. Ed. at the University of Florida, where he is currently teaching writing, one of his tamer pursuits.

We would like to thank Michael Hargraves for permission to use his excellent bibliography.

REFERENCES:

(a) Hargraves, Michael, HARRY CREWS: A Bibliography, Meckler Publ., 11 Ferry Lane West, Westport, CT 06880 (1986). In-print @ $19.50.

(b) Inventory.

001a: THE GOSPEL SINGER Morrow NY 1968 [0] 4,000 cc $100/600

002a: NAKED IN GARDEN HILLS Morrow NY 1969 [0] 5,500 cc (a & b). First issue dustwrapper with reviews of 001a on back in full green cloth. There is also light green simulated cloth binding (Joseph The Provider 10/92 mentions this as the usual binding) but our copy of the first printing is in full medium to dark green cloth and our second printing is in the light green simulated cloth binding, which would indicate that the light green is a second state/issue $35/175

002b: NAKED IN GARDEN HILLS Morrow NY 1969 [0] Second issue dustrapper with reviews of this book on back $35/75

Note: Second printing has two dots at foot of copyright page otherwise no difference

002c: NAKED IN GARDEN HILLS Charisma Books London 1973 [1] Wraps $60.

003a: THIS THING DON'T LEAD TO HEAVEN Morrow NY 1970 [0] 7,500 cc $35/175

004a: KARATE IS A THING OF THE SPIRIT Morrow NY 1971 [0] 5,942 cc $30/150

004b: KARATE IS A THING OF THE SPIRIT Secker & Warburg London (1972) [1] $30/150

005a: CAR Morrow NY 1972 [0] Uncorrected proof in white wraps (H.E. Turlington 9/90) $200.

005b: CAR Morrow NY 1972 [0] 5,005 cc $35/175

005c: CAR Car Productions L.A. 1972 [] A screenplay by Crews. 114 pages. Unproduced (Pepper & Stern 5/90) $150.

005d: CAR Secker & Warburg London (1973) [1] $25/100

006a: THE HAWK IS DYING Knopf NY 1973 [1] Approximately 5,000 cc $15/75

006b: THE HAWK IS DYING Secker & Warburg London (1974) [1] $12/60

007a: THE GYPSY'S CURSE Knopf NY 1974 [1] 6,000 cc $12/60

007b: THE GYPSY'S CURSE Secker & Warburg London (1975) [1] $12/60

008a: A FEAST OF SNAKES Atheneum NY 1976 [] Uncorrected proof in green wraps (Ken Lopez 9/90) $12/60

008b: A FEAST OF SNAKES Atheneum NY 1976 [1] 6,000 cc $15/75

008c: A FEAST OF SNAKES Secker & Warburg London (1977) [1] $12/60

009a: A CHILDHOOD: THE BIOGRAPHY OF A PLACE Harper NY [] Uncorrected proof in red wraps (Waverly Books 2/91) $75.

009b: A CHILDHOOD: THE BIOGRAPHY OF A PLACE Harper NY (1978) [3] 6,500 cc. Also states "First Edition" $10/50

009c: A CHILDHOOD: THE BIOGRAPHY OF A PLACE Secker & Warburg London (1979) [1] $10/50

010a: BLOOD AND GRITS Harper NY (1979) [] Uncorrected proof in red wraps (Waverly Books 3/89) $125.

010b: BLOOD AND GRITS Harper NY (1979) [3] 6,500 cc. Also states "First Edition" $10/50

Note: Second printing of 2,000 cc corrects an error on copyright page

011a: THE ENTHUSIAST Palaemon Press (Winston-Salem 1981) [2] 50 sgd no. cc

(Roman). Issued without dustwrapper or slipcase $200.

011b: THE ENTHUSIAST Palaemon Press (Winston-Salem 1981) [2] 150 sgd no. cc $100.

012a: FLORIDA FRENZY Univ. of Florida Gainesville (1982) [0] 1,500 cc (ref.a) (2,070 cc according to publisher in correspondence with Steven Bernard 6/20/82). Wraps. First appearance of one essay, most of the others are first book appearances $50.

013a: 2 BY CREWS Lord John Press Northridge 1984 [2] 26 sgd ltr cc. Issued without dustwrapper or slipcase $200.

013b: 2 BY CREWS Lord John Press Northridge 1984 [2] 200 sgd no. cc. Issued without dustwrapper or slipcase $100.

014a: ALL WE NEED OF HELL Harper NY 1987 [] Uncorrected proof in printed red wraps $75.

014b: ALL WE NEED OF HELL Harper NY 1987 [3] Also states "First Edition." (Published January 28, 1987 @ $14.95) $5/30

015a: BLOOD ISSUE: A DRAMA IN TWO ACTS No-publisher or place 1988 [] 107 page playscript. Loose xeroxed paper in brads (Pepper & Stern 8/90) $75.

016a: THE KNOCKOUT ARTIST Harper NY (1988) [] Uncorrected proof in printed yellow wraps with front and spine lettering unset, assume first (Beasley Books #39-1988) $125.

016b: THE KNOCKOUT ARTIST Harper NY (1988) [] Uncorrected proof in printed tan wraps with front and spine lettering typeset $75.

016c: THE KNOCKOUT ARTIST Harper NY (1988) [3] Also states "First Edition." (Published April 1988 @ $17.95) $5/25

017a: BODY Poseidon Press (NY 1990) [0] "Advance Uncorrected Proof" in wraps. Includes an excerpt along with excerpts from books by Mary Gaitskill and Patrick McGrath $25.

017b: BODY Poseidon Press NY (1990) [2] 10 sgd ltr cc in full leather. Issued by Ultramarine Press using Poseidon sheets $350.

017c: BODY Poseidon Press NY (1990) [2] 50 sgd no. cc in decorated paper boards with leather spine. Issued by Ultramarine Press using Poseidon sheets $200.

017d: BODY Poseidon Press NY (1990) [3] Signed on tipped in leaf (Waverly Books 4/92) $40/65

017e: BODY Poseidon Press NY (1990) [3] $5/25

018a: MADONNA AT RINGSIDE Lord John Press Northridge 1991 [2] 26 sgd ltr cc $150.

018b: MADONNA AT RINGSIDE Lord John Press Northridge 1991 [2] 275 sgd no. cc $75.

019a: SCARLOVER Poseidon Press NY (1992) [] Uncorrected proof in blue wraps $75.

019b: SCARLOVER Poseidon Press NY (1992) [3] (Published February 1992 @ $19.00)

JOAN DIDION

Didion was born in Sacramento, California in 1934. She received a B.A. from the University of California, Berkeley. She worked as a columnist or editor at *Vogue*, *Saturday Evening Post* and *The National Review*; and has written a number of film scripts. She is married to the writer, John Gregory Dunne.

REFERENCES:

(a) Bruccoli & Clark, FIRST PRINTINGS OF AMERICAN AUTHORS, Volume 2, Gale Research, Detroit, (1978).

(b) Inventory.

(c) CUMULATIVE BOOK INDEX.

(d) Dealer catalogs.

(e) BRITISH BOOKS IN PRINT - 1983.

001a: RUN RIVER Obolensky NY (1963) [1] $25/125

001b: RUN RIVER Jonathan Cape London (1964) [1] "Proof Only" on back dustwrapper flap. Dustwrapper about 1/2 inch taller than book. Publication date estimated at January 1, 1964 (ref.b) $15/125

001c: RUN RIVER Jonathan Cape London (1964) [1] (ref.b) $15/75

002a: SLOUCHING TOWARDS BETHLEHEM Farrar, Straus & Giroux NY (1968) [] Uncorrected proof in spiral bound wraps (Wm. Reese Co. 5/89) $250.

002b: SLOUCHING TOWARDS BETHLEHEM Farrar, Straus & Giroux NY (1968) [1] $15/75

002c: SLOUCHING TOWARDS BETHLEHEM A. Deutsch (London 1969) [] (ref.c) $15/75

003a: PLAY IT AS IT LAYS Farrar, Straus NY (1970) [] Uncorrected proof in salmon colored ring bound wraps (Waverly Books #50) $150.

003b: PLAY IT AS IT LAYS Farrar, Straus NY (1970) [1] $10/50

003c: PLAY IT AS IT LAYS Weidenfeld & Nicolson London (1971) [1] (ref.b) $8/40

003d: PLAY IT AS IT LAYS : A SCREENPLAY F.P. Films NY/LA (1971) [0] 130 pages punch bound in printed wraps. Written with John Gregory Dunne (Joseph The Provider 9/89) $125.

004a: A BOOK OF COMMON PRAYER Simon & Schuster NY (1977) [3] "Uncorrected Proofs" in tall printed pad-bound yellow wraps $100.

004b: A BOOK OF COMMON PRAYER Simon & Schuster NY (1977) [3] $8/40

004c: A BOOK OF COMMON PRAYER Weidenfeld & Nicolson London (1977) [1] (U.S. plates.) "First Publihsed in Great Britain By Weidenfeld..." (no date) assume 1977. Noted in two dustwrappers, one copper printed in light blue and black, the other pink printed in blue and dark pink (Arundel Press 10/91) $8/40

004d: A BOOK OF COMMON PRAYER Franklin Library Franklin Ctr. 1981 [2] sgd ltd edition in full leather with special message from author $60.

005a: TELLING STORIES Friends of Bancroft Library Berkeley 1978 [] Wraps. "Not For Sale" (ref.d) $75.

006a: THE WHITE ALBUM Simon & Schuster NY (1979) [3] (ref.b) $5/25

006b: THE WHITE ALBUM Weidenfeld & Nicolson London (1979) [] (ref.e) $5/25

007a: SALVADOR Simon & Schuster NY (1983) [3] "Advance Uncorrected Proof" in yellow printed wraps (ref.b) $75.

007b: SALVADOR Simon & Schuster NY (1983) [3] $5/25

007c: SALVADOR Chatto & Windus London (1983) [ ] $5/25

008a: DEMOCRACY Simon & Schuster NY (1984) [3] "Advance Uncorrected Proof" in yellow printed wraps (ref.b) $50.

008b: DEMOCRACY Simon & Schuster NY (1984) [3] (ref.b) $5/25

008c: DEMOCRACY Chatto & Windus/Hogarth London (1984) [] (ref.d) $5/25

008d: DEMOCRACY Dennys (Toronto 1984) [0] (ref.b) $5/20

009a: ESSAYS AND INTERVIEWS Ontario Review Press Princeton 1984 [] Edited by Ellen G. Friedman $6/30

010a: MIAMI Simon & Schuster NY no-date (cover) [0] Manuscript (8 1/2" x 11") sheets with black cloth spine. Reported to be limited to a few copies $75.

010b: MIAMI Simon & Schuster NY (1987) [] Uncorrected Proofs in yellow or ochre printed wraps $50.

010c: MIAMI Simon & Schuster NY (1987) [] (Published October 9, 1987 at $17.95, about 50,000 cc) $5/25

010d: MIAMI Dennys T (1987) [] $5/20

011a: AFTER HENRY Simon & Schuster NY 1992 [] Uncorrected Proof in yellow wraps $60.

011b: AFTER HENRY Simon & Schuster NY 1992 [] (Published May 1992 @ $22)

JOHN DOS PASSOS
1896 - 1970

John (Roderigo) Dos Passos was born in Chicago. He received his B.A. degree "cum Laude" from Harvard in 1916. During WWI he served with the Red Cross and U.S.A. Ambulance Services which gave him the material for his first book. During the 1920's he traveled around Spain, Mexico and the Middle East as a free-lance writer and journalist. In Paris he associated with e.e. cummings, Fitzgerald, Hemingway and other expatriates. Increasingly left wing in political views he became actively involved in social struggles and wrote articles and plays of social protest.

His literary success started with the first volume of the U.S.A. trilogy, *The 42nd Parallel*, in 1930. The trilogy won for him a reputation as one of the finest novelists of the 1930's.

By the end of the 1930's he had broken with communism and was disillusioned by the Spanish Civil War. He began to write critically of proletarianism and as time went on he started espousing conservatism.

We would like to thank Jeff Klaess for preparing the draft of this guide; and Richard Layman for providing further details on first edition identification of the British editions (which were not covered at all in any of the other references).

REFERENCES:

(a) Potter, Jack A BIBLIOGRAPHY OF JOHN DOS PASSOS Normandie House, Chicago, 1950. Used for all entries, unless otherwise indicated, up to 1949.

(b) Bruccoli & Clarke FIRST PRINTINGS OF AMERICAN AUTHORS Volume 1, Gale Research, Detroit (1977). Used for all U.S. entries from 1950 to 1974 unless otherwise indicated.

(c) Sanders, David JOHN DOS PASSOS - A COMPREHENSIVE BIBLIOGRAPHY Garland Publishing Inc., New York, 1987. Used for the quantities from 1950 to 1975, and as indicated.

(d) Information supplied by Richard Layman, inventory, dealer catalogs, etc.

001a: ONE MAN'S INITIATION - 1917 George Allen & Unwin Ltd. London (1920) [1] 750 cc (additional 500 copies shipped to Doran for U.S. edition). Pale blue mesh cloth. First state has a broken "d" and the word "flat" obliterated at p.35:32. Although not necessarily issued before second state in all cases as the sheets were used at random including those sent to the U.S. $150/750

001b: ONE MAN'S INITIATION - 1917 George Allen & Unwin Ltd. London (1920) [1] Pale blue mesh cloth. Second state has perfect "d" and "flat" at p.35:32 $100/600

001c: ONE MAN'S INITIATION - 1917 George H. Doran New York 1922 [0] 500 cc. Title page is a cancel on a stub, verso of title page blank. Shiny smooth maroon cloth, cream colored paper label on spine, top-edge trimmed and stained maroon (ref.b). Ref.d calls for red cloth. First state has broken "d" and obliterated "flat" at p.36:32 $150/750

001d: ONE MAN'S INITIATION - 1917 George H. Doran New York 1922 [0] Second state: perfect "d" and "flat" on p.35:32 $100/600

001e: FIRST ENCOUNTER Philosophical Library New York (1945) [0] 2,000 cc. New title. Contains new introduction by Dos Passos $15/75

001f: ONE MAN'S INITIATION - 1917 Cornell University Press Ithaca, New York (1969) [] 1,008 cc. Reprinted from the "Original uncorrected page proofs" per Dos Passos. Described by Publishers as "complete and unexpergated." Contains a new 34 page introduction by Dos Passos, a 5 page publisher's note, and 6 drawings by Dos Passos (Ref.b&c) $25/75

001g: ONE MAN'S INITIATION - 1917 Cornell University Press Ithaca, New York (1970) [] 3,948 cc. Wraps (Ref.c) $25.

002a: THREE SOLDIERS George H. Doran New York (1921) [] Advance copy in tan wrappers $2,000.

002b: THREE SOLDIERS George H. Doran New York (1921) [0] Approx 2-3,000 cc printed. Publisher's colophon not found in any state of first printing. Three blank integral leaves at front, none at back, endpapers front and back (ref.b). "Signing" for "singing" at p.231:13. First state dustwrapper has publisher's blurb on front, spine and back (ref.a) $75/600

002c: THREE SOLDIERS George H. Doran New York (1921) [0] Two blank integral leaves in front, none in back. Endpapers front and back. Pages 9-10 tipped onto pages 11-12 (ref.b. Not mentioned in ref.a); "signing" for "singing" p.213:31. Dustwrapper has a quotation from the *Brooklyn Daily Eagle* as last item on front panel (ref.a) $75/500

002d: THREE SOLDIERS George H. Doran New York (1921) [0] Third state, like first, has three blank integral leaves in front and none in back, endpapers front and back, "signing" has been corrected to "singing." Dustwrapper same as 002c except the quote from the *Brooklyn Daily Eagle* has been replaced by one from *Stars and Stripes* (ref.a&b) $35/300

002e: THREE SOLDIERS George H. Doran New York (1921) [0] Fourth state. Two integral blank leaves at front and three at back, no endpapers (the first and last leaves being pastedowns); "singing" at p.213:31. Dustwrapper as 002d but with price on spine blacked over (ref.a&b) $35/250

002f: THREE SOLDIERS George H. Doran New York (1921) [0] Fifth state. Three blank integral leaves in front and four in back, endpapers in front and back (ref.b) $35/250

Note: Precedence of third, fourth and fifth states unknown (ref.b). Ref.a only mentions 002b and later state with "singing." Ref.c doesn't mention any states/points. Also noted with 3 blank integral leaves in front and two in back (Waiting For Godot 4/90)

002g: THREE SOLDIERS Hurst and Blackett London (1922) [0] p.383 "Printed by Anchor Press Ltd..." (ref.d) $100/400

002h: THREE SOLDIERS Modern Library New York 1932 [0] Modern Library edition. Contains a new introduction and minor textual revisions (ref.a&b) $15/60

003a: ROSINANTE TO THE ROAD AGAIN George H. Doran New York (1922) [5] Yellow boards and dustwrapper. Quantity unknown. 2,359 cc sold $60/350

004a: A PUSHCART AT THE CURB George H. Doran New York (1922) [5] 1,313 cc printed of which 544 were remaindered. Colored pictorial cloth, cream colored paper label on black cloth spine. (Two copies know with labels on front cover as well as on spine.) Cover painting and dustwrapper art by Dos Passos

$60/350

005a: STREETS OF NIGHT George H. Doran New York (1923) [5] Erratum: p.300:8 "horeshoe" for "horseshoe" (ref.a. Not mentioned in ref.b&c). Quantity unknown. 3,414 copies sold

$50/300

005b: STREETS OF NIGHT Martin Secker London (1923) [] $50/300

006a: MANHATTAN TRANSFER Harper & Bros. New York (1925) [1] 4,000 cc. "K-Z" on copyright page. Earliest copies have a perfect "p" in "Ferryship", the running headband, p.9; a perfect "2" in folio, p.298; and an almost obliterated "i" in "telling" p.328:22. There are two types of bindings and two dws: 1) yellow paper label on front cover and publishers device blind-stamped in lower right-hand corner, back cover plain, issued in dustwrapper with a montage of urban scenes on front panel; and 2) pasted over black cloth, a pictorial paper reproduction of N.Y. Harbor and skyline, on front and back covers, tips of corners black cloth, issued in matching pictorial dw. Artwork by Dos Passos. Of the 4,000 copies printed, 2,000 issued in each binding with no priority. All copies bound and issued simultaneously $100/500

006b: MANHATTAN TRANSFER Constable London (1927) [1] (ref.b) $50/250

007a: THE GARBAGE MAN Harper & Bros. New York (1926) [1] 1,000 cc in first state of binding: chocolate brown boards, paper labels on front cover and spine, top-edge trimmed. Code

"F-A" on copyright page. Dustwrapper art by Dos Passos $75/300

007b: THE GARBAGE MAN Harper & Bros. New York, (1926) [1] 500 cc (balance of original printing) in second state binding: shiny dark blue cloth, paper label on spine only. Dustwrapper as in 007a $40/250

007c: THE GARBAGE MAN Constable London 1929 [] Excludes Author's Note on early productions of the play (ref.b) $50/250

007d: THE GARBAGE MAN Constable London 1929 [] In decorated wraps (Nicholas Pounder 6/90) 100.

008a: ORIENT EXPRESS Harper & Bros. New York (1927) [1] 1,000 cc. Issued in lavender boards and lavender paper label on shiny blue cloth spine, top-edge trimmed and stained wine-colored maroon. Code "M-A" on copyright page. 7 illustrations and dustwrapper art by Dos Passos $75/300

008b: ORIENT EXPRESS Harper & Bros. New York (1927) [1] 1,500 cc (balance of original printing) in second state binding: blue cloth with paper label on spine. Dustwrapper and illustrations remained the same $30/250

008c: ORIENT EXPRESS Jonathan Cape London (1928) [1] "First issued in Traveler's Library" (ref.b, not mentioned in a or c) $30/200

008d: ORIENT EXPRESS Cape & Smith New York 1928 [0] Cape and Smith Traveller's Library (ref.d). Also noted in dustwrapper with imprint at bottom of spine of "Galaxy"? Remainder? $15/75

009a: FACING THE CHAIR Sacco Vanzetti Defense Committee Boston 1927 [0] Stiff olive drab wraps (facsimile publication by Decapo in 1970) $200.

010a: AIRWAYS, INC. Macaulay Co. New York (1928) [0] Approx. 1,000 - 1,500 cc printed (ref.a&b) $60/300

011a: METROPOLIS (T.S. Book Co.) New York 1929 [0] Wraps. Translation of Manuel Maples Arce's work by Dos Passos (ref.a&b) $175.

012a: THE 42ND PARALLEL Harper & Bros. New York (1930) [1] 7,500 cc. Code "A-E" on copyright page. Variant bindings of paper covered boards but no priority. First volume of *U.S.A.* trilogy $60/350

012b: THE 42ND PARALLEL Constable London (1930) [0] Also noted in wraps with dustwrapper as cover. Could have been an advance copy or simultaneous paperwraps issue (ref.d) $40/250

012c: THE 42ND PARALLEL Modern Library (New York 1937) [] Adds introduction by Dos Passos $12/60

013a: PANAMA, OR THE ADVENTURES OF MY SEVEN UNCLES by Blaise Cendrars Harper & Bros. New York 1931 [2] 300 no. cc signed by Cendrars and Dos Passos (translation and introduction). In stiff cream colored pictorial wrappers. Contains 12 reproductions of paintings by Dos Passos. In slipcase with title, author... and copy number on spine (not mentioned in any of the references) $200/300

013b: PANAMA, OR THE ADVENTURES OF MY SEVEN UNCLES by Blaise Cendrars

Harper & Bros. New York 1931 [1] Code "M-E" on copyright page.Same as above without limitation page. Slipcase? $125.

014a: **1919** Harcourt, Brace New York (1932) [1] 10,250 cc printed. Second volume of the *U.S.A.* trilogy $60/300

014b: **1919** Constable London (1932) [1] Also noted in wraps with dustwrapper as cover. Could have been an advance copy or simultaneous paperwraps issue (ref.d) $40/200

015a: HARLAN MINERS SPEAK... Harcourt, Brace New York (1932) [] A report on terrorism in Kentucky coal fields prepared for the defense of political prisoners. Contains "Continuity and Explanatory" paragraphs throughout by Dos Passos) $200.

016a: CULTURE AND CRISIS... League of Professional Groups for Foster and Ford New York 1932 [0] Wraps (ref.b) $200.

017a: IN ALL COUNTRIES Harcourt, Brace New York (1934) [1] 1,500 cc printed $35/175

017b: IN ALL COUNTRIES Constable London (1934) [1] (ref.d) $25/125

018a: THREE PLAYS Harcourt, Brace New York (1934) [0] 1,500 cc. This is the first appearance of *Fortune Heights* $50/200

018b: THREE PLAYS McLeod Toronto 1934 [] (ref.c) $35/150

019a: THE BIG MONEY Harcourt, Brace New York (1936) [1] 10,000 cc. Third volume of the *U.S.A.* trilogy $40/200

019b: THE BIG MONEY Constable (London 1936) [1] Also noted in wraps with dustwrapper as cover. Could have been an advance copy of a simultaneous paperwraps issue (ref.d) $30/150

020a: THE VILLAGES ARE THE HEART OF SPAIN Esquire-Coronet Chicago (1937) [2] 1,200 no. cc. Issued without dustwrapper $200.

021a: U.S.A. Harcourt, Brace New York, (no-date {1938}) [0] 5,200 cc. One volume trilogy (includes *The 42nd Parallel*, *1919*, and *The Big Money*). First appearance of short sketch by Dos Passos. Last copyright date 1937, but not published until January 1938. None of the references indicated this edition states "first edition" so, we assume it does not $35/150

021b: U.S.A. Constable London (1938) [1] "Published... 1938" (ref.d) $25/125

021c: U.S.A. Houghton, Mifflin Boston 1946 [2] 365 no. cc signed by Dos Passos and Reginald Marsh, the illustrator. 3 volumes in slipcase $750/1000

021d: U.S.A. Houghton, Mifflin Boston (1946) [0] 36 page prospectus for illustrated edition with one plate mounted on front cover (Watermark West 11/90) $75.

021e: U.S.A. Houghton, Mifflin Boston 1946 [0] 3 vols. Illustrated by Reginald Marsh. In cellophane and paper dustwrappers and slipcase $150/600

022a: JOURNEYS BETWEEN WARS Harcourt, Brace New York (1938) [1] 2,500 cc $25/100

022b: JOURNEYS BETWEEN WARS Constable London (1938) [1] (ref.d) $20/75

023a: MAN WITH A WATCH IN HIS HAND Sherwood and Katharine Grover/Grabhorn Press San Francisco 1938 [2] 25 no. cc (Reprinted from *The Big Money* where it was titled *The American Plan*) $500.

024a: ADVENTURES OF A YOUNG MAN Harcourt, Brace New York (1939) [1] 10,000 cc. Ref.b mentions that the published reprinted this title in 1952 without date on title page but with "First Printing" on copyright page $20/100

024b: ADVENTURES OF A YOUNG MAN Constable London (1939) [] (ref.b) First issue in purple buckram (Peter Jolliffe #36) $15/75

025a: THE BITTER DRINK Sherwood and Katharine Grover/Grabhorn Press San Francisco 1939 [2] 35 no. cc (Reprinted from *The Big Money*) (ref.b. - Ref.a has 25 copies, which we believe is wrong as auction records also show 35cc) $500.

026a: HENRY AND WILLIAM FORD AND HEARST... Sherwood and Katharine Grover/Grabhorn Press San Francisco 1940 [2] 35 cc. Wraps. (*Tin Lizzie* and *Poor Little Rich Boy* retitled and reprinted from *The Big Money*) (Also noted in unbound sheets completely untrimmed) $500.

027a: THE LIVING THOUGHTS OF TOM PAINE Longmans Green New York 1940 [1] $30/150

027b: THE LIVING THOUGHTS OF TOM PAINE Cassell London (1940) [] (ref.b) $20/100

028a: THE GROUND WE STAND ON Harcourt, Brace New York (1941) [1] 3,000 cc $20/100

028b: THE GROUND WE STAND ON Geo. Routledge London (1942) [1] Adds an introduction by Dos Passos (ref.d) $15/75

029a: NUMBER ONE Houghton, Mifflin Boston 1943 [0] 15,000 cc. Date on title page. Rear panel of dustwrapper has statement by Dos Passos urging readers to buy War bonds. Ref.b mentions that the publisher reprinted the title in 1952 without a date on title page but with "First Printing" on copyright page $15/75

029b: NUMBER ONE Thomas Allen Toronto 1943 [] (ref.c) $15/75

029c: NUMBER ONE Constable London (1944) [1] (ref.d) $10/50

030a: STATE OF THE NATION Houghton, Mifflin Boston 1944 [0] 7,500 cc Date on title page $12/60

030b: STATE OF THE NATION Routledge London (1945) [1] (ref.d) $10/50

030c: STATE OF THE NATION Thomas Allen Toronto 1945 [] (ref.c) $15/60

031a: TOUR OF DUTY Houghton Mifflin Boston 1946 [0] 8,000 cc Date on title page $12/60

032a: THE GRAND DESIGN Houghton Mifflin Boston 1949 [0] 15,000 cc. Date on title page. Ref.b mentions that the publisher reprinted this title in 1952 without a date on the title page but with "First Printing" on copyright page $10/50

032b: THE GRAND DESIGN John Lehmann London (1949) [1] (ref.d) $8/40

032c: THE GRAND DESIGN Thomas Allen Toronto 1949 [] (ref.c) $10/50

033a: THE PROSPECT BEFORE US Houghton Mifflin Boston 1950 [0] 5,000 cc. Date on title page. Number of gatherings (4 -pp. 91-218 vs. 3 -pp.123-218) and printed on lighter colored paper, priority unknown $12/60

033b: THE PROSPECT BEFORE US John Lehmann London (1951) [1] (ref.d) $10/50

034a: LIFE'S PICTURE HISTORY OF WORLD WAR II Time / Simon & Schuster New York 1950 [0] (Each section has full-page article by Dos Passos.) Assume issued without dustwrapper $50.

035a: CHOSEN COUNTRY Houghton Mifflin Boston 1951 [0] 400 cc with tipped-in "Complimentary Edition For the Book-sellers ... " and Dos Passos signature $100/125

035b: CHOSEN COUNTRY Houghton Mifflin Boston 1951 [0] 10,000 cc (total a&b). Date on title page $8/40

035c: CHOSEN COUNTRY John Lehmann London (1952) [1] "This Edition First Published in 1952" $8/40

035d: CHOSEN COUNTRY Thomas Allen Toronto 1952 [] (ref.c) $10/50

036a: DISTRICT OF COLUMBIA Houghton Mifflin Boston 1952 [0] 3,000 cc. Date on title page. One volume edition containing *Adventures of a Young Man*, *Number One* and *The Grand Design* $15/75

037a: THE HEAD AND HEART OF THOMAS JEFFERSON Doubleday Garden City 1954 [1] $20/75

037b: THE HEAD AND HEART OF THOMAS JEFFERSON Robert Hale London (1955) [1] (ref.d) $15/60

038a: MOST LIKELY TO SUCCEED Prentice-Hall New York (1954) [2] 1000 signed cc. Limitation printed on half-title $50/75

038b: MOST LIKELY TO SUCCEED Prentice-Hall New York (1954) [0] Quantity is 7,539 per ref.c which we assume is for both a&b. Ref.a doesn't mention the signed copies $8/40

038c: MOST LIKELY TO SUCCEED Robert Hale London (1955) [] $8/40

039a: THE THEME IS FREEDOM Dodd Mead New York 1956 [0] 3,000 cc $15/60

040a: THE MEN WHO MADE THE NATION Doubleday Garden City 1957 [1] $8/40

041a: THE GREAT DAYS Sangamore Press New York (1958) [0] $10/50

041b: THE GREAT DAYS McClelland & Stewart Toronto 1958 [] $10/40

041c: THE GREAT DAYS Robert Hale London (1959) [1] $8/40

042a: PROSPECTS OF A GOLDEN AGE Prentice-Hall Englewood Cliffs (1959) [0] 9,995 cc $15/75

043a: U.S.A. / A DRAMATIC REVUE with Paul Shyre Samuel French New York (1960)

[0] Wraps. First has copyright of 1960 and $1.25 price on cover $30.

044a: MIDCENTURY Houghton Mifflin Boston 1961 [1] 10,000 cc $10/50

044b: MIDCENTURY Thomas Allen Toronto 1961 [] $8/40

044c: MIDCENTURY Deutsch (London 1961) [1] (ref.d) $8/40

045a: MR. WILSON'S WAR Doubleday Garden City 1962 [1] $10/50

045b: MR. WILSON'S WAR Hamish Hamilton London (1963) [1] $8/40

046a: BRAZIL ON THE MOVE Doubleday Garden City 1963 [1] $15/75

046b: BRAZIL ON THE MOVE Sidgwick & Jackson (London) 1963 [1] "First published ... 1964" (but it does have 1963 on title page) $12/60

047a: THOMAS JEFFERSON: THE MAKING OF A PRESIDENT Houghton Mifflin Boston 1964 [0] Date on title page. Two bindings: cloth 6,000 copies and 4,000 copies in library binding, assume both had dustwrappers (source: Houghton Mifflin records) $30/150

048a: OCCASIONS AND PROTESTS Henry Regnery Chicago 1964 [0] Uncorrected galley spiral bound in plain wraps (William Reese Co. 10/90) $125.

048b: OCCASIONS AND PROTESTS Henry Regnery Chicago 1964 [0] $8/40

049a: THE SHACKLES OF POWER: THREE JEFFERSONIAN DECADES Edited by Lewis

Gannett Doubleday Garden City 1966 [1] $10/50

050a: WORLD IN A GLASS Houghton Mifflin Boston 1966 [] "Revised" galley proofs spiral bound in printed wraps (William Reese Co. 10/92) $125.

050b: WORLD IN A GLASS Houghton Mifflin Boston 1966 [1] 3,500 cc (ref.c) Edited by Kenneth S. Lyon $15/60

051a: AN INFORMAL MEMOIR: THE BEST TIMES New American Library New York (1966) [1] Spiral bound uncorrected proof (Pepper & Stern 11/86) $100.

051b: AN INFORMAL MEMOIR: THE BEST TIMES New American Library New York (1966) [1] $7/35

051c: AN INFORMAL MEMOIR: THE BEST TIMES Deutsch London (1968) [] Deletes Author's Note $7/35

051d: AN INFORMAL MEMOIR: THE BEST TIMES General Publishing Co. Toronto 1968 [] $8/40

052a: THE PORTUGAL STORY: THREE CENTURIES OF EXPLORATION AND DISCOVERY Doubleday Garden City 1969 [1] $10/50

052b: THE PORTUGAL STORY: THREE... Robert Hale London (1970) [1] $8/40

053a: AN INTERVIEW WITH JOHN DOS PASSOS Edited by Frank Gado Union College Press Schenectady (1969) [0] Pamphlet. Verso of front cover has "Copyright 1969 by The Idol..." $40.

054a: EASTER ISLAND: ISLAND OF ENIGMAS Doublday Garden City 1971 [1] $10/50

055a: THE FOURTEENTH CHRONICLE: LETTERS AND DIARIES OF JOHN DOS PASSOS Gambit Boston 1973 [] Edited by Townsend Ludington. Uncorrected proof in bright red wraps (Waiting For Godot #15) $60.

055b: THE FOURTEENTH CHRONICLE: LETTERS AND DIARIES OF JOHN DOS PASSOS Gambit Boston 1973 [2] 300 sgd no cc. Edited by Townsend Ludington. Signed by editor with facsimile of a Dos Passos' signed note $60/100

055c: THE FOURTEENTH CHRONICLE: LETTERS AND DIARIES OF JOHN DOS PASSOS Gambit Boston 1973 [1] 10,000 cc. Edited by Townsend Ludington $7/35

055d: THE FOURTEENTH CHRONICLE... Deutsch London (1974) [] Edited by Townsend Ludington $7/35

056a: CENTURY'S EBB THE THIRTEENTH CHRONICLE Gambit Boston 1975 [1] 4,500 cc (ref.c) $7/35

057a: THE MAJOR NONFICTIONAL PROSE Wayne State Press Detroit 1988 [3] Wraps. Edited by Donald Pizer. Contains a number of previously uncollected pieces $30.

058a: AFTERGLOW AND OTHER UNDERGRADUATE WRITINGS Omnigraphics Detroit 1990 [0] Dos Passos first novel, a facsimile of the typescript and other early works from his Harvard days. Edited by

Richard Layman. Issued without dustwrapper

$100.

WILLIAM EASTLAKE

Eastlake was born in New York City in 1917. He served in the Army during WWII and then moved to an isolated area in New Mexico where he operated a small ranch. Although born in New York, his writing has been principally about his adopted region.

REFERENCES:

(a) FIRST PRINTINGS OF AMERICAN AUTHORS, Vol. 2, Matthew J. Bruccoli and C.E. Frazer Clark, Jr., editors, Gale Research Co., Detroit, Michigan (1978).

(b) Inventory.

001a: GO IN BEAUTY Harper NY (1956) [1]
$35/175

001b: GO IN BEAUTY Secker & Warburg London 1957 [] $20/100

002a: THE BRONC PEOPLE Harcourt NY (1958) [1] $25/125

002b: THE BRONC PEOPLE A. Deutsch London 1958 [] $15/75

003a: PORTRAIT OF AN ARTIST WITH TWENTY-SIX HORSES Simon & Schuster NY 1963 [1] $10/50

003b: PORTRAIT OF AN ARTIST WITH TWENTY-SIX HORSES Michael Joseph London 1965 [] $8/40

004a: CASTLE KEEP Simon & Schuster NY (1965) [1] $8/40

004b: CASTLE KEEP Michael Joseph London (1966) [] $8/40

005a: THE BAMBOO BED Simon & Schuster NY (1969) [1] $7/35

005b: THE BAMBOO BED Michael Joseph London (1970) [1] (ref.b) $7/35

006a: A CHILD'S GARDEN OF VERSES FOR THE REVOLUTION Grove NY (1970) [1] $8/40

007a: 3 BY EASTLAKE Simon & Schuster NY (1970) [1] Wraps $25.

008a: DANCERS IN THE SCALP HOUSE Viking NY (1975) [1] (ref.b) $8/40

009a: THE LONG, NAKED DESCENT INTO BOSTON Viking NY (1977) [] Unrevised proof in pictorial wraps (Wm. Reese Co. 5/92) $50.

009b: THE LONG, NAKED DESCENT INTO BOSTON Viking NY (1977) [1] (ref.b) $5/25

010a: JACK ARMSTRONG IN TANGIER Bamberger Books Flint, Mich. 1984 [2] 50 sgd no. cc. Issued in cloth in dustwrapper. There were also 25 copies "Not For Sale" (ref.b) $50/75

010b: JACK ARMSTRONG IN TANGIER Bamberger Books Flint, Mich. 1984 [2] 125 cc. Cloth in dustwrapper $20/40

010c: JACK ARMSTRONG IN TANGIER Bamberger Books Flint, Mich. 1984 [2] 300 cc. Wraps $20.

011a: PRETTYFIELDS : A WORK IN PROGRESS Capra Press Santa Barbara 1987 [] Wraps. Bound with a Gerald Haslam title (Watermark West 12/89) $15.

F.SCOTT FITZGERALD
1896-1940

Fitzgerald was born in St. Paul, Minnesota. He attended Princeton and served in the Army during the teens. *This Side of Paradise* was published in 1920 and it was a great financial and critical success. He married Zelda the same year and they lived the "good" life, with homes on the Riviera, and in Paris, New York, Long Island and Washington.

He was very productive in the early 1920's, and by 1926 he had written seven of the nine books he would see published during his lifetime. After 1926, the financial and emotional demands on Fitzgerald increased as each year went by and as Zelda's mental state deteriorated.

The primary reference used for this guide is Matthew J. Bruccoli's bibliography which is an excellent one.

Ref.a is the source unless otherwise noted.

REFERENCE:

(a) Bruccoli, Matthew J., F. SCOTT FITZGERALD A DESCRIPTIVE BIBLIOGRAPHY, Revised Edition. Univ. of Pittsburgh Press, 1972.

001a: FIE! FIE! FI-FI! John Church Co. (Cincinnati/NY/L on cover) 1914 [0] Copyright notice on p.3 hand-corrected in ink "MCMXIV." White boards printed in black and orange. (Note: ref.a also notes (as Item A1) acting scripts in two volumes (Acts 1 & 2) in wraps with "Property of The Triangle Club Season 1914-15" which would precede this one volume edition)

$1,750.

002a: THE EVIL EYE John Church Co. (Cincinnati/NY/L on cover) 1915 [0] White boards printed in black and orange. Some copies may have been bound in limp leather (ref.b)

$1,750.

003a: SAFETY FIRST John Church Co. Cincinnati/NY/L (1916) [0] White boards printed in black, orange, red and blue $1,500.

004a: THIS SIDE OF PARADISE Charles Scribner's Sons NY 1920 [1] 3,000 cc. "Published April, 1920." Dustwrapper price: $1.75 also "$1.75 net" (ref.b). Priority undetermined. Green cloth. Scribner's seal on copyright page

$750/7,500

004b: THIS SIDE OF PARADISE Charles Scribner's Sons NY 1920 [0] approximately 500 cc (ref.b) with signed "Author's Apology" tipped in. This is 3rd printing: "Reprinted May 1920"

$1500/2,000

004c: THIS SIDE OF PARADISE W. Collins Sons L (1921) [0] Blue cloth. Text varies unauthoritatively from the U.S. edition in some 850 readings $250/2,500

005a: FLAPPERS AND PHILOSOPHERS Charles Scribner's Sons NY 1920 [1] 5,000 cc. "Published September, 1920." Green linen-like grain cloth or vertical lines, priority undetermined. Scribner's seal on copyright page

$350/2,500

005b: FLAPPERS AND PHILOSOPHERS W. Collins & Sons L (1922) [0] Blue cloth. Numerous textual differences $150/1,250

006a: THE SAINT PAUL DAILY DIRGE (no-publisher no-place no-date) [0] Broadside written and privately printed as a joke. Distributed in 1922 in St. Paul, Minnesota $NVA

006b: THE SAINT PAUL DAILY DIRGE (Fitzgerald Newsletter Colum-bus 1968) [] 200 cc. Facsimile $100.

007a: THE BEAUTIFUL AND DAMNED Charles Scribner's Sons NY 1922 [1] 20,600 cc. "Published March, 1922." First printing of dustwrapper has book title on front in white outlined in black. Scribner's seal not on copyright page $250/2,750

007b: THE BEAUTIFUL AND DAMNED Charles Scribner's Sons NY 1922 [1] 19,750 cc. "Published March, 1922." Second printing has same title and copyright page except the latter has the Scribner seal. The second printing dustwrapper with the front title letters in black is a later dustwrapper per Bruccoli $100/1,500

007c: THE BEAUTIFUL AND DAMNED W. Collins L (1922) [0] Blue cloth $75/750

008a: TALES OF THE JAZZ AGE Charles Scribner's Sons NY 1922 [1] 8,000 cc. "Published September, 1922." Green cloth. Scribner's seal on copyright page. There were three printings in 1922 and the only major difference was "an" for "and" at p232.6 in the third printing (ref.b). Later printings were 3,000 copies each $250/2,500

008b: TALES OF THE JAZZ AGE W. Collins London/Glasgow... (1923) [0] Blue cloth $75/850

009a: THE VEGETABLE Charles Scribner's Sons NY 1923 [1] 7,650 cc. "Published April, 1923." Green cloth. Scribner's seal on copyright page $150/750

009b: THE VEGETABLE Charles Scribner's Sons NY (1976) [3] Includes unpublished scenes and corrections (ref.b) $20/75

009c: THE VEGETABLE Charles Scribner's Sons NY (1976) [3] Wraps $20.

010a: THE GREAT GATSBY Charles Scribner's Sons NY 1925 [0] 20,870 cc. (a & b) Green cloth. First state of dustwrapper on back blurb line 14 has lowercase "j" in "jay Gatsby" which is hand-corrected in ink in most copies. First state of book includes the following differences: on p.60:16 "chatter" vs "echolalia", p.119:22 "northern" vs "southern", p.205:9-10 "sick in tired" vs"sickantired", and p.211:7-8 "Union Street Station" vs "Union Station". Scribner's seal on copyright page $750/15,000

010b: THE GREAT GATSBY Charles Scribner's Sons NY 1925 [0] Second state of dustwrapper has back blurb line 14 corrected to uppercase "J" in "Jay Gatsby" 750/5,000

010c: THE GREAT GATSBY Charles Scribner's Sons NY 1925 [0] 3,000 cc. Second printing corrects the textual errors listed in 010a; otherwise, no difference in book. Dustwrapper has reviews on back flap and panel $75/1,500

010d: THE GREAT GATSBY Chatto & Windus L (1926) [0] "Published 1926." Primary binding: dark blue cloth, spine stamped in gold.

Also seen in tan cloth, stamped in black; also light blue cloth-like boards stamped in black, thought to be remainder binding. Also see Item 046a $150/1,750

010e: THE GREAT GATSBY Modern Library NY (1934) [1] Approximately 5,000 cc. New introduction by author $25/125

010f: THE GREAT GATSBY Limited Editions Club NY (1980) [2] 2,000 no. cc. sgd by Fred Meyer (illustrator). Issued in slipcase $150/200

010g: THE GREAT GATSBY Arion Press SF 1984 [2] 400 sgd no. cc. Illustrated and signed by Michael Graves $400.

Note: Also see 046a

011a: ALL THE SAD YOUNG MEN Charles Scribner's Sons NY 1926 [0] 10,100 cc. Green cloth. Earliest state of dustwrapper has woman's lips on front unbattered. Three printings in 1926 with no differences except type at p.38:6-9 (left), p.248:21-24 (right) and p.90 (folio) are more battered on later printings. About 3,000 copies each in later printings $250/1,500

012a: JOHN JACKSON'S ARCADY Walter H. Baker B (1928) [0] Wraps $2,000.

013a: TENDER IS THE NIGHT Charles Scribner's Sons NY 1934 [5] 7,600 cc. Green cloth. Dustwrapper (front flap) blurbs by Eliot, Mencken and Rosenfeld. Ref.b notes later dustwrapper with blurbs by Mary Colum, Gilbert Seldes and M.J. Rawlings. Terrell Wright noted a copy of the first edition in this later dustwrapper, which means it is a second issue dustwrapper (or somebody switched the dustwrapper) $400/4,500

013b: TENDER IS THE NIGHT Chatto & Windus L 1934 [0] Uncorrected proof bound in brown paperwraps. White label printed in black on front cover $3,500.

013c: TENDER IS THE NIGHT Chatto & Windus L 1934 [0] Blue cloth printed in yellow $100/1000

013d: TENDER IS THE NIGHT Charles Scribner's Sons NY 1951 [0] 5,075 cc (d & e) with author's final revisions and preface by Malcolm Cowley. Copyright page has seal and 1948/51 dates but no "A". Tan cloth stamped in black and red. First state has the following errors: p.xi:18 "xett"; p.xiv:19 "tsandards"; p.xviii:23 "b each"; p.xviii:24 "accompanied". A publisher errata sheet was enclosed in review copies $75/250

013e: TENDER IS THE NIGHT Charles Scribner's Sons NY 1951 [0] Errors in text (see 013d) corrected on 3 cancel leaves. (One catalog {Puffer} noted a 1953 Scribner edition with all the errors but ref.a indicates this edition contained all the corrections) $30/150

013f: TENDER IS THE NIGHT The Grey Walls Press L (1953) [0] "This new edition published in 1953." Pinkish tan cloth or gold paper-covered boards. Priority undetermined $25/125

013g: TENDER IS THE NIGHT Limited Editions Club NY 1983 [2] 2,000 no. cc signed by Fred Meyer (illustrator). Issued in slipcase $125/175

014a: THE TRUE STORY OF APPOMATTOX (no publisher, place or date) [0] A 38-line newspaper clipping made up for Fitzgerald by the *Baltimore Sun* in 1934 as a joke. May only be 3 copies (ref.b) $NVA

015a: TAPS AT REVEILLE Charles Scribner's Sons NY 1935 [5] 5,100 cc (a & b). Price rubberstamped on front flap of some copies in two sizes: 3/16" and 1/8" high. First state pp.349-352 not cancelled and p.351:29-30 reads "Oh, catch it - oh, catch it..." $300/1,500

015b: TAPS AT REVEILLE Charles Scribner's Sons NY 1935 [5] Dustwrapper price printed. Second state: pp.349-352 cancelled; p.351:29-30 reads "Oh, things like that happen..." $150/1,000

016a: THE LAST TYCOON Charles Scribner's Sons NY 1941 [5] Blue cloth stamped in gold $75/500

016b: THE LAST TYCOON Grey Walls Press L (1949) [1] Yellow cloth, spine stamped in gold $50/250

017a: THE CRACK-UP New Directions (no-place) (1945) [0] 2,520 cc. Paper covered boards with cloth spine. Title page printed in red-brown and black. Later printings have title page printed in black only and no colophon on p.348 $50/250

017b: THE CRACK-UP New Directions (no-place no-date) [0] First English issue of American copies. Paper label pasted on p.2 "This is a New Directions Book distributed through the British Empire..." $40/150

017c: THE CRACK-UP Penguin Books (Harmondsworth 1965) [0] 35,000 cc. Wraps. "Published by Penguin Books 1965." Cover price: "3'6". First actual printing in England $30.

018a: THE PORTABLE F. SCOTT FITZGERALD Viking NY 1945 [1] "Published ... Sept 1945." Selected by Dorothy Parker, introduction by John O'Hara. No new material $15/75

019a: THE DIAMOND AS BIG AS THE RITZ Armed Services Edition NY (1946) [0] Wraps $100.

020a: THE STORIES OF F. SCOTT FITZGERALD Charles Scribner's NY 1951 [5] 7,510 cc. (28 stories.) Edited by Malcolm Cowley. First issue has Malcolm misspelled "Malcom" on spine $20/100

020b: THE STORIES OF F. SCOTT FITZGERALD Charles Scribner's NY 1951 [5] Second issue, "Malcolm" corrected $15/75

021a: BORROWED TIME Grey Walls Press L 1951 [1] Edited by Alan and Jennifer Ross. 9 stories $15/75

022a: BABYLON REVISITED AND WINTER DREAMS Kenkyusha Tokyo (1955) [] Wraps. First separate edition with introduction and notes by Ikuo Uemura $125.

022b: BABYLON REVISITED + Scribner NY (1960) [5] "A-8.60 (C)" Wraps. No new material $50.

023a: AFTERNOON OF AN AUTHOR Princeton Univ Library Princeton 1957 [0] 1,500 cc $30/150

023b: AFTERNOON OF AN AUTHOR Charles Scribner's Sons NY (1958) [5] "A-2.58 [MH]" $15/75

023c: AFTERNOON OF AN AUTHOR The Bodley Head L (1958) [1] 5,000 cc $15/75

024a: SIX TALES OF THE JAZZ AGE Scribner NY (1960) [5] "A-1.60(H)." Includes *Stories From The Jazz Age* and *All The Sad Young Men*. No new material $20/100

025a: THE MYSTERY OF THE RAYMOND MORTGAGE Random House NY 1960 [2] 750 cc. Grey-blue wraps (Pepper & Stern (List R 11/86) mentions publisher's letter and mailing envelope. Letter is dated September 2, 1960 - "An F. Scott Fitzgerald first edition..." $250.

026a: THE PAT HOBBY STORIES Charles Scribner's Sons NY (1962) [] Uncorrected galley proofs. Loose sheets punched at top and string tied in plain wraps with printed label (Wm. Reese Co. 2/90) $1,250.

026b: THE PAT HOBBY STORIES Charles Scribner's Sons NY (1962) [5] 8,000 cc. "A-6.62(V)" $20/100

026c: THE PAT HOBBY STORIES Penguin Books (Harmondsworth 1967) [0] 30,000 cc. Wraps. "Published by Penguin Books 1967" Price: "4s 6d" $35.

027a: THE FITZGERALD READER Scribners NY 1963 [] Galley proof in plain wraps spiral bound at top (Wm. Reese Co. 5/92) $400.

027b: THE FITZGERALD READER Scribners NY 1963 [0] "3.63(H)." Edited by Arthur Mizener $15/75

028a: LETTER TO MAXWELL PERKINS (Scribner's NY 1963) [0] Facsimile letter from Fitzgerald to Maxwell Perkins, 18 Sept. 1919.

Four leaves printed in blue ink on white wove paper. Promotion for item 029a. Also see 1967 and 1978 entries $100.

029a: THE LETTERS OF F. SCOTT FITZGERALD Charles Scribner's Sons NY (1963) [] Galley proof in two volumes spiral bound with paper label and introduction by Andrew Turnbull laid in (Wm. Reese Co. 11/90) $750.

029b: THE LETTERS OF F. SCOTT FITZGERALD Charles Scribner's Sons NY (1963) [5] 10,000 cc. "A-9.63(V)." Edited and introduction by Andrew Turnbull $12/60

029c: THE LETTERS OF F. SCOTT FITZGERALD Bodley Head L (1964) [1] 4,000 cc $10/50

030a: TURKEY REMAINS (Cooper & Beatty Toronto 1965) [0] 2,000 cc. Wraps $75.

031a: THE APPRENTICE FICTION OF F. SCOTT FITZGERALD 1909-1917 Rutgers Univ Press New Brunswick (1965) [0] 5,000 cc $15/75

032a: THOUGHTBOOK OF FRANCIS SCOTT KEY FITZGERALD Princeton Univ Library Princeton 1965 [2] 300 cc in glassine dustwrapper $125.

033a: LETTERS TO HIS DAUGHTER Scribners NY (1965) [5] "A-8.65(V)." Introduction by Scottie Fitzgerald $10/60

034a: EXHIBITION CATALOGUE Ohio State Univ Library (no-place) 1965 [2] 25 sgd no. cc. Published in 1965 (December). An exhibition catalog marking the 25th anniversary of Fitzgerald's death. A single sheet folded twice to make 6 pages. Assume signed by Bruccoli since it is his collection. First printing of 4 Fitzgerald inscriptions $175.

034b: EXHIBITION CATALOGUE Ohio State Univ Library (no-place) 1965 [2] 225 cc $40.

035a: LETTER TO PERKINS Charles Scribner's Sons (no-place) 1967 [0] Broadside which prints facsimile of Fitzgerald letter to Maxwell E. Perkins, March 1920. Printed in black on gray wove paper. Distributed at fiftieth reunion of Fitzgerald's class. Not included in *The Letters...* (item 028a) $200.

036a: DEARLY BELOVED Windhover Press/Univ.Iowa Iowa City 1969 [2] 30 sgd no. cc. Signed by the artist, B. Burford. Copies numbered 1-30. Issued without dustwrapper $250.

036b: DEARLY BELOVED Windhover Press/Univ. Iowa Iowa City 1969 [2] 270 no. cc. Copies numbered 31-270. Issued without dustwrapper $100.

037a: "AND A FEW MISSING WORDS WOULD MEAN SO MUCH" Privately printed L 1970 [2] 200 sgd cc. Single sheet folded, signed (initialed) by Bruccoli $50.

038a: F SCOTT FITZGERALD IN HIS OWN TIME Kent State Univ Press (no-place 1971) [1] 2,500 cc. Edited by M.J. Bruccoli and Jackson Bryer. Issued without dustwrapper $60.

039a: CRAZY SUNDAYS : F. SCOTT IN HOLLYWOOD Viking 1971 [1] By Aaron Latham. Includes previously unpublished material from letters, notes and scripts $10/50

039b: CRAZY SUNDAYS : F. SCOTT IN HOLLYWOOD Secker & Warburg L (1972) $10/50

040a: DEAR SCOTT/DEAR MAX Chas. Scribner's Sons NY (1971) [5] 6,000 cc. "A-10.71(H)." Edited by John Kuehl and Jackson Bryer $10/50

040b: DEAR SCOTT/DEAR MAX Cassell L (1973) [1] 3,000 cc $10/50

041a: F. SCOTT FITZGERALD AND ERNEST HEMINGWAY IN PARIS AN EXHIBITION Bruccoli-Clark Bloomfield Hills/Columbia 1972 [0] Wraps. Introduction by Scottie (Frances Scott Fitzgerald Smith) $60.

042a: AS EVER, SCOTT FITZ Lippincott Phila/NY (1972) [ ] 22 cc in printed wraps for review. Edited by M.J. Bruccoli $250.

042b: AS EVER, SCOTT FITZ Lippincott Phila/NY (1972) [1] 5,000 cc. Edited by M.J. Bruccoli with Jennifer Atkinson. Foreword by Scottie Fitzgerald Smith $10/50

042c: AS EVER, SCOTT FITZ Woburn Press L 1973 [1] 2,000 cc $12/60

043a: THREE HOURS BETWEEN PLANES (Book Society of Canada, Ltd. no-place 1970) [0] Folio punched for loose leaf binding. pp.1-3 text; p.4 teaching material. Accompanied by single-leaf commentary $NVA

044a: THE BASIL AND JOSEPHINE STORIES (Charles Scribner's Sons NY 1973) [5] Wraps. Xeroxed galleys bound in very light blue-green wraps with white label on front printed in black $300.

044b: THE BASIL AND JOSEPHINE STORIES (Charles Scribner's Sons NY 1973) [3] 10,000 cc. Edited and introduction by Jackson R. Bryer and John Kuehl $15/60

045a: F. SCOTT FITZGERALD'S LEDGER NCR/Microcard Washington, DC (1972) (Actually published September 1973 although 1972 stated.) [2] 1,000 no. cc. Issued in coated black paper slipcase without dustwrapper. Introduction by Matthew J. Bruccoli $100.

046a: THE GREAT GATSBY A FACSIMILE OF THE MANUSCRIPT Microcard Editions Washington, DC 1973 [2] 2,000 no cc in white cloth slipcase with dustwrapper. Edited and introduction by M.J. Bruccoli $150.

047a: BITS OF PARADISE Bodley Head L/Sydney/Toronto (1973) [1] 5,000 cc. Selected by M.J. Bruccoli and Scottie Fitzgerald, who also contributed a foreword $15/75

047b: BITS OF PARADISE Chas. Scribner's Sons NY (1974) [3] 6,000 cc $15/75

048a: PREFACE TO THIS SIDE OF PARADISE Windhover Press Iowa City 1975 [2] 150 cc. Assume issued without dustwrapper $275.

049a: TRIMALCHIO Grolier Club NY 1975 [2] 300 cc Long broadside printed on both sides reproducing a page of the galley proof of *The Great Gatsby* under original title on one side and Bruccoli's collection on the other side $75.

050a: THE CRUISE OF THE ROLLING JUNK Bruccoli Clark Bloomfield Hills/Columbia 1976 [0] 1,000 cc $25/100

051a: F. SCOTT FITZGERALD'S SCREENPLAY FOR THREE COMRADES by Erich Maria Remarque Southern Illinois Univ Press Carbondale/ Edwardsville (1978) [0] 2,000 cc in cloth. $25/75

051b: F SCOTT FITZGERALD'S SCREENPLAY FOR THREE COMRADES by Erich Maria Remarque Southern Illinois Univ Press Carbondale/ Edwardsville (1978) [0] 3,000 cc in wraps. Published simultaneously $25.

052a: THE NOTEBOOKS OF F. SCOTT FITZGERALD Harcourt Brace/Bruccoli Clark NY (1978) [4] 5,000 cc $10/50

053a: LETTER TO PERKINS (M.J. Bruccoli Columbia, S.C. 1978) [2] 500 cc. Single sheet printed on both sides $50.

054a: F. SCOTT FITZGERALD'S ST. PAUL PLAYS 1911-1914 Princeton Univ Library Princeton 1978 [0] 2,500 cc. Edited and introduction by Alan Margolies $12/60

055a: THE PRICE WAS HIGH Harcourt Brace/Bruccoli Clark NY/L (1979) [] Uncorreced proof in blue wraps (Waiting For Godot 2/90) $125.

055b: THE PRICE WAS HIGH Harcourt Brace/Bruccoli Clark NY/L (1979) [4] 15,000 cc. Edited by M.J. Bruccoli $8/40

055c: THE PRICE WAS HIGH Quartet Books L/Melbourne/NY (1979) [1] 5,000 cc (a & b). First state: p.177 duplicated p.162 $20/50

055d: THE PRICE WAS HIGH Quartet Books L/Melbourne/NY (1979) [1] Second state: corrects above error $6/30

056a: CORRESPONDENCE OF F. SCOTT FITZGERALD Random House NY (1980) [] (Phoenix Bookshop #188) $10/40

057a: POEMS 1911-1940 Bruccoli Clark (Bloomfield Hills 1981) [2] 100 sgd no. cc. Edited and signed by James Dickey $150.

057b: POEMS 1911-1940 Bruccoli Clark (Bloomfield Hills 1981) [] Trade edition $10/40

058a: CHRISTMAS RECALLED Arion Press SF 1983 [] Single sheet folded, issued as Season's Greeting (Chloe's Books #27) $40.

059a: F. SCOTT FITZGERALD ON WRITING Scribner's NY (1985) [] Edited by Larry Phillips. (Pepper & Stern List T) $6/30

060a: ON WRITING Equation L 1988 [] $7/35

061a: THE SHORT STORIES OF F. SCOTT FITZGERALD : A NEW COLLECTION Scribners NY (1989) [] Edited by Matthew Bruccoli. Uncorrected proof in two volumes. Yellow-gold wraps (Waiting For Godot 2/92) $100.

061b: THE SHORT STORIES OF F. SCOTT FITZGERALD : A NEW COLLECTION Scribners NY (1989) [] $10/25

061c: THE SHORT STORIES OF F. SCOTT FITZGERALD : A NEW COLLECTION Scribners L 1989 [] Scribner proofs in blue wraps. "Printed in Great Britain" and giving provisional price in pounds (Alphabet Books 8/92) $100.

061d: THE SHORT STORIES OF F. SCOTT FITZGERALD : A NEW COLLECTION Scribners L 1989 [] $10/30

IAN FLEMING
1908-1964

Fleming was born in London, educated at Eton College and the Royal Military Academy; and studied at the University of Munich and the University of Geneva.

He was Moscow Correspondent for Reuters and later *The Times* from 1929 to 1933. He worked for a firm of merchant bankers and as a stock broker from 1933 to 1939. He served as personal assistant to the Director of Naval Intelligence from 1939 to 1945.

After the war he worked as Foreign Manager for *Kemsley* (later *Thomson*) *Newspapers* and from 1949 to 1964 published the *Book Collector* (London).

The continued interest in the Bond books may be based on the fact that the:

> "..novels are a perfect example of the right thing at the right time, as appropriate an expression and index of their age as, for example, the Sherlock Holmes stories or the novels of Dashiell Hammett... his powerful influence over writers who follow him, and his union of the fantastic and the absolutely real deserve serious and careful study... (which) may eventually establish Ian Fleming as one of the most appropriate writers of his time."
>
> -George Grella (ref.c)

(The movies haven't hurt either.)

REFERENCE:

(a) Penzler, Otto, "James Bond - Collecting Mystery Fiction" in *The Armchair Detective*, Fall 1984 (no first edition identification included).

(b) Campbell, Iain, IAN FLEMING: A Catalogue of A Collection.

(c) TWENTIETH CENTURY CRIME AND MYSTERY WRITERS edited by John M. Reilly, St. Martin's Press, New York (1985).

001a: CASINO ROYALE Cape London (1953) [1] 4,750 cc. Bottom front flap of dustwrapper blank except for price (later printings had a review from the *Sunday Times* $400/2,500

001b: CASINO ROYALE Cape London (1953) [ ] "Second Printing" $50/300

001c: CASINO ROYAL Macmillan NY 1954 [1] Complete front dustwrapper flaps $60/450

001d: CASINO ROYAL Macmillan NY 1954 [1] Front dustwrapper flaps have corners cut off $60/400

001e: YOU ASKED FOR IT Popular Library NY 1955 [] Wraps. New title $50.

002a: LIVE AND LET DIE Cape London (1954) [1] 7,500 cc $150/1,000

002b: LIVE AND LET DIE Macmillan NY 1955 [1] $50/300

003a: MOONRAKER Cape London (1955) [1] $150/950

003b: MOONRAKER Macmillan NY 1955 [1] $50/300

003c: TOO HOT TO HANDLE Permabooks NY 1957 [ ] Wraps. New title $40.

004a: DIAMONDS ARE FOREVER Cape London (1956) [1] 12,500 cc $125/650

004b: DIAMONDS ARE FOREVER Macmillan NY 1956 [1] $40/250

005a: FROM RUSSIA WITH LOVE Cape London (1957) [1] Noted with gilt lettering on spine (Edna Whiteson #118 "true first"). Also with title in red and name and Cape logo in silver $60/450

005b: FROM RUSSIA WITH LOVE Macmillan NY 1957 [1] $40/200

006a: THE DIAMOND SMUGGLERS Cape London (1957) [1] Most with white lettering on spine. Few with gilt lettering (Maurice Neville 2/89) $30/150

006b: THE DIAMOND SMUGGLERS Macmillan NY 1958 [1] $20/100

007a: DR. NO Cape London (1958) [] Uncorrected proof with woman's figure/silhouette on cover. "It was feared that this silhouette proof might be taken for a paperback so they abandoned it for a standard Cape proof format." (Ergo Books) $1,250.

007b: DR. NO Cape London (1958) [] Uncorrected proof with standard Cape wraps with logo design $650.

007c: DR. NO Cape London (1958) [1] Front cover stamped with woman's figure or blank, no clear priority. Ref.a states that both bindings occur on the later printings and the blank cover seems to be scarcer, while Ref.b states that the silhouette is scarcer and later impressions all have plain front covers (at least one second printing has been seen with silhouette). Noted without a period after "DR" on title page (all copies?) $50/300

007d: DR. NO Macmillan NY 1958 [1] $35/175

008a: GOLDFINGER Cape London (1959) [1] $40/275

008b: GOLDFINGER Macmillan NY 1959 [1] Printed and bound in England (thus, for what it's worth, the Book Club is actually the first American printing!) $30/175

009a: THE EDUCATION OF A POKER PLAYER Cape L 1959 [1] Introduction by Fleming to Herbert Yardley's book $35/150

010a: FOR YOUR EYES ONLY: Five Secret Occasions In The Life Of James Bond Cape London (1960) [1] $40/225

010b: FOR YOUR EYES ONLY: Five Secret Occasions In The Life Of James Bond Viking NY 1960 [] $30/150

011a: THUNDERBALL Cape London (1961) [1] First state in blind stamped boards (Broadhurst & Co. 9/92)?? $35/175

011b: THUNDERBALL Viking NY 1961 [1] "Published in 1961 by.." $20/100

012a: GILT-EDGED BONDS Macmillan NY 1961 [1] Contains *Casino Royale*, *From Russia With Love* and *Dr. No*. Introduction by Paul Gallico $15/75

013a: THE SPY WHO LOVED ME Cape London (1962) [1] "Published in 1962 by ..." Presumed first issue with printer's error on title page. Line between "e" and "m" in "Fleming" $60/200

013b: THE SPY WHO LOVED ME Cape London (1962) [1] Printer's error corrected $30/150

013c: THE SPY WHO LOVED ME Viking NY (1962) [1] $15/75

014a: AIRLINE DETECTIVE Collins London 1962 [0] Donald Fish's first book with foreword by Fleming $15/75

014b: THE LAWLESS SKY Putnam NY (1962) [1] Fish's book, new title $12/60

015a: ON HER MAJESTY'S SECRET SERVICE Cape London (1963) [2] 250 sgd no. cc in black cloth with a white leather spine, issued in plain plastic/acetate dustwrapper without a slipcase $2,750.

015b: ON HER MAJESTY'S SECRET SERVICE Cape London (1963) [1] $25/125

015c: ON HER MAJESTY'S SECRET SERVICE New American Library (NY 1963) [1] $15/75

016a: THRILLING CITIES Cape London (1963) [0] Erratum slip tipped in at end $15/75

016b: THRILLING CITIES New American Library (NY 1964) [1] $10/50

017a: ALL NIGHT AT MR. STANYHURST'S Cape London 1963 [] Reissue of Hugh Edward's book with introduction by Fleming $12/60

017b: ALL NIGHT AT MR. STANYHURST'S Macmillan NY (1963) [1] English sheets without price on dustwrapper $8/40

018a: THE IVORY HAMMER: The Year At Sotheby's Longmans Green (London 1963) [1] "The Property of a Lady" a specially commissioned James Bond story is included. Issued in dustwrapper (story is included in the Signet edition of *Octopussy*. See 023c) $40/125

018b: THE IVORY HAMMER: The Year At Sotheby's Holt NY (1964) [1] $30/100

019a: YOU ONLY LIVE TWICE Cape London (1964) [1] First issue with "First published 1964" (Alan Smith #4) $35/100

019b: YOU ONLY LIVE TWICE Cape London (1964) [1] Second issue with "First published in March 1964" $15/75

019c: YOU ONLY LIVE TWICE New American Library (NY 1964) [1] $12/60

020a: CHITTY-CHITTY-BANG-BANG The Magical Car Adventure Number 1 (Cape London 1964) [1] $25/100

020b: CHITTY-CHITTY-BANG-BANG The Magical Car Adventure Number 2 (Cape London 1964) [1] $25/100

020c: CHITTY-CHITTY-BANG-BANG The Magical Car Adventure Number 3 (J. Cape London 1965) [1] $25/100

The three volumes together $75/350

020d: CHITTY-CHITTY-BANG-BANG Random House NY (1964) [1] 3 volumes in one. Presumed first issue in red cloth stamped in gold, pictorial endpapers, "A Random House Book" on back of dustwrapper, 6 line entry on copyright page and 21 line dedication including "PS."

Dustwrapper priced $3.50. There are reprints without "First Printing" $25/75

020e: CHITTY-CHITTY-BANG-BANG Random House NY (1964) [1] Presume second issue/printing in red cloth stamped in either gold or black, priced at either $3.50 or $3.95, 5 or 6 line entry on copyright page (no Library of Congress) and 16 line dedication without "PS" $7/35

020f: THE COMPLETE ADVENTURES OF THE MAGICAL CAR (Cape London 1971 [1] "Omnibus Edition First Published 1971" $15/75

021a: THE MAN WITH THE GOLDEN GUN Cape London (1965) [1] With gilt embossed gun on front cover said to be rarest of all Bond first editions $1,500/1,550

021b: THE MAN WITH THE GOLDEN GUN Cape London (1965) [1] Second issue without gun on front cover, patterned white endpapers and title in one line on half-title. Also reported with white endpapers and title in two lines on half title (Steven Temple 12/88) $25/75

021c: THE MAN WITH THE GOLDEN GUN New American Library (NY 1965) [1] $10/50

022a: MORE GILT-EDGES BONDS Macmillan NY (1965) [1] Contains *Live and Let Die*, *Moonraker* and *Diamonds Are Forever* $10/50

023a: BONDED FLEMING... Macmillan NY 1965 [] (No English edition) contains *For Your Eyes Only*, *Thunderball* and *The Spy Who Loved Me*. (The Viking edition is later per Book Stalker) $10/50

024a: IAN FLEMING INTRODUCES JAMAICA Hawthorne NY (1965) [0] Edited by Morris Cargill $12/60

024b: IAN FLEMING INTRODUCES JAMAICA Deutsch Jamaica (1965) [1] Edited by Morris Cargill. U.S. sheets? $10/50

025a: OCTOPUSSY AND THE LIVING DAYLIGHTS Cape London (1966) [] Uncorrected proof in printed wraps in dustwrapper. "Proof Only" with provisional publication date of 6/23/66 (Michael Thompson 7/91) $300.

025b: OCTOPUSSY AND THE LIVING DAYLIGHTS Cape London (1966) [1] Sticker price of "16s in U.K. only 80p net" added later $8/50

025c: OCTOPUSSY New American Library (NY 1966) $8/40

025d: OCTOPUSSY Pan Toronto 1967 [] Wraps. First edition to add "The Property of A Lady" $35.

025e: OCTOPUSSY Signet Books NY 1967 [] Wraps. Also contained first U.S. book appearance of "The Property of a Lady" $35.

026a: A JAMES BOND OMNIBUS Cape London 1973 [1] Includes *Live and Let Die*, *Diamonds Are Forever* and *Dr. No* $10/50

027a: (FLEMING) OMNIBUS EDITION Heineman / Octopus London 1978 [] Includes *Moonraker*, *From Russia With Love*, *Dr. No*, *Goldfinger*, *Thunderball* and *On Her Majesty's Secret Service* $8/40

027b: JAMES BOND 007 Avenel NY 1988 []
Contains six books $5/25

For the "Bond" completist, James Bond "books" are noted:

Amis, Kingsley THE JAMES BOND DOSSIER Cape London (1965)

Markham, Robert (Kingsley Amis) COLONEL SUN Cape London / Harper NY 1968

John Gardner (Cape/Hodder & Stoughton London or Putnam NY):

LICENSE RENEWED 1981
FOR SPECIAL SERVICES 1982
ICEBREAKER 1983
ROLE OF HONOUR 1984
NOBODY LIVES FOREVER 1986
NO DEALS MR. BOND 1987
SCORPIUS 1988
WIN, LOSE OR DIE 1989
BROKEN CLAW 1990
THE MAN FROM BARBAROSSA 1991
DEATH IS FOREVER 1992

DICK FRANCIS

Francis was born in Temby, Pembrokeshire, England in 1920. He served as a flying officer in the Royal Air Force during World War II. He was an Amateur National Hunt steeplechase jockey from 1946 to 1948, when he turned professional. Francis was a professional jockey from 1948 to 1957 and then Racing Correspondent for the London *Sunday Express* from 1957 to 1973.

001a: THE SPORT OF QUEENS M. Joseph L (1957) [] $60/300

001b: THE SPORT OF QUEENS M. Joseph L (1968) [1] "This Revised Edition 1968" $25/125

001c: THE SPORT OF QUEENS Harper NY 1969 [1] $35/175

001d: THE SPORT OF QUEENS Pan L (1974) [] Wraps. Second revised edition $25.

002a: DEAD CERT M. Joseph L 1962 [] $250/1,250

002b: DEAD CERT Holt NY (1962) [1] $150/750

002c: DEAD CERT The Armchair Detective NY 1989 [2] 26 sgd ltr cc (Buckingham Books 4/91) $200/225

002d: DEAD CERT The Armchair Detective NY 1989 [2] 100 sgd no. cc. Issued in slipcase (Vagabond 9/89) $35/75

003a: NERVE M. Joseph L (1964) [1] $150/850

003b: NERVE Harper NY (1964) [1] $60/300

003c: NERVE The Armchair Detective NY 1990 [2] 26 sgd ltr cc. Issued without dustwrapper in slipcase $200/225

003d: NERVE The Armchair Detective NY 1990 [2] 100 sgd no. cc $35/75

004a: FOR KICKS M. Joseph L (1965) [] $60/350

004b: FOR KICKS Harper NY (1965) [1] $40/200

004c: FOR KICKS The Armchair Detective NY 1990 [2] 26 sgd ltr cc Issued without dustwrapper in slipcase $150/175

004d: FOR KICKS The Armchair Detective NY 1990 [2] 100 sgd no. cc. Issued without dustwrapper in slipcase $35/75

005a: ODDS AGAINST M. Joseph L (1965) [] Uncorrected proof in buff wraps (Robert Temple 12/90) $600.

005b: ODDS AGAINST M. Joseph L (1965) [1] $60/300

005c: ODDS AGAINST Harper NY (1966) [1] First printing dustwrapper does not have 3 reviews on front flap (Else Fine List 21) $35/175

006a: FLYING FINISH M. Joseph L (1966) [1] $50/250

008b: FLYING FINISH Harper NY (1967) [] Uncorrected proof in blue printed wraps with plastic spiral spine (Serendipity 5/89) $225.

006c: FLYING FINISH Harper NY (1967) [1] $25/125

007a: BEST RACING AND CHASING STORIES Vol. I Faber L 1966 [] Edited by Francis and John Welcome $25/100

008a: BLOOD SPORT M. Joseph L (1967) [1] $40/225

008b: BLOOD SPORT Harper NY (1967) [1] $20/100

009a: FORFEIT M. Joseph L (1968) [] $35/175

009b: FORFEIT Harper NY 1969 [1] $20/90

010a: ENQUIRY M. Joseph L (1969) [1] $30/150

010b: ENQUIRY Harper NY 1969 [1] $15/75

011a: BEST RACING AND CHASING STORIES Vol. II Faber L (1969) [1] Edited by Francis and John Welcome $15/75

012a: THE RACING MAN'S BEDSIDE BOOK Faber L (1969) [1] Edited by Francis and John Welcome $25/100

013a: THREE TO SHOW Harper NY (1970) [1] Includes *Dead Cert*, *Nerve* and *Odds Against* $10/50

014a: RAT RACE M. Joseph L (1970) [1] $25/125

014b: RAT RACE Harper NY (1971) [1] Also has series of numbers "71 72 73 74 10 ...1" on last blank page $15/75

015a: BONECRACK M. Joseph L (1971) [1] $20/100

015b: BONECRACK Harper NY (1972) [1] Also has series "72....321" on last page. (Published May 1972 @ $5.95) $12/60

016a: SMOKESCREEN M. Joseph L (1972) [1] $20/100

016b: SMOKESCREEN Harper NY (1973) [1] Also has numbers on back page "...76 77 10 9...1" $12/60

017a: SLAY-RIDE M. Joseph L (1973) [1] $20/100

017b: SLAY RIDE Harper NY (1974) [1] Also has numbers on back page "...76 77 10 9...1" $12/60

018a: KNOCK DOWN M. Jospeh L (1974) [1] $15/75

018b: KNOCKDOWN Harper NY (1975) [] Uncorrected proof in red wraps $100.

018c: KNOCKDOWN Harper NY (1975) [3] Also states "First Edition." Published April 1975 @ $6.95 $10/50

019a: HIGH STAKES M. Joseph L (1975) [1] $15/75

019b: HIGH STAKES Harper NY (1976) [] Uncorrected proof in red wraps (Waverly Books 1/89) $90.

019c: HIGH STAKES Harper NY (1976) [3] Also states "First Edition." Noted with both red endpapers and blue endpapers. Front dustwrapper flap has "0576" $10/50

020a: ACROSS THE BOARD Harper NY (1975) [1] Includes *Flying Finish*, *Blood Sport* and *Enquiry* $8/40

021a: IN THE FRAME M. Joseph L (1976) [1] $15/75

021b: IN THE FRAME Harper NY (1976) [3] Also states "First U.S. Edition" $10/50

022a: RISK M. Joseph L (1977) [1] $15/75

022b: RISK Harper NY (1978) [3] Also states "First U.S. Edition." (Published May 1978 @ $8.95) $10/50

023a: TRIAL RUN M. Joseph L (1978) [1] $15/75

023b: TRIAL RUN Harper NY 1979 [3] Also states "First U.S. Edition" $10/50

024a: WHIP HAND M. Joseph L (1979) [1] $12/60

024b: WHIP HAND Harper NY (1980) [3] (Copyright in 1979 but published April 1980 @ $9.95.) Also states "First U.S. Edition" $8/40

025a: REFLEX M. Joseph L (1980) [] Uncorrected proof in printed boards (Ronald Levine 6/89) $75.

025b: REFLEX M. Joseph L (1980) [1] $12/60

025c: REFLEX Putnam NY (1981) [0] 50,000 cc $8/40

026a: TWICE SHY M. Joseph L (1981) [1] $12/60

026b: TWICE SHY Putnam NY (1982) [0] 60,000 cc $8/40

027a: BANKER M. Joseph L (1982) [1] $10/50

027b: BANKER Putnam NY (1983) [1] 75,000 cc $7/35

028a: TWO BY FRANCIS Harper NY (1983 {1982?}) [3] Includes *Forfeit* and *Slay Ride* $7/35

029a: THE DANGER M. Joseph L (1983) [1] $10/50

029b: THE DANGER Putnam NY (1984) [0] 100,000 cc $6/30

030a: PROOF M. Joseph L 1984 [1] Noted with edges stained sand-colored and unstained $8/40

030b: PROOF Putnam NY (1985) [3] 110,000 cc $6/30

031a: BREAK IN M. Joseph L (1985) [1] $8/40

031b: BREAK IN Putnam NY (1986) [3] $/6/30

032a: LESTER THE OFFICIAL BIOGRAPHY M. Joseph L (1986) [1] $8/40

032b: A JOCKEY'S LIFE : THE BIOGRAPHY OF LESTER PIGGOTT Putnam NY (1986) [3] $6/35

033a: BOLT M. Joseph L (1986) [1] $8/40

033b: BOLT Putnam NY (1986) [] Uncorrected proof in printed white wraps (Bev Chaney 9/89) $35.

033c: BOLT Putnam NY (1987) [3] 140,000 cc $6/30

034a: HOT MONEY M. Joseph L (1987) [] Uncorrected proof in white wraps (Alphabet Books 11/91) $75.

034b: HOT MONEY M. Joseph L (1987) [1] $8/40

034c: HOT MONEY Putnam NY (1988) [3] Uncorrected proof in flint gray printed wraps $60.

034d: HOT MONEY Putnam NY (1988) [3] Advance reading copy in pictorial wraps $35.

034e: HOT MONEY Putnam NY (1988) [2] 250 sgd no. cc. Issued without dustwrapper in slipcase. Published March 1988 @ $75.) $100/150

034f: HOT MONEY Putnam NY (1988) [3] 155,000 cc (Published March 1988 @ $17.95) $5/25

035a: THE EDGE Joseph L (1988) [1] $7/35

035b: THE EDGE Putnam NY 1989 [] Advance reading copy in pictorial wraps $30.

035c: THE EDGE Putnam NY 1989 [] 60,000 cc (PW) (Published February 1989 @ $18.95) $5/25

036a: STRAIGHT Michael Joseph L 1989 [2] 500 sgd no. cc. Issued without dustwrapper in slipcase (Mordida Books 7/90) $100/125

036b: STRAIGHT Michael Joseph L 1989 [] $7/35

036c: STRAIGHT Putnam NY 1989 [] Uncorrected proof in red wraps $50.

036d: STRAIGHT Putnam NY 1989 [] 225,000 cc (Published November 1989 @ $18.95) $5/20

037a: LONGSHOT Michael Joseph L 1990 [] $7/35

037b: LONGSHOT Putnam NY (1990) [3] Uncorrected proof in orange-yellow wraps $30.

037c: LONGSHOT Putnam NY (1990) [3] (Published October 17, 1990 @ $19.95) $5/20

038a: DRIVING FORCE Michael Joseph L 1992 [] $7/35

038b: DRIVING FORCE Putnam NY 1992 [] (Published October 1992 @ $21.95)

Robert Frost

ROBERT FROST
1874-1963

Robert Frost was born in San Francisco but moved to his grandfather's house in Lawrence, Massachusetts after his father's death. He graduated from the local high school in 1892. A few of his poems had appeared in the high school bulletin, but his first published poem was "My Butterfly" in the *New York Independent* in 1894.

He studied at Dartmouth and Harvard without graduating. He worked in Lawrence at a woolen mill, on a newspaper and at other odd jobs, but continued to write poems. In 1900, Frost settled on a farm in Derry, New Hampshire and taught at the Academy there. He sold the farm in 1912 and moved his family to England where his first two books were published.

The first two books brought him recognition on both sides of the Atlantic and upon his return to New Hampshire in 1915, he found himself in demand for public readings and teaching positions.

Frost taught at Amherst from 1926 to 1938, Harvard from 1939 to 1943, Dartmouth from 1943 to 1949 and finally received a permanent appointment at Amherst.

He was award Pulitzer Prizes in 1924, 1931, 1937 and 1943; and is, or course, well remembered by our generation as the poet at the inauguration of President Kennedy.

Note on Pricing:

- Prices before 1920 are for very good to fine copies without dustwrapper

- Prices estimated for 1920 and later are for very good copies without/with dustwrapper

- Christmas cards are in wraps and would normally only have one estimated price but as the quantities differ so much, we have used a range showing an estimate of the card with the imprint that has the largest quantity to the imprint that has the smallest quantity

REFERENCES:

(a) Clymer, W.B. Shubrick and Charles B. Green ROBERT FROST A BIBLIOGRAPH Jones Library, Amherst (1937) Used through *Selected Poems* in 1936, unless otherwise noted.

(b) Crane, Joan St. C., ROBERT FROST: A DESCRIPTIVE CATALOGUE OF BOOKS AND MANUSCRIPTS IN THE CLIFTON WALLER BARRETT LIBRARY UNIVERSITY OF VIRGINIA, University Press of Virginia, Charlottesville, 1974. Used from 1936 through 1962 unless otherwise noted.

(c) Broccoli & Clarke, FIRST PRINTINGS OF AMERICAN AUTHORS Volume 1, Gale Research, Detroit (1977). Used from 1963 through 1972, unless otherwise noted.

(d) Inventory or dealer catalogs.

001a: TWILIGHT (American Printing House (?) Lawrence, MA 1894) [0] 2 cc printed, one destroyed by Frost, one known to survive. Wraps $60,000.

001b: TWILIGHT Clifton Waller Barrett Library/Reynolds Co. University of Virginia 1966 [2] 20 cc on handmade Maidstone paper for presentation. Facsimile. Wraps (Robert Frost Books 5/91) $250.

001c TWILIGHT Clifton Waller Barrett Library/Reynolds Co. University of Virginia 1966 [2] 170 no. cc. Wraps. Facsimile (ref.b) $125.

002a: A BOY'S WILL David Nutt London 1913 [0] (Estimated at 1,000 to 1,100 copies for A thru E.) First issue, binding A: bronzed brown pebbled cloth. Gilt stamped $4,500.

002b: A BOY'S WILL David Nutt London 1913 [0] First issue, binding B: cream vellum-paper boards stamped in red (including border rule) $2,250.

002c: A BOY'S WILL David Nutt London 1913 [0] Second issue, binding C: cream linen-paper wrappers, stamped in black without a border rule. 70 cc rubber-stamped on p.iv (ref.b) $1,500.

002d: A BOY'S WILL David Nutt London 1913 [0] Second issue, binding D: cream linen-paper wrappers, stamped in black. The difference is 4-petaled flowers (preceding bindings have 8-petaled flowers) (ref.b) $1,250.

002e: A BOY'S WILL David Nutt London 1913 [2] 135 sgd no. cc in wraps (binding D) (ref.b) $1,750.

002f: A BOY'S WILL Henry Holt New York 1915 [0] Blue fine linen cloth and white endpapers (later copies incoarse blue linen cloth with buff endpapers). "Aind" for "And" on last line of p.14. (corrected in second printing). Glassine dustwrapper $600.

002g: A BOY'S WILL Henry Holt New York 1915 [0] Second printing with "and" correct $250.

003a: NORTH OF BOSTON David Nutt London (1914) [1] 350 cc. There were 1,000 sets of sheets printed and from 1914 to 1923. These sets were bound in various bindings. First issue, binding A: coarse green cloth measuring 195 x 154 mm $2,750.

003b: NORTH OF BOSTON Henry Holt New York 1914 [1] 150 cc. The U.K. sheets with Holt title page. Drab gray-brown boards backed with brown cloth. (Actually sold in 1915) $1,750.

003c: NORTH OF BOSTON David Nutt London (1914) [1] 200 cc. Fine green cloth measuring 189 x 145 mm (first issue sheets bound ca. 1917) (ref.b) $1,500.

003d: NORTH OF BOSTON David Nutt London (1914) [1] 41 cc. Blue cloth (first issue sheets bound ca. 1922) (ref.b) $1,000.

003e: NORTH OF BOSTON David Nutt London (1914) [1] 59 cc re-bound 003c in coarse green cloth, rubber-stamp on p.iv (first issue sheets bound ca. 1923). 200 x 145 mm (ref.b) $850.

003f: NORTH OF BOSTON David Nutt London (1914) [1] 200 cc in coarse green cloth, rubber-stamp on p.iv (first issue sheets bound ca. 1923). 195 x 150 mm (ref.b) $650.

003g: NORTH OF BOSTON Henry Holt New York 1915 [0] "Second Edition, 1915." 1,300 cc. Includes one poem "Good Hours" not in first (not included in Contents) $350.

003h: NORTH OF BOSTON Henry Holt New York (no-date, 1919) [0] 500 cc. First Illustrated Edition $300.

004a: MOUNTAIN INTERVAL Henry Holt New York (1916) [0] 4,000 cc (a&b). First state: p.88:6 and 7 repeated lines; "'Come'" for "'Gone'" p.93 line 6 from bottom $250.

004b: MOUNTAIN INTERVAL Henry Holt New York (1916) [0] Second state: errors corrected $125.

005a: MY NOVEMBER GUEST (Poet's Guild New York 1922) [] 5 x 7 1/2 inch broadside. Fewer than 300 cc (Pharos 7/85) $150.

006a: A HILLSIDE THAW (Poet's Guild New York 1922) [] 5 x 7 1/2 inch broadside. About 200 cc (Pharos 7/92) $125.

007a: SELECTED POEMS Henry Holt New York 1923 [0] 1,025 cc. "March, 1923" on copyright page $150/750

007b: SELECTED POEMS Heinemann London (1923) [1] $100/500

008a: NEW HAMPSHIRE Henry Holt New York 1923 [2] 350 sgd no. cc. Issued in white slipcase. Pulitzer Prize in Poetry for 1924 $600/750

008b: NEW HAMPSHIRE Henry Holt New York 1923 [0] 5,350 cc $100/450

008c: NEW HAMPSHIRE Grant Richards Ltd London 1924 [0] 150 cc of the U.S. sheets with cancel title page $100/400

008d: NEW HAMPSHIRE New Dresden Press Hanover, NH 1955 [2] 750 sgd and no. cc. First separate edition of the poem. In semitransparent rough white Japanese paper dustwrapper $400/450

009a: AN OLD MAN'S WINTER NIGHT Hampshire Bookshop Northampton 1924 [2] 175 cc. Folded sheet $250.

010a: SEVERAL SHORT POEMS Holt (New York 1924) [0] 2,000 cc. Wraps $450.

011a: SELECTED POEMS Holt New York (1928) [1] 3,475 cc. Revised/Expanded of the 1923 edition $100/400

012a: WEST-RUNNING BROOK Holt New York (1928) [0] 8,400 cc (est.). Lacks "First Edition" statement. Ref.a assumes the publisher ran off most of the copies before noticing the ommission of the "First Edition" statement $50/250

012b: WEST-RUNNING BROOK Holt New York (1928) [1] 1,000 cc (est.). States "First Edition" $40/200

012c: WEST-RUNNING BROOK Holt New York (1928) [2] 1,000 no. cc sgd by Frost and frontis and 3 plates pencil signed by artist J.J. Lankes. Slipcase. This issue used entirely different type and pagination than the trade edition $300/400

013a: A WAY OUT: A ONE ACT PLAY Harbor Press New York 1929 [2] 485 sgd no. cc. Issued without dustwrapper $500.

014a: THE LOVELY SHALL BE CHOOSERS Random House NY 1929 [2] 475 cc. Wrappers. (Sold in a set with 11 other poet's work as *The Poetry Quartos*) $150.

015a: THE COW'S IN THE CORN: A ONE-ACT IRISH PLAY IN RHYME Slide Mountain Press Gaylordsville 1929 [2] 91 sgd and no. cc.

Issued in flexible paper covered boards without dustwrapper $1,250.

016a: CHRISTMAS TREES (Spiral Press New York 1929) [0] 275 cc. Wraps. The first of the Christmas cards with four imprints (quantities vary from 50 to 100) $400-500

017a: COLLECTED POEMS OF ROBERT FROST Random House New York 1930 [2] 1,000 sgd and no. cc. Ref.a & b do not mention a dustwrapper, Van Allen Bradley (*Handbook of Values* 1982 edition) shows with dustwrapper. Plain unprinted glassine dustwrapper (Bert Babcock 5/ 88) $400.

017b: COLLECTED POEMS OF ROBERT FROST Henry Holt NY (1930) [1] 3,870 cc. "First Trade Edition." Pulitzer Prize for Poetry for 1931" $60/300

017c: COLLECTED POEMS OF ROBERT FROST Longmans, Green London 1930 [ ] 1,000 cc. Holt's sheets with Longmans, Green title page. Also noted with Book Society wrap-around band (Hawthorn Books 4/90) $50/250

018a: WILFRED DAVISON MEMORIAL LIBRARY BREAD LOAF (Middlebury College Middlebury, VT) 1930 [] 16 page pamphlet published as *Bread Loaf Folder No.8* $350.

019a: THE FOUR BELIEFS (Dartmouth College 1931) [] 250 cc. One sheet folded $300.

020a: EDUCATION BY POETRY - A MEDITATIVE MONOLOGUE Amherst 1931 [0] 16 page pamphlet issued as supplement to Alumni Council News $300.

021a: TWO LETTERS WRITTEN ON HIS UNDERGRADUATE DAYS AT

DARTMOUTH COLLEGE IN 1892 The Printer's Devil Press Hanover 1931 [2] 10 no. cc. Wraps (ref.b) $2,000.

022a: THE AUGUSTAN BOOKS OF POETRY ROBERT FROST Benn London (1932) [0] Wraps $150.

023a: THE LONE STRIKER (Knopf New York 1933) [0] 2,000 cc. Wraps. Issued in envelope. (Some used as a Christmas card by Frost) $100.

024a: TWO TRAMPS IN MUD-TIME (Spiral Press New York) 1934 [0] 775 cc. Wraps. (Christmas poem: 6 imprints with quantities varying from 25 to 200 cc) $200-350

025a: THREE POEMS Baker Library Press Hanover (1935) [2] 125 no. cc. Wraps $750.

026a: THE GOLD HESPERIDEE (Bibliophile Press Cortland 1935) [] Tan wraps. 500 cc printed, all but 37 copies were withdrawn. Colophon page has "Cortland NY/A." Pg.7 second line from bottom "Twas Sunday and Square Hale was dressed for meeting." Unnumbered on limitation page. Leaves measure 162x114 mm $900.

026b: THE GOLD HESPERIDEE (Bibliophile Press Cortland 1935) [2] 200 no. cc. Colophon page has "Cortland NY/B." Yellow wraps. Line noted in 021a has been reset so that "for meeting" is on separate line. Leaves measure 183x127 mm $600.

026c: THE GOLD HESPERIDEE (Bibliophile Press Cortland 1935) [] Reportedly 67 cc. Same as 020a but in pale yellow wraps with the word "English" stamped under "copy number" on p.2

$750.

027a: NEITHER OUT FAR NOR IN DEEP (Spiral Press New York) 1935 [0] 1,235 cc. Wraps. (Christmas poem: 8 imprints with quantities varying from 25 to 450 cc) $100-250

028a: FROM SNOW TO SNOW Henry Holt New York (1936) [0] 300 cc. Light-tan mottled wraps with a 4 page insert before half-title from The Hampshire Bookshop. Paper water-marked "Champlain / Text" (later watermarked "Warren's / Olde Style") (Some copies issued in envelope with "...Compliments of Henry Holt and Company" printed in gray) $250.

028b: FROM SNOW TO SNOW Henry Holt New York (1936) About 1,200 copies. Bound in rough tan line cloth lettered in dark brown. Issued without dustwrapper $100.

028c: FROM SNOW TO SNOW Henry Holt New York (1936) [0] 3,000 cc. Second printing in fine green linen cloth stamped in silver, issued in dustwrapper. (There was also another printing of 1,200 copies which may be exactly the same) $15/75

029a: A FURTHER RANGE Henry Holt New York (1936) [2] 803 sgd and no. cc. Issued in glassine dustwrapper in slipcase $300/400

029b: A FURTHER RANGE Henry Holt New York (1936) [1] 4,000 cc. Pulitzer Prize for Poetry in 1937 $25/125

029c: A FURTHER RANGE Jonathan Cape London (1937) [1] $20/100

030a: SELECTED POEMS Jonathan Cape London (1936) [1] Contains comments by Auden, Engle, C. Day-Lewis and Muir $40/200

031a: EVERYBODY'S SANITY (no-publ {Dahlstrom}) L.A. 1936 [0] About 100-150 cc Wraps $300.

032a: TO A YOUNG WRETCH (Spiral Press New York 1937) [0] 820 cc. Wraps. (Christmas poem: 7 imprints with quantities varying from 25 to 275 copies) $150-250

032b: TO A YOUNG WRETCH (Barrett Library-University of Va. Charlottesville no-date, 1970) [0] Wraps $35.

033a: CARPE DIEM (Spiral Press New York 1938) [0] 230 cc. Wraps. (Christmas poem: 3 imprints, quantities of 30, 50 and 150) $250-350

034a: WHAT BECAME OF NEW ENGLAND? Oberlin College 1938 [0] One sheet folded to make 4 pages. Reprinting Frost's June 1937 commencement address, which had been published in the Oberlin alumni magazine for May 1938. First separate edition (Black Sun 5/87) $250.

035a: COLLECTED POEMS OF ROBERT FROST Henry Holt New York 1939 [1] 3,750 cc (a&b) $40/200

035b: COLLECTED POEMS OF ROBERT FROST Henry Holt New York 1939 [1] Signed on tipped-in sheet $175/300

035c: COLLECTED POEMS OF ROBERT FROST Longmans, Green London (1939) [ ] American sheets (ref.c). Not listed in ref.b $40/200

036a: A CONSIDERABLE SPECK (Colonial Society of Mass. 1939) [0] Less than 100 cc. Single sheet folded to 4 pages $600.

037a: TRIPLE PLATE (Spiral Press New York 1939) [0] 1,825 cc. Wraps. Decorated by Fritz Eichenberg (Christmas poem: 8 imprints with quantities varying from 25 to 900 cc) $60-250

038a: OUR HOLD ON THE PLANET (No publisher or place) 1940 [0] 975 cc. Wraps. (Christmas poem: 3 imprints, quantities of 125, 250 and 600 cc) $100-300

039a: I COULD GIVE ALL TO TIME (No publisher or place) 1941 [0] 1,000 cc. Wraps. (Christmas poem: 3 imprints, quantities of 150, 180 and 770 cc) $100-250

040a: A WITNESS TREE Henry Holt New York (1942) [2] 735 sgd no cc in slipcase $275/350

040b: A WITNESS TREE Henry Holt New York (1942) [1] 8,500 cc Pulitzer Prize for 1943 $20/100

040c: A WITNESS TREE Jonathan Cape London (1943) [1] $15/75

041a: THE GIFT OUTRIGHT (No publisher or place) 1942 [0] 1,250 cc. Wraps. (Christmas poem: 3 imprints, quantities of 100, 150 and 1000 cc) 100/250

042a: COME IN AND OTHER POEMS Henry Holt New York (1943) [1] Edited by Louis Untermeyer $20/100

042b: COME IN AND OTHER POEMS Jonathan Cape London (1944) [1] $15/75

043a: THE GUARDEEN (Ward Ritchie L.A.) 1943 [2] 96 no. cc. Wraps. Printed for Earle J. Bernheimer $400.

044a: TWO LEADING LIGHTS (Ward Ritchie L.A.) 1944 [2] 52 no. cc. Wraps. Printed for Earle J. Bernheimer $450.

045a: FIFTY YEARS OF ROBERT FROST Hanover 1944 [] Boards. Includes first appearance of "In England" (Pharos 5/90) $250.

045b: FIFTY YEARS OF ROBERT FROST Hanover 1944 [] Wraps. Regular issue (Pharos 1988) $100.

046a: AN UNSTAMPED LETTER IN OUR RURAL LETTER BOX (Spiral Press New York) 1944 [0] 2,050 cc. Wraps. (Christmas Poem: 6 imprints, quantities vary from 100 to 1250 cc) $75-200

047a: A MASQUE OF REASON Henry Holt New York (1945) [2] 800 sgd no. cc. Issued without dustwrapper in slipcase $275/350

047b: A MASQUE OF REASON Henry Holt New York (1945) [1] 15,000 cc $15/75

047c: A MASQUE OF REASON, A MASQUE OF MERCY AND STEEPLE BUSH Jonathan Cape London (1948) [1] $15/75

048a: A MOOD APART Duke University 1945 [] Broadside (Heritage Bookshop 6/92) $300.

049a: ON MAKING CERTAIN ANYTHING HAS HAPPENED (Spiral Press New York 1945) [0] 2,600 cc. Wraps. (Christmas poems: 8 imprints, quantities vary from 100 to 1050 cc) $60/200

050a: THE COURAGE TO BE NEW Orris Manning Memorial Ripton 1946 [0] Broadside $175.

051a: THE POCKET BOOK OF ROBERT FROST'S POEMS Pocket Books New York (1946) [] Wraps. Enlarged edition of *Come in...*, Edited by Louis Untermeyer (ref.c) $40.

052a: THE POEMS OF ROBERT FROST Modern Library New York (1946) [1] $15/75

053a: A YOUNG BIRCH (Spiral Press New York) 1946 [0] 3,445 cc. Wraps. (Christmas poems: 10 imprints, quantities vary from 50 to 1160 cc) $60-200

054a: STEEPLE BUSH Henry Holt New York (1947) [2] 751 sgd and no. cc. Issued without dustwrapper in slipcase $275/350

054b: STEEPLE BUSH Henry Holt New York (1947) [0] 7,500 cc. (See 047c for English publication) $20/100

055a: A MASQUE OF MERCY Henry Holt New York (1947) [2] 751 sgd and no. cc. Issued without dustwrapper in slipcase $275/350

055b: A MASQUE OF MERCY Henry Holt New York (1947) [1] 7,500 cc (See 047c for English publication) $15/75

056a: TWO POEMS ON REVOLUTION... Bookbuilders Boston 1947 [0] about 25-30 cc. Wraps. Also includes poem by Oscar Williams $400.

057a: A SERMON Rockdale Temple Cincinnati (1947) [2] 500 cc. Wraps $350.

058a: ONE STEP BACKWARD TAKEN (Spiral Press New York 1947) [0] 3,050 cc. Wraps. (Christmas poem: 10 imprints, quantities vary from 50 to 1200 cc) (Also a unique trial proof, with substantial differences, in pale yellow wraps catalogued by George Houle in 1988 for $1,250.) $60-200

059a: THE FALLS (Ward Ritchie L.A. 1947) [] "First Proof" in stapled pale blue wraps printed in red (Glenn Horowitz 3/91) $500.

059b: THE FALLS (Ward Ritchie L.A. 1947) [2] 60 no. cc. Wrappers. Printed for Earle J. Bernheimer $500.

060a: ON THE INFLATION OF THE CURRENCY Earle J. Bernheimer 1948 [2] 60 no. cc. Wraps $450.

061a: CLOSED FOR GOOD (Spiral Press New York 1948) [0] 2,275 cc. Wraps. (Christmas poems: 8 imprints, quantities vary from 75 to 1,050 cc) $60-175

062a: GREECE Black Rose Press Chicago (1948) [2] 47 no. cc were printed but only 26 sent out $750.

063a: ON A TREE FALLEN ACROSS THE ROAD (Spiral Press New York 1949) [0] 3,060 cc. Wraps. (Christmas poem: 14 imprints plus 50 copies left blank for Lesley Frost. Quantities vary from 50 to 935 cc) $60-200

064a: COMPLETE POEMS OF ROBERT FROST 1949 Henry Holt New York (1949) [2] 500 sgd and no. cc. Issued in glassine dustwrapper and slipcase $400/500

064b: COMPLETE POEMS OF ROBERT FROST 1949 Henry Holt New York (1949) [1] 7,325 cc $25/125

064c: COMPLETE POEMS OF ROBERT FROST 1949 Limited Editions Club NY 1950

[2] 1,500 sgd no cc. 2 volumes in slipcase $450/600

064d: COMPLETE POEMS OF ROBERT FROST 1949 Jonathan Cape London (1951) [1] $25/125

065a: DOOM TO BLOOM (Spiral Press New York 1950) [0] 3,750 cc. Wraps. (Christmas poems: 16 imprints, quantities vary from 75 to 1,050 cc) $50-175

066a: HARD NOT TO BE KING House of Books NY 1951 [2] 300 sgd no cc $500.

067a: THE ROAD NOT TAKEN Henry Holt New York (1951) [0] Further enlargement of *Come In* and *The Pocket Book...* with new title (ref.c). Edited by Louis Untermeyer $12/60

068a: A CABIN IN THE CLEARING (Spiral Press New York 1951) [0] 3,750 cc. Wraps. (Christmas poem: 14 imprints, quantities vary from 75 to 1,325 cc) $50-175

069a: DOES NO ONE AT ALL... (Spiral Press New York 1952) [0] 3,875 cc. Wraps. (Christmas poem: 14 imprints, quantities vary from 50 to 1,300 cc.) Beige wraps with design in dark green. Variant in light blue gray wraps with design in dark red $50-200

070a: AMHERST COLLEGE AMHERST, MASSACHUSETTS 1953 Amherst College Amherst 1953 [] New Year's greeting card from Frost (Robert Frost Books 5/91) $150.

071a: ONE MORE BREVITY (Spiral Press New York) 1953 [0] 4,501 cc. Wraps. (Christmas poem: 15 imprints, quantities vary from 75 to 1,575 cc) $50-175

072a: AFORESAID Henry Holt New York (1954) [2] 650 no. cc. Issued without dustwrapper in slipcase. No trade edition. Not sure if this was issued signed $350/450

073a: FROM A MILKWEED POD (Spiral Press New York 1954) [0] 5,076 cc. Wraps. (Christmas poem: 18 imprints, quantities vary from 32 to 1,767 cc) $50-250

074a: ROBERT FROST SELECTED POEMS Penguin Books Harmondsworth (1955) [1] Wraps. Penguin Poets D 27. Introduction by C. Day Lewis $40.

NEW HAMPSHIRE see item 007d

075a: SOME SCIENCE FICTION (Spiral Press New York 1955) [0] 5,650 cc. Wraps. (Christmas poem: 17 imprints, quantities vary from 50 to 2,000 cc.) Variant in gray laid paper (Robert Frost Books 5/91) $40-200

076a: KITTY HAWK (Spiral Press New York 1956) [0] 7,000 cc. Wraps. (Christmas poem: 21 imprints, quantities vary from 25 to 2,950 cc) $40-250

077a: A TALK FOR STUDENTS Fund For The Republic NY (1956) [0] Wraps $100.

078a: MY OBJECTION TO BEING STEPPED ON (Spiral Press New York 1957) [0] 8,290 cc. Wraps. (Christmas poem: 21 imprints, quantities vary from 70 to 3,675 cc.) Page 3 either has a red-orange floral ornament or an olive green 8-pointed star, no priority $40-175

079a: AWAY! (Spiral Press New York 1958) [0] 9,155 cc Wraps (Christmas poem: 22 imprints, quantities vary from 35 to 4,550 cc) $35-250

080a: A REMEMBERANCE COLLECTION OF NEW POEMS (Holt NY 1959) [2] 150 cc. Wraps (ref.d). First appearance of all 8 poems (Robert Frost Books 5/91) $200.

081a: YOU COME TOO Henry Holt New York (1959) [1] $12/60

081b: YOU COME TOO Bodley Head London (1964) [] Advance uncorrected proof in blue wraps (Dalian Books 7/91) $75.

081c: YOU COME TOO Bodley Head London (1964) [] Ref.c (not in ref.b) $12/60

082a: FRESHMAN DAYS... Dartmouth (Hanover) 1959 [0] Off-print in pictorial stapled wraps, from the March 1959 alumni magazine (Waiting For Godot 2/87) $125.

083a: A-WISHING WELL (Spiral Press New York 1959) [0] 10,760 cc. Wraps. (Christmas poem: 20 imprints, quantities vary from 50 to 6,870 cc) $35-175

084a: ACCIDENTALLY ON PURPOSE (Spiral Press New York) 1960 [0] 10,600 cc. Wraps. (Christmas poem: 20 imprints, quantities vary from 50 to 6,600 cc) $35-175

085a: THE WOOD-PILE (Spiral Press New York) 1961 [0] 15,060 cc. Wraps. (Christmas poem: 21 imprints, quantities vary from 50 to 10,265 cc) $30-175

086a: MY BUTTERFLY. AN ELEGY California Friends of Robert Frost (Huntington Library?) Pasadena (no-date) 1960s? [] 14" x 18" broadside. First separate edition of Frost's first published poem for pay (Waiting For Godot 10/90) $75.

087a: SIX POEMS New York Public Library NY 1961 [0] Wraps. Includes three poems by Frost and three by Carl Sandburg $40.

088a: DEDICATION THE GIFT OUTRIGHT THE INAUGURAL ADDRESS Washington, D.C. 1961 [2] 250 no. cc of total printing of 500 (numbered 1-250). The Inaugural Address. "Printed for the friends of Holt, Rinehart..." on p.4. Ref.a notes a "pamphlet edition from the same type was later printed by Holt as a keepsake for the dinner..." later given to Frost $400.

088b: DEDICATION THE GIFT OUTRIGHT THE INAUGURAL ADDRESS Washington, D.C. 1961 [2] 250 no. cc of total printing of 500 (numbered 251-500). "Printed for friends of the Spiral Press..." on p.4 $350.

089a: IN THE CLEARING Holt, Rinehart & Winston New York (1962) [] Tall spiral bound uncorrected proof (Pharos Books 1/90) $400.

089b: IN THE CLEARING Holt, Rinehart & Winston New York (1962) [2] 1,500 sgd and no. cc. Issued without dustwrapper in slipcase $200/275

089c: IN THE CLEARING Holt, Rinehart & Winston New York (1962) [1] Back panel of dustwrapper noted in two states: white with black lettering; and black with white lettering. Priority unknown (Am Here Books 6/89) $12/60

089d: IN THE CLEARING Holt, Rinehart & Winston London (1962) [1] Introduction by Robert Graves not in U.S. edition $15/75

090a: THE PROPHETS REALLY PROPHESY AS MYSTICS THE COMMENTATORS MERELY BY STATISTICS (Spiral Press New

York) 1962 [0] 17,055 cc. Wraps. (Christmas poem: 21 imprints, quantities vary from 50 to 12,500 cc) $30-175

091a: THE CONSTANT SYMBOL Cornelia & Waller Barrett 1962 [0] 500 cc. Wraps. Printed by Spiral Press, New York $100.

092a: ROBERT FROST ON "EXTRAVAGANCE" Dartmouth (Hanover) 1963 [] An off-print, in printed wraps, from the alumni magazine (Waiting For Godot 2/87) $100.

093a: THE LETTERS OF ROBERT FROST TO LOUIS UNTERMEYER Holt, Rinehart & Winston New York (1963) [] Uncorrected proof in sprial bound printed wraps (Wm. Reese Co. 6/92) $150.

093b: THE LETTERS OF ROBERT FROST TO LOUIS UNTERMEYER Holt, Rinehart & Winston New York (1963) [1] Edited by Louis Untermeyer $10/50

093c: THE LETTERS OF ROBERT FROST TO LOUIS UNTERMEYER Jonathan Cape London (1964) [1] $12/60

094a: ROBERT FROST: FARM POULTRYMAN Dartmouth Publications Handover, NH 1963 [0] $12/60

095a: ROBERT FROST AND JOHN BARTLETT: THE RECORD OF A FRIENDSHIP Holt, Rinehart & Winston New York (1963) [1] $10/50

096a: ROBERT FROST : HIS AMERICAN SEND-OFF - 1915 Stinehour Press Lunenberg, Vt. (1963) [] Wraps $100.

097a: IN MEMORY OF ROBERT FROST Amherst 1963 [0] Wraps. Memorial service at the Johnson Chapel on February 17, 1963 with 11 poems by Frost. 10 pages including cover $75.

098a: WILD GRAPES Scott, Foreman & Co. (Chicago 1963) [0] Wraps. The poem with questions for students and short biography $75.

099a: SELECTED POEMS OF ROBERT FROST Holt, Rinehart & Winston New York (1963) [0] Introduction by Robert Graves $15/75

100a: SELECTED LETTERS OF ROBERT FROST Holt, Rinehart & Winston New York (1964) [] Galley proofs in two spiral bound volumes (Wm. Reese Co. 6/92) $175.

100b: SELECTED LETTERS OF ROBERT FROST Holt, Rinehart & Winston New York (1964) [1] Edited by Lawrence Thompson $12/60

100c: SELECTED LETTERS OF ROBERT FROST Jonathan Cape L (1965) [1] $12/60

101a: AN UNCOMPLETED REVISION OF "EDUCATION BY POETRY" (Dartmouth Hanover 1966) [] Wraps. Facsimile of Frost's holograph corrections to text, with a note by Edward Connery Lathem $75.

102a: INTERVIEWS WITH ROBERT FROST Holt, Rinehart & Winston New York (1966) [1] Edited by Edward Connery Lathem $10/50

102b: INTERVIEWS WITH ROBERT FROST Jonathan Cape London (1967) [] $10/50

103a: ROBERT FROST AND THE LAWRENCE, MASS. "HIGH SCHOOL BULLETIN..." Grolier Club New York 1966 [ ] Edited by Lathem and Thompson $75.

104a: SELECTED PROSE OF ROBERT FROST Holt, Rinehart & Winston New York (1966) [1] Edited by Hyde Cox and Edward Connery Lathem $10/50

105a: FROST: THE POET AND HIS POETRY Holt, Rinehart & Winston New York (1967) [0] Wraps with record by Frost in back pocket. Edited by David Sohn and Richard Tyre $60.

106a: THE POETRY OF ROBERT FROST Holt, Rinehart & Winston New York (1969) [1] Edited by Edward Connery Lathem. Two volumes $15/75

106b: THE POETRY OF ROBERT FROST Holt, Rinehart & Winston New York (1969) [1] One volume in dustwrapper priced $10.95 and with "1169" at bottom of text on front flap (also noted without price or "1169" on front flap, assume book club edition) $10/50

106c: THE POETRY OF ROBERT FROST Imprint Society Barre, Mass. 1971 [2] 1,950 sgd cc. Signed by the designer, Ruzicka. Two volumes. New introduction by Edward Connery Lathem $150/200

107a: ONE FAVORED ACORN Middlebury College Ripton 1969 [2] 400 cc. Wraps (ref.b) $150.

108a: STOPPING BY THE WOODS ON A SNOWING EVENING Castalia Press Easthampton 1970 [2] 40 cc. Broadside. First separate printing (In Our Time, 1988) $500.

109a: HOLIDAY GREETINGS FROM ROBERT FROST New Hampshire Historical Society Concord 1971 [2] 750 cc. Wraps. Reprints Frost's first Christmas poem/card

"Christmas Trees" and briefly describes the various poems/cards issued between 1929 and 1963 $40.

110a: FAMILY LETTERS OF ROBERT AND ELINOR FROST State University of New York Press Albany, NY 1972 [1] Foreword by Lesley Frost, edited by Arnold Grade $10/40

111a: ROBERT FROST: POETRY AND PROSE Holt, Rinehart & Winston New York (1972) [0] Edited by Edward Lathem and Lawrance Thompson $10/40

112a: ROBERT FROST ON WRITING Rutgers University Press New Brunswick (1972) [0] Edited by Elaine Barry $10/40

113a: A TIME TO TALK CONVERSATIONS & INDISCRETIONS Robson (London 1973) [1] Recorded by Robert Francis (Robert Loren Link 6/90) $10/40

114a: ROBERT FROST 1874-1963 A REMEMBRANCE Amherst College 1974 [0] 500 cc. Wraps with facsimile of a handwritten fragment $75.

115a: TRIBUTE TO E.A. ROBINSON Godine Boston 1974 [2] 1,000 cc. Wraps. Facsimile of the original holograph manuscript (ref.d) $35.

116a: THE POETRY OF ROBERT FROST Holt, Rinehart New York (1976) [] (ref.d) $8/40

117a: FOREST FLOWERS Amherst College Library Amherst 1978 [2] 400 cc. Wraps. Laid-in is one sheet with history and first form of this poem as "Tutelary Elves" $60.

118a: ROBERT FROST AND SIDNEY COX FORTY YEARS OF FRIENDSHIP University

Press of New England Hanover 1981 [0] The letters with a foreword by James M. Cox. Connecting text by William R. Evans $8/40

119a: PROSE JOTTINGS OF ROBERT FROST Stinehour Press Lunenberg (1982) [] Quarter cloth in slipcase. Edited by Edward Connery Lathem and Hyde Cox $125.

120a: (poems) 5 volumes MOWING; NEITHER FAR OUT; THE MID-DLENESS OF THE ROAD; STORM FEAR and DESIGN Prometheus Press Grasse 1983 [2] Wraps. Each pamphlet limited to 5 copies signed and illustrated by Frederic Prokosch. Sold originally as a set $200.

121a: BIRCHES Holt New York 1988 [] $7/35

122a: ROBERT FROST : TOWARD THE SOURCE, AGAINST THE STREAM Writers In Performance New York 1990 [2] 350 cc. Wraps $40.

123a: TWO WINTERY POEMS Brookhaven Press (no place or date) [] Illustrated folded card (Chloe's Books) $25.

124a: SOME PEOPLE SEEM TO THINK Quintessence Press (no place or date) [] Illustrated broadside $25.

William Goyen

WILLIAM GOYEN
(1915-1984)

Goyen was born in Trinity, Texas. He was educated at Rice University and then served in the U.S. Navy throughout World War II. He was a critic and reviewer for the *New York Times* from 1950 to 1965, and senior editor at McGraw Hill from 1966 to 1972. During and after this period he taught at various universities.

Ref.c includes 10 plays adapted by Goyen from his own or other writers works which have not been included herein. These are mimeographed sheets for the most part and we have only seen one set catalogued, that was "Christy" (NY 1964) by Glenn Horowitz, Catalog 11 at $225.

REFERENCES:

(a) Lepper, Gary M., A BIBLIOGRAPHICAL REFERENCE TO SEVENTY-FIVE MODERN AMERICAN AUTHORS, Serendipity Books, Berkeley, 1976

(b) Bruccoli & Clark, FIRST PRINTINGS OF AMERICAN AUTHORS, Gale Research, Detroit, (1979), Volume 4

(c) Wright, Stuart, WILLIAM GOYEN A DESCRIPTIVE BIBLIOGRAPHY 1938-1985, Meckler Publ., Westport, Ct. (1986)

001a: THE HOUSE OF BREATH Random House NY (1950) [1] 4,000 cc (quanity-ref.c). One of Greene's *Fifty Best Books on Texas*. (A variant with top edge gray noted by Wm. Reese Co. Cat. 63) $25/100

001b: THE HOUSE OF BREATH Chatto & Windus L 1951 [0] 3,000 cc (quanity-ref.c) $15/75

001c: THE HOUSE OF BREATH Random House/Bookworks NY/Berkeley (1975) [2] 1,500 cc. Adds note by Goyen, 25th Anniversary Edition, quantity stated on copyright page $6/35

001d: THE HOUSE OF BREATH Random House/Bookworks NY/Berkeley (1975) [2] 7,500 cc. Wraps. Issued simultaneously. Quantity stated on copyright page $15.

002a: GHOST AND FLESH STORIES AND TALES Random House NY (1952) [1] 2,000 cc (quanity-ref.c) $15/75

003a: THE LAZY ONES New Directions (Norfolk 1952) [0] Translation of Cossery's book (ref.b) $12/50

003b: THE LAZY ONES Peter Owen L 1952 [] $10/50

004a: A SHAPE OF LIGHT Southwest Review No-place 1952 [] Off-print from Winter issue. Stapled on left margin (H.E. Turlington 9/90) $50.

005a: THE PEOPLE OF JOSEPH GLASSCO C. Viviano NY (1953) [0] Wraps. All text by Goyen $75.

006a: IN A FARTHER COUNTRY Random House NY (1955) [0] 2,500 cc (quanity-ref.c) $15/75

006b: IN A FARTHER COUNTRY Owen L (1962) [1] $10/40

006c: IN A FARTHER COUNTRY Owen L 1962 [0] about 100 cc of 5b stamped "...Dufour Editions.." on copyright page and distributed in U.S. $20/50

007a: THE FACES OF BLOOD KINDRED Random House (NY 1960) [1] $12/60

008a: THE FAIR SISTER Doubleday GC (1963) [1] $12/60

008b: SAVATA, MY FAIR SISTER Owen L (1963) [0] New title $10/40

009a: SHORT STORIES Vandenhoeck & Ruprecht Gottingen (Germany 1964) [0] Includes first publication of "The Thief Coyote" $40.

010a: JOTTINGS FROM A DUBLIN JOURNAL (Show no-place 1965) [0] 4 page off-print from magazine (H.E. Turlington 6/91) $50.

011a: MY ANTONIA A CRITICAL COMMENTARY Amer.R.D.M. NY (1966) [0] Wraps $35.

012a: RALPH ELLISON'S INVISIBLE MAN A CRITICAL COMMENTARY Amer. R.D.M. NY (1966) [0] Yellowish green, light grayish blue and white wraps (second printing in red, white and black wraps) (ref.c) $30.

013a: A BOOK OF JESUS Doubleday GC 1973 [] Long printer's galley proofs (H.E. Turlington 9/90) $200.

013b: A BOOK OF JESUS Doubleday GC 1973 [1] Uncorrected proof in mustard card covers, ring bound and with cover label (Serendipity Books #40) $100.

013c: A BOOK OF JESUS Doubleday GC 1973 [1] 5,500 cc (quanity-ref.c). Also noted in wrap-around band (H.E. Turlington 9/90) $7/35

014a: SELECTED WRITINGS OF WILLIAM GOYEN Random House NY/Berkeley (1974) [] Uncorrected proofs in string tied signatures. Laid in sample dustwrapper (H.E,. Turlington 9/90) $50.

014b: SELECTED WRITINGS OF WILLIAM GOYEN Random House NY/ Berkeley (1974) [1] 1,500 cc (quanity on copyright page) $8/40

014c: SELECTED WRITINGS OF WILLIAM GOYEN Random House, NY/Berkeley (1974) [1] Wraps. 7,500 cc (quanity on copyright page) $7.

015a: COME, THE RESTORER Doubleday GC 1974 [1] 6,000 cc (quanity-ref.c). Published 10/4/74 @ $5.95) $7/35

016a: THE COLLECTED STORIES OF WILLIAM GOYEN Doubleday GC 1975 [] Long sheets of galley proofs (H.E. Turlington 9/90) $150.

016b: THE COLLECTED STORIES OF WILLIAM GOYEN Doubleday GC 1975 [] Uncorrected proofs in red wraps $75.

016c: THE COLLECTED STORIES OF WILLIAM GOYEN Doubleday GC 1975 [1] (ref.b.) 4,000 cc (ref.c) $6/30

017a: NINE POEMS Albondocani NY 1976 [2] 26 sgd ltr cc. Wraps (ref.b) $125.

017b: NINE POEMS Albondocani NY 1976 [2] 200 sgd no cc. Wraps (ref.b) $50.

018a: WHILE YOU WERE AWAY-A TALK DELIVERED BY WM. GOYEN AT HOUSTON PUBLIC LIB+ Houston Public Lib. (Houston 1978) [0] Wraps (ref.b) $50.

019a: SIMON'S CASTLE + Deutscher... Munich (1978) [] Wraps. English and German text (H.E. Turlington 9/90) $25.

020a: ARTHUR BOND Palaemon (Winston-Salem 1979) [2] 30 cc. Marbled wraps. Numbered in Roman. For distribution by author and publisher (out of 230 cc) (ref.c states 226 copies in total were issued so perhaps this was only 26 cc) $100.

020b: ARTHUR BOND Palaemon (Winston-Salem 1979) [2] 200 sgd no cc (out of 230 cc.) Wraps (ref.c) $50.

021a: WONDERFUL PLANT Palaemon (Winston-Salem 1980) [2] 60 sgd no cc (Roman numerals). Not For Sale. Issued in acetate dustwrapper without slipcase (ref.c) $125.

021b: WONDERFUL PLANT Palaemon (Winston-Salem 1980) [2] 100 sgd no. cc. Issued in acetate dustwrapper (ref.c) $60.

022a: PRECIOUS DOOR Red Ozier Press 1981 [2] 115 sgd no cc. Issued without dustwrapper or slipcase. Signed by Goyen and the artist John DePol (ref.c) $125.

023a: NEW WORK AND WORK IN PROGRESS Palaemon (Winston-Salem 1983) [2] 40 sgd no cc. Issued without dustwrapper. Signed by Goyen and Reginald Gibbons (interviewer) (ref.c) $100.

023b: NEW WORK AND WORK IN PROGRESS Palaemon (Winston-Salem 1983) [2] 160 sgd cc (not numbered) $40.

024a: ARCADIO Potter NY (1983) [] Uncorrected proofs in pumpkin wraps (Bev Chaney 9/91) $40.

024b: ARCADIO Potter NY (1983) [3] Also states "First Edition" $4/20

025a: HAD I A HUNDRED MOUTHS Potter NY (1985) [3] Also states "First Edition." New and selected stories 1947-1983 with introduction by Joyce Carol Oates. Uncorrected proof in gray wraps (H.E. Turlington #28) $50.

025b: HAD I A HUNDRED MOUTHS Potter NY (1985) [3] Also states "First Edition" $5/15

Zane Grey.

ZANE GREY
(1875 - 1939)

Zane Grey was born in Zanesville, Ohio in 1875 and graduated from the University of Pennsylvania in 1896. He was a prolific writer of adventure stories taking place in the West and Southwest. All of his stories contain vivid topographical detail. Grey is best known for *Riders of The Purple Sage* (1912).

We wish to thank Edward and Judith Myers of Country Lane Books for allowing us to use their bibliographic work in the preparation of this guide.

REFERENCES:

(a) Myers, Edward and Judith. A BIBLIOGRAPHICAL CHECKLIST OF THE WRITINGS OF ZANE GREY. Collinsville, CT., 1986 (available for $12.50). The prices before 1920 are for fine copies without dustwrappers as dustwrappers before 1920 are rare. Nice copies in dustwrappers would probably be two to five times the prices shown.

(b) Eppard, Philip B. (editor). FIRST PRINTINGS OF AMERICAN AUTHORS, Volume 5. Gale Research, Detroit (1987). Used for English editions; however, no first edition identification was provided.

(c) Wheeler, Dr. Joe L. ZANE GREY'S WEST, Volume I through Volume VII, (Texas/Annapolis) 1989-1991.

001a: BETTY ZANE Charles Francis Press NY (1903) [0] No mention of the edition on the title page. Issued without dustwrapper $1,750.

001b: BETTY ZANE Charles Francis Press NY (1903) [] States "Second Edition" in small letters near the center of the title page. Issued without dustwrapper $750.

001c: BETTY ZANE Hodder & Stoughton L 1920 [] $150/600

001d: BETTY ZANE Saalfield Akron (1940) [] Abridge edition (George Houle 11/89) $35.

002a: THE SPIRIT OF THE BORDER A.L. Burt NY (1906) [0] With 4 pages of advertisements and Burt's address listed as 52-58 Duane Street (ref.a). Ref.b states earliest copies have ads at back headed "Good fiction worth reading." First page begins "Colonial Free Lance." Second page begins "Darnley." Third page begins "Guy Fawkes." Fourth page begins "Winsor Castle." Also, first page lists 5 books, other pages no more than 3 books $500.

002b: THE SPIRIT OF THE BORDER Laurie L. (1921) [] (Although ref.c shows 1920 using U.S. sheets) $100/500

003a: TARPON THE SILVER KING (New York and Cuba Mail Steamship Co. NY 1906) [0] Wraps. Grey's name on third page at bottom (ref.c). Not in ref. a $850.

004a: THE LAST OF THE PLAINSMEN Outing Publishing Co. NY 1908 [0] $250.

004b: THE LAST OF THE PLAINSMEN Hodder & Stoughton L 1908 [] Ref.b had 1909 but assume ref.c is correct as 1908 $200.

005a: THE LAST TRAIL A.L. Burt NY (1909) [0] With two pages of advertisements listing 52-58 Duane Street as Burt's address. The address would also appear on dustwrapper (ref.a).

Ref.b&c call for six pages of ads with page 1 beginning with "Abner Daniel," page 2 "The Circle," page 3 "The House on Cherry Street," page 4 "Max," page 5 "The Reconstructed Marriage," page 6 "Susan Clegg..." and ends with "The Younger Set." Ref.b&c go on to identify the second printing as having 9 pages of ads and the third printing having 11 pages of ads. Ed Myers believes that the address on Duane Street is important as Burt moved about 1910 $600.

005b: THE LAST TRAIL Laurie L (1920) [] $100/600

006a: NASSAU CUBA YUCATAN MEXICO A PERSONAL NOTE OF APPRECIATION OF THESE NEARBY FOREIGN LANDS New York and Cuba Mail Steam Ship Co. NY 1909 [0] Wraps. (Not in ref.a) $1000.

006b: NASSAU CUBA YUCATAN MEXICO A PERSONAL NOTE OF APPRECIATION OF THESE NEARBY FOREIGN LANDS Zane Grey Collector Williamsport, Md. 1976 [] 500 cc. Wraps. A facsimile edition edited by G.M. Farley $40.

007a: THE SHORT STOP A.C. McClure NY 1909 [1] "Published June, 1909" $500.

007b: THE SHORT STOP Laurie L (1920) [] $100/600

008a: THE HERITAGE OF THE DESERT Harper's NY 1910 [1] "Published September 1910." No code letters on copyright page $250.

008b: THE HERITAGE OF THE DESERT Nelson L (1918) [] $60.

008c: DESERT HERITAGE World L 1965 [] Wraps. New title $20.

009a: THE YOUNG FORESTER Harper & Bros. NY 1910 [1] "Published October 1915." No code letters on copyright page $400.

009b: THE YOUNG FORESTER Nelson L (1922) [] $150.

010a: THE YOUNG PITCHER Harper & Bros. NY 1911 [1] "Published March, 1911." No code letters on copyright page $500.

010b: THE YOUNG PITCHER Lloyds L (1919) [] $200.

011a: THE YOUNG LION HUNTER Harper & Bros. NY 1911 [1] "Published October 1911." No code letters on copyright page $250.

011b: THE YOUNG LION HUNTER Lloyds L (1919) [1] "Published October, 1911" $200.

012a: RIDERS OF THE PURPLE SAGE Harper & Bros. NY 1912 [] Red boards with printed label on cover and binding sample glued to back of front cover. "Advance copy for private distribution. Not for sale." (George R. Minkoff 11/90) $2,000.

012b: RIDERS OF THE PURPLE SAGE Harper & Bros. NY 1912 [1] "Published January 1912." No code letters on copyright page. (Noted with "H-M" on copyright page but this is a later printing) $350.

012c: RIDERS OF THE PURPLE SAGE Harper & Bros. NY (1921) [0] Contains code letters "K-V." Color plates by W. Herbert Dunton $150/500

013a: KEN WARD IN THE JUNGLE Harper & Bros. NY 1912 [1] "Published September

1912." Code letters "H-M" on copyright page $400.

013b: KEN WARD IN THE JUNGLE Nelson L (1919) [] $150.

014a: DESERT GOLD Harper & Bros. NY 1913 [0] Code letters [0] "C-N" on copyright page $125.

015a: THE LIGHT OF WESTERN STARS Harper & Bros. NY 1914 [1] "Published January 1914" and code letters "M-N" on copyright page $150.

015b: THE LIGHT OF WESTERN STARS Nelson L (1918) [] $100.

016a: THE LONE STAR RANGER Harper & Bros. NY 1915 [1] "Published January 1915" and code letters "M-O" on copyright page $150.

017a: THE RAINBOW TRAIL Harper & Bros. NY (1915) [1] "Published August 1915" and code letters "F-P" on copyright page $100.

018a: THE BORDER LEGION... Harper & Bros. NY (1916) [1] "Published May 1916" and code letters "E-Q" on copyright page $100.

019a: WILDFIRE Harper & Bros. NY (1917) [1] "Published January 1917" and code letters "L-Q" on copyright page $75.

019b: WILDFIRE Nelson L (1920) [] $50/300

020a: THE U.P. TRAIL Harper & Bros. NY (1918) [1] "Published January 1918" and code letters "A-S" on copyright page $75.

020b: THE ROARING U.P. TRAIL Hodder & Stoughton L (1918) [] $75.

021a: THE DESERT OF WHEAT Harper & Bros. NY (1919) [1] "Published January 1919" and code letters "A-T" on copyright page $75.

021b: THE DESERT OF WHEAT Hodder & Stoughton L (1919) [] $60.

022a: TALES OF FISHES Harper & Bros. NY (1919) [1] "Published June 1919" and code letters "F-T" on copyright page $150.

022b: TALES OF FISHES Hodder & Stoughton L (1920) [] $100/450

023a: GREAT GAME FISHING AT CATALINA Santa Catalina Island Co. 1919 [0] Pictorial stiff wraps. Issued in envelope $750.

024a: THE MAN OF THE FOREST Harper & Bros. NY (1920) [1] "Published January 1920" and code letters "A-U" on copyright page $60/350

025a: THE REDHEADED OUTFIELD AND OTHER STORIES Grosset & Dunlap NY (1920) [0] Copies have been noted with and without a frontis but Mr. Myers believes that copies with the frontispiece are later. 11 titles should be listed on first page of ads with the last being *The Last of The Great Scouts*. 18 titles on rear of dustwrapper excluding *Tales of Fishes* and *The Man of The Forest*. Bindings have been noted in both tan and green cloth $100/500

026a: THE MYSTERIOUS RIDER Harper & Bros. NY (1921) [1] "Published January 1921" and code letters "I-U" on copyright page $75/450

026b: THE MYSTERIOUS RIDER Hodder & Stoughton L (1921) [] $50/250

027a: TO THE LAST MAN Harper & Bros. NY (1921) [1] Also has code letters "K-V" on copyright page $75/450

027b: TO THE LAST MAN Hodder & Stoughton L (1922) [] $50/250

028a: THE DAY OF THE BEAST Harper & Bros. NY (1922) [1] Also has code letters "G-W" on copyright page $125/600

029a: TALES OF LONELY TRAILS Harper & Bros. NY (1922) [1] Also contains code letters "G-W" on copyright page $75/400

029b: TALES OF LONELY TRAILS Hodder & Stoughton L (1922) [] $50/250

030a: THE BONEFISH BRIGADE Zane Grey (Pasadena) 1922 [0] Wraps "Christmas 1922" on title page. Illustrated by Bessie Bethal Crank $1,000.

031a: WANDERER OF THE WASTELAND Harper & Bros. NY (1923) [1] Also contains code letters "L-W" on copyright page $50/200

031b: WANDERER OF THE WASTELAND Hodder & Stoughton L (1923) [] $25/125

032a: TAPPAN'S BURRO Harper & Bros. NY (1923) [1] Also contains code letters "I-X" on copyright page $60/350

032b: TAPPAN'S BURRO Hodder & Stoughton L (1923) [] $30/150

033a: CALL OF THE CANYON Harper & Bros. NY 1924 [1] Also contains code letters "K-X" on copyright page $40/200

034a: ROPING LIONS IN THE GRAND CANYON Harper & Bros. NY (1924) [0] Code letters "B-Y" on copyright page $150/500

034b: ROPING LIONS IN THE GRAND CANYON Hodder & Stoughton L (1924) [] $75/300

035a: TALES OF SOUTHERN RIVERS Harper & Bros. NY (1924) [1] Also contains code letters "H-Y" on copyright page $175/500

035b: TALES OF SOUTHERN RIVERS Harper(?) L (1924) [0] "H-Y" on copyright page. U.S. sheets $60/300

036a: THE THUNDERING HERD Harper & Bros. NY 1925 [1] Also contains code letters "L-Y" on copyright page $50/250

036b: THE THUNDERING HERD Hodder & Stoughton L (1925) [] $25/125

037a: THE VANISHING AMERICAN Harper & Bros. NY 1925 [1] Also contains code letters "I-Z" on copyright page $50/250

037b: THE VANISHING INDIAN Hodder & Stoughton L (1926) [] $25/125

038a: TALES OF FISHING VIRGIN SEAS Harper & Bros. NY 1925 [1] Also contains code letters "K-Z" on copyright page $175/500

038b: TALES OF FISHING VIRGIN SEAS Hodder & Stoughton L (1926) [] $100/300

039a: UNDER THE TONTO RIM Harper & Bros. NY 1926 [1] Also contains code letters "F-A" on copyright page $50/250

039b: UNDER THE TONTO RIM Hodder & Stoughton L (1927) [] $25/125

040a: TALES OF AN ANGLER'S ELDORADO Harper & Bros. NY/New Zealand 1926 [1] Also contains code letters "G-A" $175/500

040b: ANGLER'S ELDORADO... Rosyln NY (1982) [] Adds several chapters not in original (Country Lane Books 11/90) $15/40

041a: TALES OF SWORDFISH AND TUNA Harper & Bros NY 1927 [1] Also contains code letters "H-B" on copyright page $200/600

041b: TALES OF SWORDFISH AND TUNA Hodder & Stoughton L (1927) [] $125/300

042a: FORLORN RIVER Harper & Bros. NY 1927 [1] Also contains code letters "H-B" on copyright page $50/250

042b: FORLORN RIVER Hodder & Stoughton L (1928) [] $25/125

043a: NEVADA Harper & Bros. NY 1928 [] Publisher's dummy. 2pp publisher's synopsis, 4pp text in dustwrapper (George Houle 6/91) $300.

043b: NEVADA Harper & Bros. NY 1928 [1] also contains code letters "B-C" on copyright page $50/250

043c: NEVADA Hodder & Stoughton L 1928 [] $25/125

044a: TALES OF FRESH WATER FISHING Harper & Bros. NY 1928 [1] Code letters "F-C" $200/500

044b: TALES OF FRESH WATER FISHING Hodder & Stoughton L (1928) [] $150/300

045a: WILD HORSE MESA Harper & Bros. NY 1928 [1] Also contains code letters "G-C" $40/200

045b: WILD HORSE MESA Hodder & Stoughton L (1928) [] $25/125

046a: DON THE STORY OF A LION DOG Harper & Bros. NY 1928 [1] Also has code letters "G-C" $150/500

047a: ZANE GREY: THE MAN AND HIS WORK Harper NY (1928) [] 8vo leatherette. Published for Friends of the Author. Assume issued without dustwrapper (Len Unger 12/90) $200.

048a: FIGHTING CARAVANS Harper & Bros. NY 1929 [1] Also has code letters "H-D" $50/250

048b: FIGHTING CARAVANS Hodder & Stoughton L (1930) [] $25/125

049a: THE WOLF TRACKER Harper & Bros. NY 1930 [1] Code letters "C-E" $250/750

050a: THE SHEPHERD OF GUADALOUPE Harper & Bros. NY 1930 [1] Also has code letters "C-E" $60/300

050b: THE SHEPHERD OF GUADALOUPE Hodder & Stoughton L (1930) [] $30/150

051a: ZANE GREY'S BOOK OF CAMPS AND TRAILS Harper & Bros. NY 1931 [0] Code letters "G-F" $275/900

052a: TALES OF TAHITIAN WATERS Harper & Bros. NY 1931 [1] Also has code letters "I-F" $300/1,000

052b: TALES OF TAHITIAN WATERS Hodder & Stoughton L (1931) [] $200/600

053a: SUNSET PASS Harper & Bros. NY 1931 [1] Also has code letters "K-F" $40/200

053b: SUNSET PASS Hodder & Stoughton L (1931) [] $30/150

054a: ARIZONA AMES Harper & Bros. NY 1932 [1] Also has code letters "I-F" $35/175

054b: ARIZONA AMES Hodder & Stoughton L (1932) [] $20/100

055a: ROBBER'S ROOST Harper & Bros. NY 1932 [1] Also has code letters "F-G" $35/175

055b: ROBBER'S ROOST Hodder & Stoughton L (1932) [] $20/100

055c: THIEVES' CANYON World L 1965 [0] Wraps. New title $20.

056a: THE DRIFT FENCE Harper & Bros. NY 1933 [1] Also has code letters "K-G" $35/175

056b: THE DRIFT FENCE Hodder & Stoughton L (1933) [] $25/125

057a: THE HASH KNIFE OUTFIT Harper & Bros. NY 1933 [1] Also has code letters "G-H" $50/250

057b: THE HASH KNIFE OUTFIT Hodder & Stoughton L (1933) [] $30/150

058a: THE GREAT MAKO American Museum of Natural History NY 1934 [] Offprint of article from Vol. 34 No. 3 of *Natural History* with eleven black and white photos by Grey. Issued in lime white paperwraps stapled on left (George Houle 11/89) $150.

059a: THE CODE OF THE WEST Harper & Bros. NY 1934 [1] Also has code letters "B-I" $35/175

059b: THE CODE OF THE WEST Hodder & Stoughton L (1934) [] $20/100

060a: THUNDER MOUNTAIN Harper & Bros. NY 1935 [1] Also has code letters "B-K" $35/175

060b: THUNDER MOUNTAIN Hodder & Stoughton L (1935) [] $20/100

060c: THUNDER MOUNTAIN Grosset & Dunlap NY (n-d) [] Signed edition $125/150

061a: THE TRAIL DRIVER Harper & Bros. NY 1936 [1] Also has code letters "M-K" $40/200

061b: THE TRAIL DRIVER Hodder & Stoughton L (1936) [] $25/125

062a: FLY FISHING Ibbetson Horrocks 1936 [] Wraps $350.

063a: THE LOST WAGON TRAIN Harper & Bros. NY 1936 [1] Also has code letters "G-L" $50/250

063b: THE LOST WAGON TRAIN Hodder & Stoughton L (1936) [] $25/125

064a: AN AMERICAN ANGLER IN AUSTRALIA Harper & Bros. NY 1937 [1] Also has code letters "B-M" $250/750

064b: AN AMERICAN ANGLER IN AUSTRALIA Hodder & Stoughton L (1937) [] $200/500

065a: WEST OF THE PECOS Harper & Bros. NY 1937 [1] Also has code letters "C-M" $40/200

065b: WEST OF THE PECOS Hodder & Stoughton L (1937) [] $20/100

066a: RAIDERS OF SPANISH PEAKS Harper & Bros. NY 1938 [1] Also has code letters "D-N" $40/200

066b: RAIDERS OF SPANISH PEAKS Hodder & Stoughton L (1938) [] $20/100

067a: KNIGHTS OF THE RANGE Harper & Bros. NY 1939 [1] Also has code letters "M-N" $40/200

067b: KNIGHTS OF THE RANGE Hodder & Stoughton L (1939) [] $25/125

068a: WESTERN UNION Harper & Bros. NY 1939 [1] Also has code letters "I-O" $40/200

068b: WESTERN UNION Hodder & Stoughton L (1939) [] $20/100

069a: THIRTY THOUSAND ON THE HOOF Harper & Bros. NY (1940) [1] Also has code letters "G-P" $25/175

069b: THIRTY THOUSAND ON THE HOOF Hodder & Stoughton L (1940) [] $15/75

070a: TWIN SOMBREROS Harper & Bros. NY (1940) [1] Also has code letters "C-Q" $25/175

070b: TWIN SOMBREROS Hodder & Stoughton L (1942) [] $15/75

071a: MAJESTY'S RANCHO Harper & Bros. NY (1942) [1] Also has code letters "C-R." (Note: copyrighted in 1938 but published in 1942 25/175

071b: MAJESTY'S RANCHO Harper & Bros. NY (1942) [1] Variant of first on thinner paper. First stated. "Service Edition" on front panel of plain printed dustwrapper $50/150

072a: ZANE GREY OMNIBUS Harper & Bros. NY (1943) [0] Code letters "B-S." Issued without dustwrapper $300.

072b: ZANE GREY OMNIBUS Harper & Bros. NY (1943) [0] Code letters "C-S." The second edition issued as a textbook for the schools. Also issued without dustwrapper $100.

072c: ZANE GREY ROUND UP Grosset & Dunlap NY (1943) [0] New title with pictorial dustwrapper $25/100

073a: STAIRS OF THE SAND Harper & Bros. NY (copyright 1928, actually published in 1943) [1] Also has code letters "C-S" $40/200

073b: STAIRS OF THE SAND Hodder & Stoughton L (1943) [] $25/125

074a: THE WILDERNESS TREK Harper & Bros. NY (1944) [1] Also has code letters "E-T" $40/200

074b: THE WILDERNESS TREK Hodder & Stoughton L (1945) [] $30/150

075a: SHADOWS ON THE TRAIL Harper & Bros. NY (1946) [1] Also has code letters "A-V" $30/150

075b: SHADOWS ON THE TRAIL Hodder & Stoughton L (1947) [] $20/100

076a: VALLEY OF WILD HORSES Harper & Bros. NY (1947) [1] Also has code letters "B-W" $30/150

076b: VALLEY OF WILD HORSES Hodder & Stoughton L (1947) [] $20/100

077a: KING OF THE ROYAL MOUNTED and GHOST GUNS OF ROARING RIVER Whitman Racine (Wisc.) (1946) [0] "Based on famous newspaper strip" $15/75

078a: ROGUE RIVER FEUD Harper & Bros. NY (1930 but actually published in 1948) [0] Code letters "C-X." Mr. Myers notes that this is rarely seen $60/300

078b: ROGUE RIVER FEUD Hodder & Stoughton L (1949) [] $30/150

079a: THE DEER STALKER Harper & Bros. NY (copyright 1925 but actually published in 1949) [1] Also has code letters "D-Y." First printing dustwrapper without *Christian Herald* announcement (Country Lane Books 11/90) $25/125

079b: THE DEER STALKER Hodder & Stoughton L (1950) [] $12/60

080a: THE MAVERICK QUEEN Harper & Bros. NY (1950) [1] Also has code letters "D-Z" $25/125

081a: THE DUDE RANGER Harper & Bros. NY (1951) [1] Also has code letters "F-A" $25/125

081b: THE DUDE RANGER Hodder & Stoughton L (1952) [] $12/60

082a: CAPTIVES OF THE DESERT Harper & Bros. NY (copyright 1926 but actually published in 1952) [0] Code letters "B-B" $50/175

082b: CAPTIVES OF THE DESERT Hodder & Stoughton L (1953) [] $30/150

083a: ZANE GREY'S ADVENTURES IN FISHING Harper & Bros. NY (1952) [1] Also has code letters "I-B." Edited by Ed Zern (Ref.b has 1953 but code would indicate this was wrong) $50/175

084a: WYOMING Harper & Bros. NY (copyright 1932, actually published in 1953) [1] Also has code letters "F-C" $25/125

084b: WYOMING Hodder & Stoughton L (1954) [] $12/60

085a: LOST PUEBLO Harper & Bros. NY (1954) [1] Also has code letters "H-D" $25/100

085b: LOST PUEBLO Hodder & Stoughton L (1955) [] $10/50

086a: BLACK MESA Harper & Bros. NY (1955) [1] Also has code letters "H-E" $25/100

086b: BLACK MESA Hodder & Stoughton L (1956) [] $10/50

087a: STRANGER FROM THE TONTO Harper & Bros. NY (1956) [0] Code letters "G-F" $25/125

087b: STRANGER FROM THE TONTO Hodder & Stoughton L (1957) [] $12/60

088a: THE FUGITIVE TRAIL Harper & Bros. NY (1957) [0] No code letters $30/150

088b: THE FUGITIVE TRAIL Hodder & Stoughton L (1958) [] $12/65

089a: ARIZONA CLAN Harper & Bros. NY (1958) [1] Also has code letters "H-H" $25/100

089b: ARIZONA CLAN Hodder & Stoughton L (1959) [] $12/60

090a: HORSE HEAVEN HILL Harper & Bros. NY (1959) [1] Also has code letters "F-I" $25/100

090b: HORSE HEAVEN HILL Hodder & Stoughton L (1960) [] $10/50

091a: THE RANGER AND OTHER STORIES Harper & Bros. NY (1960) [1] Also has code letters "E-K" $25/100

091b: THE RANGER AND OTHER STORIES Hodder & Stoughton L (1963) [] $10/50

092a: BLUE FEATHER AND OTHER STORIES Harper & Bros. NY (1961) [1] Also has code letters "I-L" $20/100

092b: BLUE FEATHER AND OTHER STORIES Hodder & Stoughton L (1962) [] $10/50

093a: BOULDER DAM Harper & Bros. NY (1963) [1] Also has code letters "G-N" $20/100

093b: BOULDER DAM Hodder & Stoughton L (1965) [] $10/50

094a: THE ADVENTURES OF FINSPOT D.J. Books San Bernardino 1974 [2] 950 cc. Tipped in color plates. Edited by G. M. Farley and Betty Zane Grosso $15/75

095a: THE RUSTLERS OF PECOS COUNTY and SILVERMANE Belmont Tower NY (1974) [0] Wraps $20.

096a: ZANE GREY'S SAVAGE KINGDOM Belmont Tower NY (1975) [0] Wraps. Edited by Loren Grey (ref.b) $25.

097a: SHARK! ZANE GREY'S TALES OF MAN-EATING SHARKS Belmont Tower NY (1976) [0] Wraps. Edited by Loren Grey (ref.b) $25.

098a: THE TRAIL OF THE JAGUAR Zane Grey Collector Williamsport, MD (1976) [1] 500 cc. Wraps. Edited by G.M. Farley (ref.b) $40.

099a: THE WESTERNER Belmont Tower NY (1977) [0] Wraps. Edited by Loren Grey (ref.b) $25.

100a: THE REEF GIRL Harper NY (1977) [3] Also states "First Edition" $7/35

101a: THE BUFFALO HUNTER Belmont NY (1978) [0] Wraps. Edited by Loren Grey $20.

102a: ZANE GREY: OUTDOORSMAN Prentice-Hall Englewood Cliffs, N.J. (1972) [] Edited by George Reiger $20/50

103a: ZANE GREY'S GREATEST ANIMAL STORIES Belmont Tower NY (1975) [] Wraps. Edited by Loren Grey $25.

104a: ZANE GREY'S GREATEST WESTERN STORIES Belmont Tower NY (1975) [] Wraps. Edited by Loren Grey $25.

105a: ZANE GREY'S GREATEST INDIAN STORIES Belmont Tower NY (1975) [] Wraps. Edited by Loren Grey $25.

106a: ROUND-UP Manor Books (NY 1976) [] Wraps. Edited by Loren Grey $20.

107a: YAQUI AND OTHER GREAT INDIAN STORIES Belmont Tower NY (1976) [] Wraps. Edited by Loren Grey $20.

108a: THE BIG LAND Belmont Tower NY (1976) [] Wraps. Edited by Loren Grey $20.

109a: TENDERFOOT Belmont Tower NY (1977) [] Wraps. Edited by Loren Grey $20.

110a: THE CAMP ROBBER Walter J. Black Roslyn, NY (1979) [] Edited by Loren Grey $6/30

111a: LORD OF LACKAWAXEN CREEK (Lime Rock Press Salisbury, Ct. 1981) [2] A miniature book illustrated and signed by Catryna Ten Eyck (2 7/8" x 2 1/2") $35.

112a: ANGLER'S ELDORADO, ZANE GREY IN NEW ZEALAND Roslyn, NY (1982) [] Several chapters printed for first time $7/35

113a: THE WESTERN MOTION-PICTURE Arundel Press L.A. 1984 [2] 25 numbered large paper copies on handmade paper with check signed by Grey tipped in back. Bound in 1/2 morocco (Pepper & Stern 12/89) $250.

Note: There were a number of "King of the Royal Mounted" and "Tex Thorne" titles published by the Whitman Publishing Co. as "Big Little Books" but there are so many copies of them that the value is nominal.

MARTHA GRIMES

Martha Grimes, a native of Garrett County, Maryland, taught English at Montgomery College in Takoma Park, Maryland. She occasionally teaches detective fiction at Johns Hopkins University and lives in Washington, D.C. The following information is from our personal collection with the quantities supplied by Little Brown, one of the few cooperative publishers.

001a: THE MAN WITH A LOAD OF MISCHIEF Little, Brown B (1981) [1] 5,171 cc. Noted with two different dustwrappers $30/150

1: ISBN number on back panel in black letters, backed in white, the initials "FPT" on upper left corner and "00001545" in lower left corner of front flap; and

2: ISBN number printed in white on back panel, "FPT" not on front flap. Priority unknown

001b: THE MAN WITH A LOAD OF MISCHIEF Michael O'Mara L 1990 [1] "First published in Great Britain in 1990" $8/40

002a: THE OLD FOX DECEIV'D Little, Brown B (1982) [1] "Uncorrected Advance Proof" in printed red wraps $200.

002b: THE OLD FOX DECEIV'D Little, Brown B (1982) [1] 7,328 cc. (Published August 1982 @ $13.95) $20/100

002c: THE OLD FOX DECEIV'D Michael O'Mara L 1990 [] $8/40

003a: THE ANODYNE NECKLACE Little, Brown B (1983) [1] "Uncorrected Advance Proof" in printed flint gray wraps announcing a price of $13.95 $175.

003b: THE ANODYNE NECKLACE Little, Brown B (1983) [1] 8,546 cc. (Published June 27, 1983.) $14.95 price on dustwrapper $20/100

003c: THE ANODYNE NECKLACE Michael O'Mara L 1989 [] $8/40

004a: THE DIRTY DUCK Little, Brown B (1984) [1] "Uncorrected Advance Proof" in printed dark green wraps $150.

004b: THE DIRTY DUCK Little, Brown B (1984) [1] 20,075 cc. (Published April 26, 1984 @ $14.95) $12/60

004c: THE DIRTY DUCK Michael O'Mara Books (London) no-date (lists U.S. copyright of 1984) [1] "First Published in Great Britain..." $8/40

005a: JERUSALEM INN Little, Brown B (1984) [1] "Uncorrected Advance Proofs" in printed dark green wraps calling for price of $14.95 $125.

005b: JERUSALEM INN Little, Brown B (1984) [1] 24,766 cc. (Published November 7, 1984.) Dustwrapper price of $15.95 $10/50

005c: JERUSALEM INN Michael O'Mara L 1987 [] $8/40

006a: HELP THE POOR STRUGGLER Little, Brown B (1985) [1] "Uncorrected Advance Proof" in printed green wraps $125.

006b: HELP THE POOR STRUGGLER Little, Brown B (1985) [1] 24,839 cc. (Published May 1, 1985 @ $15.95) $10/50

006c: HELP THE POOR STRUGGLER Michael O'Mara L 1987 [] $8/40

007a: MARTHA GRIMES SAMPLER Dell NY 1986 [0] Wraps $15.

008a: THE DEER LEAP Little, Brown B (1985) [1] "Uncorrected Advance Proof" in printed orange-brown wraps $100.

008b: THE DEER LEAP Little, Brown B (1985) [1] 27,566 cc. (Published November 6, 1985 @ $15.95) $8/40

008c: THE DEER LEAP Michael O'Mara L 1988 [] $8/40

009a: I AM THE ONLY RUNNING FOOTMAN Little, Brown B (1986) [1] "Uncorrected Advance Proof" in printed dark green wraps $100.

009b: I AM THE ONLY RUNNING FOOTMAN Little, Brown B (1986) [1] 31,954 cc. (Published November 4, 1986 @ $15.95) $8/40

009c: I AM THE ONLY RUNNING FOOTMAN Michael O'Mara Books (L) no-date (has U.S. copyright of 1986)) [1] "First published in Great Britain..." $7/35

010a: THE FIVE BELLS AND BLADEBONE Little, Brown B (1987) [1] "Uncorrected Advance Proof" in printed orange brown wraps $100.

010b: THE FIVE BELLS AND BLADEBONE Little, Brown B (1987) [1] (Published August 25, 1987 @ $15.95) $5/35

010c: THE FIVE BELLS AND BLADEBONE Michael O'Mara L 1986 [] $8/40

011a: THE OLD SILENT Little Brown B 1989 [] Advance Reading Copy in pictorial Wraps $60.

011b: THE OLD SILENT Little Brown B 1989 [1] 100,000 cc (PW). (Published September 1989 @ $16.95) $6/30

011c: THE OLD SILENT Headline (L 1990) [3] Also says "First published in Great Britain..." $6/30

012a: SEND BYGRAVES Putnam NY (1989) [] Advance reading copy in pictorial wraps $30.

012b: SEND BYGRAVES Putnam NY (1989) [3] 36,000 cc (PW). (Published November 1989.) Illustrated by Devis Grebu. Issued without dustwrapper $20.

013a: THE OLD CONTEMPTIBLES Little Brown B (1991) [] Advance reading copy in pictorial wraps $50.

013b: THE OLD CONTEMPTIBLES Little Brown B (1991) [3] Also states "First Edition." (Published January 1991 @ $19.95) $5/20

014a: THE END OF THE PIER Knopf NY 1992 [] Uncorrected proof in pictorial wraps $50.

014b: THE END OF THE PIER Knopf NY 1992 [1] 100,000 cc (PW). (Published April 1992 @ $20.)

DORIS GRUMBACH

Doris Grumbach was born in New York City in 1918. She graduated from New York University in 1939 and received a masters degree from Cornell University in 1940. Since that time, in addition to being a novelist and biographer and mother of four, she has been active as a writer and educator. She was a Professor of English at the College of St. Rose until 1972; literary editor for the New Republic from 1972 to 1974, Professor at American University from 1974 to 1983 and taught at Johns Hopkins. During this period, she also worked as a columnist/critic/reviewer for various newspapers/news shows including the *Washington Star*, *Washington Post*, *L.A. Times*, *Chicago Tribune*, *New York Times Book Review*, *Fine Print*, *Saturday Review*, National Public Radio and MacNeil-Lehrer News Hour. In her spare time, she has taught at Empire State and the Iowa Writer's Workshop. Doris and her long time friend, Sybil Pike, maintain a residence in Washington, D.C. but spend much of their time at their home in Sargentsville, Maine where they run an antiquarian bookstore, Wayward Books.

001a: THE SPOIL OF THE FLOWERS Doubleday Garden City, NY 1962 [1] $40/150

002a: THE SHORT THROAT, THE TENDER MOUTH Doubleday Garden City, NY 1964 [1] $40/150

003a: LORD, I HAVE NO COURAGE Venerini Publications Worcester (1964) [0] Heavy (cardboard) cover with label on front. The author believes there were about 500 copies. The life story of Rosa Venerini who established a school for women in the early 18th Century. Prepared for "young readers" $350.

004a: THE COMPANY SHE KEPT Coward McCann NY (1967) [0] A portrait of Mary McCarthy $10/50

004b: THE COMPANY SHE KEPT Bodley Head London (1967) [1] $8/40

005a: LETTER TO A WOULD-BE WRITER *Fiction I* Empire State College Saratoga Springs 1973 [0] Wraps. 8"x11" sheets in clamp binder (easily reproduced) $NVA

006a: LETTER TO A WOULD-BE WRITER - *Journalism III* Empire State College Saratoga Springs 1973 [0] Wraps. 8"x11" sheets in clamp binder (easily reproduced) $NVA

Note: written for use in class. William Kennedy wrote *Fiction II* and *Journalism IV*

007a: CHAMBER MUSIC E.P. Dutton NY (1979) [] Uncorrected proof in tall gray wraps (Second Life Books 3/90) $60.

007b: CHAMBER MUSIC E.P. Dutton NY (1979) [3] Also states "First Edition". Advance reading copy in pictorial wraps $35.

007c: CHAMBER MUSIC E.P. Dutton NY (1979) [3] $8/40

007d: CHAMBER MUSIC (Hamish Hamilton London {no-date}) [0] Advance uncorrected proof in gray printed wraps $75.

007e: CHAMBER MUSIC Hamish Hamilton London (1979) [1] $7/35

008a: THE MISSING PERSON Putnam NY (1981) [0] "Uncorrected proof" in blue printed wraps $50.

008b: THE MISSING PERSON Putnam NY (1981) [0] (Published March 31, 1981 @ $11.95) $5/25

008c: THE MISSING PERSON Hamish Hamilton London (1981) [1] $7/35

009a: THE LADIES Dutton NY (1984) [3] Also states "First edition". "Advance Uncorrected Proofs" in tan wraps with picture from subsequent dustwrapper on front panel $50.

009b: THE LADIES Dutton NY (1984) [3] (Published September 27, 84 @ $14.95) $5/25

009c: THE LADIES Hamish Hamilton London (1985) [1] $6/30

010a: THE MAGICIAN'S GIRL Macmillan NY (1987) [3] "Uncorrected Proof" in printed creme colored wraps $50.

010b: THE MAGICIAN'S GIRL Macmillan NY (1987) [3] (Published January 5, 1987 @ $16.95) $5/20

010c: THE MAGICIAN'S GIRL Hamish Hamilton London (1987) [1] $6/30

011a: COMING INTO THE END ZONE: A MEMOIR Norton NY (1991) [3] Also States "First Edition" $5/20

JIM HARRISON

Harrison was born in Grayling, Michigan in 1937. He received a B.A. and M.A. in comparative literature from Michigan State University. He was an Assistant Professor of English at the State University of New York, Stony Brook for a time before resigning to write full time.

001a: PLAIN SONG Norton NY (1965) [1] 1,500 cc $50/250

001b: PLAIN SONG Norton NY (1965) [1] 1,500 cc. Wraps. Issued simultaneously $50.

002a: WALKING Pym Randall Press Cambridge (1967) [2] 26 sgd ltr cc $850.

002b: WALKING Pym Randall Press Cambridge (1967) [2] 100 sgd no cc. Oblong wraps $500.

003a: LOCATIONS Norton NY (1968) [3] 1,250 cc $40/200

003b: LOCATIONS Norton NY (1968) [3] 1,250 cc. Wraps $40.

004a: FIVE BLIND MEN Sumac Press Fremont 1969 [2] 26 sgd ltr cc. Harrison is one of five poets. Issued without dustwrapper $400.

004b: FIVE BLIND MEN Sumac Press Fremont 1969 [2] 100 cc. Harrison has indicated that none were numbered (although called for) in correspondence with Steven C. Bernard, but numbered copies have been seen $100.

004c: FIVE BLIND MEN Sumac Press Fremont 1969 [] 1,000 cc. Wraps. Issued simultaneously (Pettler & Lieberman 8/88) $40.

005a: OUTLYER AND GHAZALS Simon & Schuster NY (1971) [1] Scarcest trade book $60/300

005b: OUTLYER AND GHAZALS Simon & Schuster NY (1971) [1] Wraps $40.

006a: WOLF Simon & Schuster NY (1971) [1] $20/100

007a: A GOOD DAY TO DIE Simon & Schuster NY 1973 [3] $50/250

007b: A GOOD DAY TO DIE W.H. Allen L 1975 [] $35/175

008a: LETTERS TO YESENIN Sumac Press Fremont 1973 [2] 26 sgd ltr cc $850.

008b: LETTERS TO YESENIN Sumac Press Fremont 1973 [2] 100 sgd no cc $600.

008c: LETTERS TO YESENIN Sumac Press Fremont 1973 [] 1,000 cc. Wraps. Also see 011b $50.

009a: SERGE, YESENIN 1895-1925 Sumac Press Fremont no-date [] 33 cc. Small (6" x 9") broadside. Copy inscribed to Howard Moss by Harrison "1 of 33 handset" (Phoenix #210). We assume it was issued around time of *Letters...* (008a) $250.

010a: FARMER Viking NY (1976) [1] 7,500 cc $15/75

011a: RETURNING TO EARTH Ithaca House (Ithaca 1977) [0] Wraps. "A Court Street Chapbook." Reportedly only 500 copies $250.

011b: LETTERS TO YESENIN AND RETURNING TO EARTH POEMS Center Publ. (L.A.) 1979 [0] Wraps. (Also 35 sgd cc {Watermark West #2}. Assume unnumbered) $40.

012a: LEGENDS OF THE FALL Delacorte NY (1979) [] White pad-bound Advance uncorrected proof. Less than 15 cc (Beasley Books #31) $300.

012b: LEGENDS OF THE FALL Delacorte NY (1979) [] Uncorrected Proof in printed red wraps (Beasley Books #31) $200.

012c: LEGENDS OF THE FALL Delacorte NY (1979) [2] 250 sgd no. cc. Three volumes issued without dustwrappers in slipcase $275/350

012d: LEGENDS OF THE FALL Delacorte NY (1979) [1] 1,000 cc. Three volumes issued without dustwrappers in slipcase $75/125

012e: LEGENDS OF THE FALL Delacorte NY (1979) [1] 15,000 cc. One volume edition $10/50

012f: LEGENDS OF THE FALL Collins L 1980 [1] $8/40

013a: WARLOCK Delacorte (NY 1981) [] Uncorrected proof in yellow wraps, laid in proof dustwrapper (Ken Lopez 7/91) $150.

013b: WARLOCK Delacorte (NY 1981) [2] 250 sgd no. cc. Issued without dustwrapper in slipcase $125/200

013c: WARLOCK Delacorte (NY 1981) [1] 19,000 cc (Published October 1981 @ $13.95) $10/50

013d: WARLOCK Collins L 1981 [1] Printed in U.S. $8/40

014a: SELECTED AND NEW POEMS 1961-1981 Delacorte (NY 1982) [2] 250 sgd no cc. Issued without dustwrapper in slipcase $100/175

014b: SELECTED AND NEW POEMS 1961-1981 Delacorte (NY 1982) [1] 2,500 cc $7/35

014c: SELECTED AND NEW POEMS 1961-1981 Delacorte (NY 1982) [1] Wraps. Issued simultaneously $20.

015a: NATURAL WORLD A BESTIARY Open Book (Barrytown, NY 1981) [2] 100 sgd no. cc. Poems by Harrison and sculptures by Diana Guest. Signed by both. Issued without dustwrapper or slipcase $300.

016a: SUNDOG Dutton NY (1984) [] Uncorrected proof in orange wraps $100.

016b: SUNDOG Dutton NY (1984) [2] 250 sgd no. cc. Issued without dustwrapper in slipcase $75/150

016c: SUNDOG Dutton NY (1984) [3] Also states "First Edition" $6/30

016d: SUNDOG Heinemann L (1985) [1] $6/30

017a: THE THEORY AND PRACTICE OF RIVERS Winn Books Seattle 1986 [2] 350 sgd cc. Illustrated by Russell Chatham. Issued without dustwrapper in slipcase. Published with a portfolio of Chatham works at $350 and sold separately at $85. Many were not numbered. The publisher informed us that only 175 copies were printed. However, two dealers have catalogued copies numbered as one of 350, thus the confusion on quantity. It may be that Winn sold 175 with the portfolios and 175 without $175.

017b: THE THEORY AND PRACTICE OF RIVERS Winn Books Seattle 1986 [0] 3,000 cc. Wraps. Issued in dustwrapper $15/25

018a: DALVA Dutton NY (1988) [] Uncorrected proof in printed tan wraps $75.

018b: DALVA Dutton NY (1988) [3] (Published March 1988 @ $18.45) $5/25

018c: DALVA Jonathan Cape L 1989 [] $6/30

019a: BETWEEN WARS Columbia Pictures Burbank 1989 [] A screenplay in printed studio wraps $75.

020a: THEORY AND PRACTICE OF RIVERS AND NEW POEMS Clark City Press Livingston, Montana (1987) [1] Illustrated by Russell Chatham. "First Clark City Press Edition July 1989" $7/35

020b: THEORY AND PRACTICE OF RIVERS AND NEW POEMS Clark City Press Livingston, Montana (1987) [] Wraps $15.

021a: THE WOMAN LIT BY FIREFLIES Houghton Mifflin B 1990 [] Uncorrected proof in yellow wraps $75.

021b: THE WOMAN LIT BY FIREFLIES Houghton Mifflin B 1990 [2] 150 sgd no. cc. Issued without dustwrapper in slipcase $100/150

021c: THE WOMAN LIT BY FIREFLIES Houghton Mifflin B 1990 [3] (Published August 1990 @ $19.95) $5/25

021d: THE WOMAN LIT BY FIREFLIES (publisher ?) L 1991 [] $5/25

022a: BOOK FOR SENSEI Big Bridge Press Pacifica, Calif. 1990 [2] 26 sgd ltr cc. Signed by Harrison, Rothenberg, McClure Whalen, Kyger, Codrescu and the illustrator, Nancy Davis. Issued in slipcase $300.

022b: BOOK FOR SENSEI Big Bridge Press Pacifica, Calif. 1990 [2] 74 no. cc. Issued in boards in slipcase $150.

023a: KOBUN. A POEM Dim Gray Bar Press 1990 [2] 100 sgd no. cc. 11"x13" broadside $60.

024a: JUST BEFORE DARK. THE COLLECTED NONFICTION Clark City Press Livingston, Montana (1991) [2] 26 sgd ltr cc. Issued without dustwrapper in slipcase $450.

024b: JUST BEFORE DARK. THE COLLECTED NONFICTION Clark City Press Livingston, Montana (1991) [2] 250 sgd no. cc. Issued without dustwrapper in slipcase $100/175

024c: JUST BEFORE DARK. THE COLLECTED NONFICTION Clark City Press Livingston, Montana (1991) [1] Trade $5/25

025a: THE RAW & THE COOKED Dim Gray Bar Press NY 1992 [2] 26 sgd ltr cc. Bound in quarter morocco $250.

025b: THE RAW & THE COOKED Dim Gray Bar Press NY 1992 [2] 100 sgd no. cc $125.

Robert A. Heinlein

ROBERT HEINLEIN
(1907 - 1988)

Robert Heinlein was born in Butler, Missouri, one of seven children. He attended high school in Kansas City, Missouri and college at the U.S. Naval Academy in Annapolis, Maryland, graduating in 1929. From 1929 to 1934 he served on aircraft carriers and destroyers but was retired in the latter year due to physical disabilities. He started graduate school at UCLA, studying mathematics and physics, but his health never allowed him to finish. He worked at various jobs including real estate, mining and architecture until 1939 when he began writing full time. His writing career was interupted by the war which he spent as a mechanical engineer at the Naval Aircraft factory in Philadelphia.

He wrote for magazines, radio, television, and motion pictures in addition to his books. The winner of four Hugo Awards, among many awards during his lifetime, he was always highly regarded in the field. In 1954, the *New York Herald Tribune* wrote of *The Star Beast*: "Regularly every year Robert Heinlein produces the best juvenile science fiction novel - and in so doing creates a work more satisfying than ninety per cent of adult science fiction."

His own view - "My stories have been speculations about the future and what mankind will make of it...My writing has been strongly affected by Rudyard Kipling, Winston Churchill, H.G. Wells, et al... I enjoy life and believe man will live forever and spread out through the universe." (*Contemporary Novelists*, St. Martin's Press, NY 1976)

REFERENCES:

(a) Currey, L.W. SCIENCE FICTION AND FANTASY AUTHORS G.K. Hall Boston (1979).

(b) Smith, Curtis C. (Editor) TWENTIETH-CENTURY SCIENCE FICTION WRITERS St. Martin's Press NY (1981). Used for titles printed in Great Britain not covered in Ref.a.

(c) The information provided by Joel Sattler, would apply to all entries after 1980. Also includes a few entries derived from inventory or dealer catalogs.

Note: We have included the published prices on the Scribner books, because it is probable the publisher printed new dustwrappers with higher prices; and certainly the publisher price clipped some jackets and rubber stamped new prices, which would indicate books that were sold later, although still first edition books and jackets.

The order of publications within each year is arbitrary as we have not looked up the publication dates and do not have an accurate chronological list of the titles.

We wish to thank Joel Sattler, John Knott and particularly Lloyd Currey, the preeminent science fiction bibliographer not only for ref.a, but also for providing updated information on a number of the entries.

001a: THE DISCOVERY OF THE FUTURE... Speech Delivered by Guest of Honor at Third World Science Fiction Convention A Novacious Publication (LA 1941) [2] Stapled wraps. "Limited First Edition (200)" on front wrapper. Printed in green ink. Issued in mailing envelope

$1,500

001b: THE DISCOVERY OF THE FUTURE... A Novacious Publication (LA 1941) [2] Wraps. Adds "Reprint (100)" under original limitation. Second printing with peach colored front cover, 18pp including covers (Ref.c) $600

002a: ROCKET SHIP GALILEO Scribner's NY (1947) [5] Also has publisher's seal on copyright page. Illustrated by Thomas W. Voter. Published at $2.00 $150/750

002b: ROCKET SHIP GALILEO New English Library L 1971 [] Ref.b $25/125

003a: SPACE CADET Scribner's NY (1948) [5] Also has publisher's seal on copyright page. Illustrated by Clifford N. Geary. Published at $2.50 $100/450

003b: SPACE CADET Gollancz L 1966 [1] (Ref.c) $30/150

004a: BEYOND THIS HORIZON Fantasy Press Reading, PA 1948 [2] 500 sgd no. cc. Brick red cloth $750/1,000

004b: BEYOND THIS HORIZON Fantasy Press Reading, PA 1948 [1] Brick red cloth or medium blue cloth. Both stamped in gilt on spine. Priority unknown (Currey 4/90). (The variant blue dustwrapper in Ref.a is a proof dw.) There is also a variant without rear endpaper and final blank is used as pastedown (Lloyd Currey 9/90) $250/450

005a: RED PLANET Scribner's NY 1949 [5] Also has seal on copyright page. Illustrated by Clifford N. Geary. Published at $2.50 $100/450

005b: RED PLANET Gollancz L 1963 [0] Copy seen had "I-5.61[V]" on copyright page. Red cloth (simulated?) stamped in gold on spine $30/150

006a: SIXTH COLUMN Gnome Press NY (1949) [1] $100/400

006b: THE DAY AFTER TOMORROW (Mayflower Books L 1962) [] New title (Ref.b) $35/175

007a: THE MAN WHO SOLD THE MOON Shasta Chicago (1950) [1] Signed on tipped-in page (reportedly about 200 cc) $450/600

007b: THE MAN WHO SOLD THE MOON Shasta Chicago (1950) [1] His Future History Series. Introduction by John W. Campbell, Jr. $50/250

007c: THE MAN WHO SOLD THE MOON New American Lib (NY 1951) [1] Wraps. "First printing, March 1951." Signet #847 at 25 cents. Abridged edition $35

007d: THE MAN WHO SOLD THE MOON Sidgwick & Jackson L (1953) [] $20/100

008a: FARMER IN THE SKY Scribner's NY 1950 [5] Also has publisher's seal on copyright page. Illustrated by Clifford N. Geary. Published at $2.50. "Published in condensed form in *Boy's Life* magazine under the title: Satellite Scout" $60/350

008b: FARMER IN THE SKY Gollancz L 1962 [0] Illustrated by Clifford N. Geary. Red cloth printed in gold on spine $20/100

009a: WALDO AND MAGIC, INC. Doubleday Garden City 1950 [1] Published at $2.50 $60/300

009b: WALDO AND MAGIC INC Pan Books L 1969 [] (Pan Science Fiction) (Ref.c) $20/100

010a: UNIVERSE Dell NY (1951) [0] Dell Book 36 (10 cents). Pictorial wraps. *Adventure on A Gigantic Spaceship* at head of title $100

011a: BETWEEN PLANETS Scribner's NY 1951 [5] Also has publisher's seal on copyright page. Illustrated by Clifford N. Geary. Published at $2.50. "A condensed version under the title Planets In Combat appeared in ... the *Blue Book* magazine" $75/350

011b: BETWEEN PLANETS Gollancz L 1968 [] Illustrated by Clifford N. Geary (Ref.b) $20/100

012a: THE GREEN HILLS OF EARTH Shasta Chicago (1951) [1] Signed on tipped-in page (reportedly 200 cc) $450/650

012b: THE GREEN HILLS OF EARTH Shasta Chicago (1951) [1] (Ref.c) $50/250

012c: THE GREEN HILLS OF EARTH Sidgwick & Jackson L 1954 [1] (Ref.c) $25/125

013a: THE PUPPET MASTERS Doubleday Garden City 1951 [1] (Doubleday Science Fiction) Published at $2.75 $100/450

013b: THE PUPPET MASTERS Pan Books L (1969) [] Assume wraps $35

014a: TOMORROW, THE STARS Doubleday Garden City 1952 [1] A science fiction anthology edited by Heinlein and including his preface $25/125

015a: THE ROLLING STONES Scribner's NY (1952) [5] Also has publisher's seal on copyright page. Illustrated by Clifford N. Geary. Published at $2.50. "A condensed version ... was published in *Boy's Life* under the title Tramp Space Ship" $100/400

015b: SPACE FAMILY STONE Gollancz L 1971 [] New title (Ref.b) $30/150

016a: REVOLT IN 2100 Shasta Chicago (1953) [1] Signed on tipped-in page (reportedly 200 to 300 cc) $450/650

016b: REVOLT IN 2100 Shasta Chicago (1953) [1] $50/250

016c: REVOLT IN 2100 Gollancz L (1964) [] $25/125

017a: ASSIGNMENT IN ETERNITY Fantasy Press Reading, PA (1953) [2] 500 no. cc signed on tipped-in page $450/650

017b: ASSIGNMENT IN ETERNITY Fantasy Press Reading, PA (1953) [1] First binding: brick red cloth, gilt. "Heinlein" 3mm high on spine $60/300

017c: ASSIGNMENT IN ETERNITY Fantasy Press Reading, PA (1953) [1] Second binding (Greenberg variant): green boards, spine lettered in black $40/200

017d: ASSIGNMENT IN ETERNITY Fantasy Press Reading, PA (1953) [1] Third binding (Grant variant) Red cloth. "Heinlein" 2mm high on spine. Also noted in dark blue cloth stamped in black (Beasley Books 4/90) $25/125

017e: ASSIGNMENT IN ETERNITY Science Fiction Club (Museum Press) L (1955) [] (Ref.b) $35/175

Also see 031a

018a: STARMAN JONES Scribner's NY (1953) [5] Also has publisher's seal on copyright page. Illustrated by Clifford N. Geary. Published at $2.50 $60/300

018b: STARMAN JONES Sidgwick & Jackson L (1954) [1] (Ref.b) Blue cloth printed in dark blue on spine $25/125

019a: THE STAR BEAST Scribner's NY (1954) [5] Also has publisher's seal on copyright page. Published at $2.50 $60/300

020a: TUNNEL IN THE SKY Scribner's NY (1955) [5] Published at $2.50 $60/350

020b: TUNNEL IN THE SKY Gollancz L 1965 [] (Ref.b) $20/100

021a: DOUBLE STAR Doubleday GC 1956 [1] Heinlein's scarcest juvenile; won 1956 Hugo (his first). Published at $2.95 $250/1,250

021b: DOUBLE STAR Joseph L (1958) [] (Ref.b) $60/300

022a: TIME FOR THE STARS Scribner's NY (1956) [5] "A-8.56[v]." Published at $2.75 $75/350

022b: TIME FOR THE STARS Gollancz L 1963 [1] (Ref.c) $15/75

023a: CITIZEN OF THE GALAXY Scribner's NY (1957) [5] "A:7.57v." Published at $2.95 $100/450

023b: CITIZEN OF THE GALAXY Gollancz L 1969 [] (Ref.b) $20/100

024a: THE DOOR INTO SUMMER Doubleday GC 1957 [1] Published at $2.95 $150/750

024b: THE DOOR INTO SUMMER Panther L 1960 [] Assume wraps (Ref.b) $35

024c: THE DOOR INTO SUMMER Gollancz L 1967 [] (Robert Gavora 5/91) First U.K. hardback $30/150

025a: A ROBERT HEINLEIN OMNIBUS The Science Fiction Book Club by arrangement with Sidgwick & Jackson L 1958 [0] Collects *The Man Who Sold The Moon* and *The Green Hills of Earth*. On copyright page: ("This Science Fiction Book Club edition was produced in 1958 for sale to it's members only") $15/75

026a: METHUSELAH'S CHILDREN Gnome Press Hicksville, NY (1958) [0] 7,500 cc for all issues but many were probably never bound. Rear panel of dustwrapper lists 35 titles and publisher's address as "80 East 11th St, NY 3." Black boards, spine printed in red (Currey 4/90) $60/300

026b: METHUSELAH'S CHILDREN Gnome Press Hicksville, NY (1958) [0] Gray cloth, spine printed in red. Second issue dustwrapper lists 35 titles but "3" is dropped from address on rear panel (Currey 4/90) $40/200

026c: METHUSELAH'S CHILDREN Gnome Press Hicksville, NY (1958) [0] Red boards, spine printed in black. May have a third dustwrapper which lists 32 titles on rear panel and has publisher's address as "Box 161, Hicksville, NY" $25/125

026d: METHUSELAH'S CHILDREN Gnome Press Hicksville, NY (1958) [0] Lime green boards, spine printed in black (Currey 4/90) $25/125

026e: METHUSELAH'S CHILDREN Gnome Press Hicksville, NY (1958) [0] Red cloth (not seen) (Currey 4/90) $25/125

026f: METHUSELAH'S CHILDREN Gollancz L 1963 [0] (Ref.b) Red cloth stamped in gold on spine $25/125

027a: HAVE SPACE SUIT - WILL TRAVEL Scribner's NY (1958) [5] 1958 Hugo Nominee. Illustrated. 276 pp, 21 cm. "A.9-58 [MJ]." Published at $2.95 $100/450

027b: HAVE SPACE SUIT - WILL TRAVEL Gollancz L 1970 [] (Ref.b) $15/75

028a: STARSHIP TROOPERS Putnam's NY (1959) [0] "A much abridged version...was published in *Fantasy and Science Fiction* magazine under the title Starship Soldier." Won Hugo in 1960 $200/1,000

028b: STARSHIP TROOPERS (New English Library L 1961) [] (Ref.b) $25/125

029a: THE MENACE FROM EARTH Gnome Press Hicksville, NY (1959) [1] $60/300

030a: THE UNPLEASANT PROFESSION OF JONATHAN HOAG Gnome Press Hicksville, NY (1959) [1] Reissued by Pyramid Books in 1961 as "6xH" $30/150

030b: THE UNPLEASANT PROFESSION OF JONATHAN HOAG D. Dobson L (1964) [1] $15/75

031a: LOST LEGACY Brown, Watson L (1960) [0] Pictorial wraps. Digit Books D386 (2/-). Reprints two stories from *Assignment in Eternity* $40.

032a: STRANGER IN A STRANGE LAND Putnam's NY (1961) [0] 1962 Hugo winner. Dustwrapper priced $4.50. P.408 has "C22" (L.W. Currey 4/90) $250/1,250

032b: STRANGER IN A STRANGE LAND New English Library L 1965 [ ] Wraps $35.

032c: STRANGER IN A STRANGE LAND New English Library (L 1975) [1] First U.K. hardback edition. Green Cloth $60/300

032d: STRANGER IN A STRANGE LAND The Original Uncut Version Putnam NY 1990 [] Uncorrected proof in blue wraps $125.

032e: STRANGER IN A STRANGE LAND The Original Uncut Version Putnam NY 1990 [] The 30th Anniversary Edition with 50,000 words restored. (Published January 1991 @ $24.95) $5/25

033a: PODKAYNE OF MARS, HER LIFE AND TIMES Putnam's NY (1963) [0] Dustwrapper flap "POM | $3.50 | YA" (Currey 4/90) $150/750

033b: PODKAYNE OF MARS New English Library L 1969 [] (Ref.b) $25/125

034a: GLORY ROAD Putnam's NY (1963) [0] $125/600

034b: GLORY ROAD New English Library (L 1965) [] (Ref.b) $25/125

035a: ORPHANS OF THE SKY Gollancz L 1963 [0] Precedes American publication. Issued with wrap-around band. Reportedly the brown cloth preceded the red (Hawthorn Books 1/91) $150/650

035b: ORPHANS OF THE SKY Putnam's NY (1964) [1] Note: The Book Club also has "First American Edition" on the copyright page $75/350

036a: FARNHAM'S FREEHOLD Putnam's NY (1964) [0] "A short version of this novel...appeared in *Worlds of Science Fiction* magazine, 1964." Published at $4.95 $125/500

036b: FARNHAM'S FREEHOLD Dobson L (1965) [1] (Ref.c) $25/125

037a: THREE BY HEINLEIN Doubleday GC 1965 [0] Code "G39" at base of page 426 $15/75

037b: A HEINLEIN TRIAD Gollancz L 1966 [0] $15/75

038a: THE MOON IS A HARSH MISTRESS Putnam's NY (1966) [0] Hugo Award for 1967 $200/1,000

038b: THE MOON IS A HARSH MISTRESS Dobson L 1967 [ ] (Ref.b) $75/400

039a: THE WORLDS OF ROBERT A. HEINLEIN Ace Books NY (1966) [0] Wraps. Ace Book F-375 (40 cents). First thus $35

039b: THE WORLDS OF ROBERT A. HEINLEIN New English Library (L 1970) [] Wraps (Ref.c) $35

040a: THE PAST THROUGH TOMORROW Putnam's NY (1967) [0] Reprint collection of "Future History" stories $60/300

040b: THE PAST THROUGH TOMORROW New English Library (L 1977) [1] Two volumes. Black cloth (simulated?) $25/100

041a: I WILL FEAR NO EVIL Putnam's NY (1970) [0] $30/150

041b: I WILL FEAR NO EVIL New English Library (L 1971) [0] Dark blue cloth stamped in gold on spine $15/75

042a: TIME ENOUGH FOR LOVE Putnam's NY (1973) [0] $20/100

042b: TIME ENOUGH FOR LOVE New English Library L 1974 [] (Ref.b) $10/50

043a: THE BEST OF ROBERT HEINLEIN Sidgwick & Jackson L (1973) [1] Edited by Angus Wells $10/50

044a: ARE YOU A 'RARE BLOOD?' Horizon (no-place) 1976 [] Off-print from *Horizon Magazine*, stapled sheets (Barry Levin 1/90) $250

045a: THE NOTEBOOKS OF LAZARUS LONG Putnam's NY (1978) [0] Written with D.F. Vassallo (illuminations). Pictorial wraps $40

046a: DESTINATION MOON Gregg Press B 1979 [] With a new introduction by David G. Hartwell. [The Gregg Press Science Fiction Series]; "...photographic reprint of *Destination Moon* and his article "Shooting Destination Moon," which originally appeared in *Astounding Science Fiction*, July 1950. Issued without dustwrapper (Ref.c) $50

047a: EXPANDED UNIVERSE: The New Worlds of Robert A. Heinlein. Grosset & Dunlap NY (1980) [1] (Ref.c) $25/75

047b: EXPANDED UNIVERSE... Grosset & Dunlap NY (1980) [1] Wraps. Simultaneously issued (Ref.c) $25

048a: THE NUMBER OF THE BEAST New English Library (L 1980) [1] $15/75

048b: THE NUMBER OF THE BEAST Fawcett Columbine NY (1980) [] First US hard cover edition; reportedly published in small quantity and sold only to US library market. US text is different and adds illustrations by Richard M. Powers $15/75

048c: THE NUMBER OF THE BEAST Fawcett Columbine NY 1980 [] Wraps. Illustrated by Richard M. Powers $15

049a: FRIDAY Holt, Rinehart, Winston NY (1982) [2] 500 sgd no. cc. Issued without dustwrapper in slipcase $150/250

049b: FRIDAY Holt, Rinehart Winston NY (1982) [3] Also states "First Edition" $8/40

050a: JOB: A COMEDY OF JUSTICE Del Ray/Ballantine Books NY (1984) [] Uncorrected proof in white wraps $150.

050b: JOB: A COMEDY OF JUSTICE Del Ray/Ballantine Books NY (1984) [2] 26 sgd ltr cc (Barry Levin 11/91) $400/500

050c: JOB: A COMEDY OF JUSTICE Del Ray/Ballantine Books NY (1984) [2] 750 sgd and no. cc. Issued without dustwrapper in slipcase $150/225

050d: JOB: A COMEDY OF JUSTICE Del Ray/Ballantine Books NY (1984) [3] Also states "First Edition - September 1984" $7/35

050e: A COMEDY OF JUSTICE New English Library (L 1984) [] Note: Mistitled. Advance copy (uncorrected proof); printed wraps $75

050f: JOB: A COMEDY OF JUSTICE New English Library (L 1984) [] $7/35

051a: THE CAT WHO WALKS THROUGH WALLS Putnam's NY (1985) [2] 350 sgd no. cc. Issued without dustwrapper in slipcase $200/300

051b: THE CAT WHO WALKS THROUGH WALLS Putnam's NY (1985) [3] 115,000 cc (b&c) First issue with text in line 3 starting "Enterprise ..." on p.300 and erratum slip laid in $50/75

051c: THE CAT WHO WALKS THROUGH WALLS Putnam's NY (1985) [3] Second state: Error on p.300 corrected so that line 3 starts "Ignate universes ..." $7/35

051d: THE CAT WHO WALKS THROUGH WALLS New English Library L 1985 [] $7/35

052a: TO SAIL BEYOND THE SUNSET Ace/Putnam NY (1987) [3] 115,000 cc (Published 7/7/87 at $18.95) $6/30

052b: TO SAIL BEYOND THE SUNSET Michael Joseph L 1987 [] $6/30

053a: GRUMBLES FROM THE GRAVE Del Rey NY 1989 [3] Also states "First Edition" $5/25

054a: REQUIEM New Collected Works By and Tributes To The Grand Master Tor/St. Martin's Press NY (1992) [] Uncorrected proof in white wraps with image of dustwrapper on front cover $50.

054b: REQUIEM New Collected Works By and Tributes To The Grand Master Tor/St. Martin's Press NY (1992) [1] "First Edition, February 1992." (Published February 1992 @ $21.95)

055a: TRAMP ROYALE Berkeley/Ace NY (1992) [3] Also states "First Edition, April 19, 1992." (Published April 1992 @ $18.95)

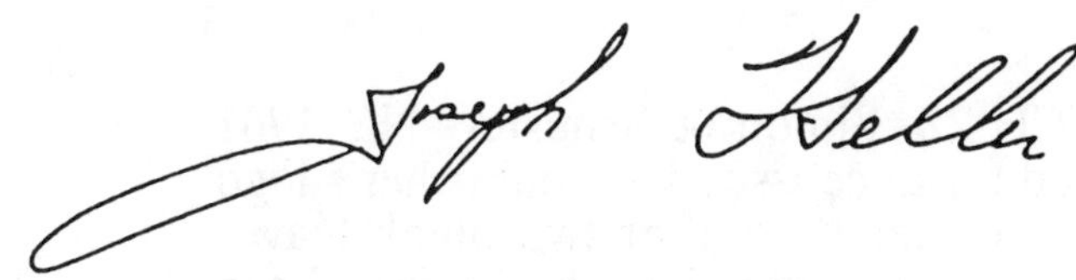

JOSEPH HELLER

Heller was born in Brooklyn in 1923. He received his B.A. from N.Y. University, his M.A. at Columbia and attended Oxford on a Fulbright Scholarship. He served in the Army Air Force during WWII and taught and worked in advertising and promotion for *Time*, *Look* and *McCall's* before becoming a full time writer.

REFERENCES:

(a) Lepper, Gary M., A BIBLIOGRAPHICAL REFERENCE TO SEVENTY-FIVE MODERN AMERICAN AUTHORS, Serendipity Books, Berkeley, 1976.

(b) Inventory.

(c) Bruccoli & Clark, FIRST PRINTINGS OF AMERICAN AUTHORS, Gale Research, Detroit, (1977), Volume 2.

001a: CATCH-22 Simon & Schuster NY 1961 []
Galley proofs in tall spiral bound pink wraps (Pharos #6) $1,000.

Note: the first chapter appeared as a novel in progress in *New World Writing* under the title Catch 18. New American Library (NY 1955) [1] Wraps $20.

001b: CATCH-22 Simon & Schuster NY 1961 []
Advance Review copy in white pictorial wraps printed in blue. (Publisher's prospectus laid in some copies {Joseph The Provider #31}) $850.

001c: CATCH-22 Simon & Schuster NY 1961 [1] Presumed advance issue with publisher's logo on first page rather than after two blank leaves as in normal trade editions; and in first issue dustwrapper without reviews on back (Waiting For Godot 10/90) $250/750

001d: CATCH-22 Simon & Schuster NY 1961 [1] In first issue dustwrapper without reviews on back $125/600

001e: CATCH-22 Simon & Schuster NY 1961 [1] In second issue dustwrapper with reviews by Algren, Jones, Shaw, et al on back $125/250

001f: CATCH-22 Jonathan Cape L (1961?) [] Pre-publication extract in 16 page booklet in green printed wraps (Dalian Books 11/88) $150.

001g: CATCH-22 Jonathan Cape L (1962) [1] With top edge stained green. Presumed first issue (Robert Dagg 11/89) $40/200

001h: CATCH-22 A Dramatization French NY (1971) [0] Wraps $40.

001i: CATCH-22 A Dramatization Delacorte NY (1973) [1] New foreword by Heller $15/75

001j: CATCH-22 Franklin Press Franklin Ctr 1978 [2] Signed "Limited Edition" in leather without dustwrapper or slipcase $100.

002a: WE BOMBED IN NEW HAVEN (Priv. Printed NY) 1968 [] Xeroxed copies for production "in a Theatre in New York" $60.

002b: WE BOMBED IN NEW HAVEN Knopf NY 1968 [1] $15/75

002c: WE BOMBED IN NEW HAVEN Jonathan Cape L 1969 [] (ref.c) $10/50

002d: WE BOMBED IN NEW HAVEN Dell NY (1970) [1] Wraps. Revised (ref.b) $25.

003a: CLEVINGER'S TRIAL French NY (1973) [0] Wraps (ref.c) $50.

004a: SOMETHING HAPPENED Knopf NY 1974 [] Uncorrected proof in mustard colored wraps (Waiting For Godot 10/90) $75.

004b: SOMETHING HAPPENED Knopf NY 1974 [2] 350 sgd no. cc. Issued in cream colored dustwrapper and slipcase $75/150

004c: SOMETHING HAPPENED Knopf NY 1974 [1] $6/30

004d: SOMETHING HAPPENED Jonathan Cape L (1975) [1] (ref.b) $8/40

005a: DIRTY DINGUS MAGEE Metro-Goldwyn-Mayer NY (1978) [] Folio wraps. Screenplay written with Tom and Frank Waldman (Joseph The Provider 8/90) $175.

006a: GOOD AS GOLD Simon & Schuster NY (1979) [] Uncorrected proofs in printed yellow wraps (H.E. Turlington #28) $75.

006b: GOOD AS GOLD Simon & Schuster NY (1979) [2] 500 sgd no. cc. Issued in acetate dustwrapper in slipcase $50/100

006c: GOOD AS GOLD Simon & Schuster NY (1979) [2] 1,000 cc. "Specially bound for friends..." Issued in acetate dustwrapper $35.

006d: GOOD AS GOLD Simon & Schuster NY (1979) [3] $5/25

006e: GOOD AS GOLD Jonathan Cape L 1979 [1] $7/35

006f: GOOD AS GOLD Franklin Press Franklin Ctr. 1979 [2] Signed "Limited Edition" with Special Message by Heller. Issued in leather without dustwrapper or slipcase $50.

007a: GOD KNOWS Knopf NY 1984 [] Uncorrected proof in yellow wraps (Bert Babcock 5/89) $50.

007b: GOD KNOWS Franklin Library (Pa.) 1984 [2] "Limited Signed" edition with Special Message by Heller. Issued in leather without dustwrapper or slipcase. $75.

007c: GOD KNOWS Knopf NY 1984 [2] 350 sgd no. cc in special dustwrapper and slipcase $50/100

007d: GOD KNOWS Knopf NY 1984 [1] (Published October 8, 1984 @ $16.95) $6/30

007e: GOD KNOWS Jonathan Cape L (1984) [1] Uncorrected proof in printed red wraps. "Provisional publication date 11/1/84 @ £8.95." (Also noted in rust colored wraps. assume the same) $60.

007f: GOD KNOWS Jonathan Cape L (1984) [1] $8/40

008a: NO LAUGHING MATTER Putnam NY 1986 [] Written with Speed Vogel. (Published @ $18.95) $6/30

008b: NO LAUGHING MATTER Jonathan Cape L (1986) [] $7/35

009a: PICTURE THIS Putnam NY 1988 []
Uncorrected proof in printed red wraps $50.

009b: PICTURE THIS Putnam NY 1988 [2]
250 sgd no. cc. Issued in slipcase $75.

009c: PICTURE THIS Putnam NY 1988 []
86,000 cc. (Published September, 1988 @ $19.95) $2/25

009d: PICTURE THIS Macmillan L (1988) [0]
24 pages in paper wraps. A "sample." Around 500 copies (Nicholas Burrows 1/89) $25.

009e: PICTURE THIS Macmillan L (1988) []
(Published October 17, 1988 @ $12.95) $25.

ZORA NEALE HURSTON
1891 - 1960

Zora Neale Hurston was born in Eatonville, Florida, the first incorporated Black town in America. Her first years are described in *Dust Tracks On A Road*. After her mother died she characterized her life as "a series of wanderings" until she enrolled as a full-time student at Baltimore's Morgan Academy. She moved to Washington, D.C. in 1918 and became a part-time student at Howard University and began to write. Hurston moved to New York in 1925 and broadened her contacts with the major figures of the Harlem Renaissance and the white literary community. She received a scholarship to Barnard College where she studied Cultural Anthropology. After graduating in 1928 she spent four years doing research on folklore in the South which she used in a number of her books.

Hurston's standing as a major writer has endured to the present although she herself withdrew from public life by the 1950's. Her argument that the pressure for integration denied the value of existing black institutions and other views did not endear her to many people. She spent the last years of her life in ill health and proverty and died in Port Pierce, Florida.

The bibliographical information herein was based on the collection of Charles Dickison, who we thank for his assistance; and Bruccoli/Clark's FIRST PRINTINGS OF AMERICAN AUTHORS, Volume I, 1978.

001a: JONAH'S GOURD VINE Lippincott Phila. 1934 [0] $350/2,000

001b: JONAH'S GOURD VINE Ducksworth London 1934 [] $200/1,250

002a: MULES AND MEN Lippincott Phila. 1935 [0] Illustrated by Miguel Covarrubias, introduction by Franz Boaz $200/1,250

002b: MULES AND MEN Kegan, Paul London 1936 [] $100/600

003a: THEIR EYES WERE WATCHING GOD Lippincott Phila. (1937) [0] $200/1,000

003b: THEIR EYES WERE WATCHING GOD Dent London 1938 [] $75/400

004a: TELL MY HORSE Lippincott Phila. (1938) [0] $200/1,000

004b: VOODOO GODS; AN INQUIRY INTO NATIVE MYTHS AND MAGIC IN JAMAICA AND HAITI Dent London 1939 [] New title $150/750

005a: MOSES, MAN OF THE MOUNTAINS Lippincott Phila. (1939) [1] Reddish-brown cloth $150/750

005b: MOSES, MAN OF THE MOUNTAINS Lippincott Phila. (1939) [1] Green cloth $60/450

005c: THE MAN OF THE MOUNTAIN Dent London 1941 [] $40/200

006a: DUST TRACKS ON A ROAD, AN AUTOBIOGRAPHY Lippincott Phila. (1942) [1] $100/450

006b: DUST TRACKS ON A ROAD, AN AUTOBIOGRAPHY Hutchinson London 1944 [] $50/250

006c: DUST TRACKS ON A ROAD, AN AUTOBIOGRAPHY Virago (London 1986)

[1] Wraps. "Published by Virago..." "several chapters restored that were either substantially altered or cut from the orignial." New introduction by Dellita Martin $35.

007a: SERAPH ON THE SUWANEE Scribner NY 1948 [5] Uncorrected proof in blue printed wraps to be "Published October 11, 1948 @ $3.00" $600.

007b: SERAPH ON THE SUWANEE Scribner NY 1948 [5] $75/350

008a: I LOVE MYSELF WHEN I'M LAUGHING Feminist Press Old Westbury, NY 1979 [] A Hurston reader edited by Alic Walker (James Jaffe 2/92) $50/150

008b: I LOVE MYSELF WHEN I'M LAUGHING Feminist Press Old Westbury, NY 1979 [] Wraps $50.

009a: THE SANCTIFIED CHURCH Turtle Island Berkeley 1981 [0] Cloth in acetate (?) dustwrapper $100.

009b: THE SANTIFIED CHURCH Turtle Island Berkeley 1981 [0] Wraps $40.

010a: SPUNK SELECTED SHORT STORIES Turtle Island Berkeley (1985) [0] Wraps $40.

011a: THE GILDED SIX-BITS Redpath Press Minn (1986) [0] Wraps. 5,000 copies. Issued in envelope $35.

JOHN IRVING

Irving was born in 1942 in Putney, Vermont. He graduated from the University of New Hampshire, received an M.F.A. from the University of Iowa and studied further at the University of Pittsburgh and the University of Vienna. The latter experience (or at least the area) was used in his first book, which received some good critical but not public attention. The latter acclaim was reserved for *The World According To Garp*, which put him "on the map" so to speak.

The information in this guide on the American firsts was based on information provided by Jackson Bryer, who we thank for his assistance; and "A John Irving Bibliography" by Edward C. Reilly in the *Bulletin of Bibliography*, Vol 42, No. 1, March, 1985. The latter was used for the British editions, but provided only the publisher and date, therefore, we assumed the first book by Corgi was in wraps. The quantities sold for the first three books were obtained from Scott Haller's "John Irving's Bizarre World" which appeared in *Saturday Review*, September 1981. This article did not state if these quantities covered more than one printing or if they included remainder sales.

We would also like to thank David Potter of St. Petersburg for providing additional listings and information.

001a: SETTING FREE THE BEARS Random House NY (1968) [1] 6,228 cc sold $75/400

001b: SETTING FREE THE BEARS Corgi Books L 1968 [] Assume issued in wraps $50.

002a: THE WATER METHOD MAN Random House NY (1972) [4] 6,906 cc sold. Although the quantity would indicate that this title would be more common than item 003a, this does not seem to be case $35/175

002b: THE WATER METHOD MAN Corgi Books L 1980 [] Wraps $35.

003a: THE 158-POUND MARRIAGE Random House NY (1974) [4] 2,560 cc sold. "...published 1980" $30/150

003b: THE 158-POUND MARRIAGE Corgi (L 1980) [1] Wraps. "First published in Great Britain." No U.K. hardback edition $40.

004a: THE WORLD ACCORDING TO GARP Dutton NY (1978) [3] "Uncorrected Proof" in bright yellow-green wraps indicating a first printing of 25,000 copies. Also noted in blue-green wraps (Serendipity) $300.

004b: THE WORLD ACCORDING TO GARP Dutton NY (1978) [3] 1,500 cc. Advance copy in white wraps with red letters $175.

004c: THE WORLD ACCORDING TO GARP Dutton NY (1978) [3] 25,000 cc. Also states "First Edition" $15/75

004d: THE WORLD ACCORDING TO GARP Gollancz L 1978 [0] $15/75

005a: THREE BY IRVING Random House NY (1980) [1] The first three novels $10/50

006a: THE PENSION GRILLPARZER (Tale Blazer Logan 1980) [] Wraps. First separate edition (Ampersand #67) $35.

007a: THE HOTEL NEW HAMPSHIRE Dutton NY (1981) [3] Uncorrected proof in tan wraps. (There is also an uncorrected proof from corrected typescript. Bound? Size? {Joseph The

Provider 9/90}. Also perfect bound in white card binding duplicating dustwrapper on front. Appeared to be a photocopy of an uncorrected proof, perhaps for use in Canada {Steven Temple 6/92}) $100.

007b: THE HOTEL NEW HAMPSHIRE Dutton NY (1981) [2] 550 sgd no. cc. Issued in full leather without dustwrapper in slipcase $75/150

007c: THE HOTEL NEW HAMPSHIRE Dutton NY (1981) [3] 175,000 cc. Also states "First Edition" $8/40

007d: THE HOTEL NEW HAMPSHIRE Cape L (1981) [1] Black boards stamped in gold on spine $8/40

008a: HOW TO SPELL (International Paper Co. NY 1983) [] 11" x 8 1/4" broadside printed on both sides with three photos of Irving. May also be a 11" x 17" format (David Potter) $60.

009a: THE CIDER HOUSE RULES Morrow NY (1985) [0] Uncorrected proof in yellow wraps $100.

009b: THE CIDER HOUSE RULES Morrow NY (1985) [0] Advance copies "Special Signed Edition" (Bev Chaney 11/89) $100.

009c: THE CIDER HOUSE RULES Franklin Library Franklin, PA 1985 [2] Signed limited edition in full leather, reportedly preceding other editions $75.

009d: THE CIDER HOUSE RULES (offered by the Book-of-the-Month Club) [2] 795 sgd no. cc. Off-yellow spine, dark green boards in glassine jacket and dark green slipcase (David Potter) $100/150

009e: THE CIDER HOUSE RULES Morrow NY (1985) [2] 750 sgd no. cc. Issued in glassine dustwrapper in slipcase $100/150

009f: THE CIDER HOUSE RULES Morrow NY (1985) [2] With signed tipped-in leaf (Watermark West #2) $50/75

009g: THE CIDER HOUSE RULES Morrow NY (1985) [0] 250,000 cc (published June 17, 1985 @ $18.95) $6/30

009h: THE CIDER HOUSE RULES Jonathan Cape L (1985) [] Uncorrected proof in red printed wraps ("Provisional publication date: 20 June 1985"). (Dalian #46 included an advance uncorrected proof in brown printed wraps?) $75.

009i: THE CIDER HOUSE RULES J. Cape L (1985) [1] Black cloth stamped in gold on spine $7/35

010a: A PRAYER FOR OWEN MEANY Dennys (Toronto 1989) [] Reportedly preceded U.S. editions $8/40

010b: A PRAYER FOR OWEN MEANY Franklin Library Franklin Center 1989 [2] Signed limited edition $60.

010c: A PRAYER FOR OWEN MEANY Morrow NY 1989 [2] 250 sgd no cc (Published @ $150). Issued in acetate dustwrapper in slipcase $125/200

010d: A PRAYER FOR OWEN MEANY Morrow NY 1989 [3] 300,000 cc (PW). (Published March 1989 @ $19.95) $5/30

010e: A PRAYER FOR OWEN MEANY Bloomsbury L (1989) [] Uncorrected proof in glossy pictorial wraps (Waiting For Godot 4/90) $60.

010f: A PRAYER FOR OWEN MEANY Bloomsbury L (1989) [] $10/40

011a: MASS APPEAL LETTER FROM NARAL Naral 1989 [] Wraps. Issued in envelope $25.

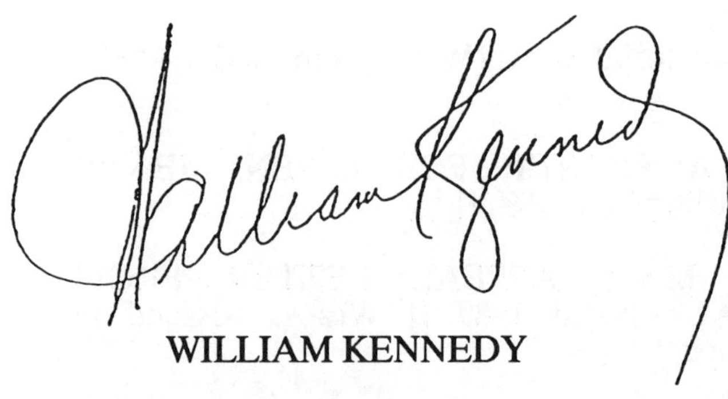

WILLIAM KENNEDY

Kennedy was born in 1928 and worked as a movie critic and reporter for the Albany Times Union. His book *Ironweed*, which was reportedly rejected by a number of publishers, won the Pulitzer Prize in 1984.

001a: THE INK TRUCK Dial NY 1969 [1]
$75/350

001b: THE INK TRUCK Macdonald & Co. L (1970) [1] Published price 1.50 (pounds) or 30s. Black cloth stamped in silver on spine only
$30/150

001c: THE INK TRUCK Viking NY (1984) [] 13,000 cc. Reissue with short author's note $7/35

002a: LETTER TO A WOULD-BE WRITER - *Fiction II* Empire State College Saratoga Springs 1973 [0] Wraps. 8"x 11" sheets in clamp binder (easily reproduced) $NVA

003a: LETTER TO A WOULD-BE WRITER - *Journalism IV* Empire State College Saratoga Springs 1973 [0] Wraps. 8" x 11" sheets in clamp binder (easily reproduced) $NVA

Note: written for use in class. Doris Grumbach wrote *Fiction I* and *Journalism III*

004a: LEGS Coward-McCann NY (1975) [0] $50/200

004b: LEGS Cape L (1976) [1] $20/100

005a: BILLY PHELAN'S GREATEST GAME Viking NY (1978) [1] 9,000 cc $30/150

005b: BILLY PHELAN'S GREATEST GAME Penguin L 1984 [1] Wraps. "Published...in Great Britain 1984" $35.

006a: IRONWEED Viking NY (1983) [] Uncorrected proof in yellow wraps (Lame Duck 9/91) $300.

006b: IRONWEED Viking NY (1983) [1] 6,500 cc. P.205:22 "perceivced" vs. "perceived." Assume all copies (error still in fifth printing - Jeff Klaess). Pulitzer Prize in 1984 $30/150

006c: IRONWEED Viking NY (L) (1983) [1] Same as Viking NY edition with two changes: "Printed in Great Britain" on copyright page and price of 7.95 (pounds) added at bottom of front dustwrapper flap, which still has $14.95 on upper corner $15/75

Note: The first copies actually sold in England were later Viking NY printings with the price sticker "7.95" (pounds)

006d: IRONWEED Viking NY (L) (1983) [1] Same as 006b with 7.95 clipped and sticker with 8.95 (pounds) pasted at bottom of dustwrapper $8/40

007a: O ALBANY Viking Press NY 1983 [0] "Unpublished Proofs" in blue printed wraps $150.

007b: O ALBANY Viking Press NY 1983 [0] 5,000 cc $20/100

008a: CHARLEY MALARKEY AND THE BELLY BUTTON MACHINE Atlantic Monthly Press B (1986) [1] Written with his son Brendan. Illustrated by Glen Baxter. (Published September 1986 @ $10.95) $6/30

008b: CHARLEY MALARKEY AND THE BELLY BUTTON MACHINE Jonathan Cape L 1987 [] Laminated pictorial boards. Issued without dustwrapper $30.

009a: THE COTTON CLUB St. Martin's Press NY (1986) [3] Wraps. Also states "First U.S. Edition." Reproduces original script by Kennedy and Francis Coppola $75.

010a: THE MAKING OF IRONWEED (Movie) Viking NY 1988 [] Uncorrected Proof in stapled wraps with eight pages of photographs from the movie $50.

010b: THE MAKING OF IRONWEED (Movie) Viking NY 1988 [] Wraps. Introduction and afterword by Kennedy as well as text for screenplay to go along with the 100+ photographs $50.

011a: QUINN'S BOOK Viking (NY 1988) [1] Unrevised and unpublished proof in dark green wraps $75.

011b: QUINN'S BOOK Viking (NY 1988) [2] 500 sgd no. cc. Issued without dustwrapper in slipcase $50/75

011c: QUINN'S BOOK Viking (NY 1988) [1] 150,000 cc (PW). (Published May 1988 @ $18.95) $5/25

011d: QUINN'S BOOK Jonathan Cape L (1988) [1] $7/35

012a: VERY OLD BONES Viking NY 1992 [] Uncorrected proof in tan-gray wraps $50.

012b: VERY OLD BONES Viking NY 1992 [] 60,000 cc (PW). (Published April 1992 @ $23.)

JOHN LeCARRE

John LeCarre is the pseudonym for David John Moore Cornwell. He was born in Poole, Dorset, England in 1931 and was a member of the British Foreign Service from 1959-64 serving as the Second Secretary at the Bonn Embassy from 1961-64.

001a: A CALL FOR THE DEAD Gollancz London 1961 [] $400/2,500

001b: A CALL FOR THE DEAD Walker NY 1962 [1] Issued in white pictorial dustwrapper. Name of British publisher misspelled on copyright page as "Gollanez." (All copies?) The edition with the color printed dustwrapper which also states "First published by Walker in 1962" is a later printing $100/500

001c: THE DEADLY AFFAIR Penguin L 1966 [] New title $30.

002a: A MURDER OF QUALITY Gollancz L 1962 [0] Red cover, variant in brown issued for libraries (Bell, Book & Radmall 6/92) $300/2,000

002b: A MURDER OF QUALITY Walker NY (1963) [1] $75/400

002c: A MURDER OF QUALITY Hodder & Stoughton L (1991) [] Wraps. Novel and complete film script, with new introduction by author $35.

003a: THE SPY WHO CAME IN FROM THE COLD Gollancz L 1963 [] (Also with Coward-McCann label pasted over Gollancz on title page, assume advance copy {Firsts & Co. 1986 $400}) $100/450

003b: THE SPY WHO CAME IN FROM THE COLD Coward-McCann NY (1964) [] Uncorrected proof in blue wraps (Chapel Hill Rare Books 6/91) $300.

003c: THE SPY WHO CAME IN FROM THE COLD Coward-McCann NY (1964) [1] First edition priced at $4.50 and without "W" on copyright page (Booksearch - AB ad). First issue dustwrapper with only three blurbs on rear panel (Joseph Dermont 3/90). Also noted with orange wrap-around band with Graham Green blurb "The best spy story I have ever read" $25/125

004a: THE LeCARRE OMNIBUS Gollancz L 1964 [] Contains *Call For The Dead* and *A Murder of Quality* $15/75

004b: THE INCONGROUS SPY Walker NY (1964) [1] States "First published in U.S..." under each title $12/60

005a: THE LOOKING GLASS WAR Heinemann L (1965) [1] (Dustwrapper spine usually faded) $25/125

005b: THE LOOKING GLASS WAR Coward McCann NY (1965) [] Uncorrected proof in spiral bound wraps (Ken Lopez 12/91) $200.

005c: THE LOOKING GLASS WAR Coward McCann NY (1965) [1] $12/60

006a: A SMALL TOWN IN GERMANY Heinemann L (1968) [0] $15/75

006b: A SMALL TOWN IN GERMANY Coward McCann NY (1968) [2] 500 sgd no. cc. In tissue dustwrapper (Maurice Neville List 0) $350.

006c: A SMALL TOWN IN GERMANY Coward McCann NY (1968) [1] Noted with spine lettering on author, title and publisher in pink, white and blue, respectively; or, in red, yellow and green, respectively. Priority unknown $12/60

007a: PHILBY: THE SPY WHO BETRAYED A GENERATION Andre Deutsch (L 1968) [1] Book by Bruce Page, David Leitch and Phillip Knightly with 15 page introduction by LeCarre $15/75

008a: THE NAIVE AND SENTIMENTAL LOVER Hodder & Stoughton L (1971) [1] $25/100

008b: THE NAIVE AND SENTIMENTAL LOVER Knopf NY 1972 [] Uncorrected proof in tall red wraps (Ken Lopez 9/91) $200.

008c: THE NAIVE AND SENTIMENTAL LOVER Knopf NY 1972 [1] $15/75

009a: TINKER, TAILOR, SOLDIER, SPY Hodder & Stoughton L (1974) [1] $20/100

009b: TINKER, TAILOR, SOLDIER, SPY Knopf NY 1974 [1] $8/40

010a: THE HONOURABLE SCHOOLBOY (Hodder & Stoughton L 1977) [] Uncorrected proof in white glazed card wraps with map endpapers tipped to flys (Alan Smith 2/91) $150.

010b: THE HONOURABLE SCHOOLBOY Hodder & Stoughton L 1977 [] 120,000 cc (Nicholos Burrows 5/92) $12/60

010c: THE HONOURABLE SCHOOLBOY Knopf NY 1977 [1] $8/40

010d: THE HONOURABLE SCHOOLBOY Franklin Library Franklin Center 1977 [2] Full leather with Special Message from LeCarre not in trade edition $75.

011a: SMILEY'S PEOPLE Hodder & Stoughton L (1980) [1] Priced £5.95 and unpriced. The latter probably for export $12/60

011b: SMILEY'S PEOPLE Knopf NY 1980 [1] With signed tipped in leaf $100/125

011c: SMILEY'S PEOPLE Knopf NY 1980 [1] $7/35

012a: QUEST FOR KARLA Hodder & Stoughton L 1982 [1] Includes *Tinker...*, *Honourable...* and *Smiley's...* $10/50

012b: QUEST FOR KARLA Knopf NY 1982 [1] $8/40

013a: THE LITTLE DRUMMER GIRL Knopf NY 1983 [] Uncorrected proof in blue wraps (Waiting For Godot 10/90) $175.

013b: THE LITTLE DRUMMER GIRL Knopf NY 1983 [1] With an extra leaf signed by author. About 200 cc (Mordida Books 5/90) $175/200

013c: THE LITTLE DRUMMER GIRL Knopf NY 1983 [1] $7/35

013d: THE LITTLE DRUMMER GIRL (Book of Month Club) NY 1983 [2] 1,048 sgd no. cc. Green cloth with tan buckram spine in acetate dustwrapper and slipcase. Issued by BOMC $175/225

013e: THE LITTLE DRUMMER GIRL Hodder & Stoughton L (1983) [2] 739 sgd cc. Pre-publication in white wraps signed by author on upper cover (R. Gekoski) $150.

013f: THE LITTLE DRUMMER GIRL Hodder & Stoughton L 1983 [1] "Reproduced from original setting by Knopf." Noted with top edge stained either gray or dark brown. Priority uncertain but Alphabet Books believes gray is first (5/92) $12/60

014a: A PERFECT SPY Hodder & Stoughton L (1986) [2] 250 sgd no. cc. Specially bound for London Limited Editions. Issued in glassine wrapper, no slipcase $225.

014b: A PERFECT SPY Hodder & Stoughton L (1986) [1] $10/50

014c: A PERFECT SPY Knopf NY 1986 [] Uncorrected proof. First in white wraps $125.

014d: A PERFECT SPY Knopf NY 1986 [] Uncorrected proof. Second issue in red wraps $75.

014e: A PERFECT SPY Knopf NY 1986 [1] Signed on tipped in leaf $100/125

014f: A PERFECT SPY Knopf NY 1986 [1] (Copies without printed price on dustwrapper are for export to Canada, unless they have a Book-of-the-Month stamp on back cover) $6/30

015a: THE CLANDESTINE MUSE Seluzicki Fine Books Portland, Oregon (1986) [2] 250 sgd no. cc. Issued in stiff wraps (plus 10 copies Hors Commerce) $250.

016a: JOHN LeCARRE SAMPLER (Bantam NY 1987) [3] Wraps. No title page but complete copyright page. Excerpts from seven novels $10.

017a: THE RUSSIA HOUSE Knopf NY 1989 [1] Uncorrected proof in creme colored wraps $125.

Note: Reportedly the U.S. edition of RUSSIA HOUSE was published three weeks before the English edition (Monroe Stahr 6/92)

017b: THE RUSSIA HOUSE Knopf NY 1989 [1] With signed tipped in leaf (about 400 cc per Ken Lopez 12/91) $100/125

017c: THE RUSSIA HOUSE Knopf NY 1989 [1] 350,000 cc (PW). (Published June 9, 1989 @ $19.95 $5/20

017d: THE RUSSIA HOUSE Hodder & Stoughton L (1989) [] Uncorrected proofs in white or tan wraps (Monroe Stahr 3/90). Priority uncertain $125.

017e: THE RUSSIA HOUSE Hodder & Stoughton/London Limited Editions L (1989) [2] 150 sgd no. cc in tissue dustwrapper $225.

017f: THE RUSSIA HOUSE Hodder & Stoughton L (1989) [1] About 500 special bound (not signed) copies in gray cloth with leather spine in slipcase (Ken Lopez 9/89) $50/75

017g: THE RUSSIA HOUSE Hodder & Stoughton L (1989) [1] $6/30

018a: THE SECRET PILGRIM Knopf NY 1991 [1] Uncorrected proof in tan or beige wraps. (Precedes U.K. but reportedly the Sydney, Australia edition was published on December 10, 1990 {Monroe Stahr 5/91}) $100.

018b: THE SECRET PILGRIM Knopf NY 1991 [1] Signed tipped in page (about 700 copies {Ken Lopez 3/92}) $100/125

018c: THE SECRET PILGRIM Knopf NY 1991 [1] 350,000 cc (PW). (Published January 1991 @ $21.95) $5/20

018d: THE SECRET PILGRIM Hodder & Stoughton L 1991 [] Uncorrected proof. First issue in printed wraps lacking full British cataloging data and proof dustwrapper without author photograph on back. (About 80 copies {Hartley Moorhouse 4/92}) $100.

018e: THE SECRET PILGRIM Hodder & Stoughton L 1991 [] Second issue uncorrected proof, bound signatures without covers, laid in proof dustwrapper with author's picture on back $75.

018f: THE SECRET PILGRIM Hodder & Stoughton L 1991 [] (Published January 17, 1991) $6/30

THE LIMITED EDITIONS CLUB

LIMITED EDITIONS CLUB

The Limited Editions Club (LEC) was founded in 1929 by George Macy, to publish finely printed and well illustrated books for a small number of members (1,500). To select texts the membership would consider worth republishing, edit them, contract with sympathetic typographers, and successful illustrators, have them printed and bound by the best available craftsmen, and turn out 12 books a year was not an easy task. However, the LEC was successful until 1971, under George Macy and his wife Helen who ran the business after his death.

From 1971 to 1978 the ownership changed five times and by the end of the decade the club was left in the red and without the Heritage Press which had published the "trade editions" of the books; and presumedly made more money for Macy than the LEC (Heritage had been sold off in the mid-1970's to raise money).

During the first few years of the 1980's the club stayed with the 2,000 copy printing, which the various owners had moved to in the 1970's, but by 1983 the club was back to the quantity of 1,500 copies, which had been used throughout the Macy's tenure. And by 1986, the quantity had moved down to 1,000 copies or less.

We believe that the LEC produced and still produces beautiful books. we've always been amazed that people are paying $40 or more for leather bound Franklin Press books "limited" to 4,000 to 15,000 copies (our best guess based on the few titles on which we've been able to obtain the quantities), when the LEC books, limited to 1,500 signed and numbered copies, were selling for under $40 in the 1970's. The recent ones, we admit have gotten much more expensive, but the current owners seem to be moving toward more expensive artist books with small limitations.

We have arranged this guide chronologically but have included an alphabetical index of the authors, illustrators, etc. for your convenience. All titles were issued in boxes or slipcases. Nearly all of the books are signed by the illustrator, and occasionally by the author or others.

Estimated value is based on slipcase being present. If they are lacking, prices would probably be lowered 10-20% on the more valuable ones and perhaps as much as 40-50% on the less valuable ones.

All are limited to 1,500 numbered copies unless otherwise stated. In some instances, the date of publication may not be in proper chronological order as we assume that they experienced printing delays after the publications were announced. We kept this guide in the same order as the primary reference through 1985. All were issued with slipcases unless noted otherwise, and estimated prices assume both the books and slipcases are in fine condition.

We wish to thank Alfred Regan for his help identifying the recent titles.

NOTE: for your convenience, an index of the authors, illustrators, etc. follows the Limited Editions Club entries.

REFERENCES:

(a) BIBLIOGRAPHY OF THE FINE BOOKS PUBLISHED BY THE LIMITED EDITIONS CLUB 1929-1985 (Limited Editions Club, New York, 1985).

(b) Haveles, Paul J. & David P. LIMITED EDITIONS CLUB GUIDE (Extensive Search Service, Danielson, Ct., 1976).

(c) Prospectus from the LEC were used from 1985 to date.

(d) Inventory, dealer catalogs, etc. were necessary, as the first three references were deficient in many ways for our purposes.

001: Swift, Jonathan THE TRAVELS OF LEMUEL GULLIVER NY 1929. Signed and illustrated by Alexander King. Introduction by Shane Leslie $250.

002: Whitman, Walt LEAVES OF GRASS Mt. Vernon, NY 1929. Signed by Frederic Warde, the designer. Introduction by Carolyn Wells $175.

003: Raspe, Rudolphe E. THE TRAVELS OF BARON MUNCHAUSEN Chicago 1929. Signed and illustrated by John Held, Jr. Introduction by Carl Van Doran $150.

004: Whittier, John Greenleaf SNOW-BOUND NY 1930. Signed by Purlington Rollins, the designer. Introduction by George S. Bryan; vignette by Alice Hubbard Stevens $100.

005: Poe, Edgar Allen THE NARRATIVE OF ARTHUR GORDON PYM Portland 1930. Signed by Rene Clarke, the designer. Introduction by Joseph Wood Krutch $150.

006: Stevenson, Robert Louis TWO MEDIAEAVAL TALES (NY) 1930. Signed and illustrated by C.B. Falls. Introduction by Clayton Hamilton $100.

007: Boccaccio, Giovanni THE DECAMERON NY 1930. 2 vols. Signed by T.M. Cleland, the designer and illustrator. Translated by Frances Winwar, introduction by Burton Rascoe $150.

008: Irving, Washington RIP VAN WINKLE NY 1930. Signed by Frederic Goudy, the designer. Introduction by Mark Van Doren $125.

009: Daudet, Alphonse TARTARIN OF TARASCON Westport 1930. 2 vols. Signed by W.A. Dwiggins, the designer and illustrator. Translated and introduction by Jacques Le Clercq $100.

010: LaMotte-Fouque, F. de UNDINE NY 1930. Signed by Allen Lewis, the illustrator. Translated by Edmund Gosse $100.

011: Defoe, Daniel ROBINSON CRUSOE NY 1930. Signed by Edward A. Wilson, the illustrator. Introduction by Ford Madox Ford $150.

012: La Fontaine, Jean De THE FABLES OF JEAN DE LA FONTAINE NY 1930. 2 vols. Signed by Rudolph Ruzicka, the illustrator. Translated and with introductions by Joseph Auslander and Jacques Le Clercq $125.

013: Hugo, Victor NOTRE-DAME DE PARIS Paris 1930. 2 vols. Signed by Masereel, the illustrator. Translated by Jessie Haynes, introduction by Andrew Lang $175.

014: DeQuincey, Thomas CONFESSIONS OF AN ENGLISH OPIUM EATER Oxford 1930. 1,520 cc. Signed by Zhenya Gay, the illustrator and B.H. Newdigate, the printer. Introduction by William Bolitho $125.

015: Homer THE ODYSSEY Haarlem 1930. Signed by J. Van Drimpen, the designer. Translated by Alexander Pope, introduction by Carl Van Doren $150.

016: Moliere TARTUFFE, or THE HYPOCRITE Leipzig 1930. Signed by Hugo Steiner-Prag, the illustrator. Translated by Curtis Hidden Page, introduction by Brander Matthews $100.

017: THE LITTLE FLOWERS OF SAINT FRANCIS OF ASSISI NY 1930. Signed by Paolo Molnar, the illustrator. The first English translation (1864), revised, by Dom Roger Hudleston. Introduction by Arthur Livingston $125.

018: Carlyle, Thomas SARTOR RESARTUS London 1931. Signed by Oliver Simon, the printer. Introduction by Bliss Perry $60.

019: AUCASSIN & NICOLETTE Prague 1931. Signed by Vojtech Preissig, the designer and illustrator. Translation and introduction by Andrew Lang $75.

020: Grimm, J.L. and W.K. GRIMM'S FAIRY TALES Offenbach 1931. Signed by Fritz Kredel, the illustrator and Rudolf Koch, the designer. Introduction by Harry Hansen $150.

021: Loti, Pierre AN ICELAND FISHERMAN Stockholm 1931. Signed by Yngve Berg, the illustrator. Introduction by Guy Endore $75.

022: Thackeray, William Makepeace VANITY FAIR Oxford 1931. 2 vols. Signed by John Austen, the illustrator. Introduction by G.K. Chesterton $125.

023: Hawthorne, Nathaniel MARBLE FAUN or THE ROMANCE OF MONTE BENI Zurich 1931. 2 vols. Signed by Carl Straus, the illustrator. Introduction by Herbert Gorman $75.

024: Homer ILIAD Haarlem 1931. Signed by J. Van Krimpen, the illustrator. Introduction by Alexander Pope. Note by Carl Van Doren $125.

025: Fielding, Henry HISTORY OF TOM JONES NY 1931. Signed by Alexander King, the illustrator. Introduction by J.B. Priestley $125.

026: Franklin, Benjamin THE AUTOBIOGRAPHY OF BENJAMIN FRANKLIN S.F. 1931. Signed by John Henry Nash, the printer. Introduction and marginal glosses by Edward F. O'Day $175.

027: Dickins, Charles THE CHIMES London 1931. Signed by Arthur Rackham, the illustrator. Introduction by Edward Wagenknecht $600.

028: Surtees, R.S. THE JAUNTS & JOLLITIES OF MR. JOHN JORROCKS Boston 1932. Signed by Gordon Ross, the illustrator. Introduction by A. Edward Newton $100.

029: Balzac, Honore de DROLL STORIES (30 Tales) Portland 1932. 3 vols. Signed by W.A. Dwiggins, the designer. Translation and preface by Jacques Le Clercq $125.

030: Goethe, Johann Wolfgang von FAUST: A TRAGEDY NY 1932. Signed by Rene Clarke, the illustrator. Translation by Alice Raphael, introduction by Mark Van Doren $75.

031: Hearn, Lafcadio KWAIDAN Tokyo 1932. Signed by Yasumasa Fujita, the illustrator. Introduction by Oscar Lewis $250.

032: Reade, Charles CLOISTER AND THE HEARTH NY 1932. 2 vols. Signed by Lynd Ward, the illustrator. Introduction by Hendrik Willem van Loon $100.

033: Cooper, James Fenimore THE LAST OF THE MOHICANS Rochester 1932. Signed by E.A. Wilson, the illustrator. Introduction by Edward Everett Hale. Designed by Will Ransom

$125.

034: Douglas, Norman SOUTH WIND NY 1932. Signed by Carlotta Petrina, the illustrator. Introduction by Carl Van Doren $75.

035: Maran, Rene BATOUALA NY 1932. Signed by Miguel Covarrubias, the illustrator. Translated and introduction by Alvah C. Bessie

$225.

036: Carroll, Lewis (Charles L. Dodgson) ALICE'S ADVENTURES IN WONDERLAND NY 1932 Approximately 1,200 of the 1,500 copies were signed by Alice Hargreaves, the original "Alice." Introduction by Henry Seidel Canby, illustrations by John Tenniel (ABPC Vol. 95 states 500 copies signed)

Signed: $850.
Unsigned: $300.

(Also see 065)

037: Apuleius, Lucius GOLDEN ASSE NY 1932. Signed by Percival Goodman, the illustrator. Translated and introduction by Jack Lindsay $125.

038: Dumas, Alexandre THE THREE MUSKETEERS Maastricht 1932. 2 vols. Signed by Pierre Falke, the illustrator. Translated by Wm. Robson, introduction by Ben Ray Redman $75.

039: THE FOUR GOSPELS According to Matthew, Mark, Luke & John Leipzig 1932. Signed by Emil Rudolf Weiss, the illustrator

$175.

040: Twain, Mark THE ADVENTURES OF HUCKLEBERRY FINN NY 1933. Signed by Carl Purington, the designer. Introduction by Booth Tarkington, includes the original illustrations by E.W. Kemble $150.

041: Alighieri, Dante THE DIVINE COMEDY Verona 1932. Signed by Hans Mardersteig, the designer and printer. Translated and annotated by Melville Best Anderson, introduction by Arthur Livingston $250.

042: Confucius THE ANALECTS OF CONFUCIUS Shanghai 1933. Translated with an introduction by Lionel Giles. In special Chinese redwood box $250.

043: Villon, Francois THE LYRICS OF FRANCOIS VILLON NY 1933. Signed by Howard Simon, the illustrator. Translations by Swinburne, Rossetti, Henley, Payne, and Leonie Adams. Introduction by Leonie Adams $100.

044: Shakespeare, William THE TRAGEDY OF HAMLET, PRINCE OF DENMARK High Wycombe 1933. Signed by Eric Gill, the illustrator. Introduction by Gilbert Murray $500.

045: Dickens, Charles THE POSTHUMOUS PAPERS OF THE PICKWICK CLUB Oxford 1933. 2 vols. Signed by John Austen, the illustrator. Introduction by G.K. Chesterton $150.

046: Tolstoy, Leo ANNA KARENIA Moscow 1933. 2 vols. Signed by Nikolas Piskariov, the illustrator. Translated by Constance Garnett, edited by Bernard Guilbert Guerney and Gustavus Spett, introduction by Anatole Lunacharsky $100.

047: AESOP'S FABLES Oxford 1933. Signed by Bruce Rogers, the designer and illustrator. Translation by Samuel Croxall, bibliographical note by Victor Scholderer $200.

048: Cervantes, Miguel de DON QUIXOTE OF LA MANCHA Barcelona 1933. 2 vols. Signed by Enric-Cristobal Ricart, the illustrator. Translated and introduction by John Ormsby $175.

049: France, Anatole AT THE SIGN OF QUEEN PEDAUQUE Chicago 1933. Signed by Sylvain Sauvage, the illustrator. Translated by Mrs. Wilfrid Jackson, introduction by Ernest Boyd $75.

050: Dostoevsky, Fyodor THE BROTHERS KARAMAZOV Boston 1933. 3 vols. Signed by Alexander King, the illustrator. Translation of Constance Garnett revised by and with an introduction by Avrahm Yarmolinsky $150.

051: Dickens, Charles THE CRICKET ON THE HEARTH Oxford 1933. Illustrated by Hugh Thomson, introduction by Walter de la Mare $175.

052: Longus THE PASTORAL LOVES OF DAPHNIS AND CHLOE NY 1934. Signed by Ruth Reeves, the illustrator. Translated and introduction by George Moore $100.

053: Shelley, Mary Wollstonecraft FRANKENSTEIN, or THE MODERN PROMETHEUS NY 1934. Signed by Everett Henry, the illustrator. Introduction by Edmund Lester Pearson $250.

054: Butler, Samuel EREWHON NY 1934. Signed by Rockwell Kent, the illustrator. Introduction by Aldous Huxley $150.

055: de Coster, Charles THE GLORIOUS ADVENTURES OF TYL ULENSPEIGL 1934. Signed by Richard Floethe, the illustrator. Translated by Allan Ros MacDougall, introduction by Romain Rolland $75.

056: Marco Polo THE TRAVELS OF MARCO POLO NY 1934. 2 vols. Signed by Nikolai Fyodorovitch Lapshin, the illustrator. The Marsden translation revised and edited, with an introduction by Manuel Komroff $125.

057: Aristophanes LYSISTRATA Westport 1934. Signed by Pablo Picasso, the illustrator. Translated and introduction by Gilbert Seldes. 150 copies also had a set of 6 proofs of the original Picasso etchings, each signed by Picasso (ref.b)

With the 6 proofs: $10,000.
Without the 6 proofs: $4,500.

058: Sheridan, Richard Brinsley THE SCHOOL FOR SCANDAL Oxford 1934. Signed by Rene Ben Sussan, the illustrator. Introduction by Carl Van Doren $125.

059: THE BOOK OF THE THOUSAND NIGHTS AND A NIGHT NY 1934. 6 vols. Signed by Valenti Angelo, the illustrator. Translation, notes, introduction (etc.) by Sir Richard Burton. Edited by Emile Van Vliet $150.

060: Emerson, Ralph Waldo THE ESSAYS OF RALPH WALDO EMERSON The First and Second Series S.F. 1934. Signed by John Henry Nash, the printer. Introduction by Edward F. O'Day $125.

061: Dickens, Charles A CHRISTMAS CAROL Boston 1934. Signed by Gordon Ross, the illustrator. Introduction by Stephen Leacock $150.

062: Chauncer, Geoffrey THE CANTERBURY TALES London 1934. 2 vols. Signed by George Jones, the printer. Introduction by Frank Ernest Hill $150.

063: More, Sir Thomas UTOPIA NY 1934. Signed by Bruce Rogers, the printer. Introduction by H.G. Wells $150.

064: Hudson, W.H. GREEN MANSIONS NY 1935. Signed by Edward A. Wilson, the illustrator. Introduction by William Beebe $75.

065: Carroll, Lewis THROUGH THE LOOKING-GLASS NY 1935. Most of the 1,500 copies were signed by Alice Hargreaves, the original "Alice." Introduction by Carl Van Doren, illustrations by John Tenniel. (Ref.b states that only 200 copies were signed by Hargreaves?)

Signed: $1,000.
Unsigned: $350.

(Also see 036)

066: Hawthorne, Nathaniel THE HOUSE OF THE SEVEN GABLES NY 1935. Signed by Valenti Angelo, the illustrator. Introduction by Van Wyck Brooks $100.

067: Henry, O. (Wm. Sydney Porter) THE VOICE OF THE CITY NY 1935. Signed by George Grosz, the illustrator. Introduction by Clifton Fadiman $350.

068: Hoffman, Dr. Heinrich SLOVENLY PETER NY 1935. Translated into English jingles by Mark Twain. Foreword by Clara Clemens, introduction by Philip Hofer, illustrated by Fritz Kredel $200.

069: Melville, Herman TYPEE: ROMANCE OF SOUTH SEAS NY 1935. Signed by Miguel Covarrubias, the illustrator. Introduction by Raymond Weaver $175.

070: Sterne, Laurence THE LIFE & OPINIONS OF TRISTRAM SHANDY, GENTLEMAN NY 1935. 2 vols. Signed by T.M. Cleland, the illustrator. Introduction by Christopher Morley $125.

071: Joyce, James ULYSSES NY 1935. All copies signed by Henri Matisse, the illustrator. 250 copies (ref.b) were also signed by Joyce. Introduction by Stuart Gilbert

Signed by Joyce and Matisse: $10,000.
Signed by Matisse: $5,000.

072: Smollett, Tobias THE ADVENTURES OF PEREGRINE PICKLE Oxford 1935. 2 vols. Signed by John Austen, the illustrator. Introduction by G.K. Chesterton $100.

073: THE HOLY BIBLE: THE KING JAMES VERSION New Haven 1935. 5 vols. Designed by George Macy $150.

074: Khayyam, Omar THE RUBAIYAT OF OMAR KHAYYAM (Westport) 1935. Signed by Valenti Angelo. Definitive text selected from the five editions of Edward FitzGerald's translation $175.

075: Butler, Samuel THE WAY OF ALL FLESH New Haven 1936. 2 vols. Signed by Robert Ward Johnson, the illustrator. Introduction by Theodore Dreiser $100.

076: Landor, Walter Savage IMAGINARY CONVERSATIONS Verona 1936. Signed by

Giovanni Mardersteig, the designer-printer. Introduction by R.H. Boothroyd $150.

077: Borrow, George LAVENGRO London 1936. 2 vols. Signed by Barnett Freedman, the illustrator. Introduction by Hugh Walpole $100.

078: Thoreau, Henry David WALDEN, or LIFE IN THE WOODS NY 1936. Signed by Edward Steichen, the photographer. Introduction by Henry Seidel Canby $900.

079: Hale Edward Everett THE MAN WITHOUT A COUNTRY NY 1936. Signed by Edward A. Wilson, the illustrator. Introduction by Carl Van Doren $75.

080: Rostand, Edmond CYRANO DE BERGERAC Windham 1936. Signed by Sylvain Sauvage, the illustrator. Translated, with an introduction by Brian Hooker $75.

081: Sterne, Laurence A SENTIMENTAL JOURNEY THROUGH FRANCE AND ITALY High Wycombe 1936. Signed by Denis Tegetmeier, the illustrator and Eric Gill, the designer $175.

082: Rabelais, Francois GARGANTUA AND PANTAGRUEL Portland 1936. 5 vols. Signed by W.A. Dwiggins, the designer and decorator. Introduction by Jacques Le Clercq $175.

083: Malory, Sir Thomas LE MORTE D'ARTHUR London 1936. 3 vols. Signed by Robert Gibbings, the illustrator. Preface by William Caxton, bibliographical note by A.W. Pollard. Printed by the Golden Cockerel Press $275.

084: Milton, John PARADISE LOST and PARADISE REGAIN'D S.F. 1936. Signed by

Carlotta Petrina, the illustrator. Introduction by William Rose Benet. Designed by John Henry Nash $125.

085: Aristophanes THE FROGS Haarlem 1937. Signed by John Austen, the illustrator. Translated by William James Hickie, introduction by Gilbert Seldes $100.

086: Cellini, Benvenuto THE LIFE OF BENVENUTO CELLINI Verona 1937. Signed by Fritz Kredel, the illustrator. Translated by John Addington Symonds, introduction by Thomas Craven. Printed by Hans Mardersteig $150.

087: Wilde, Oscar THE BALLAD OF READING GAOL NY 1937. Signed by Zhenya Gay, the illustrator. Introduction by Burton Rascoe $125.

088: Collodi, Carlo PINOCCHIO, THE ADVENTURES OF A MARIONETTE NY 1937. Signed by Richard Floethe, the illustrator. Introduction by Carl Van Doren $150.

089: Lewis, Sinclair MAIN STREET Chicago 1937. Signed by Grant Wood, the illustrator. Contains a special introduction by the author $600.

090: Gay, John THE BEGGAR'S OPERA Lyon 1937. Signed by Mariette Lydis, the illustrator. Preface by A.P. Herbert $60.

091: Dickens, Charles GREAT EXPECTATIONS Edinburgh 1937. Signed by Gordon Ross, the illustrator. With the original "honest ending" (original ending which had not appeared in book form previously). Preface by Bernard Shaw $175.

092: Burton, Richard F. THE KASIDAH OF HAJI ABDU EL-YEZDI New Haven 1937. Signed by Valenti Angelo, who did the designs, decorations and hand-illuminations $125.

093: Dumas, Alexandre CAMILLE London 1937. Signed by Marie Laurencin, the illustrator. Translation and introduction by Edmund Gosse $750.

094: Allen, Hervey ANTHONY ADVERSE Mount Vernon 1937. 3 vols. Signed by Edward A. Wilson, the illustrator. Special introduction by the author $100.

095: Collier, John Payne PUNCH AND JUDY NY 1937. Introduction by Paul McPharlin, illustrated by George Cruikshank $125.

096: France, Anatole THE CRIME OF SYLVESTRE BONNARD NY 1937. Signed by Sylvain Sauvage, the illustrator. Translated by Lafcadio Hearn, introduction by A.S.W. Rosenbach $100.

097: Stowe, Harriet Beecher UNCLE TOM'S CABIN NY 1938. Signed by Miguel Covarrubias, the illustrator. Introduction by Raymond Weaver $400.

098: Le Sage, Alain Rene THE ADVENTURES OF GIL BLAS OF SANTILLANE Oxford 1937. 2 vols. Signed by John Austen, the illustrator. Translated by Tobias Smollett, introduction by J.B. Priestley $125.

099: Maugham, W. Somerset OF HUMAN BONDAGE New Haven 1938. 2 vols. Signed by John Sloan, the illustrator. Introduction by Theodore Dreiser $600.

100: Peattie, Donald Culross AN ALMANAC FOR MODERNS Washington 1938. Signed by Asa Cheffetz, the illustrator. Special introduction by the author $60.

101: Flaubert, Gustave MADAME BOVARY Zurich 1938. Signed by Gunther Boehmer, the illustrator. Translated by Eleanor Marx Aveling, introduction by Andre Maurois $125.

102: THE SONG OF ROLAND Windham 1938. Signed by Valenti Angelo, the illustrator. Translated by C.K. Scott-Moncrieff, introduction by Hamish Miles $150.

103: Boswell, James THE LIFE OF SAMUEL JOHNSON, LL.D. London 1938. 3 vols. Designed by Oliver Simon. Introduction by Edward Fletcher $200.

104: Wilde, Oscar SALOME Paris/London 1938. 2 vols. Signed by Andre Derain, the illustrator. First volume is the original French version, the seconnd volume is the English version translated by Lord Alfred Douglas, introduction by Holbrook Jackson with illustrations by Aubrey Beardsley (contains 4 not in first edition) $500.

105: Tolstoy, Leo WAR AND PEACE Glasgow 1938. 6 vols. Signed by Barnett Freedman, the illustrator. Introduction by Aylmer Maude $250.

106: Gray, Thomas ELEGY WRITTEN IN A COUNTRY CHURCH-YARD London 1938. Signed by Agnes Miller Parker, the illustrator. Introduction by Hugh Walpole $250.

107: Stevenson, Robert Louis KIDNAPPED NY 1938. Signed by Hans Alexander Mueller, the illustrator. Introduction by Christopher Morley $75.

108: Hugo, Victor LES MISERABLES Mount Vernon 1938. 5 vols. Signed by Lynd Ward, the illustrator. Introduction by Andre Maurois $175.

109: Wharton, Edith ETHAN FROME Portland 1939. Signed by Henry Varnum Poor, the illustrator. Introduction by Clifton Fadiman $100.

110: Dreiser, Theodore SISTER CARRIE NY 1939. Signed by Reginald Marsh, the illustrator. Introduction by Burton Rascoe $200.

111: Browne, Sir Thomas RELIGIO MEDICI Univ. of Oregon 1939. Signed by John Henry Nash, designer and printer. Introduction by Geoffrey Keynes $75.

112: Shaw, Bernard BACK TO METHUSELAH NY 1939. Signed by John Farleigh, the illustrator. New introduction by the author $75.

113: Chaucer, Geoffrey TROILUS AND CRESSIDA London 1939. Signed by George W. Jones, the designer. Rendered in modern English verse by George Philip Krapp $100.

114: Twain, Mark THE ADVENTURES OF TOM SAWYER Cambridge 1939. Signed by Thomas Hart Benton, the illustrator. Introduction by Bernard De Voto $500.

115: Austen, Jane PRIDE AND PREJUDICE Boston 1940. Signed by Helen Sewell, the illustrator. Preface by Frank Swinnerton $125.

116: Casanova, Jacques THE MEMOIRS OF JACQUES CASANOVA DE SEINGALT Edinburgh 1940. 8 vols. Translated by Arthur Machen, introduction by Francis Meynell $125.

117: Baudelaire, Charles LES FLEURS DU MAL / FLOWERS OF EVIL Paris/London 1940. 2 vols. The French original, illustrated by Auguste Rodin, preface by Camille Mauclair; and the English version, signed by Jacob Epstein, the illustrator. Introduction by James Laver. (Distribution of the French volume was delayed until 1947 by WWII)

Both volumes: $250.
French version alone: $100.
English version alone: $100.

118: Shakespeare, William THE COMEDIES, HISTORIES & TRAGEDIES OF WILLIAM SHAKESPEARE NY 1939-1940. 37 vols. 1,950 copies. Signed by Bruce Rogers. Illustrated by various artists $1,500.

(Also see 122)

119: Cooper, James Fenimore THE PRAIRIE NY 1940. Signed by John Steuart Curry, the illustrator. Introduction by Harry Hansen $150.

(Also see special editions at end of listing)

120: Scott, Sir Walter IVANHOE NY 1940. 2 vols. Signed by Allen Lewis, the illustrator. Introduction by the author $125.

121: Brooks, Van Wyck FLOWERING OF NEW ENGLAND Boston 1941. Signed by Raymond J. Holden, the illustrator. Introduction by M.A. DeWolfe Howe. Some copies also signed by author

Signed by both: $100.
Signed only by Holden: $75.

122: Shakespeare, William POEMS AND SONNETS NY 1941. 2 vols. Signed by Bruce

Rogers, the designer. Introduction by Louis Untermeyer

2 vols: $250.
with 37 vols of Plays (118): $1,750.

(Also see 118)

123: Stevenson, Robert Louis TREASURE ISLAND NY 1941. Illustrated by Edward A. Wilson, introduction by the author $150.

124: Merimee, Prosper CARMEN NY 1941. Signed by Jean Charlot, the illustrator. Introduction by Konrad Bercovici $125.

125: Poe, Edgar Allan TALES OF MYSTERY AND IMAGINATION Baltimore 1941. Signed by William Sharp, the illustrator. Introduction by Vincent Starrett $150.

126: Bellamy, Edward LOOKING BACKWARD L.A. (1941). Signed by Elise (Cavanna), the illustrator. Introduction by Irwin Edman $125.

127: Dumas, Alexandre THE COUNT OF MONTE CRISTO Mount Vernon 1941. 4 vols. Signed by Lynd Ward, the illustrator. Introduction by Andre Maurois $125.

128: Plutarch THE LIVES OF THE NOBLE GRECIANS AND ROMANS Portland 1941. 8 vols. Signed by W.A. Dwiggins, the designer. Introduction by Emil Ludwig $225.

129: Bunyan, John THE PILGRIM'S PROGRESS NY 1941 Introduction by Geoffrey Keynes, illustrated by William Blake $150.

130: Bennett, Arnold THE OLD WIVES' TALE Oxford 1941. 2 vols. Signed by John Austen, the illustrator. Preface by the author, introduction by Frank Swinnerton $100.

131: Hawthorne, Nathaniel THE SCARLET LETTER NY 1941. Signed by Henry Varnum Poor, the illustrator. Introduction by Dorothy Canfield $100.

132: Twain, Mark ADVENTURES OF HUCKLEBERRY FINN (New Haven) 1942. Signed by Thomas Hart Benton, the illustrator. Introduction by Bernard De Voto $500.

133: Adams, Henry THE EDUCATION OF HENRY ADAMS Boston 1942. Signed by Samuel Chamberlain, the illustrator. Introduction by Henry Seidel Canby $100.

134: Masters, Edgar Lee SPOON RIVER ANTHOLOGY NY 1942. Signed by the author and Boardman Robinson, the illustrator. New introduction by the author $225.

135: Pepys, Samuel THE DIARY OF SAMUEL PEPYS Mt. Vernon 1942. 10 vols. Signed by William Sharp, the illustrator. Introduction by Henry B. Wheatley $150.

136: Stephens, James THE CROCK OF GOLD NY 1942. Signed by Robert Lawson, the illustrator. Introduction by Clifton Fadiman $100.

137: Lincoln, Abraham THE LITERARY WORKS OF ABRAHAM LINCOLN NY 1942. Signed by John Steuart Curry, the illustrator. Introduction and notes by Carl Van Doren $175.

138: Andersen, Hans Christian FAIRY TALES NY 1942. 2 vols. Signed by Fritz Kredel, the illustrator and Jean Hersholt, the translator $125.

139: Hemingway, Ernest FOR WHOM THE BELL TOLLS Princeton 1942. Signed by Lynd Ward, the illustrator. Introduction by Sinclair Lewis $250.

140: Diaz del Castillo, Bernal THE DISCOVERY AND CONQUEST OF MEXICO 1517-1521 Mexico City 1942. Signed by Miguel Covarrubias, the illustrator. Also signed by Harry Block, the editor and Rafael Loera Y Chavez, the printer $300.

141: Whitman, Walt LEAVES OF GRASS NY 1942. 2 vols. Signed by Edward Weston, the photographer. Introduction by Mark Van Doren $1,000.

142: Thackeray, William Makepeace THE ROSE AND THE RING NY 1942. Illustrated by Fritz Kredel. Dedicatory introduction by George Macy $75.

143: Flaubert, Gustave THE TEMPTATION OF SAINT ANTHONY NY 1943. Signed by Warren Chappell, the illustrator. Translated by Lafcadio Hearn $125.

144: Erasmus, Desiderius THE PRAISE OF FOLLY (MORIAE ENCOMIUM) Harrisburg 1943. Signed by Lynd Ward, the illustrator. Translated by Harry Carter, introduction by Hendrik Willem van Loom $125.

145: Fielding, Henry THE HISTORY OF THE LIFE OF THE LATE MR. JONATHAN WILD THE GREAT NY 1943. Signed by T.M. Cleland, the illustrator. Introduction by Louis Kronenberger $125.

146: Hoffman, Ernest THE TALES OF HOFFMANN NY 1943. Signed by Hugo

Steiner-Prag, the illustrator. Introductory essay by Arthur Ransom $100.

147: Puskin, Alexander EUGENE ONEGIN NY 1943. Signed by Fritz Eichenberg, the illustrator. Translation by Babette Deutsch, introduction by Avrahm Yarmolinsky $100.

148: Melville, Herman MOBY DICK, or THE WHALE Brattleboro 1943. 2 vols. Signed by Boardman Robinson, the illustrator. Introduction by Clifton Fadiman $250.

149: Parkman, Francis THE OREGON TRAIL Brattleboro 1943. Signed by Maynard Dixon, the illustrator. Introduction by Mason Wade $150.

150: Cable, George Washington OLD CREOLE DAYS Together with "The Scenes of Cable's Romances" by Lafcadio Hearn NY 1943. Signed by John O'Hara Cosgrave, the illustrator $100.

151: Bierce, Ambrose TALES OF SOLDIERS AND CIVILIANS NY 1943. Signed by Paul Landacre, the illustrator. Introduction by Joseph Henry Jackson $125.

152: Hudson, W.H. FAR AWAY AND LONG AGO Buenos Aires 1943. Signed by Raul Rosarivo, the illustrator and Alberto Kraft, the designer $175.

153: Poe, Edgar Allan THE POEMS OF EDGAR ALLAN POE NY 1943. 1,100 cc. Signed by Hugo Steiner-Prag, the illustrator. Commentary by Louis Untermeyer $200.

154: Gautier, Theophile MADEMOISELLE DE MAUPIN NY 1943. Signed by Andre Dugo, the illustrator. Introduction by Jacques Barzun $75.

155: Crane, Stephen THE RED BADGE OF COURAGE NY 1944. 1,000 cc. Signed by John Steuart Curry, the illustrator. Introduction by Carl Van Doren $200.

156: Stevenson, Robert Louis A CHILD'S GARDEN OF VERSES NY 1944. 1,100 cc. Signed by Roger Duvoisin, the illustrator. Introduction by William Rose Benet $150.

157: Bacon, Sir Francis THE ESSAYS OF FRANCIS BACON NY 1944. 1,100 cc. Signed by Bruce Rogers, the designer. Introduction by Christopher Morley, bibliographical note by A.S.W. Rosenbach $175.

158: Twain, Mark LIFE ON THE MISSISSIPPI NY 1944. 1,200 cc. Signed by Thomas Hart Benton, the illustrator. Introduction by Edward Wagenknecht. Adds a number of previously suppressed passages printed for the first time $450.

159: Willkie, Wendell L. ONE WORLD NY 1944. 1,500 cc. Signed by Willkie. Illustrated with photographs $75.

160: Harte, Bret TALES OF THE GOLD RUSH NY 1944. 1,200 cc. Signed by Fletcher Martin, the illustrator. Introduction by Oscar Lewis $100.

161: Plato THE REPUBLIC NY 1944. 2 vols. 1,200 sets (ref.b states 1,500 sets). Signed by Fritz Kredel, the illustrator and Bruce Rogers, the designer. Translation, introduction, etc. by Benjamin Jowett $125.

162: Longfellow, Henry Wadsworth THE POEMS OF HENRY WADSWORTH LONGFELLOW Brattleboro 1944. 1,100 cc.

Signed by Boyd Hanna, the illustrator. Commentary by Louis Untermeyer $100.

163: Virgil THE AENEID Brattleboro 1944. 1,100 cc. Signed by Carlotta Petrina, the illustrator. Translated and introduction by John Dryden $100.

164: Gogol, Nikolai CHICHIKOV'S JOURNEYS (DEAD SOULS) Brattleboro 1944. 2 vols. 1,200 sets. Signed by Lucille Corcos, the illustrator. Translated by Bernard Guilbert Guerney, introduction by Avrahm Yarmolinsky $125.

165: Hughes, Richard THE INNOCENT VOYAGE (A HIGH WIND IN JAMAICA) Brattleboro 1944. Signed by Lynd Ward, the illustrator. Introduction by Louis Untermeyer $100.

166: Beckford, William VATHEK, AN ARABIAN TALE NY 1945. Signed by Valenti Angelo, the designer. Translated and introduction by Herbert Grimsditch $75.

167: Untermeyer, Louis THE WONDERFUL ADVENTURES OF PAUL BUNYAN NY 1945. Retold and with a foreword by Untermeyer. Signed by Everett Gee Jackson, the illustrator $75.

168: Emerson, Ralph Waldo THE POEMS OF RALPH WALDO EMERSON NY 1945. Signed by Richard and Doris Beer, the illustrators. Commentary by Louis Untermeyer $125.

169: Hamilton, Alexander and James Madison and John Jay THE FEDERALIST NY 1945. 2 vols. Signed by Bruce Rogers, the designer. Introduction by Carl Van Doren $150.

170: Coleridge, Samuel Taylor THE RIME OF THE ANCIENT MARINER New Haven 1945. Signed by Edward A. Wilson, the illustrator. Introduction by John Livingston Lowes $90.

171: Whittier, John Greenleaf THE POEMS OF JOHN GREENLEAF WHITTIER NY 1945. Signed by Raymond J. Holden, the illustrator. Commentary by Louis Untermeyer $75.

172: Addison, Joseph with Richard Steele and Eustace Budgell THE SIR ROGER DE COVERLEY PAPERS NY 1945. Signed by Gordon Ross, the illustrator. Prefatory notes by William Makepeace Thackeray $75.

173: THE BOOK OF JOB NY 1946. 1,950 cc. Signed by Arthur Szyk, the illustrator. Introduction by Mary Ellen Chase $350.

174: Gibbon, Edward THE HISTORY OF THE DECLINE AND FALL OF THE ROMAN EMPIRE Brattleboro 1946. 7 vols $150.

175: Chaucer, Geoffrey THE CANTERBURY TALES London 1946. Signed by Arthur Szyk, the illustrator. Put into modern English verse by Frank Ernest Hill $300.

176: Montaigne, Michel de THE ESSAYS OF MICHEL DE MONTAIGNE NY 1946. 4 vols. Signed by T.M. Cleland, the designer. Introduction by Andre Gide and a Handbook to the Essays by Grace Norton $75.

177: Bryant, William Cullen THE POEMS OF WILLIAM CULLEN BRYANT NY 1947. Signed by Thomas W. Nason, the illustrator. Comentary by Louis Untermeyer $75.

178: Nordoff, Charles and James Norman Hall MUTINY ON THE BOUNTY NY 1947. Signed by Fletcher Martin, the illustrator. With a preface by the authors and an appendix containing the true story of Peter Heywood $200.

179: Morier, J.J. THE ADVENTURES OF HAJJI BABA OF ISPAHAN NY 1947. 2 vols. Signed by Honore Guilbeau, the illustrator. Introduction by E.G. Browne $100.

180: Stendhal (Marie-Henri Beyle) THE RED AND THE BLACK NY 1947. Signed by Rafaello Busoni, the illustrator. Translated by C.K. Scott-Moncrieff, introduction by Hamilton Basso $75.

181: France, Anatole PENGUIN ISLAND NY 1947. Signed by Malcolm Cameron, the illustrator. Translated by A.W. Evans, introduction by Carl Van Doren $60.

182: Kingsley, Charles WESTWARD HO! NY 1947. 2 vols. Signed by Edward A. Wilson, the illustrator. Introduction by John T. Winterich $100.

183: Epicurus THE EXTANT WORKS OF EPICURUS NY 1947. Signed by Bruce Rogers, the designer. Translation by Cyril Bailey, introduction by Irwin Edman $175.

184: THE BOOK OF RUTH NY 1947. 1,950 cc (ref.b). Signed by Arthur Szyk, the illustrator. Preface by Mary Ellen Chase $300.

185: Dana, Richard Henry TWO YEARS BEFORE THE MAST NY 1947. Signed by Hans Alexander Mueller, the illustrator. Introduction by William McFee $125.

186: Browning, Elizabeth Barrett SONNETS FROM THE PORTUGUESE NY 1948. Signed by Valenti Angelo, the illustrator. Introduction by Louis Untermeyer $125.

187: Walton, Izaak and Charles Cotton THE COMPLEAT ANGLER NY 1948. Signed by Douglas Gorsline, the illustrator. Introduction by James Russell Lowell $200.

188: Zola, Emile NANA NY 1948. Signed by Bernard Lamotte, the illustrator. Translated by E. A. Vizetelly, preface by Henry James (from the first English edition) and a new introduction by Lewis Galantiere $100.

189: Dostoevsky, Fyodor CRIME AND PUNISHMENT Brattleboro 1948. 2 vols. Signed by Fritz Eichenberg, the illustrator. Translated by Constance Garnett, introduction by Laurence Irving $125.

190: Balzac, Honore de OLD GORIOT London 1948. Signed by Rene ben Sussan, the illustrator. Translated by Ellen Marriage, introduction by Francois Mauriac $60.

191: Chuan, Shui Hu ALL MEN ARE BROTHERS NY 1948. 2 vols. Signed by Miguel Covarrubias, the illustrator. English version by Pearl Buck, introduction by Lin Yutang $200.

192: Benet, Stephen Vincent JOHN BROWN'S BODY London 1948. Introduction by Douglas Southall Freeman, illustrated by John Steuart Curry $75.

193: *The Evergreen Tales* NY 1948. 3 vols. (Series I) 2,500 cc.

ALADDIN AND THE WONDERFUL LAMP Retold by Jean Hersholt. Illustrated by Fritz Kredel

Southey, Robert THE THREE BEARS Edited by Jean Hersholt, illustrated by William Moyers

THE STORY OF JOSEPH AND HIS BROTHERS Edited by Jean Hersholt, illustrated by Arthur Szyk

The three: $200.

(Also see 202, 203, 222, 228)

194: Browning, Robert THE RING AND THE BOOK L.A. 1949. 2 vols. Signed by Carl Schultheiss, the illustrator. Introduction by Edward Dowden $75.

195: Anderson, Hans Christian THE COMPLETE ANDERSEN NY (1949). 6 vols. 168 stories. Signed by Fritz Kredel and Jean Hersholt, the translator $250.

196: Clemens, Samuel Langhorne (Mark Twain) A CONNECTICUT YANKEE IN KING ARTHUR'S COURT NY 1949. Signed by Honore Guilbeau, the illustrator. Introduction by Carl Van Doren $100.

197: Dostoevsky, Fyodor THE BROTHERS KARAMAZOV Brattleboro 1949. 2 vols. Signed by Fritz Eichenberg, the illustrator. Translation by Constance Garnett revised and introduced by Avrahm Yarmolinsky $125.

198: THE SEVEN VOYAGES OF SINDBAD THE SAILOR NY 1949. Signed by Edward A. Wilson, the illustrator. Introduction by C.S. Forester $150.

199: James, Henry THE TURN OF THE SCREW L.A. 1949. Introduction by Carl Van Doren, Illustrated by Mariette Lydis $100.

200: France, Anatole CRAINQUEBILLE NY 1949. Signed by Bernard Lamotte, the illustrator. Translation and introduction by Jacques Le Clercq $60.

201: Brillat-Savarin, Jean Anthelme THE PHYSIOLOGY OF TASTE NY 1949. Translated by M.F.K. Fisher, illustrations by Sylvain Sauvage $175.

202: *The Evergreen Tales* NY 1949. 3 vols. (Series II) 2,500 cc.

SAINT GEORGE AND THE DRAGON Retold by William H.G. Kingston, illustrated by Edward Shenton

Beaumont, Mme. Le Prince de BEAUTY AND THE BEAST Translated by P.H. Muir, illustrated by Edy Legrand

DICK WHITTINGTON AND HIS CAT Retold and illustrated by Robert Lawson

The three: $150.

(Also see 193, 203, 222, 228)

203: *The Evergreen Tales* NY 1949. 3 vols. (Series III) 2,500 cc.

THE TALE OF ALI BABA AND THE FORTY THIEVES Translated into English by E.Powys Mathers, illustated by Edward Ardizzone

Perrault, Charles THE SLEEPING BEAUTY IN THE WOOD Translated by P.H. Muir, illustrated by Sylvain Sauvage

Andersen, Hans Christian THE UGLY DUCKLING Translated by Jean Hersholt, illustrated by Everett Gee Jackson

The three: $150.

(Also see 193, 202, 222, 228)

204: Swift, Jonathan A VOYAGE TO LILLIPUT BY DR. LEMUEL GULLIVER NY 1950. A minature book 2 1/4 x 3 1/2 inches. In compartmented slipcase with A VOYAGE TO BROBDINGNAG MADE BY LEMUEL GULLIVER (13 1/4 x 18 1/2 inches). Designed by Bruce Rogers $250.

205: Pushkin, Alexander THE GOLDEN COCKEREL NY (1949). Signed by Edmund Dulac, the illustrator $225.

206: Flaubert, Gustave MADAME BOVARY NY 1950. Signed by Pierre Brissaud, the illustrator. Introduction by Jacques de Lacretelle $75.

207: Doyle, Arthur Conan THE ADVENTURES OF SHERLOCK HOLMES Mount Vernon 1950. 3 vols. Illustrated by Frederic Dorr Steele, Sidney Paget, and others. Introduction by Vincent Starrett $300.

208: Frost, Robert THE COMPLETE POEMS OF ROBERT FROST NY 1950. 2 vols. Signed by Frost and Thomas W. Nason, the illustrator. Designed by Bruce Rogers $600.

209: Cervantes Saavedra, Miguel de DON QUIXOTE, THE INGENIOUS GENTLEMAN OF LA MANCHA Mexico City 1950. 2 vols. Translated by John Ormsby, introduction by Irwin Edman, illustrated by Edy Legrand $200.

210: Apuleius, Lucius THE MARRIAGE OF CUPID AND PSYCHE NY 1951. Signed by Edmund Dulac, the illustrator. Retold by Walter Pater $250.

211: Scott, (Sir) Walter IVANHOE NY 1951. 2 vols. Signed by Edward A. Wilson, the illustrator $75.

212: Turgenev, Ivan FATHERS AND SONS NY 1951. Signed by Fritz Eichenberg, the illustrator. Translated by Constance Garnett, preface by John T. Winterich $75.

213: Tolstoy, Leo ANNA KARENINA London 1951. 2 vols. Signed by Barnett Freedman, the illustrator. Introduction by Lionel Trilling $125.

214: Shakespeare, William THE LIFE OF KING HENRY V NY 1951. Illustrated by Fritz Kredel. Introduction by Herbert Arthur Evans and prefatory note by Mark Van Doren $100.

215: Wister Owen THE VIRGINIAN L.A. 1951. Signed by William Moyers, the illustrator. Introduction by Struthers Burt $100.

216: Schiller, Johann Christoph Friedrich von WILLIAM TELL Zurich 1951. Signed by Charles Hug, the illustrator. Introductory essay by Thomas Carlyle $75.

217: Manzoni, Alessandro THE BETROTHED (I PROMESSI SPOSI) Verona 1951. Signed by Bruno Bramanti, the illustrator and Giovanni Mardersteig, the printer. Introduction by Ronald H. Boothroyd $150.

218: Stevenson, Robert Louis STRANGE CASE OF DR. JEKYLL AND MR. HYDE NY 1952. Signed by Edward A. Wilson, the illustrator. Introduction by John Mason Brown $125.

219: Dumas, Alexandre THE BLACK TULIP Haarlem 1951. Signed by Jan van Krimpen, the designer and Franz Lammers the illustrator. Introduction by Ben Ray Redman $125.

220: Fielding, Henry THE HISTORY OF TOM JONES, A FOUNDLING NY 1952. 2 vols. Signed by T.M. Cleland, the illustrator. Introduction by Louis Kronenberger $125.

221: Raspe, Rudolph and others THE SINGULAR ADVENTURES OF BARON MUNCHAUSEN NY 1952. Signed by Fritz Kredel, the illustrator. Introduction by John Carswell $75.

222: *The Evergreen Tales* NY 1952. 3 vols. (Series IV) 2,500 cc.

Anderson, Hans Christian THE EMPEROR'S NEW CLOTHES Translated by Jean Hersholt, illustrated by Ervine Metzl

Hawthorne, Nathaniel PANDORA'S BOX Illustrated by Rafaello Busoni

Hawthorne, Nathaniel KING MIDAS AND THE GOLDEN TOUCH Illustrated by Fritz Eichenberg

The three: $150.

(Also see 193, 202, 203, 228)

223: Doyle, Arthur Conan THE LATER ADVENTURES OF SHERLOCK HOLMES Mt. Vernon 1952. 3 vols. Illustrated by Frederic Dorr Steele, Sidney Paget and others.

Introductions by Elmer Davis, Fletcher Pratt and Rex Stout $250.

(Also see 207 and 224, the companion volumes)

224: Doyle, Arthur Conan THE FINAL ADVENTURES OF SHERLOCK HOLMES Mt. Vernon 1953. 2 vols. Illustrated by Frederic Dorr Steele, Sidney Paget and others. Introductions by Christopher Morley and Anthony Boucher $200.

The set (207, 223 and 224): $750.

225: BEOWUF NY 1952. Translated, with introduction, by William Ellery Leonard. Illustrated by Lynd Ward. Not signed $75.

226: Maupassant, Guy de A WOMAN'S LIFE (UNE VIE) NY 1952. Signed by Edy Legrand, the illustrator. Translated by Marjorie Laurie. Introduction by Edmond Jaloux $50.

227: Dickenson, Emily POEMS OF EMILY DICKINSON NY 1952. Signed by Helen Sewell, the illustrator. Commentary by Louis Untermeyer $100.

228: *The Evergreen Series* NY 1952. 3 vols. (Series V) 2,500 cc.

Perrault, Charles BLUEBEARD Translated by Arthur Quiller-Couch, illustrated by Hans Bendix

Grimm, Jacob and Wilhelm HANSEL AND GRETEL Translated by P.H. Muir, illustrated by Henry C. Pitz

JACK AND THE BEANSTALK Retold by Jean Hersholt, illustrated by Malcolm Cameron

The three: $150.
The set (193, 202, 203, 222, 228): $850.

229: Virgil (Publius Virgilius Maro) THE GEORGICS Verona 1952. Signed by Bruno Bramanti, the illustrator and Giovanni Mardersteig, the printer. Translated by John Dryden, introduction by George F. Whicher $150.

230: Tennyson, Alfred Lord IDYLLS OF THE KING New Haven 1953. Introduction by Henry Van Dyke, illustrated by Lynd Ward $75.

231: Doughty, Charles M. TRAVELS IN ARABIA DESERTA NY 1953. Introduction by T.E. Lawrence, illustrated by Edy Legrand. Not signed. Text abridged and arranged by Edward Garnett $150.

232: Tegner, Esaias FRITHIOF'S SAGA Stockholm 1953. Signed by Eric Palmquist, the illustrator. General introduction by Bayard Taylor $60.

233: Voltaire (Francois Marie Arouet) THE HISTORY OF ZADIG, OR DESTINY Paris 1952. Translated by R. Bruce Boswell. Introduction by Rene de Messieres, translated by Jacques Le Clercq. Illustrated by Sylvain Sauvage $125.

234: Spenser, Edmund THE FAERIE QUEENE Oxford 1953. 2 vols. Signed by Agnes Miller Parker, the illustrator. Introduction by John Hayward $175.

235: Eliot, George SILAS MARNER, THE WEAVER OF RAVELOE London 1953. Signed by Lynton Lamb, the illustrator. Introduction by John T. Winterich $75.

236: Jonson, Ben VOLPONE, or THE FOX Oxford 1952. Signed by Rene ben Sussan, the illustrator. Introduction by Louis Kronenberger $125.

237: Dumas, Alexandre THE THREE MUSKETEERS NY 1953. Illustrated by Edy Legrand $60.

238: Sheridan, Richard Brinsley THE RIVALS London 1953. Signed by Rene ben Sussan, the illustrator. Introduction by John Mason Brown $75.

239: France, Anatole THE REVOLT OF THE ANGELS NY 1953. Translated by Mrs. Wilfrid Jackson, introduction by Desmond MacCarthy, illustrated by Pierre Watrin $60.

240: Rostand, Edmond CYRANO DE BERGERAC NY 1954. Signed by Pierre Brissaud, the illustrator. Introduction by Louis Untermeyer $75.

241: Machiavelli, Niccolo THE PRINCE NY 1954. Translated by Hill Thompson, preface by Irwin Edman, designed by George Macy $100.

242: Goethe, Johann Wolfgang von THE STORY OF REYNARD THE FOX NY 1954. Signed by Fritz Eichenberg, the illustrator. Introduction by Edward Lazare. Translated by Thomas James Arnold $75.

243: Defoe, Daniel THE FORTUNES AND MISFORTUNES OF THE FAMOUS MOLL FLANDERS Mt. Vernon 1954. Signed by Reginald Marsh, the illustrator. Introduction by John T. Winterich $100.

244: Proust, Marcel SWANN'S WAY NY 1954. Signed by Bernard Lamotte, the illustrator.

Translated by C.K. Scott-Moncrieff, introduction by Justin O'Brien $125.

245: Grammaticus, Saxo THE HISTORY OF AMLETH, PRINCE OF DENMARK Copenhagen 1954. Signed by Sigurd Vasegaard, the illustrator. Translated by Oliver Elton, introduction by Israel Gollancz, prefatory note by Henrik de Kauffmann $75.

246: Milton, John L'ALLEGRO and IL PENSEROSO NY 1954. Introductory essays by W.P. Trent and Chauncey B. Tinerk. Illustrations by William Blake $150.

247: Dreiser, Theodore AN AMERICAN TRAGEDY NY 1954. Introduction by Harry Hansen, illustrated by Reginald Marsh but not signed (his final work, issued posthumously) $125.

248: Riggs, Lynn GREEN GROW THE LILACS Univ. of Oklahoma Press (Norman, OK) 1954. Signed by Thomas Hart Benton, the illustrator. Introduction by Brooks Atkinson $400.

249: Caesar, Julius THE GALLIC WARS Verona 1954. Signed by Bruno Bramanti, the illustrator and Giovanni Mardersteig, the printer. Introduction by John Warrington, preface by John Mason Brown $200.

250: Milton, John THE MASQUE OF COMUS Cambridge 1954. Poem by John Milton, songs by Henry Lawes. Prefatory by Mark Van Doren and Hubert Foss. Illustrated by Edmund Dulac $175.

251: Popol Vuh THE BOOK OF THE PEOPLE Los Angeles 1954. Signed by Everett Gee Jackson, the illustrator. Translated from the ancient Maya, with an introduction, by Delia Goetz and Sylvanus Morley $75.

252: Thackeray, William Makepeace THE NEWCOMBES Cambridge 1954. 2 vols. Signed by Edward Ardizzone, the illustrator. Introduction by Angela Thirkell $125.

253: Rousseau, Jean-Jacques THE CONFESSIONS OF JEAN-JACQUES ROUSEEAU Mt. Vernon 1955. Signed by William Sharp, the illustrator. Introduction by A.S.B. Glover $75.

254: THE ARABIAN NIGHTS ENTERTAINMENTS Ipswich 1954. 4 vols. Illustrated by Arthur Szyk. Translation and explanatory notes by Richard Burton. Unsigned as Szyk died before this work, his last, was printed $250.

255: Hugo, Victor NOTRE-DAME DE PARIS NY 1955. Signed by Bernard Lamotte, the illustrator. Translated by Jessie Haynes, introduction by Justin O'Brien $75.

256: Sophocles OEDIPUS REX Haarlem 1955. Signed by Demetrios Galanis, the illustrator. Translated by Francis Storr $100.

257: Holmes, Oliver Wendell THE AUTOCRAT OF THE BREAKFAST TABLE New Haven 1955. Signed by Raymond J. Holden, the illustrator. Introduction by Van Wyck Brooks $75.

258: Dumas, Alexandre CAMILLE (LA DAME AUX CAMELIAS) Baltimore 1955. Signed by Bernard Lamotte, the illustrator. Translated by Edmund Gosse, introduction by Andre Maurois $100.

259: Ibsen, Henrik PEER GYNT Oslo 1955. Signed by Per Krohg, the illustrator. Translated by William and Charles Archer, introduction by William Archer $60.

260: Meredith, George SHAVING OF SHAGPAT NY 1955. Signed by Honore Guilbeau, the illustrator. Introduction by Sir Francis Meredith Meynell $75.

261: Stendhal THE CHARTERHOUSE OF PARMA NY 1955. Signed by Rafaello Busoni, the illustrator. Introductory essay by Honore de Balzac $60.

262: Hardy, Thomas TESS OF THE D'URBERVILLES NY 1956. Signed by Agnes Miller Parker, the illustrator. Introduction by Robert Cantwell $150.

263: Trollope, Anthony THE WARDEN NY (1955). Signed by Fritz Kredel, the illustrator. Introduction by Angela Thirkell $90.

264: Dostoevsky, Fyodor THE IDIOT NY 1956. Signed by Fritz Eichenberg, the illustrator. Introduction by Avrahm Yarmolinski $125.

265: Carlyle, Thomas THE FRENCH REVOLUTION NY 1956. Signed by Bernard Lamotte, the illustrator. Introduction by Cecil Brown $75.

266: Darwin, Charles THE VOYAGE OF H.M.S. BEAGLE Cambridge 1956. Signed by Robert Gibbings, the illustrator. Introduction by Sir Gavin de Beer $250.

267: Thackeray, William Makepeace THE HISTORY OF HENRY ESMOND, ESQ. Cambridge 1956. Signed by Edward Ardizzone, the illustrator. Introduction by Laura Benet $90.

268: Verne, Jules TWENTY THOUSAND LEAGUES UNDER THE SEA Los Angeles 1956. Signed by Edward A. Wilson, the illustrator. Introduction by Fletcher Pratt $75.

269: Aurelius, Marcus MEDITIATIONS OF MARCUS AURELIUS Mt. Vernon 1956. Signed by Hans Alexander Mueller, the illustrator. Translated by Meric Casaubon $60.

270: Bulwer-Lytton, Edward THE LAST DAYS OF POMPEII Verona 1956. Signed by Kurt Craemer, the illustrator and Mardersteig, the printer. Introduction by Edgar Johnson $75.

271: Stevenson, Robert Louis THE BEACH OF FALESA Los Angeles 1956. Signed by Millard Sheets, the illustrator. Introduction by J.C. Furnas $75.

272: Austen, Jane SENSE AND SENSIBILITY New Haven 1957. Signed by Helen Sewell, the illustrator. Introduction by Stella Gibbons $75.

273: Heine, Heinrich POEMS OF HEINRICH HEINE NY 1957. Signed by Fritz Kredel, the illustrator. Introduction by Louis Untermeyer $75.

274: Dickens, Charles DOMBEY AND SON Mt. Vernon 1957. 2 vols. Signed by Henry C. Pitz, the illustrator. Introduction by John T. Winterich $75.

275: Prescott, Willian Hickling HISTORY OF THE CONQUEST OF PERU Mexico City 1957. Signed by Everett Gee Jackson, the illustrator and Harry Block, the printer. Introduction by Samuel Eliot Morison $150.

276: Adams, Henry MONT-SAINT-MICHEL AND CHARTRES Mt. Vernon 1957. Signed by Samuel Chamberlain, the photographer. Introduction by Francis Henry Taylor $125.

277: Stevenson, Robert Louis TRAVELS WITH A DONKEY IN THE CEVENNES Los Angeles 1957. Signed by Roger Duvoisin, the illustrator. Introduction by Andre Chamson $75.

278: Carus, Titus Lucretius OF THE NATURE OF THINGS NY 1957. Signed by Paul Landacre, the illustrator. Translated by William Ellery Leonard, introduction by Charles E. Bennett $75.

279: Cook, Capt. James THE EXPLORATIONS OF CAPTAIN JAMES COOK IN THE PACIFIC Adelaide, Australia 1957. Signed by Geoffrey C. Ingleton, the illustrator and Douglas Dunstan, the designer. Taken from Cook's journals 1768-1779 $200.

280: Hersey, John THE WALL NY 1957. Signed by William Sharp, the illustrator. Introduction by George N. Shuster $75.

281: Wilde, Oscar THE PICTURE OF DORIAN GRAY NY 1957. Signed by Lucille Corcos, the illustrator. Introduction by Andre Maurois $125.

282: Harris, Joel Chandler UNCLE REMUS: HIS SONGS AND SAYINGS NY 1957. 1,000 cc. Introduction by Marc Connelly, illustrated by Seong Moy $125.

283: Dumas, Alexandre TWENTY YEARS AFTER NY 1958. Signed by Edy Legrand, the illustrator. Introduction by Ben Ray Redman $60.

284: THE KORAN: SELECTED SURAS NY 1958. Signed by Valenti Angelo, the illustrator. Translated and introduction by Arthur Jeffrey $100.

285: Rhodius, Apollonius THE ARGONAUTICA Athens 1957. Signed by A. Tassos, the illustrator. The text first in Greek and then the translation "Jason and The Golden Fleece" by Edward P. Coleridge with introduction by Moses Hadas $125.

286: Bulfinch, Thomas THE AGE OF FABLE NY 1958 Signed by Joe Mugnaini, the illustrator. Introduction by Dudley Fitts $60.

287: Hardy, Thomas FAR FROM THE MADDING CROWD Cambridge 1958. Signed by Agnes Miller Parker, the illustrator. Introduction by Robert Cantwell $125.

288: Alain-Fournier THE WANDERER NY 1958. Signed by Andre Dignimont, the illustrator. Translated by Francois Delisle, introduction by Henri Peyre $60.

289: CHRONICLE OF THE CID New Haven 1958. Signed by Rene ben Sussan, the illustrator. Translated by Robert Southey, introduction by V.S. Pritchett $75.

290: Ovid METAMORPHOSES Verona 1958. Signed by Hans Erni, the illustrator and Hans Mardersteig, the printer. Introduction by Gilbert Highet $250.

291: Gilbert and Sullivan THE FIRST-NIGHT GILBERT AND SULLIVAN NY 1958. Edited and introduced by Reginal Allen, foreword by Bridget D'Oyly Carte. Illustrated with contemporary drawings $150.

292: Trollope, Anthony BARCHESTER TOWERS Mt. Vernon 1958. 2 vols. Signed by Fritz Kredel, the illustrator. Introduction by Angela Thirkell $100.

293: THE HISTORIES OF HERODOTUS OF HALICARNASSUS NY 1958. Signed by Edward Bawden, the illustrator. Introduction by Harry Carter $200.

294: QUARTO-MILLENARY: THE FIRST 250 PUBLICATIONS AND THE FIRST 25 YEARS (1929 - 1954) OF THE LIMITED EDITIONS CLUB NY 1959. 2,250 cc. Contains critiques by John T. Winterich and others $300.

295: Verne, Jules THE MYSTERIOUS ISLAND Baltimore 1959. Signed by Edward A. Wilson, the illustrator. Translated by W.H.G. Kingston, introduction by Ray Bradbury $125.

296: Goethe, Johann Wolfgang von WILHELM MEISTER'S APPRENTICESHIP NY 1959. Signed by William Sharp, the illustrator. Translated by Thomas Carlyle, introduction by Franz Schoenberner $100.

297: Saint-Simon, Due de MEMOIRS OF THE DUC DE SAINT-SIMON NY 1959. 2 Vols. Signed by Pierre Brissaud, the illustrator. Introduction, etc. by Desmond Flower $75.

298: Jackson, Helen Hunt RAMONA L.A. 1959. Signed by Everett Gee Jackson, the illustrator. Introduction by J. Frank Dobie $60.

299: Aristophanes THE BIRDS NY 1959. Signed by Marian Parry, the illustrator. Introduction by Dudley Fitts $90.

300: Conrad, Joseph LORD JIM New Haven 1959. Signed by Lynd Ward, the illustrator. Introduction by Nicholas Monsarrat $125.

301: Congreve, William THE WAY OF THE WORLD Mt. Vernon 1959. Signed by T.M. Cleland, the illustrator. Introduction by Louis Kronenberger $60.

302: Sienkiewicz, Henryk QUO VADIS? Verona 1959. Signed by Salvatore Fiume, the illustrator and Giovanni Mardersteig, the printer. Issued in dustwrapper printed on spine only $150.

303: Collins, Wilkie THE MOONSTONE NY 1959. Signed by Andre Dignimont, the illustrator. Introduction by Vincent Starrett $75.

304: Dostoevsky, Fyodor THE POSSESSED Hartford 1959. 2 vols. Signed by Fritz Eichenberg, the illustrator. Translated by Constance Garnett, introduction by Marc Slonim $100.

305: Alarcon, Pedron Antonio de THE THREE-CORNERED HAT L.A. 1959. Signed by Roger Duvoisin, the illustrator. Translated by Martin Armstrong, introduction by Gerald Brenan $60.

306: Froissard, Jean THE CHRONICLES OF ENGLAND NY 1959. Signed by Henry C. Pitz, the illustrator. Translated by Lord Berners, introduction by Sidney Painter $90.

307: Wells, H.G. TONO-BUNGAY NY 1960. Signed by Lynton Lamb, the illustrator. Introduction by Norman Strouse $90.

308: London, Jack THE CALL OF THE WILD L.A. 1960. Signed by Henry Varnum Poor, the illustrator. Introduction by Pierre Berton $150.

309: Flaubert, Gustave SALAMMBO Cambridge 1960. Signed by Edward Bawden, the illustrator. Translated by J.S. Matthews, introduction by Justin O'Brien $125.

310: THE ECLOGUES OF VIRGIL NY 1960. Signed by Marcel Vertes, the illustrator. Translated by C.S. Calverley, introduction by Moses Hadas $125.

311: THE NIBELUNGENLIED NY 1960. Signed by Edy Legrand, the illustrator. Translated by Margaret Armour, introduction by Franz Schoenberner $125.

312: Wallace, Lew BEN-HUR Hartford 1960. Signed by Joe Mugnaini, the illustrator. Introduction by Ben Ray Redman $75.

313: Beerbohm, Max ZULEIKA DOBSON Baltimore 1960. Signed by George Him, the illustrator. Introduction by Douglas Cleverdon $75.

314: Hugo, Victor THE TOILERS OF THE SEA Verona 1960. Signed by Tranquillo Marangoni, the illustrator and Giovanni Mardersteig, the printer. Introduction by Matthew Josephson $150.

315: THE LIVING TALMUD: THE WISDOM OF THE FATHERS NY 1960. Signed by Ben-Zion, the illustrator. Introduction by Judah Goldin $200.

316: THE ROMANCE OF TRISTAN AND ISEULT NY 1960. Signed by Serge Ivanoff, the illustrator. Retold by Joseph Bedier, introduction

Padraic Colum, translated by Hilaire Belloc and Paul Rosenfield $100.

317: Balzac, Honore de EUGENIE GRANDET London 1960. Signed by Rene ben Sussan, the illustrator. Translated by Ellen Marriage, introduction by Richard Aldington $75.

318: THE BOOK OF PSALMS NY 1960. Signed by Valenti Angelo, the illustrator. Introduction by Mark Van Doren $175.

319: Cooper, James Fenimore THE DEERSLAYER (Hartford) 1961. Signed by Edward A. Wilson, the illustrator. Introduction by John T. Winterich $75.

320: Melville, Herman OMOO Oxford 1961. Signed by Reynolds Stone, the illustrator. Introduction by Van Wyck Brooks $125.

321: Paine, Thomas RIGHTS OF MAN Lunenburg, VT 1961. Signed by Lynd Ward, the illustrator. Introduction by Howard Fast $150.

322: Schreiner, Olive THE STORY OF AN AFRICAN FARM (NY) 1961. Signed by Paul Hogarth, the illustrator. Introduction by Isak Dinesen $100.

323: Conrad, Joseph NOSTROMO S.F. 1961. Signed by Lima de Freitas, the illustrator. Introduction by Rupert Croft-Cooke $100.

324: Howells, William Dean THE RISE OF SILAS LAPHAM Phila. 1961. Signed by Mimi Korach, the illustrator. Introduction by Henry Steele Commager $75.

325: ODES AND EPODES OF HORACE NY 1961. 2 vols. Translated and introduction by Louis Untermeyer. Second volume contains facsimile pages with bibliographic preface by John T. Winterich $100.

326: London, Jack THE SEA WOLF Hartford 1961. Signed by Fletcher Martin, the illustrator. Introduction by Edmund Gilligan $100.

327: Thackeray, William Makepeace THE HISTORY OF PENDENNIS Ipswich 1961. 2 vols. Signed by Charles Steward, the illustrator. Introduction by Robert Cantwell $75.

328: Aeschylus THE ORESTEIA NY 1961. Signed by Michael Ayrton, the illustrator. Translated by E.D.A. Morstead, introduction by Rex Warner $100.

329: Tarkington, Booth MONSIEUR BEAUCAIRE NY 1961. Signed by T.M. Cleland, the illustrator. Introduction by Donald Adams $75.

330: Scott, Sir Walter WAVERLEY (NY) 1961. Signed by Robert Ball, the illustrator. Introduction by Andrew Lang $75.

331: Wilder, Thornton THE BRIDGE OF SAN LUIS REY NY 1962. Signed by Jean Charlot, the illustrator. Introduction by Granville Hicks $125.

332: Twain, Mark THE INNOCENTS ABROAD NY 1962. Signed by Fritz Kredel, the illustrator. Introduction by Edward Wagenknecht $125.

333: Mann, Thomas THE MAGIC MOUNTAIN NY 1962. 2 vols. Signed by Felix Hoffman, the illustrator. Translated by H.T. Lowe-Porter $150.

334: Shaw, George Bernard MAN AND SUPERMAN Mt. Vernon 1962. Signed by Charles Mozley, the illustrator. Introduction by Sir Lewis Casson. Also includes *The Revolutionist's Handbook...* by John Tanner (Member of The Idle Rich Class) $125.

335: THE CONFESSIONS OF ST. AUGUSTINE Ipswich 1962. Signed by Edy Legrand, the illustrator. Introduction by George N. Shuster $125.

336: Lewis and Clark THE JOURNALS OF THE EXPEDITION OF CAPTAINS MERIWETHER LEWIS AND WILLIAM CLARK Hartford 1962. 2 vols. Introduction by John Bakeless. Edited by J.G. Pilkington $250.

337: Kipling, Rudyard KIM NY 1962. Signed by Robin Jacques, the illustrator. Introduction by Charles Edmund Carrington $75.

338: Plato THE TRIAL AND DEATH OF SOCRATES Verona 1962. Signed by Hans Erni, the illustrator and Giovanni Mardersteig, the printer. Translated, introduction, etc. by Benjamin Jowett $225.

339: Verne, Jules AROUND THE WORLD IN EIGHTY DAYS L.A. 1962. Signed by Edward A. Wilson, the illustrator. Introduction by Ray Bradbury $100.

340: Grimm, J.L. and W.K. GRIMM'S FAIRY TALES NY 1962-63. 4 vols. Signed by Lucille Corcos, the illustrator. Introduction by Louis Untermeyer, essay by Andrew Lang $150.

341: Cooper, James Fenimore THE SPY NY 1963. Signed by Henry C. Pitz, the illustrator. Introduction by John T. Winterich $75.

342: Moliere TARTUFFE and THE WOULD-BE GENTLEMAN NY 1963. Signed by Serge Ivanoff, the illustrator. Introduction by Henri Peyre $75.

343: Wyss, Johann David THE SWISS FAMILY ROBINSON Ipswich 1963. Signed by David Gentleman, the illustrator. Introduction by Robert Cushman Murphy $100.

344: Darwin, Charles ON THE ORIGIN OF SPECIES Adelaide, Austrailia 1963. Illustrated by Paul Landacre $250.

345: Eliot, George THE MILL ON THE FLOSS Mt. Vernon 1963. Signed by Wray Manning, the illustrator. Introduction by David Daiches $75.

346: de Maupassant, Guy THE TALES OF GUY DE MAUPASSANT London 1963. Signed by Gunther Boehmer, the illustrator. Translations by Lafcadio Hearn and others. Introduction by Justin O'Brien $75.

347: Suetonius Tranquillus, Gaius THE LIVES OF THE TWELVE CAESARS Verona 1963. Signed by Salvatore Flume, the illustrator and Giovanni Mardersteig, the printer. Introduction by Moses Hadas $175.

348: Tolstoy, Leo RESURRECTION NY 1963. Signed by Fritz Eichenberg, the illustrator. Introduction by Ernest J. Simmons $150.

349: JOURNALS AND OTHER DOCUMENTS ON THE LIFE AND VOYAGES OF CHRISTOPHER COLUMBUS NY 1963. Signed by Lima de Freitas, the illustrator. Translated and edited by Samuel Eliot Morison $175.

350: du Maurier, George PETER IBBETSON Hartford 1963. 1,600 cc. Not signed. Introduction by Daphne du Maurier. Illustrated by the author $75.

351: James, Henry THE AMBASSADORS (NY) 1963. Signed by Leslie Saalburg, the illustrator $75.

352: THE BOOK OF PROVERBS NY 1963. Signed by Valenti Angelo, the illustrator. Introduction by Dr. Robert Gordis $100.

353: Hardy, Thomas THE MAYOR OF CASTERBRIDGE NY 1964. Signed by Agnes Miller Parker, the illustrator. Introduction by Frank Swinnerton $125.

354: Wells, H.G. THE WAR OF THE WORLDS and THE TIME MACHINE NY 1964. 2 vols. Signed by Joe Mugnaini, the illustrator. Introduction by J.B. Priestley $125.

355: Aristotle THE POLITICS and THE POETICS Lunenburg 1964. Signed by Leonard Baskin, the illustrator. Introduction by Horace M. Kallen $250.

356: Galsworthy, John THE MAN OF PROPERTY NY 1964. Signed by Charles Mosley, the illustrator. Introduction by Evelyn Waugh $75.

357: Collins, Wilkie THE WOMAN IN WHITE Woodstock, VT 1964. Signed by Leonard Rosoman, the illustrator. Introduction by Vincent Starrett $75.

358: Goldsmith, Oliver SHE STOOPS TO CONQUER NY 1964. Signed by T.M. Cleland, the illustrator. Introduction by Louis

Kronenberger. (There were also 15 copies for presentation to Alfred Knopf) $75.

359: Austen, Jane EMMA NY 1964. Signed by Fritz Kredel, the illustrator. Introduction by Stella Gibbons $75.

360: THE SATYRICON OF PETRONIUS ARBITER NY 1964. Signed by Antonio Sotomayer, the illustrator. Introduction by Gilbert Bagnani $75.

361: Twain, Mark THE PRINCE AND THE PAUPER Westerham 1964. Signed by Clarke Hutton, the illustrator. Introduction by Edward Wagenknecht $100.

362: Franklin, Benjamin POOR RICHARD'S ALMANACKS FOR THE YEARS 1733-1758 Phila. 1964. Signed by Norman Rockwell, the illustrator. Introduction by Van Wyck Brooks $350.

363: Nietzsche, Friedrich THUS SPAKE ZARATHUSTRA NY 1964. Translated by Thomas Common, introduction by Henry David Aiken $75.

364: Ibsen, Henrik THREE PLAYS OF HENRIK IBSEN: AN ENEMY OF THE PEOPLE, THE WILD DUCK, and HEDDA GABLER Oslo 1964. Signed by Fredrik Matheson, the illustrator. Introduction by John Gassner $60.

365: Dumas, Alexandre THE MAN IN THE IRON MASK NY 1965. Signed by Edy Legrand, the illustrator. Introduction by Andre Maurois $60.

366: Stevenson, Robert Louis THE MASTER OF BALLANTRAE (NY) 1965. Signed by

Lynd Ward, the illustrator. Introduction by G.B. Stern $75.

367: Melville, Herman BILL BUDD and BENETO CERENO NY 1965. Signed by Robert Shore, the illustrator. Introduction by Maxwell Geismar $75.

368: Burns, Robert THE POEMS OF ROBERT BURNS Glasgow 1965. Signed by Joan Hassall, the illustrator. Introduction by DeLancey Ferguson $75.

369: BHAGAVAD GITA: THE SONG CELESTIAL Bombay 1965. Signed by Y.G. Srimati, the illustrator. Translation by Edwin Arnold. Introduction by Shri Sri Prakasa $75.

370: Aeschylus PROMETHEUS BOUND and Percy Bysshe Shelley's PROMETHEUS UNBOUND NY 1965. Introduction by Rex Warner, plates by John Farleigh $100.

371: Cooper, James Fenimore THE PATHFINDER Luxenberg, VT 1965. Signed by Richard M. Powers, the illustrator. Introduction by Robert E. Spiller $60.

372: Conrad, Joseph THE NIGGER OF "NARCISSUS" L.A. 1965. Signed by Millard Sheets, the illustrator. Introduction by Howard Mumford Jones $100.

373: Sinclair, Upton THE JUNGLE Baltimore 1965. Signed by the author and Fletcher Martin, the illustrator $125.

374: Porter, William Sydney THE STORIES OF O. HENRY Burlington 1965. Signed by John Groth, the illustrator. Introduction by Harry Hansen $100.

375: Petrarch THE SONNETS OF PETRARCH Verona 1965. Signed by Aldo Salvadori, the illustrator and Giovanni Mardersteig, the printer. Introduction by Thomas G. Bergin $150.

376: Stoker, Bram DRACULA NY 1965. Signed by Felix Hoffman, the illustrator. Introduction by Anthony Boucher $175.

377: Marlowe, Christopher FOUR PLAYS OF CHRISTOPHER MARLOWE: TAMBURLAINE I, II, DR. FAUSTUS and EDWARD II NY 1966. Signed by Albert Decaris, the illustrator. Introduction by Havelock Ellis $100.

378: Hope, Anthony THE PRISONER OF ZENDA Baltimore 1966. Signed by Donald Spencer, the illustrator. Introduction by Sir Sydney Roberts $75.

379: Epictetus THE DISCOURSES AND MANUAL OF EPICTETUS Berne 1966. Signed by Hans Erni, the illustrator. Introduction by P.E. Mattheson $125.

380: Dickens, Charles HARD TIMES NY 1966. Introduction by John T. Winterich. Illustrated by Charles Raymond $100.

381: Shaw, George Bernard TWO PLAYS FOR PURITANS NY 1966. Signed by George Him, the illustrator $75.

382: Keats, John THE POEMS OF JOHN KEATS Cambridge 1966. Signed by David Gentleman, the illustrator. Introduction by Aileen Ward $100.

383: Scott, Sir Walter KENILWORTH Burlington 1966. Signed by Clarke Hutton, the illustrator. Introduction by David Daiches $75.

384: Twain, Mark A TRAMP ABROAD Hartford (1966). Signed by David Knight, the illustrator. With reproductions of drawings made by Mark Twain "without help" for the first edition. Introduction by Edward Wagenknecht $125.

385: Chekhov, Anton TWO PLAYS OF ANTON CHEKHOV: THE CHERRY ORCHARD and THREE SISTERS NY 1966. Signed by Lajos Szalay, the illustrator. Translated by Constance Garnett, introduction by Sir John Gielgud $60.

386: THE DEAD SEA SCROLLS Kent, England 1966. Signed by Shraga Weil, the illustrator. Translated, introduction etc. by Geza Vermes $225.

387: Verne, Jules A JOURNEY TO THE CENTER OF THE EARTH NY 1966. Signed by Edward A. Wilson, the illustrator. Introduction by Isaac Asimov $100.

388: Hawthorne, Nathaniel TWICE-TOLD TALES NY 1966. Signed by Valenti Angelo, the illustrator. Introduction by Wallace Stegner $75.

389: Vasari, Giorgio LIVES OF THE MOST EMINENT PAINTERS Verona 1966. 2 vols. Signed by Giovanni Mardersteig, the printer. Introduction by Marilyn Aronberg Lavin $225.

390: THE MONK AND THE HANGMAN'S DAUGHTER NY 1967. Signed by Michel Ciry, the illustrator. (Written by Herr Richard Voss, although not mentioned in ref.a or b.) Adapted from the German by Ambrose Bierce, with introductions by Maurice Valency and Bierce $75.

391: James, Henry THE PORTRAIT OF A LADY (NY) 1967. Signed by Colleen Browning, the illustrator. Introduction by Robert W. Stallman $100.

392: Dostoevsky, Fyodor THE GAMBLER and NOTES FROM UNDER-GROUND Bloomfield 1967. Signed by Alexandre Alexeieff, the illustrator. Translated by Constance Garnett, introduction by George Steiner $90.

393: Euripides THREE PLAYS OF EURIPIDES: MEDEA, HIPPOLYTUS, and THE BACCHAE London 1967. Signed by Michael Ayrton, the illustrator. Introduction by Philip Vellacott $75.

394: THE BOOK OF BALLADS (NY) 1967. Signed by Fritz Kredel, the illustrator. Edited, with introduction, by MacEdward Leach $75.

395: Wells, H.G. THE INVISIBLE MAN NY 1967. Signed by Charles Mozley, the illustrator. Introduction by Bernard Bergonzi $100.

396: Alcott, Louisa May LITTLE WOMEN NY 1967. Signed by Henry C. Pitz, the illustrator. Introduction by Edward Weeks $100.

397: Jefferson, Thomas THE WRITINGS OF THOMAS JEFFERSON Luxenburg, VT 1967. Signed by Lynd Ward, the illustrator. Selected and introduction by Saul K. Padover $150.

398: Shakespeare, William THE POEMS OF WILLIAM SHAKESPEARE Cambridge 1967. Signed by Agnes Miller Parker, the illustrator. Introduction etc. by Peter Alexander $125.

399: Prescott, William H. THE HISTORY OF THE REIGN OF FERDINAND AND ISABELLA THE CATHOLIC NY 1967. Signed by Lima de Freitas, the illustrator. Introduction by C. Harvey Gardiner $100.

400: Mitchell, Margaret GONE WITH THE WIND NY 1968. 2 vols. Signed by John Groth, the illustrator. Introduction by Henry Steele Commager $225.

401: Defoe, Daniel A JOURNAL OF THE PLAGUE YEAR Bloomfield 1968. Signed (or initialed) by Domenico Gnoli, the illustrator. Introduction by J.R. Sutherland $75.

402: Joyce, James A PORTRAIT OF THE ARTIST AS A YOUNG MAN NY 1968. Signed by Brian Keogh, the illustrator. Introduction by Hugh Kenner $125.

403: Kipling, Rudyard THE JUNGLE BOOKS Luxenburg, VT 1968. Signed by David Gentleman, the illustrator. Introduction by Bonamy Dobree $125.

404: THE BOOK ECCLESIASTES NY 1968. Signed by Edgar Miller, the illustrator. Introduction by Kenneth Rexroth $125.

405: Maupassant, Guy de BEL-AMI NY 1968. 2,000 cc. Signed by Bernard Lamotte, the illustrator. Introduction by Alec Waugh $60.

406: Wilde, Oscar THE SHORT STORIES OF OSCAR WILDE (NY) 1968. Signed by James Hill, the illustrator. Introduction by Robert Gorham Davis $75.

407: Donne, John THE POEMS OF JOHN DONNE Cambridge 1968. Signed by Imre

Reiner, the illustrator. Introduction by Frank Kermode $90.

408: Thoreau, Henry David CAPE COD Portland 1968. Signed by Raymond J. Holden, the illustrator. Introduction by Joseph Wood Krutch $125.

409: Plato THREE DIALOGUES OF PLATO: LYSIS, THE SYMPOSIUM, and PHAEDRUS (NY) 1968. Signed by Eugene Karlin, the illustrator. Introduction by Whitney J. Oates $100.

410: Cooper, James Fenimore THE PILOT (Baltimore) 1968. Signed by Robert Quackenbush, the illustrator. Introduction by John T. Winterich $60.

411: AMERICAN INDIAN LEGENDS L.A. 1968. Signed by Everett Gee Jackson, the illustrator. Selected, edited and introduction by Allan A. Macfarlan $100.

412: Remarque, Erich Maria ALL QUIET ON THE WESTERN FRONT (NY) 1969. Signed by John Groth, the illustrator. Introduction by Harry Hansen $100.

413: Conrad, Joseph HEART OF DARKNESS NY 1969. Signed by Robert Shore, the illustrator. Introduction by Leo Gurko $75.

414: Dumas, Alexandre MARGUERITE DE VALOIS NY 1969. Signed by Edy Legrand, the illustrator. Introduction by Henri Peyre $60.

415: Scott, Sir Walter THE TALISMAN Ipswich 1968. Signed by Federico Castellone, the illustrator. Introduction by Thomas Caldecot Chubb $75.

416: Browning, Robert THE POEMS OF ROBERT BROWNING Cambridge 1969. Signed by Peter Reddick, the illustrator. Introduction by C. Day Lewis $100.

417: Creasey, Sir Edward S. THE FIFTEEN DECISIVE BATTLES OF THE WORLD (NY 1969). Signed by Joseph Domjan, the illustrator. Introduction by Hanson W. Baldwin $75.

418: Hardy, Thomas JUDE THE OBSCURE NY 1969. Signed by Agnes Miller Parker, the illustrator. Introduction by John Bayley $150.

419: Aquinas, Thomas THE WRITINGS OF ST. THOMAS AQUINAS Chatham, Eng. 1969. Signed by Reynolds Stone, the illustrator. Selected and with introduction by George N. Shuster $125.

420: Xenophon THE ANABASIS Athens 1969. Signed by A. Tassos, the illustrator. Translated by Henry G. Dakyns, introduction by Robert Payne $125.

421: James, Henry DAISY MILLER Cambridge 1969. Signed by Gustave Nebel, the illustrator. Introduction by John Holloway $125.

422: Irving, Washington THE ALHAMBRA (NY) 1969. Signed by Lima de Freitas, the illustrator. Introduction by Angel Flores $75.

423: Steinbeck, John OF MICE AND MEN NY 1970. Signed by Martin Fletcher, the illustrator. Introduction by John T. Winterich $175.

424: Frazer, Sir James George THE GOLDEN BOUGH NY 1970. 2 vols. Signed by James Lewicki, the illustrator. Introduction by Stanley Edgar Hyman $125.

425: Yeats, W.B. THE POEMS OF W.B. YEATS NY 1970. Signed by Robin Jacques, the illustrator. Introduction by William York Tindall $175.

426: Washington, Booker T. UP FROM SLAVERY NY 1970. Signed by Denver Gillen, the illustrator. Introduction by Booker T. Washington III $100.

427: Livy THE HISTORY OF EARLY ROME Verona 1970. Signed by Raffaele Scorzelli, the illustrator and Giovanni Mardersteig, the printer $150.

428: THE ANALECTS OF CONFUCIUS L.A. 1970. Signed by Tseng Yu-Ho, the illustrator. Translated, annotated and introduction by Lionel Giles $125.

429: Verne, Jules FROM THE EARTH TO THE MOON and AROUND THE MOON NY 1970. 2 vols. Signed by Robert Shore, the illustrator. Introduction by Jean Jules-Verne $125.

430: Addison, Joseph THE SPECTATOR London 1970. Signed by Lynton Lamb, the illustrator. Introduction by Robert Halsband $75.

431: Twain, Mark THE NOTORIOUS JUMPING FROG AND OTHER STORIES NY 1970. Signed by Joseph Low, the illustrator. Introduction by Edward Wagenknecht. Assume first of this selection $75.

432: RUSSIAN FOLK TALES NY 1970. Signed by Teje Etchemendy, the illustrator. Selected, edited and introduction by Albert B. Lord $75.

433: Pushkin, Alexander THE CAPTAIN'S DAUGHTER AND OTHER STORIES (NY) 1971. Signed by Charles Mozley, the illustrator. Translated by Ivy and Tatiana Litvinov. Introduction by Kathryn Feuer $75.

434: Dickens, Charles THE SHORT STORIES OF CHARLES DICKENS NY 1971. Signed by Edward Ardizzone, the illustrator and Joseph Blumenthal, the designer. Introduction by Walter Allen $125.

435: Darwin, Charles THE DESCENT OF MAN and SELECTION IN RELATION TO SEX Adelaide, So. Australia 1971. Signed by Fritz Kredel, the illustrator. Introduction by Ashley Mantagu $175.

436: Austen, Jane NORTHANGER ABBEY (NY) 1971. Signed by Clark Hutton, the illustrator. Introduction by Sylvia Townsend Warner $90.

437: Baudelaire, Charles THE FLOWERS OF EVIL NY 1971. 2 vols. Signed by Pierre-Yves Tremois, the illustrator. Introduction by James Laver $100.

438: Camus, Albert THE STRANGER (NY) 1971. Signed by Daniel Maffia, the illustrator. Translated by Stuart Gilbert, introduction by Wallace Fowlie $100.

439: James, Henry WASHINGTON SQUARE NY 1971. Signed by Lawrence Beall Smith, the illustrator. Introduction by Louis S. Auchincloss $75.

440: Ovidius Naso, P. (Ovid.) THE ART OF LOVE (NY) 1971. Signed by Eric Fraser, the illustrator. Translated, with introduction and notes, by B.P. Moore $100.

441: Pascal, Blaise LES PENSEES Bloomfield 1971. Signed by Ismar David, the illustrator. Translated and introduction by Martin Turnell $60.

442: SIR GAWAIN AND THE GREEN KNIGHT NY 1971. Signed by Cyril Satorsky, the illustrator. Modern translation and introduction by James L. Rosenberg $175.

443: Shelley, Percy B. THE POEMS OF PERCY BYSSHE SHELLEY Cambridge 1971. Signed by Richard Shirley Smith, the illustrator. Introduction by Stephen Spender $100.

444: Mann, Thomas DEATH IN VENICE NY 1972. Signed by Felix Hoffmann, the illustrator. Translated by Kenneth Burke, introduction by Erich Heller $125.

445: O'Neill, Eugene AH, WILDERNESS! NY 1972. Signed by Shannon Stirweiss, the illustrator. Introduction by Walter Kerr $100.

446: Conrad, Joseph YOUTH, TYPHOON, and THE END OF THE TETHER L.A. 1972. Signed by Robert Shore, the illustrator and Ward Ritchie, the printer/designer $75.

447: Tolstoy, Leo CHILDHOOD, BOYHOOD, YOUTH NY 1972. Signed by Fritz Eichenberg, the illustrator. Introduction by John Bayley $75.

448: Twain, Mark ROUGHING IT NY 1972. Signed by Noel Sickles, the illustrator. Introduction by Edward Wagenknecht $100.

449: White, Gilbert THE NATURAL HISTORY OF SELBORNE Ipswich 1972. Signed by John Nash, the illustrator. Introduction by the Earl of Cranbrook $150.

450: THE MEMOIRS OF CASANOVA Haarlem 1972. Signed by Rene ben Sussan, the illustrator. Introduction by J. Rives Childs $90.

451: Bierce, Ambrose THE DEVIL'S DICTIONARY NY 1972. Signed by Fritz Kredel, the illustrator. Introduction by Louis Kronenberger $125.

452: THE ORATIONS AND ESSAYS OF CICERO Verona 1972. Signed by Salvatore Fiume, the illustrator. Introduction by Reginald H. Barrow. Printed by Hans Martersteig $125.

453: THE BOOK OF THE DEAD NY (1972). 2 vols. Translation and introduction by Raymond O. Faulkner. Accompanied by a volume of photographs by Peter Parkinson, mounted accordian-style to form strip 16' 5" long $125.

454: THE PANCHANTANTRA NY 1972. Signed by Y.G. Srimati, the illustrator. Introduction by Arthur W. Ryder $75.

455: Blake, William THE POEMS OF WILLIAM BLAKE Cambridge 1973. Introduction by Aileen Ward, illustrated with Blake's colored engravings $200.

456: Voltaire CANDIDE, or OPTIMISM NY 1973. Signed by May Neama, the illustrator. Introduction by Anatole Broyard $75.

457: Wilde, Oscar LADY WINDERMERE'S FAN and THE IMPORTANCE OF BEING EARNEST London 1973. Signed by Tony Walton, the illustrator. Introduction by Sir John Gielgud $75.

458: Dumas, Alexandre THE QUEEN'S NECKLACE NY 1973. Signed by Edy Legrand

and Cyril Arnstram, the illustrators. Introduction by Henri Peyre $60.

459-465: LEC skipped 7 numbers at this point "to conform with the number of the corresponding Monthly Letter"

466: Chekhov, Anton THE SHORT STORIES OF ANTON CHEKHOV Avon, CT 1973. 2,000 cc. Signed by Lajos Szalay, the illustrator. Introduction by Helen Muchnic $75.

467: IRISH FOLK TALES Avon, CT 1973. 2,000 cc. Signed by Ted Gensamer, the designer/decorator. Introduction by William Butler Yeats, illustrated by Rowel Fries $125.

468: London, Jack WHITE FANG Lunenburg, VT 1973. 2,000 cc. Signed by Lydia Dabcovich, the illustrator. Introduction by Ray Gardner $75.

469: Wharton, Edith THE AGE OF INNOCENCE Avon, CT 1973. 2,000 cc. Signed by Lawrence Beall Smith, the illustrator. Introduction by W.B. Lewis $100.

470: Wordsworth, William THE POEMS OF WILLIAM WORDSWORTH Cambridge 1973. 2,000 cc. Signed by John O'Connor, the illustrator $90.

471: Kipling, Rudyard TALES OF EAST AND WEST Avon, CT 1973. 2,000 cc. Signed by Charles Raymond, the illustrator. Introduction by Bernard Bergonzi $60.

472: Huxley, Aldous BRAVE NEW WORLD (Avon, CT) 1974. 2,000 cc. Signed by Mary McAfee, the illustrator. Introduction by Ashley Montagu $125.

473: GILGAMESH Avon, CT 1974. 2,000 cc. Signed by Irving Amen, the illustrator. Translated by William Ellery Leonard, introduction by Leonard Cottrell $75.

474: Boswell, James JOURNAL OF A TOUR TO THE HEBRIDES WITH SAMUEL JOHNSON, LL.D Bloomfield 1974. 2,000 cc. Illustrated by Thomas Rowlandson, introduction by Robert Halsband $125.

475: Weems, Mason L. THE LIFE OF WASHINGTON (NY) 1974. 2,000 cc. Signed by Robert Quackenbush, the illustrator. Introduction by Henry Steele Commager $75.

476: Thucydides THE HISTORY OF THE PELOPONNESIAN WAR Avon, CT 1974. 2 vols. 2,000 sets. Signed by A. Tassos, the illustrator. Introduction by Peter Pouncey $100.

477: Twain, Mark PUDD'NHEAD WILSON Avon, CT 1974. 2,000 cc. Signed by John Groth, the illustrator. Introduction by Edward Wagenknecht. Also a separate small volume in wraps PUDD'NHEAD WILSON'S CLENDAR also illustrated by Garth $100.

478: Shaw, George Bernard PYGMALION and CANDIDA Avon, CT 1974. 2,000 cc. Signed by Clarke Hutton, the illustrator. Introduction by Alan Strachan $90.

479: Crane, Stephen MAGGIE: A GIRL OF THE STREETS (NY) 1974. 2,000 cc. Signed by Sigmund Abeles, the illustrator. Introduction by Shirley Ann Grau $90.

480: Bradbury, Ray THE MARTIAN CHRONICLES Avon, CT 1974. 2,000 cc. Signed by the author and Joseph Mugnaini, the illustrator. Introduction by Martin Gardner $300.

481: Wilder, Thornton OUR TOWN Avon, CT 1974. 2,000 cc. Signed by the author and Robert J. Lee, the illustrator. Introduction by Brooks Atkinson $150.

482: Dostoevsky, Fyodor A RAW YOUTH Verona 1974. 2 vols. 2,000 cc. Signed by Fritz Eichenberg, the illustrator. Introduction by Konstantin Mochulsky $100.

483: Tennyson, Alfred Lord THE POEMS OF ALFRED, LORD TENNYSON Cambridge 1974. 2,000 cc. Signed by Reynolds Stone, the illustrator. Introduction by John D. Rosenberg $125.

484: Dickens, Charles AMERICAN NOTES Avon, CT 1975. 2,000 cc. Signed by Raymond F. Houlihan, the illustrator. Introduction by Angus Wilson $75.

485: Wharton, Edith THE HOUSE OF MIRTH (NY) 1975. 2,000 cc. Signed by Lily Harmon, the illustrator. Introduction by Arthur Mizener $90.

486: Conrad, Joseph THE OUTCAST OF THE ISLANDS Avon, CT 1975. 2,000 cc. Signed by Robert Shore, the illustrator. Introduction by Clifton Fadiman $75.

487: Jerome, Jerome K. THREE MEN IN A BOAT Ipswich 1975. 2,000 cc. Signed by John Griffiths, the illustrator. Introduction by Stella Gibbons $60.

488: Thoreau, Henry David A WEEK ON THE CONCORD AND MERRIMACK RIVERS Lunenburg 1975. 2,000 cc. Signed by Raymond J. Holden, the illustrator. Introduction by Charles R. Anderson $90.

489: Sophocles ANTIGONE Haarlem 1975. 2,000 cc. Signed by Harry Bennett, the illustrator. Introduction by D.S. Carne-Ross $90.

490: Walpole, Hugh THE CASTLE OF OTRANTO Westerham 1975. 2,000 cc. Signed by W.S. Lewis, the editor/introduction. Contemporary illustrations $100.

491: Burke, Edmund ON CONCILIATION WITH AMERICA AND OTHER PAPERS ON THE AMERICAN REVOLUTION Lunenburg, VT 1975. 2,000 cc. Signed by Lynd Ward, the illustrator. Introduction and prefaces by Peter J. Stanlis $100.

492: Fernandez de Oviedo y Valdes, Capt. Gonzalo THE CONQUEST AND SETTLEMENT OF THE ISLAND OF BORIQUEN or PUERTO RICO Lunenburg 1975. 2,000 cc. Signed by Jack and Irene Delano, the illustrators. Introduction and notes by E. Daymond Turner $75.

493: Lawrence, D.H. SONS AND LOVERS Avon, CT 1975. 2,000 cc. Signed by Sheila Robinson, the illustrator. Introduction by Robert Gorham Davis $90.

494: Bligh, William A VOYAGE TO THE SOUTH SEAS Adelaide, So. Australia 1975. 2,000 cc. Signed by Geoffrey C. Ingleton, the illustrator and Douglas Dunstan, the designer. Introduction by Alan Villiers $175.

495: Kafka, Franz THE TRIAL Avon, CT 1975. 2,000 cc. Signed by Alan E. Cober, the illustrator. Introduction by Erich Heller (full leather) $175.

496: Pater, Walter THE RENAISSANCE Verona 1976. 2,000 cc. Signed by Martino

Mardersteig, the designer. Introduction by Kenneth Clarke $200.

497: Arnold, Sir Edwin THE LIGHT OF ASIA Avon, CT 1976. 2,000 cc. Illustrated by Ayres Houghtelling. Introduction by Melford E. Spiro $60.

498: Defoe, Daniel ROXANA, THE FORTUNATE MISTRESS Avon, CT 1976. 2,000 cc. Illustrated and signed by Bernd Kroeber. Introduction by James R. Sutherland $75.

499: Stevenson, Robert Louis NEW ARABIAN NIGHTS Avon, Ct 1976. 2,000 cc. Signed by Clarke Hutton, the illustrator. Introduction by Norman H. Strouse $90.

500: Gogol, Nikolai THE OVERCOAT and THE GOVERNMENT INSPECTOR Westport, CT 1976. 2,000 cc. Signed by Saul Field, the illustrator. Introduction by Alfred Kazin $60.

501: Cabell, James Branch JURGEN: A COMEDY OF JUSTICE Westport, CT (1976). 2,000 cc. Signed and illustrated by Virgil Burnett. Introduction by Edward Wagenknecht $75.

502: Turgenev, Ivan THE TORRENTS OF SPRING Westport, CT 1976. 1,600 cc. Signed by Lajos, the illustrator. Introduction by Alec Waugh $75.

503: Austen, Jane PERSUASION Westport, CT 1977. 1,600 cc. Signed and illustrated by Tony Buonpastore. Introduction by Louis Auchincloss $90.

504: Hesse, Herman STEPPENWOLF Westport, CT 1977. 1,600 cc. Signed by Helmut Ackermann, the illustrator $125.

505: Hugo, Victor THE BATTLE OF WATERLOO Westport, CT 1977. 1,600 cc. Illustrated by Edouard Detaille. Introduction by Drew Middleton. Epilogue by Reginald Colby $75.

506: Sasson, Siegfried MEMOIRS OF A FOX-HUNTING MAN (London) 1977. 1,600 cc. Signed by Paul Hogarth, the illustrator. Introduction by Geoffrey Keynes $100.

507: THE SERMON ON THE MOUNT NY 1977. 1,600 cc. Commentaries and introduction by Roman A. Greer. Decorated by Leo Watt, designed by John Dreyfus $75.

508: THE BALLADS OF ROBIN HOOD Cambridge 1977. 1,600 cc. Illustrated by David Gentleman. Introduction by Jim Lees. Designed by John Dreyfus $75.

509: (this number was not used by LEC)

510: Anderson, Sherwood WINESBURG, OHIO Lunenburg 1978. 1,600 cc. Signed by Ben F. Stahl, the illustrator. Introduction by Malcolm Cowley $125.

511: Flaubert, Gustave THREE TALES NY 1978. 1,600 cc. Signed by May Neama, the illustrator. Introduction by Guy de Maupassant $75.

512: THE BOOK OF THE PROPHET ISAIAH NY 1979. 2,000 cc. Signed by Chaim Gross, the illustrator. Introduction by Franklin H. Littell $175.

513: Villon, Francois THE LYRICAL POEMS OF FRANCOIS VILLON NY 1979. 2,000 cc. Signed by Stephen Harvard, the designer. Introduction by Robert Louis Stevenson. Poems in French and English, with the latter versions by A.C. Swinburne, Dante Gabriel Rossetti, W.E. Henley, John Payne and Leonie Adams (who selected the poems for inclusion) $100.

514: Singer, Isaac Bashevis THE GENTLEMAN FROM CRACOW and THE MIRROR NY 1979. 2,000 cc. Signed by the author and Raphael Soyer, the illustrator $175.

515: Carson, Rachel THE SEA AROUND US NY 1980. 2,000 cc. Signed by Alfred Eisenstaedt, the photographer $200.

516: Fitzgerald, F. Scott THE GREAT GATSBY (NY 1980). 2,000 cc. Signed by Fred Meyer, the illustrator. Introduction by Charles Scribner III $150.

517: Graves, Robert POEMS BY ROBERT GRAVES Lunenburg 1980. 2,000 cc. Signed by Paul Hogarth, the illustrator $100.

518: Rilke, Rainer Maria SELECTED POEMS OF RAINER MARIA RILKE NY 1981. 2,000 cc. Signed by Robert Kipniss, the illustrator. Translated by C.F. MacIntyre. Preface by Harry T. Moore $125.

519: Sassoon, Siegfried MEMOIRS OF AN INFANTRY OFFICER Portland 1981. 2,000 cc. Signed by Paul Hogarth, the illustrator. Introduction by David Daiches $100.

520: Crane, Hart THE BRIDGE NY 1981. 2,000 cc. Signed by Richard Mead Benson, the photographer. Introduction by Malcolm Cowley $150.

521: Homer THE ODYSSEY (NY) 1981. 2,000 cc. Signed by Barry Moser, the illustrator. Translated by T.E. Shaw (Lawrence). Preface by Jeremy M. Wilson $225.

522: Grimmelshausen, Johann von THE ADVENTURES OF SIMPLICUSSIMUS Charlotte 1981. 2,000 cc. Signed by Fritz Eichenberg, the illustrator. Translation and introduction by John Spielman $100.

523: Cowley, Malcolm EXILE'S RETURN NY 1981. 2,000 cc. Signed by the author and Bernice Abbott, the photographer. Includes photographs by Abbott, Man Ray and Andre Kertesz, et al. Introduction by Leon Edel $250.

524: Fitzgerald, F. Scott TENDER IS THE NIGHT Lunenburg (1982). 2,000 cc. Signed by Fred Meyer, the illustrator and Charles Scribner III (the publisher) $150.

525: O'Neill, Eugene THE ICEMAN COMETH Lunenburg 1982. 2,000 cc. Signed by Leonard Baskin, the illustrator. Introduction by Irma Jaffe. Includes an original lithograph (signed in the stone) bound at rear $250.

526: Dostoevsky, Fyodor THE HOUSE OF THE DEAD Boston 1982. 2,000 cc. Signed by Fritz Eichenberg, the illustrator. Foreword by Boris Shragin $125.

527: Bradbury, Ray FAHRENHEIT 451 NY 1982. 2,000 cc. Signed by the author and Joe Mugnaini, the illustrator $250.

528: Finney, Charles G. THE CIRCUS OF DR. LAO Lunenburg 1982. 2,000 cc. Signed by Claire Van Vliet, the illustrator. Introduction by Edward Hoagland $150.

529: Brecht, Bertolt THE THREEPENNY OPERA (NY 1982). 2,000 cc. Signed by Jack Levine (illustrator) and Eric Bentley (introduction) $125.

530: Heaney, Seamus POEMS AND A MEMOIR BY SEAMUS HEANEY (NY 1982). 1,500 cc. Signed by the author (who also contributes a preface), Henry Pearson (illustrator) and Thomas Flanagan (introduction). A first edition of this selection including eight "early uncollected poems." In print at $300 $300.

531: Williams, Tennessee A STREETCAR NAMED DESIRE NY 1982. 2,000 cc. Signed by Al Hirshfeld, the illustrator. Foreword by Jessica Tandy, introduction by the author (an essay that appeared in "The New York Times: drama section on November 30, 1947) $200.

532: Marquez, Garcia Garcia ONE HUNDRED YEARS OF SOLITUDE (NY 1982). 2,000 cc. Signed by Rafael Ferrer, (illustrator), Alastair Reid (introduction) and Gregory Rabassa (translator). An original graphic is laid-in $250.

533: Walcott, Derek POEMS OF THE CARIBBEAN NY (1982). 2,000 cc. Signed by the author and Romare Bearden, the illustrator. Introduction by Joseph Brodsky. An numbered lithograph is laid-in $350.

534: Colette BREAK OF DAY NY 1983. 2,000 cc. Signed by Francoise Gilot, the illustrator. Introduction by Robert Phelps. In print at $150 $150.

535: Hersey, John HIROSHIMA NY 1983. 1,500 cc. Signed by the author, Robert Penn

Warren (poem), and Jacob Lawrence (illustrator). In print at $1,000 $1,000.

536: Cather, Willa A LOST LADY NY 1983. 1,500 cc. Signed by William Bailey, the illustrator. Introduction by John Hollander. In print at $400 $400.

537: Milosz, Czeslaw THE CAPTIVE MIND NY (1983). 1,500 cc. Signed by the author (who adds a new preface for this edition) and Janusz Kapusta, the illustrator $125.

538: Singer, Isaac Bashevis THE MAGICIAN OF LUBLIN NY 1984. 1,200 cc. Signed by the author and Larry Rivers, the illustrator. In print at $400 $400.

539: Kafka, Franz METAMORPHOSIS NY (1984). 1,500 cc. Signed by Jose Luis Cuevas, the illustrator. Introduction by Robert Coles $275.

540: Miller, Arthur DEATH OF A SALESMAN NY (1984). 1,500 cc. Signed by the author, who adds a new foreword, and Leonard Baskin, the illustrator $450.

541: Borges, Jore Luis FICCIONES NY (1984). 1,500 cc. Signed by Sol LeWitt, the illustrator. Introduction by Alexander Coleman. Trnslated by Anthony Kerrigan and others. In print at $1,000 $450.

542: Poe, Edgar Allan THE FALL OF THE HOUSE OF USHER NY 1985. 1,500 cc. Signed by Raphael Soyer, who did a tribute to Alice Neel, the illustrator died before the book was published; however, she did sign some sheets and copies with her signature would be about $1,500. In print without Neel's signature at $700 $700.

543: Conrad, Joseph THE SECRET SHARER NY (1985). 1,500 cc. Signed by Bruce Chandler, the illustrator. Introduction by Ian Watt. In print at $200 $200.

544: Grass, Gunter THE FLOUNDER NY 1985. 1,000 cc. 3 vols. Signed by the author, who also illustrated the book. Translated by Ralph Mannheim. In print at $400 $400.

545: Rimbaud, Arthur A SEASON IN HELL NY (1986). 1,000 cc. Signed Robert Mapplethorpe, the artist and Paul Schmidt, translation/introduction. In print at $3,000. There were also 40 signed numbered portfolios of the illustrations sold separately $2,500.

546: Joyce, James DUBLINERS (NY 1986). 1,000 cc. Signed by Robert Ballagh (photogravures) and Tom Flanagan (introduction). In print at $600 $600.

547: Bernanos, Georges THE DIARY OF A COUNTRY PRIEST (NY 1986). 1,000 cc. Signed by Fritz Eichenberg, the illustrator. Introduction by Robert Coles. In print at $150 $150.

548: Kafka, Franz IN THE PENAL COLONY NY (1987). 800 cc. Signed by Michael Hofftka, the illustrator. Translation by Willa and Edwin Muir. In print at $400 $400.

549: Ionesco, Eugene JOURNEYS AMONG THE DEAD Munich (1987). 1,000 cc. Signed by the author, who also illustrated the book. Translation by Barbara Wright. Also includes a new preface in the form of a "Conversation with Ionesco | Eugene Ionesco and Verena Heyden-Rynsch | Paris, March 14, 1987." In print at $400 $400.

550: Rilke, Rainer Maria THE NOTEBOOKS OF MALTE LAURIDS BRIGGE (NY 1987). 800 cc. Translated by Stephen Mitchell. Not signed. (This book was substituted by the club but never advertised) $200.

551: Faulkner, William HUNTING STORIES (NY 1988). 850 cc. Signed by Neil Welliver, the illustrator. Although announced to be signed by Cleanth Brooks (introduction), it was not. In print at $300 $300.

552: Carpentier, Alejo THE KINGDOM OF THIS WORLD (NY 1987). 750 cc. Signed Roberto Juarez (illustrations) and John Hersey (introduction). In print at $600. There was also twenty signed numbered sets of the illustrations sold separately $400.

553: Paz, Octavio THREE POEMS (NY 1988). 750 cc. Signed by the author and Robert Motherwell, the artist. In print at $8,000. There were also 20 signed numbered exhibition sets of the illustations; and 50 signed numbered portfolios. Both in wooden boxes $4,500.

554: Lampedusa, Giuseppe di THE LEOPARD (no-place 1988). 750 cc. Signed by the artist Piero Guccione and Leonard Sciascia, introduction. Translated by Archibald Colquhoun. In print at $150 $150.

555: Durrenmatt, Friedrich OEDIPUS (NY 1989). 650 cc. 2 vols. Signed by the author and Marie Casindas (photogravures). Translated by Leila Vennewitz. Foreword by the author. In print at $400 $400.

556: Warren, Robert Penn ALL THE KING'S MEN (NY 1989). 550 cc. 2 vols. Signed by the author and the artist Hank O'Neal (photogravures). New introduction. In print at $1,200. There were also 30 signed numbered sets of the photogravures sold separately $1,200.

557: GENESIS (NY) 1989. 425 cc. Signed by the artist Jacob Lawrence. In print at $2,500. There were also 22 signed numbered exhibition sets; and 50 signed numbered portfolios of the illustrations sold separately $1,500.

558: Beckett, Samuel NOHOW ON (NY) 1989. 550 cc. Signed by Beckett and the illustrator Robert Ryman. In print at $8,000. $NVA

559: Hemingway, Ernest THE OLD MAN AND THE SEA (NY 1990). 600 cc. Signed by Alfred Eisenstaedt (photogravures). Oblong size in clam shell box. In print at $1,500. There were also 30 signed numbered sets of the photogravures sold separately $1,500.

560: Whitman, Walt THE SONG OF THE OPEN ROAD (NY) 1990. 550 cc. Illustrated with photogravures by Aaron Sisking and Signed by him. In print at $1,500. There were also 12 signed numbered exhibition sets; and 30 signed numbered sets of the photogravures sold separately $1,500.

561: O'Hara, Frank POEMS NY 1990. 500 cc. Illustrated with 17 lithographs by Willem de Kooning. Introduction by Riva Castleman. In print at $8,000. There were also 12 numbered exhibition sets; and 60 numbered portfolios

$NVA

562: Kawabata, Yasunari SNOW COUNTRY NY 1990. 375 cc. Signed by the illustrator, Tadakki Kuwayama, and translator, Edward Seidensticker. In print at $2,000. There were also 40 signed numbered sets of the illustrations

$NVA

563: Mann, Thomas THE BLACK SWAN NY 1990. 375 cc. Signed by the illustrator, John Hejduk. Afterword by David Shapiro. In print at $1,500 $NVA

564: Mitchell, Joseph THE BOTTOM OF THE HARBOR NY 1991. 250 cc. With photographs by Berenice Abbott. Signed by Mitchell. In print at $2,000

565: Pasternak, Boris MY SISTER/LIFE NY 1992. 250 cc. Illustrated and signed by Yuri Kuper. In print at $2,000. There were also 40 signed numbered sets of the etchings sold separately

Planned for 1992/3:

Pound, Ezra CATHAY NY 1990. 250 cc. Illustrated with etchings by Francesco Clements.

SPECIAL PUBLICATIONS:

S1a: Dill, Francis P. and Porter Garnett THE IDEAL BOOK LEC (NY) 1931. 2,600 cc. Wraps. Two essays. Jointly awarded the prize offered by LEC for Best Essay on subject $35.

S1b: Dill, Francis P. and Porter Garnett THE IDEAL BOOK LEC NY 1932. 500 cc. The second printing, the first in cloth (issued without dustwrapper). Prepared as a keepsake for The American Institute of Graphic Arts $30.

S2: Dwiggins, W.A. TOWARDS A REFORM OF THE PAPER CURRENCY NY 1932. 452 cc. Signed by Dwiggins $450.

S3: THE DOLPHIN, *A Journal of the Making of Books* No.1 1933. 1,200 cc $125.

S4: THE DOLPHIN, *A Journal of the Making of Books* No.2 1935. 2,000 cc $100.

S5: THE DOLPHIN, *A History of the Printed Book* No.3 1938. 1,800 cc. Edited by Lawrence C. Wroth $200.

S6: Jackson, Holbrook OF THE USES OF BOOKS (1937). 1,500 cc. 30 pages in boards $40.

S7: THE LEC INC : YOU FAVORITE BOOKS... The Tenth Anniversary Series (no-date). Paperwraps. Prospectus and history $20.

S8: THE DOLPHIN, *A Periodical for All People Who Find Pleasure in Fine Books* No.4. Designed by W.A. Dwiggins

Part I: Fall, 1940 500 cc in green buckram: $150.
11,500 cc in wraps: $35.
Part II: Winter 1941 3,000 cc bound in green buckram: $40.
Part III: Winter 1941 3,000 cc bound in green buckram: $40.

S9: Boccaccio, Giovanni THE DECAMERON NY 1940. 2 vols. 530 cc. Illustrated by Fritz Kredel, introduction by Edward Hutton $350.

S10: Grahame, Kenneth THE WIND IN THE WILLOWS 1940. 2,020 cc. Signed by Bruce Rogers, the designer. Introduction by A.A. Milne, illustrated by Arthur Rackham $1000.

S11: Steinbeck, John THE GRAPES OF WRATH 1940. 2 vols. 1,146 cc. Signed by

Thomas Hart Benton, the illustrator. Introduction by Joseph Henry Jackson and Thomas Craven $800.

S12: Jackson, Joseph Henry WHY STEINBECK WROTE *THE GRAPES OF WRATH* Booklets For Bookman LEC NY (1940) [0] Wraps. Also includes essays by Carter Meredith and A.A. Milne $30.

S13: TEN YEARS AND WM. SHAKESPEARE, *A Survey of The Publishing Activities of The Limited Editions Club From October 1929 to October 1940* (1940) $25.

S14: A RECORD OF THE PROCEEDINGS AT THE LIMITED EDITIONS CLUB'S DINNER TO CELEBRATE THE TWENTY-FIRST BIRTHDAY OF THE CLUB & THE FIFTIETH BIRTHDAY OF IT'S FOUNDER 1950. 3,000 cc. Includes photographs of dinner $20.

S15: Robert, Maurice and Frederic Warde A CODE FOR THE COLLECTOR OF BEAUTIFUL BOOKS 1936 $50.

S16: TO EDWARD F. FOLLEY, THE LEC ON THE OCCASION OF IT'S 21ST BIRTHDAY PRESENTS THIS GREETING IN TOKEN OF IT'S APPRECIATION FOR AND ADMIRATION OF THE BIBLIOGRAPHICAL ACTIVITIES OF THIS HONORED CHARTER MEMBER DURING ALL OF THE CLUB'S 21 YEARS 1950. Laminated plastic broadside printed in two colors enclosed in a special marbled paper covered box $40.

S17: BIBLIOGRAPHY OF THE FINE BOOKS PUBLISHED BY THE LIMITED EDITIONS

CLUB 1929-1985 New York City (1985) 800 no. cc. In print at $300 $300.

Following is an index of the authors, illustrators, etc. for your convience

INDEX

JACK LONDON
(1876 - 1916)

John Griffith London was born in San Francisco, the illegitimate son of an itinerant Irish astrologer (W.H. Chaney) whom London never met. His mother married John London when Jack was eight months old.

London grew up along the Oakland waterfront but was a heavy reader at an early age. He was guided to better literature by the librarian of the Oakland Public Library, Ina Coolbrith (Poet Laureate of California).

At fifteen he went on the road as a tramp. At sixteen he was an oyster-pirate and longshoreman near San Francisco Bay; and then a seaman on a sealing schooner in the north Pacific. He joined Coxey's Army at eighteen and went East by hopping freight trains. He spent 30 days in jail for vagrancy in Pennsylvania.

He returned to California and joined the Socialist Labor Party. When gold was discovered in the Klondike he was off to find it but only brought back material for later books.

In 1899 the "Atlantic Monthly" bought a long story "An Odssey of the North" and Houghton Mifflin offered him a contract for a volume of short stories (*The Son of The Wolf*). He married Bessie Maddern in 1900 and divorced her in 1905 to marry Charmian Kittredge.

The Call of The Wild was the first book to bring him broad recognition, which was to lead to his being called the highest paid, best-known and most popular writer in the world by 1913. His 50 books made him over a million dollars which he managed to spend on lavish hospitality and building (or rebuilding after a fire destroyed) his Wolf House, among other extravagances.

On slow days he covered the Russo-Japanese War, ran for mayor of Oakland on the Socialist ticket, sailed the "Snark" to Hawaii; and pioneered in agriculture and livestock breeding at Wolf House.

He died of a morphine overdose in 1916 at the age of 40.

REFERENCES:

The primary reference for this guide was ref.a which carried through 1965 and contains detailed bibliographical descriptions including the first print run quantities.

(a) Blanck, Jacob BIBLIOGRAPHY OF AMERICAN LITERATURE Vol. 5 Yale University Press New Haven 1969 (through 1965 unless otherwise stated).

(b) Sisson, James E. III & Robert W. Martens JACK LONDON FIRST EDITIONS Star Rover House Oakland 1979.

(c) Inventory, dealer catalogs, etc.

Note: Estimated prices are for fine copies without dustwrapper until 1920. Dustwrappers would, of course, increase the values shown substantially.

001a: THE SON OF THE WOLF ... Houghton, Mifflin Boston/NY 1900 [0] Three trial bindings are known (No priority):

Binding A: Rough grass-green V cloth, stamped in silver (one known copy) $3,500.

Binding B: Greenish-black V cloth, stamped in silver $3,500.

Binding C: White buckram stamped in red only $3,500.

001b: THE SON OF THE WOLF ... Houghton, Mifflin Boston/NY 1900 [0] Wraps. 19cc possibly for review $7,500.

001c: THE SON OF THE WOLF ... Houghton, Mifflin Boston/NY 1900 [0] 2,028 cc First printing. Gray cloth stamped in silver. Pagination (i-viii); no blank leaf following p(252); collation: 1(4), 2-22(6) $1,000.

001d: THE SON OF THE WOLF ... Houghton, Mifflin Boston/NY 1900 [0] 1,010 cc. Second printing. Gray cloth stamped in silver. Pagination: (i-vi) blank leaf following p(252) $600.

001e: THE SON OF THE WOLF ... Houghton, Mifflin Boston/NY 1900 [0] 763 cc of third printing. Same as second except collation differs: 1-21(6), 22(4) $350.

001f: THE SON OF THE WOLF ... Houghton, Mifflin Boston/NY 1900 [0] 241 cc of third printing. Cover in green V cloth stamped in white and red with illustration of man in arctic dress on front cover $350.

001g: THE SON OF THE WOLF ... A.P. Watt London 1900 [0] 6cc. Cancel title page of first printing $1,500.

001h: THE SON OF THE WOLF ... Isbister & Co. London 1902 [0] Copyright page blank. Red cloth stamped in gold on front and spine, spine imprint "Pitman," gold stamped design on spine, blind stamp design on front. Collation: (i-viii), (1)-251, (251-253) ads including *God of His Father* and Gorky's *Three Men*. (Ref.c) $600.

001i: AN ODYSSEY OF THE NORTH Mills & Boon London 1913 [0] $150.

001j: AN ODYSSEY OF THE NORTH Mills and Boon London (no-date) [] Published 1915 $100.

001k: AN ODYSSEY OF THE NORTH Haldemann Julius Co. Gerard, KS (1920) [0] Wraps. "Little Blue Book No. 1022." Cover title "A Heroic Tale of The Far North" (ref.c) $35.

001l: THE SON OF THE WOLF ... Haldemann Julius Co. Girard, KS (1920) [0] Wraps. "Little Blue Book No. 152" $35.

002a: THE GOD OF HIS FATHERS + McClure, Phillips NY 1901 [0] $750.

002b: THE GOD OF HIS FATHERS Isbister London 1902 [] $300.

002c: THE GOD OF HIS FATHERS Mills and Boon London 1915 [] $100.

003a: CHILDREN OF THE FROST Macmillian NY/London 1902 [0] Wraps. Pagination: (i-iv), (1)-263. Printed for copyright purposes $2,500.

003b: CHILDREN OF THE FROST Macmillan NY/London 1902 [1] 3,466 cc. "Set Up And Electrotyped September, 1902" $650.

003c: CHILDREN OF THE FROST Macmillan London 1902 [] $250.

003d: CHILDREN OF THE FROST Mills & Boon London (1915) [] 1915 (ref.a). (Boston Book Annex catalogued a copy with a 1917 copyright?) $100.

004a: THE CRUISE OF THE DAZZLER Century Co. NY 1902 [1] "Published October, 1902" $1,750.

004b: THE CRUISE OF THE DAZZLER Hodder & Stoughton London 1906 [] $450.

004c: THE CRUISE OF THE DAZZLER Mills & Boon London 1915 [] $125.

005a: A DAUGHTER OF THE SNOWS J.B. Lippincott Phila. 1902 [1] "Published October, 1902." Another copy noted exactly the same except the words "Second Edition" added on first half title (ref.c) $600.

005b: A DAUGHTER OF THE SNOWS Isbister London 1904 [] $150.

006a: THE KEMPTON - WACE LETTERS Macmillan NY/L 1903 [1] "Set Up And Electrotyped May 1903." Anonymous, neither London's nor co-author Anna Strunsky's name appears $600.

006b: THE KEMPTON - WACE LETTERS Macmillan NY/L 1903 [] Second printing had author's names on title page $250.

006c: THE KEMPTON - WACE LETTERS Isbister London 1903 [] $250.

006d: THE KEMPTON - WACE LETTERS Mills and Boon London 1921 [] $150.

007a: THE CALL OF THE WILD Macmillan NY/L 1903 [0] Wraps. 2 known copies. Presumably issued to secure copyright $4,000.

007b: THE CALL OF THE WILD Macmillan NY/L 1903 [1] 71,584 cc. "Set Up, Electrotyped and Published July 1903." Top edge gilt in all references, but we had one without gilt, no priority. (Catalogued at $1,500 to $2,250 in dustwrapper) $750.

007c: THE CALL OF THE WILD Heinemann London 1903 [0] $400.

007d: THE CALL OF THE WILD George N. Morang Toronto 1903 [0] Blue green cloth. Macmillan bought Morang in 1906 and reissued the Morang 1905 sheets in binding stamped "Macmillan" at foot of spine, which may have been the first book issued by Macmillan (David Mason 10/89) $350.

007e: THE CALL OF THE WILD Limited Editions Club NY 1960 [2] 1,500 sgd no. cc. Illustrated and signed by Henry Varnum Poor, issued without dustwrapper in slipcase $75/150

007f: THE CALL OF THE WILD Franklin Library Franklin Center 1977 [2] "Limited Edition" in full leather. One of the 100 Greatest Masterpieces... Illustrated by David J. Passalacqua $50.

008a: THE PEOPLE OF THE ABYSS Macmillan NY/L 1903 [1] 3,982 cc. "Published October, 1903" 850.

008b: THE PEOPLE OF THE ABYSS Isbister London 1903 [] $250.

009a: THE FAITH OF MEN + Macmillan NY/L 1904 [1] 6,802 cc. "Set Up, Electrotyped, and Published April, 1904" $500.

009b: THE FAITH OF MEN + Heinmann London 1904 [] $175.

010a: THE BANKS OF THE SACRAMENTO Daily Mail Publishing Office London 1904 [0]

Wraps. 12 leaves prepared for copyright purposes $1,500.

011a: THE TRAMP Wilshire's Magazine NY no-date [0] Published in 1904. Earliest issue with publisher's addresses 125 E. 2304 St, NY Later issue gives publisher's address as 200 Williams St., NY (not before 1905) $450.

011b: THE TRAMP Charles Kerr Chicago (no-date circa 1904) [] Wraps. (Maurice F. Neville List K) $200.

012a: THE SEA-WOLF Macmillan NY/L 1904 [0] Title-page not a cancel; copyright notices dated 1904 only. Only one copy of this state $3,000.

012b: THE SEA-WOLF Macmillan NY/L 1904 [1] 63,339 cc. Title page is a cancel; copyright notices dated 1903 and 1904. "Published October, 1904." Some copies stamped in gold on spine - some in white (includes a copy of 012a. MacDonnell Rare Books 12/90). No known priority $350.

012c: THE SEA-WOLF Heinemann London 1904 [0] $125.

012d: THE SEA-WOLF Limited Editions Club Hartford 1961 [2] 1,500 sgd and no. cc. Illustrated and signed by Fletcher Martin. Issued without dustwrapper in slipcase $50/100

013a: THE SCAB Charles H. Kerr Chicago (no-date) [0] Wraps. Published in 1905, reprinted from the *Atlantic Monthly*. Reprinted several times; earliest issue has publisher's address as 56 5th Ave., Chicago. Later printings have other addresses or none on title page $400.

014a: WAR OF THE CLASSES Macmillan NY/L 1905 [1] 2,530 cc. "Published April, 1905" $650.

014b: WAR OF THE CLASSES Macmillan NY/L 1905 [0] Wraps. Presumes simultaneous issue $500.

014c: WAR OF THE CLASSES Heinemann L 1905 [] $250.

014d: WAR OF THE CLASSES Mills & Boon L (1905) Actually published in 1920 [] $100.

015a: THE GAME Macmillan NY/L 1905 [1] 26,420 cc (a&b) "Published June 1905." First issue does not have *Metropolitan Magazine* rubber stamp on copyright page. (4 copies with dustwrappers were catalogued 1990-1992 at $1,000, $1,750, $2,400 and $3,500) $250.

015b: THE GAME Macmillan NY/L 1905 [0] "Published June 1905." Rubber stamped on copyright page "Copyright, 1905, by the *Metropolitan Magazine* Co." Two forms of stamp known, no priority: 1/16" tall and 3/32" tall $150.

015c: THE GAME Heinemann L 1905 [] $175.

015d: THE GAME Morang & Co. Toronto 1905 [] $150.

016a: TALES OF THE FISH PATROL. Macmillan NY/L 1905 [1] 8,392 cc. "Published September, 1905" $450.

016b: TALES OF THE FISH PATROL Heinemann L 1906 [] $150.

017a: WHITE FANG Macmillan NY/L 1905 [0] Gray paper wraps. "Printed for copyright purposes only" $1,500.

017b: WHITE FANG Macmillan NY/L 1906 [1] 48,195cc (b&c). "Published October, 1906." Presumed earliest state with title-leaf integral (One copy in dustwrapper catalogued at $1850.) $250.

017c: WHITE FANG Macmillan NY/L 1906 [1] "Published October, 1906." Presumed later state with title leaf tipped-in $150.

017d: WHITE FANG Methuen L 1907 [] $125.

017e: WHITE FANG Limited Editions Club Lutenburg, Vt. 1973 [2] 2,000 sgd no. cc Illustrated and signed by Lydia Dabcovich. Issued without dustwrapper in slipcase $40/75

018a: WHAT COMMUNITIES LOSE BY THE COMPETATIVE SYSTEM Twentieth Century Press London (no-date) [] Wraps. Published 1906 $350.

019a: CIRCULATE "THE JUNGLE" DEAR COMRADES: HERE IT IS AT LAST! Jungle Publishing Co. NY (1906) [0] Open letter urging support for Sinclair's *The Jungle*. Single leaf, 6" x 3 1/2", printed on verso only $250.

019b: THE BOOKS OF UPTON SINCLAIR... Jungle Publishing Co. NY (no-date) [0] Wraps. Published in 1906. Single sheet folded to 8 pages. Pale yellow paper. 6 5/16" x 4 1/2". Full text of an open letter $150.

019c: A TERRIBLE BOOK...APPEAL TO REASON Girard, KS (no-date) [0] Wraps. Single sheet folded to 6 pages. 5 7/8" x 3 7/16". Contains full text of open letter $75.

019d: THE JUNGLE... (Jungle Publishing Co. NY) (no-date) [0] Wraps. 1906? single sheet folded to 4 pages. 6 1/4" x 3 1/2" 1st printing: Price of *The Jungle* on p.(4) given as $1.35 Extract of open letter on p.(1) $100.

019e: THE JUNGLE...(Jungle Publishing Co. NY) (no-date) [0] Wraps. 1906? Single sheet folded to 4 pages. 6 1/4" x 3 1/2" 2nd printing: Price of *The Jungle* on p.(4) given as $1.20. Extract of open letter on p.(1) $75.

019f: A NEW EDITION OF THE JUNGLE (Upton Sinclair) (Pasendena, CA) (no-date) [0] Wraps. Circa 1920. Single sheet folded to 4 pages. Brown paper. 1st printing: London's open letter on p.(4); imprint on p.(3) $40.

019g: A NEW EDITION OF THE JUNGLE (Upton Sinclair) (Pasendena, CA) (no-date) [0] Wraps. Circa 1920. Single sheet folded to 4 pages. Brown paper. 2nd printing: London's open letter on pp.(3-4); imprint on p.(4) $30.

019h: A NEW EDITION OF THE JUNGLE (Upton Sinclair) (Pasadena, CA) (no-date) [0] Wraps. A Single sheet folded to 4 pages. Brown paper. 6 3/4" x 4 7/16". Full text of open letter on pp.(2-3); imprint on p.(4) $25.

019i: "THE JUNGLE IS GOING SPLENDIDLY..." Jungle Publishing Co. Princeton, NJ (no-date) [0] Single sheet. Printed on verso only. 5 13/16" x 3 7/16" Private letter. 1st printing $25.

019j: "THE JUNGLE IS GOING SPLENDIDLY..." Jungle Publishing Co. NY (no-date) [0] Single sheet printed on verso only. 5 3/4" x 3 9/16". Private letter. 2nd printing $25.

020a: MOONFACE + Macmillan NY/L 1906 [1] Wraps. "Published (blank), 1906" Printed for copyright purposes. Printed tan paperwraps $1,000.

020b: MOONFACE + Macmillan NY/L 1906 [1] 8,400 cc. "Published September, 1906" $350.

020c: MOONFACE + Heinemann L 1906 [] $150.

020d: MOONFACE + Regent Press NY (1906) Actually published 1915 Reprint/reissue $50.

021a: LOVE OF LIFE + Macmillan NY/L 1906 [1] Wraps. Prepared for copyright purposes only. On copyright page: "Published (blank), 1906" $1,000.

021b: LOVE OF LIFE + Macmillan NY/L 1907 [1] 7,973 cc. "Published September, 1907" $350.

021c: LOVE OF LIFE + Everett & Co. L 1908 [] $125.

021d: LOVE OF LIFE + Mills & Boon L 1916 [] $60.

022a: BEFORE ADAM Macmillan L/NY 1906 [1] Wraps. Prepared for copyright purposes. Tan paperwraps. "Published (blank), 1906" on copyright page $1,000.

022b: BEFORE ADAM Macmillan NY/L 1907 [1] "Published February, 1907." (One copy in dustwrapper catalogued for $3,000.) $200.

022c: BEFORE ADAM Werner Laurie L (1908) [] $75.

023a: THE APOSTATE ... APPEAL TO REASON Girard, KS 1906 [0] Wraps. Salmon colored wraps $300.

023b: THE APOSTATE... Charles H. Kerr Chicago (no-date) [0] $75.

023c: THE APOSTATE... Haldeman-Julius Co. Girard, KS (no-date) [0] Wraps. Published 1924? Little Blue Book No. 640 $30.

023d: HE RENOUNCED THE FAITH People's Pocket? Girard, KS (no-date) [0] Wraps. Published 1920. People's Pocket Series No. 47 $30.

024a: SCORN OF WOMEN Macmillan NY/L 1906 [1] 920 cc. "Published November, 1906." Top edges gilt. "The Macmillan Company" on spine $2,000.

024b: SCORN OF WOMEN Macmillan NY/L 1906 [0] "Published November, 1906." Variant binding with top edges plain; "Macmillan" on spine. Remainder binding? $1,500.

024c: SCORN OF WOMEN Macmillan L 1907 [0] $450.

025a: JACK LONDON HIS LIFE & LITERARY WORK Macmillan NY 1906 [] Wraps. Text entirely written by London (Pepper & Stern List N) $200.

026a: WHAT LIFE MEANS TO ME (Intercollegiate Socialist Society Princeton, NJ) (no-date) [0] Wraps. Published 1906. On p.(4) is imprint of Appeal to Reason Press, Girard, KS $400.

026b: WHAT LIFE MEANS TO ME Charles Kerr Chicago (no-date) [0] Wraps. Not issued before 1912 $175.

026c: JACK LONDONS WHAT LIFE MEANS TO ME (no-publisher San Fran. 1916) [0] Wraps. "Memorial Edition" $150.

026d: WHAT LIFE MEANS TO ME Haldeman & Julius Co. Girard, KS (1924) [0] Wraps. Little Blue Book No. 30 $25.

027a: THE IRON HEEL Macmillan NY/L 1907 [1] Wraps. Tan paper dustwrapper printed for copyright purposes only $1,000.

027b: THE IRON HEEL Macmillan NY/L 1908 [1] 12,472 cc. "Published February, 1908" $400.

027c: THE IRON HEEL Appeal to Reason Girard, KS 1908 [1] "Published February, 1908." Macmillan sheets with tipped in title page and spine without Macmillan although otherwise the same $250.

027d: THE IRON HEEL Wilshire Book Co. NY 1908 [0] $60.

027e: THE IRON HEEL Everett L 1908 [] $100.

027f: THE IRON HEEL Mills & Boon L 1916 [] $50.

028a: THE ROAD Macmillan NY 1907 [1] 5,360 cc (a&b). "Published November, 1907." Gray cloth stamped in gold and black $500.

028b: THE ROAD Macmillan NY 1907 [0] "Published November 1907." Variant binding (possible remainder) stamped in black only, top edges not gilt $350.

028c: THE ROAD Mills & Boon L 1914 [] $150.

029a: MARTIN EDEN Macmillan NY 1908 [1] Wraps. Printed for copyright purposes only. Tan paper dustwrapper. "Published (blank), 1908" on copyright page $1,000.

029b: MARTIN EDEN M.A. Donohue Co. Chicago 1908 [] (ref.c) $300.

029c: MARTIN EDEN Macmillan NY 1909 [1] 17,309 cc. "Published September 1909" $400.

029d: MARTIN EDEN Heineman L 1910 [] $125.

030a: A BRIEF EXPLANATION (no-publisher Hobart, Tasmania? 1909?) [0] Wraps. Mimeographed (press release?) statement $300.

031a: REVOLUTION Charles H. Kerr Chicago (1909) [0] Wraps. Ads on p.(32) headed: "A Socialist Success" Publisher's address: 118 Kinzie Street. Terminal ads $350.

031b: REVOLUTION Charles H. Kerr Chicago (1909) [0] Wraps. Ads on p.(32) headed: "Pocket Library of Socialism." Publishers address in terminal ads: 118 W. Kinzie Street $300.

031c: REVOLUTION Charles H. Kerr Chicago (1909)[] P.32 headed "Socialist Periodicals" address is "118 West Kinsie" (Kevin MacDonnell #1) $250.

031d: REVOLUTION Charles H. Kerr Chicago (1909) [0] Wraps. Ads on p.(32) Headed: "Study Socialism" $175.

031e: REVOLUTION Charles H. Kerr Chicago (1909) [0] Wraps. Ads on p.32 headed: "Socialist Literature" $125.

032a: GLEN ELLEN, SONOMA CO., CA... (Prison Reform League L.A. 1910) [0] Single leaf letter printed on letterhead of Prison Reform League 8 7/16" x 5 1/2" $300.

033a: LOST FACE Macmillan NY 1910 [1] 6,954 cc. "Published March, 1910" $300.

033b: LOST FACE Mills & Boon. L (no-date) (1915) [] $75.

034a: REVOLUTION + Macmillan NY 1910 [1] 2,130 cc (a&b). "Published March, 1910." Maroon cloth stamped in gold and blind stamped. "The Macmillan Company" on spine. Terminal ads (priority listed as probable in BAL) $450.

034b: REVOLUTION + Macmillan NY 1910 [0] "Published March 1910." Variant: brown cloth, stamped in black, "Macmillan" on spine, no ads $300.

034c: REVOLUTION + Mills & Boon L 1920 [] $125.

035a: BURNING DAYLIGHT Macmillan NY 1910 [1] 27,108 cc (a&b). "Published October 1910." First printing: One blank leaf follows P(374); At foot of spine "Macmillan" or "The|Macmillan|Company" - no clear priority. The latter reported by Merle Johnson but no copy seen by Blanck. Blanck felt this might have been an advance printing rather than the first. (Two copies in dustwrapper catalogued at $675 and $1,100) $300.

035b: BURNING DAYLIGHT Macmillan NY 1910 [1] "Published October 1910." Second printing: 3 blank leaves follow p.(374); at foot of spine "Macmillan" or "The | Macmillan Company" - No clear priority $150.

035c: BURNING DAYLIGHT Heinemann L 1911 [] $100.

035d: BURNING DAYLIGHT Land's End... (Chicago 1911) [0] Wraps. A synopsis and reprint of portions of novel with letter from London granting permission to publish $100.

036a: THEFT Macmillan NY/L 1910 [1] 990 cc. "Published November 1910." Maroon cloth sides, white cloth shelfback, top edges gilt. Variant: Olive and red cloth, front cover plain, author's name and book title in rectangular box at top of spine. Also noted in plain gray cloth, lettered in black on spine (Calif. Book auction 2/89) and yellow-tan cloth (ref.c). Also in pale lavender cloth with plain top edges and front unstamped (Robert Dagg 3/91) and "pinkish T" cloth (Waiting For Godot 9/92) $1,750.

037a: BUNCHES OF KNUCKLES (The New York Herald Paris 1910) [0] Wraps. Christmas Supplement. Sunday December 18, 1910 $350.

038a: WHEN GOD LAUGHS + Macmillan NY 1911 [1] 3,758 cc. "Published January 1911" $450.

038b: THE CHINAGO + Leslie-Judge Co. NY (1911) [] Reprints seven stories from 38a under new title $100.

038c: WHEN GOD LAUGHS + Mills & Boon L 1912 [] $150.

039a: ADVENTURE Thomas Nelson & Sons L | Edinburgh | Dublin | Leeds | NY | Leipzig | Paris (1911) [1] "First published in 1911." (February) $600.

039b: ADVENTURE Macmillan NY 1911 [1] 14,600 cc. "Published March 1911." Blue cloth stamped in white and Blue. Variant: red cloth stamped in white $300.

039c: ADVENTURE Mills & Boon L 1916 [] $100.

040a: THE CRUISE OF THE SNARK Macmillan NY 1911 [1] 4,265 cc. "Published June 1911" $450.

040b: THE CRUISE OF THE SNARK Mills & Boon L 1913 [] $150.

041a: THE STRENGTH OF THE STRONG Charles H. Kerr & Co Chicago (1911) [0] First book edition (also see 059). White paperwraps printed in blue, publisher's address: 118 West Kinzie Street, Chicago. Note: Reprints can be identified by the following - 1912 date on title, or with publisher's address as 341-349 E. Ohio Street and/or text ending on p.29 (vs. 30 in first) $125.

041b: THE STRENGTH OF THE STRONG Haldeman-Julius Girard, Ks. (no-date) [0] Wraps. Little Blue Book 148. 64 pages without title page (Watermark West 11/90) $25.

042a: SOUTH SEA TALES Macmillan NY 1911 [1] 4,974 cc. "Published October, 1911" $400.

042b: SOUTH SEA STORIES Heinemann L 1911 [ ] Listed, but ever published? $NVA

042c: SOUTH SEA TALES Mills & Boon L 1912 [] $100.

042d: SOUTH SEA TALES World Cleveland|NY (1946) [1] "First Printing March 1946" $15/60

043a: NORTH OF BAY COUNTIES CALIFORNIA... (no-publisher, place or date) [0] Wraps. Circa 1911. 9 3/8" x 6 1/2". Illustrated $250.

044a: JACK LONDON GLEN ELLEN SONOMA CO., CALIF..U.S.A.... (no-publisher, place or date) [0] Single cut sheet folded to make 4 pages. Printed in blue on blue-gray paper. Page size 6 5/16" x 3 1/2". (Directions for getting to Glen Ellen etc) $250.

045a: THE HOUSE OF PRIDE + Macmillan NY 1912 [1] 4,340 cc. "Published March 1912." Fern green cloth. Variant: Dark green cloth $450.

045b: THE HOUSE OF PRIDE + Mills & Boon L 1914 [] $125.

046a: A SON OF THE SUN Doubleday, Page GC, NY 1912 [0] $300.

046b: A SOUVENIR CHAPTER OF ... A SUN OF THE SON Mills & Boon L (1913) [0] Wraps. First eight pages of text $100.

046c: A SON OF THE SUN. Mills & Boon L 1913 [] $75.

046d: THE ADVENTURES OF CAPTAIN GRIEF (World Cleveland|NY 1954) [0] A reprint under a different title $10/40

047a: WONDER OF A WOMAN A "Smoke Bellew" Story International Magazine Co. NY (1912) [0] Wraps. The text of the magazine appearance slightly altered in the book (next entry) $400.

047b: WONDER OF A WOMAN ... (Wolf House Books Michigan 1975) [] 1,000 cc in stapled wraps (Waiting For Godot L-1) $35.

048a: SMOKE BELLEW The Century Co. NY 1912 [1] "Published, October 1912." Blue-green pictorial cloth. Variant: in plain gray-blue cloth $350.

048b: SMOKE BELLEW Mills & Boon L 1913 [] $100.

049a: THE SCARLET PLAGUE Paul R. Reynolds NY 1912 [0] Printed blue paperwraps. Presumably printed for copyright purposes $1,000.

049b: THE SCARLET PLAGUE Macmillan NY 1915 [1] 5,105 cc. "Published May 1915" $300.

049c: THE SCARLET PLAGUE. Mills & Boon, L 1915 [] $100.

050a: THE DREAM OF DEBS. A STORY OF INDUSTRIAL REVOLT. BY JACK LONDON Charles H. Kerr Chicago (no-date) (not before 1912) [0] Wraps. 7 1/4" x 5" Presumed first issue. Back wrappers "History of the Supreme Court ..." Inner wrappers unprinted $250.

050b: THE DREAM OF DEBS BY JACK LONDON Charles H. Kerr Chicago (no-date) [0] Wraps. Circa 1912. 5 13/16" x 5 1/8" Presumed second issue. Back wrapper: "Books by Jack London..." Note: Later printing(s): p.(32)

has publisher's ads; outer back wrapper headed: "Study Socialism" $175.

051a: THE NIGHT-BORN.... Century Co. NY 1913 [1] "Published February, 1913." First printing: 1 blank leaf follows p.(292); bound in polished gray-blue cloth, gold stamped on front and spine except for black stamped totem poles $200.

051b: THE NIGHT-BORN... Century Co. NY 1913 [1] "Published February 1913." Second printing: 2 blank leaves follow p.(292); bound in unpolished blue-gray cloth, stamped in blue, totem poles blind stamped on front and spine $75.

051c: THE NIGHT-BORN... Century Co. NY 1913 [1] "Published February 1913." Third printing: 2 blank leaves follow p.(292); binding as in first printing. Variant: 2 blank leaves follow p.(292); bound in light gray cloth, blind stamped totem poles on front cover and with letters on front cover, spine printed in black (ref.c) $40.

051d: THE NIGHT-BORN... Mills & Boon L 1916 [] $75.

052a: HOW WILL YOUR VOTE EFFECT THIS BOY? (no-publisher Fresno, CA 1913) [0] Wraps. Single sheet folded to make 4 pages, 8 1/2" x 5 1/2" $300.

053a: THE VALLEY OF THE MOON Reprinted from *Cosmopolitan Magazine* for April NY 1913 [0] Wraps. First installment of novel, not located by BAL $450.

053b: THE VALLEY OF THE MOON Macmillan NY 1913 [1] 23,779 cc. "Published October 1913" $200.

053c: THE VALLEY OF THE MOON (Mills & Boon L 1914) [1] Noted in both green and blue cloths First edition states "Published 1914" (Glyn's 9/91). Reprints read "Published in 1914" (Robert Temple 11/91) $100.

053d: THE VALLEY OF THE MOON (publisher?) Santa Barbara 1975 [] $25.

054a: THE ABYSMAL BRUTE The Century Co. NY 1913 [1] "Published May 1913." Smooth olive-green cloth stamped in black (deep-green?) and yellow. (4 copies in dustwrapper catalogued in 1990 at $1000, $1250, $1500 and $2200) $200.

054b: THE ABYSMAL BRUTE The Century Co. NY 1913 [0] Variant binding in rough green cloth stamped in black and green $175.

055a: JOHN BARLEYCORN The Century Co. NY 1913 [1] "Published August, 1913." First printing: 1 blank leaf follows p.(343). Also noted with 2 blank leaves in front and 2 in back (Greg Brumfield) $175.

055b: JOHN BARLEYCORN The Century Co. NY 1913 [0] "Published August, 1913." Second printing: 3 blank leaves follow p.(343) $60.

055c: JOHN BARLEYCORN Mills & Boon L (1914) [] $75.

056a: JACK LONDON BY HIMSELF... Macmillan NY (no-date) [0] Printed self-wrapper. Published 1913. Cover title printed black and red 7 1/4" x 5 5/16" $200.

056b: JACK LONDON BY HIMSELF Mills & Boon L 1913 [] Wraps. Primarily promotes *The Valley of the Moon*. Later printing primarily promotes *The Mutiny of the Elsinore* $150.

056c: JACK LONDON: THE AUTHOR WITH SALES Mills & Boon L (circa 1915) [] 8 stapled pages recycling material from a&b above (Waiting for Godot 10/89) $75.

057a: JACK LONDON SAYS: (Hellier Denslow Studio L 1913) [0] Wraps. Single leaf folded to make 4 pages. Page size: 5 7/16" x 3 11/16". Issued as an advertisement. Includes comments on bookplate design $200.

058a: A LETTER FROM JACK LONDON Glen Ellen Sonoma County, Ca. April 15, 1913 (no-publisher, place or date) [0] 1913? Single cut sheet. 8 3/16" x 7 1/8". Testimonial for an antiseptic $100.

059a: THE STRENGTH OF THE STRONG Macmillan NY 1914 [1] 3,948 cc. "Published May 1914." Also see 041 $450.

059b: THE STRENGTH OF THE STRONG Mills & Boon L 1917 [0] $125.

060a: THE GOOD SOLDIER (no-publisher, place or date) (circa 1914?) [] Broadside urging young men not to enlist. London denied authorship (catalogued by Waiting For Godot 4/89) $175.

061a: THE MUTINY OF THE ELSINORE Macmillan NY 1914 [1] 16,884 cc. "Published September, 1914." Also noted with front board unstamped (Katie Books 11/91) $400.

061b: THE MUTINY OF THE ELSINORE Mills & Boon L (1915) [] $150.

061c: THE MUTINY OF THE ELSINORE Nelson L 1916 [] $40.

THE SCARLET PLAGUE see 1912 entry (item 049)

062a: THE JACKET (THE STAR ROVER) Mills & Boon L (1915) [1] "Published 1915" $350.

062b: JACK LONDON : THE AUTHOR WITH THE SALES Mills & Boon Ltd. L 1915 [] 8 pages. Illustrated with photographs $125.

062c: THE STAR ROVER Macmillan (NY 1915) [] Wraps. Prospectus. 8 page booklet (Bert Babcock 6/89) $125.

062d: A NEW IDEA IN FICTION: THE STAR ROVER Macmillan NY (no-date) (1915) [] Pictorial wraps (London photo). 4 pages. Sketch of London's life with blurbs on 28 of his books (Joseph The Provider 3/89) $125.

062e: THE STAR ROVER Macmillan NY 1915 [1] 13,021 cc. "Published October, 1915." (Two copies in dustwrapper catalogued in 1990-92 at $3,500 and $4,500) $350

062f: THE STAR ROVER AUTOBIOGRAPHICAL INTRO Macmillan/Collier: Macmillan NY/L (1963) [] Same as *Jack London By Himself* (056) $40.

063a: THE ACORN-PLANTER Macmillan NY 1916 [1] 1,350 cc. "Published February, 1916." Three forms of binding, no known priority. (A copy in dustwrapper, binding unspecified, catalogued for $3,850)

Spine lettered: THE | ACORN | PLANTER | JACK | LONDON | The | Macmillan | Company. Top edges gilt $1,250.

Spine lettered: THE | ACORN | PLANTER | JACK | LONDON Top edges gilt (publisher's spine imprint worn away?) $1,250.

Spine lettered: THE | ACORN | PLANTER | (3 dots) | JACK | LONDON | The | Macmillan | Company. Top edges gilt $1,250.

063b: THE ACORN-PLANTER Mills & Boon L (1916) [] $300.

064a: THE RESIGNATION OF JACK LONDON DEAR COMRADES: (no-publisher, place or date) [0] Single cut sheet. 1916. 11" x 8 1/2" printed in imitation of typewritten letter. (Text of his resignation from Socialist Party) $200.

065a: THE LITTLE LADY OF THE BIG HOUSE Macmillan NY 1916 [1] 18,448 cc. "Published April 1916." Variant: Copyright notices read "Copyright 1915 | by Jack London | copyright, 1916 | by Jack London." BAL also notes a "variant" with 1915 on title page. This would seem to us to be an advance copy and would be worth considerably more than the 1916 $250.

065b: THE LITTLE LADY OF THE BIG HOUSE Mills & Boon L (1916) [] $100.

065c: THE LITTLE LADY OF THE BIG HOUSE Nelson L 1916 [] $50.

066a: AN OLD LIE FINALLY NAILED (no-publisher, place or date) [0] Wraps. Published 1916. Single sheet folded to make 4 pages 7 1/16" x 4" $300.

067a: THE TURTLES OF TASMAN Macmillan NY 1916 [1] 5,914 cc. "Published September, 1916." $500.

067b: THE TURTLES OF TASMAN Mills & Boon L (1916) [] $150.

068a: THE HUMAN DRIFT Macmillan NY 1917 [1] 3,056 cc. "Published, February, 1917." Red-brown cloth stamped on spine and front. Also in reddish brown cloth stamped in gold on spine but with blank front cover (Robert Dagg 3/91). Ref.a notes a variant in smooth red linen stamped on spine only but in black $500.

068b: THE HUMAN DRIFT Mills & Boon L (1919) [] $200.

069a: JERRY: JACK LONDON'S LAST GREAT STORY (Cosmopolitan Magazine, no-place, Feb. 1917) [] 8 pages in stapled wraps. First separate appearance of the first installment of *Jerry of The Islands*, which was serialized from January to April 1917 (Waiting For Godot 2/90) $400.

070a: JERRY OF THE ISLANDS Macmillan NY 1917 [1] 13,024 cc. "Published, April, 1917." (Two copies in dustwrapper catalogued 1990-92 at $600 and $970) $175.

070b: JERRY OF THE ISLANDS Mills & Boon L (1917) [] $75.

071a: MICHAEL BROTHER OF JERRY Macmillan NY 1917 [1] 10,320 cc. "Published, November, 1917." $200.

072a: EIGHT GREAT FACTORS OF LITERARY SUCCESS (no-publisher, place or date) [0] Single cut sheet 8 7/16" x 6" printed on recto only. Published 1917. Includes a holograph facsimile signature of London $350.

073a: THE RED ONE Macmillan NY 1918 [1] 5,342 cc. "Published, October, 1918." (One copy in dustwrapper catalogued for $2500) $750.

073b: THE RED ONE Mills & Boon L (1919) [] $250.

074a: HEARTS OF THREE Mills & Boon L (no-date) [] Published 1918. Note: Later printing on p.(iv) under "Books by Jack London" lists *Island Tales* $200.

074b: HEARTS OF THREE Macmillan NY 1920 [0] 4,990 cc. "Published, September, 1920" $450.

074c: HEARTS OF THREE Macmillan NY 1928 [] ("The Sonoma Edition." Reprint) (Alphabet Bookshop cat 18) $50.

075a: ON THE MAKALOA MAT Macmillan NY 1919 [1] 4,972 cc. "Published, September 1919" $400.

075b: ISLAND TALES Mills & Boon L (1920) [0] "Published 1920" $175.

076a: SMOKE AND SHORTY Mills & Boon L (1920) [1] "Published 1920" $200/600

077a: HE RENOUNCED THE FAITH Appeal to Reason (no-date) [0] Wraps. "People's Pocket Series No. 47." Published 1920 $150.

078a: BROWN WOLF AND OTHER STORIES.. Macmillan NY 1920 [0] $250/750

079a: TALES OF THE FAR NORTH Haldeman-Julius Girard, KS (1920) [0] Wraps. "Little Blue Book No. 288" $40.

080a: DUTCH COURAGE + Macmillan NY 1922 [1] 4,348 cc. "Published September 1922" $400/1,750

080b: DUTCH COURAGE + Mills & Boon L (1923) [] $200/1,000

081a: STORIES OF SHIPS AND THE SEA Haldeman & Julius Co. Girard, KS (1922) [0] Wraps. Little Blue Book No. 1169 (cover title *Tales of Ships and Seas* ref.c). Printed blue paperwraps. Earliest printing has date "1922" present in copyright notice. Date absent in later printing(s). All stories are also in *Dutch Courage* +, priority unknown $75.

082a: TALES OF THE WHITE SILENCE Haldeman-Julius Girard, KS (no-date) [0] Wraps. Little Blue Book No. 1024" Published 1926? $35.

083a: THE WIFE OF A KING Haldeman-Julius Girard, KS (no-date) [0] Wraps. "Little Blue Book No. 233." Published 1926? $35.

084a: THE CALL OF THE WILD + Macmillan NY 1926 [0] Leather shelfback $25/125

084b: THE CALL OF THE WILD + Dodd, Mead NY (1960) [] $10/50

084c: THE CALL OF THE WILD, THE CRUISE OF THE DAZZLER + Platt & Munk NY (1960) [] $10/50

085a: LONDON'S ESSAYS OF REVOLT Vanguard NY 1926 [0] Edited and introduction by Leonard D. Abbott. First thus. Includes *Apostate*, *Dream of Debs*, *How I Became A Socialist*, *What Life Means To Me*, *The Scab* and *Revolution* $40/200

086a: STORIES OF ADVENTURE Haldeman-Julius Girard, KS [0] Wraps. "Little Blue Book NO. 1168." Published 1927? $40.

087a: SELECTED STORIES OF JACK LONDON World Syndicate | Three Pay Sales | NY | Cleveland 1930 [] $40/200

087b: SELECTED STORIES OF JACK LONDON World Publ | Leslie Publ | Cleveland | B 1930 [] In tissue and printed dustwrapper. No publisher but has "NY | 1933" on spine (Joseph The Provider 3/88). Also noted in unprinted brown paper dustwrapper and printed dustwrapper with "1933" on spine (Beasley Books 2/90) $25/125

088a: THE SEA SPRITE AND THE SHOOTING STAR. (Privately Published, no-place, 1932) [0] Single cut sheet folded to make 4 pages 10 3/4" x 5 3/4" cream-white paper $150.

089a: THE LETTERS OF WESTERN AUTHORS NUMBER 12 December 1935 Jack London with comment by Charmain Kittredge London, Book Club of California (SF 1935) [0] Wraps. Single cut sheet folded to 4 pages 9 15/16" x 8 1/4". Pasted to p.(3) is envelope containing a facsimile Jack London letter printed on sleaves $75.

090a: CHAPTER V OF *THE IRON HEEL*... Socialist Labor Party of Australia Sydney 1936 [] Wraps. First separate edition $150.

091a: JACK LONDON'S STORIES FOR BOYS Cupples & Leon NY (1936) [] $15/60

092a: BEST SHORT STORIES OF JACK LONDON Sun Dial Press Garden City, NY (1945) [] $15/60

093a: LOVE OF LIFE + Paul Gleck L (1946) [0] Introduction by George Orwell. "1946 | Catalogue No. 159/9" on copyright page (ref.c) $30/150

094a: JACK LONDON AMERICAN REBEL Citadel Press NY 1947 [0] Contains first book appearance of some of the essays (ref.c) $25/100

095a: FOUR SHORT STORIES Longmans Green L/NY/Toronto (1949) [] Wraps $40

096a: THE SUN-DOG TRAIL + World Cleveland/NY (1951) [1] $15/75

097a: JACK LONDON'S TALES OF ADVENTURE Hanover House Garden City (1956) [] (Waiting For Godot Cat.15) $15/75

098a: SHORT STORIES Hill & Wang NY (1960) [] Wraps $25.

099a: THE BODLEY HEAD JACK LONDON The Bodley Head L (1963) [] $15/75

100a: WHITE FANG + Dodd, Mead NY (1963) [] $12/60

101a: THE ASSASSINATION BUREAU, LTD. McGraw-Hill NY/Toronto/L (1963) [] Gally in loose sheets, ring bound in plain boards (William Reese Co. 11/91) $500.

101b: THE ASSASSINATION BUREAU, LTD. McGraw-Hill NY/Toronto/L (1963) [1] 2,500 cc $15/75

101c: THE ASSASSINATION BUREAU, LTD. McGraw-Hill NY/Toronto/L (1963) [1] 10,000 cc. Wraps $25.

101d: THE ASSASSINATION BUREAU, LTD. Deutsch L (1964) [] (Maurice Neville List Q) $15/75

102a: THE SEA-WOLF SELECTED STORIES New American Library (NY 1964) [1] Wraps $25.

103a: STORIES OF HAWAII Appleton-Century NY (1965) [1] $12/60

104a: LETTERS FROM JACK LONDON CONTAINING AN UNPUBLISHED CORRESPONDENCE BETWEEN LONDON AND SINCLAIR LEWIS... Odyssey Press NY (1965) [0] $15/75

104b: LETTERS FROM JACK LONDON ... L 1966 [] Edited by Ring Hendricks and Irving Shepard (Peter Ellis 12/89) $12/60

105a: GREAT SHORT WORKS Harper & Row NY (1965) [] $10/50

106a: TO BUILD A FIRE Evelyn Woods Reading Dynamics (no-place, 1966) [] Wraps. (Waiting For Godot Cat L-1) $30.

106b: TO BUILD A FIRE (Tales For Travelers Napa, CA 1986) [] Single sheet folded map style (Boston Book Annex Cat. 31) $30

107a: JACK LONDON REPORTS Doubleday Garden City, NY 1970 [1] 4,109 cc. Edited by Ring Hendricks and Irving Shepard (ref.b) $15/75

108a: DAUGHTERS OF THE RICH Holmes Book Co Oakland 1971 [1] 1,000 cc (Pepper & Stern) $25/75

108b: DAUGHTERS OF THE RICH Holmes Book Co Oakland 1971 [1] 2,900 cc. Wraps (ref.b) $30.

109a: JACK LONDON'S ARTICLES AND SHORT STORIES IN THE (OAKLAND) HIGH SCHOOL REGIS THE LONDON COLLECTOR Cedar Springs 1971 [1] 300 cc. Wraps. Issued as "The London Collector No. 3." Errata slip attached to Front page of first printing (ref.b) $60.

110a: GOLD. A PLAY IN THREE ACTS Holmes Book Co. Oakland 1972 [1] 1,000 cc. Written with Herbert Heron (ref.b) $10/40

110b: GOLD Holmes Book Co. Oakland 1973 [2] 100 cc. "Illustrated Limited Issue" (ref.c) $175.

111a: JACK LONDON AT YALE (Wolf House Books Michigan 1972) [] Facsimile of 1906 edition. 28 pages in stapled wraps (Waiting For Godot L-1) $30.

112a: GOLIAH: A UTOPIAN ESSAY Thorp Springs Press Berkeley, CA (no-date) [] Wraps. Published 1973 (first published in *Revolution* ++). Edited by Dale L. Walker. Preface by Philip Jose Farmer (Watermark West Cat.8) $40.

113a: CURIOUS FRAGMENTS... Kennkat Press Port Washington 1975 [] (Pepper & Stern List M) $40.

114a: THE SCIENCE FICTION OF JACK LONDON Gregg Press B 1975 [] 400 cc. Issued without dustwrapper (L.W. Currey 8/92) $65.

115a: DEAR MATE Holmes Book Co. Oakland 1976 [2] 300 cc. Wraps. London's inscriptions to Charmain in his books $75.

116a: SELECTED SCIENCE FICTION & FANTASY STORIES Fictioneer Books (Lakemont, GA 1978) [0] Annotated by Dick Weiderman, illustrated by Philip Craig Russell (ref.c) $10/40

117a: JACK LONDON ON THE ROAD: THE TRAMP DIARY + Utah State Univ. Press. Logan, Utah (1979) [] (Waiting For Godot L-1) $10/40

118a: NO MENTOR BUT MYSELF A COLLECTION OF ARTICLES, ESSAYS, REVIEWS ... Kennikat Press. Port Washington 1979 [] Edited by Dale L. Walker $12/60

119a: IF JAPAN WAKENS CHINA Modern Times Takoma 1979 [] Wraps (Maurice F. Neville List K) $40.

120a: SPORTING BLOOD Presidio Press (Novato, CA 1981) [0] Selections of London's sprots writings edited by Howard Lachtman (ref.c) $10/40

121a: DEAREST GREEK Eureka Publ Cupertino, CA (1983) [] 500 cc in stapled wraps. Jack and Charmain's presentation inscriptions to George Sterling. Edited and introduction by Stanley Wertheim and Sal Noto (Waiting For Godot L-1) $30.

122a: LEARNING HAWAIIAN SURFING Boom Enterprises Hawaii 1983 [] Wraps. "Hawaiian Memorial Edition" (Waiting For Godot L-1) $35.

123a: A KLONDIKE TRILOGY ... Neville Santa Barbara 1983 [2] 26 ltr cc. Bound in full leather with autographed check of Jack London tipped-in $750.

123b: A KLONDIKE TRILOGY ... Neville Santa Barbara 1983 [2] 300 cc. Issued without dustwrapper $75.

124a: TOLD IN THE DROOLING WARD Jack London Research Center Glen Ellen, Ca 1984 [2] 1,000 signed cc. Wraps. Signed by the editor (Waiting For Godot) $30.

125a: FIVE POEMS Quintessence Amador City? 1984 [2] 250 cc. Wraps (Maurice Neville List Q) $60.

126a: WITH A HEART FULL OF LOVE... Two Windows Press Berkeley, Ca 1986 [2] 351 cc. Issued without dustwrapper (Pepper & Stern List U) $75.

127a: JACK LONDON'S CALIFORNIA: THE GOLDEN POPPY + Beaufort Books NY (1986) [] (Beasley Books Cat. 36) $10/35

128a: IN FAR COUNTRY... Jameson Books Ottawa, Il 1986 [] (Beasley Books Cat. 36) $10/35

129a: THE LETTERS OF JACK LONDON Stanford Univ. Press Stanford 1988 [] Advance proofs in three spiral bound volumes (James Dourgarian 5/90) $150.

129b: THE LETTERS OF JACK LONDON 1896-1916 Stanford Univ. Press Stanford 1988 [] Edited by E. Labor, R.C. Leitz and I.M. Shepard $10/50

130a: TO BUILD A FIRE and THE MEXICAN Engdahl Typegraphy Vineland, CA 1989 [2] 200 sgd cc (Signed by Lee Engdahl, printer) $60.

131a: THE JACK LONDON CREDO Quintessence Press Amador City 1991 [2] 200 cc. Illustrated broadside (Chloe's Books 12/91) $25.

ROBERT LUDLUM

Ludlum was born in New York City in 1927 and served in the Marine Corps from 1945 to 1947. He graduated from Wesleyan University in 1951. Ludlum acted on the stage and television, as well as producing stage plays through 1969 when he took up writing full-time. He also writes as Jonathan Ryder and Michael Shepherd.

001a: THE SCARLATTI INHERITANCE World NY (1971) [1] Printed acetate dustwrapper. (The Book-of-the-Month Club edition states "First..." It does have a blind stamp on back cover right corner but it is easy to overlook). First has "A3696" on back of dustwapper and Book Club has "0360" on back. Also text on first dustwrapper starts 1/4 inch from top of front flap while Book Club starts 3/4 inch from the top (Allan Asselstine) $35/175

001b: THE SCARLATTI INHERITANCE Hart Davis London (1971) [] $20/100

001c: THE SCARLATTI INHERITANCE Armchair Detective NY 1991 [2] 26 sgd ltr cc. Issued without dustwrapper in slipcase $125.

001d: THE SCARLATTI INHERITANCE Armchair Detective NY 1991 [2] 100 sgd no cc. Issued without dustwrapper in slipcase $75.

002a: THE OSTERMAN WEEKEND World NY (1972) [1] Printed acetate dustwrapper, priced $6.95 with "A 3918" on bottom right corner of back panel. Also noted "First Printing" copies with "7452" where price should be and same number (A 3918) on back; and "First Printing" copies with no price and "7452" at bottom right corner of back panel of dustwrapper. The latter two editions do not have Book-of-the-Month dots but the covers of the book are smoother and lighter blue than the true first. $25/125

002b: THE OSTERMAN WEEKEND Hart Davis London 1972 [] $15/75

002c: THE OSTERMAN WEEKEND Armchair Detective NY 1991 [2] 100 sgd no cc. Issued without dustwrapper in slipcase $75.

003a: THE MATLOCK PAPER Dial Press NY 1973 [1] $15/75

003b: THE MATLOCK PAPER Hart Davis MacGibbon London (1973) [1] $12/60

004a: TREVAYNE Delacorte NY (1973) [1] Written as Jonathan Ryder $40/200

004b: TREVAYNE Weidenfeld & Nicolson London 1974 [] $25/125

005a: THE CRY OF THE HALIDON Delacorte NY (1974) [1] Written under the name Jonathan Ryder $15/75

005b: THE CRY OF THE HALIDON Weidenfeld & Nicolson London 1974 [] Written under the name Jonathan Ryder $12/60

006a: THE RHINEMANN EXCHANGE Dial Press NY 1974 [1] $12/60

006b: THE RHINEMANN EXCHANGE Hart Davis MacGibbon London 1975 [] $10/50

007a: THE ROAD TO GANDOLFO Dial Press NY 1975 [1] Written as Michael Shepherd. Generally seen with three dustwrappers designed by Tom Upshur (blue), Jack Ribik (dark blue), and David Holzman (purple-plum). The latter seems more common to us, but have no idea of priority.

One jacket	$15/50
Two jackets	$15/60
Three jackets	$15/100

007b: THE ROAD TO GANDOLFO Hart Davis MacGibbon London 1976 [] $15/75

008a: THE GEMINI CONTENDERS Dial Press NY 1976 [1] $10/50

008b: THE GEMINI CONTENDERS Hart Davis MacGibbon London 1976 [] $8/40

009a: THE CHANCELLOR MANUSCRIPT Dial Press NY 1977 [] Uncorrected proof in brown printed wraps (Bev Chaney 2/89) $90.

009b: THE CHANCELLOR MANUSCRIPT Dial Press NY 1977 [1] $10/50

009c: THE CHANCELLOR MANUSCRIPT Hart Davis MacGibbon London 1977 [ ] $8/40

010a: THE HOLCROFT COVENANT Marek NY (1978) [] Uncorrected proof in green wraps $75.

010b: THE HOLCROFT COVENANT Marek NY (1978) [1] $10/50

010c: THE HOLCROFT COVENANT Hart Davis Granada / MacGibbon London 1978 [] $8/40

011a: THE MATARESE CIRCLE Marek NY (1979) [1] $8/40

011b: THE MATARESE CIRCLE Granada London 1979 [ ] $7/35

012a: THE BOURNE IDENTITY Marek NY (1980) [0] $8/40

012b: THE BOURNE IDENTITY Granada London 1980 [1] "Published by ... 1980" $7/35

013a: THE PARSIFAL MOSAIC Random House NY (1982) [4] Signed tipped in sheet $40/75

013b: THE PARSIFAL MOSAIC Random House NY (1982) [4] $7/35

013c: THE PARSIFAL MOSAIC Granada London (1982) [1] "Published by Granada Publishing 1982" $7/35

014a: VIEWPOINT: UNRAVELING THE MYSTERIES OF TRAVELS American Express Member Only Newsletter For Oct. 1982 [0] Wraps. Front page and part of last page (of 4 pages). For the completist $15.

015a: THE AQUITAINE PROGRESSION Random House NY (1984) [4] $7/35

015b: THE AQUITAINE PROGRESSION Granada London (1984) [1] "Published by Granada ... 1984" $7/35

016a: THE ROBERT LUDLUM SAMPLER (Bantam NY 1984) [3] Wraps. No title page.

Excerpts from nine novels. Short note to the reader from Ludlum on first page $10.

017a: THE BOURNE SUPREMACY Random House NY (1986) [] Uncorrected proof in yellow wraps (Wavery Books 4/89) $75.

017b: THE BOURNE SUPREMACY Franklin Press Franklin Center 1986 [2] "Limited Signed Edition". Full leather with special message $60.

017c: THE BOURNE SUPREMACY Random House NY (1986) [4] $6/30

017d: THE BOURNE SUPREMACY Grafton London (1986) [1] "Published by Grafton ... 1986" $6/30

018a: THE ICARUS AGENDA Random House NY (1988) [] Uncorrected proof in yellow wraps (Waverly Books 3/89) $50.

018b: THE ICARUS AGENDA Random House NY (1988) [4] 500,000 cc (PW). (Published 3/88 @ $19.95) $6/30

019a: THE BOURNE ULTIMATUM Random House NY 1990 [] Uncorrected proof in yellow wraps (Waverly Books 3/90) $50.

019b: THE BOURNE ULTIMATUM Random House NY 1990 [2] 350 sgd no cc. Issued without dustwrapper in slipcase $75/125

019c: THE BOURNE ULTIMATUM Random House NY 1990 [] $5/25

NORMAN MAILER

Norman Mailer was born in Long Branch, New Jersey on January 31, 1923. He obtained an engineering degree from Harvard University in 1943; and attended the Sorbonne, Paris in 1947. He served in the Army in WWII (1944 to 1946). As well as writing, he was the Co-Editor of *Dissent* magazine from 1952 to 1963 (and is still a contributing editor); and Co-Founding Editor of the *Village Voice*. He ran for mayor of New York City in 1968. He won a Pulitzer Prize and National Book Award for non-fiction with *The Armies of The Night* in 1969; and a Pulitzer in fiction for *The Executioner's Song* in 1980.

There is much more that could be said about the man so many expected would write the "Great American Novel;" but most of this man's accomplishments and failures have been highlighted by either himself or the press; probably highlighted more than any other writer of the second half of this century.

The bulk of the bibliographical information furnished herein was provided by J. Michael Lennon, Director and Professor of English at Sangamon State University, who edited *Conversations With Norman Mailer* (entry no. 047). The printing quantities are estimates furnished by Mailer. We would also like to thank Thomas Fiske and Charles Michaud for their assistance.

In addition to these items there are a number of publicity handouts, position papers and notes to workers that were generated during the NYC mayoral campaign. We have seen these catalogued in the $50 to $100 range. How many of these, if any, were actually written by Mailer is unclear but they would certainly reflect his thoughts and opinions and would presumedly have been approved by him.

REFERENCES:

(a) Lennon, J. Michael. Collection.

(b) FIRST PRINTINGS OF AMERICAN AUTHORS Vol.5 Matthew J. Bruccoli and E.E. Frazer Clark, Jr., editors Gale Research Co. Detroit, Michigan (1987).

(c) Inventory, dealer catalogs, etc.

001a: THE FOUNDATION Privately published California 1943-44 [] Wraps. Mimeographed. Also published as "A Calculus at Heaven" in *Cross-Section: A Collection of American Writing*, edited by Edwin Seaver. N.Y., L.B. Fisher, 1944. Later reprinted in *Advertisements For Myself* $750.

Mailer APG 114.1 copr. Dec. 1992 [page 1]

002a: THE NAKED AND THE DEAD Rinehart NY 1948 [5] Advance Reading Copy bound in red and black wrappers with flaps as in final dustwrapper $750.

002b: THE NAKED AND THE DEAD Rinehart NY/T (1948) [5] 25,000 cc. Black boards with white lettering, in red and black dustwrapper priced $4.00 with Mailer's picture on back panel $100/500

002c: THE NAKED AND THE DEAD Wingate L 1949 [2] Collector's Book Club issue, using sheets of first English edition and issued simultaneously with it. 253 copies with 240 numbered. In full leather, issued without dustwrapper $600.

002d: THE NAKED AND THE DEAD Wingate L (1949) [1] $40/200

002e: THE NAKED AND THE DEAD Franklin Library Franklin Center, PA 1979 [2] 10,000 cc. Signed by Mailer, Includes "A special message to subscriber from Norman Mailer" $100.

003a: BARBARY SHORE Rinehart NY 1951 [5] Advance copy. Perfect bound in wraps used for trade edition dustwrapper. Copies with both variants of dustwrapper also noted (see below) $450.

003b: BARBARY SHORE Rinehart NY/T (no-date) [5] 20,000 cc Black boards with white lettering. Two dustwrappers on first edition apparently issued simultaneously: red and black; red and green $50/250

003c: BARBARY SHORE Cape L (1952) [] (ref.b) $20/100

003d: BARBARY SHORE Cape L (1971) [ ] Adds "Note from the Author" by Mailer reprinted from *Advertisements for Myself* $10/40

004a: THE DEER PARK Putnam NY (1955) [] Uncorrected galley proofs in narrow 4to wraps with printed label $400.

004b: THE DEER PARK Putnam NY (1955) [0] 25,000 cc. Black cloth with green lettering. Two dustwrappers noted on first editions: author's name in orange, word "Park" in green; reverse of this. Priority unknown $40/200

004c: THE DEER PARK Wingate L (1957) [1] $20/100

004d: THE DEER PARK (Berkley NY 1976) [] Wraps. "Berkley Windhover Edition, NOVEMBER, 1976" A 3264. New preface and notes by Mailer. The "Notes" consist of "Fourth Advertisement For Myself: The Last Draft of *The Deer Park*" and "Postscript to the Fourth Advertisement For Myself", both reprinted from *Advertisements For Myself* $35.

005a: THE WHITE NEGRO City Lights Books (SF 1957) [0] Black and white wrappers. 8 5/8" x 5 3/4". Front cover: 35 cents $200.

005b: THE WHITE NEGRO City Lights Books (SF 1957) Later printings (front cover): 50 cents $40.

006a: ADVERTISEMENTS FOR MYSELF Putnam NY (1959) [0] Advance uncorrected proof (galleys). Perfect bound in tall dark green wraps with label on front $400.

006b: ADVERTISEMENTS FOR MYSELF Putnam NY (1959) [0] 10,000 cc. Red and black cloth, red and gold lettering $25/125

006c: ADVERTISEMENTS FOR MYSELF Deutsch (L 1961) [ ] New edition. Abridged (by about 40 pages). Black cloth with gold lettering, in red, black and orange dustwrapper $15/75

006d: ADVERTISEMENTS FOR MYSELF Berkley (NY 1976) [] Wraps. Copyright page: "G.P. Putnam/Berkley Windhover Edition, DECEMBER 1976" B 3282. New edition with a new preface by Mailer $30.

007a: DEATHS FOR THE LADIES AND OTHER DISASTERS Putnam NY (1962) [0] 5,000 cc. Black and white cloth with white lettering in black and white dustwrapper $50/250

007b: DEATHS FOR THE LADIES AND OTHER DISASTERS Putnam NY (1962) [0] Simultaneously published in wraps $50.

007c: DEATHS FOR THE LADIES AND OTHER DISASTERS Deutsch (L 1962) [] Wraps. No hardbound U.K. edition (David Rees 2/92) $50.

007d: DEATHS FOR THE LADIES AND OTHER DISASTERS New American Library (NY 1971) [1] Wraps. Signet Book W4853. Adds an intro by Mailer $25.

008a: THE PRESIDENTIAL PAPERS Putnam NY (1963) [0] Advance edition dustwrapper is purple and white with orange and white lettering; no blurbs, text (except title, author) or photos $25/200

008b: THE PRESIDENTIAL PAPERS Putnam's NY (1963) [0] 10,000 cc. First and second impression dustwrappers have photo of Mailer in J.F.K. style rocker $25/75

008c: THE PRESIDENTIAL PAPERS Deutsch (L 1964) [] New preface by Mailer, probably the special preface to Bantam edition $15/60

008d: THE PRESIDENTAL PAPERS Bantam NY (1964) [1] Wraps. Copyright page: "A Bantam Book|published May 1964." S2727. Contains "Special Preface to Bantam Edition" (noting J.F.K.'s death) $30.

008e: THE PRESIDENTIAL PAPERS "Berkley Windhover Edition, OCTOBER, 1976" [] Wraps. A 3243. New edition. Adds another new preface by Mailer $20.

009a: GARGOYLE, GUIGNOL, FALSE CLOSET (Dolmen Press Dublin 1964) [2] 2 pages. 100 cc. Scarce. Reprinted from *Architectural Forum, 120* (April 1964), pp.96-97 $300.

010a: AN AMERICAN DREAM Dial Press NY 1965 [0] 50,000 cc. Red, white and blue dustwrapper containing head shot of Mailer's fourth wife, Beverly Bentley. Blue cloth spine and gray boards, silver lettering; or full blue cloth. (Thomas Fiske believes that blue cloth is second. Charles Michaud has seen a blue cloth first that was inscribed in month of publication {3/65}) $12/60

010b: AN AMERICAN DREAM Deutsch (L 1965) [] Advance uncorrected proof in blue printed wraps (Dalian 5/90) $150.

010c: AN AMERICAN DREAM Deutsch (L 1965) [] (ref.b) $12/60

010d: AN AMERICAN DREAM Warner Brothers (LA 1966) [] Screenplay by Mann Rubin based on the novel by Mailer . Pinned self-wraps with printed label dated 3/1/66 (Serendipity) $400.

011a: CANNIBALS AND CHRISTIANS Dial Press NY 1966 [0] Review cc consisting of gathered signatures, ring bound, preceded publication. Also spiral bound 4to printed galleys with changes on slips pasted over original (Joseph The Provider 9/90. The same?) $400.

011b: CANNIBALS AND CHRISTIANS Dial Press NY 1966 [0] 10,000 cc. First issue has color photograph of Vertical City (Lego Block architectural model built by Mailer), same as on dustwrapper, tipped-in on page opposite title page (frontis) $30/75

011c: CANNIBALS AND CHRISTIANS Dial Press NY 1966 [0] Photograph frontis is printed $10/40

011d: CANNIBALS AND CHRISTIANS Deutsch (L 1967) [] Maroon cloth, gold lettering (ref.b) $10/50

011e: CANNIBALS AND CHRISTIANS Granada L/T/S/NY (1979) [] Wraps. Panther book. Abridged edition (ref.b) $20.

012a: THE DEER PARK A PLAY Dell NY (1967) [1] Wraps. $60.

012b: THE DEER PARK A PLAY Dial NY 1967 [1] Black cloth, gold lettering in red, white and black dustwrapper $20/100

012c: THE DEER PARK A PLAY Weindenfeld & Nicolson L (1970) [1] (ref.c) $12/60

013a: THE BULLFIGHT CBS Legacy Collection/MacMillan (NY 1967) [0] 5,000 cc Maroon boards, gold lettering, white dustwrapper and housed in a clear plastic box. Accompanied by 33 1/3 r.p.m. record of Mailer reading from the text and a poem by Garcia Lorca. Text contains bullfight photos. Very scarce with record. (Full leather burgundy binding in dustwrapper. Fine Books 1/92) $150/250

013b: THE BULLFIGHT CBS Legacy Collection/MacMillan (NY 1967) [0] Without record $35/125

014a: THE SHORT FICTION OF NORMAN MAILER Dell (NY 1967) [1] Wraps. 10,000 cc. "First Dell Printing - May 1967." #7850 $40.

014b: THE SHORT FICTION OF NORMAN MAILER Weidenfeld & Nicolson L 1969 [] (Charles Michaud has seen a listing for this but never seen the book and we haven't either $NVA

015a: WHY ARE WE IN VIETNAM? Putnam NY (1967) [1] 50,000 cc. Blue cloth, gold lettering, red, white and black dustwrapper. Includes a dedication to six of Mailer's friends. The name of one of these friends, Buzz Farber, was misspelled as Buzz Farbar? This edition was apparently recalled and the dedication page excised. The dedication was restored in three American paperback reprintings but does not appear in the hardback "first" editions per ref.a. However, corrected tipped-in dedications do show up in some copies (see below) $200/225

015b: WHY ARE WE IN VIETNAM? Putnam NY (1967) [1] With tipped-in corrected dedication page (Thomas Fiske and Charles Michaud) $100/125

015c: WHY ARE WE IN VIETNAM? Putnam's NY (1967) [1] Without dedication page $10/40

015d: WHY ARE WE IN VIETNAM? Weidenfeld & Nicolson L (1969) [] (ref.b) $10/50

015e: WHY ARE WE IN VIETNAM? Putnam/Berkely (NY 1977) [] Wraps. " G.P. Putnam's Sons|Berkley Windhover Edition, January, 1977." Adds a new preface by Mailer (ref.b) $25

016a: TRIAL OF THE WARLOCK Playboy Shueisha, Japan 1977 [] Screenplay adaption of J.K. Husyman's 1891 novel *La-Bas*. The Japanese volume was translated from the *Playboy* issue of December 1976. Gray brown cloth, red and white dustwrapper. The only cloth bound edition $50/200

017a: THE ARMIES OF THE DEAD New American Library NY (1968) [] Narrow galleys, ring bound, with original title $300.

017b: THE ARMIES OF THE NIGHT. HISTORY AS A NOVEL, THE NOVEL AS HISTORY New American Library (NY 1968) [1] 35,000 cc. Published May 6, 20 years to the day after *The Naked and The Dead*. Black cloth, white lettering, in white, red and black dustwrapper. Pulitzer Prize and National Book Award for non-fiction in 1969 $12/60

017c: THE ARMIES OF THE NIGHT Weidenfeld & Nicolson L (1968) [1] Light green cloth with black lettering, in white and black dustwrapper $15/50

018a: THE IDOL AND THE OCTOPUS POLITICAL WRITINGS... ON THE KENNEDY AND JOHNSON ADMINISTRATIONS Dell (NY 1968) [1] Wraps. 10,000 cc. "First Printing - June, 1968." #3952 $40.

019a: MIAMI AND THE SEIGE OF CHICAGO AN INFORMAL HISTORY OF THE REPUBLICAN AND DEMOCRATIC CONVENTIONS OF 1968 New American Library (NY 1968) [1] Wraps. "First Printing, October 1968." Signet Special Q3785 $40.

019b: MIAMI AND THE SIEGE OF CHICAGO AN INFORMAL HISTORY OF THE REPUBLICAN AND DEMOCRATIC CONVENTIONS OF 1968 World NY/Cleveland (1968) [1] 15,000 cc. "First printing, October 1968." Black cloth with red lettering, in red,white and blue dustwrapper. Assume issued simultaneously $15/75

019c: MIAMI AND THE SIEGE OF CHICAGO AN INFORMAL HISTORY OF THE AMERICAN POLITICAL CONVENTIONS OF 1968 Weidenfeld & Nicolson L (1968) [] New title (ref.b) $15/60

020a: NATIONAL BOOK AWARD IN ARTS & lETTERS 1969 ACCEPTANCE SPEECH (National Book Awards NY 1969) [0] Two sheets, stapled $125

021a: RUNNING AGAINST THE MACHINE Doubleday Garden City, NY 1969 [] Edited by Peter Manso. Compilation of papers and articles from the Norman Mailer-Jimmy Breslin New York Democratic mayoral primary. Several speeches and articles by Mailer not published elsewhere. Also one paragraph dedication by Mailer to campaign staff. Simultaneously published in cloth and wrappers. Red cloth with black lettering, in black dustwrapper with red and white lettering $30/100

021b: RUNNING AGAINST THE MACHINE Doubleday Garden City, NY 1969 [] Wraps $35.

022a: A FIRE ON THE MOON Weidenfeld & Nicholson L (1970) [0] $15/50

022b: OF A FIRE ON THE MOON Little, Brown Boston/T (1971) [1] 25,000 cc. Green cloth with gold lettering $10/40

022c: OF A FIRE ON THE MOON Little, Brown Boston/T (1971) [] With a signed tipped-in leaf (Waiting For Godot 4/90) $50/75

023a: KING OF THE HILL New American Library (NY 1971) [1] Wraps. "First Printing, April 1971." Signet Special N 4787 $40.

024a: MAIDSTONE. A MYSTERY New American Library (NY 1971) [1] Wraps. "FIRST PRINTING, OCTOBER 1971." Signet Film Series W4782 $35.

025a: THE PRISONER OF SEX Little, Brown Boston/T (1971) [] Uncorrected proof in printed wrappers preceded publication (ref.c) $250.

025b: THE PRISONER OF SEX Little, Brown Boston/T (1971) [1] 10,000 cc. Green boards, gold lettering,in gold and white dustwrapper. Note: inside front flap of dustwrapper contains price ($5.95 on first edition only) $10/40

025c: THE PRISONER OF SEX Weidenfeld & Nicholson L (1971) [] (ref.b) $10/40

026a: THE LONG PATROL, 25 YEARS OF WRITING ... World/Times Mirror NY (1971) [1] Edited by Robert F. Lucid. Selections from 13 of Mailer's works $15/50

027a: EXISTENTIAL ERRANDS Little, Brown Boston/T (1972) [1] 10,000 cc. Yellow and black boards with gold lettering, in white dustwrapper $10/40

028a: ST. GEORGE AND THE GODFATHER New American Library (NY 1972) [1] Wraps. "First printing, September, 1972." Signet special W5122 $35.

028b: ST. GEORGE AND THE GODFATHER Arbor House NY (1983) [3] First hardback edition. Copyright 1972 but rear flap of dustwrapper has "9-83" so, assume 1983 publication $10/35

029a: MARILYN, A PREVIEW Grosset & Dunlap NY (1972) [] 12 page promotional pamphlet (Astoria Books 4/90) $40.

029b: MARILYN, A BIOGRAPHY Grosset & Dunlap NY 1973 [2] Limited signed edition in white cloth and publisher's black clam shell case. Signed by Lawrence Shiller (the book's "producer") as well as Mailer. No limitation quantity stated $200/300

029c: MARILYN, A BIOGRAPHY (Grosset & Dunlap NY 1973) [1] 100,000 cc. Tan cloth with gold lettering. (There were also 125,000 Book Club copies) $20/60

029d: MARILYN, A BIOGRAPHY (Grosset & Dunlap NY 1973) [] Second printing in white plastic(?) Signed by Mailer but no limitation (Charles Michaud) $40/60

029e: MARILYN, A BIOGRAPHY (Hodder & Stoughton L 1973) [] (ref.b) $20/60

029f: MARILYN, A BIOGRAPHY Warner NY 1975 [1] Wraps. Includes new final chapter "The Murder File" $40.

030a: THE 1974 MARILYN MONROE DATEBOOK Alskog (LA 1973) [0] Spiral bound wraps $40

031a: THE FAITH OF GRAFFITI Praeger NY 1974 [2] Limited to 350 cc. signed by all three contributors (Mailer, Mervyn Kurlansky and Jon Naar, photographers). 14 inch folio in cloth slipcase $75/150

031b: THE FAITH OF GRAFFITI Alskog/Praeger NY (1974) [1] Brown cloth in green dustwrapper. The title and copyright page are the same and appear twice, on the verso of the front free endpaper and the recto of the rear free endpaper $20/75

031c: THE FAITH OF GRAFFITI Alskog/Praeger NY (1974) [1] Wraps $20.

031d: WATCHING MY NAME GO BY (Mathews Miller Dunbar L 1974) [1] $15/75

031e: WATCHING MY NAME GO BY (Mathews Miller Dunbar L 1974) [1] Wraps $20.

032a: THE FIGHT Little, Brown Boston/T (1975) [1] 20,000 cc. Black cloth, silver lettering $10/40

032b: THE FIGHT Hart-Davis, MacGibbon L (1976) [0] $10/40

033a: GENUIS AND LUST. A JOURNEY THROUGH THE MAJOR WRITINGS OF HENRY MILLER Grove NY (1976) [1] Tan cloth, blue lettering. 80 pages of commentary by Mailer, 500 pages of Miller excerpts. Dustwrapper drawing of Miller by Norris Church Mailer (his sixth wife) $20/50

034a: SOME HONORABLE MEN POLITICAL CONVENTIONS 1960-1972 Little, Brown Boston/T [1] 10,000 cc. Original preface, rest of book reprinted for *Presidential Papers*, *Cannibals*, *Miami* and *St. George*. Blue cloth with silver lettering, in black and white dustwrapper $8/40

035a: A TRANSIT TO NARCISSUS Howard Fertig NY 1978 [1] Uncorrected proof in creme colored wraps $150

035b: A TRANSIT TO NARCISSUS Howard Fertig NY 1978 [1] 1,000 cc. Tan cloth with black lettering $12/60

036a: THE EXECUTIONERS SONG Little, Brown Boston/T (1979) [1] Uncorrected Advance Proof in blue wrappers $200.

036b: THE EXECUTIONERS SONG Little, Brown Boston/T (1979) [1] 100,000 copies. Blue cloth, silver and gold lettering in blue, black and gold dustwrapper. Pulitzer Prize in Fiction for 1980 $10/40

036c: THE EXECUTIONERS SONG Hutchison (L 1979) [] (ref.b) $10/40

036d: THE EXECUTIONER'S SONG The Execution's Song Production Co. LA 1981 [0] 197 pages (only recto numbered). Green wrappers, pin bound. Shooting draft of screenplay, September 25 $300.

036e: THE EXECUTIONER'S SONG Lawrence Schiller Productions Hollywood 1981 [] 4to punch bound sheets in printed covers (Antic Hay 5/91)

i. 150 pages. Feature draft $250.
ii. 196 pages. Corrected second draft $250.
iii. 197 pages. Shooting draft $250.

037a: OF A SMALL AND MODEST MALIGNANCY WICKED AND BRISTLING WITH DOTS Lord John Press Northridge 1980 [2] 100 sgd no. cc. Deluxe edition on Curtis Rag and bound in leather. Issued without dustwrapper in slipcase. First appeared in *Esquire* Nov. 1977 $150/250

037b: OF A SMALL AND MODEST MALIGNANCY WICKED AND BRISTLING WITH DOTS Lord John Press Northridge 1980 [2] 300 sgd no cc on Mohawk Superfine and bound in cloth. Issued without dustwrapper in slipcase $50/100

038a: OF WOMEN AND THEIR ELEGANCE Simon & Schuster NY (1980) [] Loose pages with sample photograph laid in publisher's box with differences from published book (George Robert Minkoff 6/90) $300.

038b: OF WOMEN AND THEIR ELEGANCE Simon & Schuster NY (1980) [3] Photographs by Milton H. Greene $20/60

038c: OF WOMEN AND THEIR ELEGANCE Hodder & Stoughton L / Sydney / Auckland / Toronto (1980) [] Sheets of the American edition (ref.b) $20/50

039a: PIECES AND PONTIFICATIONS Little, Brown Boston/T (1982) [1] Uncorrected proof in blue wraps with "Pontification" misspelled on title page $200

039b: PIECES AND PONTIFICATIONS Little, Brown Boston/T (1982) [1] Bound uncorrected proof in tan wrappers with price ($22.95) and 448 pages. Also noted in creme wraps (Lame Duck Books 9/91) $100.

039c: PIECES AND PONTIFICATIONS Little, Brown Boston/T (1982) [1] Purple cloth with silver lettering in white, green and purple dustwrapper $10/35

039d: PIECES Little, Brown Boston/T (1982) [1] Blue wraps. Republished in two volumes $20.

039e: PONTIFICATIONS Little, Brown Boston/T (1982) [1] White wraps. Edited by Michael Lennon $20.

039f: PIECES AND PONTIFICATIONS New English Library (L 1983) [1] Black cloth with gold lettering in red, tan, white and black dustwrapper (ref.b) $10/35

040a: THE ESSENTIAL MAILER New English Library Kent 1982 [] First Bristish edition of *The Short Fiction of Norman Mailer* and *Existential Errands*, which are combined in this edition. Green-blue cloth with silver lettering in red, white, blue and black dustwrapper $10/35

041a: ANCIENT EVENINGS Little, Brown Boston/T (1983) [] Uncorrected proof. Two volumes offset from typescript. 1,746 pages (Christoper Stephens 11/91) with many differences from final book $250.

041b: ANCIENT EVENINGS Little, Brown Boston/T (1983) [ ] Uncorrected proof in yellow wraps with $19.95 price and 704 pages noted on cover $100.

041c: ANCIENT EVENINGS Little, Brown Boston/T (1983) [2] 350 sgd no. cc. Issued without dustwrapper in slipcase $75/150

041d: ANCIENT EVENINGS Little, Brown Boston/T (1983) [1] 100,000 cc. Black cloth with gold and red lettering in red, black and gold dustwrapper $6/30

041e: ANCIENT EVENINGS Macmillan L 1983 [] Advance uncorrected proof in yellow wraps (Dalian 5/90) $75.

041f: ANCIENT EVENINGS Macmillan L 1983 [] $10/40

042a: THE LAST NIGHT Targ Editions NY 1984 [2] 250 sgd no. cc. Black and white boards in plain white dustwrapper $125/150

043a: TOUGH GUYS DON'T DANCE Random House NY (1984) [4] Uncorrected proof in yellow wraps $100.

043b: TOUGH GUYS DON'T DANCE Franklin Library Franklin Center 1984 [2] Signed "limited" first edition in full brown leather with "Special Message From The Author" not in Random House edition $75.

043c: TOUGH GUYS DON'T DANCE Random House NY (1984) [2] 350 sgd no. cc. Issued without dustwrapper in slipcase $60/125

043d: TOUGH GUYS DON'T DANCE Random House NY (1984) [4] 100,000 cc. Black cloth with gold lettering in black, yellow and gold dustwrapper $10/25

043e: TOUGH GUYS DON'T DANCE Joseph L (1984) [] (ref.b) $10/40

043f: TOUGH GUYS DON'T DANCE: A SCREENPLAY Cannon Films (no-place) 1986 [] 116 pp. (only recto numbered) Blue wrappers, pin bound. Draft 4.2 by Mailer, October 11, 1986 $250.

044a: FRAGMENT FROM VIETNAM: A PLAY IN ONE ACT Eurographica Helsinki (1985) [2] 12 author's copies. Edited by Rolando Pieraccini. Blue-gray wrappers. Also contains Mailer's self-interview from the *New York Times Book Review* (17 September 1967, 4-5, 40) $300.

044b: FRAGMENT FROM VIETNAM: A PLAY IN ONE ACT Eurographica Helsinki (1985) [2] 350 no. cc as above $175.

045a: HUCKLEBERRY FINN, ALIVE AT 100 Caliban Press (Montclair) 1985 [2] 50 no. cc casebound in boards $200.

045b: HUCKLEBERRY FINN, ALIVE AT 100 Caliban Press (Montclair) 1985 [2] 200 no. cc sewn in red crimson wraps $100.

046a: 48TH INTERNATION PEN CONGRESS PRESS KIT NY 1986 January 12-18 [] Includes 11 page speech by Mailer. Loose sheets stapled in gray folder $50.

047a: CONVERSATIONS WITH NORMAN MAILER University Press of Miss. Jackson/L (1988) [3] 1,500 cc. Edited by J. Michael Lennon $15/30

047b: CONVERSATIONS WITH NORMAN MAILER University Press of Miss. Jackson/L (1988) [3] 3,500 cc. Wraps. Issued simultaneously $20.

048a: HARLOT'S GHOST Random House NY 1991 [2] 300 sgd no. cc. Issued without dustwrapper in slipcase. Published at $200

048b: HARLOT'S GHOST Random House NY 1991 [1] 186,000 cc (PW). Issued in two dustwrappers (gray and red), reportedly there were only 250 of the red dustwrapper (Bev Chaney 2/92). However, an article in PW states Mailer "had approved the original gray dustwrapper. It continued to outsell the strawberry four to one..." If this is true, there must have been more red copies. Published August 1991 at $30

049a: HOW THE WIMP WON THE WAR Lord John Press Northridge 1992 [2] 26 sgd ltr cc. Issued without dustwrapper $150.

049b: HOW THE WIMP WON THE WAR Lord John Press Northridge 1992 [2] 275 sgd no cc. Issued without dustwrapper $75.

INTRODUCTIONS:

050a: VIEWS OF A NEARSIGHTED CANNONEER Excelsior Press NY (1961) [] Wraps. Foreword by Mailer, written by Seymour Krim. Krim's first book $10/40

051a: THE BEARD Coyote (SF) 1967 [2] 40 specially bound copies signed by the author, Michael McClure. Foreword by Mailer $150.

051b: THE BEARD Coyote (SF) 1967 [1] 5,000 cc. Wraps $20.

052a: THE END OF OBSCENITY | THE TRIALS OF LADY CHATTERLEY, TROPIC OF CANCER and FANNY HILL Deutsch (L 1969) [0] Foreword by Mailer written by Charles Rembar $10/40

052b: THE END OF OBSCENITY | THE TRIALS OF LADY CHATTERLEY, TROPIC OF CANCER and FANNY HILL Bantam T/NY/L (1969) [1] Wraps. Copyright page: "Bantam edition published September 1969." Q5236. New edition $15.

053a: STING LIKE A BEE THE MUHAMMAD ALI STORY Abelard-Schuman L/NY/T 1971 [0] Preface by Mailer written by Jose Torres $15/40

053b: STING LIKE A BEE THE MUHAMMAD ALI STORY Curtis Books NY 1971 [] Wraps $15.

054a: THE JOKER Warner (NY 1974) [1] Wraps. Introduction by Mailer, written by Jean Malaquais and translated by Herma Briffault $20.

055a: FICTION WRITER'S HANDBOOK Harper & Row NY/Evanston/SF/L (1975) [1] Preface by Mailer, written by Hallie and Whit Burnett $10/35

056a: ST. PATRICK'S DAY WITH MAYOR DALEY AND OTHER THINGS TOO GOOD TO MISS Seabury, NY (1976) [0] Foreward by Mailer, written by Eugene Kennedy $10/25

057a: PAPA A PERSONAL MEMOIR Houghton Mifflin Boston 1976 [3] Preface by Mailer, written by Gregory H. Hemingway $10/35

058a: FIRST FLOWERING THE BEST OF THE HARVARD ADVOCATE Addison-Wesley, Mass / Ca / L / Amsterdam / Ontario / Sydney (1977) [3] Preface by Mailer, edited by Richard M. Smoley $10/30

059a: SOON TO BE A MAJOR MOTION PICTURE Putnam's NY (1980) [0] Introduction by Mailer, written by Abbie Hoffman $15/40

059b: SOON TO BE A MAJOR MOTION PICTURE Putnam's NY (1980) [0] Wraps. Issued simultaneously $15.

060a: IN THE BELLY OF THE BEAST LETTERS FROM PRISON Random House NY (1981) [3] (Also states "First Edition.") Introduction by Mailer, written by Jack Henry Abbott $10/30

060b: IN THE BELLY OF THE BEAST LETTERS FROM PRISON Hutchison L 1982 [] Introduction by Mailer, written by Jack Henry Abbott (ref.b) $10/30

061a: DEAR MUFFO: 35 YEARS IN THE FAST LANE Stein and Day NY (1982) [1] Foreward by Mailer, written by Harold Conrad $10/25

062a: AFTER THE LAST GENERATION: A CRITICAL STUDY OF THE WRITERS OF TWO WARS Arbor House NY (1985) [3] Wraps. Written by John W. Aldridge, with an introduction by Mailer $15.

063a: DISCRIMINATIONS: ESSAYS & AFTERTHOUGHTS DaCapo Press (NY 1985) [] Wraps. Introduction by Norman Mailer, written by Dwight MacDonald (originally by Grossman in 1974. This the first with Mailer introduction) $15.

Bernard Malamud

BERNARD MALAMUD

Malamud was born in Brooklyn in 1914. He graduated from the City College of New York and received a M.A. from Columbia. He taught at various New York high schools in the 1940's and at Oregon State from 1949 to 1961. He received a National Book Award for *The Magic Barrel* and a Pulitzer Prize for *The Fixer.*

REFERENCES:

(a) Lepper, Gary M. A BIBLIOGRAPHICAL REFERENCE TO SEVENTY-FIVE MODERN AMERICAN AUTHORS, Serendipity Books, Berkeley, 1976.

(b) Kosofsky, Rita N. BERNARD MALAMUD: AN ANNOTATED CHECK-LIST, Kent State, (1969).

(c) CONTEMPORARY NOVELISTS, Second Edition, St. Martin's Press, NY, (1976), edited by James Vinson.

(d) Eppard, Philip B., Editor FIRST PRINTINGS OF AMERICAN AUTHORS, Vol. 5, Gale Research, Detroit (1987).

(e) Inventory.

001a: THE NATURAL Harcourt NY (1952) [1] The latest thinking seems to be that there is no priority among red, blue and gray bindings $100/600

001b: THE NATURAL Eyre & Spottiswode L 1963 [1] "Uncorrected proof" in printed tan wraps "To Be Published March 1963 at 21s Net." Includes 10 pages of notes on baseball not in U.S. edition $350.

001c: THE NATURAL Eyre & Spottiswode L 1963 [1] Contains 10 pages of notes on baseball not included in U.S. edition $40/200

002a: THE ASSISTANT Farrar Straus NY 1957 [1] Reviews of *The Natural* on back panel $35/175

002b: THE ASSISTANT Farrar Straus NY 1957 [1] Reviews of this title on back panel $35/100

002c: THE ASSISTANT Eyre & Spottiswode L 1959 [1] First book published in England (ref.b) $15/75

003a: MAGIC BARRELL + Farrar Straus NY (1958) [] Uncorrected galley in narrow sheets punched at top and string tied into plain wraps with typed label and front panel of dustwrapper art mount thereon (William Reese Co. 5/89) $1,000.

003b: MAGIC BARRELL + Farrar Straus NY (1958) [1] Winner of the National Book Award for 1959 $15/75

003c: MAGIC BARRELL + Jewish Publ. Soc. Ph. 1958 [1] No priority (ref.a) but this issue is noted as the first issue (Sylvester & Orphanos #41) $20/100

003d: MAGIC BARRELL+ Eyre & Spottiswode L 1960 [1] $12/60

003e: MAGIC BARREL AND IDIOT'S FIRST Franklin Library Franklin Center 1978 [2] "Limited Edition" in full leather (ref.c) $60.

003f: MAGIC BARREL + Tales for Travellers (Napa, Calif. 1985) [0] 15,000 cc. Wraps map folded. First separate edition. (Later printing overstamped on back with eith "Parke-Davis" or "Dermik") $20.

004a: NATIONAL BOOK AWARD ACCEPTANCE SPEECH (Privately Printed NY) 1959 [0] Wraps. Two mimeographed sheets $50.

005a: A NEW LIFE Farrar Straus NY (1961) [1] $12/60

005b: A NEW LIFE Eyre & Spottiswode L 1962 [] Uncorrected proof in printed green wraps (Dalian 5/90) $125.

005c: A NEW LIFE Eyre & Spottiswode L 1962 [] (ref.b) $10/50

006a: IDIOT'S FIRST Farrar Straus NY (1963) [] Uncorrected galley proofs in plain wraps with typed label (William Reese Co. 5/89) $500.

006b: IDIOT'S FIRST Farrar Straus NY (1963) [1] $10/50

006c: IDIOT'S FIRST Eyre & Spottiswode L 1964 [] $10/50

Also see 003d

007a: TWO NOVELS BY BERNARD MALAMUD... Random House NY 1964 [] First two books (ref.b) $8/40

008a: THE FIXER Farrar Straus NY (1966) [1] Winner of Pulitzer Prize for 1967 $12/60

008b: THE FIXER Eyre & Spottiswode L (1967) [] (ref.b) $10/50

008c: THE FIXER Franklin Library Franklin Center 1978 [2] "Limited Edition" in full leather $50.

009a: A MALAMUD READER Farrar Straus NY (1967) [] Uncorrected galley proofs punched at left and string tied in plain wraps with typed label (William Reese Co. 5/89) $150.

009b: A MALAMUD READER Farrar Straus NY (1967) [0] Edited by Philip Rahv $10/50

010a: PICTURES OF FIDELMAN Farrar Straus NY (1969) [] Uncorrected proofs in tall, thin, spiral bound, pale blue wraps (James Jaffe 5/92) $200.

010b: PICTURES OF FIDELMAN Farrar Straus NY (1969) [1] $8/40

010c: PICTURES OF FIDELMAN Eyre & Spottiswode L 1970 [] (ref.c) $8/40

011a: THE TENANTS Farrar Straus NY (1971) [1] Approximately 250 copies with signed tipped in sheet. In orange cloth $50/75

011b: THE TENANTS Farrar Straus NY (1971) [1] First binding in orange cloth (Caney Booksellers 5/88) $15/40

011c: THE TENANTS Farrar Straus NY (1971) [1] Second binding in dark red $5/30

011d: THE TENANTS Metheun L (1972) [1] (ref.e) (Published February 23, 1972 at £1.95) $7/35

012a: REMBRANDT'S HAT Farrar Straus NY (1973) [] Uncorrected proofs in green wraps (William Reese 5/89) $125.

012b: REMBRANDT'S HAT Farrar Straus NY (1973) [1] $8/40

012c: REMBRANDT'S HAT Eyre & Methuen L 1973 [] (ref.c) $7/35

013a: TWO FABLES Bennington/Banyon Benn./Pawlet (1978) [2] 320 sgd no cc. Issued without dustwrapper. Excerpt from *The Magic Barrel* $125.

014a: DUBIN'S LIVES Farrar Straus NY (1979) [1] Wraps. Uncorrected page proofs in peach colored printed wraps which differs from published version, but with the 5 words (see below) (ref.d) $125.

014b: DUBIN'S LIVES Farrar Straus NY (1979) [1] Missing the last five words on bottom of p.231 "When he asked her why," (ref.c) $150/175

014c: DUBIN'S LIVES Farrar Straus NY (1979) [1] Approximately 70cc sent out for review with 5 words in last line p.231 written in (Jos. the Prov. Cat. 24) (ref.d calls this second state) $125/150

014d: DUBIN'S LIVES Franklin Press Franklin Ctr 1979 [2] "Limited Edition" in full leather, special message $50.

014e: DUBIN'S LIVES Farrar Straus NY (1979) [2] 750 cc "For friends of..." issued in plain glassine dustwrapper (with p.231 tipped in) (ref.d - third state) $35/40

014f: DUBIN'S LIVES Farrar Straus NY (1979) [1] With p.231 tipped in (ref.d) $6/30

014g: DUBIN'S LIVES Chatto & Windus L 1979 [] (ref.d) $6/30

015a: GOD'S GRACE Farrar Straus NY (1982) [2] 300 sgd no. cc. Issued without dustwrapper in slipcase $50/100

015b: GOD'S GRACE Farrar Straus NY (1982) [1] $6/30

015c: GOD'S GRACE Chatto & Windus L 1982 [] $6/30

016a: THE STORIES Farrar Straus NY (1983) [] Uncorrected proofs in blue wraps $75.

016b: THE STORIES Farrar Straus NY (1983) [2] 300 sgd no. cc. Issued without dustwrapper in slipcase $50/100

016c: THE STORIES Farrar Straus NY (1983) [1] $6/30

016d: THE STORIES Chatto & Windus/Hogarth L 1984 [] Advance proof in plain wraps. Bound in proof dustwrapper (Ian McKelvie 2/90) $60.

016e: THE STORIES Chatto & Windus/Hogarth L 1984 [1] "Published in 1984 by ..." $6/30

017a: ON BEING ACQUAINTED WITH EUDORA WELTY Stuart Wright (no-place) 1984 [2] Wraps. 5 sgd no cc (Black Sun Books #71) $250.

018a: LONG WORK, SHORT LIFE (Bennington College Bennington, VT) 1984 [2] Wraps. 1,000 no. cc (Glenn Horowitz #13) $40.

019a: THE PEOPLE AND OTHER UNCOLLECTED FICTION Farrar Straus NY 1989 [] Uncorrected proof in green wraps $50.

019b: THE PEOPLE AND OTHER UNCOLLECTED FICTION Farrar Straus NY 1989 [] Edited by Robert Giroux. Published November 1989 at $18.95 $5/20

019c: THE PEOPLE AND OTHER UNCOLLECTED FICTION Chatto & Windus L (1990) $6/30

020a: THE MAGIC BARREL TALES FOR TRAVELLERS (Napa, Calif. 1985) [0] Single sheet map folded. First separate edition $25.

021a: CONVERSATIONS WITH BERNARD MALAMUD University Press of Mississippi Jackson (1991) [] Interviews from 1958-1986. Edited by Lawrence Lasher $10/30

021b: CONVERSATIONS WITH BERNARD MALAMUD University Press of Mississippi Jackson (1991) [] Wraps $15.

DAVID MARKSON

Markson was born in Albany, New York, in 1927 and educated at Union College and Columbia; his master's thesis was the first extended critical treatment of Malcolm Lowry's *Under The Volcano*. The "spiritual son" of Lowry and Conrad Aiken, Markson also associated with the Beats in the late '50s and early '60s. He has spent long periods in England, Spain, and Mexico, but considers Greenwich Village home.

We would like to thank Steven Moore for the preparation of the bibliographical information herein.

001a: THE LOVE-MAKERS Lion Books NY (1956) [] Wraps. Edited by "Mark Merrill" $40.

002a: WOMEN AND VODKA Pyramid NY (1956) [] Wraps. Edited by "Mark Merrill." (Reissued as *Great Tales of Old Russia* under Markson's real name in 1963) $35.

003a: EPITAPH FOR A TRAMP Dell (NY 1959) [1] Wraps. (Reissued as *Fannin* in 1971) $30.

004a: EPITAPH FOR A DEAD BEAT Dell (NY 1961) [1] Wraps $25.

005a: MISS DOLL, GO HOME Dell (NY 1965) [1] Wraps $25.

006a: THE BALLAD OF DINGUS MAGEE Bobbs-Merrill Indianapolis (1965) [1] Wraps. Advance copy in white wraps $50.

006b: THE BALLAD OF DINGUS MAGEE Bobbs-Merrill Indianapolis (1965; actually spring of 1966) [1] $7/35

007a: GOING DOWN (Holt, Rinehart NY 1970) [1] $6/30

008a: SPRINGER'S PROGRESS Holt, Rinehart NY (1977) Wraps. Uncorrected proofs in printed wraps $50.

008b: SPRINGER'S PROGRESS Holt, Rinehart NY (1977) [1] $5/25

009a: MALCOLM LOWRY'S *VOLCANO* Times Books (NY 1978) [0] $5/25

010a: WITTGENSTEIN'S MISTRESS Dalkey Archive Elmwood Park (1988) $5/20

Paule Marshall

PAULE MARSHALL

Marshall was born in 1929 in Brooklyn, the setting for her first book about a West Indian girl transplanted to Brooklyn. She graduated from Brooklyn College in 1953 and has been writing full-time since her first book.

We appreciate the assistance of Charles Dickison for bibliographical information on a number of these books.

001a: BROWN GIRL, BROWNSTONES Random House NY (1959) [1] $60/350

001b: BROWN GIRL, BROWNSTONES W.H. Allen L 1960 [ ] $35/175

001c: BROWN GIRL, BROWNSTONES Black Oak Books Berkeley 1991 [] "They danced near the edge of the circle ..." 6 1/2" x 11" broadside (Ken Lopez 1/92) $25.

002a: SOUL CLAP HANDS AND SING Atheneum NY 1961 [1] $30/150

002b: SOUL CLAP HANDS AND SING W.H. Allen L 1962 [1] $15/75

003a: THE CHOSEN PLACE, THE TIMELESS PEOPLE Harcourt Brace NY (1969) [1] $20/100

003b: THE CHOSEN PLACE, THE TIMELESS PEOPLE Longmans L 1970 [1] $12/60

004a: REENA Feminist Press Old Westbury, NY (1983) [3] Wraps $60.

004b: MERLE Virago (L 1985) [0] Advance proof in blue printed wraps with publication date of 2/21/85 at £9.95. No place or date in book except copyright 1983 by Feminist Press. New title $75.

004c: MERLE Virago (L 1985) [] $10/35

004d: MERLE Virago (L 1985) [] Wraps $15.

005a: PRAISESONG FOR THE WIDOW Putnam NY (1983) [0] Uncorrected proof in orange wraps (Lame Duck Books 9/91) $100.

005b: PRAISESONG FOR THE WIDOW Putnam NY (1983) [0] $5/15

006a: DAUGHTERS Atheneum NY 1991 [] Advance excerpt. 25 pages, pictorial wraps $25.

006b: DAUGHTERS Atheneum NY 1991 [] (Published October 1991 @ $19.95)

William Maxwell

WILLIAM MAXWELL

William Maxwell was born in Lincoln, Illinois in 1908. He received his undergraduate degree from the University of Illinois and his masters from Harvard. He taught for a short period and then spent his entire working career as a member of the staff of *The New Yorker* magazine.

001a: BRIGHT CENTER OF HEAVEN Harper NY 1934 [1] $100/500

001b: BRIGHT CENTER OF HEAVEN Musson Toronto 1934 [] $40/200

002a: THEY CAME LIKE SWALLOWS Harper NY 1937 [1] Noted with the numbers "1186" and "1213" at bottom of back panel of dustwrapper. "1188" is assumed to be the first $50/250

002b: THEY CAME LIKE SWALLOWS Musson Toronto 1937 [] $20/100

002c: THEY CAME LIKE SWALLOWS M. Joseph L 1937 [] $25/125

002d: THEY CAME LIKE SWALLOWS Vintage NY 1960 [1] Wraps. Slightly revised by author $25.

003a: THE FOLDED LEAF Harper NY 1945 [1] $40/200

003b: THE FOLDED LEAF Faber L (1946) [] 5,579 cc $25/125

003c: THE FOLDED LEAF Vintage NY 1959 [1] Slightly revised by author $25.

004a: HEAVENLY TENANTS Harper NY (1946) [0] Pictures by Ilonka Karasz. Dark blue cloth, dustwrapper priced at $2.00 with "6317" at bottom of front flap $35/175

004b: HEAVENLY TENANTS Musson Toronto 1946 [] $20/100

005a: TIME WILL DARKEN IT Harper NY 1948 [1] $20/100

005b: TIME WILL DARKEN IT Musson Toronto 1948 [] $12/60

005c: TIME WILL DARKEN IT Faber L 1949 [] 3,500 cc $12/60

005d: TIME WILL DARKEN IT Vintage (NY 1962) [1] Wraps. Revised edition $25.

006a: THE WRITER AS ILLUSIONIST Smith College (Northampton) (1955) [0] Wraps (in dustwrapper -Waiting For Godot #13) $100/125

007a: STORIES Farrar Straus NY (1956) [1] With Cheever, Stafford and Daniel Fuchs $12/60

008a: THE ANXIOUS MAN PAX NY 1957 [] Large folio sheet folded twice (Waiting For Godot #L-One) $60.

009a: THE CHATEAU Knopf NY 1961 [1] $12/60

009b: THE CHATEAU McClelland Toronto 1961 [] $8/40

010a: THE OLD MAN AT THE RAILROAD CROSSING Knopf NY 1966 [] Galley proofs in spiral bound printed wraps (William Reese Co. 11/90) $150.

010b: THE OLD MAN AT THE RAILROAD CROSSING Knopf NY 1966 [1] $10/50

011a: ANCESTORS Knopf NY 1971 [1] $8/40

012a: OVER BY THE RIVER+ Knopf NY 1977 [] Uncorrected proof in tall brick red wraps $75.

012b: OVER BY THE RIVER+ Knopf NY 1977 [1] $8/40

013a: SO LONG, SEE YOU TOMORROW Knopf NY 1980 [1] $7/35

013b: SO LONG, SEE YOU TOMORROW Secker L (1988) [1] $7/35

014a: LETTERS/SYLVIA TOWNSEND WARNER Viking NY (1983) [1] "Published in 1983 by ..." Edited by Maxwell $6/30

014b: LETTERS/SYLVIA TOWNSEND WARNER Chatto & Windus L 1982 [] $6/30

015a: FIVE TALES Cummington Press Omaha 1988 [2] 60 no. cc $100.

015b: FIVE TALES Cummington Press Omaha 1988 [2] 160 no. cc. Hors Commerce $100.

016a: THE OUTERMOST DREAM Knopf NY 1989 [] Uncorrected proof in orange wraps (Bev Chaney 2/89) $40.

016b: THE OUTERMOST DREAM Knopf NY 1989 [1] Essays and reviews. (Published April 1989 @ $19.95) $5/20

017a: BILLY DYER + Knopf NY 1992 [] Uncorrected proof in yellow wraps (Bev Chaney 11/91) $40.

017b: BILLY DYER + Knopf NY 1992 [1]

Joe McElroy

JOSEPH McELROY

McElroy was born in Brooklyn in 1930. He graduated from William and Mary and received a masters from Columbia University. He has taught English at various universities.

001a: A SMUGGLER'S BIBLE Harcourt Brace & World NY (1966) [] Uncorrected proof in yellow printed wraps. May have been as many as 200 copies (Glenn Horowitz #7). (Also an advance reading copy catalogued by Joseph The Provider -same?) $400.

001b: A SMUGGLER'S BIBLE Harcourt Brace & World NY (1966) [1] (Published September 28, 1966) $60/300

001c: A SMUGGLER'S BIBLE Longmans Toronto 1966 [] $25/125

001d: A SMUGGLER'S BIBLE A. Deutsch (L 1968) $30/150

002a: HIND'S KIDNAP Harper NY (1969) [1] $25/125

002b: HIND'S KIDNAP Anthony Blond (L 1970) [1] $15/75

003a: ANCIENT HISTORY Knopf NY 1971 [1] (Published May 21, 1971) $15/60

004a: LOOKOUT CARTRIDGE Knopf NY 1974 [] Uncorrected proof in light blue wraps (Serendipity 2/89) $150.

004b: LOOKOUT CARTRIDGE Knopf NY 1974 [1] Cloth spine and paper covered boards first issue (Christopher Stevens) $15/60

004c: LOOKOUT CARTRIDGE Knopf NY 1974 [1] Full cloth binding $10/40

005a: PLUS Knopf NY 1977 [1] $20/60

005b: PLUS Knopf NY 1977 [1] Wraps (simultaneous issue) $20.

006a: SHIP ROCK. A PLACE Wm. Ewert Concord, NH (1980) [2] 13 cc. Specially bound for presentation, quarter leather and boards (James Jaffe #12) $300.

006b: SHIP ROCK. A PLACE Wm. Ewert Concord, NH (1980) [2] 26 sgd ltr cc $175.

006c: SHIP ROCK. A PLACE Wm. Ewert Concord, NH (1980) [2] 200 (of 220) sgd no. cc $75.

007a: WOMEN AND MEN Ultramarine Hastings-on-Hudson 1987 [2] 99 sgd no. cc. Issued in half-leather $175.

007b: WOMEN AND MEN Knopf NY 1987 [] Uncorrected proofs in two volumes in yellow wraps (Lame Duck Books 4/90) $125.

007c: WOMEN AND MEN Knopf NY 1987 [1] 7,000 cc (Published February 27, 1987). Incorrect copyright on first state J&J Hanrahan 2/89)? Bev Chaney states "reportedly 2,500 cc" 2/92 $10/35

008a: THE LETTER LEFT TO ME Knopf NY 1988 [] Uncorrected proof in red wraps (Bev Chaney List C) $75.

008b: THE LETTER LEFT TO ME Knopf NY 1988 [] 8,500 cc (Published October 1988 @ $16.95) $6/30

THOMAS McGUANE

McGuane was born in Michigan in 1939. He received a B.A. at Michigan State University and a Masters in Drama from Yale. He has been writing full-time since the success of his first book.

Bibliographic information supplied by Jack Mullenax and Michael Raskin.

001a: THE SPORTING CLUB Simon & Schuster NY (1968) [1] Advance uncorrected proof in tall yellow wraps $300.

001b: THE SPORTING CLUB Simon & Schuster NY (1968) [1] Red cloth, gilt lettering $30/150

001c: THE SPORTING CLUB Andre Deutsch (L 1969) [1] Green boards, gilt lettering $20/100

001d: THE SPORTING CLUB Doubleday Toronto (1969) [] $12/60

002a: THE BUSHWHACKED PIANO Simon & Schuster NY (1971) [] Uncorrected proof in tall pad bound yellow wraps $250.

002b: THE BUSHWHACKED PIANO Simon & Schuster NY (1971) [1] Brown cloth, black title letters $20/100

003a: NINETY-TWO IN THE SHADE Farrar, Straus & Giroux NY (1973) "Uncorrected page proofs" in yellow wraps $200.

003b: NINETY-TWO IN THE SHADE Farrar, Straus & Giroux NY (1973) [1] Cloth in two shades of blue with silver lettering $15/60

003c: NINETY-TWO IN THE SHADE Collins L (1974) [] Advance copy in red wraps $125.

003d: NINETY-TWO IN THE SHADE Collins L 1974 [1] Red boards, silver title letters $10/50

004a: THE MISSOURI BREAKS Ballantine NY (1976) [1] Paper-back originial "First Edition: June 1976." No.25218-7 with $1.75 price $40.

005a: THE ANGLER'S COAST Doubleday NY 1976 [1] Introduction by McGuane to Russell Chatham's book $8/40

006a: PANAMA Farrar, Straus & Giroux NY (1978) [] Tall narrow gray-green wraps (Ken Lopez 10/91) $100.

006b: PANAMA Farrar, Straus & Giroux NY (1978) [1] Green cloth spine, green boards, silver title letters $6/30

006c: PANAMA McGraw-Hill Ryerson Toronto (1978) [] $6/30

006d: PANAMA Penguin Books Harmondsworth 1979 [1] Wraps $20.

007a: AN OUTSIDE CHANCE+ Farrar, Straus & Giroux NY (1980) [1] Uncorrected proof in green wraps $75.

007b: AN OUTSIDE CHANCE+ Farrar, Straus & Giroux NY (1980) [1] Creme cloth spine and brown boards with bronze title letters $8/40

007c: AN OUTSIDE CHANCE+ McGraw-Hill Ryerson Toronto (1980) [] $7/35

007d: AN OUTSIDE CHANCE+ Penquin Books Harmondsworth (1982) [1] Wraps $20.

007e: AN OUTSIDE CHANCE+ Houghton Mifflin Boston 1990 [3] 4,200 cc. 4 new essays and introduction by Geoffrey Wolff. (Published October 1990 @ $19.95) $10/20

007f: AN OUTSIDE CHANCE+ Houghton Mifflin Boston 1990 [] 7,000 cc. Wraps $10.

008a: NOBODY'S ANGEL Random House NY 1982 [] Uncorrected proof in red wraps $100.

008b: NOBODY'S ANGEL Random House NY (1982) [4] 5,000 cc. Brown cloth spine and tan boards with gilt letters $10/30

008c: NOBODY'S ANGEL Random House NY (1982) [4] Wraps Issued simultaneously $15.

008d: NOBODY'S ANGEL Random House of Canada Ltd T (1981) [] $6/30

009a: THE VANISHING BREED New York Graphic Society/Little Brown Boston (1982) [2] 750 sgd no cc. Leather spine. Issued in slipcase. Short introduction by McGuane. Signed by McGuane and William Albert Allard, a photographer $150/225

009b: THE VANISHING BREED New York Graphic Society/Little Brown Boston (1982) [1] 17,500 cc $20/50

009c: THE VANISHING BREED New York Graphic Society/Little Brown Boston (1982) [1] 10,000 cc. Wraps $20.

010a: DEEP CREEK Winn Seattle 1984 [2] 150 sgd cc. Paintings by Russell Chatham and signed by him (not by others), text by McGuane, Hunter Thompson and Jim Harrison. Includes 2 of Chatham's signed plates in rear pocket. There is no limitation page. Plates are numbered and signed. Issued without dustwrapper or slipcase. (Published October 1984 @ $175) $250.

010b: RUSSELL CHATHAM Clark City Press Livingston, Montana 1987 [3] Wraps. Adds 4 full page photographs in front (pages 6 through 9 unnumbered) and changed two in back; otherwise, exactly the same as 010a but no acknowledgment that it was ever published before $20.

011a: IN THE CRAZIES Winn Seattle 1985 [2] 185 sgd no cc (190 copies in total). With large portfolio of 10 various sized plates signed and numbered by artist Russell Chatham. Book signed by both McGuane and Chatham. Book has leather spine and cloth covered boards in gray cloth slipcase. Portfolio is in matching gray cloth. Published at $1,500. $1,500.

012a: SOMETHING TO BE DESIRED Random House NY (1984) [4] Uncorrected proof in yellow wraps (Bert Babcock 2/92) $75.

012b: SOMETHING TO BE DESIRED Random House NY (1984) [4] Blue cloth spine and white boards with silver title letters. (Published October 29, 1984 @ $14.95) $6/30

012c: SOMETHING TO BE DESIRED Random House of Canada Toronto (1984) [] $6/30

012d: SOMETHING TO BE DESIRED Secker & Warburg L 1985 [1] Red boards and gilt letters $6/30

013a: TO SKIN A CAT Dutton NY (1986) [] Advance uncorrected proof in mint green wraps $60.

013b: TO SKIN A CAT Dutton NY (1986) [2] 250 sgd no cc of an advance excerpt in wraps (Beasley Books #34) $40.

013c: TO SKIN A CAT Dutton NY 1986 [3] Also states "First Edition." (Published October 1986 @ $16.95) $5/25

013d: TO SKIN A CAT Dutton NY (1987) [3] Wraps. Also states "First Edition" $10.

013e: TO SKIN A CAT Secker & Warburg L (1987) [1] Red boards, gilt letters $5/25

014a: KEEP THE CHANGE Houghton Mifflin Boston 1989 [3] Advance Reading Copy in decorated wraps $40.

014b: KEEP THE CHANGE Houghton Mifflin Boston 1989 [2] 150 sgd no cc. Issued without dustwrapper in slipcase $50/100

014c: KEEP THE CHANGE Houghton Mifflin Boston 1989 [3] 30,000 cc. Tan cloth spine and green boards with green title letters and gilt signature on front cover. (Published September 1989 @ $18.95) $5/25

014d: KEEP THE CHANGE Secker & Warburg L 1989 [0] $6/30

015a: NOTHING BUT BLUE SKIES Houghton Mifflin Boston 1992 [3] Advance uncorrected proof in pictorial wraps $60.

015b: NOTHING BUT BLUE SKIES Houghton Mifflin Boston 1992 [2] 200 sgd no. cc $50/100

015c: NOTHING BUT BLUE SKIES Houghton Mifflin Boston 1992 [3] 50,000 cc (PW)

LARRY McMURTRY

Larry McMurtry was born in Wichita Falls, Texas in 1936. He spent most of his early years in the ranching country of north-central Texas. He holds a master's degree from Rice University. He received a Wallace Stegner Fellowship at Stanford and was awarded a Guggenheim Fellowship for creative writing in fiction. *Horseman Pass By* (Hud), *The Last Picture Show*, and *Terms of Endearment* were made into successful movies with the latter receiving the Academy Award for the Best Picture of 1983.

McMurtry is a prolific book reviewer, essayist and screen writer and operates antiquarian bookstores in Texas and in the Georgetown section of Washington, D.C. with his partner, Marcia Carter. His book, *Lonesome Dove*, won the Pulitzer Prize for Fiction for 1986.

REFERENCES:

(a) Lepper, Gary M., A BIBLIOGRAPHICAL INTRO-DUCTION TO SEVENTY-FIVE MODERN AMERI-CAN AUTHORS, Serendipity Books, Berkeley, 1976.

(b) FIRST PRINTINGS OF AMERICAN AUTHORS, Volume 4, Bruccoli, et al, Gale Research, Detroit (1979).

(c) Inventory, catalogs, publishers' records. Used for all entries after 011.

001a: HORSEMAN, PASS BY Harper NY (1961) [1] Approximately 5,000 cc. One of A.C. Greene's *50 Best Books on Texas* $250/1,250

001b: HUD Popular Library NY (1963) [1] Wraps. Movie title of *Horseman Pass By*. No. SP 218 $40.

001c: HORSEMAN, PASS BY Sphere L 1971 [1] (Ref.c) $75.

002a: TEXAS INSTITUTE... AWARDS... SPEECH (Texas Institute Dallas 1962) [0] Wraps. Ditto sheets of text of speech $350.

003a: LEAVING CHEYENNE Harper & Row NY (1963) [1] Approximately 3,500 cc. One of A.C. Greene's *50 Best Books on Texas*. Dustwrapper priced at $4.50, changed to $4.95 after publication (reportedly printed but we've only seen with gummed sticker over old price) $200/1,000

003b: LEAVING CHEYENNE Sphere L 1972 [] Ref.b. Although the only edition we've seen is Penguin Books (Harmondsworth 1979) [1] "Published in Penguin Books 1979" in wraps $75.

004a: DAUGHTER OF THE TEJAS NY Graphic Greenwich, CT (1965) [1] Ghostwritten for Orphelia Ray. In gray dustwrapper. Although this was ghosted by McMurtry, he believes it's possible it may have been rewritten by someone else before publication $35/175

004b: DAUGHTER OF THE TEJAS NY Graphic Greenwich, CT (1965) [1] White dustwrapper. We assume this is a remainder dustwrapper $35/125

005a: THE LAST PICTURE SHOW Dial NY 1966 [] Uncorrected galley proof (7 1/2" x 12") punched at top and string tied with printed cover sheet (William Reese 5/89) $4,000.

005b: THE LAST PICTURE SHOW Dial NY 1966 [1] Wraps. Spiral-bound reading copies in plain stiff olive covers (Joseph The Provider 9/89). (Green card covers -Ken Lopez 4/92) $2,000.

005c: THE LAST PICTURE SHOW Dial NY 1966 [1] $75/350

005d: THE LAST PICTURE SHOW Dial NY (1966?) [0] "Book Club Edition" stated on bottom corner of front dustwrapper flap, no price on top of front dustwrapper flap. Does not state "First Edition" on copyright page $5/25

005e: THE LAST PICTURE SHOW Sphere L 1972 [] (ref.b) Although the only edition we've seen is Penguin Books (Harmonsworth 1979) [1] "Published in Penguin Books 1979" in wraps $60.

005f: THE LAST PICTURE SHOW Simon & Schuster NY (no-date {1989}) [3] Hardback reprint published at $18.95 but could be confusing because it has the number "1" in series and is not clearly marked as a reprint $5/25

006a: IN A NARROW GRAVE Encino Austin 1968 [0] 845 cc. With "skycrappers" vs "skyscrappers" on p.105:12 and many other errors. All but 15 were reportedly destroyed but seems more common $1,200/1,500

006b: IN A NARROW GRAVE Encino Austin 1968 [2] 250 sgd no cc. Issued in slipcase $1,000/1,250

006c: IN A NARROW GRAVE Encino Austin 1968 [0] $100/400

006d: IN A NARROW GRAVE Encino Austin 1968 [0] Has "B" on copyright page (second printing) $25/100

006e: IN A NARROW GRAVE Simon & Schuster NY (1989) [3] Wraps. Also states "First Touchstone Edition." Includes new preface $15.

007a: MOVING ON Simon & Schuster NY (1970) [1] 22,500 cc $40/200

007b: MOVING ON Weidenfeld L (1971) [1] (ref.c) $25/125

007c: MOVING ON Simon & Schuster NY (1987) [3] Wraps. Also states "First Touchstone Edition." Includes new preface $15.

008a: "TEXAS IS RICH IN UNREDEMMED DREAMS" Texas Library Association Austin (1971) [0] Broadside using quote from *In A Narrow Grave...* The majority of these are printed on tan stock, but there are a few on white which were (reportedly) done initially and rejected in favor of the tan. These are valued higher having sold for $300 to $700 in the past $175.

009a: ALL MY FRIENDS ARE GOING TO BE STRANGERS Simon & Schuster NY (1972) [] Uncorrected proof, pad bound, in tall yellow wraps (Ken Lopez 12/90) $500.

009b: ALL MY FRIENDS ARE GOING TO BE STRANGERS Simon & Schuster NY (1972) [1] 10,000 cc $30/150

009c: ALL MY FRIENDS ARE GOING TO BE STRANGERS Secker & Warberg L (1972) [1] (ref.c) $15/75

009d: ALL MY FRIENDS ARE GOING TO BE STRANGERS Simon & Schuster NY (1989) [3] Wraps. Also states "First Touchstone Edition." Includes new preface $15.

009e: ALL MY FRIENDS ARE GOING TO BE STRANGERS Book of Month Club NY (1989) [1] "This edition was specially created in 1989 for BOMC." Also includes *Terms of Endearment* and new prefaces for each which are the only hardback appearances of the prefaces $5/25

010a: IT'S ALWAYS WE RAMBLED... Hallman NY 1974 [2] 300 sgd no cc. Issued without dustwrapper or slipcase $300.

011a: TERMS OF ENDEARMENT Simon & Schuster NY (1975) [3] Advance uncorrected proofs in tall yellow printed wraps (ref.c) $500.

011b: TERMS OF ENDEARMENT Simon & Schuster NY (1975) [3] 16,500 cc. One of those Simon & Schustered aged page editions. Price would be for better than usual copies $25/125

011c: TERMS OF ENDEARMENT Allen L 1977 [1] 2,000 cc $15/60

011d: TERMS OF ENDEARMENT Allen L 1977 [1] 100,000 cc. Wraps $15.

011e: TERMS OF ENDEARMENT Simon & Schuster NY (1989) [3] Wraps. Also states "First Touchstone Edition." Includes new preface (ref.c) $15.

012a: SOMEBODY'S DARLING Simon & Schuster NY (1978) [3] Wraps. Advance uncorrected roof in yellow wraps (ref.c) $400.

012b: SOMEBODY'S DARLING Simon & Schuster NY (1989) [3] $10/50

012c: SOMEBODY'S DARLING Simon & Schuster NY (1987) [3] Wraps (ref.c). Also states "First Touchstone Edition." New preface $10.

013a: CADILLAC JACK Simon & Schuster NY (1982) [3] Advance uncorrected proof in yellow wraps (ref.c) $200.

013b: CADILLAC JACK Simon & Schuster NY (1982) [2] 250 sgd no cc. Issued without dustwrapper in slipcase (ref.c) $175/250

013c: CADILLAC JACK Simon & Schuster NY (1982) [3] 22,500 cc (ref.c) $10/50

013d: CADILLAC JACK Simon & Schuster NY (1985) [3] Wraps. Also states "First Touchstone Edition." ISBN numbers would indicate a hardback edition, but none published. Includes new preface $15.

013e: CADILLAC JACK W.H. Allen L 1986 [0] $15/60

014a: THE DESERT ROSE Simon & Schuster NY (1983) [3] Wraps. Advance uncorrected proof in yellow wraps (ref.c) $175.

014b: THE DESERT ROSE Simon & Schuster NY (1983) [2] 250 sgn no cc. Issued without dustwrapper in slipcase (ref.c) $175/250

014c: THE DESERT ROSE Simon & Schuster NY (1983) [3] 19,800 cc (ref.c) $10/50

014d: THE DESERT ROSE W.H. Allen L 1985 [1] $10/50

014e: THE DESERT ROSE Simon & Schuster NY (1985) [3] Wraps. Also states "First Touchstone Edition." Includes new preface. ISBN numbers would indicate there was a hardback edition, but none published $15.

015a: LONESOME DOVE Simon & Schuster NY (1985) [3] Approximately 500 cc. Advance uncorrected proof in yellow printed wraps $400.

015b: "PIGS ON THE PORCH" Simon & Schuster (NY 1985) [0] 500 cc. Promotional broadside for book, which starts "When Augustus came out on the porch..." 500 copies were printed for bookstore promotion, but not too many seemed to have survived $150.

015c: LONESOME DOVE Simon & Schuster NY (1985) [3] 41,000 cc. P.621.16 "none" vs. "done" (presume all copies - Jenkins #187). Pulitzer Prize in 1986 $40/200

015d: LONESOME DOVE Pan Books L 1986 [] Wraps. No hardcover edition $50.

016a: TENT LIFE IN SIBERIA Peregrine Smith Salt Lake City (1986) [3] Wraps. 3,000 cc. McMurtry introduction to this reprint of George Kennan's book $30.

017a: A WALK IN PASADENA WITH DIANNIE AND MARY ALICE (no-publisher, place or date) [0] Published about 1987. Oversize heavy paper wraps. Author retained 8 copies and the others were given to Dianne Keaton. Total number unknown but we have never seen a copy offered for sale $750.

018a: TEXASVILLE Simon & Schuster NY (1987) [0] Xerox copy of manuscript, cheaply bound in two volumes with black cloth spine $250.

018b: TEXASVILLE Simon & Schuster NY (1987) [3] 367 cc. Uncorrected proof in yellow wraps $150.

018c: TEXASVILLE Simon & Schuster NY (1987) [3] 100,000 cc. (Published April 1987 @ $18.95) $6/30

018d: TEXASVILLE Sidgewick & Jackson L (1987) [1] $7/35

019a: FILM FLAM Simon & Schuster NY (1987) [0] Xerox copy of manuscript with "The Hired Man" as "The Hired Pen" and without "A Walk In Pasadena With ..." (Bev Chaney #47) $200.

019b: FILM FLAM Simon & Schuster NY (1987) [3] Uncorrected proof in yellow wraps $175.

019c: FILM FLAM Simon & Schuster NY (1987) [3] 15,000 cc (Published June 5, 1987 @ $16.95) $8/40

020a: COWBOYS Wind River Press For The Book Club of Texas (Austin) 1988 [0] 14" x 20" poster with one drawing by Barbara Holman (ref.c) $100.

021a: ANYTHING FOR BILLY Simon & Schuster NY (1988) [3] Uncorrected proof in yellow wraps $125.

021b: ANYTHING FOR BILLY Simon & Schuster NY (1988) [3] 201,000 cc (Published October 1988 @ $18.95.) Also have seen one copy of a proof dustwrapper that is very similar to the *Lonesome Dove* dustwrapper. Reportedly there were a number sent to sales force but have never seen it offered for sale $7/35

021c: ANYTHING FOR BILLY Collins L 1989 [1] $8/40

022a: SOME CAN WHISTLE Simon & Schuster NY (1989) [] Uncorrected proof in yellow wraps $125.

022b: SOME CAN WHISTLE Simon & Schuster NY (1989) [3] (Published October 1989 @ $19.95) $5/20

022c: SOME CAN WHISTLE Century L (1990) [1] $7/35

023a: BUFFALO GIRLS Simon & Schuster NY 1990 [] Unbound sheets with holographic changes reproduced $150.

023b: BUFFALO GIRLS Simon & Schuster NY (1990) [] Uncorrected proof in yellow wraps $150.

023c: BUFFALO GIRLS Simon & Schuster NY (1990) [3] $5/20

023d: BUFFALO GIRLS Century L (1991) [2] 500 no. cc of proof in wraps $75.

023e: BUFFALO GIRLS Century L (1991) [] $7/35

024a: THE EVENING STAR Simon & Schuster NY (1992) [] 8 1/2" x 11" reproduced manuscript sheets $150.

024b: THE EVENING STAR Simon & Schuster NY (1992) [] Uncorrected proof in yellow wraps $125.

024c: THE EVENING STAR Simon & Schuster NY (1992) [3] (Published June 1992 @ $23)

VLADIMIR NABOKOV
1899-1977

Nabokov was born in St. Petersburg, Russia, of aristocratic parents in 1899. After the Russian Revolution, he emigrated to England where he graduated from Cambridge in 1922. He came to the United States in 1940 and became a naturalized citizen in 1945. He was a professor of Russian literature at Cornell University from 1948 to 1959.

We have concerned ourselves with only those books of the author published in English. There are 22 other Nabokov items (in Russian) not included here, but which are included in Ref.a.. We have listed them chronologically as they appeared in translation before 1941. Nabokov's first book *Stikhi* was a collection of 68 poems published in Russia in 1916 but never translated into English. His first book to be translated was *Camera Obscura* and was published in England in 1936. We have included some of the scientific off-prints; there were 18 in total. We left out those that had little or no bibliographical information in the primary reference or were single sheets.

We wish to thank Michael Juliar for permission to use his bibliography, and for the updates and editing that he was kind enough to provide. This guide reflects Juliar's updates as of October 1992 and therefore do not coincide completely with his bibliography as published in 1986.

REFERENCES:

(a) Juliar, Michael VALADIMIR NABOKOV: A DESCRIPTIVE BIBLIO-GRAPHY, Garland, NY, 1986 (an excellent reference).

(b) Bruccoli & Clark FIRST PRINTINGS OF AMERICAN AUTHORS Vol. 5, Gale Research, Detroit, (1987).

(c) Inventory or dealer catalogs.

001a: CAMERA OBSCURA John Long L (1936) [0] Author's last name listed on book as "Nabokoff-Sirin." Translated by Winifred Roy
$1,500/15,000

001b: LAUGHTER IN THE DARK Bobbs-Merrill Ind./NY (1938) [1] New title. Author's last name listed as "Nabokoff." Translated into English by Nabokov. The presumed first issue binding is green (based on the two copyright deposit copies at the Library of Congress)
$150/750

001c: LAUGHTER IN THE DARK Bobbs-Merrill Ind./NY (1938) [1] Variant bindings: orange, brown or red $50/600

001d: LAUGHTER IN THE DARK New Directions (NY 1960) [1] "New Edition 1960." Two variants, one has two extra lines at bottom of copyright page "New Directions... New York 14," the other does not. Ref.a gives no priority, but states about 1,490 copies in variant without address and 1,468 copies in the other. Publisher records show 1,492 copies bound November 10, 1960; and 1,409 copies bound later $12/60

001e: LAUGHTER IN THE DARK Weidenfeld & Nicolson L (1961)[0] $30/150

002a: DESPAIR John Long L (1937) [1] Author's last name listed as "Nabokoff-Sirin." Black cloth stamped in gilt (ref.a). Also noted in orange cloth lettered in black (Joseph The Provider 9/90) $2,000/20,000

002b: DESPAIR G.P. Putnam NY (1966) [0] Author's last name listed as "Nabokov." Revised with new material and new foreword. The first issue dustwrapper has the title in reddish-pink on front dustwrapper flap $25/150

002c: DESPAIR G.P. Putnam NY (1966) [0] Title on front flap in black $25/100

002d: DESPAIR Weidenfeld & Nicolson L 1966 [1] $15/75

003a: THE REAL LIFE OF SEBASTIAN KNIGHT New Directions Norfolk, Ct. (1941) [0] 1,500 cc (total a&b, approximately 750 in each binding). First issue binding: woven red burlap $200/600

003b: THE REAL LIFE OF SEBASTIAN KNIGHT New Directions Norfolk, Ct. (1941) [0] Bound in smooth red cloth with two dustwrapper variants, author's name spelled "Nabokov" and Nabokoff." No priority although 003a is shown with "Nabokov" spelling, which would seem to indicate it was first; and the feeling is that the "Nabokoff" was printed first but set aside and only used on the later second issue copies when they ran out of the other dustwrappers $50/250

003c: THE REAL LIFE OF SEBASTIAN KNIGHT Editions Poetry L (1945) [1] First issue dustwrapper in red with gold and black lettering $35/175

003d: THE REAL LIFE OF SEBASTIAN KNIGHT Editions Poetry L (1945) [1] Dustwrapper yellow with red and black lettering. Note: both priced 8s.6d $35/125

004a: THE NEARCTIC FORMS OF LYCAEIDES HUB... Museum of Com-parative Zoology (Cambridge 1943) [0] 100 cc. Off-print from *Psyche* in stapled wraps $1,000.

005a: NOTES ON THE MORPHOLOGY OF THE GENUS LYCAEIDES Psyche (Cambridge 1944) [0] 100 cc. Off-print in stapled wraps $1,000.

006a: NIKOLAI GOGOL New Directions Norfolk, Ct. (1944) [0] Tan cloth with brown lettering, 5 titles listed on verso of half-title. Dustwrapper priced $1.50. (Illustration of hand holding a pen) $50/250

006b: NIKOLAI GOGOL New Directions Norfolk, Ct. (1944) [0] Tan cloth with blue stamping and 14 titles listed on verso of half-title. Dustwrapper price $2.00 and 14 titles listed on back flap $30/150

006c: NIKOLAI GOGOL Editions Poetry L (1947) [1] Noted in tan or green cloth, priority unknown $30/150

007a: THREE RUSSIAN POETS Selections from Pushkin, Lermontov and Tyutchev New Directions Norfolk, Ct. (1944) [0] Translation by Nabokov. Part of the Poets of the Year series. Plain gray paper boards. Dustwrapper gray with brown lettering and $1.00 upper corner of front flap $100/300

007b: THREE RUSSIAN POETS Selections from Pushkin, Lermontov and Tyutchev New Directions Norfolk, Ct. (1944) [0] Tan stapled pamphlet. Dustwrapper bluish gray with brown lettering and $0.50 in lower right corner of front flap $25/150

007c: PUSHKIN LERMONTOV TYUTCHEV Lindsay Drummond Ltd L 1947 [1] This edition includes 11 poems not in the American edition (007a) $50/200

008a: NOTES ON NEOTROPICAL PLEBEJINAE (Museum of Comparative Zoology Cambridge 1945) [0] 100 cc Off-print from *Psyche* in stapled wraps $850.

009a: A THIRD SPECIES OF ECHINARGUS NABOKOV Museum of Com-parative Zollogy (Cambridge 1945) [0] 100 cc. Single leaf. Note on an article that appeared in *Psyche* $600.

010a: BEND SINISTER Henry Holt NY (1947) [1] $50/250

010b: BEND SINISTER Weidenfeld & Nicolson L (1960) [1] $35/175

010c: BEND SINISTER Time NY (1964) [0] Wraps. 75,000 cc. First edition has one "X" in colophon on last page. Adds new foreword by Nabokov $30.

011a: NINE STORIES (New Directions NY 1947) [0] Wraps. Published as *Direction Two*. This issue was devoted entirely to Nabokov. (Probably a few copies in cloth, perhaps black, would be worth quite a bit more) $250.

012a: A NEW SPECIES OF CYCLARGUS NABOKOV Cornell Univ. Ithaca (1948) [0] Wraps. Cover has "Reprinted From *The Entomologist...*" $500.

013a: THE NEARCTIC MEMBERS OF THE GENUS LYCAEIDES HUBNER (LYCAENIDAE LEPIDOPTERA) Museum of Comparative Zoology Cambridge 1949 [] Wraps. The article occupies the entire issue of this bulletin (Vol. 101, No. 4) $500.

014a: CONCLUSIVE EVIDENCE A MEMOIR Harper New York (1951) [1] Also has "A-A" on copyright page $50/250

014b: SPEAK, MEMORY A MEMOIR Gollancz L 1951 [0] First issue in blue-green cloth with black stamping. In dustwrapper without *Daily Mail* device on spine and at bottom of front flap $60/300

014c: SPEAK, MEMORY A MEMOIR Gollancz L 1951 [0] Second issue in blue cloth and gilt stamping in dustwrapper with *Daily Mail* device on spine and at bottom of front flap ("Daily Mail Book of the Month" wrap-around band on some copies) $40/200

014d: SPEAK, MEMORY AN AUTOBIOGRAPHY REVISED G.P. Putnam NY (1966) [0] 5,000 cc. States "Revised Edition" on copyright. Revised and adds new foreword $25/100

014e: SPEAK, MEMORY AN AUTOBIOGRAPHY REVISED Weidenfeld & Nicolson L (1967) [1] $25/100

015a: LOLITA Olympia Paris (1955) [0] Approximately 5,000 cc. Wraps. Two volumes.

Printed price "Francs : 900" on back cover $1,500.

015b: LOLITA G.P. Putnam NY (1958) [0] One volume. Adds afterword by Nabokov $30/150

Note: book club copies have "Book Club Edition" on the corner of front flap (Cannot be distinguished from the trade edition without dustwrapper)

015c: LOLITA Weidenfeld & Nicolson L (1959) [1] Black cloth stamped in silver $25/125

015d: THE ANNOTATED LOLITA McGraw-Hill NY/Toronto (1970) [1] Edited by Alfred Appel. Putnam text with many corrections $12/60

015e: THE ANNOTATED LOLITA Weidenfeld & Nicolson L (1971) [1] $12/60

015f: LOLITA: A SCREENPLAY McGraw-Hill NY (1974) [3] $10/50

015g: LOLITA Franklin Library Franklin Ctr. 1979 [2] "Limited edition" in full leather. Illustrated by Herbert Tauss $75.

015h: LOLITA Franklin Library Franklin Ctr. 1981 [2] "Limited Edition." Illustrated by Jerry Pinkney $60.

016a: PNIN Doubleday GC 1957 [1] Noted with "46946" above or below price on dustwrapper flap (priority unknown) $35/175

016b: PNIN Heineman Melbourne/L/T (1957) [] Uncorrected proof in orange wraps with author, title and month of publication typed on front cover (Nicholas Pounder 5/90). Ref.a has white label on front $300.

016c: PNIN Heinemann Melbourne/L/T (1957) [1] $25/125

017a: A HERO OF OUR TIME Doubleday Anchor GC 1958 [1] Wraps. Written by Mihail Lermontov and translated by Vladimir Nabokov with Dmitri Nabokov. Cover illustration and topography by Edward Gorey $50.

017b: A HERO OF OUR TIME Oxford Univ. Press Oxford 1984 [1] (Ref.c) $35/100

017c: A HERO OF OUR TIME Oxford Univ. Press Oxford 1984 [1] Wraps $25.

018a: NABOKOV'S DOZEN Doubleday GC 1958 [1] A collection of 13 stories $30/150

018b: NABOKOV'S DOZEN Heineman L/M/T (1959) [1] $25/125

019a: INVITATION TO A BEHEADING G.P. Putnam NY (1959) [0] Translated with Dimitri Nabokov $25/100

019b: INVITATION TO A BEHEADING Weidenfeld & Nicolson L (1960) [1] $25/100

020a: POEMS Doubleday GC 1959 [1] The Library of Congress deposit copy has "A25" on lower right corner of p.44 $35/175

020b: POEMS Doubleday GC 1959 [1] "A26" on lower right corner of p.44 (priority unknown, we assume this is a later issue) $25/125

020c: POEMS Weidenfeld & Nicolson L (1961) [1] $5/125

021a: THE SONG OF IGOR'S CAMPAIGN Random House NY (1960) [1] Wraps. Translated by Nabokov $50.

021b: THE SONG OF IGOR'S CAMPAIGN Weidenfeld & Nicolson L (1961) [1] $30/150

022a: PALE FIRE G.P. Putnam NY (1962) [1] "First Impression" also on front dustwrapper flap. Red endpapers $35/175

022b: PALE FIRE Weidenfeld & Nicolson L (1962) [] Uncorrected proof in brown wraps (Thomas Goldwasser 6/92) $250.

022c: PALE FIRE Weidenfeld & Nicolson L (1962) [1] $20/100

023a: NOTES ON PROSODY Bollingen Series LXXII (Bollingen NY 1963) [0] 200 cc 30 copies of which went to Nabokov to give as Christmas gifts. This is an off-print taken from his translation of Pushkin's *Eugene Onegin* to be published later that same year. Wraps and dustwrapper $250/350

023b: NOTES ON PROSODY Pantheon (NY 1964) [0] 3,500 cc. Wraps and dustwrapper which is glued at spine to the wrappers. Appendix II to 025a below $75.

023c: NOTES ON PROSODY Routledge & Kegan Paul L (1965) [1] 500 cc $40/125

024a: THE GIFT G.P. Putnam NY (1963) [0] Book bulks 3.3 cm. Dustwrapper priced $5.95 (priority assumed) $25/125

024b: THE GIFT G.P. Putnam NY (1963) [0] Book 3.8 cm wide. Dustwrapper priced $6.95. Assume a second issue $25/100

024c: THE GIFT Weidenfeld & Nicolson L (1963) [] Uncorrected proof in gray wraps (Waiting For Godot 7/90) $250.

024d: THE GIFT Weidenfeld & Nicolson L (1963) [0] $20/100

025a: EUGENE ONEGIN, A NOVEL IN VERSE by Aleksandr Pushkin Pantheon (NY 1964) [0] 4 volumes. Translation, introduction and commentary by Nabokov. In dustwrappers and slipcase. Earliest sets have ribbon place markers $150/300

025b: EUGENE ONEGIN, A NOVEL IN VERSE Pantheon (NY 1964) [0] Without ribbons $125/250

025c: EUGENE ONEGIN, A NOVEL IN VERSE Routledge & Kegan Paul L (1964) [1] 4 volumes $125/250

025d: EUGENE ONEGIN, A NOVEL IN VERSE Revised Edition Princeton University Press (1975) [0] 2,856 cc. 4 volumes. Bollingen Series LXXII $75/150

025e: EUGENE ONEGIN, A NOVEL IN VERSE Revised Edition Routledge & Kegan Paul L (1975) [1] 1,000 cc. 4 volumes. (Sheets imported) $75/150

026a: THE RETURN OF PUSHKIN Edition N.P. Belaieff L 1964? [] Wraps? Translated by Nabokov $75.

027a: THE DEFENSE G.P. Putnam NY (1964) [0] $20/100

027b: THE DEFENSE Weidenfeld & Nicolson L (1964) [0] $15/75

028a: THE EYE Phaedra NY (1965) [1] Advance review copy in plain white wraps and cloth spine with publisher's address on copyright page. Dustwrapper printed on white laid uncoated paper with Trident Press mentioned at bottom of back flap $75/125

028b: THE EYE Phaedra NY (1965) [1] Publisher's address on copyright page. Dustwrapper printed on white laid uncoated paper with Trident Press mentioned at bottom of back flap. Although Ref.a does not assign a priority to this issue, we believe it would be first as it matches the advance copy $10/60

028c: THE EYE Phaedra NY (1965) [1] Assume second issue without publisher's address on copyright page. Dustwrapper printed on white smooth coated paper without Trident mentioned $8/40

028d: THE EYE Weidenfeld & Nicolson L (1966) [] Advance uncorrected proof in orange printed wraps $100.

028e: THE EYE Weidenfeld & Nicolson L (1966) [1] $12/60

029a: THE WALTZ INVENTION Phaedra (NY) 1966 [1] A play in three acts

Variant a: blue cloth. Bound in 4 signatures, 1st is on an unacidic paper, the other 3 are on acidic bulky paper (such as newsprint). White endpapers. Dustwrapper has "New York 17, N.Y." on back flap. Bulks about 10mm $10/50

Variant b: as variant a except all 4 signatures are on a non-acidic paper $10/50

Variant c: as variant b except with red endpapers. Bulks 8.5mm $10/50

Variant d: as variant c except back flap of dustwrapper lacks "New York 17, N.Y." Bulks 8.5mm $10/50

Variant e: as variant a except dark blue cloth, 8 extra blank pages after text, and has a dustwrapper totally different from other variants (most notable difference if you do not have two dustwrappers to compare is that this variant has a blue background). Back flap has publisher at 27 Washington Square (in lieu of 220 East 22nd St.). We assume this is not a variant but a later issue, as 22nd Street was an earlier address $5/25

029b: THE WALTZ INVENTION Weidenfeld & Nicolson (L 1967) [1] dw $10/60

030a: NABOKOV'S QUARTET Phaedra (NY) 1966 [1]

Variant a: green endpapers; pages bulk about 10.5mm $15/75

Variant b: white endpapers; pages bulk about 8.5mm $12/60

Variant c: white endpapers; pages bulk about 8.5mm. Two different kinds of paper used (one for the first signature and another for the second and third signatures) $10/50

030b: NABOKOV'S QUARTET Weidenfeld & Nicolson L (1967) [1] $10/60

031a: KING, QUEEN, KNAVE McGraw-Hill NY/T (1968) [1] "First Edition 45715." Bottom edge rough-trimmed. Many of this state were destroyed by the publisher $75/100

031b: KING, QUEEN, KNAVE McGraw-Hill NY/T (1968) [1] "First Edition 45715." Bottom edge smoothly trimmed $10/50

032a: KING, QUEEN, KNAVE Weidenfeld & Nicolson L (1968) [1] $10/50

033a: NABOKOV'S CONGERIES Viking NY (1968) [1] selected with a critical introduction by Page Stegner, an extensive bibliographical essay by Stegner; and an essay by Nabokov "Reply To My Critics" not published before $12/60

034a: NOTES ON PROSODY AND ABRAM GANNIBAL Princeton Univ. Press (Princeton, NJ 1969) [0] 5015 cc. Wraps. Bollingen Series. Extract from *Eugene Onegin* $75.

035a: ADA OR ARDOR: A FAMILY CHRONICLE McGraw-Hill NY/T (1969) [] Uncorrected proof in olive printed wraps with mimeographed title page (Thomas Goldwasser 2/91) $300.

035b: ADA OR ARDOR: A FAMILY CHRONICLE McGraw-Hill NY/T (1969) [1] "First Edition 45720" $10/50

035c: ADA OR ARDOR: A FAMILY CHRONICLE Weidenfeld & Nicolson (1969) [1] $8/40

035d: ADA OR ARDOR: A FAMILY CHRONICLE Penguin (Harmondsworth 1970 [0] Wraps. Adds "Notes to Ada by Vivian Darkbloom" by Nabokov $30.

036a: MARY McGraw-Hill NY/T (1970) [1] Translated by Michael Glenny, in collaboration with Nabokov (original in Russian in 1926) $10/50

036b: MARY Weidenfeld & Nicolson L (1971) [1] $10/50

037a: ANNIVERSARY NOTES Northwestern Univ. Press (Evanston, IL) 1970 [0] Wraps. "Supplement to Triquarterly 17." 16-page stapled pamphlet with Nabokov's response to the Triquarterly tribute for his 70th birthday. Written in March 1970 but published winter 1970 $100.

038a: POEMS AND PROBLEMS McGraw-Hill NY/T (1971) [1] copyright 1970, published March 1971 $15/75

038b: POEMS AND PROBLEMS Weidenfeld & Nicolson L (1972) [1] $12/60

039a: GLORY McGraw-Hill NY/T (1971) [1] Translated by Dmitri Nabokov in collaboration with the author (original in Russian in 1932) $8/40

039b: GLORY McGraw-Hill Weidenfeld & Nicolson L (1972) [1] $8/40

040a: TRANSPARENT THINGS McGraw-Hill NY/St.L/S.F./T (1972) [3] $10/40

040b: TRANSPARENT THINGS Weidenfeld & Nicolson L (1973) [1] $10/40

041a: A RUSSIAN BEAUTY AND OTHER STORIES McGraw-Hill NY/T (1973) [3] also states "First Edition" $12/60

041b: A RUSSIAN BEAUTY AND OTHER STORIES Weidenfeld & Nicolson L (1973) [1] $10/50

042a: STRONG OPINIONS McGraw-Hill NY/St.L/SF/T (1973) [3] $10/40

042b: STRONG OPINIONS Weidenfeld & Nicolson L (1974) [1] $10/40

043a: LOLITA A SCREENPLAY McGraw-Hill NY/St.L/SF/T (1974) [3] (The original screenplay by Seven Arts Productions {1961}, punchbound mimeographed sheets, was catalogued by Jos. the Provider 2/90 for $650.) Nabokov was nominated for an Academy Award for his screenplay $15/75

044a: LOOK AT THE HARLEQUINS! McGraw-Hill NY/St.L/SF/T (1974) [3] $8/40

044b: LOOK AT THE HARLEQUINS! Weidenfeld & Nicolson L (1975) [1] $8/40

045a: TYRANTS DESTROYED AND OTHER STORIES McGraw-Hill NY/T (1975) [3] $8/40

045b: TYRANTS DESTROYED AND OTHER STORIES Weidenfeld & Nicolson L (1975) [1] $8/40

046a: DETAILS OF A SUNSET AND OTHER STORIES McGraw-Hill NY/St.L/SF/T (1976) [3] $15/60

046b: DETAILS OF A SUNSET AND OTHER STORIES Weidenfeld & Nicolson L (1976) [1] $15/60

047a: THE NABOKOV-WILSON LETTERS Harper & Row NY/H/SF/L (1979) [3] Also states "First Edition." 15,000 cc. Edited by Simon Karlinsky $10/40

047b: THE NABOKOV-WILSON LETTERS Weidenfeld & Nicolson L (1979) [1] $8/40

047c: THE NABOKOV-WILSON LETTRS Harper Colophon NY (1980) [3] Wraps. Also states "First Harper ... published 1980." Corrected edition $15.

048a: LECTURES ON LITERATURE Harcourt Brace Janovich/Bruccoli Clark NY/L (1980) [4] Edited by Fredson Bowers $10/50

048b: LECTURES ON LITERATURE Weidenfeld & Nicolson L (1980) [1] $10/50

049a: LECTURES ON ULYSSES A FACSIMILE OF THE MANUSCRIPT Bruccoli Clark Bloomfield Hills/Columbia 1980 [2] 20 cc numbered I-XX (reserved for the publisher). (Also 20 copies of letter "A" reserved for the publisher? -Fine Books 5/92) $250.

049b: LECTURES ON ULYSSES A FACSIMILE OF THE MANUSCRIPT Bruccoli Clark Bloomfield Hills/Columbia 1980 [2] 480 no. cc. Bound in natural buckram, in glassine dustwrapper (ref.c). Note: publisher offered copies in custom bindings $125.

050a: LECTURES ON RUSSIAN LITERATURE Harcourt Brace Jovanovich/Bruccoli Clark NY/L (1981) [4] Edited by Fredson Bowers $10/50

050b: LECTURES ON RUSSIAN LITERATURE Weidenfeld & Nicolson L (1982) [1] $10/50

051a: LECTURES ON DON QUIXOTE Harcourt Brace/Bruccoli Clark SD/NY/L 1983 [] Uncorrected proof (calling for "foreword to come" by Reynolds Price) $125.

051b: LECTURES ON DON QUIXOTE Harcourt Brace/Bruccoli Clark SD/NY/L 1983 [4] Foreword by Guy Davenport (the dustwrapper lists it as a preface, the title page as an introduction) $10/40

051c: LECTURES ON DON QUIXOTE Weidenfeld & Nicolson L (1983) [1] $10/40

052a: THE MAN FROM THE U.S.S.R. AND OTHER PLAYS Harcourt Brace/Bruccoli Clark San Diego (1984) [3] "First Edition ABCDE." (Published December 14, 1984 @ $24.95.) Introduction and translation by Dmitri Nabokov) $10/40

052b: THE MAN FROM THE U.S.S.R. AND OTHER PLAYS Harcourt ... San Diego (1985) [3] Wraps. "First Harvest ... 1985/ABC..." $15.

052c: THE MAN FROM THE U.S.S.R. AND OTHER PLAYS Weidenfeld & Nicolson L (1985) [] (Ref.b) $10/40

053a: THE ENCHANTER Putnam NY (1986) [3] Wraps. Uncorrected proof in orange printed wraps (Ref.c) $100.

053b: THE ENCHANTER Putnam NY (1986) [3] (Published October 1986 @ $16.95) (Ref.b) $7/35

053c: THE ENCHANTER Picador (L 1987) [] (I.D. Edrich 6/91) $10/30

054a: CARROUSEL | THREE TEXTS BY VLADIMIR NABOKOV Spectatorpers Aartswoud, The Netherlands 1987 [2] 40 no. cc (1 to 40). Natural white boards. Issued without dustwrapper. Not for sale $200.

054b: CARROUSEL | THREE TEXTS BY VLADIMIR NABOKOV Spectatorpers Aartswoud, The Netherlands 1987 [2] 60 no. cc (41 to 100). Plain rust wraps in white dustwrapper $125/150

054c: CARROUSEL | LAUGHTER AND DREAMS | PAINTED WOOD | THE RUSSIAN SONG Spectatorpers Aartswoud, The Netherlands 1987 [2] 40 no. cc in Roman numerals. Includes introduction by Dmitri Nabokov not in first two issues. Natural white boards. Issued without dustwrapper $125

054d: CARROUSEL | LAUGHTER AND DREAMS | PAINTED WOOD | THE RUSSIAN SONG Spectatorpers Aartswoud, The Netherlands 1987 [2] 110 no. cc in plain rust colored wraps and white dustwrapper $35/75

054e: CARROUSEL | LAUGHTER AND DREAMS | PAINTED WOOD | THE RUSSIAN SONG Spectatorpers Aartswoud, The Netherlands 1987 [] Unspecified number of copies marked "H.C." (hors commerce) $30/60

055a: VLADIMIR NABOKOV: SELECTED LETTERS 1940-1977 Harcourt Brace San Diego 1989 [1] Also states "First Edition." Edited by Dmitri Nabokov and Matthew Bruccoli (published September 1, 1989 @ $29.95) (Ref.c) $7/35

055b: VLADIMIR NABOKOV: SELECTED LETTERS 1940-1977 Weidenfeld & Nicolson L (1990) [1] $7/35

FLANNERY O'CONNOR
(1925-1964)

Flannery O'Connor was born in Georgia in 1925. She graduated from Georgia State College for Women and studied writing for two years at the State University of Iowa. Sixteen years after her death, her first book, *Wise Blood*, was made into a movie directed by John Huston. That same year, she was given a special award from the National Book Award Committee for the significant body of writing she produced in her short writing career. She is considered one of the best short story writers of the post war generation. She is probably one of the best, certainly one of the strongest, of the century.

REFERENCES:

(a) Bruccoli & Clarke FIRST PRINTINGS OF AMERICAN AUTHORS Volume 1, Gale Research, Detroit (1977). Used through 1971 for U.S. editions.

(b) Farmer, David FLANNERY O'CONNOR A DESCRIPTIVE BIBLIOGRAPHY Garland Publishing, New York, 1981. Used through 1980 for U.K. editions and quantities for both U.S. and U.K. editions.

(c) Inventory, dealer catalogs, etc.

001a: WISE BLOOD Harcourt Brace New York (1952) [1] 3,000 cc $250/1,250

001b: WISE BLOOD Neville Spearman London (1955) [1] 3,000 cc $75/400

001c: WISE BLOOD Farrar, Straus & Cudahy New York (1962) [0] Includes "Author's Note to the Second Edition" $30/150

001d: WISE BLOOD Faber & Faber London (1968) [1] 3,000 cc. "First published in Great Britain in mcmlxviii." Also includes author's note (ref.b) $25/125

002a: A GOOD MAN IS HARD TO FIND Harcourt Brace New York (1955) [1] 2,500 cc (a&b). First issue dustwrapper has *Wise Blood* on rear panel. Dustwrapper spine usually faded, the estimated price would be for unfaded one $150/750

002b: A GOOD MAN IS HARD TO FIND Harcourt Brace New York (1955) [1] In second issue dustwrapper with this title on back panel (ref.c) $150/500

002c: THE ARTIFICIAL NIGGER AND OTHER TALES Neville Spearman L (1957) [1] 2,000 cc. New title $100/400

002d: A GOOD MAN IS HARD TO FIND Faber & Faber London (1968) [] (Joseph Dermont 1/92) $20/100

003a: THE VIOLENT BEAR IT AWAY Farrar, Straus & Cudahy New York (1960) [0] $60/300

003b: THE VIOLENT BEAR IT AWAY Longmans, Green & Co. (London 1960) [1] 3,500 cc. "This edition first published 1960." Red cloth reportedly scarcer than orange $40/200

004a: SOME ASPECTS OF THE GROTESQUE IN SOUTHERN FICTION (Wesleyan College Macon, Georgia 1960) [0]

Ref.a lists this item as being published in 1960 in an edition of 20 copies. Back in 1985 we tried to find out who put this entry in ref.a, but we were never successful. We did find out, indirectly, from Ms Ann Munck, Chairman of the English Department at Wesleyan, that O'Connor's speech on October 27, 1960 (during the Eugenia Dorothy Blount Lamar Lecture Series) was taped. She also believes that Mercer University borrowed the tape to transcribe the speech for their literary magazine, where it did appear. A copy was catalogued by Henry Turlington with the following comments:

"Five single-spaced mimeographed pages from typscript. Copy of the speech as O'Connor presented it at Wesleyan College, October 27, 1960. It seems pretty clear that this is what FPAA refers to in its bibliographical entry on O'Connor, although many have regarded it as a ghost. The mimeograph was made by O'Connor's friend, Thomas Gossett from a manuscript which she sent him for review. In a letter to this cataloguer, Dr. Gossett wrote that O'Connor 'did send me a copy of her article...I am fairly sure she sent it in 1961 or 1962. At the time she was using the article...for lectures she gave at various colleges over the country. She explained that if she published the article at that time she would not have been able to use it for her lectures.' Dr. Gossett goes on to say that he typed a copy of the article, returned the original to O'Connor, and gave copies to his students in San Antonio. It should be noted that there are a number of differences between this version of O'Connor's most famous essay and the published version." $1,250.

005a: A MEMOIR OF MARY ANN Farrar, Straus & Cudahy New York (1961) [1] Written by the Domincan Nuns of Our Lady of Perpetual Help Home. Introduction by O'Connor. Noted with top edge stained blue and unstained. Priority unknown (Chapel Hill Rare Books 1/90) $20/100

005b: DEATH OF A CHILD Burns & Oates London (1961) [0] New title. Edited and introduction by Flannery O'Connor. (Also issued by Catholic Book Club in 1961, but ref.b would seem to indicate that this was later) $15/75

006a: THREE BY FLANNERY O'CONNOR New American Library/Signet (New York 1964) [1] Wraps. 109,000 cc. First thus. First three books $35.

007a: EVERYTHING THAT RISES MUST CONVERGE Farrar, Straus & Giroux New York (1965) [1] $40/200

007b: EVERYTHING THAT RISES MUST CONVERGE Faber & Faber London (1966) [] Uncorrected proof in unprinted blue wraps (Waiting For Godot 10/90) $300.

007c: EVERYTHING THAT RISES MUST CONVERGE Faber & Faber London (1966) [1] 2,470 cc $25/125

007d: EVERYTHING THAT RISES MUST CONVERGE (Tales For Travelers Napa, CA 1985) [0] 15,000 cc. Wraps. Single sheet folded to make 24 pages (map style). First separate edition (later printings were overstamped on the back with either "Parke-Davis" or "Dermik" $25.

008a: THE ADDED DIMENSION The Art and The Mind of Flannery O'Connor Fordham University Press New York (1966) [] Contains the first publication of a selection of letters and first book appearances of some of the essays. Edited by Melvin J. Friedman and Lewis A. Lawson $25/100

009a: MYSTERY AND MANNERS Farrar, Straus & Giroux New York (1969) [1] $30/150

009b: MYSTERY AND MANNERS Faber & Faber London (1972) [1] 1,000 cc. First state without author's name on spine of book $100/150

009c: MYSTERY AND MANNERS Faber & Faber London (1972) [1] 1,000 cc. Second state with author's name on spine of book $15/75

010a: THE COMPLETE STORIES Farrar, Straus & Giroux New York (1971) [1] $20/100

010b: THE COMPLETE STORIES Franklin Library Franklin Ctr 1980 [] Full leather (Pharos 1/91) $75.

010c: THE COMPLETE STORIES Franklin Library Franklin Ctr 1983 [] Full leather (Pharos 11/89) $75.

011a: THREE SHORT STORIES (World Today Press Hong Kong 1975) [] Wraps. First thus. In English and Chinese (Henry Turlington 1/90) $75.

012a: THE HABIT OF BEING Farrar, Straus & Giroux New York (1979) [] Uncorrected proof in mauve wraps (Nouveau Books 2/91) $150.

012b: THE HABIT OF BEING Farrar, Straus & Giroux New York (1979) [1] Letters edited by Sally Fitzgerald $15/75

012c: THE HABIT OF BEING Faber & Faber London 1980 [] $12/60

013a: HIGHER EDUCATION Palaemon Press (Winston-Salem, NC 1980) [2] 26 ltr cc. 8x10 broadside $125.

013b: HIGHER EDUCATION Palaemon Press (Winston-Salem, NC 1980) [2] 100 no. cc. 8x10 broadside $60.

014a: HOME OF THE BRAVE Albondocani New York 1981 [2] 26 ltr cc. Wraps $200.

014b: HOME OF THE BRAVE Albondocani New York 1981 [2] 200 no. cc $100.

015a: THE PRESENCE OF GRACE AND OTHER BOOK REVIEWS Univ. of Georgia Press Athens (1983) [3] Compiled by Leo J. Zuber. Introduction by Carter W. Martin $10/40

016a: THE CORRESPONDENCE OF FLANNERY O'CONNOR AND THE BRAINARD CHANEYS Univ. Press of Mississippi Jackson (1986) [] Proof in spiral bound plain wraps with printed label (William Reese Co. 2/92) $100.

016b: THE CORRESPONDENCE OF FLANNERY O'CONNOR AND THE BRAINARD CHANEYS Univ. Press of Mississippi Jackson (1986) [3] 188 previously unpublished letters (117 by O'Connor), edited by C. Ralph Stephens $15/40

016c: THE CORRESPONDENCE OF FLANNERY O'CONNOR AND THE BRAINARD CHANEYS Univ. Press of Mississippi Jackson (1986) [3] Wraps $15.

017a: CONVERSATIONS WITH FLANNERY O'CONNOR Univ. Press of Mississippi Jackson (1987) [] Uncorrected proof in spiral bound printed wraps (William Reese Co. 2/92) $75.

017b: CONVERSATIONS WITH FLANNERY O'CONNOR Univ. Press of Mississippi Jackson (1987) [] $15/40

017c: CONVERSATIONS WITH FLANNERY O'CONNOR Univ. Press of Mississippi Jackson (1987) [] Wraps $15.

018a: REVELATION Tales For Travellers (Napa, Calif. 1987) [0] 15,000 cc. Wraps (map folded). First separate edition. (Later printings were overstamped on back with either "Parke-Davis" or "Dermik" $25.

019a: COMPLETE WORKS Library of America (New York 1988) [] Includes a few stories not in book form before and 21 unpublished letters (Ampersand 7/92) $20/40

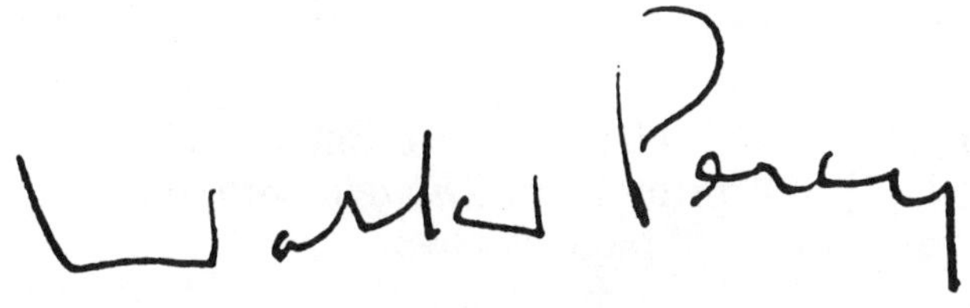

WALKER PERCY
1916-1990

Percy was born in Birmingham, Alabama in 1916. He received his B.A. from the University of North Carolina in Chapel Hill and a M.D. from Columbia University. Percy interned at Bellevue in 1942. He contracted tuberculosis and after recovering he decided to give up medicine and become a full-time writer.

> "Percy finds the modern world in a state of moral confusion, the values of the past no longer work and the majority of the men are spiritually dead, abstracted and if sensitive, ingrown and cut off from life outside themselves... (in spite of this) his rendering of characters and scenes is strikingly fresh, vivid and bitingly satirical. He is a moral and, ultimately, a religious writer, but he is also a novelist of manners who can delineate with remarkable skill the contrasts between certain kinds of Northerners, Southerners and Middle Westerners..."

-W. S.Stuckey in *Contemporary Novelists*,
St. Martins Press (1976)

REFERENCES:

(a) Wright, Stuart WALKER PERCY A BIBLIOGRAPHY: 1930-1984 Meckler Publishing (Connecticut 1986)

(b) Hobson, Linda Whitney WALKER PERCY: A COMPREHENSIVE DESCRIPTIVE BIBLIOGRAPHY Faust publishing Company New Orleans 1988.

(c) Inventory or dealer/publisher catalogs.

001a: SYMBOL AS NEED Fordham Univ. (NY) 1954 [0] Offprint from *Thought*. Stapled printed wraps with title page as cover $850.

002a: SYMBOL AS HERMENEUTIC IN EXISTENTIALISM Philosophy and Phenomenological Research (cover title) no-place 1956 [0] Wraps. An offprint, apparently without the title on cover $400.

003a: SEMIOTIC AND A THEORY OF KNOWLEDGE (Modern Schoolman no-place 1957) [0] Wraps. An offprint, assume without a cover $400.

004a: SYMBOL, CONSCIOUSNESS AND INTERSUBJECTIVITY The Journal of Philosophy (Lancaster) 1958 [0] Wraps. An offprint $400.

005a: CULTURE: THE ANTIMONY OF THE SCIENTIFIC METHOD New Scholasticism no-place 1958 [0] Wraps. An offprint $400.

006a: THE MESSAGE IN THE BOTTLE Thought Magazine no-place 1959 [0] Wraps. An offprint from the *Fordham University Quarterly* (for published book of same title see item 016 below) $350.

007a: NAMING AND BEING (The Personalist Bruges 1960) [0] Wraps. An offprint, assume in plain wraps $300.

008a: THE SYMBOLIC STRUCTURE OF THE INTERPERSONAL PROCESS Pyschiatry Journal... Washington, D.C. 1961 [0] Wraps. An offprint $300.

009a: THE MOVIEGOER Knopf NY 1961 [1] 3,000 cc. National Book Award for 1962. (Ref.b stated 1,500 copies; but the Knopf records at

Humanities Research Center indicate 3,000.) There is a Book Club edition (we assume) exactly like the first but states "Published..." vs. "First Edition: on copyright page and lacks price and "0561" on front dustwrapper corners $250/1,250

009b: THE MOVIEGOER Eyre & Spottiswoode L 1963 [1] $40/200

009c: THE MOVIEGOER Franklin Library Franklin Ctr 1980 [2] Signed limited edition. Issued in full leather. Incudes special message by the author $125.

010a: THE LAST GENTLEMAN Farrar Straus NY (1966) [1] $30/150

010b: THE LAST GENTLEMAN Eyre & Spottiswoode L (1967) [1] $20/100

011a: LOVE IN THE RUINS Farrar Straus NY (1971) [1] $15/75

011b: LOVE IN THE RUINS Eyre & Spottiswoode L (1971) [1] $15/75

012a: WHY DON'T YOU LINGUISTS HAVE AN EXPLANATORY THEORY OF LANGUAGE? no-publisher or place 1972 [2] 7 cc. "Original edition... consists of an original and six (6) copies of which this is no..." Xerox pages in 3-ring binder (Library of Congress) $NVA

013a: TOWARD A TRIADIC THEORY OF MEANING Psychiatry Journal.. No-place 1972 [0] No cover. 10 leaves with "Reprinted from..." top of first page $300.

014a: REVIEWS (no-publisher, place or date) [0] Tear sheets from Tulane Law Review 1972, reportedly 10 copies $NVA

015a: LANTERNS ON THE LEVEE Louisiana State Univ. Baton Rouge (1973) [0] Wraps. Introduction to William Alexander Percy's book $30.

016a: THE MESSAGE IN THE BOTTLE Farrar Straus NY (1975) [1] 8,000 cc. Top edge stained orange (Nouveau Rare Books, Steve Silberman talked to publisher and obtained quantity) $25/75

016b: THE MESSAGE IN THE BOTTLE Farrar Straus NY (1975) [1] 2,000 cc. Top edge unstained (Nouveau Rare Books) $12/60

017a: LANCELOT Farrar Straus NY (1977) [1] $6/30

017b: LANCELOT Secker & Warburg L (1977) [1] $10/50

018a: GOING BACK TO GEORGIA Univ of Ga. no-place 1978 [0] Wraps. The Ferdinand Phinizy Lecture $150.

019a: BOURBON Palaemon Press Winston-Salem (1979) [2] 5 sgd ltr (A to E) copies in full green leather $750.

019b: BOURBON Palaemon Press Winston-Salem (1979) [2] 50 sgd no. cc (Roman numerals) for use of author and publisher. Marbled wraps and dustwrapper $200/250

019c: BOURBON Palaemon Press Winston-Salem (1979) [2] 200 sgd no. cc. Marbled wraps and dustwrapper $100/150

019d: BOURBON Palaemon Press (Winston-Salem 1981) [2] 26 sgd ltr cc. Cloth spine and boards issued without dustwrapper or slipcase.

Second edition adding Percy's favorite drink $300.

019e: BOURBON Palaemon Press (Winston-Salem 1981) [2] 50 sgd no. cc (Roman numerals). Cloth spine and boards issued without dustwrapper or slipcase. Limitation states one of 150 copies but ref.a indicates that less than 100 copies, including 019d, were actually bound $150.

020a: QUESTIONS THEY NEVER ASKED ME Lord John Press Northridge 1979 [2] 50 sgd no. cc. Bound in full blue leather $250.

020b: QUESTIONS THEY NEVER ASKED ME Lord John Press Northridge 1979 [2] 300 sgd no. cc. Patterned paper covered boards with blue cloth spine $125.

021a: A CONFEDERACY OF DUNCES Louisiana State Univ. Baton Rouge 1980 [0] 2,500 cc. Percy's foreword to John Kennedy Toole's book $75/400

021b: A CONFEDERACY OF DUNCES Allen Lane (London 1981) [1] Reportedly 1,500 copies $30/150

022a: THE SECOND COMING Franklin Library Franklin Ctr 1980 [2] Signed limited first edition in full leather with special message from the author $150.

022b: THE SECOND COMING Farrar Straus NY (1980) [2] 450 sgd no. cc. Issued without dustwrapper in slipcase $75/150

022c: THE SECOND COMING Farrar Straus NY (1980) [1] $8/40

022d: THE SECOND COMING Secker & Warburg L (1981) [] (Ref.b) $8/40

023a: SEWANEE Frederic C. Beil NY 1982 [0] 3,000 cc. First separate appearance of this chapter from *Lanterns On The Levee*. Percy introduction the same as in 015a. Issued without dustwrapper $25.

024a: LOST IN THE COSMOS Farrar Straus NY (1983) [] Uncorrected proof in printed blue wraps (Bev Chaney #7) $250.

024b: LOST IN THE COSMOS Farrar Straus NY (1983) [2] 350 sgd no. cc. Issued without dustwrapper in slipcase $100/200

024c: LOST IN THE COSMOS Farrar Straus NY (1983) [1] $7/35

024d: LOST IN THE COSMOS Arrow Books L 1984 [] Wraps. No U.K. hardback (Ian McKelvie 6/91) $35.

025a: THE CITY OF THE DEAD Lord John Press Northridge 1984 [2] 26 sgd ltr cc. Broadside illustrated by Lyn Hill $200.

025b: THE CITY OF THE DEAD Lord John Press Northridge 1984 [2] 100 sgd no. cc. Broadside illustrated by Lyn Hill $125.

026a: DIAGNOSING THE MODERN MALAISE Faust Publ. New Orleans 1985 [2] 50 sgd no. cc. Specially bound (ref.c) $200.

026b: DIAGNOSING THE MODERN MALAISE Faust Publ. New Orleans 1985 [2] 250 sgd no. cc. Issued without dustwrapper or slipcase $125.

027a: CONVERSATIONS WITH WALKER PERCY Univ. Press of Mississippi Jackson

(1985) [3] Edited by Lewis A. Lawson and Victor A. Krammer (ref.c) $15/40

027b: CONVERSATIONS WITH WALKER PERCY Univ. Press of Mississippi Jackson (1985) [3] Wraps $15.

028a: NOVEL WRITING IN AN APOCALYPTIC TIME Faust Publ. New Orleans 1986 [2] 100 sgd no. cc. Afterword by Eudora Welty. Signed by both. Deluxe edition (Published July 1986 @ $150.) (ref.c) $250.

028b: NOVEL WRITING IN AN APOCALYPTIC TIME Faust Publ. New Orleans 1986 [2] 300 sgd no. cc. (Published July 1986 @ $75.) (ref.c) $125.

Note: There were also 60 unnumbered copies reserved for presentation (Lemuria List J)

029a: THE THANATOS SYNDROME Farrar Straus NY [] Uncorrected proof in printed red wraps (Bev Chaney #7) $125.

029b: THE THANATOS SYNDROME Farrar Straus NY (1987) [2] 250 sgd no. cc. In slipcase. (Published April 1987 @ $75.) (ref.c) $75/150

029c: THE THANATOS SYNDROME Farrar Straus NY (1987) [0] 75,000 cc (PW). (Published April 1987 @ $17.95) $6/30

029d: THE THANATOS SYNDROME Deutsch L (1987) [] $7/35

030a: THE STATE OF THE NOVEL: DYING ART OR NEW SCIENCE Faust Publ. New Orleans 1988 [2] 75 sgd no. cc. Deluxe edition $175.

030b: THE STATE OF THE NOVEL: DYING ART OR NEW SCIENCE Faust Publ. New Orleans 1988 [2] 250 sgd no. cc $100.

031a: SIGNPOSTS IN A STRANGE LAND Farrar Straus NY (1991) [] Uncorrected proof in blue wraps (Bev Chaney 9/91) $75.

031b: SIGNPOSTS IN A STRANGE LAND Farrar Straus NY (1991) [] 12,500 cc. Essays (some first appearances) edited by Patrick Samwau, S.J.

REYNOLDS PRICE

Reynolds Price was born in Macon, North Carolina in 1933. He graduated from Duke in 1955, then studied for three years as a Rhodes Scholar at Merton College, Oxford. In 1958 he returned to Duke, where he is now James B. Duke Professor of English. *A Long and Happy Life* received the William Faulkner Foundation Award for the most notable first novel of the year (1962). Price's books have received numerous other awards and have been translated into fourteen languages.

REFERENCES:

(a) Wright, Stuart and James L.W. West, REYNOLDS PRICE: A BIBLIOGRAPHY 1949-1984, University Press of Virginia, Charlottesville (1986).

(b) Ray A. Roberts, "Reynolds Price: A Bibliographical Checklist" in AMERICAN BOOK COLLECTOR, July / August 1981, pp.15-23.

(c) Gary M. Lepper, A BIBLIOGRAPHICAL INTRODUCTION TO SEVENTY-FIVE MODERN AMERICAN AUTHORS, Serendipity Books, Berkeley 1976, pp.349-352.

(d) FIRST PRINTINGS OF AMERICAN AUTHORS, Volume 1, Gale Research/Bruccoli Clark, Detroit (1977), pp.301-303 (compiled by Clayton S. Owens).

We wish to express our appreciation to D. Edmond Miller who prepared the original bibliographic portion of this guide with the generous assistance of Reynolds Price, Lawrence McIntyre of Atheneum Publishers, and the staff of the Rare Book Room of Perkins Library, Duke University.

001a: ONE SUNDAY IN LATE JULY (Encounter Magazine L 1960) [0] 50 cc. Wraps. Offprint, creme colored wrappers state "Reprinted from Encounter, March, 1960" $2,500.

002a: A LONG AND HAPPY LIFE Atheneum NY 1961 [1] Plastic ring-bound, light blue wrappers. Uncorrected proof, paper label on cover gives tentative publication date of September 13, 1961 and tentative price of $3.50 $400.

002b: A LONG AND HAPPY LIFE Atheneum NY 1962 [1] 500 cc. Advance reading copy in yellow wraps, cover states "This is an advance copy..." and gives tentative publication date of January 5, 1962 and price of $3.95 (ref.c notes a later issue bound in the dustwrapper for the finished book) $250.

002c: A LONG AND HAPPY LIFE Atheneum NY 1962 [1] 5,500 cc (c&d). First state dustwrapper: rear panel prints names of those providing blurbs in pale yellowish-green. (Published March 19, 1962) $15/100

002d: A LONG AND HAPPY LIFE Atheneum NY 1962 [1] Second state dustwrapper: rear panel prints names of those providing blurbs in darker bluish-green. (Published March 19, 1962) $15/75

002e: A LONG AND HAPPY LIFE Chatto & Windus L 1962 [0] 4,900 cc. (Published March 22, 1962) $15/75

Note: A LONG AND HAPPY LIFE was published in its entirety in a special section of *Harper's Magazine*, April 1962.

	Price
003a: THE NAMES AND FACES OF HEROES Atheneum NY 1963 [1] 6,000 cc (Published June 25, 1963)	$15/75
003b: THE NAMES AND FACES OF HEROES Chatto & Windus L 1963 [0] 2,750 cc (Published September 29, 1963)	$15/75
004a: A GENEROUS MAN Atheneum NY 1966 [1] Plastic ring-bound wraps. Uncorrected proof in light blue wraps, cover has paper label, text printed on rectos only	$350.
004b: A GENEROUS MAN Atheneum NY 1966 [1] 500 cc. Wraps. Advance reading copy, bound in the dustwrapper for the finished book	$125.
004c: A GENEROUS MAN Atheneum NY 1966 [1] 9,500 cc. (Published March 25, 1966)	$10/50
004d: A GENEROUS MAN Chatto & Windus L 1967 [0] 4,000 cc. (Published January 12, 1967)	$10/50

Note: A LONG AND HAPPY LIFE and A GENEROUS MAN were issued in a combined edition by the Quality Paperback Book Club in 1976. The text was offset from the second printing of each book.

005a: THE THING ITSELF (Duke Univ. Library Durham, NC 1966) [0] 750 cc (estimated). White wraps. (ref.c states 500 cc.) (Probably published June 1966)	$125.
006a: LOVE AND WORK Atheneum NY 1968 [1] Plastic ring-bound wraps. Uncorrected proof, light-blue cover has paper label	$250.

006b: LOVE AND WORK Atheneum NY 1968 [1] 10,000 cc. (Published May 29, 1968) $10/50

006c: LOVE AND WORK Chatto & Windus L 1968 [0] 1,250 cc. (Published October 24, 1968) $12/60

007a: LATE WARNING Albondocani Press NY 1968 [2] 26 sgd ltr cc. Wraps. (Published December 26, 1968) $250.

007b: LATE WARNING Albondocani Press NY 1968 [2] 150 sgd no. cc. Wraps. (Published December 26, 1968) $150.

008a: TORSO OF AN ARCHAIC APOLLO (Albondocani Press & Ampersand Books NY 1969) [2] Wraps. States "three hundred copies," but 110 copies with Albondocani Press and Ampersand Books mentioned on first page and 210 cc with the greeting only on first page (no priority). Price's Christmas greeting for 1969. (Published December 12, 1969) $60.

009a: PERMANENT ERRORS Atheneum NY 1970 [1] 5,000 cc. (Published September 23, 1970) $10/50

009b: PERMANENT ERRORS Chatto & Windus L 1971 [0] 1,500 cc. (Published March 25, 1971) $12/60

010a: TWO THEOPHANIES (Privately printed Durham, NC 1971) [2] 200 cc (a&b). Wraps. First state wrapper: purple printed in silver. Most copies are first state. Price's Christmas greeting for 1971 $100.

010b: TWO THEOPHANIES (privately printed Durham, NC 1971) [2] Second state wrapper: grey printed in black $75.

011a: FOR ERNEST HEMINGWAY New American Review (NY 1972) [0] Wraps. Offprint, grey-blue wrappers state "Reprinted From New American Review 14." (Probably published April 1972) $75.

012a: THINGS THEMSELVES Atheneum NY 1972 [1] 3,500 cc. (Published May 22, 1972) $10/50

013a: THE FOURTH ECLOGUE OF VERGIL (Privately printed Durham, NC 1972) [2] 225 cc. Tan wraps printed in brown, Price's Christmas greeting for 1972. (Published December 15, 1972) $75.

014a: AN APOCRYPHAL HYMN OF JESUS (Privately printed Durham, NC 1973) [2] 215 cc. Creme wraps printed in purple. Price's Christmas greeting for 1973. (Published December 15, 1973) $75.

015a: PRESENCE AND ABSENCE Bruccoli Clark Bloomfield Hills, MI & Columbia, SC 1973 [2] 300 sgd no. cc. Three unsewn signatures laid into a brown cloth clam-shell box stamped in gold. There was a substantial overrun of this publication. Although the title page states 1973, the copyright notice contains the dates 1970, and 1974, and the book was actually issued in June, 1974 $75.

016a: A NATIVITY FROM THE APOCRYPHAL BOOK OF JAMES (Privately printed Durham, NC 1974) [2] 225 cc. Brown wraps printed in black. Price's Christmas greeting for 1974. (Published December 15, 1974) $75.

017a: THE SURFACE OF EARTH Atheneum NY 1975 [1] Wraps. Uncorrected proof in dark blue wraps, paper label on cover gives tentative publication date of May 23, 1975 $175.

017b: THE SURFACE OF EARTH Atheneum NY 1975 [1] 15,000 cc. (Published 14, 1975) $8/40

017c: THE SURFACE OF EARTH Arlington Books L (1977) [1] 10,000 cc. (Published February 27, 1978) $8/40

018a: ANNUNCIATION (Privately printed Durham, NC 1975) [2] 225 cc. Tan wraps printed in black. Price's Christmas greeting for 1975. (Published December 15, 1975) $75.

019a: "A GREAT DEAL MORE": Une Interview de Reynolds Price Recherches Anglaises et Americaines Strasbourg, France 1976 [0] Wraps. Offprint of a 1974 interview conducted by Georges Gary, blue and white wrappers state "Extrait" $75.

020a: CONVERSATIONS: REYNOLDS PRICE & WILLIAM RAY Memphis State Univ. 1976 [0] 500 cc. Light green wraps. Bulletin #9 (Fall, 1976) of the Mississippi Valley Collection at Memphis State's John Willard Brister Library, comprising interviews from 1973-75 $60.

021a: THE GOOD NEWS ACCORDING TO MARK (Privately printed Durham, NC 1976) [2] 250 cc. Pictorial creme colored wraps printed in black and rust. Price's Christmas greeting for 1976. (Published November 15, 1976) $60.

021b: THE GOOD NEWS ACCORDING TO MARK (Privately printed Durham, NC 1976) 50 sgd no. cc. Wraps. For sale in 1977 $175.

	Price
022a: EARLY DARK Atheneum NY 1977 [1] Mustard colored wraps. Uncorrected proof	$200.
022b: EARLY DARK Atheneum NY 1977 [1] 3,000 cc (b & c). First state dustwrapper omits the author's name on the spine. (Published July 25, 1977)	$15/60
022c: EARLY DARK Atheneum NY 1977 [1] Second state dustwrapper includes the author's name on the spine	$15/40
023a: ORACLES Friends of Duke Univ. Library Durham, NC 1977 [2] 300 sgd no. cc. Signed by Price and the illustrator, Jacob Roquet. (Published October 1977)	$75.
023b: ORACLES Friends of Duke Univ. Libary Durham, NC 1977 [2] 6 sgd no. cc. These 6 overrun copies lack Roquet's etchings, containing instead original drawings by Price	$200.
024a: LESSONS LEARNED Albondocani Press NY 1977 [2] 26 sgd ltr cc. Wraps. (Published December 21, 1977)	$200.
024b: LESSONS LEARNED Albondocani Press NY 1977 [2] 200 sgd no. cc. Wraps	$60.
025a: THE DREAM OF A HOUSE (Palaemon Press Winston-Salem, NC 1977) [0] Broadside. Uncorrected proof, lacking the poem's title and printed on heavier stock than the published broadside	$150.
025b: THE DREAM OF A HOUSE (Palaemon Press Winston-Salem, NC 1977) [2] 26 sgd ltr cc. Broadside. (Published December 22, 1977)	$175.

025c: THE DREAM OF A HOUSE (Palaemon Press Winston-Salem, NC 1977) [2] 100 sgd no. cc. Broadside. (Published December 22, 1977) $90.

026a: A PALPABLE GOD Atheneum NY 1978 [1] 15 cc. Uncorrected proof in mustard colored wraps $300.

026b: A PALPABLE GOD Atheneum NY 1978 [1] 4,000 cc. (Published February 17, 1978) $8/40

027a: DEAD MAN, DYING GIRL Phosphenes (Walnut Creek, CA) 1978 [2] 30 cc. Broadside. Imprinted "Presentation Copy" (not for sale) $100.

027b: DEAD MAN, DYING GIRL Phosphenes (Walnut Creek, CA) 1978 [2] 26 sgd ltr cc. Broadside. Signed by Price and the illustrator, Chuck Miller. (Published April 15, 1978) $175.

027c: DEAD MAN, DYING GIRL Phosphenes (Walnut Creek, CA) 1978 [2] 200 sgd no. cc. Broadside. Signed by Price and the illustrator, Chuck Miller. (Published April 15, 1978) $75.

028a: PURE BOYS AND GIRLS (Palaemon Press Winston-Salem, NC 1978) [2] 28 sgd Roman numberal copies. Broadside. Issued as part of a folio entitled "For Aaron Copland." (Published November 14, 1978.) Price for entire protfolio $500.

028b: PURE BOYS AND GIRLS (Palaemon Press Winston-Salem, NC 1978) [2] 50 sgd no. cc. Broadside. Issued as part of a folio entitled "For Aaron Copland." (Published November 14, 1978.) Price for entire folio $350.

Price

029a: CHRIST CHILD'S SONG AT THE END OF THE NIGHT (Albondocani Press & Ampersand Books NY 1978) [2] Wraps. States "four hundred copies," but 155 copies with Albondocani Press and Ampersand Books mentioned on first page and 255 copies with the greeting only on first page (no priority). Price's Christmas greeting for 1978 (Published December 19, 1978) $50.

030a: FOR LEONTYNE AFTER ARIADNE (privately printed Durham, NC 1979) [2] 100 sgd no. cc. Broadside. (Published April 5, 1979) $125.

031a: THE LINES OF LIFE (Stuart Wright Winston-Salem, NC 1979) [2] 2 sgd Roman numberal copies. Broadside. (Published June 8, 1979) $NVA

031b: THE LINES OF LIFE (Stuart Wright Winston-Salem, NC 1979) [2] 6 sgd ltr cc. Broadside. (Published June 1979) $NVA

032a: QUESTION AND ANSWER The Baylor School Chattanooga 1979 [0] 500 cc. Wraps. The Second Archibald Yell Smith IV Lecture, given April 26, 1979 (this date appears on the cover) and published December 1, 1979 in white wraps $50.

033a: NINE MYSTERIES Palaemon Press (Winston-Salem, NC 1979) [2] 9 sgd ltr cc. Deluxe issue binding: dark grey cloth with a black leather spine. Each copy contains on the title page an original color drawing by Price. (Published December 15, 1979) $500.

033b: NINE MYSTERIES Palaemon Press (Winston-Salem, NC 1979) [2] 300 sgd cc. Regular issue binding: black cloth. (Published February 1, 1980) $60.

034a: SOCRATES AND ALCIBIADES (Palaemon Press Winston-Salem, NC 1980) [2] 75 sgd no. cc. Broadside. Issued as part of a folio entitled "For Robert Penn Warren." (Published April 24, 1980.) Price for entire folio $350.

035a: THE ANNUAL HERON Albondocani Press NY 1980 [2] 300 sgd no. cc. Wraps. (Published December 17, 1980) $50.

036a: A FINAL LETTER Sylvester & Orphanos L.A. 1980 [2] 4 sgd "Special Presentation" copies, each bearing the printed name of the recipient. (Also 30-35 overrun copies imprinted "Presentation Copy.") (Published February 6, 1981) $NVA

036b: A FINAL LETTER Sylvester & Orphanos L.A. 1980 [2] 26 sgd ltr cc. These copies are in black cloth slipcases and have not yet been offered for sale $200.

036c: A FINAL LETTER Sylvester & Orphanos L.A. 1980 [2] 300 sgd no. cc in glassine wraps. (Published February 6, 1981) $75.

037a: THE SOURCE OF LIGHT Atheneum NY 1981 [1] 50 cc. Uncorrected proof in yellow wraps $150.

037b: THE SOURCE OF LIGHT Atheneum NY 1981 [1] 10,000 cc. (Published April 23, 1981) $8/40

038a: COUNTRY MOUSE, CITY MOUSE (Friends of the Library N.C. Wesleyan College 1981) [2] 50 sgd no. cc. Pictorial wraps. (Published October 11, 1981) $100.

038b: COUNTRY MOUSE, CITY MOUSE (Friends of the Library N.C. Wesleyan College

1981) [2] 450 cc. Pictorial wraps. (Published October 11, 1981) $40.

039a: A START Palaemon Press (Winston-Salem, NC 1981) [2] 8 cc. Left unbound $NVA

039b: A START Palaemon Press (Winston-Salem, NC 1981) [2] 75 sgd no. cc. Bound in marbled boards with a brown leather spine. (Published December 30 1981) $150.

040a: LOVE ACROSS THE LINES South Atlantic Modern Language Association University, AL 1982 [0] Creme colored wraps. Off-print from the *South Atlantic Review*, May 1982 $75.

041a: VITAL PROVISIONS Atheneum NY 1982 [1] Wraps. Uncorrected proof $200.

041b: VITAL PROVISIONS Atheneum NY 1982 [1] 1,000 cc in cloth. (Published November 30, 1982) $25/75

041c: VITAL PROVISIONS Atheneum NY 1982 [1] 2,000 cc in wraps. (Published November 30, 1982) $25.

042a: MUSTIAN Atheneum NY 1983 [1] Uncorrected proof in light blue wraps $125.

042b: MUSTIAN Atheneum NY 1983 [1] 4,000 cc. (Published April 25, 1983) $8/40

043a: A FAIRLY CRUCIAL CHOICE (Office of the President of Duke Univ. Durham, NC) 1983 [0] 6,000 cc. Blue wraps printed in gray. Number 11 in the *How to Think Straight Series*. (Published November 1983) $50.

044a: A CHAIN OF LOVE Nan'un-do Tokyo (1984) [0] Wraps. Prints in English the text of

2 Price stories, along with commentary in Japanese. (Published February 2, 1984) $50.

045a: PRIVATE CONTENTMENT Atheneum NY 1984 [1] 3,000 cc. (Published March 26, 1984) $7/35

046a: KATE VAIDEN Atheneum NY 1986 [1] 144 cc. Wraps. Uncorrected proof in buff colored wraps (made in December 1985) $100.

046b: KATE VAIDEN Atheneum NY 1986 [1] 15,000 cc. National Book Critics Circle Award for 1986. (Published June 23, 1986) $7/35

046c: KATE VAIDEN Chatto & Windus L (1987) [1] "Published in 1987 by ..." $7/35

047a: THE LAWS OF ICE Atheneum NY 1986 [] (Published October 1986 @ $17.95) $5/25

048a: HOUSE SNAKE Lord John Press Northridge 1986 [2] 26 sgd ltr cc $150.

048b: HOUSE SNAKE Lord John Press Northridge 1986 [2] 150 sgd no. cc $50.

049a: A COMMON ROOM : ESSAYS 1954-1987 Atheneum NY 1987 [] $6/30

050a: UNBEATEN PLAY FOR ROSE QUAINTANCE Hawk Hill no-place (1987) [2] 10 sgd no. cc. Wraps $150.

050b: UNBEATEN PLAY FOR ROSE QUAINTANCE Hawk Hill no-place [2] 65 cc $40.

051a: GOOD HEARTS Atheneum NY 1988 [] Uncorrected proof in red wraps $50.

	Price
051b: GOOD HEARTS Atheneum NY 1988 []	$5/25
052a: CLEAR PICTURES Atheneum NY 1989 [] (Published June 1989 @ $19.95)	$5/25
053a: BACK BEFORE DAY North Carolina Wesleyan College Press Rockymount 1989) [2] 60 specially bound copies issued without dustwrapper or slipcase, with signed poem "Spring Takes The Home Place" laid in	$75.
053b: BACK BEFORE DAY North Carolina Wesleyan College Press Rocky Mount 1989) [2] 400 copies in cloth issued without dustwrapper or slipcase	$30.
054a: THE TONGUES OF ANGELS Atheneum NY 1990 [] Uncorrected proof in red wraps	$50.
054b: THE TONGUES OF ANGELS Atheneum NY / Ultramarine Hastings-on-Hudson 1990 [2] 26 sgd ltr cc. Bound in leather	$325.
054c: THE TONGUES OF ANGELS Atheneum NY / Ultramarine Hastings-on-Hudson 1990 [2] 100 sgd no. cc	$150.
054d: THE TONGUES OF ANGELS Atheneum NY 1990 [] With signed tipped-in sheet (Bert Babcock 5/91)	$35/50
054e: THE TONGUES OF ANGELS Atheneum NY 1990 [] (Published May 16, 1990 @ $18.95)	$5/20
055a: HOME MADE North Carolina Wesleyan College Rocky Mount 1990 [2] 26 sgd ltr cc. Illustrated with photographs by Roger Manley	

and signed by both. Issued in cloth without dustwrapper $175.

055b: HOME MADE North Carolina Wesleyan College Rocky Mount 1990 [2] 200 sgd no. cc. Issued in cloth without dustwrapper $60.

055c: HOME MADE North Carolina Wesleyan College Rocky Mount 1990 [] 300 cc. Wraps $25.

056a: THE USE OF FIRE Atheneum NY 1990 [] Uncorrected proof in orange wraps $40.

056b: THE USE OF FIRE Atheneum NY 1990 [] (Published December 1990 @ $19.95) $5/20

057a: LOST HOMES Mud Puppy Press Chapel Hill (1990) [2] 26 sgd ltr cc. $150.

057b: LOST HOMES Mud Puppy Press Chapel Hill (1990) [2] 100 sgd no. cc. Issued in oblong wraps in dustwrapper $50.

058a: THE FORESEEABLE FUTURE: THREE LONG STORIES Atheneum NY 1991 [] Uncorrected advance proof in white wraps $50.

058b: THE FORESEEABLE FUTURE: THREE LONG STORIES Atheneum NY 1991 [3] (Published May 1991 @ $19.95)

059a: CONVERSATIONS WITH REYNOLDS PRICE University of Mississippi Jackson (1991) [] $15/30

059b: CONVERSATIONS WITH REYNOLDS PRICE University of Mississippi Jackson (1991) [] Wraps $15.

060a: BLUE CALHOUN Atheneum NY 1992 [] Advance reading copy in pictorial wraps $50.

060b: BLUE CALHOUN Atheneum NY 1992 [] (Published May 1992 @ $22.95)

061a: "AND WAY IN THE NIGHT" Black Oak Books Berkeley 1992 [] 13 1/4" x 6 1/2" broadside $20.

Notes:

Price's Christmas greetings were generally mailed in white envelopes, some with cardboard stiffeners. *A Fairly Crucial Choice* was also issued in a white envelope, by the Office of the President of Duke University.

Price has written or collaborated on several screenplays of *A Long and Happy Life*; he completed one version in 1965. In 1970, a screenplay he wrote with Richard Neubert was done up in conventional binders by Rubin Productions in Beverly Hills to be distributed among potential producers in Hollywood. Aside from the scenes included in *Things Themselves* (1972), none of these dramatic versions has been published.

Acting scripts were done up for the various productions of Price's play *Early Dark* and for the television production of his play *Private Contentment*, which preceded book publication by two years.

In 1985-86, Price circulated copies of three new plays among friends and potential producers. Approximately 50 copies each of *August Snow*, *New Music*, and *Better Days* were done up in conventional binders for this purpose. There were two issues of *August Snow*: a first draft, and a revised version following the premiere production of the play in Arkansas in 1985.

Mustian (1983) collects the novels *A Long and Happy LIFE* and *A Generous Man* and the story "A Chain of Love." A new introduction is added, called "A Place to Stand."

The following books by Price have been reprinted in one or more paperback editions:

A Long and Happy Life
The Names and Faces of Heroes
A Generous Man
Love and Work
Permanent Errors
The Surface of Earth
A Palpable God
Vital Provisions
Mustian

Henry Roth

HENRY ROTH

Roth was born in Austria-Hungary in 1906. He graduated from the City College of New York in 1928. His first book *Call it Sleep* was well received by the critics and sold reasonably well, but it was not until it was reissued in 1960 that the book was recognized as one of the finest novels of the century and one of the best novels about childhood ever written by an American.

Roth worked for the WPA and as a teacher, metal-grinder, a hospital attendant, and waterfowl farmer. He wrote a second novel and started a third but was not satisfied with either and only published seven stories from 1938 to 1969.

001a: CALL IT SLEEP Ballou NY (1934) [] $500/2500

001b: CALL IT SLEEP Pageant Book Paterson, NJ 1960 [1] "Published 1960 by..." Introduction by Maxwell Geismar, appreciation by Meyer Levin $25/100

001c: CALL IT SLEEP Michael Joseph London (1963) [1] $25/100

002a: NATURE'S FIRST GREEN Targ Editions NY 1979 [2] 300 sgd no. cc. issued in plain unprinted yellow dustwrapper $60/75

003a: SHIFTING LANDSCAPE: A Composite 1925-1987 Jewish Publ. Soc. Phila. 1987 [1] Uncorrected proof in printed yellow mustard wraps $40.

003b: SHIFTING LANDSCAPE: A Composite 1925-1987 Jewish Publ. Soc. Phila. 1987 [1]

Edited and with introduction by Mario Materassi. (Published November 1987 @ $19.95)

$6/30

004a: BOUNDARIES OF LOVE British American Publ. NY 1990 [] Uncorrected proof in light blue wraps (Waverley Books 7/90) $35.

004b: BOUNDARIES OF LOVE British American Publ. NY 1990 [] $5/25

Evelyn Scott

EVELYN SCOTT
(1893-1963)

Scott was born in Tennessee and educated by tutors in New Orleans and at Newcomb College and Newcomb School of Art. She states:

> "I educated myself...which inspired me with simultaneous ambitions to become a writer, a painter, an actress and a disciple of Pavlowa, Tolstoy, Schopenhauer, Nietzsche, Bergson and Karl Marx, all at once... I rejected the idea of being a Southern belle...and ran away from home..."
>
> -*Twentieth Century Authors*, Kunitz & Haycroft, Wilson, NY 1942

She was married to Cyril Kay Scott (original name - Frederick Creighton Wellman) in 1913 and to John Metcalfe in 1928.

Although at the time of her death she had not published a book in over twenty years and was, by most people, entirely forgotten, during her active career between the wars she participated in the major American literary movements, first in Greenwich Village and then as an expatriate in North Africa and Europe. She experimented with every form of literature, but her primary contributions were as the author of the first book of criticism of William Faulkner *On William Faulkner's The Sound and The Fury* (1929) and as the author of *The Wave*, which some consider to be the best Civil War novel ever written and the first book published by the firm of Jonathan Cape & Harrison Smith in 1929.

REFERENCES:

We wish to thank Henry Turlington (ref.a) whose collection was used for the majority of the bibliographical information here-in.

(b) FIRST PRINTINGS OF AMERICAN AUTHORS, Volume 5, edited by Philip B. Eppard, Bruccoli Clark Layman, Gale Research, Detroit (1987).

001a: PRECIPITATIONS Nicholas L. Brown NY 1920 [0] Blue-green cloth with labels $40/200

001b: PRECIPITATIONS Nicholas L. Brown NY 1920 [0] Red cloth (priority assumed) $30/150

002a: THE NARROW HOUSE Boni & Liveright NY (1921) [0] Black cloth with blue lettering $60/300

002b: THE NARROW HOUSE Duckworth L (1921) [1] Orange paper boards (dustwrapper not seen). (Published October 6, 1921) $30/150

002c: THE NARROW HOUSE Harcourt Brace NY 1922 [0] Assume Boni & Liveright sheets were used for this printing $25/125

003a: NARCISSUS Harcourt Brace NY (1922) [0] Black cloth with gray lettering $50/250

003b: BEWILDERMENT Duckworth L (1922) [1] New title, dark gray cloth with yellow/gold lettering $50/250

004a: ESCAPADE Seltzer NY 1923 [0] black cloth $50/500

004b: ESCAPADE : A FRAGMENT OF AUTOBIOGRAPHY Cape L 1930 [] (Ref.b) $50/250

005a: THE GOLDEN DOOR Seltzer NY 1925 [0] Tan cloth spine and purple paper covered boards $30/150

006a: IN THE ENDLESS SANDS : A CHRISTMAS BOOK FOR BOYS AND GIRLS Holt NY (1925) [0] Written with C. Kay Scott. Pictorial cloth with lettering printed in red. Tipped-in frontis (ref.b) $50/250

007a: MIGRATIONS AN ABABESQUE IN HISTORIES Albert & Charles Boni NY 1927 [0] Green cloth with black stamping $25/125

007b: MIGRATIONS AN ABABESQUE IN HISTORIES Duckworth L 1927 [] (ref.b) $20/100

008a: IDEALS A BOOK OF FARCE & COMEDY Albert & Charles Boni NY 1927 [0] Gray binding $20/100

008b: IDEALS A BOOK OF FARCE & COMEDY Albert & Charles Boni NY 1927 [0] Green (remainder) binding $15/100

009a: ON LOLA RIDGE Payson & Clarke NY (1929) [] 2-page mimeographed news release (distributed with review copies of Ridge's *Firehead*) (ref.b) $75

010a: ON WILLIAM FAULKNER'S "THE SOUND AND THE FURY" (Cape & Smith NY 1929) [2] 1,000 cc in wraps resembling *The Sound and The Fury* endpapers $250.

011a: THE WAVE Cape & Smith NY (1929) [1] Blue cloth with gray lettering (also noted in Grosset & Dunlap dustwrapper which would constitute another issue) $25/125

011b: THE WAVE Cape L 1929 [] ref.b $20/100

012a: WITCH PERKINS A STORY OF THE KENTUCKY HILLS Holt NY (1929 [0] Green cloth printed with red $30/150

013a: BLUE RUM Cape & Smith NY (1930) [1] Written as Ernest Souza. Proof dustwrapper has no printing on flaps or back panel $75/400

013b: BLUE RUM Cape L 1930 [] (ref.b) $25/125

014a: THE WINTER ALONE Cape & Smith NY (1930) [1] Black cloth spine in Lynd Ward pictorial boards (and endpapers). Cellophane dustwrapper with flaps $35/175

015a: A CALENDAR OF SIN AMERICAN MELODRAMAS Cape & Smith NY (1931) 2 volumes in dustwrappers and unmarked cardboard slipcase $35/200

Without slipcase $35/150

016a: EVA GAY A ROMANTIC NOVEL Smith & Haas NY (1933) [0] Brown cloth with gold lettering $40/200

016b: EVA GAY A ROMANTIC NOVEL Lovat Dickson L (1934) [1] Blue cloth spine printed in red $25/125

017a: BILLY THE MAVERICK Holt NY (1934) [0] $30/150

018a: BREATHE UPON THESE SLAIN Smith & Haas NY 1934 [0] Blue cloth with silver, blue and black decorated spine $50/250

018b: BREATHE UPON THESE SLAIN Lovat Dickson L 1934 [] (ref.b) $30/150

019a: BACKGROUND IN TENNESSEE McBride NY (1937) [1] Rust colored cloth with blue lettering (priority assumed). (Published October 13, 1937) $10/50

019b: BACKGROUND IN TENNESSEE McBride NY (1937) [1] Also noted in dark blue cloth with black lettering and green cloth with black lettering $8/40

020a: BREAD AND A SWORD Scribners NY 1937 [5] Orange cloth with black lettering $25/125

021a: THE SHADOW OF THE HAWK Scribners NY 1941 [5] Gray cloth with blue lettering $20/100

Sincerely
Thorne Smith

THORNE SMITH
(1892-1934)

James Thorne Smith, Jr. was born in Annapolis, Maryland in 1892. He attended Dartmouth and then served in the Navy for two years, until 1919. For the next ten years he wrote copy for advertising agencies. He became a full-time writer in 1928. In 1930, Ogden Nash signed Smith to a contract with Doubleday, Doran for which he produced a number of books before his untimely death in 1934.

The bibliographical information herein is based on an article on Smith by George H. Scheetz and Rodney N. Henshaw in the *Bulletin of Bibliography* (41/1-March 1984). Reference has also been made to E.F. Bleiler's *Checklist of Science Fiction & Supernatural Fiction*, Firebell Books, Glen Rock N.J. (1978) and Allen J. Hubin's *Crime Fiction 1749-1980, A Comprehensive Bibliography*, Garland Publishing, NY/L, 1984. The estimates are certainly no more than that for, with the exception of the first book, *The Stray Lamb* and *The Passionate Witch*, very few of the titles have been catalogued.

The signature of Thorne Smith is published with the permission of the Houghton Library, Harvard University, Cambridge, Mass.

001a: BILTMORE OSWALD: THE DIARY OF A HAPLESS RECRUIT Stokes NY (1918) [0] Pictorial boards and dustwrapper $50/250

002a: HAUNTS AND BY PATHS AND OTHER POEMS Stokes NY (1919) [] Advance dummy in pictorial paper covered boards. 87 pages with 60 blank (Waiting For Godot 7/90) $750.

002b: HAUNTS AND BY PATHS AND OTHER POEMS Stokes NY (1919) [0] $100/500

003a: OUT O'LUCK: BILTMORE OSWALD VERY MUCH AT SEA Stokes NY (1919) [0] $60/300

004a: TOPPER: AN IMPROBABLE ADVENTURE McBride NY 1926 [1] "First Published February 1926." Bleiler (Ghosts) p.182 $150/750

004b: TOPPER: AN IMPROBABLE ADVENTURE Robert Holden L 1926 [] $75/350

004c: THE JOVIAL GHOSTS: THE MIS-ADVENTURE OF TOPPER Arthur Barker L 1933 [] $50/200

005a: DREAM'S END McBride NY 1927 [1] "First Published March 1927." Blieler (Ghosts) p.182 $60/300

005b: DREAM'S END Jarrolds L (1928) [] $40/200

006a: THE STRAY LAMB Cosmopolitan NY 1929 [0] Bleiler (Fantasy, Theriomorphy) p.182 $60/300

006b: THE STRAY LAMB Heinemann L 1930 [] $30/150

007a: DID SHE FALL? Cosmopolitan NY 1930 [0] Hubin (Crime Fiction) p.373 $60/300

007b: DID SHE FALL? Doubleday Doran GC 1932 [0] $15/75

007c: DID SHE FALL? Arthur Barker L (1936) [1] $25/125

008a: LAZY BEAR LANE Doubleday Doran GC 1931 [1] $100/500

009a: THE NIGHT LIFE OF THE GODS Doubleday Doran GC 1931 [1] Bleiler (Pagan Gods, Fantasy) p.182 $60/300

009b: THE NIGHT LIFE OF THE GODS Arthur Barker L 1934 [0] $35/175

010a: TURNABOUT Doubleday Doran GC 1931 [1] Bleiler (Personality Change) p.182 $60/300

010b: TURNABOUT Arthur Barker L 1933 [0] $35/175

011a: TOPPER TAKES A TRIP Doubleday Doran GC 1932 [1] Bleiler (Ghosts) p.182 $60/300

011b: TOPPER TAKES A TRIP Arthur Barker L 1935 [0] $30/150

012a: THE BISHOP'S JAEGERS Doubleday Doran GC 1932 [1] $50/250

012b: THE BISHOP'S JAEGERS Arthur Barker L 1934 [0] $35/175

012c: THE BISHOP'S JAEGERS Pocket Books NY 1945 [1] Wraps. Includes afterword by author "What Thorne Smith..." $35.

013a: RAIN IN THE DOORWAY Doubleday Doran GC 1933 [1] Bleiler (Fantasy) p.182 $30/150

013b: RAIN IN THE DOORWAY Arthur Barker L 1933 [0] $20/100

014a: SKIN AND BONES Doubleday Doran GC 1933 [1] Bleiler (Fantasy) p.182 $40/200

014b: SKIN AND BONES Arthur Barker L (1936) [1] $25/125

015a: THE GLORIOUS POOL Doubleday Doran GC 1934 [1] Bleiler (Fantasy) p.182 $35/175

015b: THE GLORIOUS POOL Arthur Barker L 1935 [0] $25/125

015c: THE GLORIOUS POOL Pocket Books NY 1946 [1] Wraps. Includes afterword as in 12c, but retitled $25.

016a: THORNE SMITH, HIS LIFE AND TIMES Doubleday GC 1934 [] Wraps. Written by Roland Young, with some portions by Smith (listed as co-author). (Beasley Books 3/89) $12/60

017a: THE THORNE SMITH 3-DECKER Doubleday Doran GC 1936 [1] Bleiler (Fantasy) p.182 $15/75

018a: THE THORNE SMITH TRIPLETS Doubleday Doran GC 1938 [0] Bleiler (Fantasy) p.182 $15/75

019a: THE PASSIONATE WITCH Doubleday Doran GC 1941 [1] Completed by Norman Matson $25/100

019b: THE PASSIONATE WITCH Methuen L (1942) [1] Gray cloth with red lettering on spine. Dustwrapper price "7s6d net" $15/75

019c: THE PASSIONATE WITCH Pocket Books NY 1946 [1] Wraps. Includes an afterword "About Thorne Smith" $25.

020a: THE THORNE SMITH THREE-BAGGER Doubleday Doran GC 1943 [1] Bleiler (Supernatural) p.182 $15/75

021a: BATS IN THE BELFRY Doubleday Doran GC 1943 [1] Written by Norman Batson. A sequel to *The Passionate Witch*, which Matson completed $15/75

W.M. Spackman

W.M. SPACKMAN

William Mode Spackman was born May 20, 1905 in Coatesville, Pennsylvania and was a graduate of Princeton University and a Rhodes Scholar at Balliol College, Oxford. He was a radio writer, public-relations executive, and literary critic. He taught at both New York University and the University of Colorado. He was awarded the Harold D. Vursell Memorial Award by the American Academy and Institute of Arts and Letters in 1984; and the University Medal by the University of Colorado in 1985.

The bibliographical portion of this guide was prepared by Maurice B. Cloud and he wishes to thank Mr. Spackman for both his patience and assistance.

001a: HEYDAY Ballantine Books NY 1953 [0] $25/75

001b: HEYDAY Ballantine Books NY 1953 [0] Wraps $20.

001c: HEYDAY Frederick Muller, Ltd. L 1954 [0] Red cloth boards. Dustwrapper contains numerous changes and omissions from the Ballantine edition $20/60

002a: TWENTY-FIVE YEARS OF IT Perros-Guirec (Paris) 1967 [0] 6 cc (total edition 250 copies). Bound in cloth $150.

002b: TWENTY-FIVE YEARS OF IT Perros-Guirec (Paris) 1967 [0] 250 cc. Wraps $60.

003a: ON THE DECAY OF HUMANISM Rutgers Univ. Pr. New Brunswick, NJ 1968 [0]

2,500 cc. Contains misprint: "dis-like" for "distaste" p.101:5/6 $10/40

004a: AN ARMFUL OF WARM GIRL Realforms Co. (Canto Review of The Arts) Andover, MA 1977 [0] 3,000 cc. Wraps. Contains line: "What, dear?" p.77:39 $20.

004b: AN ARMFUL OF WARM GIRL Alfred A. Knopf NY 1978 [1] 14,616 cc. Dropped line "What, dear?" p.79:39 $7/35

004c: DIE UNSCHULD DER FUNFZIGER (The Innocence of the Fifties. German language edition of *An Armful of Warm Girl*) Claassen Dusseldorf 1981 [1] 5,000 cc. Brown beveled boards and dustwrapper. Contains line "Aber wieso denn, Liebste?" ("What, dear?") dropped in Knopf edition p.125:10 $10/40

004d: AN ARMFUL OF WARM GIRL Van Vactor & Goodheart Cambridge, MA 1981 [0] 4,500 cc (combined printings). Both printings contain line "What, Dear?" p.79:39. (Note: reprinted in 1982 [0]) $15.

005a: A PRESENCE WITH SECRETS Alfred A. Knopf NY 1980 [] Uncorrected proof in tall salmon colored wraps $40.

005b: A PRESENCE WITH SECRETS Alfred A. Knopf NY 1980 [1] 6,000 cc. Contains misprints "this" for "his" p.75:13 and "steaks" for "streaks" p.137:24 $10/30

005c: A PRESENCE WITH SECRETS Dutton Obelisk NY 1982 [1] 6,000 cc. Wraps. Contains introduction by Edmund White. Knopf misprints corrected $15.

006a: A DIFFERENCE OF DESIGN Alfred A. Knopf NY 1983 [] Uncorrected proof in yellow printed wraps (Bert Babcock #48) $35.

006b: A DIFFERENCE OF DESIGN Alfred A. Knopf NY 1983 [1] 6,500 cc $5/25

007a: A LITTLE DECORUM, FOR ONCE Alfred A. Knopf NY 1985 [] Uncorrected proof in creme colored wraps $30.

007b: A LITTLE DECORUM, FOR ONCE Alfred A. Knopf NY 1985 [1] 5,000 cc $5/20

WILLIAM STYRON

William Styron was born in Virginia in 1925. He served in the Marine Corps from 1943 to 1945, he attended Duke University and graduated in 1947. After being fired from the only job he ever held, a mauscript reader at McGraw-Hill Publishing Company, he began writing. He received a Pulitzer Prize in 1968 for his book *The Confessions of Nat Turner*.

REFERENCES:

(a) West, James L. III, WILLIAM STYRON: A Descriptive Bibliography, G. K. Hall & Co., Boston, Mass. (1977).

(b) Lepper, Garry M., A BIBLIOGRAPHICAL INTRODUCTION TO SEVENTY-FIVE MODERN AMERI-CAN AUTHORS, Serendipity Books, Berkeley, 1976.

(c) FIRST PRINTINGS OF AMERICAN AUTHORS Vol. 4, Bruccoli Clark/Gale Research, Detroit (1979).

(d) Dermont, Joseph A., PALAEMON PRESS CATALOG 40, March, 1989.

We would also like to thank D. Edmond Miller for providing some of the detailed information herein.

001a: LIE DOWN IN DARKNESS Bobbs-Merrill Ind. (1951) [1] Uncorrected proof in paperwraps (ref.b) $600.

001b: LIE DOWN IN DARKNESS Bobbs-Merrill Ind. (1951) [1] Some copies have unlettered bindings, no priority. (Published September 10, 1951) $50/250

001c: LIE DOWN IN DARKNESS Hamilton L (1952) [1] $50/200

001d: LIE DOWN IN DARKNESS Franklin Library Franklin Ctr. (Pa.) 1982 [2] Full leather "Limited Edition" signed by Styron $75.

002a: THE LONG MARCH Modern Library NY (1956) [0] Wraps. Number p22 - 95 cents (published october 29, 1956). ("Vintage Book" edition was published in 1960.) First appeared as "Long March" in *Discovery*, No. 1, New York (1953) $175.

002b: THE LONG MARCH Hamish Hamilton L (1962) [] Uncorrected proof in yellows wraps $250.

002c: THE LONG MARCH Hamish Hamilton L (1962) [1] (Remainder of this edition reissued in 1970 in Jonathan Cape dustwrapper) $25/125

002d: THE LONG MARCH Random House NY (1968) [0] First U.S. hardbound edition. Three printings, no differences noted in ref.b but the dustwrappers may provide definite clues on the later printings: the first has "$3.95" and "3/68" at the top and bottom, respectively, of the front flap and mentions "*Confessions*..." on back panel $15/60

003a: SET THIS HOUSE ON FIRE Random House NY (1960) [1] Light green dustwrapper lettered in red, title and publisher's information on flaps, but no text. West believes there were less than 12 copies in this dustwrapper, although this seems low. Ken Lopez catalogued (4/92) a copy in pale blue dustwrapper printed in red (same?) $15/850

003b: SET THIS HOUSE ON FIRE Random House NY (1960) [1] Dark green dustwrapper lettered in white, with additional text on flaps. Published May 4, 1960 $15/75

003c: SET THIS HOUSE ON FIRE Hamilton L (1961) [1] $15/75

004a: THE FOUR SEASONS Penna. State Univ. Press 1965 [2] 75 sgd no. cc. Boxed set of four etchings signed by the artist Harold Altman. Styron introduction $1500.

005a: THIS QUIET DUST (Random House NY 1967) [0] 500 cc. Promotional pamphlet for "Nat Turner" (quantity per Chapel Hill Rare Books 5/88) $250.

006a: THE CONFESSIONS OF NAT TURNER Random House NY (1967) [2] 500 sgd no. cc. Issued in slipcase $175/275

006b: THE CONFESSIONS OF NAT TURNER Random House NY (1967) [1] Trade edition with extra leaf signed $100/150

006c: THE CONFESSIONS OF NAT TURNER Random House NY (1967) [1] (Published October 9, 1967) $12/60

006d: THE CONFESSIONS OF NAT TURNER Cape L (1968) [1] Review copies "Proof Only" in red printed wraps in proof dustwrapper giving provisional publication date of May 2, 1968 on rear flap $250.

006e: THE CONFESSIONS OF NAT TURNER Cape L (1968) [1] (Also noted with Pulitzer Prize wrap-around band) $15/75

006f: THE CONFESSIONS OF NAT TURNER Franklin Press Franklin Ctr 1976 [2] "Limited" edition in full leather (not signed - part of Pulitzer series) $75.

006g: THE CONFESSIONS OF NAT TURNER Franklin Library Franklin Ctr. 1979 [2] Signed limited edition in full leather $75.

007a: IN THE CLAP SHACK Random House NY (1973) [0] Uncorrected proof in printed red wraps $150.

007b: IN THE CLAP SHACK Random House NY (1973) [0] (Published June 15, 1973) $15/75

008a: CHRISTCHURCH, AN ADDRESS... Briarpatch Press Davidson (1977) [2] 26 sgd ltr cc. Wraps $250.

008b: CHRISTCHURCH, AN ADDRESS... Briarpatch Press Davidson (1977) [2] 350 no. cc $100.

009a: ADMIRAL ROBERT PENN WARREN... Palaemon Winston-Salem (1978) [2] 26 sgd ltr cc in wraps (ref.c) $300.

009b: ADMIRAL ROBERT PENN WARREN... Palaemon Winston-Salem (1978) [2] 200 sgd no. cc (ref.c) $75.

009c: ADMIRAL ROBERT PENN WARREN... Palaemon Winston-Salem (1981) [2] 50 sgd no. (Roman) cc in cloth and decorated paper covered boards. New edition signed by both Styron and Warren (ref.d) $125.

009d: ADMIRAL ROBERT PENN WARREN... Palaemon Winston-Salem (1981) [2] 26 sgd ltr cc (signed by both). Bound in decorated paperwraps (ref.d) $175.

009e: ADMIRAL ROBERT PENN WARREN... Palaemon Winston-Salem (1981) [2] 74 sgd no. cc (signed by both) in wraps (ref.d) $125.

010a: SOPHIE'S CHOICE Random House NY (1979) [1] Uncorrected proof in red wraps. (Issued February 15, 1979) $175.

010b: SOPHIE'S CHOICE Random House NY (1979) [2] 500 sgd no. cc. Issued without dustwrapper in slipcase $175/250

010c: SOPHIE'S CHOICE Random House NY 1979 [1] The trade edition with extra leaf "Advance Presentation Edition" bound in. Light blue cloth in tissue dustwrapper. (Issued April 27, 1979) $20/60

010d: SOPHIE'S CHOICE Franklin Library Franklin Ctr. 1979 [2] "Limited Edition" bound in full leather $60.

010e: SOPHIE'S CHOICE Random House NY (1979) [1] 125,000 cc. Maroon cloth. (Published June 11, 1979) $8/40

010f: SOPHIE'S CHOICE Jonathan Cape L 1979 [] Uncorrected proof in red wraps $175.

010g: SOPHIE'S CHOICE Jonathan Cape L (1979) [1] Two variants noted: light brown endpapers and dustwrapper not priced; and white endpapers and priced dustwrapper (priority unknown) (Robert Temple #37). (Our experience indicates that unpriced copies usually are meant for export to Canada, Australia, etc.) $8/40

011a: SHADRACH Sylvester & Orphanos L.A. 1979 [2] 4 sgd cc with name of recipient $NVA

011b: SHADRACH Sylvester & Orphanos L.A. 1979 [2] 26 sgd ltr cc. Issued without dustwrapper $300.

011c: SHADRACH Sylvester & Orphanos L.A. 1979 [2] 300 sgd no. cc. Issued without dustwrapper $75.

012a: THE MESSAGE OF AUSCHWITZ Press de la Warr (Blacksburg) 1979 [2] 26 sgd ltr cc. Wraps $300.

012b: THE MESSAGE OF AUSCHWITZ Press de la Warr (Blacksburg) 1979 [2] 200 sgd no. cc. Wraps $75.

013a: AN ADDRESS AT THE 204th COMMENCEMENT OF HAMPDON SYDNEY COLLEGE (Hampdon-Sydney 1980) [2] 50 sgd no. cc. Wraps $175.

013b: AN ADDRESS AT THE 204th COMMENCEMENT OF HAMPDON SYDNEY COLLEGE (Hampdon-Sydney 1980) [2] 950 no. cc. Wraps $50.

014a: AGAINST FEAR Palaemon Winston-Salem (1981) [2] 50 sgd no. cc in blue wraps for private distribution (ref.d) $175.

014b: AGAINST FEAR Palaemon Winston-Salem (1981) [2] 250 sgd no. cc in grey wraps (ref.d) $75.

015a: AS HE LAY DEAD, A BITTER GRIEF Albondocani NY 1981 [2] 26 sgd ltr cc $300.

015b: AS HE LAY DEAD, A BITTER GRIEF Albondocani NY 1981 [2] 300 sgd no. cc. Wraps $75.

016a: THIS QUIET DUST + Random House NY (1982) [4] Advance uncorrected proof in red printed wraps $150.

016b: THIS QUIET DUST + Random House NY (1982) [2] 250 sgd no. cc. Issued without dustwrapper in slipcase $100/200

016c: THIS QUIET DUST + Random House NY (1982) [4] (Published November 30, 1982) $7/35

016d: THIS QUIET DUST + Jonathan Cape L (1983) [] $8/40

017a: MR. JEFFERSON AND OUR TIMES Stuart Wright (Winston-Salem 1984) [2] 14 sgd no. cc in Japanese decorated paperwraps (ref.d) $300.

017b: MR. JEFFERSON AND OUR TIMES Stuart Wright (Winston-Salem 1984) [2] 61 sgd cc in marbled wraps (ref.d) $150.

018a: CONVERSATIONS WITH WILLIAM STYRON Univ. Press of Mississippi Jackson (1985) [] Uncorrected proof. Oblong folio. Spiral bound wraps with paper label $100.

018b: CONVERSATIONS WITH WILLIAM STYRON Univ. Press of Mississippi Jackson (1985) [] Edited by James West III $10/30

018c: CONVERSATIONS WITH WILLIAM STYRON Univ. Press of Mississippi Jackson (1985) [] Wraps $15.

019a: LETTER TO THE EDITOR OF THE PARIS REVIEW Press de la Warr no-place 1986 [2] 6 specially bound sgd ltr cc. Wraps (Edmond Miller) $150.

019b: LETTER TO THE EDITOR OF THE PARIS REVIEW Press de la Warr no-place 1986 [2] 20 sgd ltr cc. Wraps $125.

019c: LETTER TO THE EDITOR OF THE PARIS REVIEW Press de la Warr no-place 1986 [2] 100 sgd no. cc. Wraps (Bert Babcock 5/91) $75.

020a: BLANKENSHIP Press de la Warr State College 1988 [2] 26 sgd ltr cc. Wraps $175.

020b: BLANKENSHIP Press de la Warr State College 1988 [2] 100 sgd no. cc. Wraps $75.

021a: DARKNESS VISIBLE Random House NY (1990) [] Unrevised proofs, 83 pages, in yellow wraps (Edmond Miller) $75.

021b: DARKNESS VISIBLE Random House NY (1990) [] Unrevised proofs, 84 pages, in yellow wraps. Issued June 1990 (Edmond Miller) $60.

021c: DARKNESS VISIBLE Random House NY (1990) [1] Some copies signed on half title for sales force (Waverly Books 1/92) $50/75

021d: DARKNESS VISIBLE Random House NY (1990) [1] 75,000 cc (PW). (Published September 4, 1990 @ $15.95) $5/20

Peter Taylor

PETER TAYLOR

Taylor was born in Trenton, Tennessee in 1917. He graduated from Kenyon College in 1940 and served in the Army during WWII. In addition to his writing career, Taylor was a Professor of English at the University of Virginia and has been a visiting lecturer at Indiana, University of Chicago, Oxford, Ohio State and Harvard among others.

001a: A LONG FOURTH + Harcourt, Brace NY (1948) [1] $75/350

001b: A LONG FOURTH + Routledge L 1949 [] $50/250

002a: A WOMAN OF MEANS Harcourt, Brace NY (1950) [] Uncorrected proof in bound signatures laid in proof dustwrapper (Joseph The Provider 9/92) $1,500.

002b: A WOMAN OF MEANS Harcourt, Brace NY (1950) [1] $60/300

002c: A WOMAN OF MEANS Routledge L 1950 [] $40/200

003a: THE WIDOWS OF THORNTON Harcourt NY (1954) [1] $50/250

004a: TENNESSEE DAY IN ST. LOUIS Random House NY (1957) [0] Also noted without dustwrapper price (Pharos Books) $30/150

005a: HAPPY FAMILIES ARE ALL ALIKE McDowell-Obolensky NY (1959) [1] $25/125

005b: HAPPY FAMILIES ARE ALL ALIKE Macmillan L 1960 [] Yellow cloth with brown lettering (Henry Turlington) $35/125

005c: HAPPY FAMILIES ARE ALL ALIKE Macmillan L 1960 [] Variant bindings $15/100

006a: MISS LENORA WHEN LAST SEEN + Obolensky NY (1963) [1] $40/200

007a: THE COLLECTED STORIES OF PETER TAYLOR Farrar, Straus & Giroux NY (1969) [1] $15/75

008a: LITERATURE, SEWANEE AND THE WORLD (Univ. of the South Sewanee 1972) [] Wraps. Eight pages plus cover title (H.E. Turlington #34) $250.

009a: PRESENCES SEVEN DRAMATIC PIECES Houghton Mifflin B 1973 [1] 1,750 cc $50/150

009b: PRESENCES SEVEN DRAMATIC PIECES Houghton Mifflin B 1973 [1] 2,500 cc. Wraps $40.

010a: IN THE MIRO DISTRICT+ Knopf NY 1977 [1] Uncorrected proofs in printed yellow wrapper $175.

010b: IN THE MIRO DISTRICT+ Knopf NY 1977 [1] $15/75

010c: IN THE MIRO DISTRICT+ Knopf NY 1977 [1] Wraps $15.

010d: IN THE MIRO DISTRICT+ Chatto & Windus L 1977 [0] "Published by Chatto & Windus Ltd." 1,750 cc (Chapel Hill Rare Books 1/91). First issue dustwrapper priced in pounds (Bert Babcock 12/90) $10/50

011a: THE ROAD AND OTHER MODERN STORIES Cambridge Univ. Press Cambridge 1979 [] Wraps. Edited by Taylor $20.

012a: THE EARLY GUEST Palaemon Winston-Salem (1982) [2] 26 sgd ltr cc. Wraps in dustwrapper $200.

012b: THE EARLY GUEST Palaemon Winston-Salem (1982) [2] 140 sgd ltr cc $100.

013a: EUDORA WELTY Stuart Wright no-place 1984 [2] 5 cc. Stiff white printed wraps. An off-print from *Eudora Welty: A Tribute* $250.

014a: THE OLD FOREST+ Dial NY 1985 [] Uncorrected proofs in printed decorated tan wrappers $125.

014b: THE OLD FOREST+ Dial NY 1985 [1] (Published February 8, 1985 @ $16.95) $12/60

014c: THE OLD FOREST+ Chatto & Windus/Hogarth L (1985) [1] "Published in 1985 by ..." (Published August 15, 1985 @ $9.95) $10/50

015a: A STAND IN THE MOUNTAINS Beil NY 1985 [0] 1,000 cc. Issued without dustwrapper in plain cardboard mailing box/slipcase which was not used on all copies. Colophon states "Verona. March 1986" $40/60

016a: A SUMMONS TO MEMPHIS Knopf NY 1986 [1] Uncorrected proof in blue wraps $125.

016b: A SUMMONS TO MEMPHIS Knopf NY 1986 [1] (Published October 6, 1986 @ $15.95.) Winner of the Pulitzer prize for 1986 $12/60

016c: A SUMMONS TO MEMPHIS Chatto & Windus L 1987 [] $10/40

017a: "A WALLED GARDEN" Tales For Travellers Napa, Calif. 1987 [0] Map fold wraps with a story by John Galsworthy $15.

018a: CONVERSATIONS WITH PETER TAYLOR Univ. Press of Mississippi Jackson (1987) [] Uncorrected proof in spiral bound plain wraps with printed label (William Reese Co. 2/92) $50.

018b: CONVERSATIONS WITH PETER TAYLOR Univ. Press of Mississippi Jackson (1987) [3] $10/30

018c: CONVERSATIONS WITH PETER TAYLOR Univ. Press of Mississippi Jackson (1987) [3] Wraps $10.

DYLAN THOMAS
(1914 - 1953)

Thomas was born in Swansea, Glamorganshire, South Wales and educated at Swansea Grammar School, where he contributed to (and for a good while edited) the *Swansea Grammar School Magazine* (1925-1934). He appeared in 15 issues in all including his first published poem "The Song of A Mischievous Dog" in the December 1925 issue (value about $500). He was a reporter for the Swansea evening newspaper for about a year. In 1934 the *Sunday Referee* chose him as its prize poet for the year and published, along with the Parton Bookshop, his first collection of verse *(18 Poems)*. His first book appearance was in *The Years Poetry*, John Lane, London (1934), which preceded *18 Poems* by just a few days.

In 1936, Edith Sitwell favorably reviewed his second book, *Twenty-Five Poems* for the *Sunday Times* and his reputation started to expand. In the late 1940's he started working for B.B.C. and subsequently his radio and poetry readings in England and the U.S. brought him wide recognition. But financial problems and drinking plagued him most of his life and the drinking finally caught up with him in New York at the age of only 39.

We would like to thank Jeff Towns (Dylan's Book Shop, Swansea) for his review and assistance on this update.

REFERENCES

(a) Rolph, J. Alexander, DYLAN THOMAS A BIBLIOGRAPHY, Dent New Directions, London/New York (1956).

(b) Maud, Ralph, DYLAN THOMAS IN PRINT A Bibliographical History, J.M. Dent, London (1970).

(c) Provided by New Directions.

(c) Provided by New Directions.

(d) Inventory, dealer catalogs, Library of Congress.

Ref.a was used for items up to 020, unless otherwise noted. It is an excellent bibliography. Ref.b was used for items 021 through 031, unless otherwise noted. Ref.b is basically a check-list with no title page, copyright page or quantity information; and did not even include (except for printing quantities) the basic bibliographical information so well presented in ref.a. Therefore any information included on title page content or first edition identification after item 020 came from other sources.

001a: 18 POEMS Sunday Referee & Parton Bookshop L (1934) [1] 250 cc. Black cloth, flat spine, lacks leaf between half-title and title pages, front edge roughly trimmed. Pale Gray dustwrapper lettered in darker gray $500/2,500

001b: 18 POEMS Sunday Referee & Parton Bookshop L (1936) [1] 250 cc. Rounded spine, has leaf between half-title and title pages advertising this book and titles by George Barker and David Gascoyne. Front edge cut evenly. Same sheets as 001a, 500 in total $150/750

001c: 18 POEMS The Fortune Press L (circa 1942) [1] Verso of title page still states "First Published in 1934..." Red buckram, lettered in gold (many later printings in various bindings). Yellow dustwrapper lettered in red. D'Arch Smith in his bibliography of the Fortune Press breaks down this title as follows:

-First issue (1942). Printer's imprint is Knole Park Press $30/150

-Second issue (1946?). Printers imprint is Poole J. Looker $25/125

-Third issue (1954?). Also Knole Park Press but with 5 misprints (which would suggest it was reset): p.12:8 "no" for "nor", p.20:7 "fist" for "Fists", p.23:7 "word" for "world", p.23:27 "may" for "my" and p.30:12 "guns" for "guns."

$20/100

002a: TWENTY-FIVE POEMS J.M. Dent L (1936) [1] 730 cc $150/750

003a: THE HAND Frederic Prokosch Venice 1939 [2] Wraps. Colored frontis by Prokosch (Van Allen Bradley 1982-83 lists this "One of 3 (of 10) on Arches paper. $1,500 - $2,000") $NVA

004a: THE MAP OF LOVE J.M. Dent L (1939) [] Uncorrected proof in drab wraps. The trade edition was entirely corrected and reset prior to publication (R.A. Gekoski) $1,250.

004b: THE MAP OF LOVE J.M. Dent L (1939) [1] 1,000 cc. first issue in fine grained mauve cloth, an almost silky texture; title blocked in gold on front cover; title and author's name in gold on spine; "Dent" blind-stamped at foot of spine; top edge stained dark-purple. 2,000 sets of sheets printed, balance used on other issues $100/500

004c: THE MAP OF LOVE J.M. Dent L (1939) [1] 250 cc. Second issue bound in coarser and plum-colored cloth, else same as 004a

$50/250

004d: THE MAP OF LOVE J.M. Dent L (1939) [1] 250 cc. Third issue purple cloth intermediate between fine and coarse grained; blocked in blue including "Dent" at foot of spine; top edge stained purple. Issued in February 1948 $25/125

004e: THE MAP OF LOVE J.M. Dent L (1939) [1] 500 cc. Fourth issue bound as 003c but top edge unstained. Issued between December 1948 and February 1949 $20/100

005a: THE WORLD I BREATHE New Directions Norfolk, Ct. (1939) [0] 700 cc (a & b) with one star on either side of author's name on title page and spine (Van Allen Bradley 1982-83, not in ref.a or b). Also noted with one star on either side of name on title page and five stars on either side on spine (Jeff Towns) $200/850

005b: THE WORLD I BREATHE New Directions Norfolk, Ct. (1939) [0] With five stars on either side of author's name on title page and spine $150/750

006a: THE RULERS Koppel (L 1940?) [] Wraps. 22 pages. Music with words by Thomas (Waiting For Godot #10) $350.

007a: PORTRAIT OF THE ARTIST AS A YOUNG DOG Dent L (1940) [1] 1,500 cc $100/400

007b: PORTRAIT OF THE ARTIST AS A YOUNG DOG New Directions Norfolk, Ct. (1940) [0] 1,000 cc. "Printed for New Directions ... September 1940" 60/300

007c: PORTRAIT OF THE ARTIST AS A YOUNG DOG Guild Books/Dent L (1948) [1] 40,250 cc. Wraps. Actually published in March 1949, total quantity 50,250 cc, see next entry $25.

007d: PORTRAIT OF THE ARTIST AS A YOUNG DOG Guild Books/Dent L (1948) [1] 10,000 cc. During 1952 a four-color dustwrapper was added to the book until they ran out $25/75

008a: FROM IN MEMORY OF ANN JONES Caseg Press Llanllechid, Caernarvonshire (1942) [0] 500 cc. Caseg Broadsheet No. 5 $300.

009a: NEW POEMS New Directions Norfolk, Ct. (1943) [0] 1,000 cc. Issued in paper boards. Ref.a notes that the true first printing of this title was completely destroyed as the size differed from the other volumes in the "Poet of The Month" series, so there may be some unbound sheets somewhere $75/300

009b: NEW POEMS New Directions Norfolk, Ct. (1943) [0] 1,500 cc. Wraps. (Issued simultaneously.) Also in dustwrapper. (Have a note that dustwrapper with reviews would be later. But not sure of source of this) $25/125

010a: DEATHS AND ENTRANCES J.M. Dent & Sons Ltd. L (1946) [1] 3,000 cc. One of Cyril Connolly's 100 key books in *The Modern Movement* $60/300

010b: DEATHS AND ENTRANCES Gregynog (Newtown) 1984 [2] 28 no. (Roman) cc. Bound in a special designer binding by James Brockman (also 2 unnumbered copies) $1,500.

010c: DEATHS AND ENTRANCES Gregynog (Newtown) 1984 [2] 250 no. cc. Illustrated by John Piper. Dark green leather spine and blue gray cloth. Issued in slipcase. (Also 20 unnumbered copies) $300/350

011a: SELECTED WRITINGS New Directions (NY 1946) [0] 4,000 cc. "Reprints are identifiable only by the dustwrapper which has printing number stated on front flap" and in mauve cloth (ref.a). However, we believe Jeff Towns is correct in believing Rolph was looking at a later printing. The first is in green cloth, with the title on a double page spread and copyright pages starting "Copyright 1946..." Later printings have a single page title page and "Copyright 1939 / By New Directions / Copyright 1946." "Other New Directions Books..." on back panel. Address "500 Fifth Avenue." Later dustwrappers have "The New Classics Series..." on back, address "333 Sixth Avenue" $30/150

012a: TWENTY-SIX POEMS (New Directions Norfolk, Ct. 1950) [2] 8 sgd no. cc on Japanese vellum. Copies numbered III-X. In slipcase. (American issue preceded English by 3 months.) (Brought $6,500. at auction in 1986 and has been catalogued at $9,500 and $13,000) $10,000.

012b: TWENTY-SIX POEMS (New Directions Norfolk, Ct. 1950) [2] 87 sgd no. cc on handmade paper. Copies numbered 61-147. In slipcase $2,250.

012c: TWENTY-SIX POEMS J.M. Dent & Sons Ltd L (1950) [2] 2 sgd no. cc on Japanese vellum. Copies numbered I-II. In slipcase $10,000.

012d: TWENTY-SIX POEMS J.M. Dent & Sons Ltd L (1950) [2] 50 sgd no. cc. Numbered 11-60 (copies 148-150 for author & publisher). In slipcase $2,250.

013a: IN COUNTRY SLEEP New Directions (NY 1952) [2] 100 sgd no. cc. Issued in dark brown slipcase $1,500/1,750

013b: IN COUNTRY SLEEP New Directions (NY 1952) [0] 5,000 cc. Reportedly the first issue has Thomas photograph tipped to title, but all copies we've seen have the photograph $40/200

014a: COLLECTED POEMS 1934-1952 J.M. Dent & Sons Ltd L (1952) [1] 68 copies of the proof in pale green wraps printed in black omitting author's prologue and introduction thereto $1,250.

014b: COLLECTED POEMS 1934-1952 J.M. Dent & Sons Ltd L (1952) [] Later proof including prologue and introduction, but the prologue is changed for the trade edition (Jeff Towns). Not clear whether this proof would be part of the 68 copies noted by Rolph but assume it may have been as the outward appearance is the same $750.

014c: COLLECTED POEMS 1934-1952 J.M. Dent & Sons Ltd L (1952) [2] 65 sgd no. cc. Full dark blue morocco in plain cellophane dustwrapper. (Brought $2,000. at auction in 1986) $2,500.

014d: COLLECTED POEMS 1934-1952 J.M. Dent & Sons Ltd L (1952) [1] 4,760 cc $35/175

014e: THE COLLECTED POEMS OF DYLAN THOMAS New Directions (NY 1953) [0] 4 page prospectus with 2 poems and reviews $40.

014f: THE COLLECTED POEMS OF DYLAN THOMAS New Directions (NY 1953) [0] 6,000 cc (a & b). The word "daughter" misspelled on p.199 (corrected in later printings) (Note: the 1956, 11th printing had the first printing of the poem "Elegy" complete by Vernon Watkins and with a note by him) $30/150

015a: THE DOCTOR AND THE DEVILS J.M. Dent & Sons Ltd L (1947) [0] 35 cc in stiff cork colored wraps. Proofs with the character "Salter" which was changed to "Rock" in final version. "1947" on verso of title page (The book was not produced until 1953) $1,250.

015b: THE DOCTOR AND THE DEVILS J.M. Dent & Sons Ltd L (1953) 97 cc. Proofs in pale green wraps $600.

015c: THE DOCTOR AND THE DEVILS J.M. Dent & Sons Ltd L (1953) [1] 4,000 cc $20/100

015d: THE DOCTOR AND THE DEVILS New Directions (Norfolk 1953) [0] 1,500 cc. English sheets measuring 7 1/4" x 4 3/4" (second printing was 8" x 5 1/4") (Published October 8, 1953 @ $2.50) $15/75

016a: UNDER MILK WOOD J.M. Dent & Sons Ltd L (1954) [1] 6,400 cc. (Note: first separate appearance of this BBC commissioned work preceded the Book by a month. This script offered by Beasley Books for $1,000. 8/91) $50/250

016b: UNDER MILK WOOD New Directions (NY 1954) [0] 6,000 cc. (Ref.c shows only 2,149 copies bound) 25/125

016c: UNDER MILK WOOD (Acting Edition) J.M. Dent & Sons Ltd L (1958) [1] Wraps (ref.b). Preface and musical settings by Daniel Jones $50.

016d: UNDER MILK WOOD (Acting Edition) (New Directions NY 1958) [0] (Ref.b) Wraps. English sheets $40.

016e: UNDER MILK WOOD Timon Film circa 1970 [] First draft screenplay by Andrew Sinclair in black wraps (Jeff Towns) $500.

016f: UNDER MILK WOOD Timon Film circa 1970 [] Release script by Andrew Sinclair in red wraps (Jeff Towns) $500.

016g: UNDER MILK WOOD Folio Society L 1972 [] Lithographs by Ceri Richards. First illustrated edition. Issued without dustwrapper in slipcase (ref.d) $40/75

017a: QUITE EARLY ONE MORNING... J.M. Dent & Sons Ltd L 1954 [] Proof copy in plain gray wraps laid in dustwrapper of published edition (ref.d) $450/500.

017b: QUITE EARLY ONE MORNING... J.M. Dent & Sons Ltd L 1954 [1] 10,000 cc. First issue has full stop after "sailors" at end of verse 5 on pages 3 and 11 (comma added in subsequent printings) $25/100

017c: QUITE EARLY ONE MORNING New Directions (NY 1954) [0] 3,200 cc. Wrap-around band (Boston Book Annex #23). Later printings only identifiable by note on front dustwrapper flap. Contents differ from English edition $15/75

018a: CONVERSATION ABOUT CHRISTMAS New Directions no-place 1954 [0] 2,000 cc. Wraps. Christmas greeting, 8 stapled pages plus covers in mailing envelope for "The Friends of J. Laughlin..." $150.

019a: MEMORIES OF CHRISTMAS J.M. Dent Don Mills, Ontario (1954) [] Christmas keepsake issued in Canada only. Priority of this and previous entry unknown (Letters 5/91) $200.

020a: TWO EPIGRAMS OF FEALTY (no publisher or place 1953) [2] 30 no. cc. Wraps. "Printed for members of the Court of the Realm of Redonda" (John Gawsworth). Each a single printed sheet folded into quarters enclosed in cloth folders and slipcase. 1953 appears at bottom of poems, but ref.b&d give 1954 as date $500.

020b: GALSWORTHY AND GAWSWORTH (no publisher or place 1953) [2] 30 no. cc. wr "Printed for members of the Court of the Realm of Redonda" (John Gawsworth). Each a single printed sheet folded into quarters enclosed in cloth folders and slipcase. 1953 appears at bottom of poems, but ref.b&d gives 1954 as date

$500.

021a: ADVENTURES IN THE SKIN TRADE + New Directions (NY 1955) [0] 5,000 cc

$15/75

021b: ADVENTURES IN THE SKIN TRADE Putnam L (1955) [] Proof copy in manilla wraps (Jeff Towns) $400.

021c: ADVENTURES IN THE SKIN TRADE Putnam L (1955) [1] 6,900 cc. Title story (unfinished novel) only $20/100

021d: ADVENTURES IN THE SKIN TRADE Studio Services NY (1966) [] Film script by Andrew Sinclair (Jeff Towns) $400.

021e: ADVENTURES IN THE SKIN TRADE J.M. Dent L 1967 [] A dramatization by Andrew Sinclair $8/40

021f: ADVENTURES IN THE SKIN TRADE New Directions NY 1968 [] A dramatization by Andrew Sinclair $7/35

022a: A PROSPECT OF THE SEA + J.M. Dent & Sons Ltd L (1955) [1] 8,000 cc $15/75

023a: A CHILD'S CHRISTMAS IN WALES New Directions Norfolk, Ct. (1955) [0] 10,000 cc. Published in 1955, although copyright page states 1954. 7 1/4" x 5" in pale gray boards with title in red and author's name in black. First Separate edition $15/75

023b: A CHILD'S CHRISTMAS IN WALES J.M. Dent & Sons Ltd L (1968) [1] Wraps. Noted in yellow with red lettering and red with black lettering (priority unknown) $7/35

023c: A CHILD'S CHRISTMAS IN WALES New Directions (NY 1959) [1] This edition first published 1959. Woodcuts by Ellen Raskin $6/30

023d: A CHILD'S CHRISTMAS IN WALES New Directions NY 1969 [2] 100 sgd (artist) no. cc with 5 original prints by Fritz Eichenberg. Leather backed boards in black portfolio. Also "stiff card folder with printed labels (William Reese Co. 12/91) (Published October 15, 1969 @ $200.) (ref.c) $750/850

023e: A CHILD'S CHRISTMAS IN WALES New Directions NY 1969 [] 15,197 cc. (Published October 15, 1969 @ $4.00) (ref.c) $8/40

024a: LETTERS TO VERNON WATKINS J.M. Dent/Faber & Faber L (1957) [1] Edited with introduction by Watkins $10/50

024b: LETTERS TO VERNON WATKINS New Directions (NY 1957) [0] 5,051 cc. (Published December 11, 1957 @ $3.00) (ref.c) $10/40

025a: THE BEACH OF FALESA Stein & Day NY (1963) [0] (ref.b&d) $8/40

025b: THE BEACH OF FALESA Jonathan Cape L (1964) [1] (ref.d) $8/40

026a: MISCELLANY: POEMS STORIES BROADCASTS J.M. Dent & Sons Ltd L (1963) [] Aldine Paperback #13 (ref.d) $35.

027a: TWENTY YEARS A-GROWING J.M. Dent & Sons Ltd L (1964) [1] Film script based on Maurice O'Sullivan's story (ref.d) $8/40

028a: REBECCA'S DAUGHTERS Triton (L 1965) [1] (ref.d) $8/40

028b: REBECCA'S DAUGHTERS Little, Brown B (1965) [1] (ref.b&d) $8/40

029a: ME AND MY BIKE MacDonald L (1964) [] Uncorrected proofs in brown wraps with label on front (Ken Lopez 1/89) $150.

029b: ME AND MY BIKE Triton (L 1965) [2] 500 no cc. Issued in slipcase (ref.d) $25/100

029c: ME AND MY BIKE Triton (L 1965) [1] (ref.d) $12/60

029d: ME AND MY BIKE McGraw-Hill NY (1965) [] Illustrated by Leonora Box (ref.d). English sheets $8/40

030a: THE DOCTOR AND THE DEVILS AND OTHER SCRIPTS New Directions (NY 1966) [1] 3,485 cc. First dustwrapper has ad for *Collected Poems* on back. Second printing dustwrapper has ads for 9 other books by Thomas (ref.c&d) $8/40

031a: MISCELLANY TWO J.M. Dent L (1966) [] Wraps. Aldine Paperback No. 49 (ref.d) $30.

032a: SELECTED LETTERS OF DYLAN THOMAS J.M. Dent L (1966) [1] $10/50

032b: SELECTED LETTERS OF DYLAN THOMAS New Directions (NY 1967) [0] 3,915 cc. (Published May 15, 1967 @ $8.50) (ref.b&c) $8/40

033a: THE NOTEBOOKS OF DYLAN THOMAS New Directions (NY 1967) [] 5,057 cc. (Published October 31, 1967 @ $8.50) (ref.b&c) $8/40

033b: POET IN THE MAKING J.M. Dent L (1968) [] (ref.d) $8/40

034a: TWO TALES... Sphere NY 1968 [] Contains *Me and My Bike* and *Rebecca's Daughters*. Illustrated by Leonora Box (ref.d) $12/60

035a: TWELVE MORE LETTERS (Turret Books L 1969) [2] 26 ltr cc. Dark brown cloth. Issued in glassine dustwrapper (Peter Jolliffe Cat.27) $250.

035b: TWELVE MORE LETTERS (Turret Books L 1969) [2] 175 no cc. Yellow cloth. Issued in glassine dw (Argosy Bookstore Cat. 745) $100.

036a: EARLY PROSE WRITINGS J.M. Dent L (1971) [] (Ian McKelvie Cat. 57) $12/60

036b: EARLY PROSE WRITINGS New Directions NY 1972 [1] 488 cc. (Published March 22 or April 20, 1972 @ $8.75.) (Ref.c indicates 488 copies for New Directions and 100 for Dent and that later New Directions imported copies from Dent as follows: 3/27/74 - 500 copies of which 252 damaged, 4/25/76 - 406 copies) $15/75

037a: THE OUTING Dent L (1971) [1] Wraps. Illustrated by Meg Stevens $40.

037b: THE OUTING Dent L (1985) [1] Illustrated by Paul Cox $10/40

038a: THE POEMS OF DYLAN THOMAS J.M. Dent L (1971) [] (Ian McKelvie Cat. 57) $10/50

038b: THE POEMS OF DYLAN THOMAS New Directions (NY 1971) [1] 8,118 cc. (Published September 22, 1971 @ $6.00.) (Ref.c) $8/40

039a: HOLIDAY MEMORY L (1972) [] Wraps. First separate publication (ref.d) $25.

039b: HOLIDAY MEMORY Lime Rock Press Salisbury, Ct. (1979) [2] 25 Roman no. cc signed by the publishers with four miniature mounted black and white photographs of Dylan Thomas's home $200.

039c: HOLIDAY MEMORY Lime Rock Press Salisbury, Ct. (1979) [2] 100 no. cc signed by the publishers. Miniature measuring 2"x2"x1/4" $75.

040a: SEVEN POEMS Art School Press Camberwell 1974 [2] 75 sgd no. cc. Folio cut in linoleum, signed by Keith Holmes who designed and printed the book $125.

041a: THE DEATH OF THE KING'S CANARY Hutchinson L (1976) [1] Written with John Davenport. Introduction by Constantine FizGibbon $8/40

041b: THE DEATH OF THE KING'S CANARY Viking NY (1977) [1] "Published in 1977 by..." Written with John Davenport. Errata slip laid-in $5/25

042a: THE FOLLOWERS Dent L (1976) [2] First separate edition. Text cuts by Keith Holmes, signed by him. Vellum in hinged box (Bromer #25) $350.

042b: THE FOLLOWERS L (1976) [1] Wraps (ref.d) $30.

042c: THE FOLLOWERS Raamin-Presse (Hamburg) 1977 [2] 30 sgd no cc. 1 to 20 in German and 1 to 10 in English with a numbered and signed etching by Roswitha Quadelieg $250.

042d: THE FOLLOWERS Raamin-Presse (Hamburg) 1977 [2] 90 sgd no. cc. 21 to 80 in German and 11 to 40 in English $100.

043a: FERN HILL Four Winds Press (Locust Valley) 1978 [2] 30 cc. Large 4to sheets folded and laid in stiff green wrapper folder (Wilder Books #28) $150.

044a: DRAWINGS TO POEMS BY DYLAN THOMAS Enitharmon Press (L) 1980 [] Drawings by Ceri Richards $10/50

045a: LAUGHARNE Lime Rock Press Salisbury, Ct. 1980 [2] 25 sgd ltr cc. Text by Thomas. Photographs by Tryntje Van Ness Seymour $750.

045b: LAUGHARNE Lime Rock Press Salisbury, Ct. 1980 [2] 75 cc (numbered? signed?). Published at $395 $450.

046a: THE COLLECTED STORIES Franklin Lib. Franklin Ctr. 1980 [2] "Limited Edition." 25 stories illustrated by Paul Hogarth. Blue leather (ref.d) $60.

046b: THE COLLECTED STORIES J.M. Dent L (1983) [1] 44 stories $8/40

046c: THE COLLECTED STORIES New Directions (NY 1984) [1] "First published clothbound ... 1984." 44 stories $7/35

047a: THE PEACHES (Tales For Travellers S.F. 1982) [0] Wraps (map fold). Last copyright 1982 but probably published in 1985 or later $25.

048a: The following were illustrated and signed by Frederic Prokosch using Prometheus Press, Grasse (France) 1982. [2] 5 sgd no cc. 6 1/4" x 4 1/2" (Howard Woolmer 10/90):

a. THE AIR YOU BREATHE $75.
b. CONCEIVE THESE IMAGES $75.
c. DO NOT GO GENTLE $75.
d. THE ROD $75.
e. SONG $75.
The set $400.

049a: The following were illustrated and signed by Frederic Prokosch using Prometheus Press, Grasse (France) 1983. [2] 5 sgd no cc. (Eric & Joan Stevens #131):

a. HIGH ON A HILL $75.
b. HERE LIE THE BEASTS $75.
c. POEM $75.
d. LAST NIGHT $75.
e. WAS THERE A TIME $75.
The set $400.

050a: POEM ON HIS BIRTHDAY : IN THE MUSTARDSEED SUN Tern Press (Marret Drayton 1983) [2] 85 sgd no. cc. Illustrated and signed by Nicholas Parry. Issued without dustwrapper (George Houle #39). Also "One of 60" copies (London) 1983 (Bev Chaney #6) $125.

051a: THE COLLECTED LETTERS Dent L 1985 [] Edited by Paul Ferris $8/40

051b: THE COLLECTED LETTERS Macmillan NY 1985 [] Uncorrected proof in blue wraps $60.

051c: THE COLLECTED LETTERS Macmillan NY 1985 [] $7/35

052a: THE OUTING Dent L (1985) [1] First separate and first illustrated edition $6/30

053a: THE MOUSE AND THE WOMAN Brighton Press San Diego 1988 [2] 180 sgd no. cc. Signed by the illustrator James Renner. First separate edition of a section of *The Adventures in the Skin Trade*. Issued without dustwrapper in slipcase. (Published @ $250) $250.

054a: IN MY CRAFT OR SULLEN ART L 1989 [] Broadside posted in London Subway (Bayside Books 12/89) $35.

Mark Twain

Saml. L. Clemens

MARK TWAIN
Samuel Langhorne Clemens
1835-1910

Clemens was born in 1835 in Florida, Missouri. He spent his boyhood in Hannibal, Mississippi and it was his boyhood recollections that produced his most famous stories, *The Adventures of Tom Sawyer* and *The Adventures of Huckleberry Finn*. In 1857 he became a Mississippi river pilot, an experience that gave him his pseudonym ("mark twain" was called out when the depth of water of two fathoms was reached).

He worked as a wandering printer and newspaperman ending up in San Francisco where Bret Harte encouraged him in his writing of "tall tales" and he won his first fame for his short story *The Celebrated Jumping Frog of Calaveras County*.

Clemens married and moved to Hartford, Connecticut in 1872, where his investments in printing and publishing ventures left him penniless by 1894. He began lecturing around the world to pay off these debts.

His bad investments, the death of two of his daughters and the long illness and death of his wife combined to change his writing from the humorous to the pessimistic.

Mark Twain is considered to be one of the finest writers America has produced.

The retail prices herein are our best estimates based on dealer catalog prices and auction records where available. The price(s) estimated are for fine copies without dustwrappers before 1920. Although we know the books were issued in dustwrappers from at least the 1890's on and estimated prices with dustwrapper before 1920 would be three times more at least than unjacketed copies. Starting in 1920 the two prices indicate estimates without/with dustwrappers. Truely fine or better copies of the early books are not common and should command the prices shown and conversely worn copies or those with defects would sell for considerably less. Copies bound in original publisher's leather are consistently catalogued or sold at auction for more than the cloth bound copies. We tried to mention this on each title where we knew it applied but if we missed some titles, the general rule still applies. It also should be noted that issues with gilt edges seem to consistently bring more than their plain edge counterparts.

We would like to thank Carl Hahn for his assistance in the preparation of this guide; and Ken Sanderson of the Mark Twain Project at the Bancroft Library in Berkeley.

REFERENCES:

Unless otherwise noted, information is for ref.a through 1956 and ref.b thereafter.

(a) Blanck, Jacob BIBLIOGRAPHY OF AMERICAN LITERATURE Vol. II, Yale University Press, New Haven/London (1957).

(b) McBride, William M. MARK TWAIN A Bibliography of the Collections of the Mark Twain Memorial and the Stowe-Day Foundation, McBride Publications, Hartford (1984).

(c) Fox, Alan C. CATALOGUE ONE (Sherman Oaks 1980).

(d) THE JULES L. MERRON COLLECTION OF MARK TWAIN catalogued (38) by David J. Holmes, Philadelphia (1992).

001a: THE CELEBRATED JUMPING FROG OF CALAVERAS COUNTY++ C.H. Webb NY 1867 [0] First issue has single leaf of ads on cream-yellow paper before title-page. P.66: last line "life" unbroken. P.198: last line "this" unbroken. In various cloth colors. Usually with frog in left corner of front cover, variant has frog in middle. One copy reported with p.198 unprinted, which may be earliest state $17,500.

001b: THE CELEBRATED JUMPING FROG OF CALAVERAS COUNTY++ C.H. Webb NY 1867 [0] Second printing lacks ads before title-page. Type noted above either broken or worn $2,500.

Note: Intermediate states of above exist

001c: THE CELEBRATED JUMPING FROG OF CALAVERAS COUNTY++ George Routledge & Sons London 1867 [0] Wraps $3,500.

001d: THE JUMPING FROG ++ John Camden Hotten London (n-d) [0] Wraps (pictorial? published 1867?) $1,250.

001e: THE CELEBRATED JUMPING FROG++ George Routledge & Sons London 1868 [0] Wraps $600.

001f: THE JUMPING FROG IN ENGLISH... Harper & Bros. NY 1903 [0] (Issued in dustwrapper) $125.

001g: THE NOTORIOUS JUMPING FROG... Duschnes NY 1932 [2] 200 cc in green boards. Issued without dustwrapper $100.

001h: JIM SMILEY & HIS JUMPING FROG Pocahontas Press (Chicago) 1940 [] $60.

001i: THE NORTORIOUS JUMPING FROG & OTHER STORIES Limited Editions Club NY 1970 [2] 1,500 cc Signed by Joseph Low, the illustrator. Selected and introduced by Edward Wagenknecht. Issued without dustwrapper in slipcase $40/75

001j: THE JUMPING FROG Cheloniidae Press Easthampton, Mass. (1985) [2] 15 sgd no cc. Illustrated and signed by James Alan Robinson. Bound in full leather and in tray case with an additional suite of prints with state proofs of etchings and working proofs of wood engravings $2,000.

001k: THE JUMPING FROG Cheloniidae Press Easthampton, Mass. (1985) [2] 50 sgd no cc. Illustrated and signed by James Alan Robinson. Bound in quarter leather in tray case with an additional suite of engravings $750.

001l: THE JUMPING FROG Cheloniidae Press Easthampton, Mass. (1985) [2] 250 sgd no cc. Wraps. Illustrated and signed by James Alan Robinson $150.

001m: THE JUMPING FROG Chronicle Books San Francisco (1987) Woodcuts by Alan James Robinson. Creme cloth. Issued without dustwrapper? $25.

002a: ADDRESS TO HIS IMPERIAL MAJESTY: -ALEXANDER II. EMPEROR OF RUSSIA... (no publisher?, no-place?, no-date?) [0] Broadside printed on gray paper measuring 11 1/2" x 10 3/4" $NVA

003a: THE PUBLIC TO MARK TWAIN. CORRESPONDENCE... NEW MERCANTILE LIBRARY... (no publisher) (San Francisco 1868) [0] Single sheet, 15" x 5 7/8" $NVA

004a: THE INNOCENTS ABROAD... American Publ. Co. Hartford; Bliss & Co. Newark; R.W. Bliss & Co. Toledo; F.G. Gilman Chicago; Nettleton & Co. Cincinnati; F.A. Hutchinson & Co. St. Louis; H.H. Bancroft San Francisco. Publisher's prospectus consisting of prelims, selections from text, representation illustrations, publisher advertisements and spaces for subscriber's names. Two binding backstrips (ref.d) $3,500.

004b: THE INNOCENTS ABROAD... American Publ. Co. Hartford; Bliss & Co. Newark; R.W. Bliss & Co. Toledo; F.G. Gilman Chicago; Nettleton & Co. Cincinnati; F.A. Hutchinson & Co. St. Louis; H.H. Bancroft San Francisco. 1869 [0] First issue: pp.xvii-xviii table of contents lacks page reference numbers; p.xviii the last entry reads "Thankless Devotion-A Newspaper Valedictory" <leaders>; p.129 no illustration; p.(643) Chapter "XLI"; p.(654) "Personal History ..." Bound variously in black cloth, sheep, morocco and half calf. The binding, other than cloth, would probably be worth twice as much as the cloth prices shown $1,500.

004c: THE INNOCENTS ABROAD... (publishers and places as above) 1869 [0] Second issue: pp.xvii-xviii page reference nnumbers present in table of contents; p.xviii the last entry reads "Thank-less devotion-A Newspaper Valedictory-Conclusion <leaders> 638"; p.129 portrait of Napoleon III; p.<643> Chapter XLI; p.<654> Personal History ... $750.

004d: THE INNOCENTS ABROAD ... (publishers and places as above) 1869 [0] Third issue: same as for second issue except p.<654> has ad "History of the Bible ... Album Family Bible" $400.

Note: Intermediate issues are known. Also seen, an issue with imprint: "San Francisco, Calif.: H.H. Bancroft and Company, Hartford, Conn.: American Publishing Company. 1869"

004e: THE INNOCENTS ABROAD ... American Publ. Co. Hartford 1870 [] Prospectus. 8vo, 55 leaves of text and illustrations, 3 leaves of subsciptions. Issued in black cloth with cloth and leather samples on pastedowns (Heritage Cat. #162) $2,000.

004f: INNOCENTS ABROAD ... John Camden Hotten London (no-date) [0] (Published 1870.) Cloth. First English edition. Unauthorized by Twain. (First half of *Innocents Abroad*) $450.

004g: INNOCENTS ABROAD ... John Camden Hotten London (no-date) [0] Simultaneous issue in wraps $450.

004h: THE NEW PILGRIM'S PROGRSS ... John Camden Hotten London (no-date) [0] Cloth. Published 1870. Second half of *Innocents Abroad* $350.

004i: THE NEW PILGRIM'S PROGRESS ... John Camden Hotten London (no-date) [0] Simultaneous issue in wraps $250.

004j: THE INNOCENTS ABROAD A.S. Irving Toronto 1870 [] Cloth. Redated preface 1870, but same as original preface $250.

004k: THE INNOCENTS ABROAD A.S. Irving Toronto 1870 [ ] Wraps $250.

004l: MARK TWAIN'S PLEASURE TRIP ON THE CONTINENT... John Camden Hotten London (no-date) [0] Printed boards, also issued in cloth. Published 1871. Also noted in stiff pictorial boards. 6 1/4" x 4", with 22 pages of ads dated 1871 (Ergo Books #801) New title. Reprints complete text. Also noted as "Yellow Back." Includes *Innocents Abroad* and *The New Pilgrim's Progress* (Ergo Books 12/90) $350.

004m: THE INNOCENTS ABROAD George Routledge & Sons London (1872) [0] Pictorial wrappers. First half $350.

004n: THE NEW PILGRIM'S PROGRESS... Author's English Edition George Routledge London (no-date) [0] Wraps. Published in 1872. Second half of *The Innocents Abroad*. Title page mentions Routledge is Twain's only authorized publisher. First issue has imprint of Bradbury, Evans & Company on p.255 $300.

004o: THE NEW PILGRIM'S PROGRESS... Author's English Edition George Routledge London (no-date) [0] Wraps. Published 1872. Second issue with imprint of Bradbury, Agnew & Co. on p.255 $250.

004p: THE NEW PILGRIMS PROGRESS... Author's English Edition George Routledge London (no-date) [0] Wraps. Published 1872. Thirrd issue with imprint of Woodfall & Kinder on p.255 $200.

004q: THE NEW PILGRIMS PROGRESS Joseph Knight Co. B 1895 [] 2 volumes. Issued with linen dustwrapper. Illustrations include 30 full page photogravures (Kenneth Karmiole 6/92) $150/200

004r: THE INNOCENTS ABROAD OR THE NEW PILGRIM'S PROGRESS Ltd Editions Club NY 1962 [2] 1,500 sgd cc in box. Illustrated and signed by Fritz Kredel $75/125

005a: MARK TWAIN'S (BURLESQUE) AUTOBIOGRAPHY AND FIRST ROMANCE

Sheldon & Co. NY (1871) [0] Wraps. First issue lacks ads for Ball, Black & Co. on copyright page; no priority between 005a/b i.e. cloth vs wraps $275.

005b: MARK TWAIN'S (BURLESQUE) AUTOBIOGRAPHY AND FIRST ROMANCE Sheldon & Co. NY (1871) [0] In green, terra-cotta or purple cloth. First issue lacks ads for Ball, Black & Co. on copyright page $250.

005c: MARK TWAIN'S (BURLESQUE) AUTOBIOGRAPHY AND FIRST ROMANCE Sheldon & Co. NY (1871) [0] Cloth. Second issue has ads for Ball, Black & Co. on copyright page $150.

005d: MARK TWAIN'S (BURLESQUE) AUTOBIOGRAPHY AND FIRST ROMANCE Sheldon & Co. NY (1871) [0] Wraps. Second issue has ads for Ball, Black & Co. on copyright page $100.

005e: MARK TWAIN'S (BURLESQUE)... AUTOBIOGRAPHY... ON CHILDREN John Camden Hotten London (no-date) [0] Cloth. No date, but published 1871 $300.

005f: MARK TWAIN'S (BURLESQUE)... AUTOBIOGRAPHY... ON CHILDREN John Camden Hotten London (no-date) [0] Pictorial wraps $250.

005g: MARK TWAIN'S (BURLESQUE) AUTOBIOGRAPHY AND FIRST ROMANCE George Routledge & Sons London (no-date) [] Wraps. First authorized English edition following Hotten's unauthorized edition published 2 weeks earlier $175.

005h: MARK TWAIN'S BURLESQUE AUTOBIOGRAPHY Peter Pauper Press Larchmont 1930 [2] 525 cc $50.

006a: MARK TWAIN'S MEMORANDA. FROM THE GALAXY Canadian News Toronto 1871 [0] Offered by various distributors whose imprint appears in place of publisher: A.S. Irving, Wm. Warwich, C.A. Backas, all of Toronto. Publication was unauthorized. Issued in cloth. (Brought $1,800 at auction) $2,000.

006b: MARK TWAIN'S MEMORANDA. FROM THE GALAXY Canadian News Toronto 1871 [0] Simultaneous issue in wraps $1,500.

007a: EYE OPENERS... John Camden Hotten London (no-date) [0] Cloth. First printing: p.(176) "..Special List for 1871..." $600.

007b: EYE OPENERS... John Camden Hotten London (no-date) [0] Wraps. First printing: p.(176) "..Special List for 1871..." No priority between cloth and wraps $600.

007c: EYE OPENERS... John Camden Hotten London (no-date) [0] Cloth. Second printing: p.(176) "..Special List for 1872..." $250.

007d: EYE OPENERS... John Camden Hotten London (no-date) [0] Wraps. Second printing: p.(176) "..Special List for 1872..." No priority between cloth and wraps $250.

008a: SCREAMERS... John Camden Hotten London (no-date) [0] Cloth. First issue: text ends on p.172 due to inclusion of story entitled "Vengeance." Ads dated 1871 $600.

008b: SCREAMERS... John Camden Hotten London (no-date) [0] Wraps. Same issue point as above. No priority between wraps and cloth $600.

008c: SCREAMERS... John Camden Hotten London (no-date) [0] Cloth. Second issue: text ends at p.166; ads dated 1872 $250.

008d: SCREAMERS... John Camden Hotten London (no-date) [0] Wraps. Second issue points same as above. No priority between cloth and wraps $250.

009a: "ROUGHING IT."... COPYRIGHT EDITION George Routledge London (1872) [0] Pictorial yellow boards. First half of *Roughing It* $600.

009b: THE INNOCENTS AT HOME... COPYRIGHT EDITION George Routledge London (1872) [0] First state of binding pictorial salmon or pictorial yellows boards; five titles listed on back cover. The first English edition of final portion of *Roughing It and Mark Twain's Burlesque...* Also noted in yellow pictorial wraps (ref.d) $500.

009c: THE INNOCENTS AT HOME... COPYRIGHT EDITION George Routledge London (1872) [0] Presumed second state of binding pictorial yellow boards; seven numbered titles and two unnumbered titles are listed on back cover (ref.b identified another state with 9 titles not in BAL which we assume would be an intermediate state). Eleven titles listed per ref.a $400.

009d: THE INNOCENTS AT HOME... COPYRIGHT EDITION George Routledge London (1872) [0] Presumed third state of binding pictorial yellow boards; eleven titles listed on back cover $300.

009e: ROUGHING IT American Publ., F.G. Gilman, Chicago; W.E. Bliss, Toledo; Nettleton, Cincinnati; D. Ashmead, Philadelphia; Geo. A. Smith, Boston 1872 [0] Publisher's prospectus in black cloth consisting of prelims, selections from text, representative illustrations, publisher's ads, spaces for purchasers and two binding samples (ref.d) $3,000.

009f: ROUGHING IT American Publ., F.G. Gilman, Chicago; W.E. Bliss, Toledo; Nettleton, Cincinnati; D. Ashmead, Philadelphia; Geo. A. Smith, Boston; A. Roman & Company San Francisco 1872 [0] Adds "A. Roman & Company, San Francisco, Calif.." to imprint $750.

009g: ROUGHING IT American Publ., F.G. Gilman, Chicago; W.E. Bliss, Toledo; Nettleton, Cincinnati; D. Ashmead, Philadelphia; Geo. A. Smith, Boston; A. Roman, San Francisco 1872 [0] Issued with variant imprints of agents other than those listed above. Published in black cloth, cloth with gilt edges, sheep, half morocco, half calf. Probable earliest state reads: "Premises-said he/was occupying his/" on p.242:20-21. Seen with and without ads on p.(592), priority unknown. Leather bound copies would be worth more than the cloth bound prices shown $1,250.

009h: ROUGHING IT (publishers and places as above) 1872 [0] Probable second state letters and/or words lacking on p.242:20-21 $650.

009i: THE INNOCENTS AT HOME... Robertson Melbourne 1873 [] Printed in Melbourne, copyrighted in Australia $400.

009j: ROUGHING IT IN CALIFORNIA Allen Press Kentfield 1953 [2] 200 cc per ref.c $450.

009k: ROUGHING IT Limited Editions Club NY 1972 [2] 1,500 sgd cc boxed. Illustrated and signed by Noel Sickles $75/100

010a: A CURIOUS DREAM +++ George Routledge London (1872) [0] Yellow pictorial boards. Earliest printing: endpapers blank; leaf L4 blank; "Bradbury, Evans" imprint on pp.(2) and/or p.150 $600.

011a: MARK TWAIN'S SKETCHES... George Routledge London 1872 [0] "Copyright Edition." Pictorial boards. Reprint save for author's prefatory note $500.

012a: THE CHOICE HUMOROUS WORKS OF MARK TWAIN John Camden Hotten London (no-date) [0] Published 1873 $350.

012b: THE CHOICE HUMOROUS WORKS OF MARK TWAIN Chatto & Windus London 1874 [0] Reprint of above $200.

013a: MARK TWAIN'S LETTER TO THE NEW YORK TRIBUNE (no-publisher, place or date) [0] Wraps. Issued as an advertisement for the Cunnard Line in Boston in 1873. Printed in blue and red; 4 pages size 7 3/4" x 5 1/4"; probably occurs with imprints of other agencies $600.

014a: THE GILDED AGE... American Publ. Co., Hartford/F.G. Gilman, Chicago 1873 [0] Innumerable variants of this book exist, as well as cloth and leather bindings. Leather bound copies are worth more than cloth prices shown and there were 500 copies with all edges gilt (Kevin MacDonnell) which would be worth more.

Point 1: "Everybody's Friend" described as a "truex inde" in ads at end of book, later corrected to "true index"

Point 2: Artist "White" present on title-page, deleted in later state

Point 3: Earliest printing (printings?) of p.(vii) under chapter 5 has "Eschol Sellers" (in reprints it is "Beriah Sellers")

Point 4: p.xvi the final illustration is numbered "211". Later "212

Point 5: p.246:5 (from the bottom) "Hallelujah". Later "Halleluhah,"

Point 6: p.280:18 "Dr. Jackson." Later "Dr. Jackson"

Point 7: p.351:last "would kill me if she could, thought the Colonel; but he". Line absent in later states

Point 8: p.353:1-2 "let him keep it. She looked down into his face with a pitia- / ble tenderness, and said in a weak voice,". Later state above lines absent

Point 9: p.403 no illustration. Later state illustration present

All points	$2,500.
Lacking points 7 & 8	$2,000.
Other 1873	$1,250.
1874	$350.

014b: THE GILDED AGE... in Three Volumes George Routledge London/NY 1874 [0] Includes Author's preface to London edition

$1,500.

014c: THE GILDED AGE George Routledge London (no-date) [0] (Published 1874) Cloth. First one-volume English edition (BAL 3606) although ref.c shows an 1883 edition in red cloth as possibly the first one volume edition? $500.

014d: THE GILDED AGE George Routledge London (no-date) [0] Pictorial boards issued simultaneously $500.

015a: MARK TWAIN'S SKETCHES Authorized Edition American News Co. NY (1874) [0] Wraps. Presumed earlier state: front of wraps imprinted, otherwise blank $1,000.

015b: MARK TWAIN'S SKETCHES Authorized Edition American News Co. NY (1874) [0] Wraps. Presumed later state back of wraps has ad for Aetna Life Insurance Co. $300.

016a: MARK TWAIN'S SPEECH ON ACCIDENT INSURANCE (no-publisher, place or date) [0] Wraps printed in blue. Issued as an ad by the Hartford Insurance Co., Hartford, CT, 1874. Four pages 5 3/16" x 3 1/8" $500.

017a: MARK TWAIN'S SKETCHES, NEW AND OLD... The American Publishing Co. Hartford / Chicago 1875 [0] Publisher's prospectus with 3 binding samples (ref.d) $2,000.

017b: MARK TWAIN'S SKETCHES, NEW AND OLD... The American Publishing Co. Hartford / Chicago 1875 [0] Various bindings. The earliest state: p.119 has footnote; footnote repeated on p.120; p.299 has 11 line skit headed "From Hospital Days". Leather bindings would be worth more than cloth prices shown $500.

017c: MARK TWAIN'S SKETCHES, NEW AND OLD... The American Publishing Co. Hartford/Chicago 1875 [0] Later state: p.119

footnote present; p.120 footnote not present; p.299 "From Hospital Days" not present $300.

018a: INFORMATION WANTED + George Routledge & Sons London (no-date) [0] Published 1876. First state: lacks "Honored As a Curiosity" on pp.128-130 $600.

018b: INFORMATION WANTED + George Routledge & Sons London (no-date) [0] Published 1876. Second state: includes "Honored As a Curiosity" on pp.128-130 $250.

019a: THE ADVENTURES OF TOM SAWYER Chatto & Windus London 1876 [0] $2,500.

019b: THE ADVENTURES OF TOM SAWYER Belford Brothers Toronto 1876 [0] Assumed to be set from English edition and also preceded U.S. edition $1,250.

019c: THE ADVENTURES OF TOM SAWYER The American Publishing Co. Hartford, Chicago, Cincinnati; A. Roman & Co., San Fran. 1876 [0] First printing is on wove paper. Front matter paged (I)-xvi, fly-title, p.(I). Pp.(II-III blank. Frontispiece, p.(iv). Collation: (I)-xvi, (17)-(275); blank, p.(276); 4pp ads. (Verso of half-title and preface blank)

Half-morocco (200 cc) $15,000.
Calf (1,500 cc) $12,000.
Blue cloth, edges gilt (748 cc) $9,000.
Blue cloth, edges plain (7,431 cc) $6,500.

019d: THE ADVENTURES OF TOM SAWYER The American Publishing Co. Hartford, Chicago, Cincinnati; A. Roman & Co., San Francisco 1876 [0] Second printing, issue A: printed on laid paper. Fly-title, p.(II). Pagination: (I-XII), (17)-(275); blank, p.(276); plus ads, pp.(277-280). Mispagination: p.(IX) mispaged XII; p.(X) mispaged XIII; p.(XII) mispaged XVI. Illustration of Tom on verso of half-title and contents on verso of preface. Leather bound copies on this and later issues would be worth more than cloth prices shown. $1,000.

019e: THE ADVENTURES OF TOM SAWYER The American Publishing Co. Hartford, Chicago, Cincinnati; A. Roman & Co., San Francisco 1876 [0] Second printing, issue B: same as second printing, issue A but on wove paper $850.

019f: THE ADVENTURES OF TOM SAWYER The American Publishing Co. Hartford, Chicago, Cincinnati; A. Roman & Co., San Francisco 1876 [0] Second printing, issue C: same as issue A and B but made up of both wove and laid papers within the same copy $750.

019g: THE ADVENTURES OF TOM SAWYER The American Publishing Co. Hartford, Chicago, Cincinnati: A. Roman & Co., San Francisco 1876 [0] Third printing. Printed on laid paper. Pp. (I-II) used as pastedown. Fly-title, p.(v). Frontispiece, p.(VI). Pagination: (I)-XVI, (17)-(275); blank, p.(276); ads, pp.(277-280). Note: in the front matter folio XVI is the only one present $600.

019h: THE ADVENTURES OF TOM SAWYER Random House NY 1930 [2] 2,000 sgd no cc. Signed by Donald McKay. Leather spine in slipcase $75/125

019i: THE ADVENTURES OF TOM SAWYER Limited Eds. Club Cambridge 1939 [2] 1,500 sgd no cc in slipcase. Illustrated and signed by Thomas Hart Benton $400/500

019j: THE ADVENTURES OF TOM SAWYER World Publishing Cleveland/NY (1946) [0] Illustrated by Louis Slobodkin. First thus $15/60

019k: THE ADVENTURES OF TOM SAWYER Georgetown Univ Lib/Univ Publ Washington, D.C. 1982 [2] 1,000 cc. Two volumes in slipcase. A facsimile of the author's holograph manuscript with an introduction by Paul Baender $125/150

020a: OLD TIMES ON THE MISSISSIPPI Belford Bros. Toronto 1876 [0] Wraps. Title set in Old English, upper and lower case, in a single line. No publisher's notice on title-page. Inner wrap blank (priority between 021a and b unknown) $750.

020b: OLD TIMES ON THE MISSISSIPPI Belford Bros. Toronto 1876 [0] Wraps. As above but inner wrap has published ads. Also seen in salmon cloth (priority between 021a and b unknown) $750.

020c: OLD TIMES ON THE MISSISSIPPI Belford Bros. Toronto 1876 [0] Reprint A (no priority): title-page set in Roman and Arabic; title in three lines; imprint dated 1876; page opposite title-page blank. Green cloth stamped in black. P.(160) "...The New Poems..." $400.

020d: OLD TIMES ON THE MISSISSIPPI Belford Bros. Toronto 1876 [0] Reprint B (no priority): title-page set in Roman only; title in 3 lines; Publisher's device not present; imprint dated "MDCCCLXXVI"; opposite title-page is ad for *Tom Sawyer*. Green or purple cloth; p.(160): "New and Popular Books..." $400.

020e: OLD TIMES ON THE MISSISSIPPI Belford Bros. Toronto 1876 [0] Reprint C (no priority): same as reprint B except p.(160): "Norman McLeod's Works..." $400.

020f: OLD TIMES ON THE MISSISSIPPI Belford Bros. Toronto 1876 [0] Reprint D (no priority): same as reprint B except p.(160): Common Sense in the Household..." $400.

Note: We had a variant with ads on pages (158, 159), while none of ref.a reprints had ads on page (158).

020g: THE MISSISSIPPI PILOT Ward, Lock & Tyler London (no-date) [] Wraps (published 1877). $350.

020h: THE MISSISSIPPI PILOT Grand Colosseum Warehouse Co. Glasgow, Scotland [0] Title page only lists this title but contents page also includes Bret Harte's *Two Men of Sand Bar* and *Poem* $300.

021a: A TRUE STORY, AND THE RECENT CARNIVAL OF CRIME James R. Osgood & Co.; Late Ticknor & Fields; and Fields, Osgood & Co. Boston 1877 [0] First state of binding with "JRO & Co" monogram on front cover. Green or terra-cotta cloth $1,250.

021b: A TRUE STORY, AND THE RECENT CARNIVAL OF CRIME James R. Osgood & Co.; Late Ticknor & Fields; and Fields, Osgood & Co. Boston 1877 [0] Second state of binding with "HO" (i.e. Houghton, Osgood) on front cover $850.

022a: AN IDLE EXCURSION (title page) Rose-Belford Publ. Co. Toronto 1878 [0] Brown cloth. Also green cloth per Ref.c. No priority known between wraps and cloth binding. 114 pages. Cover title *Rambling Notes of An Idle*

Excursion which causes confusion with e&f below $750.

022b: AN IDLE EXCURSION Rose-Belford Publ. Co. Toronto 1878 [0] Wraps $750.

022c: AN IDLE EXCURSION J. Ross Robertson Toronto 1878 [0] Wraps. (Gray wraps per Ref.c.) 36 pages. Title story only. May have preceded above entries per note to BAL 3377 $300.

022d: AN IDLE EXCURSION + Chatto & Windus London 1878 [0] Pictorial boards $400.

022e: RAMBLING NOTES OF AN IDLE EXCURSION Rose-Belford Toronto 1878 [0] First printing with device of the Canadian Paper Company on verso of title page (cloth or wraps) $250.

022f: RAMBLING NOTES OF AN IDLE EXCURSION Rose-Belford Toronto 1878 [0] Second printing without device (cloth or wraps) $100.

023a: PUNCH, BROTHERS, PUNCH! + Slote, Woodman & Co. NY (1878) [] Cloth. First issue: on title-page author's name printed in Roman; p.91:4 from bottom reads "health offi....could..." No priority between cloth and wraps. Undecorated cream-coated endpapers. Blue or green cloth (ref.a), brown cloth (Waiting For Godot #12 1987) $600.

023b: PUNCH, BROTHERS, PUNCH! + Slote, Woodman & Co. NY (1878) [0] Wraps. First issue: points as above. Red-coated paperwraps, spine lettered down "Mark Twain's Sketches" $600.

023c: PUNCH, BROTHERS, PUNCH! + Slote, Woodman & Co. NY (1878) [0] Cloth. Second issue: on title-page author's name is in facsimile autograph; p.91:4 from bottom reads "health officer's funeral could..."; endpapers decorated in blue with a scattering of caricatures $400.

023d: PUNCH, BROTHERS, PUNCH! + Slote, Woodman & Co. NY (1878) [0] Wraps. Second issue: on title-page author's name is in facsimile autograph; p.91:4 from bottom reads "health officer's funeral could..."; spine lettered down "Mark Twain's Punch" $350.

023e: PUNCH, BROTHERS, PUNCH! + E. & S. Livingston Edinburgh (no-date) [0] Pictorial boards, published 1878 $250.

024a: MARK TWAIN'S NIGHTMARE ... Ward, Lock & Co. (London 1878) [0] Wraps. Contains no first edition material and works by other authors. First state imprinted "Ward, Lock & Co. Warwick House, Dorset Buildings, Salisbury Square, E.C." Contains material by other authors $400.

024b: MARK TWAIN'S NIGHTMARE ... Ward, Lock & Co. London (1878) [0] Second state ? imprinted: "Ward, Lock & Co., London: Warwick House, Salisbury Square, E.C. New York:10, Bond Street" $300.

024c: MARK TWAIN'S NIGHTMARE ... Ward, Lock & Co. London (1878) [0] Wraps. Third state ? imprinted: "Ward, Lock & Co. London: Warwick House, Salisbury Square, E.C. New York: Bond Street" $300.

024d: MARK TWAIN'S NIGHTMARE ... Ward, Lock & Co. L/NY/Melbourne (1878) Wraps. A state not mentioned in BAL (ref.c) $300.

025a: SKETCHES Belfords, Clarke & Co. Toronto 1879 [0] Includes two first book appearances earliest printing(s?). The verso of title pages has "C.B. Robinson: and "Brown Bros." which are not on later printings $400.

026a: MARK TWAIN ON BABIES George B. Hatfield (London no-date) [0] Single leaf folded to four pages. Date unknown 1879? $750.

A BOY'S ADVENTURES see 1928 entry.

027a: A TRAMP ABROAD American Publishing Co. Hartford; Chatto & Windus London 1880 [0] First state: frontispiece captioned, "Moses". Priority of other points in BAL not established. Leather bindings would be worth more than the cloth prices shown $1,000.

027b: A TRAMP ABROAD American Publishing Co. Hartford; Chatto & Windus London 1880 [0] Second state: frontispiece captioned, "Titian's Moses" $400.

027c: A TRAMP ABROAD ... Chatto & Windus London 1880 [0] 2 vols. Ads dated "February, 1880" (ref.d) $1,250.

027d: A TRAMP ABROAD ... Chatto & Windus London 1880 [0] One volume edition. Ads dated August 1880 per Ref.c $150.

027e: A TRAMP ABROAD Limited Editions Club (NY 1966) [2] 1,500 sgd cc in slipcase. Illustrated and signed by David Knight with 12 illustrations by Twain made "without help." First book appearances? $75/125

028a: (1601) CONVERSATION, AS IT WAS BY THE SOCIAL FIRESIDE, IN THE TIME OF THE TUDORS (no-place or date) [0]

Wraps. 8 9/16" x 7" printed on wove paper, self-wrapper. Possibly printed for Alexander Gunn, Cleveland, Ohio, 1880 $NVA

028b: (1601) CONVERSATION, AS IT WAS BY THE SOCIAL FIRESIDE, IN THE TIME OF THE TUDORS (n-p, n-d) [0] Wraps. 8 7/16" x 7 1/16". Printed on laid paper, self-wrapper. Possibly printed for Alexander Gunn, Cleveland, Ohio, 1880 $NVA

028c: DATE 1601 CONVERSATION, AS IT WAS... ("Academie Press", West Point, NY 1882) [0] First authorized edition $1,500.

The Following are some of the editions of "1601" we've found. They are listed chronologically with the undated ones at the end:

028d: A CONVERSAZIONE IN THE YEAR MDCI... (Printed by order of the King, Bangkok 1894) [2] 20 no. cc (I-XX). Red crushed morocco, marbled endpaper, top edge gilt (ref.d) $350.

028e: A CONVERSAZIONE IN THE YEAR MDCI... (Printed by order of the King, Bankok 1894) [2] 75 no. cc. Japan vellum (ref.d) $100.

028f: 1601 ... (no publisher, place or date {circa 1903}) [0] 4to. 10 5/8" x 5 1/4". Cream-colored wraps, 32 pages, stapled, newspaper article dated 1903 (Waiting For Godot 2/91) $75.

028g: A CONVERSATION IN THE YEAR MDCI (Privated printed) 1913 [2] 75 no. cc in decorated wraps. Printed on Japan vellum $150.

028h: THIS EDITION OF MARK TWAIN'S DATE 1601 CONVERSATION... (Privately printed, NY) 1920 [2] 110 cc. Tan stapled wraps (Heritage 3/89) $150.

028i: 1601 ... Privately printed 1924 [] 35 cc. Wraps (Book Treasury 1/90) $75.

028j: "1601" ... (Grabhorn Press) S.F. 1925 [2] 100 cc. Full calf or morocco $200.

028k: FIRESIDE CONVERSATION IN 1601 ... (Privately published, no-place) 1925 [2] 500 cc. Wraps. "No. One of the Airdale Series" (ref.d) $75.

028l: 1601 ... (no publisher or place) 1926 [2] 525 no. cc. Stapled wraps. Semi-Centennial Edition (ref.d) $50.

028m: "1601" ... (Privately published) NY 1927 [2] 125 cc per Ref.c. Orange cloth backed, black and gold decorated boards in glassine dustwrapper $100.

028n: 1601 ... (Privately Printed London 1927) [2] 101 no. cc. Wraps. 7" x 5" $60.

028o: FIRESIDE CONVERSATION IN THE TIME OF QUEEN ELIZABETH OR "1601" Privately printed (no-place) 1928 [2] 1,000 no. cc. Wraps (ref.d) $40.

028p: MARK TWAIN'S DATE 1601... Privately printed (no-place) 1929 [2] 110 no. cc. Wraps (ref.d) $50.

028q: 1601 ... Printed at Ye Blew Grasse Press Louisville 1929 [2] 1,000 no. cc (First work of the Blue Grass Press). Printed blue boards (ref.d) $75.

028r: 1601, OR A FIRESIDE COMPANION (Privately printed, no-place?) 1929 [2] 40 cc (Boston Book Annex #29) Brown morocco spine over green cloth in slipcase (Kenneth Karmiole

3/90). Also in red morocco and green cloth with pencilled note "Windsor Press" (ref.d) $175.

028s: FIRESIDE CONVERSATION IN 1601 ... (no-publisher or place) 1932 [2] 1,000 cc. Wraps (ref.c) $60.

028t: MARK TWAIN'S 1601 ... Waverley Lewis Root Paris (1932) [2] 500 no. cc. Printed on Verge de Rives paper (ref.d) $50.

028u: 1601 ... Golden Hind Press (NY) 1933 [] Preface by Samuel Roth (ref.d) $15/60

028v: 1601 ... Privately Printed (no-place?) 1934 [] 250 cc. Cloth without dustwrapper (Polyanthos Park 10/90) $40.

028w: 1601 ... Black Cat Press Chicago 1936 [ ] 300 cc in red leatherette $60.

028x: MARK TWAIN'S 1601 ... Lyle Stuart NY (1938) [] Red cloth, no slipcase. Introduction, footnote and bibliography by Franklin J. Meine (Antic Hay 11/88) $40.

028y: FIRESIDE CONVERSATION IN THE TIME OF QUEEN ELIZABETH ... Privately printed no-place 1938 [0] Shimmery light blue cloth, glassine dustwrapper, slipcase (ref.d) 75.

028z: MARK TWAIN'S (1601) CONVERSATION ... Mark Twain Soc. of Chicago, Chicago 1939 [2] 550 no. cc. Red cloth in slipcase, includes bibliography of 44 editions of *1601* by Franklin J. Meine $75.

028aa: MARK TWAIN'S (1601) CONVERSATION ... Mark Twain Soc. of Chicago, Chicago 1939 [2] 1,000 cc. Unnumbered in slipcase $40.

028bb: MDCI. A FIRESIDE CHATTE ... Ye Three Astericks at Ye Signe of Ye Gaye Goose no-place 1941 [2] 300 cc. Printed boards (ref.d) $50.

028cc: MARK TWAIN'S "1601" ... Privately printed (Mexico City 1943) [2] 1,000 no. cc. Wraps (ref.d) $40.

028dd: MDCI. A FIRESIDE ... Ye Three Astericks at Ye Signe of Ye Gaye Goose (no-place) 1948 [2] 300 cc. Printed boards (ref.d) $75.

028ee: 1601 Earth Publishing Co. (no-place 1955) [] Wraps (ref.d) $35.

028ff: 1601 ... Tasmania Press Claremont, Calif October, 1957 [] One leaf, illustrated, folded to make 4 pages (ref.d) $25.

028gg: MARK TWAIN'S (1601) (Lyle Stuart) NY (circa 1961) [0] Reprint of 1939 ed. Red cloth with printed slipcase and yellow paper band stating a special pre-publication price of $4.95 (ref.b) $25/50

028hh: 1601 Black Cat Press Chicago 1962 [ ] minature book $50.

028ii: 1601 Brentano's Paris 1962 [] Blue-green cloth (J&J House 4/89) $40.

028jj: FIRESIDE CONVERSATIONS... 1601 Presse of The Indian Kidde Nappanee 1974 [ ] about 40 cc (Bookseller #21 -1986) $100.

028kk: "1601" ... (Land's End Press) London (1969) [0] "Printed for Subscribers Only ..." Cloth (ref.d) $5/25

028ll: "1601" ... (Land's End Press) London (1969) [0] "Printed for Subscribers Only ..." Pictorial boards (ref.d) $15/50

028mm: "1601" ... Merlin Verlag Hamburg (1974) [2] 300 no. cc signed by the illustrator H.G. Rauch. Decorated cloth, folio (ref.d) $150.

028nn: 1601 (no-publisher) Northampton, Mass. 1978 [2] 200 sgd no. cc. Lazarus Edition (sheets from a privately printed 1920 edition) with Barry Moser frontispiece signed by artist (ref.d) $125.

028oo: CONVERSATION AS IT WAS BY THE SOCIAL FIRE-SIDE ... Ye Puritan Presse At Ye Sign of Ye Jolly Virgin (no-place or date) [300 no. cc. Printed card wrappers with satin tie (ref.d) $75.

028pp: CONVERSATION AS IT WAS BY THE SOCIAL FIRE-SIDE ... Ye Puritan Presse At Ye Sign of Ye Jolly Virgin (no-place or date) [2] 500 no. cc. Wraps (ref.d) $25.

028qq: MARK TWAIN'S 1601 ... (Privated published. No-place or date) [2] 110 cc (ref.b) $75.

029a: A CURIOUS EXPERIENCE W.G. Gibson Toronto (no-date) [0] Wraps. Published 1881. Cream-yellow wraps (another edition printed with two columns on each page noted by BAL but the title page and cover missing) $350.

030a: THE PRINCE AND THE PAUPER ... Chatto & Windus London 1881 [0] Red cloth. Publishers catalog dated Nov. 1881 inserted at back $600.

030b: THE PRINCE AND THE PAUPER ... Dawson Bros. Montreal 1881 [0] 275 cc in gray-blue wrappers (Ref.a&c). Presumed to have been issued same time as English edition $1,250.

030c: THE PRINCE AND THE PAUPER ... Dawson Bros. Montreal 1881 [0] Blue cloth (also tan cloth per Ref.c) $600.

030d: THE PRINCE AND THE PAUPER ... Dawson Bros. Montreal 1881 [0] Title-page is a cancel with "Author's Canadian Edition..." added. Tan cloth stamped in gold and black (ref.c) $400.

030e: THE PRINCE AND THE PAUPER ... James R. Osgood & Co. Boston 1882 [0] 6-8 cc printed on China paper, bound in white linen, stamped in gold, inner hinges of blue linen $15,000.

030f: THE PRINCE AND THE PAUPER ... James R. Osgood & Co. Boston 1882 [0] First state: at front: true binder's endpapers of white, or toned white, paper. At back: leaf (26)8 used as pastedown. leaf (26)7 present as a blank. Uppermost rosette on spine 1/8" below fillet. Franklin Press imprint on copyright page. Leather binding and cloth with all edges gilt would be worth more than prices shown $600.

030g: THE PRINCE AND THE PAUPER ... James R. Osgood & Co. Boston 1882 [0] Second state: true binder's endpapers at both front and back; leaves (26)7-8 present as blanks; rosette on spine 1/16" below fillet. Franklin Press imprint on copyright page $350.

030h: THE PRINCE AND THE PAUPER ... Limited Editions Club (NY) 1964 [2] 1,500 sgd cc in slipcase. Illustrated and signed by Clarke Hutton $60/100

031a: THE STOLEN WHITE ELEPHANT Chatto & Windus London 1882 [0] Presumed first state: list of books on verso of half-title does not list *The White Elephant*; title-page has imprint on verso; foot of p.285 has one line imprint. Publisher's catalog dated May 1882 $250.

031b: THE STOLEN WHITE ELEPHANT Chatto & Windus London 1882 [0] Presumed second state: list of books on verso of half-title mentions *The White Elephant*; no imprint on verso of title-page; no imprint at foot of p.285 $150.

031c: THE STOLEN WHITE ELEPHANT James R. Osgood & Co. Boston 1882 [0] Tan cloth (or creme cloth - MacDonnell Rare Books 12/90) $350.

031d: THE STOLEN WHITE ELEPHANT + Haldeman-Julius Co. Girard, Kansas (no-date) [0] Wraps. Published 1925. "Little Blue Book No. 931" $35.

032a: LIFE ON THE MISSISSIPPI Chatto & Windus London 1883 [0] Red cloth. Advertisements dated March 1883 $900.

032b: LIFE ON THE MISSISSIPPI James R. Osgood & Co. Boston 1883 [] Publisher's prospectus with contents, list of illustrations, 39 leaves of text/illustrations, 3 pages publisher's announcements, 9 leaves of order pages, back pastedown has two leather spine examples and front pastedown has two cloth spine examples $2,000.

032c: LIFE ON THE MISSISSIPPI James R. Osgood & Co. Boston 1883 [0] 40,000 cc. Bound on date of publication. First state: p.441: present is a tail-piece depicting an urn, flames, and head of Twain; p.443: the caption reads "The

St. Louis Hotel". Leather binding would be worth more than cloth prices shown. First state sheets also noted in the Webster 1888 edition as Twain acquired the sheets after Osgood went bankrupt (Amaranth Books 3/92) $1,250.

032d: LIFE ON THE MISSISSIPPI James R. Osgood & Co. Boston 1883 [0] Second state: P.441: tail-piece not present; p.443: the caption reads "The St. Charles Hotel" $450.

Note: Intermediate states have been noted. Also see 102a

032e: LIFE ON THE MISSISSIPPI Limited Editions Club NY 1944 [0] 1,200 no. cc. Illustrated and signed by Thomas Hart Benton. Folding box, tissue dustwrapper $350/450

033a: THE ADVENTURES OF HUCKLEBERRY FINN ... Chatto & Windus London 1884 [0] Red cloth. Publisher's catalog dated October 1884 inserted at back. (A fine copy brought $2,250 at auction in 1991) $1,500.

033b: THE ADVENTURES OF HUCKLEBERRY FINN ... Dawson Bros Montreal 1885 [] Issued December 10, 1884. Copyrighted in name of Chatto, but per ref.c, obviously printed from American plates. Red or green cloth (ref.c). Has the signature mark "11" not seen on any NY 1885 edition. (Has been cataloged for $4,500)

$NVA

033c: ADVENTURES OF HUCKLEBERRY FINN ... Charles L. Webster & Co. NY 1885 [0] Publisher's prospectus. Earliest copies reportedly only advertised the book in green cloth (not blue and green) and had the copyright notice dated 1885 (ref.a) $10,000

033d: ADVENTURES OF HUCKLEBERRY FINN ... Charles L. Webster & Co. NY 1885 [0] Publisher's prospectus in green cloth with spine imprint on back cover and two samples of leather spines on front pastedown, sample text and illustrations and subscriber forms at end. Offers the book in blue or green cloth and sheep or one-half morocco binding (earliest prospectus reportedly offered only green cloth and would be worth more that the price shown) $7,500.

033e: THE ADVENTURES OF HUCKLEBERRY FINN ... Charles L. Webster & Co. NY 1885 [0] Issued in blue, and green cloth. Numerous variants exist. It has been suggested that the earliest bound copies were in leather, perhaps because of point 5 below:

Point 1: BAL's earliest state: title page with copyright notice on verso (1884) tipped-in. Later state: leaf bound-in. Some of the prospectuses had copyright as 1885, but no bound copy of the book has been seen with this copyright date. Ref.b notes that neither Merle Johnson nor Adam have a preference, perhaps because one leather bound copy (which are thought to be early) has a bound in title page.

Point 2: Earliest state: p.(13): "Him and another man" listed incorrectly at p.88. Later state: p.(13): "Him and another man" listed correctly at p.87.

Point 3: Earliest state: p.57:11 up: "...with the was..." Later state: "...with the saw..."

Point 4: Earliest state: p.155: Johnson has final 5 in page number same font in various "off-balance" position. Later state: p.155, final 5 absent. BAL lists these two states in reverse order of Johnson but indicates that he is uncertain, both agree on the latest state: p.155, final 5 present, wrong font (larger).

Point 5: Earliest state: p.283, seen only in prospectuses and leather bound copies; fly outline of trousers a pronounced curve; leaf bound in. Later state: p.283: engraving redone so fly is a straight line, leaf tipped-in. Final state: p.283: engraving redone, leaf bound-in, although there are those who argue there is no evidence to support a preference between the later two states (see ref.b pages 102-105). In addition, there is a defaced plate known as the "priapic" plate, which shows the gentleman with an erection, but no bound copy of any edition, including the prospectuses has ever been found with this plate. The latter plate was issued in a single sheet 6 9/16" x 8 1/4". Limited to 100 copies (ref.d).

Point 6: Earliest state: Portrait Frontispiece; cloth under bust visible; "Heliotype" imprint. Later state: cloth not visible; "Heliotype" imprint. Final state: cloth not visible; "Photo-gravure" imprint. Note: "Heliotype..." usually about 1/4" below line, while Kevin MacDonnell (11/91) cataloged a copy with the words 3/4" below.

Point 7: Possible point noted by McBride in ref.b as attributed to John S. Van Kohn (Seven Gables Bookshop). Earliest state: p. 143: "l" missing in "Col." that is part of the illustration at top line of text; "b" in "body", line 7, broken. Later state: p.143: period and bottom of "l" in "Col." missing; "body" perfect. Final state: p.143: "l" in "Col." replaced; "body" perfect.

Note: a signature mark "11" on p.161 of the Montreal edition has never been seen in a U.S. edition of 1885; and leaf 23(8), the final leaf, is blank leaf in leather bound copies and later issues. In all cloth bound early issues, the leaf has been excised or pasted under the terminal endpaper.

So, there we have it. General agreement on Points 1, 2, 3, and 6; uncertainty on Points 4 and 5 and Point 7 was noted only as a possible point, having been seen in a leather bound copy and corrected in obvious later states. It would appear that if you have a cloth bound copy with first state points of 1, 2, 3 and 6 and 4 and 5 in one of the first two states, no one can say it is not the earliest state. Given this, the following is a wild guess as to value of nice "first" state copies:

Leather bound with earliest state of Point 5 $12,500.

Leather bound with later state of point 5 $5,000.

Blue cloth $5,000.

Green cloth $4,000.

(you could add for gilt edges)

033f: THE ADVENTURES OF HUCKLEBERRY FINN ... Limited Editions Club NY 1933 [2] 1,500 no. cc. Includes original illustrations by E.W. Kemble. Introduction by Booth Tarkington, in slipcase $100/150

033g: THE ADVENTURES OF HUCKLEBERRY FINN ... Limited Editions Club NY 1942 [2] 1,500 sgd no cc. Illustrated and signed by Thomas Hart Benton, in slipcase $400/500

033h: ADVENTURES OF HUCKLEBERRY FINN Pennyroyal Press West Hatfield 1985 [2] 300 cc. Illustrated and signed by Barry Moser. Issued in slipcase (George Houle Cat. 32) $1,000.

033i: ADVENTURES OF HUCKLEBERRY FINN Detroit 1983 [] 1,015 cc. Facsimile of manuscript. Issued without dustwrapper in slipcase $175.

034a: CHOICE BITS FROM MARK TWAIN Diprose & Bateman London (no-date) [0] Published 1885. Issued in pictorial boards $350.

035a: THE MARK TWAIN BIRTHDAY BOOK Ward, Lock & Co. London (no-date) [0] Circa 1885 $350.

036a: ENGLISH AS SHE IS TAUGHT T. Fisher Unwin London 1887 [0] Book by Caroline Lerow with 30 page commentary by Twain (also see 1900 entry) $350.

037a: COPY OF A LETTER WRITTEN IN ANSWER TO INQUIRIES MADE BY A PERSONAL FRIEND ... (no-publisher, place or date) [0] Single leaf printed in Hartford, CT., 1887? Issued as testimonial for the Loisette School of Memory $150.

038a: MARK TWAIN'S LIBRARY OF HUMOR Chas. L. Webster & Co. NY 1888 [0] First issue with index of titles in order of appearance. Anonymously edited by William Dean Howells $250.

038b: MARK TWAIN'S LIBRARY OF HUMOR Chas. L. Webster & Co. NY 1888 [0] Second issue with index of titles in alphabetical order $200.

038c: MARK TWAIN'S LIBRARY OF HUMOR Chatto & Windus L 1888 [0] (Maurice F. Neville Cat. 15) $250.

038d: MARK TWAIN'S LIBRARY OF HUMOR Dawson Brothers Montreal 1888 [] (ref.c) $200.

039a: A YANKEE AT THE COURT OF KING ARTHUR Chatto & Windus L 1889 [0] Advertisements dated June 1889 earliest noted. We have put this edition first based on Twain's intentions. In a letter (sold at Park-Bernet in 1956), Twain had instructed Fred Hall to publish the books as follows: Great Britain Dec 6th, Canada Dec 8th and U.S. Dec 10th; and the actual publication dates appear to follow this per BAL 3429, although the books may have actually been available at different times (the Library of Congress deposit copy was received Dec 5th) $450.

039b: A CONNECTICUT YANKEE IN KING ARTHUR'S COURT G.M. Rose Toronto (1889) [0] Printed from Hartford edition (below) with "s" like ornament between "The" and "King" on p.59 (not noted in later state) $400.

039c: A CONNECTICUT YANKEE IN KING ARTHUR'S COURT Chas. L. Webster & Co. NY 1889 [] Publisher's prospectus with half title, frontis illustration, title page, contents page, page stating illustrations not complete, preface, 63 pages of text, publisher's statement regarding illustrations, 15 pages of illustrations, publisher's sample ads and 32 page subscription form section. Two samples of leather on inside front cover, while inside rear cover contains front cover sample (Eldon Steeves #1) $3,000.

039d: A CONNECTICUT YANKEE IN KING ARTHUR'S COURT Chas. L. Webster & Co. NY 1889 [0] Earliest state: p.(59) has a small "s" like ornament between "The" and "King" in the caption $750.

039e: A CONNECTICUT YANKEE IN KING ARTHUR'S COURT Chas. L. Webster & Co. NY 1889 [0] Later state/printing: p.(59) no "s" like ornament in caption "The King" $400.

039f: A CONNECTICUT YANKEE IN KING ARTHUR'S COURT Limited Editions Club NY 1949 [2] 1,500 no. cc. Signed by illustrator Honore Guilbeau. Issued in slipcase $60/100

040a: FACTS FOR MARK TWAIN'S MEMORY BUILDER Chas. L. Webster & Co. NY 1891 [0] Wraps. Designed to accompany "Mark Twain's Memory Builder," a board game (includes board and small box with *Facts...* booklet and pins) $500.

041a: THE AMERICAN CLAIMANT Chas. L. Webster & Co. NY 1892 [0] Gray-green or olive-green cloth (auction records in 1985 show a 1889 edition, but assume a typo) $175.

041b: THE AMERICAN CLAIMANT Chatto & Windus L 1892 [0] Advertisements dated "October, 1892" which is about when it was published, although ref.d notes copies with ads dated "May 1892" are known $150.

042a: MERRY TALES Chas. L. Webster & Co. NY 1892 [0] Presumed earliest state: white endpapers printed in faded olive-green with an all-over pattern of berries and thorns; also printed in faded olive-green with an over-all pattern of parsley-like leaves; no inserted portrait frontispiece $300.

042b: MERRY TALES Chas. L. Webster & Co. NY 1892 [0] Presumed later state: same as above but contains inserted portrait frontispiece of Twain $200.

042c: MERRY TALES Chas. L. Webster & Co. NY 1892 [0] Presumed final state: has inserted frontispiece; plain white endpapers $100.

043a: THE £1,000,000 BANK-NOTE + Chas. L. Webster & Co. NY 1893 [0] Publisher's prospectus with frontis and title page only, text pages blank but overall thicker than published book (ref.d) $1,500.

043b: THE £1,000,000 BANK-NOTE + Chas. L. Webster & Co. NY 1893 [0] $275.

043c: THE £1,000,000 BANK-NOTE + Chatto & Windus L 1893 [0] Advertisements dated April 1893. Also noted with ads dated March 1893 (Hermitage Bookshop 5/91) $200.

043d: THE £1,000,000 BANK-NOTE.. Harper & Bros. NY/L (1917) [0] First separate edition with publisher's code "E-R" on copyright page, indicating May 1917 $125.

044a: PUDD'NHEAD WILSON'S CALENDAR FOR 1894 (Century Co., Dawson's Landing, MO. i.e N.Y. 1893) [0] Wraps. Issued in deep buff or orange wrappers and there are 3 known variants. No priority for any variant or wrapper color. Miniature (3" x 2 1/2"), 16 pages. Issued to promote the Century Magazine serialization $2,000.

045a: TOM SAWYER ABROAD... Chas. L. Webster & Co. NY 1894 [0] $450.

045b: TOM SAWYER ABROAD... Chatto & Windus L 1894 [0] Advertisments dated February 1894. Red cloth (reissued in blue cloth) $350.

046a: PUDD'NHEAD WILSON A TALE Chatto & Windus L 1894 [0] Advertisements dated September 1894. Red cloth, although also noted in dark blue cloth with same dated ads (Sumner & Stillman 4/92) $450.

046b: THE TRAGEDY OF PUDD'NHEAD WILSON AND THE COMEDY OF THOSE EXTRAORDINARY TWINS... American Publishing Co. Hartford 1894 [0] Earliest state: sheets bulk about 1 1/8"; the title leaf is clearly joined to the next leaf. Includes *Those Extraordinary Twins*, not in English edition. Leather bound copies would be worth more than cloth price shown $450.

046c: THE TRAGEDY OF PUDD'NHEAD WILSON AND THE COMEDY OF THOSE EXTRAORDINARY TWINS... American Publishing Co. Hartford 1894 [0] Second state: sheets bulk 1 1/4"; title leaf not conjugate with next leaf and is an insert printed on paper which varies slightly from what is used in body of book $175.

046d: PUDD'NHEAD WILSON Limited Editions Club Avon, CT 1974 [2] 2,000 sgd cc. Illustrated and sigend by John Groth. Also includes *Pudd'nhead Wilson's Calendar*, small, in wraps and also illustrated by Groth. Issued in slipcase $60/100

047a: AMERICAN DROLLERIES Grand Colosseum Warehouse Co. Glasgow (no-date, circa 1895?) [] Reprints from plates of *Jumping Frog* and *Screamers* $250.

047b: AMERICAN DROLLERIES Ward, Lock & Bowden, L/NY/Melbourne (no-date) [0] Circa 1895 (ref.c). Not noted in BAL, so priority uncertain $250.

048a: PERSONAL RECOLLECTIONS OF JOAN OF ARC... Harper & Bros. NY 1896 [0] Earliest state: p.(463): "Some books for the Library The Abbey Shakespeare..." The fourth entry is for *Memoirs of Barras* described as in 4 volumes with vols. I-II offered @ $3.75 each;

vols. III-IV as "just ready". Twain's name on binding but not title page $400.

048b: PERSONAL RECOLLECTIONS OF JOAN OF ARC... Harper & Bros. NY 1896 [0] Later state: p.(463): "Some books for the Library George Washington..." On p.(464) the *Memoirs of Barras* is described as in 4 vols. @ $15 $200.

048c: PERSONAL RECOLLECTIONS OF JOAN OF ARC... Chatto & Windus L 1896 [0] Advertisments dated March 1896 $250.

048d: SAINT JOAN OF ARC... Harper & Bros. NY/L (1919) [1] "Published, May 1919." "D-T" First state: marginal decoration on p.18 in correct position; endpapers printed in green. Illustrated by Howard Pyle $75.

048e: SAINT JOAN OF ARC... Harper & Bros. NY/L (1919 [1] "Published, May 1919." "D-T" Second state: marginal decoration on p.18 is inverted; endpapers unprinted $50.

049a: TOM SAWYER ABROAD TOM SAWYER DETECTIVE + Harper & Bros. NY 1896 [0] 1,000 cc (Kevin MacDonnell 11/91) $1,000.

050a: TOM SAWYER, DETECTIVE AS TOLD BY HUCK FINN + Chatto & Windus L 1897 [0] Publisher's catalog dated September 1896 inserted at back. Contains first collected appearances of 6 stories (Fine Books 1/92). Also noted with ads dated November 1896 (Country Lane #35) $300.

051a: HOW TO TELL A STORY + Harper & Bros. NY 1897 [0] 2,000 cc (MacDonnell Rare Books 12/88) (Note: Vol. 22 of *Writings*... with this title, contains first appearances not in this edition. See BAL 3458. Also see 1921 entry) $250.

052a: IN MEMORIAM / OLIVIA SUSAN CLEMENS ... (no-publisher Lake Lucerne 1897) [0] Single sheet folded to four pages. At end: "Lake Lucerne: August 18, 1897" $300.

053a: FOLLOWING THE EQUATOR... American Publishing Co. Hartford 1897 [] Publisher's propectus. Reproduction of spine on back cover, 55 leaves of sample text and illustrations, 16 leaves of blank subscription sheets (Heritage Cat. #162 2/88). (There was also a trial binding in two volumes, perhaps unique, at auction in June 1992. It sold for $8,800.) $2,000.

053b: FOLLOWING THE EQUATOR... American Publishing Co. Hartford 1897 [0] Title-page also occurs with the following imprint: "Hartford New York/American Publishing Co. Doubleday & McClure Co./MDCCCXCVII" - no priority over single imprint. Leather bound copies would be worth more than the cloth prices shown $300.

053c: MORE TRAMPS ABROAD ... Chatto & Windus L 1897 [0] First English edition of *Following The Equator*. Advertisements dated September 1897 $200.

053d: FOLLOWING THE EQUATOR... American Publishing Co. Hartford 1898 [2] 250 sgd no. cc. Also issued with the joint imprint of the American Publishing Co. and Doubldeday and McClure. Ref.c suggests that no more than 60 copies of this were bound $5,000.

054a: THE WRITINGS OF MARK TWAIN AUTOGRAPH EDITION American Publishing Co. Hartford (1899-1907) [2] 512 no. sets in 25 volumes. Signed certificate of issue in vol. I. Ref.c indicates 1,000 copies $3,000.

054b: THE WRITINGS OF MARK TWAIN Chatto & Windus L 1899 [2] 620 sgd no. cc. 25 volumes. Vols. 24 and 25 unnumbered as they were published separately by Harpers (Maurice Neville Cat. 12) $4,500.

054c: THE WRITINGS OF MARK TWAIN Riverside Edition American Publ Co. Hartford 1901 [2] 625 sets. 25 volumes. White buckram in blue cloth dustwrapper $2,000/2,500

054d: (THE WRITINGS OF MARK TWAIN. Hillcrest Edition) Harper & Bros NY/L 1906-1907 [0] 25 volumes. Buckram with leather spine labels $1,500.

054e: THE WRITINGS OF MARK TWAIN Definitive Edition Gabriel Wells NY 1922-1925 [2] 1,024 sgd sets. 37 volumes. Author's signature in volume 1. Signed leaves prepared in 1906 $3,500.

054f: THE WRITINGS OF MARK TWAIN Harper NY 1929 [2] 90 sets, Stormfield Edition. 37 volumes with leaf of manuscript (half mororrco with gilt by Strikeman sold at auction in 1986) $8,500.

054g: THE WRITINGS OF MARK TWAIN Harper NY 1929 [] 37 volumes. Blue cloth in dustwrapper $1,500/2,000

NOTE: there have been numerous sets of Twain's Writings published over the years. The above listings are but a sample of some of the values. Many are not noted in BAL, Johnson, or McBride. We found some listed only in the auction records of *American Book Prices Current*.

055a: THE PAINS OF LOWLY LIFE (Anti-Vivisection Society L 1900) [1] Wraps. "Published for the first time, March 1900" Publisher's address corrected in some copies with pasted-in slip $500.

056a: THE MAN THAT CORRUPTED HADLEYBURG + Harper & Bros. NY/L 1900 [0] Earliest state: sheets bulk about 1 1/16"; the plate opposite p.2 has, in addition to the caption, the line: "[Page 2" $400.

056b: THE MAN THAT CORRUPTED HADLEYBURG + Harper & Bros. NY/L 1900 [0] Later state: sheets bulk about 1 3/16"; plate opposite p.2 has caption only $200.

056c: THE MAN THAT CORRUPTED HADLEYBURG + Harper & Bros. NY/L 1900 [0] Final state: sheets bulk about 1 1/4"; the plate opposite p.2 has caption only $125.

056d: THE MAN THAT CORRUPTED HADLEYBURG + Chatto & Windus L 1900 [0] Advertisements dated June, 1900. Two stories not in U.S. edition $250.

057a: A SALUTATION SPEECH FROM THE NINETEENTH CENTURY TO TWENTIETH ... (no-publisher or place) 1900 [0] Card prepared for the Red Cross Society (reprinted by Roxburghe Club San Francisco 1929) $150.

058a: ENGLISH AS SHE IS TAUGHT Mutual Book Co. B (1900) [0] Wraps or cloth. Earliest state: p.16:5 "The fivc" for "The five". First separate edition, originally published as a commentary to Caroline LeRow's book, see 1887 entry $350.

058b: ENGLISH AS SHE IS TAUGHT Mutual Book Co. B (1900) [0] Later state: p.16:5 "The five" $150.

058c: ENGLISH AS SHE IS TAUGHT Century NY 1901 [] Revised version $125.

Note: reissued in wraps imprinted A. M. Davis Co., Boston 1887 (circa 1917 to 1920?)

059a: EDMUND BURKE ON CROKER & TAMMANY (Economist Press NY 1901) [0] Wraps $500.

060a: TO THE PERSON SITTING IN DARKNESS... (Anti-Imperialist League NY 1901) [0] Wraps $600.

060b: TO THE PERSON SITTING IN DARKNESS... (Privately printed no-place) 1926 [2] 250 cc. Wraps $75.

061a: A DOUBLE BARRELLED DETECTIVE STORY Harper & Bros. NY/L 1902 [0] Red or maroon cloth, issued in dustwrapper. Variant binding: red cloth, stamped in gold on front, publisher's name not on spine. "Tabard Inn Library" book plate on front pastedown $250.

061b: A DOUBLE BARRELLED DETECTIVE STORY Chatto & Windus L 1902 [0] Advertisements dated "March, 1902" (ref.d) $175.

062a: DIRECTIONS... TELEPHONE ADDRESS: 150 KINGS BRIDGE (no-publisher) NY (no-date) [0] Card, 2 11/16" x 3 3/4". Prepared by Twain for the convenience of his guests, giving directions to his home in Riverdale, NY. 1902? $100.

063a: EXTRACT FROM LETTER OF "MARK TWAIN" TO FREDERICK W. PEABODY (no-publisher, place or date) [0] Single leaf 5 7/8" x 4 5/8". Printed in Boston, 1902? Announces Peabody's forthcoming book on Christian Science. (Reprinted and inserted in copies of later editions of Peabody's book but this issue didn't carry notice on forth-coming book) $200.

064a: "A DOGS TALE" REPRINTED BY PERMISSION FROM HARPER'S MAGAZINE... (National Anti-Vivisection Society L 1903) i.e. 1904 [0] Wraps. First separate edition $350.

064b: A DOG'S TALE Harper & Bros. NY/L 1904 [0] "Published September, 1904" $150.

065a: EXTRACTS FROM ADAM'S DIARY... Harper & Bros. NY/L 1904 [0] $150.

065b: EXTRACTS FROM ADAM'S DIARY... L/NY 1904 [] (Kevin MacDonnell Rare Books 11/89) $100.

066a: TO WHOM THIS SHALL COME... (No-publisher Florence, Italy) 1904 [0] Printed on folded sheet of mourning stationery. A 9-line acknowledgment of messages of condolence on Mrs. Clemen's death $100.

067a: AN UNEXPECTED ACQUAINTANCE Harper & Bros. NY/L 1904 [0] Wraps. Reissued without date on title page $400.

068a: KING LEOPOLD'S SOLILOQUY... P.R. Warren Co. B 1905 [0] Wraps. First published edition, first issue: (i-ii), (1)-(50); frontispiece and 5 plates inserted; other illustrations in text; 7 3/8" x 4 3/4"; white paperwraps, outside printed in green and yellow, inside blank; footnote on p.8:last line: "Jordan and other prominent citizens in a petition.."; frontispiece caption: set in 2 lines including a reference to p.25; caption on plate opposite p.8 set in 1 line including reference to p.8. The whole set 2 3/16" wide; caption on plate opposite p.28: set in 2 lines including a reference to p.27; the caption under the illustration on p.32 is set in 2 lines. The first word of text immediately below the illustration is the word "out" $600.

068b: KING LEOPOLD'S SOLILOQUY... P.R. Warren Co. B 1905 [0] Wraps. First published edition, second issue: points as above except: white paperwraps. Outside printed in dark green and yellow; inside blank. Also: white paperwraps. Outside printed in black and yellow. Inside blank; footnote on p.8:last line: "Citizens in a petition..." Frontispiece caption: set in 1 line including a reference to p.25; caption on plate opposite p.8: set in 1 line including reference to p.8. The whole set 2 11/16" wide $500.

068c: KING LEOPOLD'S SOLILOQUY... P.R. Warren Co. B 1905 [0] Wraps. First published edition, third issue: points as in 67a except: frontispiece and 5 plates inserted. Other illustrations in text. 7 7/16" x 4 3/4"; footnote on p.8:last line: "Citizens in petitions..." Frontispiece caption: set in one line including a reference to p.25; caption on plate opposite p.8: set in one line including a reference to p.8. The whole set 2 11/16" wide $400.

068d: KING LEOPOLD'S SOLILOQUY... P.R. Warren Co. B 1905 [0] Wraps. First published edition, fourth issue: (1)-(52). Frontispiece and 5 plates inserted. Other illustrations in text. 7 1/4" x 4 5/8"; white paperwraps. Outside printed in black and yellow. Inside blank; footnote on p.10:last line: "Citizens in petitions..." Frontispiece caption: set in one line including a reference to p.27; caption on plate opposite p.10: set in one line including a reference to p.10. The whole set 2 3/4" wide; caption on plate opposite p.28: set in 2 lines including a reference to p.29; the caption under the illustration on p.34 is set in one line. The last word of text immediately under the illustration is the word "pattern" $300.

Note: the second edition so states.

068e: KING LEOPOLD'S SOLILOQUY... T. Fisher Unwin L 1907 [] $400.

069a: EDITORIAL WILD OATS Harper & Bros. NY/L 1905 [1] "Published September, 1905." (Note: dustwrapper with no titles listed on back published later) $125.

070a: MARK TWAIN ON VIVISECTION... New England Anti-Vivisection Society B (no-date) [0] Single leaf of creme-yellow wove paper folded to 4 pages. Circa 1905 $350.

070b: MARK TWAIN ON VIVISECTION... New York Anti-Vivisection Society NY (no-date) [0] Single leaf of white laid paper folded to 4 pages. Also contains G.G. Vest's *Eulogy on the Dog*. Circa 1905 $250.

071a: MARK TWAIN'S LIBRARY OF HUMOR MEN AND THINGS... Harper & Bros. NY/L 1906 [1] "Published February, 1906" $150.

072a: MARK TWAIN'S LIBRARY OF HUMOR WOMEN AND THINGS... Harper & Bros. NY/L 1906 [1] "Published April, 1906" $150.

073a: MARK TWAIN'S LIBRARY OF HUMOR THE PRIMROSE WAY... Harper &

Bros. NY/L 1906 [1] "Published April, 1906" $150.

073b: MARK TWAIN'S LIBRARY OF HUMOR A LITTLE NONSENSE Harper NY 1906 [1] "Published .. July, 1906" $150.

074a: EVE'S DIARY TRANSLATED FROM THE ORIGINAL MS Harper & Bros. L/NY 1906 [1] "Published June, 1906." All copies apparently have the imprint "London and New York" $150.

075a: WHAT IS MAN? De Vinne Pr. NY 1906 [2] 250 cc. Anonymous. First issue: leaf (18)2 is not a cancel. P.131 ends: ..."thinks about/". Slipcase, tissue dustwrapper $650.

075b: WHAT IS MAN? De Vinne Pr. NY 1906 [2] 250 cc. Anonymous. Second issue: leaf (18)2 is a cancel. P.131 ends: "thinks about / it." $500.

075c: WHAT IS MAN? Watts & Co. L 1910 [0] First disclosure of authorship $250.

075d: WHAT IS MAN? + Harper & Bros. NY/L (1917) [0] Red cloth $200.

075e: WHAT IS MAN? + Harper & Bros. NY/L (1917) [0] Limp red leather $200.

075f: WHAT IS MAN? + Chatto & Windus L 1919 [0] $200.

076a: THE $30,000 BEQUEST + Harper & Bros. NY/L 1906 [0] First state: no ads on copyright page $250.

076b: THE $30,000 BEQUEST + Harper & Bros. NY/L 1906 [0] Second state: boxed ads on copyright page $125.

077a: MARK TWAIN ON SIMPLIFIED SPELLING... (The Simplified Spelling Board NY 1906) [0] "The Simplified Spelling Board Circular No. 9, Nov. 10, 1906." Single leaf folded to 4 pages. Presumed first issue: unbroken type p.1:3: "reached except thru you..." $300.

077b: MARK TWAIN ON SIMPLIFIED SPELLING... (The Simplified Spelling Board NY 1906) [0] Presumed second issue: broken type p.1:3: "reached except thru you..." $200.

078a: A BIRTHPLACE WORTH SAVING The Lincoln Farm Association (no-place or date) [0] Single sheet. 16 7/8" x 5 1/2". Printed 1906 $125.

079a: CHRISTIAN SCIENCE WITH NOTES... Harper & Bros. NY/L 1907 [0] Book has appeared in varous states (see ref.b). Advertisements on back ending with *Jumping Frog*. Second dustwrapper adds *Christian Science* to list on back.

Point 1: Earlier state: copyright page boxed ads list 17 titles.

Later state: copyright page boxed ads list 18 titles.

Point 2: Earlier state: p.(iii): type, including heading is 8 lines long.

Later state: p.(iii): type is 6 lines long.

Point 3: Earlier state: frontispiece dated (1906).

Later state: frontispiece dated (1907).

Point 4: Earlier state: p.3:9 "farmhouse."

Later state: p.3:9 "fa mhouse."

Point 5: Earlier state: p.5:14 "w" in "why" standard.

Later state: p.5:14 "w" in "why" heavy.

Earlier state $175.
Later/mixed state $125.

079b: CHRISTIAN SCIENCE WITH NOTES... Harper & Bros. L/NY 1907 [0] Same as 088a, London just list first on title page (Wm. & Victoria Dailey 3/90) $150.

080a: A HORSE'S TAIL Harper & Bros. NY/L 1907 [0] Issued in dustwrapper $100.

081a: MARK TWAIN ON THREE WEEKS (no-publisher, place or date) [0] Wraps. Privately printed for Mrs. Elinor Glyn for private distribution, probably London 1908. Printed in orchid, on pale orchid, vellum-like paper, tied with orchid cord. Mrs. Glyn's report of an interview with Twain (nine pages) and Twain's letter after reading her report (two pages) $400.

082a: TO MY GUESTS GREETING AND SALUTATION AND PROSPERITY!... (No-publisher) Redding, Conn. 1908 [0] Single leaf. 10 1/4" x 8". An appeal for contributions for the Mark Twain Public Library $200.

083a: IS SHAKESPEARE DEAD?... Harper & Bros. NY/L 1909 [1] Earliest state: with frontis portraits of Shakespeare and Bacon. "Published April, 1909," without inserted advertisement leaves either between (1)2 and (1)3 or, between (10)6 and (10)7. Issued in dustwrapper $200.

083b: IS SHAKESPEARE DEAD?... Harper & Bros. NY/L 1909 [1] "Published April, 1909." Later state: inserted between leaves (1)2-3 is a one page advertisement referring to

Greenwood's *The Shakespeare Problem Restated* $125.

083c: IS SHAKESPEARE DEAD?... Harper & Bros. NY/L 1909 [1] "Published April, 1909." Later state (no priority between b&c): inserted between (10)6-7 is 2-page advertisement for Greenwood's *The Shakespeare Problem Restated* and *In re Shakespeare Problem* $125.

084a: EXTRACT FROM CAPTAIN STORMFIELD'S VISIT TO HEAVEN Harper & Bros. NY/L 1909 [0] Printed on different paper with three different widths, no priority $125.

085a: TRAVELS AT HOME... Harper & Bros. NY/L 1910 [] Selected by Percival Chubb $150.

086a: TRAVELS IN HISTORY... Harper & Bros. NY/L 1910 [] $150.

087a: TO THE EDITOR: WE HAVE PREPARED FOR YOUR USE... Harper & Bros. (NY no-date) [0] Circa 1910. Single sheet 20 7/16" x 15 9/16". Text set in 6 columns. Promotional material $200.

088a: MARK TWAIN'S SPEECHES WITH INTRODUCTION BY WILLIAM DEAN Harper & Bros. NY/L 1910 [1] "Published June, 1910" $125.

088b: MARK TWAIN'S SPEECHES WITH INTRODUCTION BY WILLIAM DEAN Harper NY (1923) [1] Also has "D-X." Expanded to include later speeches $75/350

089a: QUEEN VICTORIA'S JUBILEE... (No-publisher, place or date) [2] 195 no. cc. Privately printed for private distribution only. Probably printed in NY, 1910. Printed white boards, cloth shelf back $600.

090a: (MARK TWAIN'S LONDON LECTURE NOTES) [title assigned] (no-publisher or place 1910) [0] 10-12 cc. Single leaf 9"x6" printed with a series of mnemonic caricatures by Clemens used as lecture aid. 10 to 12 copies printed for copyright purposes $NVA

091a: MARK TWAIN'S LETTER TO THE CALIFORNIA PIONEERS Dewitt & Snelling Oakland, CA 1911 [2] Wraps. Presumed first state with copyright notice on p(4) and copies unnumbered. Total edition 750 cc (a&b). We had a copy with copyright on page 4 and numbered "643" $100.

091b: MARK TWAIN'S LETTER TO THE CALIFORNIA PIONEERS Dewitt & Snelling Oakland, CA 1911 [2] 750 cc. Wraps. Presumed second state without copyright notice on p(4) and numbered. Seems to be scarcer, based on the fact that four 11 copies of the "first" have been catalogued in the last 10 years but none of this state $100.

092a: MARK TWAIN AND FAIRHAVEN The Millicent Library Fairhaven, Mass. (1913) [0] Wraps. Tan linen-weave paper wraps $175.

092b: MARK TWAIN AND FAIRHAVEN The Millicent Library Fairhaven, Mass. (1976) Wraps. Revised edition, introduction by Earl Dias $40.

093a: THE SUPPRESSED CHAPTER OF "LIFE ON THE MISSISSIPPI" (no-publisher) NY no date (1913) [2] 250 no cc. Single leaf folded to 4 pages $450.

094a: DEATH-DISK Edgar S. Werner NY (no-date) [0] Wraps. Circa 1913 $150.

095a: THE MYSTEROUS STRANGER... Harper & Bros. NY/L (1916) [1] "Published October, 1916" and "K-Q" on copyright page. Illustrated by N.C. Wyeth $200.

096a: HOW TO REACH THE AGE OF SEVENTY... (Edwin B. Hill Mesa, Ariz. 1916) [2] 350 cc. Wraps. Reprint of part of Twain's speech on his 70th birthday $175.

097a: SAMUEL LANGHORNE CLEMENS (no-publisher, place or date) [0] 5-7 cc. WRaps. Said to be printed at the Davis Press, Worcester, Mass. 1916. 5-7 cc printed on paper watermarked "Clemens" $750.

097b: SAMUEL LANGHORNE CLEMENS (no-publisher, place or date) [0] 30-75 cc. Wraps. Said to be printed at the Davis Press, Worcester, Mass. 1916. 30-75 cc on paper watermarked "Mark Twain" $650.

098a: WHO WAS SARAH FINDLAY? Clement Shorter L 1917 [2] 25 sgd no. cc. Wraps. With a suggested solution by J.M. Barrie. Signed by Shorter $750.

099a: MARK TWAIN'S LETTERS... Harper & Bros. NY/L (1917) [2] 350 sets. Two volumes. Limitation certificate in first volume. Uncut edges; paper labels. (Issued in dustwrappers and slipcase) $250/750

099b: MARK TWAIN'S LETTERS... Harper & Bros. NY/L (1917) [1] "Published November, 1917" and "L-R" on copyright page. Two volumes. Library edition. Red cloth stamped in gold on spine $150.

099c: MARK TWAIN'S LETTERS... Harper & Bros. NY/L (1917) [1] "Published November, 1917" and "L-R" on copyright page. Two volumes. Trade edition. Paper watermarked "Olde Style" $150/450

WHAT IS MAN? see 1906 entry

100a: IN DEFENSE OF HARRIET SHELLEY + Harper & Bros. NY/L (1918) [0] Ref.a does not indicate "First Edition" is stated. Code letters "B-S" on copyright page. Issued in limp leather series $175.

101a: MY WATCH AN INSTRUCTIVE LITTLE TALE Waltham Watch Co. Waltham, Mass. (c.1918) [0] Stapled wraps. First separate edition $250.

102a: AN ADDITION TO THE PRIVATE HISTORY OF THE "JUMPING FROG" STORY... (Privately Printed) NY 1918 [2] 10 cc

$NVA

103a: THE CURIOUS REPUBLIC OF GONDOUR + Boni & Liveright NY 1919 [0] Seems to show up in dustwrapper more than any other Twain title before 1930 $100/400

SAINT JOAN OF ARC... see PERSONAL... 1896 entry

104a: MOMENTS WITH MARK TWAIN Harper & Bros. NY/L 1920 [1] "Published March, 1920" and code letters "B-U" on copyright page. Issued in imitation leather, assume no dustwrapper (ref.d) $200.

104b: MOMENTS WITH MARK TWAIN Harper & Bros. NY/L 1920 [1] "Published March, 1920" and code letters "B-U" on copyright page $100/400

105a: MARK TWAIN ABLE YACHTSMAN... (No-publisher, place or date) [2] 12 no. cc. Bound in creme paper boards with blue line shelfback. Total edition (a&b) 109 copies. Privately printed in New York in 1920. (Merle Johnson's copy to NY Public Library, number 51, we had one numbered 49), therefore (obviously), the boards were not the first 12 copies $1,750.

105b: MARK TWAIN ABLE YACHTSMAN... (No-publisher, place or date) [2] 97 no. cc in wraps $850.

106a: THE SANDWICH ISLANDS (No-publisher) NY 1920 [2] 30 cc. Issued in 3/4 morocco $2,750.

107a: (THE MAMMOTH COD) (No publisher) NY (no-date) circa 1920 [2] 20 no. cc. 4 pages in white rough-tooth paper. 1-4 blank, 2-4 unsigned sketches by Merle Johnson. P.3 Twain's verse $750.

107b: (THE MAMMOTH COD) (No-publisher, place or date) [2] A single leaf (unillustrated) printed, 6" x 3 1/2", white paper. Printed in NY circa 1920? Merle Johnson first saw this in 1930. Ref.d had a copy with a note on back indicating it had been "given me by Bliss, son of American Publishing Co. Hartford, Connecticut 11/17/1915" $650.

107c: (THE MAMMOTH COD) (Hammer & Chisel Club NY 1937) [2] 19 cc. Stated Second Edition. On pale bluff paper $200.

107d: THE MAMMOTH COD AN ADDRESS TO THE STOMACH CLUB Maledicta (Milwaukee) 1976 [2] Unspecified number of copies (ref.b's copy is no. 1,019). Green cloth. Introduction by G. Legman $15/60

108a: (A PROSE POEM FROM HAWAII) (Mercantile Pr. Honolulu no-date) [0] Single sheet folded to 4 pages. Title at head of p.2. Circa 1920 $175.

109a: EIGHT HUMOROUS SKETCHES... Haldeman-Julius Co. Girard, Kansas (1921) [0] Wraps $40.

110a: HOW TO TELL A STORY (P.F. Collier & Son NY 1921) [0] Wraps. First printing: no boxed ad on p.(ii); inner front wrapper printed in deep purple with Twain portrait; inner back wrapper has illustration from *The Celebrated Jumping Frog*. (also see 1897 entry) $250.

110b: HOW TO TELL A STORY (P.F. Collier & Son NY 1921) Circa 1925 [0] Wraps. Second printing: boxed ad on p.(ii); inner back wrapper printed in green with picture of "Author's National Edition" $150.

110c: HOW TO TELL A STORY (P.F. Collier & Son NY 1921) Circa 1925 [0] Wraps. Third printing: on front cover is author's facsimile autograph $100.

111a: "COMING OUT" A LETTER TO A ROSEBUD... (no-publisher NY 1921) [2] 200 cc. Rose paper boards, imitation vellum shelfback $300.

112a: THE MYSTEROUS STRANGER + Harper & Bros. NY/L 1922 [1] "Also has code letters "D-W" on copyright page. First book appearance for 4 of the stories. Three spine stampings. No priority $125/500

113a: MARK TWAIN'S SPEECHES... Harper & Bros. NY/L (1923) [1] "Large Paper" edition, leaf size 8 1/8" x 5 7/16". Profile of Mark Twain blind stamped on front cover $100/400

113b: MARK TWAIN'S SPEECHES... Harper & Bros. NY/L (1923) [1] Trade edition. Red cloth, circular devise in gold on front cover. "D-X" on copyright page $60/300

114a: EUROPE AND ELSEWHERE... Harper & Bros. NY/L (1923) [1] Code letters "E-X" on copyright page $75/350

115a: ...AMUSING ANSWERS TO CORRESPONDENCE + Haldeman-Julius Co. Girard, Kansas (no-date) [0] Wraps. Published 1924. Little Blue Book No. 662 $40.

116a: ...HUMOROUS FABLES... Haldeman-Julius Girard, Kansas (no-date) [0] Wraps. Published 1924. Little Blue Book No. 668 $40.

117a: ...JOURNALISM IN TENNESSEE + Haldeman-Julius Co. Girard, Kansas (no-date) [0] Wraps. Little Blue Book No. 663 $40.

118a: MARK TWAIN'S AUTOBIOGRAPHY... Harper & Bros. NY/L 1924 [1] Two volumes. Advance copies with pages uncut. (See ref.c & d) $1,750.

118b: MARK TWAIN'S AUTOBIOGRAPHY... Harper & Bros. NY/L 1924 [1] Two volumes. Presumed earliest state with 2 pages of ads in back of vol. 2. "H-Y" on copyright page. In dustwrapper and box $100/400

118c: MARK TWAIN'S AUTOBIOGRAPHY... Harper & Bros. NY/L 1924 [1] Two volumes. "H-Y" on copyright page. Presumed later state without ads at back of vol. 2 $50/250

118d: THE AUTOBIOGRAPHY OF MARK TWAIN Harper & Bros. NY (1959) [] Contains some new material per ref.c. $15/75

119a: ...A CURIOUS EXPERIENCE + Haldeman-Julius Girard, Kansas (no-date) [0] Wraps. Published 1925. Little Blue Book No. 932 $40.

120a: S.L.C. TO C.T. (no-publisher, place or date) [2] Wraps. 100 cc. Published 1925 $400.

121a: SKETCHES OF THE SIXTIES... John Howell San Francisco 1926 [2] 250 no. cc. Printed on Strathmore Japan paper. Written with Bret Harte $100/300

121b: SKETCHES OF THE SIXTIES... John Howell San Francisco 1926 [2] 2,000 cc. Tan boards, brown-orange cloth shelfback $35/150

121c: SKETCHES OF THE SIXTIES... John Howell San Francisco 1927 [] Enlarged edition $25/100

122a: MARK TWAIN VS THE STREET RAILWAY CO. Privately Printed (no-place) 1926 [1] Wraps. "Printed November, 1926." Includes facsimiles of Twain's letters, essay by John S. Mayfield $100.

123a: MARK TWAIN IN NEVADA Nevada...Univ. Women (no-place) 1927 [] Wraps. First separate publication of section from *Roughing It*. 26 pages in white wraps and printed dustwrappers $50/150

124a: MORE MAXIMS OF MARK (No-publisher or place) 1927 [2] 50 no. cc. Privately printed in NY. Paper boards, cloth shelf-back (ref.b) $750.

125a: THE QUAKER CITY HOLY LAND... (Privately Printed no-place) 1927 [2] 200 cc. Wraps. Published by M. Harzof, NY, who claims to have destroyed all but about 50 copies. However, as seven or eight copies have been catalogued in the last six years, there would appear to be some doubt that only 50 exist $350.

126a: THE ADVENTURES OF THOMAS JEFFERSON SNODGRASS... Pascal Covici Chicago 1928 [2] 375 no. cc. Brown paper boards, tan buckram spine $100/300

127a: ...A BOY'S ADVENTURE... (No-publisher, place or date) [0] Single leaf folded to four pages. Privately printed by Merle Johnson, NY 1928. Originally in *Bazaar Budget*, 1880 $175.

128a: THE SUPPRESSED CHAPTER OF FOLLOWING THE EQUATOR (No-publisher, place or date) [2] 30 no. cc of which all but 5, including galleys, were destroyed (Nick Karanovich). Not bound, not published. Privately printed for Merle Johnson, NY 1928. (2 copies per ref.a) $3,000.

129a: A LETTER FROM MARK TWAIN TO HIS PUBLISHER, CHATTO & WINDUS... The Penguin Press SF 1929 [2] 50 cc. Wraps $400.

130a: A GREETING FROM THE NINETEENTH TO THE TWENTIETH CENTURY... James Tuft for the Roxburge Club SF 1929 [0] Wraps (ref.d) $125.

131a: INNOCENCE AT HOME (No-publisher, place or date) [0] Single leaf printed in black on pale green block, 9" x 6". Printed 1929 $250.

132a: THREE ACES JIM TODD'S EPISODE (Privately printed Westport, Conn. i.e. N.Y.,

1929 i.e. circa 1930) [2] "50 copies." Wraps. Certificate of issue is false in terms of who, where and when this was published $175.

133a: A CHAMPAGNE COCKTAIL... (Privately printed no-place 1930) [2] "Limited Edition." Wraps. (Comment above also applies to this book) $125.

134a: THE PRIVATE LIFE OF ADAM AND EVE Harper & Bros. NY/L (1931) [1] Code letters "E-F" on copyright page. First one volume edition with frontis of ALS not previously published $40/150

135a: MARK TWAIN'S EARLY WRITINGS IN HANNIBAL MISSOURI PAPERS Willard S. Morse Santa Monica 1931 [0] (ref.b) $40/150

136a: THE STORY OF ARCHIMEDES Single Tax Publ. Co. NY (c1931) [] 12 pages in white printed, stapled wraps. Reprinted from the Sydney (Australia) *Standard* (Waiting For Godot 4/89) $600.

137a: BE GOOD, BE GOOD (Privately printed NY 1931) [0] 10-12 cc. Single sheet folded to 4 pages, printed in blue on vellum. Privately printed by Merle Johnson as a Christmas token $800.

137b: BE GOOD, BE GOOD (Privately printed NY 1931) [0] Single sheet French folded to 4 pages. Printed through-out in green $350.

138a: MARK TWAIN THE LETTER WRITER Meador Publ. Co. B 1932 [0] $25/125

139a: THERE'LL BE A HOT TIME IN THE OLD TOWN TO-NIGHT Jacob Blanck NY 1932 [2] 299 cc. Christmas card greeting. Twain's statement, previously unpublished (Kevin MacDonnell Rare Books 11/89) $75.

140a: CONCERNING THE JEWS Harper & Bros. NY/L 1934 [0] Wraps. Code letters "G-I" on copyright page $150.

141a: THE FAMILY MARK TWAIN Harper & Bros. NY/L (1935) [0] $25/100

142a: THE COMPLETE SHORT STORIES AND HUMOROUS SKETCHES OF MARK TWAIN Centennial Edition 1835-1935 Wise & Co. NY 1935 [] Assume not issued in dustwrapper (Waiting For Godot 6/89) $75.

143a: SLOVENLY PETER... Limited Editions Club NY 1935 [2] 1,500 sgd no. cc. Illustrated and signed by Fritz Kredel. Pictorial cloth with tissue dustwrapper, folding box and slipcase $150/200

143b: SLOVENLY PETER... Harper & Bros. NY/L 1935 [1] Code letters "K-K" on copyright page. Illustrated by Fritz Kredel. (Pepper & Stern cataloged this as preceding the Limited Editions Club edition by 2 1/2 months, while ref.a shows the LEC deposit copy in August and the Harper in November?) $50/200

144a: MARK TWAIN'S WIT AND WISDOM Stokes NY 1935 [] Edited by Cyril Clemens, preface by Stephen Leacock (ref.b) $25/100

145a: MARK TWAIN'S NOTEBOOK... Harper & Bros. NY/L 1935 [1] "I-K" on copyright page. Prepared by Albert Bigelow Paine. Ref.a notes that Harper stopped the press in the middle of the run and changed to "Second Edition" but left the "I-K" on page $35/150

146a: MARK TWAIN'S GOOD-BYE Davis Hannibal (1935) [] Wraps. Sheet music, words by Twain, music by Paul Rottman $75.

147a: AURELIA'S UNFORTNATE YOUNG MAN Eucalyptus Press (no-place) 1936 [] Paper over flexible boards $150.

148a: LETTERS FROM THE SANDWICH ISLANDS... Grabhorn Press SF 1937 [2] 550 cc. Issued in plain green dustwrapper (ref.b) $200/250

148b: LETTERS FROM THE SANDWICH ISLANDS... Stanford Univ. Press Calif. (1938) [0] $25/100

149a: EXTRACTS FROM PUDD'NHEAD WILSON'S CALENDAR Golden Hind Press Madison, NJ 1937 [2] 110 no. cc. Wraps (Antic Hay 11/88) $75.

150a: ...HOW TO CURE A COLD (The Cloister Press) SF 1937 [2] about 200 cc $250.

151a: THE WASHOE GIANT... George Fields SF 1938 [0] $35/150

152a: THE COYOTE The Rounce & Coffin Club (no-place) 1938 [2] 25 cc. Wraps $300.

153a: MARK TWAIN'S LETTER TO WILLIAM BOWEN Book Club of Calif SF 1938 [2] 400 cc. Plain dustwrapper $100/125

153b: MARK TWAIN'S LETTER TO WILLIAM BOWEN Univ. of Texas Austin 1941 [] Wraps $50.

154a: LETTERS FROM HONOLULU... Thomas Nickerson Honolulu 1939 [2] 1,000 cc. In glassine dustwrapper? $150.

155a: MARK TWAIN'S TRAVELS WITH MR. BROWN Knopf NY 1940 [2] 1,795 no. cc. Issued in dustwrapper $40/150

156a: MARK TWAIN IN ERUPTION Harper & Bros. NY/L (1940) [1] 500 cc. On thin paper in flexible binding. Issued simultaneously with 158b, no priority. Issued without dustwrapper (Kevin MacDonnell Rare Books 11/91) $100.

156b: MARK TWAIN IN ERUPTION Harper & Bros. NY/L (1940) [1] 7,000 cc. Issued in dustwrapper. "K-P" on copyright page $50/125

157a: TOM SAWYER A DRAMA (No-publisher Washington, D.C. 1940) [2] 25 cc. Large paper edition. 9 1/4" x 6 1/4". First printing of Twain's synopsis of *The Adventures of Tom Sawyer* $600.

157b: TOM SAWYER A DRAMA (No-publisher Washington, D.C. 1940) [2] 100 cc. Small paper edition. Single sheet French folded to 4 pages. 7 7/8" x 5 3/8" $250.

158a: REPUBLICAN LETTERS... Internat'l Mark Twain Soc. Webster Groves, Mo. 1941 [0] Red cloth. Assume without dustwrapper $125.

159a: AN UNPUBLISHED MARK TWAIN LETTER (American Literature no-place no-date) [0] Single leaf folded to 4 pages. Reprinted from *American Literature*, Vol. 13, No.4, January 1942 $150.

160a: MARK TWAIN'S LETTERS IN THE MUSCATINE JOURNAL... Mark Twain Assoc. of Amer. Chicago 1942 [2] 300 no. cc. Wraps $150.

161a: WASHINGTON IN 1868... International Mark Twain Soc. / T. Werner Laurie Webster Groves/L 1943 [0] Red cloth. Assume without dustwrapper $125.

162a: A MURDER, A MYSTERY, AND A MARRIAGE... (Manuscript House NY) 1945 [2] 16 cc. Wraps $600.

163a: SELECTED SHORT STORIES OF MARK TWAIN Armed Services Editions NY (no-place circa 1945) [] Wraps (James Dourgarian Books 2/89) $75.

164a: MARK TWAIN, BUSINESS MAN... Little, Brown & Co. B 1946 [1] $35/100

165a: THE PORTABLE MARK TWAIN Viking Press NY 1946 [1] Edited by Bernard DeVoto $25/75

166a: THREE SKETCHES BY MARK TWAIN Overbrook Press Stamford, Ct. 1946 [2] 100 cc (Bromer Booksellers 10/92) $60.

167a: ...LETTERS OF QUINTUS CURTIUS SNODGRASS... Univ. Pr. SMU Dallas 1946 [0] $25/75

168a: MARK TWAIN AND HAWAII The Lakeside Pr. Chicago 1947 [2] 1,000 sgd no. cc. Issued in glassine dustwrapper. By Walter Francis Frear and signed by him. Includes much previously unpublished Twain material $150.

169a: MARK TWAIN IN THREE MOODS Friends of the Huntington Library San Marino 1948 [2] 1,200 no. cc $60.

170a: MARK TWAIN AT YOUR FINGERTIPS Beechurst Press NY (1948) [] Edited by Caroline Thomas Harnsberger $25/150

171a: MARK TWAIN Printed for C. Charles Burlingame Hartford 1948 [] Illustrated by Kathryn Howard. Pictorial boards in glassine dustwrapper. Twain aphorisms as a Christmas greeting (ref.d) $35.

172a: MARK TWAIN TO MRS. FAIRBANKS... Huntington Library San Marino 1949 [1] $12/60

173a: THE LOVE LETTERS OF MARK TWAIN... Harper & Bros. NY 1949 [2] 155 sgd no. cc. Twain signature has been in possession of publisher for 50 years. In dustwrapper and box $1,500/2,000

173b: THE LOVE LETTERS OF MARK TWAIN Harper & Bros. NY 1949 [1] $25/100

174a: THE STORY OF A BAD LITTLE BOY THAT BORE A CHARMED LIFE (Allen Press Hillsborough 1949) [] 75 cc (*American Book Prices Current* 1989) $750.

175a: SOME THOUGHTS ON THE SCIENCE OF ONANISM... (No-publisher or place) 1952 [2] 100 cc. Single sheet French folded to 4 pages $300.

175b: SOME THOUGHTS ON THE SCIENCE OF ONANISM... (Privately printed no-place) 1964 [2] 1,000 cc. Wraps (ref.b) $40.

176a: REPORT FROM PARADISE... Harper & Bros. NY 1952 [1] Code letters "F-B" on copyright page $25/100

177a: MARK TWAIN'S FIRST STORY... Prairie Press (Iowa City 1952) [0] Wraps $50.

178a: MARK TWAIN TO UNCLE REMUS... The Library of Emory Univ. Atlanta 1953 [0] Wraps $40.

179a: MARK TWAIN FOR YOUNG PEOPLE Whittier Books NY 1953 [] Compiled by Cyril Clemens, introduction by James Hilton. Assume no dustwrapper (ref.b) $40.

180a: MARK TWAIN'S LETTERS FROM HAWAII Appleton-Century NY 1956 [] (ref.b) $15/75

181a: AN OPEN LETTER TO COMMODORE VANDERBILT (No-publisher B 1956) [2] 123 cc. Wraps. "One of very few with the blank handmade envelope." Inscribed by publisher, Frank C. Wilson (In Our Time 3/92) $150.

182a: MARK TWAIN OF THE ENTERPRISE... Univ. of Calif. Press Berkeley 1957 [] (ref.b) $15/75

183a: MARK TWAIN: SAN FRANCISCO...CORRESPONDENT Book Club of Calif. SF 1957 [2] 400 cc. Cloth backed boards, tissue dustwrapper (ref.b) $350.

184a: THE COMPLETE SHORT STORIES OF MARK TWAIN Hanover House GC 1957 [] (ref.b.) Also Doubleday, Garden City (1957) (ref.d) $12/60

185a: MARK TWAIN'S JEST BOOK Mark Twain Journal Kirkwood, MO 1957 [] (ref.b) Pictorial wraps. Edited by Cyril Clemens, foreword by Carl Sandburg $75.

185b: MARK TWAIN'S JEST BOOK Mark Twain Journal Kirkwood, MO 1963 [] Second edition. Pictorial wraps (ref.b) $35.

185c: MARK TWAIN'S JEST BOOK Mark Twain Journal Kirkwood, MO 1965 [] Third edition with new material. Pictorial wraps (ref.b) $35.

186a: TRAVELLING WITH THE INNOCENTS ABROAD Univ. of Oklahoma Press Norman (1958) [] (ref.b) $12/60

187a: CONCERNING CATS... Book Club of Calif. SF 1959 [2] 450 cc. Unprinted white dustwrapper (ref.b) $275/300

188a: THE ART, HUMOR & HUMANITY OF MARK TWAIN Univ. of Oklahoma Press Norman 1959 [] (ref.b) $12/60

189a: MARK TWAIN-HOWELLS LETTERS... Belknap Press of Harvard Univ. Cambridge, Mass. 1960 [] Two volumes (ref.b) $25/75

190a: OUR MARK TWAIN. SOME WRITINGS ... Image of America NY (1960) Assume no dustwrapper (Waiting For Godot) $35.

190b: SELECTED MARK TWAIN-HOWELLS LETTERS... Belknap Press of Harvard Univ. Cambridge, Mass. 1967 [] First one volume edition (ref.b) $10/50

191a: MARK TWAIN AND THE GOVERNMENT Caxton Printers Caldwell, Idaho 1960 [] Selected and arranged by Svend Petersen $20/60

192a: MY DEAR BROTHER... The Berkeley Albion (Berkeley) 1961 [] Wraps. Letter to his brother Orion in either teal or buff wraps $40.

193a: MARK TWAIN WIT AND WISE-CRACKS Peter Pauper Press Mt.Vernon/NY (1961) [] (ref.b) $6/30

194a: MARK TWAIN'S LETTERS TO MARY Columbia Univ. Press NY 1961 [0] Edited by Lewis Leary (ref.b) $8/40

195a: MARK TWAIN: LIFE AS I FIND IT Hanover House GC (1961) [] (ref.b) $10/40

196a: "AH SIN" A DRAMATIC WORK Book Club of Calif. SF 1961 [2] 450 cc. Issued in unprinted green dustwrapper (ref.b) $250/275

197a: THE COMPLETE HUMOROUS SKETCHES AND TALES OF MARK TWAIN Hanover House GC (1961) [] (ref.b) $7/35

198a: MARK TWAIN ON THE DAMNED HUMAN RACE Hill & Wang NY (1962) [] Cloth in dustwrapper 9The Bookshop 8/92). Ref.b lists only wraps $15/50

198b: MARK TWAIN ON THE DAMNED HUMAN RACE Hill & Wang NY (1962) [] Wraps (ref.b) $25.

199a: MARK TWAIN'S BEST: EIGHT SHORT STORIES... Scholastic Book Services NY (1962) [] Wraps (ref.b) $15.

200a: MARK TWAIN, LETTERS FROM THE EARTH Harper & Row NY (1962) [] Galley proofs. Spiral bound in house logo wraps (William Reese Co. 11/90) $200.

200b: MARK TWAIN, LETTERS FROM THE EARTH Harper & Row NY (1962) [1] (ref.b) $15/75

201a: SELECTED SHORTER WRITINGS... Houghton Mifflin B (1962) [] Wraps (ref.b) $20.

202a: MARK TWAIN'S SAN FRANCISCO McGraw-Hill NY/T/L (1963) [] (ref.b) $10/50

203a: THE COMPLETE ESSAYS OF MARK TWAIN Doubleday & Co. GC 1963 [] (ref.b) $10/50

204a: AS MARK TWAIN SAYS (Printed for friends of May McNeer and Lynd Ward No-place 1963) [0] Wraps. 16 pages stapled $40.

205a: THE FORGOTTEN WRITINGS... Citadel Pr. NY (1963) [] Wraps (ref.b) $25.

205b: THE FORGOTTEN WRITINGS... Philosophical Library NY (1963) [] Blue cloth. Twain's writings for the *Buffalo Press*. Edited by Henry Duskis (The 19th Century Shop 2/90) $15/40

206a: SIMON WHEELER, DETECTIVE NY Public Library NY 1963 [2] 1,500 cc (ref.b, 1,000 ref.d). Green cloth, tissue dustwrapper $75.

207a: THE COMPLETE NOVELS... Doubleday & Co. GC 1964 [] Two volumes (ref.b) $25/75

208a: MARK TWAIN: A CURE FOR THE BLUES Charles Tuttle Co. Rutland, VT (1964) [] (ref.b) $10/50

209a: THE ADVENTURES OF COLONEL SELLERS... Doubleday & Co. GC 1965 [1] $15/75

210a: SUZY AND MARK TWAINS' FAMILY DIALOGUES Harper NY (1965) [] (ref.b) $10/50

211a: MARK TWAIN'S LETTERS FROM HAWAII Appleton-Century NY (1966) [1] (ref.c) $15/75

211b: MARK TWAIN'S LETTERS FROM HAWAII Chatto & Windus L 1967 (Dinkytown 10/91) $12/60

212a: A CURTAIN LECTURE CONCERNING SKATING Donald M. Kunde Denver 1967 [2] 50 sgd no cc. Signed by Kunde. Special presentation copy. Issued without dustwrapper? $100.

212b: A CURTAIN LECTURE CONCERNING SKATING Donald M. Kunde Denver 1967 [2] 265 no. cc. Issued without dustwrapper $60.

212c: A CURTAIN LECTURE CONCERNING SKATING AND MRS. MARK TWAIN'S SHOE Baldwin Denver 1986 [] Second edition with new material. Wraps? (Astoria Books 12/89) $35.

213a: MARK TWAIN'S WHICH WAS THE DREAM? + Univ. of Calif. Press Berkeley, CA 1967 [0] $10/50

214a: MARK TWAIN'S SATIRES & BURLESQUES Univ. of Calif. Press Berkeley/L.A. 1967 [0] $10/50

215a: THE WAR PRAYER St. Crispin/Harper & Row (NY 1968) [0] First separate edition. illustrated by John Groth $12/60

216a: MARK TWAIN'S CORRESPONDENCE WITH HENRY HUTTLESTON ROGERS 1893-1909 Univ. of Calif. Press Berkeley/L.A. 1969 [] $8/40

217a: CLEMENS OF THE CALL: MARK TWAIN IN SAN FRANCISCO Univ. of Calif. Press Berkeley 1969 [] Edited by E.M. Branch (William Reese Co. 9/89) $10/50

218a: MARK TWAIN'S HANNIBAL, HUCK & TOM Univ. of Calif. Press Berkeley/L.A. 1969 [] (ref.b) $8/40

219a: MARK TWAIN'S THE MYSTEROUS STRANGER MANUSCRIPTS Univ. of Calif. Berkeley/L.A. 1969 [] (ref.b) $10/50

220a: MARK TWAIN'S LETTERS TO THE ROGERS FAMILY Reynolds-De Walt (New Bedford, Mass.) 1970 [] Tissue dustwrapper (ref.b) $50.

221a: MAN IS THE ONLY ANIMAL THAT BLUSHES... Random House (NY 1970) [] (ref.b) $10/50

222a: MARK TWAIN ON MAN AND BEAST Lawrence & Co. NY/Westport, Ct. 1972 [] Wraps (ref.b) $20.

223a: THE GREAT LANDSLIDE CASE Univ. of Calif. Press (no-place) 1972 [] Wraps (ref.c) $40.

224a: MARK TWAIN'S FABLES OF MAN Univ. of Calif. Press Berkeley LA 1972 [] $8/40

225a: A MARK TWAIN TURNOVER: ADVICE FOR GOOD LITTLE GIRLS with MARK TWAIN AND THE DEVIL Robt. E. Massmann New Britain, CT 1972 [2] 250 cc. 1 1/2" square miniature book in slipcase $100.

226a: THE MOST PRODIGIOUS ASSET OF A COUNTRY Folger Library Washington, D.C.

1972 [0] Wraps. Reproduces a previously unpublished five page hand corrected section of Twain's *Autobiography*. Issued in folded wraps. A keepsake for an exhibition (Pepper & Stern List V-1987) $50.

227a: EVERYONE'S MARK TWAIN A.S. Barnes/Thomas Yoseloff So. Brunswick, NJ/NY/L (1972) [] Issued without dustwrapper (ref.b) $35.

228a: A PEN WARMED-UP IN HELL Harper & Row NY/Evanston/SF/L (1972) [] (ref.b) $10/50

229a: MARK TWAIN AND THE THREE R'S... Bobbs-Merrill Ind. and NY (1973) [] (ref.b) $10/50

230a: MARK TWAIN TO GENERAL GRANT (Kent State Univ. Ohio 1973) [2] 200 cc. Wraps. Facsimile of a letter. Single page folded to 4 pages (Waiting For Godot 2/91) $75.

231a: MARK TWAIN'S NOTEBOOKS & JOURNALS VOLUME I (1855-1873) Univ. of Calif. Press Berkeley/LA 1975 [] $10/40

232a: MARK TWAIN'S NOTEBOOKS & JOURNALS VOLUME II (1877-1883) Univ. of Calif. Press Berkeley/LA 1975 [] $10/40

233a: MARK TWAIN'S NOTEBOOKS & JOURNALS VOLUME III (1883-1891) Univ. of Calif. Press Berkeley/LA 1979 [] $10/40

234a: MARK TWAIN SPEAKING Univ. of Iowa Press (Iowa City 1976) [] (ref.b) $10/40

235a: THE HIGHER ANIMALS... A MARK TWAIN BESTIARY Thomas Y. Crowell NY (1976) [] (ref.b) $8/40

236a: THE UNABRIDGED MARK TWAIN Running Press Phila. (1976) [] Opening remarks by Kurt Vonnegut, Jr. (ref.b) $10/50

236b: THE UNABRIDGED MARK TWAIN Running Press Phila. (1979) [] Volume II $8/40

237a: THE COMIC MARK TWAIN READER Doubleday & Co. GC 1977 [] (ref.b) $8/40

238a: MARK TWAIN SPEAKS FOR HIMSELF Perdue Univ. Press West Lafayette 1978 [] (ref.b) $8/40

239a: EARLY TALES AND SKETCHES VOLUME I (1851-1864) Univ. of Calif. Press Berkeley/LA/L 1979 [] (see Volume II below) $8/40

240a: JIM WOLF AND THE CATS Hillside Press Buffalo 1979 [2] 225 cc. Miniature book in slipcase (ref.b), but we've had three copies and none had a slipcase $40/60

241a: THE LATE BENJAMIN FRANKLIN (Privately printed SF 1980) [2] 125 cc. Wraps. Printed by Lawton Kennedy (Geo. Houle 1985) $75.

242a: MARK TWAIN: SOCIAL CRITIC FOR THE 80's AT Press SF 1980 [] $8/40

243a: THE DEVIL'S RACE TRACK : MARK TWAIN'S GREAT DARK WRITING Univ. of Calif. Berkeley (1980) [] $8/40

243b: THE DEVIL'S RACE TRACK : MARK TWAIN'S GREAT DARK WRITING Univ. of Calif. Berkeley (1980) [] Wraps $15.

244a: A MARK TWAIN SAMPLER (Lime Rock Press Salisbury, CT 1980) [2] 1,001 cc. Wraps. Illustrated and signed by Catryna Ten Eyck. A miniture book (3x2 1/2") $30.

245a: ADAM'S DIARY (Lime Rock Press Salisbury, Ct. 1980) [2] 25 cc. Published @$195. $200.

246a: EARLY TALES AND SKETCHES VOLUME II (1864-1865) Univ. of Calif. Press Berkeley/LA/L 1981 [] $8/40

247a: THE NEW WAR-SCARE Neville Publishing SB 1981 [2] 15 lettered cc with original clipped signature, in full leather $1,250.

277b: THE NEW WAR-SCARE Neville Publ. SB 1981 [2] 100 no. cc $100.

248a: MARK TWAIN ON THE DAMED HUMAN RACE Hill/Wang NY (1981) [] Wraps $15.

249a: WAPPING ALICE Bancroft Library Berkeley 1981 [] Wraps $40.

250a: A LETTER FROM MARK TWAIN CONCERNING THE PAIGE COMPOSITOR Vance Gerry Glendale 1982 [2] 200 cc. Wraps (Pepper & Stern Cat 22) $40.

251a: THE SELECTED LETTERS OF MARK TWAIN Harper NY (1982) [3] Also states "First Edition." Edited and introduction by Charles Neider. Maroon cloth $7/35

252a: MARK TWAIN'S RUBAIYAT Jenkins/Karpeles Austin/SB (1982) [2] 20 cc. Issued in green quarter morocco (Kevin MacDonnell Rare Books 1987) $125.

252b: MARK TWAIN'S RUBAIYAT Jenkins/Karpeles Austin/SB (1983) [2] 50 editorial out-of-series cc $75.

252c: MARK TWAIN'S RUBAIYAT Jenkins/Karpeles Austin/SB (1983) [2] 600 cc of which about 50 lost in fire $75.

253a: SELECTED WRITINGS OF AN AMERICAN SKEPTIC Prometheus Bks NY (1983) [] $8/40

254a: MARK TWAIN'S WEST Lakeside Press Chicago 1983 [] Brown cloth. Selection of autobiographical writings. Issued without dustwrapper in Lakeside's Christmas series (The 19th Century Shop 2/90) $35.

255a: SAMUEL LANGHORNE CLEMENTS, PRINTER... (Privately Printed Lafayette, Calif. 1984) [] Wraps in envelope $25.

256a: MARK TWAIN COMPLIMENTS THE PRESIDENT'S WIFE Anne & David Bromer (B) 1984 [2] 50 no. cc. Miniature book (Bert Babcock Cat. 47) $125.

256b: MARK TWAIN COMPLIMENTS THE PRESIDENT'S WIFE Anne & David Bromer (B) 1984 [2] 200 no. cc. Bound in cloth. Miniature book $45.

257a: PLYMOUTH ROCK AND THE PILGRIMS AND OTHER SALUTARY PLATFORM OPINIONS Harper NY (1984) [3] Also states "First Edition." Selected and edited by Charles Neider $6/30

258a: THE GRANGERFORD - SHEPHERDSON FEUD Friends of the Bancroft Library 1985 [] Wraps. Issued as Keepsake No. 33. Not For Sale $40.

259a: CONCERNING THE JEWS Ronning Press Philadelphia (1985) [] Pictorial wraps (ref.d) $15.

260a: MARK TWAIN AT HIS BEST ... Doubleday GC 1986 [] Selected, edited and introduction by Charles Neider (ref.d) $6/30

261a: TWO STORIES Hillside Press Buffalo 1986 [2] 300 no. cc. First separate printing. Miniature book (Waiting For Godot 6/89) $60.

262a: THE OUTRAGEOUS MARK TWAIN Doubleday GC 1987 [] Selected, edited and introduction by Charles Neider (ref.d) $6/30

263a: THE WIT AND WISDOM OF MARK TWAIN Harper NY (1987) [] Edited by Alex Ayres (ref.d) $5/25

264a: MARK TWAIN'S LETTERS, Volume I: 1853-1866 Univ. of Calif. Press 1988 [] in-print @ $35.

265a: MARK TWAIN'S NICODEMUS DODGE Ash Ranch Press San Diego 1989 [2] 26 ltr cc signed by Don Hildreth, the illustrator. Deluxe editions with blue bonded leather spine in slipcase. Story from *A Tramp Abroad* (Wilder Books 11/91) $250.

266a: COLLECTED TALES, SKETCHES, SPEECHES & ESSAYS Library of America NY 1992 [] Two volumes $15/30

267a: MARK TWAIN'S WEAPONS OF SATIRE Anti-Imperialist Writings On The Philippine-American War Syracuse Univ. Press Syracuse 1992 [] (Published July 1992 @ $32.50)

Jon Updike

JOHN UPDIKE

Updike was born in 1932 in Shillington, Pennsylvania. He graduated from Harvard in 1954 and was a staff reporter on *The New Yorker* from 1955 to 1957. He won the National Book Award in 1964 and Pulitzer Prizes in 1982 and 1991.

Unless noted all entries were based on reference "a" up to 1980 and reference "b" until early 1986 which only left 24 or 25 further entries to bring it up to 1992.

REFERENCES:

(a) Roberts, Ray A., JOHN UPDIKE A Bibliographic Checklist in *American Book Collector*, January/February 1980.

(b) FIRST PRINTINGS OF AMERICAN AUTHORS, Volume 5, Gale Research, Detroit (1987).

(c) Inventory or dealer catalogs.

001a: THE CARPENTERED HEN + Harper NY (1958) [1] 2,000 cc (Fine Books Co. #31). First issue dustwrapper mentions "2 children"

$100/600

001b: THE CARPENTERED HEN + Harper NY (1958) [1] 2,000 cc. Second issue with "4 children" $100/350

001c: HOPING FOR A HOOPOE Gollancz L 1959 [0] New title and additional "Author's Note"

$15/75

001d: HOPING FOR A HOOPOE Knopf NY 1982 [] Uncorrected proof in green wraps (Waiting For Godot 2/95) $100.

001e: THE CARPENTERED HEN + Knopf NY 1982 [1] "First Knopf edition." Revised and new foreword (ref.b) $7/35

002a: THE POORHOUSE FAIR Knopf NY 1959 [1] 5,000 cc. (Note: the second printing dw has a biographical note as second paragraph on back flap which is not on first printing dustwrapper) $75/350

002b: THE POORHOUSE FAIR Gollancz L 1959 [0] $35/175

002c: THE POORHOUSE FAIR and RABBIT, RUN Modern Library NY (1965) [1] New foreword dated October 1964 $10/50

002d: THE POORHOUSE FAIR Knopf NY 1977 [0] "New Edition published Feb 1977." Contains a 14 page "Introduction to the 1977 Edition" $8/40

003a: THE SAME DOOR Knopf NY 1959 [1] First dustwrapper has "Also by John Updike *The Poorhouse Fair* (later has "The novels and Stories of John Updike" listing through *The Centaur*) $50/250

003b: THE SAME DOOR Deutsch (L 1962) [1] $30/150

004a: RABBIT, RUN Knopf NY 1960 [1] 10,000 cc. Top edge stained. Also noted without top edge stained, assume remainder? $100/450

004b: RABBIT, RUN Deutsch (L 1961) [1] $30/150

004c: RABBIT, RUN Penguin (Harmondsworth 1964) [0] "This revised edition pub...1964." Wraps $35.

004d: See 002c

004e: RABBIT, RUN Franklin Library Franklin Center 1977 [2] 12,619 copies. Limited signed edition in full leather with a "Special Message..." $100.

005a: THE FIRST AND SOUTH CONGREGATIONAL CHURCH OF IPSWICH, MASSACHUSETTS (Ipswich 1961) [0] Folded leaf (ref.b) $450.

006a: PIGEON FEATHERS + Knopf NY 1962 [1] $30/150

006b: PIGEON FEATHERS + Deutsch (L 1962) [1] $20/100

007a: THE MAGIC FLUTE Knopf NY (1962) [0] Illustrations by Warren Chappell. Mustard cloth in dustwrapper $75/300

007b: THE MAGIC FLUTE Knopf NY (1962) [] Pictorial cloth issued without dustwrapper $150.

007c: THE MAGIC FLUTE Deutsch & Ward (L 1964) [1] $30/150

008a: THE CENTAUR Knopf NY 1963 [] Uncorrected galley proofs in spiral bound plain wraps (William Reese Co. 5/89) $2,000.

008b: THE CENTAUR Knopf NY 1963 [1] National Book Award for 1964 $30/150

008c: THE CENTAUR Deutsch (L 1963) [1] $15/75

009a: TELEPHONE POLES + Knopf NY 1963 [] Uncorrected galley proofs in spiral bound plain wraps with typed label (William Reese 5/89) $1,250.

009b: TELEPHONE POLES + Knopf NY 1963 [1] $15/75

009c: TELEPHONE POLES + Deutsch (L 1964) [1] $15/75

010a: OLINGER STORIES Vintage Books NY (1964) [1] Wraps $50.

011a: THE RING Knopf NY (1964) [0] $50/150

011b: THE RING Knopf NY (1964) [0] Pictorial cloth without dustwrapper $100.

011c: THE RING Knopf NY (1964) [0] "Gibralter Library binding," issued without dustwrapper, is different from 011b (Waiting For Godot 4/90) $60.

012a: ASSORTED PROSE Knopf NY 1965 [] Uncorrected galley proofs in spiral bound printed wraps (William Reese Co. 5/89) $1,250.

012b: ASSORTED PROSE Knopf NY 1965 [1] With tipped-in slip signed by Updike $175/250

012c: ASSORTED PROSE Knopf NY 1965 [1] 10,000 cc (both a & b) $25/100

012d: ASSORTED PROSE Deutsch (L 1965) [1] First issue dustwrapper priced 25 shillings (Alphabet Books 11/91) $15/75

013a: OF THE FARM Knopf NY 1965 [] Uncorrected galley proofs in spiral bound printed wraps which was reportedly extensively revised for published version (William Reese Co. 5/89) $1,500.

013b: OF THE FARM Knopf NY 1965 [1] 15,000 cc $20/100

013c: OF THE FARM Deutsch (L 1966) [1] $15/75

014a: A CHILD'S CALENDAR Knopf NY (1965) [0] $50/175

014b: A CHILD'S CALENDAR Knopf NY (1965) [0] "Gibralter Library Binding." Issued without dustwrapper in two variants but not clear what the difference was (Waiting For Godot 4/90) $100.

015a: DOG'S DEATH Adams House (Cambridge) 1965 [2] 100 sgd no. cc. Broadside $1,250.

016a: VERSE ... Crest Books Greenwich (1965) [1] Wraps $40.

017a: THE MUSIC SCHOOL Knopf NY 1966 [] Uncorrected galley proof in spiral bound printed wraps (William Reese Co. 5/89) $1,250.

017b: THE MUSIC SCHOOL Knopf NY 1966 [1] 10,000 cc (a, b & c). P.46:15 starts "The state..." $200/250

017c: THE MUSIC SCHOOL Knopf NY 1966 [1] P.46:15 starts "The King..." on tipped-in leaf $75/125

017d: THE MUSIC SCHOOL Knopf NY 1966 [1] P.46:15 starts "The King..." on integral leaf $15/75

017e: THE MUSIC SCHOOL Deutsch (L 1967) [1] $15/75

018a: COUPLES Knopf NY 1968 [1] 25,000 cc $15/75

018b: COUPLES Deutsch (L 1968) [1] $12/60

019a: BATH AFTER SAILING Country Squire's Books Stevenson, CT (1968) [2] 125 sgd no. cc. Issued in stiff wraps $850.

020a: THE ANGELS King & Queen Press Pensacola 1968 [2] 150 cc. Sewn in wraps. Issued in mailing envelope $750.

021a: THREE TEXTS FOR EARLY IPSWICH 17th Century... Ipswich 1968 [2] 50 sgd no. cc $450.

021b: THREE TEXTS FOR EARLY IPSWICH 17th Century... Ipswich 1968 [2] 950 cc $150.

021c: THREE TEXTS FOR EARLY IPSWICH 17th Century... Ipswich 1968 [2] 26 sgd ltr cc. Issued in cloth with glassine dustwrapper. (Bound and distributed in 1978.) Also four "Author's Presentation copies" $1,000.

022a: ON MEETING AUTHORS Wickford Press Newburyport 1968 [2] 250 no. cc. Wraps $750.

023a: DECEMBER (Edward Naumberg, Jr. NY 1968) [0] 100 cc. Uncolored Christmas card in plain envelope $600.

023b: DECEMBER (Edward Naumberg, Jr. NY 1968) [0] Colored red or green Christmas card in plain envelope $400.

024a: MIDPOINT Knopf NY 1969 [2] 350 sgd no. cc. Issued in dustwrapper and slipcase (dustwrapper differs from trade edition) $175/250

024b: MIDPOINT Knopf NY 1969 [1] Preceded 024a by a few weeks -Alphabet Books 11/91) $12/60

024c: MIDPOINT Deutsch (L 1969) [1] $10/50

025a: BOTTOM'S DREAM... Knopf NY (1969) [0] Blue cloth. Issued in dustwrapper $50/150

025b: BOTTOM'S DREAM... Knopf NY (1969) [0] Pictorial cloth without dustwrapper $85.

026a: PENS AND NETTLES Gambit B 1969 [2] 300 sgd no. cc. Literary caricatures by David Levine. Selected and introduction by Updike. Signed by both $200/300

026b: PENS AND NETTLES Gambit B 1969 [] Trade edition $10/50

027a: THE DANCE OF THE SOLIDS (Scientific America NY 1969) [0] 6,200 cc. Wraps. Were to be used as a Season's Greeting (along with W.H. Auden's *A New Year Greeting*, both in cardboard sleeve $1,250.

028a: BECH: A BOOK Knopf NY 1970 [] Long folded original galley proofs (William Reese Co. 5/89) $1,250.

028b: BECH: A BOOK Knopf NY 1970 [2] 500 sgd no. cc. Issued in dustwrapper and slicpcase (dustwrapper differs from trade edition) $75/150

028c: BECH: A BOOK Knopf NY 1970 [1]
$7/35

028d: BECH: A BOOK Deutsch (L 1970) []
$7/35

029a: DIE NEVEN HEILIGEN... Fabrik Biberach an der Riss (1970) [0] Wraps. Single leaf folded for use as holiday greeting (ref.b)
$200.

030a: RABBIT REDUX Knopf NY 1971 [] Uncorrected proof in creme colored wraps (Waverly Books 5/88) $750.

030b: RABBIT REDUX Knopf NY 1971 [2] 350 sgd no cc. Issued in acetate dustwrapper and slipcase $225/300

030c: RABBIT REDUX Knopf NY 1971 [1]
$8/40

030d: RABBIT REDUX Deutsch (L 1972) [1]
$10/50

030e: RABBIT REDUX Franklin Library Franklin Ctr 1979 [2] Signed limited edition in full leather. (Also another issued in 1981?) $75.

031a: A CONVERSATION WITH JOHN UPDIKE (Union College Schenectady 1971) [0] Wraps. Edited by Frank Gado $50.

032a: THE INDIAN Blue Cloud Abbey Marvin, S.D. (book cover) no-date (1971) [0] Wraps (ref.b and c) $100.

033a: SEVENTY POEMS Penguin (Harmondsworth 1972) [1] Wraps. "Published in Penguin Books 1972" $50.

034a: MUSEUMS AND WOMEN + Knopf NY 1972 [2] 350 sgd no. cc. Issued in dustwrapper and slipcase (dustwrapper differs from trade edition) $125/200

034b: MUSEUMS AND WOMEN + Knopf NY 1972 [1] $8/40

034c: MUSEUMS AND WOMEN + Deutsch (L 1973) [ ] $8/40

035a: WARM WINE AN IDYLL Albondocani Press NY 1973 [2] 26 sgd ltr cc. Wraps $400.

035b: WARM WINE AN IDYLL Albondocani Press NY 1973 [2] 250 sgd no. cc. Wraps $175.

036a: PHI BETA KAPPA POEM Harvard Cambridge 1973 [0] Seven memeographed sheets, stapled $125.

037a: A GOOD PLACE... Aloe (NY) 1973 [2] 26 sgd ltr cc. Wraps $400.

037b: A GOOD PLACE... Aloe (NY) 1973 [2] 100 sgd no. cc. Wraps $300.

038a: SIX POEMS Aloe (NY) 1973 [2] 26 sgd ltr cc. Wraps $450.

038b: SIX POEMS Aloe (NY) 1973 [2] 100 sgd no. cc. Wraps $350.

039a: BUCHANAN DYING Knopf NY 1974 [1] $10/50

039b: BUCHANAN DYING Deutsch (L 1974) [1] $8/40

039c: BUCHANAN DYING San Diego State Univ. (San Diego) 1977 [0] 8 1/2" x 11" sheets in printed brown covers with program bound in back. Last page of play notes "...printed by ... in Limited Edition for ..." Play produced in March 1977. Both ref a & b state "1976," but copy in inventory states "1977" which would seem to be correct as it was produced then. Acting edition adapted by Robert McCoy and ref.a states approximately 36 copies were for sale $400.

040a: QUERY (Albondocani Press and Ampersand Books NY 1974) [0] 75 cc. First issue with illustration upside-down was reportedly suppressed (Phoenix Bookshop 8/88) $300.

040b: QUERY (Albondocani Press and Ampersand Books NY 1974) [0] Wraps. Holiday greeting with publishers' names on 160 copies and without names and title in lower left hand corner on 260 copies $75.

041a: CUNTS Hallman NY (1974) [2] 26 sgd ltr cc. Boards $450.

041b: CUNTS Hallman NY (1974) [2] 250 sgd no. cc. Boards. There were also 15 extra copies reserved for the editor and signed by Updike (George Robert Minkoff 1/90) $275.

041c: "CUNTS" in *The New York Quarterly* Summer 1973 [2] 26 sgd ltr cc with limitation notice and signature on page 65 $175.

041d: "CUNTS" in *The New York Quarterly* Summer 1973 [2] 457 sgd no. cc with limitation notice and signature on page 65 $50.

042a: A MONTH OF SUNDAYS Knopf NY 1975 [] Uncorrected proof in narrow blue wraps (Waiting For Godot 4/90) $300.

042b: A MONTH OF SUNDAYS Knopf NY 1975 [2] 450 sgd no. cc. Issued in dustwrapper and slipcase (dustwrapper differs from trade edition) $125/175

042c: A MONTH OF SUNDAYS Knopf NY 1975 [1] $8/40

042d: A MONTH OF SUNDAYS Deutsch (L 1975) [1] $8/40

043a: SUNDAY IN BOSTON (Rook Press Derry, Pa. 1975) [2] 100 sgd no. cc. Illustrated by Wm. Lint. Broadside (sgd by both) $275.

043b: SUNDAY IN BOSTON (Rook Press Derry, Pa. 1975) [2] 100 no. cc (101-200). Not signed or illustrated $100.

043c: SUNDAY IN BOSTON (Rook Press Derry, Pa. 1975) [2] 100 sgd no. cc (201-300). Signed by Updike, not illustrated $175.

044a: FLIRT (International Poetry Forum Pittsburgh 1975) [0] about 500 cc. Broadside issued on white, blue, salmon and purple paper (no priority) $200.

045a: PICKED-UP PIECES Knopf NY 1975 [] Uncorrected proof in narrow blue wraps (Waiting For Godot 6/89) $350.

045b: PICKED-UP PIECES Knopf NY 1975 [2] 250 sgd no. cc. Issued in dustwrapper (differs from trade dustwrapper) and slipcase $225/300

045c: PICKED-UP PIECES Knopf NY 1975 [1] $8/40

045d: PICKED-UP PIECES Deutsch (L 1976) [1] $10/50

046a: SCENIC (Roxburghe Club SF 1976) [] 150 cc. Broadside $250.

047a: COUPLES: A SHORT STORY Halty Ferguson Cambridge 1976 [2] 26 sgd ltr cc. Wraps $450.

047b: COUPLES: A SHORT STORY Halty Ferguson Cambridge 1976 [2] 250 sgd no. cc. Wraps $275.

048a: MARRY ME Franklin Library Franklin Ctr 1976 [2] 12,646 cc. "Limited Edition." in full leather with two page introductory note by Updike. Illustrated by Barbara Fox. (Black Sun #71 offered a cloth bound copy imprinted with "Record and Reference Copy" on spine and front) $60.

048b: MARRY ME Knopf NY 1976 [2] 300 sgd no. cc. Issued in dustwrapper (differs from trade dustwrapper) and slipcase $125/200

048c: MARRY ME Knopf NY 1976 [1] Dustwrapper has code "394-40856-X" on back panel (BOMC dustwrapper does not have numbers) $8/40

048d: MARRY ME Deutsch (L 1977) [1] $8/40

049a: RAINING AT MAGENS BAY John Updike Newsletter (Northridge 1977) [2] 26 ltr cc. Broadside $200.

049b: RAINING AT MAGENS BAY John Updike Newsletter (Northridge 1977) [2] 200 no. cc. Broadside $75.

050a: TOSSING AND TURNING Knopf NY 1977 [1] $8/40

050b: TOSSING AND TURNING Deutsch (L 1977) [1] $8/40

051a: HUB FANS BID KID ADIEU Lord John Press Northridge 1977 [2] 26 sgd ltr cc. Issued without dustwrapper $450.

051b: HUB FANS BID KID ADIEU Lord John Press Northridge 1977 [2] 350 sgd no. cc. Preface is new. Issued without dustwrapper $150.

052a: FROM THE JOURNAL OF A LEPER Lord John Press Northridge 1978 [2] 26 sgd ltr cc. Black cloth spine. Issued without dustwrapper (also 9 over-run copies with individual names) $450.

052b: FROM THE JOURNAL OF A LEPER Lord John Press Northridge 1978 [2] 300 sgd no. cc. Issued without dustwrapper. (Red cloth spine) $100.

053a: THE COUP Knopf NY 1978 [2] 350 sgd no. cc. Issued in dustwrapper (which differs from trade dustwrapper) and slipcase $100/175

053b: THE COUP Knopf NY 1978 [1] First issue with top edge yellow $10/50

053c: THE COUP Knopf NY 1978 [1] Second issue with top edge black. (Also noted with top edge unstained and lacking last two lines of text on last page. "This book was composed ... Vermont" which Waiting For Godot catalogued at $650.) $10/50

053d: THE COUP Deutsch (L 1979) [1] $10/50

054a: THE LOVELORN ASTRONOMER G.K. Hall (B 1978) [0] Wraps. 400 cc. Copyright notice handwritten. Issued as a Holiday Greeting $400.

054b: THE LOVELORN ASTRONOMER G.K. Hall (B 1978) [0] Wraps. 1,400 cc. Copyright notice printed $75.

055a: THE DICK CAVETT SHOW A CONVERSATION... (Waggoner Wash. DC 1979) [] Unbound xeroxed sheets (ref.b) $35.

056a: SIXTEEN SONNETS Halty Ferguson Cambridge 1979 [2] 26 sgd ltr cc. Issued in cloth without dustwrapper $500.

056b: SIXTEEN SONNETS Halty Ferguson Cambridge 1979 [2] 250 sgd no. cc. Wraps $100.

057a: TOO FAR TO GO Fawcett NY (1979) [3] Wraps. No. 2-4002-9 $35.

057b: YOUR LOVER JUST CALLED... Penguin (Harmondsworth 1980) [] Wraps (ref.b) $40.

058a: THREE ILLUMINATIONS... Targ Editions NY 1979 [2] 350 sgd no. cc. Issued with plain white tissue dustwrapper $125.

059a: AN ODDLY LOVELY DAY ALONE Waves Press Richmond 1979 [2] 26 sgd ltr cc. Broadside $250.

059b: AN ODDLY LOVELY DAY ALONE Waves Press Richmond 1979 [2] 250 sgd no. cc. Broadside $75.

060a: THE VISIONS OF MACKENZIE KING (John Updike Newsletter Northridge 1979) [2] 150 cc. Broadside $75.

061a: PROBLEMS + Knopf NY 1979 [2] 350 sgd no. cc. Issued in dustwrapper (which differs from trade dustwrapper) and slipcase $100/150

061b: PROBLEMS + Knopf NY 1979 [1] $8/40

061c: PROBLEMS + Deutsch (L 1980) [1] (ref.b) $8/40

062a: PIGEON FEATHERS (Perfection Form Co. Logan, Iowa 1979) [] Wraps. First separate edition $25.

063a: EARTHWORM (Ontario Review Princeton 1979) [] 100 cc (a & b). Postcard with earliest issue: "God Bless" stanza 3:1 $100.

063b: EARTHWORM (Ontario Review Princeton 1979) [] Stanza 3:1 changed to "God blesses" $50.

064a: TALK FROM THE FIFTIES Lord John Press Northridge 1979 [2] 75 sgd no. cc. Issued without dustwrapper $175.

064b: TALK FROM THE FIFTIES Lord John Press Northridge 1979 [2] 300 sgd no. cc. Issued without dustwrapper (ref.b) $100.

065a: THE CHASTE PLANET Metacom Press Worcester 1980 [2] 26 sgd ltr cc. Issued in cloth without dustwrapper (ref.b) $450.

065b: THE CHASTE PLANET Metacom Press Worcester 1980 [2] 300 sgd no. cc. Wraps $100.

066a: IOWA Press-22 Portland (1980) [2] 26 sgd ltr cc. Broadside (ref.b) $200.

066b: IOWA Press-22 Portland (1980) [2] 200 sgd no. cc. Broadside (ref.b) $100.

067a: EGO AND ART IN WALT WHITMAN Targ Editions NY 1980 [2] 350 sgd no. cc. Issued in plain tan dustwrapper (ref.b & c) $100.

068a: FIVE POEMS Bits Chapbook (Cleveland 1980) [2] 50 sgd no. cc (1-50). Issued on handmade paper $450.

068b: FIVE POEMS Bits Chapbook (Cleveland 1980) [2] 135 sgd no. cc (51-185). Issued in paper wallet (Bert Babcock #56) $125.

069a: PEOPLE ONE KNOWS... Lord John Press Northridge 1980 [2] 100 sgd no. cc. Issued without dustwrapper in slipcase (ref.b & c) $150.

069b: PEOPLE ONE KNOWS... Lord John Press Northridge 1980 [2] 350 sgd no. cc. Issued without dustwrapper in slipcase (ref.b & c) $100.

070a: A SENSE OF SHELTER (Perfection Form Co. Logan 1980) [] $25.

071a: HAWTHRONE'S CREED Targ Editions NY (1981) [2] 250 sgd no. cc (ref.b). Issued in unprinted pale gray/green dustwrapper $125/150

072a: INVASION OF THE BOOK ENVELOPES Wm. Ewert (Concord 1981) [2] 10 sgd cc. Leather spine, separate colophon and half-title not in 71b (description provided by publisher) $750.

072b: INVASION OF THE BOOK ENVELOPES Wm. Ewert (Concord 1981) [2] 125 cc in wraps. Issued in envelope $100.

073a: RABBIT IS RICH Knopf NY 1981 [] Uncorrected proof in salmon colored wraps (Waiting For Godot 10/90) $250.

073b: RABBIT IS RICH Knopf NY 1981 [] With signed tipped in page (Joseph the Provider #33) $100/125

073c: RABBIT IS RICH Knopf NY 1981 [2] 350 sgd no. cc. Issued in dustwrapper (which differs from trade edition) in slipcase (ref.c) $175/250

073d: RABBIT IS RICH Knopf NY 1981 [1] Pulitzer Prize in 1982 (ref.b) $10/50

073e: RABBIT IS RICH Deutsch (L 1982) [1] (ref.b) $8/40

073f: RABBIT IS RICH Franklin Library Franklin Ctr 1984 [2] "Limited Edition" in full leather (ref.c) $60.

074a: THE BELOVED Lord John Press Northridge 1982 [2] 100 sgd no. cc $150.

074b: THE BELOVED Lord John Press Northridge 1982 [2] 300 sgd no. cc $100.

075a: STYLES OF BLOOM Palaemon (Winston-Salem 1982) [2] 26 sgd no. cc. Broadside $150.

075b: STYLES OF BLOOM Palaemon (Winston-Salem 1982) [2] 55 sgd no. cc. Issued in Palaemon Broadside Folio $300.

076a: SMALL CITY PEOPLE Lord John Press Northridge 1982 [2] 100 sgd no. cc. Broadside $125.

077a: SPRING TRIO Palaemon (Winston-Salem 1982) [2] 10 sgd no. cc (Roman numerals) $350.

077b: SPRING TRIO Palaemon (Winston-Salem 1982) [2] 26 sgd ltr cc $250.

077c: SPRING TRIO Palaemon (Winston-Salem 1982) [2] 100 sgd no. cc (also 8 out-of-series copies) $125.

078a: BECK IS BACK Knopf NY 1982 [] Uncorrected proof in yellow wraps (Waiting For Godot 4/89) $200.

078b: BECH IS BACK Knopf NY 1982 [2] 500 sgd no. cc. Issued in dustwrapper (which differs from trade edition) and slipcase $75/125

078c: BECH IS BACK Knopf NY 1982 [1] $7/35

078d: BECH IS BACK Deutsch (L 1983) [1] $7/35

079a: HUGGING THE SHORE Knopf NY 1983 [] Uncorrected proof in blue printed wraps $250.

079b: HUGGING THE SHORE Knopf NY 1983 [1] $15/50

079c: HUGGING THE SHORE Deutsch (L 1984) [1] U.S. sheets (ref.b) $15/50

080a: TWO SONNETS... Palaemon Winston-Salem 1983 [2] 75 sgd no. cc. Broadside. Included in Northern Lights portfolio with other authors' broadsides (per publisher, ref.b indicated 26 sgd ltr cc). Also 15 ltr cc for contributors with 2 extra broadsides for that contributor, others unsigned (Geo. Robert Minkoff 8/90) $400.

081a: CONFESSIONS OF A WILD BORE Tamazunchale Press Newton 1984 [2] 250 no. cc. Miniature leather book issued without dustwrapper $60.

082a: JESTER'S DOZEN Lord John Press Northridge 1984 [2] 50 sgd no. cc $200.

082b: JESTER'S DOZEN Lord John Press Northridge 1984 [2] 150 sgd no. cc. Issued without dustwrapper $125.

083a: EMERSONIANISM Bits Press Cleveland (1984) [2] 203 sgd cc. Revised from *The New Yorker* appearance. (Published March 1985 @ $75) $125.

084a: THE WITCHES OF EASTWICK Knopf NY 1984 [] Uncorrected proof in red printed wraps with passages not in later proof or published version (Waiting For Godot #7) $300.

084b: THE WITCHES OF EASTWICK Knopf NY 1984 [] Uncorrected proof in Salmon-colored wraps $150.

084c: THE WITCHES OF EASTWICK Franklin Library Franklin Ctr 1984 [2] "Signed Limited" in full leather, includes "Special message" from author $75.

084d: THE WITCHES OF EASTWICK Knopf NY 1984 [2] 350 sgd no. cc $125/175

084e: THE WITCHES OF EASTWICK Knopf NY 1984 [1] 110,000 cc (PW) $7/35

084f: THE WITCHES OF EASTWICK Deutsch (L 1984) [] Uncorrected proof in blue wraps (Bev Chaney 6/91) $150.

084g: THE WITCHES OF EASTWICK Deutsch (L 1984) [1] $7/35

085a: A & P (AND) SHOULD WIZARD HIT MOMMY? Tales For Travellers S.F. (1985) [0]

Single sheet map folded to 24 pages. First separate edition $25.

086a: FACING NATURE Knopf NY 1985 [] Uncorrected proof in blue wraps (Bev Chaney List C) $200.

086b: FACING NATURE Knopf NY 1985 [1] $8/40

086c: FACING NATURE Deutsch (L 1986) $8/40

087a: IMPRESSIONS Sylvester & Orphanos L.A. 1985 [2] 4 sgd no. cc with recipient's name $NVA

087b: IMPRESSIONS Sylvester & Orphanos L.A. 1985 [2] 26 sgd ltr cc. Not For Sale $350.

087c: IMPRESSIONS Sylvester & Orphanos L.A. 1985 [2] 300 sgd no. cc (in-print) $250.

088a: SEVEN GOTHIC TALES A NEW INTRODUCTION Book-of-the-Month Club (NY 1986) [0] Wraps. Contains Updike's introduction $35.

089a: ROGER'S VERSION Knopf NY 1986 [] Uncorrected proof in ochre (Waverly 10/89), yellow (Joseph Dermott 3/90) and yellow-gold (Waiting For Godot 2/91) $150.

089b: ROGER'S VERSION Franklin Library Franklin Ctr 1986 [2] Ltd sgd edition in full leather $75.

089c: ROGER'S VERSION Knopf NY 1986 [2] 350 sgd no. cc. Issued in acetate dustwrapper and slipcase $75/125

089d: ROGER'S VERSION Knopf NY 1986 [1] (Published September 10, 1986 @ $17.95) $7/35

089e: ROGER'S VERSION Deutsch (L 1986) [1] $7/35

090a: A & P : LOST IN THE AISLES Redpath, Minn 1986 [0] 5,000 cc Wraps. Front flap blank, later printing (Bert Babcock #56) $25.

091a: A SOFT SPRING NIGHT IN SHILLINGTON Lord John Press Northridge 1986 [2] 50 sgd no. cc. Leather spine in slipcase. (In-print) $100/150

091b: A SOFT SPRING NIGHT IN SHILLINGTON Lord John Press Northridge 1986 [2] 250 sgd no. cc. Issued without dustwrapper. (In-print) $50.

092a: GETTING OLDER Eurographica Helsinki 1986 [2] 350 sgd no. cc. Issued in stiff wraps and dustrapper. Three stories $250.

093a: A PEAR LIKE A POTATO Lord John Press Northridge (1986) [2] 26 sgd ltr cc. Broadside $250.

093b: A PEAR LIKE A POTATO Lord John Press Northridge (1986) [2] 100 sgd no. cc. (In-print) $75.

094a: TRUST ME Knopf NY 1987 [1] Uncorrected proof in creme colored wraps $150.

094b: TRUST ME Knopf NY 1987 [2] 350 sgd no. cc. Issued in slipcase $100/150

094c: TRUST ME Knopf NY 1987 [1] 50,000 cc (PW). (Published May 1987 @ $17.95) $6/30

094d: TRUST ME Andre Deutsch (L 1987) [] Uncorrected proof in blue wraps (Waiting For Godot 10/89) $100.

094e: TRUST ME Andre Deutsch (L 1987) [] $7/35

095a: THE AFTERLIFE Sixth Chamber Press L 1987 [2] 26 sgd no. cc. Issued in quarter leather and slipcase (Published May 1987 @ £200) $400.

095b: THE AFTERLIFE Sixth Chamber Press L 1987 [2] 175 sgd no. cc. Issued in full cloth (Published May 1987 @ £60) $150.

096a: THE ART OF ADDING AND THE ART OF TAKING AWAY Harvard Library Cambridge 1987 [] Wraps. Reproductions of Updike's manuscripts and drawings with his introduction $30.

097a: MORE STATELY MANSIONS Nouveau Press Jackson 1987 [2] 40 sgd no. cc (Roman numberals). Not For Sale. (Published May 1987) $250.

097b: MORE STATELY MANSIONS Nouveau Press Jackson 1987 [2] 300 sgd no. cc. Issued without dustwrapper $100.

098a: HOWELLS AS ANTI-MOVELIST Wm. Dean Howells Memorial Committee Kittery Point, Maine 1987 [2] 150 cc. Issued in stiff printed wraps (Wm. Reese Co. 2/91) $75.

099a: S Knopf NY 1988 [1] Uncorrected proof in red wraps $100.

099b: S Knopf NY 1988 [2] 350 sgd no. cc. Issued in acetate dustwrapper and slipcase $100/150

099c: S Knopf NY 1988 [1] 100,000 cc (PW). (Published March 1988 @ $17.95) $5/25

099d: S Andre Deutsch (L 1988) [2] 12 sgd no. (Roman) cc. Bound in full green claf. Assume in marbled paper slipcase $350/400

099e: S Andre Deutsch (L 1988) [2] 10 sgd ltr cc in quarter leather in marbled paper slipcase. (Not for sale) $300/350

099f: S Andre Deutsch (L 1988) [2] 75 sgd no. cc. Issued in quarter leather in marbled paper slipcase $200/250

099g: S Andre Deutsch (L 1988) [] Trade edition $7/35

100a: ON THE MOVE Bits Press Cleveland (1988) [2] 120 sgd cc. Wraps $100.

101a: SELF CONSCIOUSNESS : MEMOIRS (Knopf NY 1988) [] Uncorrected proof in buff/creme colored wraps $100.

101b: SELF CONSCIOUSNESS : MEMOIRS (Knopf NY 1988) [] Promotional broadside with photograph of Updike (Henry Turlington 7/89) $50.

101c: SELF CONSCIOUSNESS : MEMOIRS Knopf NY 1989 [2] 350 sgd no. cc. Issued in acetate dustwrapper and slipcase $100/150

101d: SELF CONSCIOUSNESS : MEMOIRS Knopf NY 1989 [1] 50,000 cc (PW). Trade edition $5/25

101e: SELF CONSCIOUSNESS : MEMOIRS Andre Deutsch L (1989) [] Uncorrected proof in blue wraps $75.

101f: SELF CONSCIOUSNESS : MEMOIRS Andre Deutsch L (1989) [] Trade edition $7/35

102a: GETTING THE WORDS OUT Lord John Press Northridge 1988 [2] 50 sgd no. cc. Issued in quarter leather $150.

102b: GETTING THE WORDS OUT Lord John Press Northridge 1988 [2] 250 sgd no. cc. Issued without dustwrapper or slipcase $50.

103a: JUST LOOKING : ESSAYS ON ART Knopf NY 1989 [] Uncorrected proof in white wraps $100.

103b: JUST LOOKING : ESSAYS ON ART Knopf NY 1989 [] 8 page publicity color brochure (Bev Chaney 9/89) $50.

103c: JUST LOOKING : ESSAYS ON ART Knopf NY 1989 [2] 350 sgd no. cc. Issued in acetate dustwrapper and slipcase $100/150

103d: JUST LOOKING : ESSAYS ON ART Knopf NY 1989 [1] (Published October 1989 @ $35) $7/35

104a: IN MEMORIAM : FELIS FELIX Sixth Chamber Press Leamington Spa 1989 [2] 26 sgd ltr cc. Signed by Updike and R.R. Kitaj (illustrator). Issued in slipcase $300/400

104b: IN MEMORIAM : FELIS FELIX Sixth Chamber Press Leamington Spa 1989 [2] 200 sgd no. cc. Issued in acetate dustwrapper $100.

105a: THE COMPLETE BOOK OF COVERS FROM THE NEW YORKER 1925-1989 Knopf NY 1989 [1] (Published November 1989 @ $75) $25/75

106a: GOING ABROAD Eurographica Helsinki 1989 [2] 350 sgd no. cc. Issued in stiff wraps (Herb Yellin 3/90) $200.

107a: BROTHER GRASSHOPPER Metacom Press Worcester, Mass. 1990 [2] 26 sgd ltr cc $350.

107b: BROTHER GRASSHOPPER Metacom Press Worcester, Mass. 1990 [2] 150 sgd no. cc $125.

108a: MITES & OTHER POEMS IN MINATURE Lord John Press Northridge 1990 [2] 26 sgd ltr cc. Issued in slipcase $150.

108b: MITES & OTHER POESM IN MINATURE Lord John Press Northridge 1990 [2] 200 sgd no. cc. Issued without slipcase $50.

109a: RABBIT AT REST Knopf NY 1990 [1] Uncorrected proof in yellow wraps $150.

109b: RABBIT AT REST Knopf NY 1990 [1] Signed uncorrected proof in white wraps and publisher's green slipcase $150/175

109c: RABBIT AT REST Franklin Library Franklin Ctr. 1990 [] Signed "limited" "first edition" with special message not in trade edition $100.

109d: RABBIT AT REST Knopf NY 1990 [2] 350 sgd no. cc. Issued in slipcase $150/200

109e: RABBIT AT REST Knopf NY 1990 [1] 125,000 cc (PW). Pulitzer Prize winner. (Published October 1990 @ $21.95) $6/30

110a: "FULL FORTY YEARS ..." (Privately Printed Pennsylvania 1990) [0] 8" x 10" untitled broadside written for his high school reunion.

Reportedly 100 copies, of which 55 were given away at the event (Bert Babcock 2/91) $75.

111a: THANATOPSES Bits Press Cleveland 1991 [] 237 cc. Wraps $75.

112a: RECENT POEMS 1986-1990 Eurographica Helsinki (1991) [2] 350 sgd no. cc. Issued in stiff wraps $150.

113a: THE FIRST PICTURE BOOK Whitney Museum NY 1991 [2] 25 deluxe copies. Bound in full leather with additional photogravures, 24 offset lithographs by Mary Steichen Calderone and Edward Steichen. Afterword by Updike $1,250.

114a: ODD JOBS : ESSAYS AND CRITICISM Knopf NY 1991 [] Uncorrected proof in yellow wraps (Bert Babcock 2/92) $100.

114b: ODD JOBS : ESSAYS AND CRITICISM Knopf NY 1991 [1] (Published November 7, 1991 @ $30) $5/20

KURT VONNEGUT, JR.

Vonnegut was born in 1922 in Indianapolis, educated at Cornell and the University of Chicago. He served during World War II, and was awarded a Purple Heart. Vonnegut was a police reporter in Chicago after the war and also worked in public relations for the General Electric Company before turning to free lance writing in 1950.

Vonnegut was initially labeled a science fiction writer but he did not like the label. He preferred to think of himself as a 20th century Mark Twain. Critics consider his work, except for the earliest, predominately satire.

REFERENCES:

(a) Pieratta, Asa B., Jr. and Jerome Klinkowitz, KURT VONNEGUT, JR. A Descriptive Bibliography..., Archon Books (no-place) 1974.

(b) Currey, L.W., SCIENCE FICTION AND FANTASY AUTHORS..., G.K. Hall & Co., Boston (1979).

(c) Bruccoli, Matthew J. (editor) FIRST PRINTINGS OF AMERICAN AUTHORS, Vol. 1, Gale Research, Detroit (1977).

(d) Inventory or dealer catalogs.

001a: PLAYER PIANO Charles Scribner's Sons NY 1952 [5] 25 to 30 cc. Wraps. Advance copies for review using dustwrapper as self wraps with flaps pasted on front pastedown and endpaper $850.

001b: PLAYER PIANO Charles Scribner's Sons NY 1952 [5] 7,600 cc. Has "A" and Scribner's seal. Doubleday Book Club edition has an "A" also, but no seal $100/500

001c: PLAYER PIANO Macmillan L 1953 [] Approximately 2,000 cc. 3,000 copies were printed but approximately 1,000 were pulped $50/250

001d: UTOPIA 14 Bantam Books NY (1954) [1] Wraps. "1st printing... October 1954." New Title. "Bantam Giant A 1262" $35.

002a: THE SIRENS OF TITAN Dell (NY 1959) [1] 177,500 cc. Wraps. "First printing October, 1959" $75.

002b: THE SIRENS OF TITAN Houghton Mifflin Co. B 1961 [1] 2,500 cc $75/450

002c: THE SIRENS OF TITAN Gollancz L 1962 [0] Red cloth with spine stamped in gold $30/150

003a: CANARY IN A CAT HOUSE Gold Medal/Fawcett Greenwich, CT (1961) [1] 175,000 cc. Wraps. "First printing September 1961." Gold Medal Book S 1153. Also distributed in England. All but one story later collected in *Welcome To The Monkey House* (ref.b) $100.

004a: MOTHER NIGHT Gold Medal/Fawcett Greenwich, CT (1962) [1] 175,000 cc. Wraps. Also distributed in England $100.

004b: MOTHER NIGHT Harper & Row NY (1966) [] Uncorrected proof in spiral bound plain wraps (William Reese Co. 7/89) $750.

004c: MOTHER NIGHT Harper & Row NY (1966) [1] 5,500 cc. Adds introduction by author $30/150

004d: MOTHER NIGHT Jonathan Cape L (1968) [1] $25/125

005a: CAT'S CRADLE Holt, Rinehard & Winston NY/Ch/SF (1963) [1] 6,000 cc $75/350

005b: CAT'S CRADLE Victor Gollancz L 1963 [0] $25/125

006a: GOD BLESS YOU, MR. ROSEWATER... Holt, Rinehart & Winston NY/Ch/SF (1965) [1] 6,000 cc $75/350

006b: GOD BLESS YOU, MR. ROSEWATER... Jonathan Cape L (1965) [1] Maroon paper over boards, spine printed in gold. Later printings are black paper over boards $25/125

007a: HAVE YOU EVER BEEN TO BARNSTABLE (Venture Magazine) no-place 1966 [] 2 leaves folded to make 8 pages. An offprint (Fine Books #30) $200.

008a: WELCOME TO THE MONKEY HOUSE... Delacorte (NY 1968) [] Uncorrected proofs in spiral bound salmon colored wraps (Joseph Dermont 6/92) $750.

008b: WELCOME TO THE MONKEY HOUSE... Delacorte (NY 1968) [1] 5,000 cc $60/300

008c: WELCOME TO THE MONKEY HOUSE... Jonathan Cape L (1969) [1] $10/50

009a: SLAUGHTERHOUSE FIVE... Delacorte (NY 1969) [1] 10,000 cc $50/250

009b: SLAUGHTERHOUSE FIVE... Jonathan Cape L (1970) [1] $25/125

009c: SLAUGHTERHOUSE FIVE... Franklin Library Franklin Ctr. 1978 [2] "Signed Limited Edition" with special message not in trade edition. Issued in full leather $75.

010a: TORTURE AND BLUBBER Peoples Union no-place or date (circa 1971) [] Broadside. First separate appearances of this piece from the *New York Times* (another author on back) (Waiting For Godot 10/68) $75.

011a: HAPPY BIRTHDAY, WANDA JUNE Delacorte NY 1971 [1] 3,000 cc. Dustwrapper priced at top of front flap (Asa Pieratta). We have seen several copies with no price and clipped at bottom of front flap where "Book Club" or "Fireside Book Club" would normally be printed. The books themselves in these dustwrapper's did not look like Book Club editions and stated "First Printing." We wonder if Fireside or another club purchased the publisher's first edition and put their dustwrapper on it. Noted with both "0971" on bottom and "3456" on "Book Club" dustwrappers $75/500

011b: HAPPY BIRTHDAY, WANDA JUNE Delta NY 1971 [1] Wraps. "First Delta Printing..." Assume published simultaneously $40.

011c: HAPPY BIRTHDAY, WANDA JUNE Wanda June/Filmakers Hollywood 1971 []

Wraps. Original screenplay (Pepper & Stern #22) $200.

011d: HAPPY BIRTHDAY, WANDA JUNE Jonathan Cape L (1973) [1] (Published June 14, 1973 @ £1.95) $35/125

011e: HAPPY BIRTHDAY, WANDA JUNE French NY (1974) [0] Wraps. Drops author's note $30.

012a: BETWEEN TIME AND TIMBUKTU Delacorte (NY 1972) [1] $75/350

012b: BETWEEN TIME AND TIMBUKTU Panther (St. Albans 1975) [1] Wraps. No U.K. hardcover edition $50.

013a: BREAKFAST OF CHAMPIONS (Delacorte NY 1973) [1] Approximately 100,000 cc $12/60

013b: BREAKFAST OF CHAMPIONS Jonathan Cape L (1973) [1] $10/50

014a: ONE GREAT NOVELIST OF THE 70'S WRITES ABOUT ANOTHER... Ballantine (NY 1974) [] Vonnegut on Joseph Heller's *Something Happened. New York Times Book Review*, 8 pages in blue wraps with white and black letters. Generated in connection with the release of the paperback edition of Heller's book (Between the Covers) $125.

015a: WAMPETERS FOMA & GRANFALLOONS Delacorte (NY 1974) [1] (ref.c) $12/60

015b: WAMPETERS FOMA & GRANFALLOONS Jonathan Cape L (1975) [1] (ref.c) $12/60

016a: SLAPSTICK... (Delacorte) NY (1976) [] Uncorrected proof in gray wraps $75.

016b: SLAPSTICK... (Delacorte) NY (1976) [1] Actually issued a month before 014c & d (ref.b) $8/40

016c: SLAPSTICK... (Delacorte) NY (1976) [2] 250 sgd no. cc. Issued without dustwrapper in slipcase (ref.b) $100/175

016d: SLAPSTICK... Franklin Library Franklin Center 1976 [2] "Limited Edition" with special message by the author. Full leather binding (ref.b) $75.

016e: SLAPSTICK... Jonathan Cape L (1976) [1] (ref.d) $8/40

017a: JAILBIRD Delacorte NY (1979) [] Uncorrected proof in yellow (mustard) wraps $75.

017b: JAILBIRD (Delacorte NY 1979) [2] 500 sgd no. cc. Issued without dustwrpper in slipcase (ref.d) $75/125

017c: JAILBIRD Delacorte NY (1979) [1] (ref.d) $7/35

017d: JAILBIRD Jonathan Cape L (1979) [1] (ref.d) $8/40

018a: SUN MOON STAR Harper & Row (NY 1980) [1] $10/50

018b: SUN MOON STAR Hutchinson L (1980) [1] $8/40

019a: HOW TO WRITE WITH STYLE International Paper Co. (Elmsford, NY 1980) [0] Wraps. Single sheet, folded once. Illustrated with photos (offprint of Company's magazine ad) $40.

020a: PALM SUNDAY Delacorte NY (1981) [] Uncorrected proof in yellow wraps $75.

020b: PALM SUNDAY Delacorte NY (1981) [2] 500 sgd no. cc. Issued without dustwrapper in slipcase $75/125

020c: PALM SUNDAY Delacorte NY (1981) [1] $7/35

020d: PALM SUNDAY Jonathan Cape L (1981) [] Uncorrected proof in green wraps (Bev Chaney) $75.

020e: PALM SUNDAY Jonathan Cape L (1981) [] $8/40

021a: DEADEYE DICK Delacorte (NY 1982) [] Uncorrected proof in red wraps $75.

021b: DEADEYE DICK Delacorte (NY 1982) [2] 350 sgd no. cc. Issued without dustwrapper in slipcase $100/150

021c: DEADEYE DICK Delacorte (NY 1982) [1] $7/35

021d: DEADEYE DICK Jonathan Cape L (1983) [] $7/35

022a: BOB AND RAY / A RETROSPECTIVE Museum of Broadcasting NY (1982) [] An appreciation by Vonnegut. Folio sheet folded to make 6 pages/panels $40.

023a: FATES WORSE THAN DEATH (cover title) (Bertrand Russell Peace... Nottingham no-date) (1982) [0] Wraps. Text of Vonnegut speech $40.

(Also see item 033)

024a: NOTHING IS LOST SAVE HONOR Nouveau Jackson, Miss. 1984 [2] 40 sgd no. cc. Printed on handmade Japanese Etching. Half-bound in Nigerian Oasis goatskin and cloth $250.

024b: NOTHING IS LOST SAVE HONOR Nouveau Jackson, Miss. 1984 [2] 300 sgd no. cc. Boards. Issued without dustwrappers. (In print) $90.

025a: GALAPAGOS Delacorte NY 1985 [1] Uncorrected proof in pale blue printed wraps $75.

025b: GALAPAGOS Franklin Library Franklin Center 1985 [2] "Limited Signed Edition." Full leather, original 2-page introduction. Reported to precede Delacorte edition $75.

025c: GALAPAGOS Delacorte NY 1985 [2] 500 sgd no. cc. Issued without dustwrapper in slipcase $75/125

025d: GALAPAGOS Delacorte NY 1985 [1] (Published October 4, 1985 @ $16.95) $6/30

025e: GALAPAGOS Jonathan Cape L (1985) [] Advance uncorrected proof in publisher's brown printed wraps (Dalian 9/92) $60.

025f: GALAPAGOS Jonathan Cape L (1985) [] $7/35

026a: BLUEBEARD Delacorte (NY 1987) [] Uncorrected proof in red wraps $60.

026b: BLUEBEARD Franklin Library Franklin Ctr. 1987 [2] Signed limited edition in full leather $75.

026c: BLUEBEARD Delacorte (NY 1987) [2] 500 sgd no. cc. Issued without dustwrapper in slipcase $50/100

026d: BLUEBEARD Delacorte (NY 1987) [1] $5/25

026e: BLUEBEARD Jonathan Cape L 1988 [] $5/25

027a: VARGA, THE ESQUIRE YEARS: A CATALOGUE RAISONNE Alfred Van Der Marck Editions 1987 [2] Signed limited edition (PW) Announced for $350. Never seen. Foreword by Vonnegut

027b: VARGA, THE ESQUIRE YEARS: A CATALOGUE RAISONNE Alfred Van Der Marck Editions 1987 [] 35,000 cc (PW). Foreword by Vonnegut $10/50

028a: WHO AM I THIS TIME? Redpath Minn. 1987 [0] Wraps. Issued in plain envelope $25.

029a: PRECAUTIONARY LETTER TO THE NEXT GENERATION Volkswagon (1988) [0] Off-print of an ad in *Time* magazine (Ken Lopez 4/91) $50.

030a: CONVERSATION WITH KURT VONNEGUT Univ. of Mississippi Jacksonville (1988) [] $15/35

030b: CONVERSATION WITH KURT VONNEGUT Univ. of Mississippi Jacksonville (1988) [] Wraps $15.

031a: "TO WHOM IT MAY CONCERN" (Poetry Center of the 92nd Street Y NY 1990) [0] Wraps (Waiting For Godot 10/90) $35.

032a: HOCUS POCUS OR, WHAT'S THE HURRY, SON Putnam NY (1990) [] Uncorrected proof in gold wraps (Waiting For Godot 2/91) $60.

032b: HOCUS POCUS OR, WHAT'S THE HURRY, SON Franklin Library Franklin Ctr. 1990 [2] Signed limited edition in full leather with frontis illustration by Edith Vonnegut. Squibb and special message to readers by the author $75.

032c: HOCUS POCUS OR, WHAT'S THE HURRY, SON Putnam NY (1990) [2] 250 sgd no. cc. Issued without dustwrapper in slipcase $75/125

032d: HOCUS POCUS OR, WHAT'S THE HURRY, SON Putnam NY (1990) [] (Published June 1990 @ $19.95) $5/25

032e: HOCUS POCUS OR, WHAT'S THE HURRY, SON Jonathan Cape L 1990 [] Uncorrected proof in pictorial wraps $60.

033a: FATES WORSE THAN DEATH Putnam NY (1991) [] Uncorrected proof in red wraps $50.

(Also see item 033a)

033b: FATES WORSE THAN DEATH Putnam NY (1991) [2] 200 sgd no. cc. Issued without dustwrapper in slipcase $75/125

033c: FATES WORSE THAN DEATH Putnam NY (1991) [3] With tipped-in signed page (Bert Babcock 2/92) $35/50

033d: FATES WORSE THAN DEATH Putnam NY (1991) [3] (Published August 1991 @ $22.95) $4/20

EUDORA WELTY

Eudora Welty was born in Jackson, Mississippi in 1909. She was educated at Mississippi State College For Women, University of Wisconsin and Columbia University School of Advertising in New York. Miss Welty has been writing full-time for over 50 years. During that career she has received about all the fellowships and prizes a writer can garner, including a Pulitzer Prize for *The Optimist's Daughter* in 1973.

REFERENCES:

(a) Bruccoli Clark, FIRST PRINTINGS OF AMERICAN AUTHORS Gale Research, Detroit (1977) (for U.S. editions through 1975 unless otherwise stated).

(b) "Eudora Welty: A Bibliographical Checklist" compiled by Noel Polk in *American Book Collector*, Vol. 2, No. 1 Jan/Feb 1981 (for British editions through 1980 and U.S. editions 1975 - 1980 unless otherwise stated).

(c) Turlington, H.E. *Southern Women Writers 1922-1984*, Catalog 27 issued in March 1986

(d) Inventory, dealer catalogs, *Publishers Weekly*, etc.

001a: EUDORA WELTY: A NOTE ON THE AUTHOR AND HER WORK by Katherine Anne Porter... (Doubleday Doran GC 1941) [0] Pictorial wraps. A pre-publicity pamphlet for *A Curtain of Green* containing Welty's short story *The Key* $2,500.

002a: A CURTAIN OF GREEN Doubleday Doran GC 1941 [1] $200/1000

002b: A CURTAIN OF GREEN John Lane Bodley Head L (1943) [1] $75/300

003a: THE ROBBER BRIDEGROOM Doubleday Doran GC 1942 [1] $125/600

003b: THE ROBBER BRIDEGROOM John Lane Bodley Head L (1944) [1] Illustrated by James Holland. First illustrated $50/250

003c: THE ROBBER BRIDEGROOM Pennyroyal Press West Hatfield, MA 1987 [2] 150 no. cc. Signed by Welty and Barry Moser, the illustrator. In full red leather without slipcase $500.

003d: THE ROBBER BRIDEGROOM Harcourt Brace SD (1987) [] Illustrated by Barry Moser $10/40

004a: THE WIDE NET + Harcourt Brace NY (1943) [1] First issue with top edge stained green (source?) $125/650

004b: THE WIDE NET + John Lane Bodley Head L (1945) [1] On reverse of Welty dustwrapper is jacket for F.E. Mills Young's *Unlucky Farm* $50/350

005a: DELTA WEDDING Harcourt Brace NY (1946) [1] $60/300

005b: DELTA WEDDING Bodley Head L (1947) [1] $40/200

006a: MUSIC FROM SPAIN The Levee Press Greenville, MS 1948 [2] 750 sgd no. cc. Issued in glassine dustwrapper $650.

007a: THE GOLDEN APPLES Harcourt Brace NY (1949) [1] $35/175

007b: THE GOLDEN APPLES Bodley Head L (1950) [1] First issue in brown cloth lacking front endpapers (Peter Jolliffe 7/90) $50/200

008a: SHORT STORIES Harcourt Brace NY (1949) [2] 1,500 cc. Issued in glassine dustwrapper $150.

009a: THE PONDER HEART Harcourt Brace NY (1954) [1] $30/150

009b: THE PONDER HEART Hamish Hamilton L (1954) Advance copy in brown wraps and dustwrapper (Nicholas Pounder 12/91) $200.

009c: THE PONDER HEART Hamish Hamilton L (1954) [1] $25/100

009d: THE PONDER HEART : A PLAY Random House NY (1956) [1] Adapted by Joseph Feilds and Jerome Chodorov. (Published May 18, 1956 @ $2.95) $15/75

010a: SELECTED STORIES... Modern Library NY (1954) [1] $15/75

011a: THE BRIDE OF THE INNISFALLEN + Harcourt Brace NY (1955) [1] Copyright notice of first issue contains only one date: "copyright... 1955, by Eudora Welty." Issued in blue and green mottled boards, green cloth spine, silver stamping (Ref.b) $300/400

011b: THE BRIDE OF THE INNISFALLEN + Harcourt Brace NY (1955) [1] Second issue copyright contains 5 dates: "copyright...1949, 1951, 1952, 1954, 1955..." Copyright page tipped-in. Issued in blue and green mottled boards, green cloth spine, silver stamping (Ref.b) $75/225

011c: THE BRIDE OF THE INNISFALLEN + Harcourt Brace NY (1955) [1] Third issue and second binding: copyright notice with 5 dates as in 011b but issued in light grayish brown cloth, blue and gold stamping (Ref.b) $30/150

011d: THE BRIDE OF THE INNISFALLEN + Hamish Hamilton L (1955) [1] $30/150

012a: PLACE IN FICTION (South Atlantic Quarterly no-place or date circa 1956) [0] Printed wraps. Approximately 50 cc. An offprint from the *South Atlantic Quarterly* (Ref.c) $800.

012b: PLACE IN FICTION House of Books NY 1957 [2] 26 sgd ltr cc. Issued in glassine dustwrapper $750.

012c: PLACE IN FICTION House of Books NY 1957 [2] 300 sgd no. cc. Issued in glassine dustwrapper. Part of edition was destroyed (Joseph The Provider 3/89) $500.

013a: OCTOBER 7-25, 1958 EXHIBITION OF RECENT SCULPTURE JOHN ROOD The Contemporaries NY (1958) [0] Stiff white wraps. Welty wrote text for this art exhibition catalogue. (Pictorial wraps per William Reese Co. 1/87) $600.

014a: HENRY GREEN : A NOVELIST... (The Texas Quarterly Austin 1961) [0] 50 cc. Wraps. 12 page offprint of article which appeared in *The Texas Quarterly* Special Issue, Britain 2 Autumn 1961. (Ref.c indicates there were only 25 cc) $500.

015a: THREE PAPERS ON FICTION Smith College Northampton, MA 1962 [0] Wraps. 1,300 cc (Serendipity Cat. 43) $125.

016a: THE SHOE BIRD Harcourt Brace NY (1964) [1] $50/200

017a: THIRTEEN STORIES Harcourt Brace NY (1965) [1] Wraps. Selected and introduction by Ruth M. Van de Kieft $60.

018a: A SWEET DEVOURING Albondocani Press NY 1969 [2] 26 sgd ltr cc. Wraps $500.

018b: A SWEET DEVOURING Albondocani Press NY 1969 [2] 150 sgd no. cc. Wraps $300.

019a: LOSING BATTLES Random House NY (1970) [2] 300 sgd no. cc. Issued in acetate dustwrapper and slipcase $250/350

019b: LOSING BATTLES Random House NY (1970) [1] $10/50

019c: LOSING BATTLES Virago L (1982) [] Uncorrected proof in green and white stiff wraps and dustwrapper j(Fugitive Phoenix 5/90) $50.

019d: LOSING BATTLES Virago L (1982) [1] "Published by...1982" $8/40

020a: A FLOCK OF GUINEA HENS... (Albondocani Press NY 1970) [0] 100 cc. Wraps. Has greeting and "Albondocani Press / Ampersand Books" on first page (Ref.b). 110 copies (Beasley Books 7/92) $175.

020b: A FLOCK OF GUINEA HENS... (Albondocani Press NY 1970) [0] 210 cc. Wraps. Greeting only on first page, printed for use as Christmas card (Ref.b) $150.

021a: ONE TIME, ONE PLACE... Random House NY (1971) [2] 300 sgd no. cc. Issued in acetate dustwrapper and brown slipcase $250/350

021b: ONE TIME, ONE PLACE... Random House NY (1971) [1] $25/100

022a: THE OPTIMIST'S DAUGHTER Random House NY (1972) [2] Approximately 225 sgd no. cc. Approximately 75 copies destroyed of projected edition of 300 because of defective bindings (Ref.b). Issued without dustwrapper in slipcase $250/350

022b: THE OPTIMIST'S DAUGHTER Random House NY (1972) [1] Pulitzer Prize for 1973 $12/60

022c: THE OPTIMIST'S DAUGHTER Andre Deutsch (L 1973) [1] $10/50

022d: THE OPTIMIST'S DAUGHTER Franklin Library Franklin Ctr. 1978 [2] "Limited Edition" in brown leather $50.

022e: THE OPTIMIST'S DAUGHTER Franklin Library Franklin Ctr 1980 [2] Signed "Limited Edition." Contains 7 page special message from Welty to subscribers. Issued in maroon leather $100.

023a: SOME NOTES ON TIME IN FICTION Mississippi Quarterly Jackson, MS 1973 [0] Wraps. Offprint from *Mississippi Quarterly* Vol. XXVI, No.4 (Ref.c) $350.

024a: A PAGEANT OF BIRDS Albondocani Press NY 1974 [2] 26 sgd ltr cc. Wraps and dustwrapper $350/400

024b: A PAGEANT OF BIRDS Albondocani Press NY 1974 [2] 300 sgd no. cc. Wraps and dustwrapper $150/200

025a: IS PHOENIX JACKSON'S GRANDSON REALLY DEAD... (Critical Enquiry Chicago 1974) [0] Wraps. An off-print. Estimated at 25 to 50 copies (Glenn Horowitz #7) $350.

026a: FAIRY TALE OF THE NATCHEZ TRACE The Mississippi Historical Society Jackson, MS 1975 [0] 1,000 cc. Issued without dustwrapper (in Publisher's envelope -Joseph The Provider Cat. 24) $75.

027a: IMAGES OF THE SOUTH Center For Southern Folklore Memphis 1977 [1] Wraps. Visits with Eudora Welty and Walker Evans $50.

028a: ACROBATS IN A PARK Delta (no-place) 1977 [] Wraps. Off-print from *Delta Magazine* (Ref.c) $250.

028b: ACROBATS IN A PARK Lord John Press Northridge, CA 1980 [2] 100 sgd no. cc. Issued without dustwrapper in green cloth with brown stamping $250.

028c: ACROBATS IN A PARK Lord John Press Northridge, CA 1980 [2] 300 sgd no. cc. Issued without dustwrapper in green, gold and rust marbled boards, green cloth spine with gold stamping $175.

029a: THE EYE OF THE STORY... Random House NY (1978) [2] 300 sgd no. cc. Issued without dustwrapper in light gray slipcase $175/275

029b: THE EYE OF THE STORY... Random House NY (1978) [1] $10/50

029c: THE EYE OF THE STORY... Virago (L) 1987 [] (Ken Lopez 9/91) $8/40

030a: IDA M'TOY Univ. of Illinois Press Urbana/Chicago/L (1979) [2] 350 sgd no. cc. Issued in green or red cloth without dustwrapper (no priority). Also in black (Bert Babcock) $175.

031a: WOMEN! MAKE A TURBAN IN OWN HOME! Palaemon Press (Winston-Salem, NC 1979) [2] 35 sgd no. cc. Numbered I-XXXV $350.

031b: WOMEN! MAKE A TURBAN IN OWN HOME! Palaemon Press (Winston-Salem, NC 1979) [2] 200 sgd no. cc. Issued without dustwrapper $150.

032a: CRITICAL ESSAYS Univ. Press of Mississippi Jackson 1979 [] Edited by Peggy Whitman Prenshaw (Bev Chaney) $10/50

033a: MOON LAKE + Franklin Library Franklin Ctr 1980 [2] "Limited Edition." Issued in dark green leather. Same stories as in *Thirteen Stories* (017a) $100.

034a: TWENTY PHOTOGRAPHS Palaemon Press (Winston-Salem, NC 1980) [2] 20 sgd no. cc. (Roman) Photographs mounted on heavy rag board in clamshell folio box. Errata slip laid-in. Five of these copies were for the author's use $2,750.

034b: TWENTY PHOTOGRAPHS Palaemon Press (Winston-Salem, NC 1980) [2] 75 sgd no. cc. Issued in clam-shell box. Errata slip laid-in $2,000.

035a: THE COLLECTED STORIES... Franklin Library Franklin Ctr 1980 [2] "Limited Edition" in red leather. Includes one page special message $100.

035b: THE COLLECTED STORIES... Harcourt Brace Jovanovich NY/L (1980) [2] 500 sgd no. cc. Issued without dustwrapper in maroon slipcase with white label $150/250

035c: THE COLLECTED STORIES... Harcourt Brace Jovanovich NY/L (1980) [0] States "A limited first edition has been privately printed BCDE" on copyright page $10/50

035d: THE COLLECTED STORIES... Marion Boyars L 1981 [] Also wraps? $12/60

036a: BYE-BYE BREVOORT New Stage Theatre Jackson, MS (1980) [2] 26 sgd ltr cc. Issued without dustwrapper in boards with leather spine $400.

036b: BYE-BYE BREVOORT New Stage Theatre Jackson, MS (1980) [2] 50 sgd no cc (Roman). Issued without dustwrapper $350.

036c: BYE-BYE BREVOORT New Stage Theatre Jackson, MS (1980) [2] 400 sgd cc. Unnumbered and issued without dustwrapper $125.

037a: WHITE FRUITCAKE (Albondocani Press NY 1980) [0] 175 cc. Wraps. "Albondocani Press/Ampersand Books" and greeting printed on first page. Issued with mailing envelope $85.

037b: WHITE FRUITCAKE (Albondocani Press NY 1989) [0] 275 cc. Wraps. Greeting only printed on first page. Printed for use as Christmas card. Issued with mailing envelope $50.

038a: RETREAT Palaemon Press (Winston-Salem, NC 1981) [2] 7 sgd no. cc with signed numbered woodcut by Ann Carter Pollard tipped-in before title page. Not For Sale (Joseph Dermont #40) $500.

038b: RETREAT Palaemon Press (Winston-Salem, NC 1981) [2] 50 sgd no. cc. Each containing an original aquatint by Ann C. Pollard (Joseph Dermont #40) $500.

038c: RETREAT Palaemon Press (Winston-Salem, NC 1981) [2] 40 sgd no. cc. Numbered I-XL. Issued for the private use of the author and publisher (Joseph Dermont #40) $250.

038d: RETREAT Palaemon Press (Winston-Salem, NC 1981) [2] 150 sgd no. cc. Bound with cloth spine and light blue decorated paper-covered boards $150.

039a: ONE WRITER'S BEGINNINGS Harvard Univ. Press Cambridge 1984 [] Uncorrected proof in green wraps (Bev Chaney 9/91) $200.

039b: ONE WRITER'S BEGINNINGS Harvard Univ. Press Cambridge / London 1984 [2] 350 sgd no. cc. Issued without dustwrapper in cloth slipcase $250/350

039c: ONE WRITER'S BEGINNINGS Harvard Univ. Press Cambridge 1984 [] $12/60

039d: ONE WRITER'S BEGINNINGS Faber L (1985) [] Wraps. (No hardback in England - Maurice Neville 7/88) $40.

040a: FOUR PHOTOGRAPHS (Lord John Press Northridge, CA 1984) [2] 150 sgd no. cc. Broadside $175.

041a: THE MacNEIL / LEHRER NEW HOUR - Transcript #2230 Journal Graphics NY (1984) [0] Stapled self wraps. The transcript of a broadcast interview (on PBS) with Welty entitled "Eudora Welty at 75." Published in an edition of 300 copies (Jos. The Provider 3/89). Although in talking to *Journal Graphics* we got the impression that the copies were run off as ordered and there would be no way to differentiate later runs. This can still be ordered as far as we know $15.

042a: CONVERSATIONS WITH EUDORA WELTY Univ. Press of Mississippi Jackson (1984) [] Edited by Peggy Whitman Prenshaw $20/40

042b: CONVERSATIONS WITH EUDORA WELTY Univ. Press of Mississippi Jackson (1984) [] Wraps $20.

043a: IN BLACK AND WHITE Lord John Press Northridge 1985 [2] 100 sgd no. cc. Special binding, marbled boards with leather spine and in slipcase. Introduction by Anne Tyler. Signed by both $225/300

043b: IN BLACK AND WHITE Lord John Press Northridge 1985 [2] 300 sgd no. cc. Cloth spine, issued without dustwrapper or slipcase $175.

044a: THE LITTLE STORE Tamazunchale Press Newton, Iowa 1985 [2] 250 no. cc. Full leather, miniature book (not signed) $75.

045a: THE FAULKNER INVESTIGATION Cordelia Editions Santa Barbara 1985 [2] 500 cc. Wraps $40.

046a: MORGANA Univ. Press of Miss. Jackson (1988) [2] 26 sgd ltr cc. Two stories from *The Golden Apples*, illustrated by Mildred Nungester Wolf (signed by both). Issued without dustwrapper in slipcase $350/400

046b: MORGANA Univ. Press of Miss. Jackson (1988) [2] 250 sgd no. cc. Issued without dustwrapper in slipcase $200/250

046c: MORGANA Univ. Press of Miss. Jackson (1988) [] 3,000 cc $7/35

047a: PHOTOGRAPHS Univ. Press of Miss. Jackson (1989) [2] 52 sgd ltr cc. Foreword by Reynolds Price. Issued in full leather with separate photo. In cloth covered box (Magnum Opus 9/91) $600/700

047b: PHOTOGRAPHS Univ. Press of Miss. Jackson (1989) [2] 375 sgd no. cc. Issued without dustwrapper in slipcase $150/200

047c: PHOTOGRAPHS Univ. Press of Miss. Jackson (1989) [3] 6,500 cc (Nouveau Books 2/90) $30/60.

048a: THE WELTY COLLECTION Univ. of Miss. Jackson (1989) [] A catalog of Welty collection at the Mississippi Department of Archives & History. Includes manuscript pages and a selection of photographs. (Published @ $27.50)

WILLIAM CARLOS WILLIAMS
1883-1963

Williams was born in Rutherford, N.J. He received his M.D. from the University of Pennsylvania and did graduate work at the University of Leipzig. But aside from college he didn't travel much -"What the hell is there to see, anyway, compared with what's on the inside?" (ref.d)

He grew up in Rutherford, married a local girl, practiced medicine, wrote (in the house he bought in 1913), and died there in 1963.

He is known for his vivid, realistic and precise recording of the easily overlooked details of experience.

"There are a few things in life that one comes to want to do as one grows older, apart from turning over a little cash. I wanted to write... I've been writing, trying to get a few things said, ever since I started to study medicine. One feeds the other... Both seem necessary to me. One gets you out among the neighbors, the other permits me to express what I've been turning over in my mind as I go along." (ref.d)

REFERENCES:

(a) Wallace, Emily Mitchell, A BIBLIOGRAPHY OF WILLIAM CARLOS WILLIAMS, Wesleyan Univ. Press, Middletown, CT (1968).

(b) Bruccoli, Matthew J., et al, FIRST PRINTINGS OF AMERICAN AUTHORS, Volume 3, Gale Research, Detroit (1978).

(c) Information provided by New Directions.

(d) Kunitz & Haycraft, TWENTIETH CENTURY AUTHORS, H.W. Wilson Co., NY 1942.

Ref.a, an excellent bibliography, was used for all entries through item 059, unless otherwise noted.

001a: POEMS (Reid Howell Rutherford, NJ) 1909 [0] 100 cc. Wraps. Never published. Two copies known to have survived. Brown paper covers First state contained numerous misprints and errors, line 5 of the first poem "Innocence" reads "of youth himself,all rose-y-clad" $35,000.

001b: POEMS (Reid Howell Rutherford, NJ) 1909 [0] 100 cc. Wraps. Second state with numerous text corrections including line 5 of the poem "Innocence" which reads "of youth himself all rose-yclad." Less than 15 of this second state known $22,500.

002a: THE TEMPERS Elkin Mathews L 1913 [0] Probably 1,000 cc. Issued in glassine dustwrapper $1,000.

003a: AL QUE QUIERE! The Four Seas Co. B 1917 [0] 1,000 cc. Yellow-orange paper boards printed in black. Also variant with tan paper boards and author's name misspelled "Willams" on spine. Priority unknown $900.

004a: KORA IN HELL: IMPROVISATIONS The Four Seas Co. B 1920 [0] 1,000 cc. Orange dustwrapper printed in black. (Some copies had glassine dustwrappers) $250/850

004b: KORA IN HELL: IMPROVISATIONS City Lights Books S.F. (1957) [0] 1,500 cc. Wraps. The Pocket Poets Series No. Seven with a new prologue by Williams $40.

005a: SOUR GRAPES The Four Seas Co. B 1921 [0] 1,000 cc. Author's name on spine label only $275/950

006a: THE GREAT AMERICAN NOVEL Three Mountains Press P 1923 [2] 300 no. cc. Some copies have a rectangular slip covering name of the press (on the title page) upon which is printed "Contact Editions 29 Quai d'Anjou, Paris" -priority unknown (ref.b). Dustwrapper not mentioned $750.

007a: SPRING AND ALL (Contact Publ. Co. P 1923) [0] 300 cc. Wraps. Issued in glassine dustwrapper $750.

007b: SPRING AND ALL Frontier Press (West Newburyport, Mass.) 1970 [0] Galley proofs. 27 narrow leaves (Wm. Reese Co. #40) $200.

007c: SPRING AND ALL Frontier Press (West Newburyport, Mass.) 1970 [0] Wraps (ref.b) $35.

008a: (First printed leaf) MANIKIN NUMBER TWO (Second printed leaf) GO GO (no-publisher) NY (1923) [0] 150 cc. *Manikin Number Two* by Monroe Wheeler, *Go Go* by Williams. Gray card-board covers printed in blue, tied with blue string in stabbed holes at fold $1,000.

009a: IN THE AMERICAN GRAIN Albert & Charles Boni NY 1925 [0] Original price $3.00, but raised to $3.50 right after publication (ref.a) $125/600

009b: IN THE AMERICAN GRAIN New Directions Norfolk (1939) [0] 1,120 cc. Yellow cloth boards, lettered in red. Yellow dustwrapper printed in green and red $30/100

009c: IN THE AMERICAN GRAIN New Directions (NY 1966) [] 5,043 cc. Wraps. "Third Printing" stated. First revised edition $25.

009d: IN THE AMERICAN GRAIN New Directions (NY 1967) [] 1,000 cc. Clothbound issue of 009c $15/50

009e: IN THE AMERICAN GRAIN MacGibbon & Kee (L 1967) [1] 2,000 cc. "First published in Great Britain...1966" Actually published in March 1967 $10/50

010a: A VOYAGE TO PAGANY Macaulay Co. NY 1928 [0] $75/350

010b: A VOYAGE TO PAGANY New Directions (NY 1970) [] With an introduction by Harry Levin $8/40

011a: LAST NIGHTS OF PARIS Macaulay Co. NY 1929 [0] William's translation of the work by Philippe Soupault $75/350

011b: LAST NIGHTS OF PARIS Full Court Press NY (1982) [2] 100 sgd no. cc. Enlarged edition. New introduction by Soupault and signed by him (Joseph The Provider #31) $75.

012a: A NOVELETTE AND OTHER PROSE (1921-1931) TO Publishers (Toulon, France 1932) [0] Approximately 500 cc. Wraps $600.

013a: THE KNIFE OF THE TIMES + The Dragon Press Ithaca, NY (1932) [2] 500 cc. Some copies have tipped-in slip near foot of title page reading "The Dragon Press, Publishers, Duffield & Green, distributors" - priority unknown. Glassine dustwrapper covered by gray paper dustwrapper printed in blue $250/750

014a: THE COD HEAD Harvest Press SF (1932) [2] 125 cc. Wraps. (Geo. Robert Minkoff - List 86-F catalogued a variant without place and date on front cover and "Friends of Milton Arbenethy" in place of standard colophon. Baltimore Book Auctions lists apparenent unrecorded trial copy with second "e" in surname in wrong type and 100 cc for limitation.) Also title, colophon ("100 copies") and two pages of text, without wraps (William Reese Co. 5/91)

$600.

015a: COLLECTED POEMS 1921-1931 The Objectivist Press NY 1934 [0] 500 cc $100/500

016a: AN EARLY MARTYR + The Alcestis Press NY 1935 [2] 20 sgd cc. Numbered I-XX. Stiff yellow wraps, glassine dustwrapper and yellow slipcase $1,500/1,750

016b: AN EARLY MARTYR + The Alcestis Press NY 1935 [2] 135 sgd cc. Numbered 1-135. Yellow wraps, glassine dustwrapper and green slipcase (also 10 copies out-of-series for review)

$1,000/1,250

017a: ADAM & EVE & THE CITY The Alcestis Press Peru, VT 1936 [2] 20 sgd cc. Numbered I-XX. Olive-green wraps in green slipcase $1,750/2,000

017b: ADAM & EVE & THE CITY The Alcestis Press Peru, VT 1936 [2] 135 sgd cc. Numbered 1-135. Olive-green wraps in green slip-case (also 12 copies marked out-of-series, 2 for copyright) $1,250/1,500

018a: WHITE MULE New Directions Norfolk, CT 1937 [0] 1,100 cc. White cloth boards printed in black or gray cloth, printed in crimson on spine - priority unknown. (The second printing of 300 copies is probably indistinguishable from the first printing.) At least 445 sets of sheets not sold as they were used for 026a below $75/350

018b: WHITE MULE MacGibbon & Kee (L 1965) [1] 2,000 cc $12/60

019a: WILLIAM ZORACH TWO DRAWINGS WILLIAM CARLOS WILLIAMS TWO POEMS Stovepipe Press (no-place) 1937 [2] 500 cc (430 for sale). Wraps $175.

020a: LIFE ALONG THE PASSAIC RIVER New Directions Norfolk, CT 1938 [0] 1,006 cc $100/400

021a: THE COMPLETE COLLECTED POEMS 1906-1938 New Directions Norfolk, CT (1938) [2] 50 sgd no. cc. Dark blue cloth stamped in gold on spine in pale blue slipcase (actually 52 printed) $2,000/2,250

021b: THE COMPLETE COLLECTED POEMS 1906-1938 New Directions Norfolk, CT (1938) [0] 816 cc. Bound in dark green cloth. There were 506 copies bound in October 1938 and 310 copies in February 1939, both in dark green $100/450

021c: THE COMPLETE COLLECTED POEMS 1906-1938 New Directions Norfolk, CT (1938) [0] 650 cc. Bound in dark blue cloth in 1940 and later (same sheets as 021a & b). There were 400 copies bound in January 1940 and 250 "May" have been bound in April 1945 $60/300

022a: CHARLES SHEELER PAINTINGS DRAWINGS PHOTOGRAPHS MOMA NY 1939 [2] 5,500 cc. Wraps. Introduction by William Carlos Williams $75.

023a: IN THE MONEY/WHITE MULE Part II New Directions Norfolk, CT (1940) [0]

Approximately 1,500 cc (of which assume 445 used for 026a below) $60/300

023b: IN THE MONEY MacGibbon & Kee (L 1966) [1] 2,000 cc $12/60

024a: THE BROKEN SPAN New Directions Norfolk, CT (1941) [0] 300 cc. First binding: gray paper boards printed in black and fuchsia. Front flap of dustwrapper has comments about book, rear flap lists 12 Poet of the Month pamphlets $60/300

024b: THE BROKEN SPAN New Directions Norfolk, CT (1941) [0] 1,500 cc. Second binding: blank stiff white paper covers. Dustwrapper as in 024a $25/125

024c: THE BROKEN SPAN New Directions Norfolk, CT (1941) [0] Approximately 200 cc. Yellow paper wraps not attached at spine $100.

025a: THE WEDGE The Cummington Press (Cummington, Mass) 1944 [2] 380 cc. Glassine dustwrapper $500.

026a: FIRST ACT (IN THE MONEY/WHITE MULE) New Directions Norfolk, CT 1937/1940 (1945) [0] 445 copies of sheets of the second printing of 018a and 023a bound together, original title pages used and no additional title page added. Dustwrapper title and spine imprint is *"First Act"* $100/500

027a: THREE POEMS (General Mag & Historical Chronicle) Ph. (1945) [] Wraps. An offprint (Glenn Horowitz #9) $400.

028a: PATERSON (BOOK ONE) New Directions (Norfolk, CT 1946) [2] 1,063 cc (952 bound for publication date, 111 copies bound

April 1948). "... one thousand copies have been printed..." $75/350

029a: PATERSON (BOOK TWO) New Directions (Norfolk, CT 1948) [2] 1,009 cc (1,002 bound 4/1/48, 7 cc bound 4/13/48). "... one thousand copies have been printed ..." $50/250

030a: THE CLOUDS ... Wells College Press/The Cummington Press (no-place 1948) [2] 60 sgd cc. Numbered I-LX on English handmade paper bound in slate cloth boards in slipcase $1,500/1,750

030b: THE CLOUDS ... Wells College Press/The Cummington Press (no-place 1948) [2] 250 no. cc. Numbered 61-310 on rag paper in similar binding (to 030a) but issued without slipcase $350.

031a: A DREAM OF LOVE... (New Directions Norfolk, CT 1948) [0] 1,700 cc. Wraps. Heavy, brown paper covers printed in black $150.

032a: SELECTED POEMS (New Directions Norfolk, CT 1949) [0] 3,591 cc. Tan endpapers (second impression has white endpapers). Introduction by Randall Jarrell $25/125

Note: A later (1968) printing of the New Direction Paperbook No. 131 of this title was enlarged by the addition of 25 poems)

033a: THE PINK CHURCH Golden Goose Press Columbus, OH 1949 [2] 25 sgd no. cc. Numbered 1-25. Wraps $1,250.

033b: THE PINK CHURCH Golden Goose Press Columbus, OH 1949 [2] 375 no. cc. Numbered 26-400. Wraps $150.

034a: PATERSON (BOOK THREE) New Directions (Norfolk, Ct 1949) [2] 999 cc. "... one thousand copies have been printed ..." $40/200

035a: PICASSO THE FIGURE Louis Carre Gallery NY (1950) [0] Folio exhibition folder containing an essay by Williams $150.

036a: THE COLLECTED LATER POEMS New Directions (Norfolk, CT 1950) [2] 100 sgd no. cc. "The Rose" section loosely inserted. Issued without dustwrapper in slipcase $800/1,000

036b: THE COLLECTED LATER POEMS New Directions (Norfolk, CT 1950) [0] 1,993 cc. "The Rose" section loosely inserted. (8 leaves, stapled at fold, numbered 233-245). Total quantity (a, b & c) originally printed was 4,700 which apparently did not include the Horace Mann editions $25/125

036c: THE COLLECTED LATER POEMS New Directions (Norfolk, CT 1950) [0] Approximately 2,441 cc. Later binding of 036b with pages 233-245 correctly bound in $25/100

036d: THE COLLECTED LATER POEMS New Directions (Norfolk, CT 1950 (actually 1956) [2] 52 copies of which 50 are signed numbered copies in red. Facing title page "Horace Mann School Editions." Gray slipcase. "The Rose" section bound in. Printed from first edition plates in 1956 $800/1,000

036e: THE COLLECTED LATER POEMS New Directions (Norfolk, CT 1950 (actually 1956) [0] 522 cc. Plain brown dustwrapper with circular cut-out to reveal H. Mann School seal. "The Rose" section loosely inserted. Printed from first edition plates in 1956 $25/125

036f: THE COLLECTED LATER POEMS New Directions (Norfolk, CT 1963) [] 2,904 cc. "Revised Edition" stated. First thus $8/40

036g: THE COLLECTED LATER POEMS MacGibbon & Kee L 1965 [] 1,500 cc. (Revised edition) $10/50

037a: MAKE LIGHT OF IT COLLECTED STORIES Random House NY (1950) [1] 5,000 cc. Includes one story which had not appeared in print before ("Lena") $15/75

038a: A BEGINNING ON THE SHORT STORY The Alicat Book-Shop Pr. Yonkers, NY 1950 [2] 1,000 cc. Wraps. White or tan heavy paper covers, no priority. "This copy one of 750 offered for sale" $75.

039a: PATERSON (BOOK FOUR) New Directions (Norfolk, CT 1951) [2] 995 cc. "... one thousand copies have been printed ..." $35/175

040a: AUTOBIOGRAPHY Random House NY (1951) [1] 5,000 cc $15/75

040b: THE AUTOBIOGRAPHY OF WILLIAM CARLOS WILLIAMS MacGibbon & Kee L 1968 [] (Dalian Books 4/90.) Assume this is the same book $10/50

041a: THE COLLECTED EARLIER POEMS New Directions (Norfolk, CT 1951) [0] 5,000 cc $15/75

041b: THE COLLECTED EARLIER POEMS MacGibbon & Kee (L 1967) [1] 1,500 cc. Verso of title page states "Second printing/manufactured in the United States." Back dust-wrapper flap "Printed in Great Britain" 10/50

042a: EMANUEL RAMANO Passedoit Gallery NY (1951) [0] 500 cc. Wraps. Four page exhibition catalog with text by Williams $150.

043a: THE BUILD-UP Random House NY (1952) [1] 6,000 cc printed but sticker pasted on title page of 684 copies in 1965 when New Directions acquired plates $15/75

043b: THE BUILD-UP MacGibbon & Kee (L 1969) [] (ref.b) $8/40

044a: THE DESERT MUSIC + Random House NY (1954) [2] 111 cc of which 100 were signed and numbered. Glassine dustwrapper in slipcase $850/1,000

044b: THE DESERT MUSIC + Random House NY (1954) [0] 2,532 cc $30/150

045a: THE DOG AND THE FEVER ... The Shoe String Press Hamden CT (1954) [0] 1,000 cc. Translation of work of Francisco de Queredo (aka Pedro Espinosa) by Williams and Raquel Helene Williams $12/60

046a: SELECTED ESSAYS Random House NY (1954) [] Uncorrected galley proofs punchbound in blue wraps (Joseph The provider 12/88) $400.

046b: SELECTED ESSAYS Random House NY (1954) [1] 3,350 cc. "New Directions" sticker pasted on title page of 992 copies in June 1965 when New Directions acquired Random House plates $15/75

046c: SELECTED ESSAYS New Directions NY 1969 [1] Wraps. "New Directions Paperbook 273." Published March 26, 1969 @ $2.45 (ref.c) $15.

047a: JOURNEY TO LOVE Random House NY (1955) [0] 3,000 cc $25/100

048a: THE SELECTED LETTERS McDowell, Obolensky NY (1957) [2] 75 sgd no. cc. Issued without dustwrapper in slipcase $600/750

048b: THE SELECTED LETTERS McDowell, Obolensky NY (1957) [0] 2,000 cc $25/100

049a: THE GIFT (New Directions NY 1957) [0] 2,500 cc. Wraps. Christmas greeting (also issued as Christmas card by Hallmark in 1962) $75.

050a: SAPPHO (Poems in Folio SF 1957) [2] 150 sgd no. cc. Translation by Williams. Issued as broadside $350.

050b: SAPPHO (Poems in Folio SF 1957) [0] 1,000 cc. Translation by Williams. Issued as broadside $75.

051a: I WANTED TO WRITE A POEM Beacon Press B (1958) [] Spiral bound galley proof in gray wraps with label (Glenn Horowitz #11) $500.

051b: I WANTED TO WRITE A POEM Beacon Press B (1958) [0] 3,543 cc. Reported and edited by Edith Heal $15/75

051c: I WANTED TO WRITE A POEM Cape L 1967 [] (ref.b) Wraps in dustwrapper (David Mayou #23) $10/50

051d: I WANTED TO WRITE A POEM New Directions NY 1978 [1] 3,000 cc. New Directions Paperbook 469 (ref.c). (Published October 19, 1978 @ $3.45) $25.

052a: A NOTE ON THE TURN OF THE VIEW TOWARD POETIC TECHNIQUE Hanover Forum Hanover, Ind. (1958) [0] 8 pages in stapled wraps $125.

053a: PATERSON (BOOK FIVE) New Directions (Norfolk, CT 1958) [0] 3,000 cc 25/125

054a: W.C.W. - F.H.W. APRIL 18, 1959 (Press of Igals Roodenko 1959) [2] 100 cc. Printed for New Directions (consists of William's "To Be Recited to Flossie on Her Birthday") $100.

055a: YES, MRS. WILLIAMS... McDowell, Obolensky NY (1959) [0] $12/60

055b: YES, MRS. WILLIAMS... New Directions NY 1982 [1] New Directions Paperbook 534 (ref.c). (Published June 30, 1982 @ $5.95) $10.

056a: THE FARMERS' DAUGHTERS New Directions (Norfolk, CT 1961) [1] 1,500 cc $25/100

056b: THE FARMERS' DAUGHTERS New Directions (Norfolk, CT 1961) 10,000 cc. Wraps. On spine "ND Paperbook 106." Published simultaneously $25.

057a: MANY LOVES + New Directions (Norfolk, CT 1961) [0] 1,983 cc $25/75

057b: MANY LOVES + New Directions (Norfolk, CT 1965) [0] 2,443 cc. Wraps. On back cover "A New Directions Paperbook NDP 191." Not bound and published until 1965 $25.

058a: PICTURES FROM BRUEGHEL + New Directions Paperbook (Norfolk, CT 1962) [1] 7,500 cc. "ND Paperbook 118" Pulitzer Prize in Poetry for 1963 $50.

058b: PICTURES FROM BRUEGHEL + MacGibbon & Kee L 1963 [1] 1,500 copies printed 950 copies bound. First cloth bound edition $20/100

059a: PATERSON (COLLECTED) New Directions (NY 1963) [1] Wraps. 8,598 cc. "ND Paperbook 152." Includes first five books and notes for the sixth $30.

059b: PATERSON (COLLECTED) MacGibbon & Kee L 1964 [1] 1,500 cc $25/100

059c: PATERSON : REVISED EDITION New Directions NY 1992 [] Edited by Christopher MacGowan. (Published November 1992 @ $35)

060a: COLLECTED PLAYS Oxford L 1963 [] Introduction by John Heath-Stubbs. First appearance of two plays (Boston Book Annex #21) $12/60

061a: THE WILLIAM CARLOS WILLIAMS READER New Directions (NY 1966) [0] 3,000 cc. Yellow stamped in blind and gold (ref.a). Also yellow cloth stamped in black and blind (William Reese Co. 2/91) $12/60

061b: THE WILLIAM CARLOS WILLIAMS READER MacGibbon & Kee (L 1966) [1] 2,000 cc. Actually published 3/20/67 $10/50

THE AUTOBIOGRAPHY OF WILLIAM CARLOS WILLIAMS see 1951

062a: IMAGINATIONS New Directions NY (1970) [0] (ref.b) 3,557 cc. (Published August 24, 1970 @ $10.) ref.c $8/40

062b: IMAGINATIONS MacGibbon & Kee (L 1970) [] (ref.b) $8/40

063a: THE EMBODIMENT OF KNOWLEDGE New Directions (NY 1974) [0] 2,064 cc. Edited by Ron Loewinsohn (ref.c). (Published November 27, 1974 @ $18.75) $10/50

064a: (POEM, 1911) I WILL SING A JOYOUS SONG Lockwood Memorial Library Buffalo 1974 [2] 25 no. cc. Broadside (ref.b) $100.

064b: (POEM, 1911) I WILL SING A JOYOUS SONG Lockwood Memorial Library Buffalo 1974 [1] 2,000 cc. Broadside (apparently not for sale) ref.b $30.

065a: SELECTED POEMS Penquin L 1976 [] Wraps. Edited and introduction Charles Tomlinson (Ian McKelvie 7/89) $30.

066a: INTERVIEWS WITH WILLIAM CARLOS WILLIAMS "SPEAKING STRAIGHT AHEAD" New Directions (NY 1976) [0] Edited by Linda Welshimer Wagner (ref.c). (Published November 9, 1976 @ $8.50) $10/40

066b: INTERVIEWS WITH WILLIAM CARLOS WILLIAMS "SPEAKING STRAIGHT AHEAD" New Directions (NY 1976) [0] Wraps. "ND Paper-book 421." Simultaneously published with cloth edition (ref.c) $15.

067a: A RECOGNIZABLE IMAGE: WILLIAM CARLOS WILLIAMS ON ART & ARTISTS New Directions NY 1978 [1] 2,555 cc. (Published October 29, 1978 @ $16.00) ref.c $10/15

068a: WILLIAM CARLOS WILLIAMS AND THE AMERICAN SCENE 1920-1940 Whitney Museum (NY) 1978 [] Wraps. 11 pages. First separate edition of this selection. Selected by Dickran Tashjian (Waiting For Godot) $35.

069a: SELECTED POEMS Snake River Press (Sussex 1981) [2] 25 no. cc. Folio. Half burgandy morocco over Roma paper boards (Geo. Houle Cat. 27) $350.

070a: FLOWERS OF AUGUST Windhover Press Iowa City 1983 [2] 260 cc. (Actually published in 1984.) Issued without dustwrapper (William Reese Co. Cat. 30) $100.

071a: WILLIAM CARLOS WILLIAMS / JOHN SANFORD: A CORRESPONDENCE Oyster Press SB 1984 [2] 75 no. cc signed by John Sanford. Issued in dustwrapper $50/75

071b: WILLIAM CARLOS WILLIAMS / JOHN SANFORD: A CORRESPONDENCE Oyster Press SB 1984 [2] 425 cc. Issued in dustwrapper $20/40

071c: WILLIAM CARLOS WILLIAMS / JOHN SANFORD: A CORRESPONDENCE Oyster Press SB 1984 [2] 2,000 cc. Wraps $20.

072a: SELECTED POEMS Franklin Library Franklin Ctr 1984 [2] "Limited Edition" in full red leather (J. & J. House 4/89) $50.

073a: THE DOCTOR STORIES New Directions NY 1984 [1] (Published October 12, 1984 @ $13.50) ref.c $10/35

073b: THE DOCTOR STORIES New Directions NY 1984 [1] New Directions Paperbook 585 (ref.c) $10.

074a: SOMETHING TO SAY New Directions NY 1985 [] (Published October 10, 1985 @ $23.95) ref.c $6/30

075a: DEAR EZ: LETTERS FROM WILLIAM CARLOS WILLIAMS Friends of The Lilly Library Bloomington 1985 [2] 203 no. cc (Beasley Books #23) $75/125

076a: JANUARY MORNING (NY 1986) [] Triple fold pamphlet issued as greeting (Phoenix Book Shop 10/88) $20.

077a: COLLECTED POEMS OF WILLIAM CARLOS WILLIAMS Volume I 1909-1936 New Directions NY (1986) [] Edited by A. Walton Litz and Christopher MacGowen $7/35

078a: COLLECTED POEMS OF WILLIAM CARLOS WILLIAMS Volume II 1939-1962 New Directions NY (1988) [] $7/35

079a: THE NORMAL AND ADVENTITIOUS DANGER PERIODS FOR PULMONARY DISEASE IN CHILDREN Dim Gray Bar NY 1988 [2] 100 cc. Wraps. Williams' medical article originally published in the *Archives Pediatrics* in 1913. Signed by the publisher, Barry Magid, M.D. (William Reese Co. 7/90) $50.

080a: WILLIAM CARLOS WILLIAMS AND JAMES LAUGHLIN : SELECTED LETTERS Norton NY (1989) [] Edited by Hugh Witemeyer (Chloe's Books 9/89) $5/25

081a: THE AMERICAN IDIOM. A CORRESPONDENCE Bright Tyger Press SF 1990 [] Williams and Harold Norse. Hardbound without dustwrapper $35.

081b: THE AMERICAN IDIOM. A CORRESPONDENCE Sun Moon Press place? date? [] (Bev Chaney 1/92) $10.

082a: THE LETTERS OF WILLIAM CARLOS WILLIAMS AND CHARLES TOMLINSON Dim Gray Bar Press NY 1992 [2] 26 sgd ltr cc. Signed and preface by Tomlinson. Edited by Barry Magid and Hugh Witemeyer. Introduction by Hugh Kenner. Goatskin and handmade paperboards $300.

082b: THE LETTERS OF WILLIAM CARLOS WILLIAMS AND CHARLES TOMLINSON Dim Gray Bar Press NY 1992 [2] 124 sgd no. cc. Signed by Tomlinson. Cloth and boards $150.

REFERENCED DEALERS

ABOUT BOOKS, 83 Harbord Street, Toronto, Ontario M5S 1G4, Canada

ALPHABET BOOKSHOP, 145 Main Street West, Port Colborne, Ontario, Canada L3K 3V3

AMPERSAND BOOKS, Box 674, Cooper Station, New York City 10276

ANACAPA BOOK, 3090 Claremont Avenue, Berkeley, CA 94705

ANTIC HAY RARE BOOKS, Box 2185, Asbury Park, NJ 07712

ARGOSY BOOK STORE, 116 E. 59th Street, New York City 10022

ASPIDISTRA BOOKSHOP, 2630 North Clark, Chicago, IL 60614

THE ASSOCIATES, Box 4747, Falls Church, VA 22044

ATTIC BOOKS, Box 611136, Port Huron, MI 48061

AUTHORS OF THE WEST, 191 Dogwood Drive, Dundee, OR 97115

BAY SIDE BOOKS, Box 57, Soquel, CA 95073

BERT BABCOCK BOOKSELLER, P.O. Box 1140, 9 East Derry Road, Derry, NH 03038

BEASLEY BOOKS, 1533 West Oakdale, Chicago, IL 60657

BELL, BOOK & RADMALL, LTD., 4 Cecil Court, London WCZ 4HE, England

BERKELOUW ANTIQUARIAN BOOKSELLERS, 830 North Highland Avenue, Los Angeles, CA 90038

STEVEN C. BERNARD, 15011 Plainfield Lane, Darnestown, MD 20874

BETWEEN THE COVERS, 575 Collings Avenue, Collingwood, NJ 08107

PRESTON C. BEYER, 752A Pontiac Lane, Oronoque Village, Stratford, CT 06497

BLACK SUN BOOKS, Box 7916, FDR Station, New York, NY 10150

BOOKFINDERS, Box 13692, Atlanta, GA 30324

THE BOOKPRESS, Box KP, Williamsburg, VA 23187

THE BOOKSHOP, 400 West Franklin Street, Chapel Hill, NC 27514

BOSTON BOOK ANNEX, 705 Centre Street, Jamaica Plain, MA 02130

BOWIE & COMPANY, 314 First Avenue South, Seattle, WA 98104

MARILYN BRAITERMAN, 20 Whitfield Road, Baltimore, MD 21210

THE BRICK ROW BOOKSHOP, 278 Post Street, #303, San Francisco, CA 94108

BUDDENBROOKS, 753 Boylston Street, 2nd Floor, Boston, MA 02116

JOHN R. BUTTERWORTH, 742 West 11th Street, Claremont, CA 91711

NICHOLAS BURROWS, 30 Kenilworth Avenue, Wimbledon, London SW19 7LW, England

THE CAPTAIN'S BOOKSHELF, 31 Page Avenue, Asheville, NC 28801

NICHOLAS CERTO, Box 322, Circleville, NY 10919

BEV CHANEY, JR., 73 Croton Avenue, Ossining, NY 10562

CHAPEL HILL RARE BOOKS, P.O. Box 456, Carrboro, NC 27510

CHLOE'S BOOKS, Box 255673, Sacramento, CA 95865

CLEARWATER BOOKS, 19 Matlock Road, Ferndown, Wimborne, Dorset BH22 8Q7, England

COLD TONNAGE BOOKS, 136 New Road, Bedfont, Feltham, Middlesex TW14 8H7, England

THE COLOPHON BOOK SHOP, 117 Water Street, Exeter, NH 03833

COUNTRY LANE BOOKS, Box 47, Collinsville, CT 06022

L.W. CURREY, INC., Water Street (Box 187), Elizabethtown, NY 12932

ROBERT DAGG, Box 4758, Santa Barbara, CA 93140

W & V DAILEY, LTD. Box 69160, Los Angeles, CA 90069

DALIAN BOOKS, 81 Albion Drive, London Fields, London E8 4LT, England

DAREES BOOKS (David Rees), 22 Wanley Road, London SE5 8A7, England

JOSEPH A. DERMONT, Box 654, 13 Arthur Street, Onset, MA 02558

DETERING BOOK GALLERY, 2311 Bissonnet, Houston, TX 77005

DINKYTOWN ANTIQUARIAN BOOKSTORE, 1316 SE 4th Street, Minneapolis, MN 55414

JAMES DOURGARIAN, 1595-A Third Avenue, Walnut Creek, CA 94596

DUNN & POWELL, Box 2544, Meriden, CT 06450 and The Hideaway, Bar Harbor, ME 04609

I.D. EDRICH, 17 Selsdon Road, London E11 2QF England

PETER ELLIS, 31 Museum Street, Bloomsbury, London WC1A 1LH, England

ELSE FINE BOOKS, Box 43, Dearborn, MI 48121

ERGO BOOKS, 46 Lisburne Road, London NW3 2NR, England

EUCLID BOOKS, 227 Euclid Street, Santa Monica, CA 90402

EVLEN BOOKS, Box 42, Centerport, NY 11721

THE FINE BOOK CO., 781 East Snell Road, Rochester, MI 48064

FIRSTS & COMPANY, 25 East 83rd Street, New York, NY 10028

FIRST ISSUES LTD., 17 Alfoxton Avenue, London N15 3DD England

R.A. GEKOSKI, 33B Chalot Square, London NW1 8YA, England

GOTHAM BOOK MART, 41 West 47th Street, New York 10036, NY

HAWTHORN BOOKS, 7 College Park Drive, Westbury-on-Trym, Bristol BS10 7AN, England

HEARTWOOD BOOKS, 9 Elliewood Avenue, Charlottesville, VA 22903

SUSAN HELLER, Box 22219, Cleveland, OH 44122

HERITAGE BOOKSHOP, 8540 Melrose Avenue, Los Angeles, CA 90069

MELISSA AND MARK HIME, Box 309, Idyllwild, CA 92349

DAVID J. HOLMES AUTOGRAPHS, 230 South Broad Street, 3rd Floor, Philadelphia, PA 19102

GLENN HOROWITZ, 141 East 44th Street, Suite 808, New York, NY 10017

GEORGE HOULE, 7260 Beverly Boulevard, Los Angeles, CA 90036

IN OUR TIME, Box 386, Cambridge, MA 02139

JAMES S. JAFFE, Box 496, Haverford, PA 19041

JANUS BOOKS, P.O. Box 40787, Tucson, AZ 85717

PETER JOLLIFFE, 2 Acre End Street, Eynsham, Oxon OX8 1PA, England

JOSEPH THE PROVIDER, 10 West Michaeltorena, Santa Barbara, CA 93101

KEANE-EGAN BOOKS, Box 529, State College, PA 16804

KENNETH KARMIOLE BOOKSELLER, 1225 Santa Monica Mall, Los Angeles, CA 90401

JOHN KNOTT JR., BOOKSELLER, 8453 Early Bud Way, Laurel, MD 20707

OWEN KUBIK, 3474 Clar-Von Drive, Dayton, OH 45430

LAME DUCK BOOKS, 90 Moraine Street, Jamaica Plains, MA 02130

JAMES & MARY LAURIE, BOOKSELLERS, 251 South Snelling, St. Paul, MN 55105

LEAVES OF GRASS, 2433 Whitmore Lake Road, Ann Arbor, MI 48103

LEMURIA BOOKS, 202 Banner Hall, 4465 I-55 North, Jackson, MS 39206

LIMESTONE HILLS BOOK SHOP, Box 1125, Glen Rose, TX 76043

ROBERT LOREN LINK, BOOKSELLERS, Box 511, Las Cruces, NM 88004

KEN LOPEZ, BOOKSELLER, 51 Huntington Road, Hadley, MA 01035

MacDONNELL RARE BOOKS, 9307 Glenlake Drive, Austin, TX 78730

GEORGE S. MacMANUS CO., 1317 Irving Street, Philadelphia, PA 19107

ROBERT A. MADLE, 4406 Bestor Drive, Rockville, MD 20853

MAGNUM OPUS, Box 1301, Charlottesville, VA 22902

JEFFREY H. MARKS, 45 Exchange Street, Room 701, Rochester, NY 14614

DAVID MASON, 342 Queen Street West, 2nd Floor, Toronto M5V 2A2 Canada

WILLIAM MATTHEWS, BOOKSELLER, 16 Jarvis Street, Fort Erie, Ontario L2A 2S1 Canada

DAVID MAYOU, 103 Mill Hill Road, London W3 England

IAN McKELVIE, 45 Hertford Road, London N2 9BX England

ALLAN R. MILKERIT BOOKS, 2141 Mission, Suite 301, San Francisco, CA 94110

GEORGE ROBERT MINKOFF, 26 Rowe Road, Alford, 01230

HARTLEY MOORHOUSE, 142 Petersham Road, Richmond, Surrey TW10 6UX, England

MORDIDA BOOKS, Box 79322, Houston, TX 77279

BRADFORD MORROW, 33 West 9th Street, New York, NY 10011

MYSTERIOUS BOOKSHOP, 129 West 56th Street, New York, NY 10019

MAURICE F. NEVILLE, Box 50509, Santa Barbara, CA 93150

NOUVEAU RARE BOOKS, 5005 Meadow Oaks Park Dr., Jackson, MS 39211

THE OLD NEW YORK BOOK SHOP, 1069 Juniper Street, NE, Atlanta, GA 30309

JAMES F. O'NEIL, Box 326, Charles Street Station, Boston, MA 02114

PEPPER & STERN RARE BOOKS, 1980 Cliff Drive, Suite 224, Santa Barbara, CA 93109 and Box 160, Sharon, MA 02067

PETTLER & LIEBERMAN, 8033 Sunset Boulevard, No. 977, Los Angeles, CA 90046

PHAROS BOOKS, Box 17, Fair Haven Station, New Haven, CT 06513 and P.O. Box 18246, GR-116 10 Athens, Greece

PHOENIX BOOKSHOP, Box 1018, St. Michaels, MD 21663

PHILLIP J. PIRAGES, 965 West 11th Street, McMinnville, OR 97128

POLYANTHOS BOOKS, P.O. Box 343, Huntington, NY 11743

NICHOLAS POUNDER, BOOKSELLER, 298 Victoria Street, Box 451, Kings Cross NSW 2011, Australia

QUILL & BRUSH, Box 5365, Rockville, MD 20848

WILLIAM REESE COMPANY, 409 Temple Street, New Haven, CT 06511

L & T RESPESS BOOKS, P.O. Box 1238, Northampton, MA 01061

BOB ROSENBERG, 1955 34th Avenue, San Francisco, CA 94116

BERTRAM ROTA LTD. 9-11 Langley Court, Covent Garden, London WC2E 9RX England

SCHOYER'S BOOKS, 1404 South Negley Avenue, Pittsburgh, PA 15217

SECOND STORY BOOKS, 12160 Parklawn Drive, Rockville, MD 20852

CHARLES SELUZICK RARE BOOKS, 3733 N.E. 24th Avenue, Portland, OR 97212

SERENDIPITY BOOKS, 1201 University Avenue, Berkeley, CA 94702

ANTHONY F. SMITH, BOOKSELLER, 1414 Lynnview Drive, Houston, TX 77055

MONROE STAHR, 4420 Ventura Canyon Avenue, No. 2, Sherman Oaks, CA 91423

ERIC STEVENS, 74 Fortune Green Road, London NW6 1DS England

JOAN STEVENS, 2 Prospect Road, London NW2 2JT, England

STEVEN A. STILLWELL, 2333 Minneapolis Avenue, Minneapolis, MN 55406

SYLVESTER & ORPHANOS, Box 2567, Los Angeles, CA 90078

ROBERT TEMPLE, 65 Mildmay Road, London N1 4PU England

STEVEN TEMPLE BOOKS, 489 Queen Street West, 2nd Floor, Toronto, Ontario M5V 2B4, Canada

TRANSITION BOOKS, 2626 Filbert Street, San Frncisco, CA 94123

H.E. TURLINGTON BOOKS, Box 190, Carrboro, NC 27510

LEN UNGER, RARE BOOKS, P.O. Box 5858, Sherman Oaks, CA 91413

VAGABOND BOOKS, 2076 Westwood Boulevard, Los Angeles, CA 90025

WAITING FOR GODOT BOOKS, Box 331, Hadley, MA 01035

WATER ROW BOOKS (Jeff Weinberg), Box 438, Sudbury, MA 01776

WATERMARK WEST, 149 North Broadway, Wichita, KS 67202

WAVERLY BOOKS, 946 9th Street, #E, Santa Monica, CA 90403

JEFF WEBER RARE BOOKS, 1923 Foothill Drive, Glendale, CA 91201

J. HOWARD WOOLMER RARE BOOKS, Marienstein Road, Revere, PA 18953

WORDS ETC., Hod House, High Street, Child Okeford, Dorset DT11 8EH, England

HERB YELLIN, 19073 Los Alimos Street, Northridge, CA 91326